INDIGENOUS CONTINENT

INDIGENOUS CONTINENT

The Epic Contest for North America

Pekka Hämäläinen

LIVERIGHT PUBLISHING CORPORATION

A DIVISION OF W.W. NORTON & COMPANY

Independent Publishers Since 1923

For information about permission to reproduce selections from this book,
write to Permissions, Liveright Publishing Corporation, a division of
W. W. Norton & Company, Inc., 500 Fifth Avenue, New York, NY 10110

For information about special discounts for bulk purchases, please contact
W. W. Norton Special Sales at specialsales@wwnorton.com or
800-233-4830

Manufacturing by Lakeside Book Company
Book design by Lovedog Studio
Production manager: Anna Oler

ISBN 978-1-63149-699-8

Liveright Publishing Corporation
500 Fifth Avenue, New York, N.Y. 10110
www.wwnorton.com

W. W. Norton & Company Ltd.
15 Carlisle Street, London W1D 3BS

1 2 3 4 5 6 7 8 9 0

CONTENTS

THE MYTH OF COLONIAL AMERICA

T HERE IS AN OLD, DEEPLY ROOTED STORY ABOUT America that goes something like this: Columbus stumbles upon a strange continent and brings back stories of untold riches. The European empires rush over, eager to stake out as much of this astonishing New World as possible. Even as they clash, they ignite an era of colonial expansion that lasts roughly four centuries, from the conquest of Hispaniola in 1492 to the Wounded Knee Massacre in 1890. Between those two moments, European empires and the nascent American empire amass souls, slaves, and territory, dispossessing and destroying hundreds of Indigenous societies. The Indians fight back but cannot stop the onslaught. Resourceful and defiant though they might be, they are no match for the newcomers and their raw ambition, superior technology, and lethal microbes that penetrate Native bodies with shocking ease. Indians are doomed; Europeans are destined to take over the continent; history itself is a linear process that moves irreversibly toward Indigenous destruction.

Indigenous Continent tells a different story. It offers a new account of American history by challenging the notion that colonial expansion was inevitable and that colonialism defined the continent, as well as the experiences of those living on it. Stepping outside of such outdated assumptions, this book reveals a world that remained overwhelmingly Indigenous well into the nineteenth century. It argues that rather than a "colonial America," we should speak of an *Indigenous* America that was only slowly and unevenly becoming colonial. By 1776, various European colonial powers together claimed nearly all of the continent for themselves, but Indigenous peoples and powers controlled it. The maps in modern textbooks that paint much of early North America with neat, color-coded blocks confuse outlandish imperial claims for actual holdings. The history of the overwhelming and persisting Indigenous power recounted here remains largely unknown, and it is the biggest blind spot in common understandings of the American past.

The reality of an Indigenous continent has remained obscure because European empires, and especially the United States, invested power in the state and its bureaucracy, whereas Native nations invested power in kinship. From the beginning, European arrivals judged Indians on European terms. Later historians did the same, focusing on state power as the driving force in America. Kinship could be a source of great power, and Indigenous nations possessed advanced political systems that allowed for flexible diplomacy and war-making, even if Euro-Americans often failed to see them. Time and again, and across centuries, Indians blocked and destroyed colonial projects, forcing Euro-Americans to accept Native ways, Native sovereignty, and Native dominance. This is what the historical record shows when American history is detached from mainstream historical narratives that privilege European ambitions, European perspectives, and European sources.

The traditional master narrative is entrenched in our culture and minds. Consider how Red Cloud's War and Custer's Last Stand are usually understood. According to the conventional narrative, in a single decade between 1866 and 1876, the Lakota Indians and their Cheyenne and Arapaho allies defeated the United States in two wars—first along the Bozeman Trail in what became known as Red Cloud's War, and then in the Battle of the Little Bighorn, where they annihilated George Armstrong Custer's 7th U.S. Cavalry Regiment. Both defeats have entered American history as aberrations or flukes. The United States, after all, had already become a continent-spanning military-industrial power poised to expand beyond the West Coast. The Lakotas had humiliated the United States at a charged moment when the nation was shedding its frontier identity and entering the modern era of the corporate, the bureaucratic, and the scientific. The fiascos would be blamed on poor generalship and on a canny enemy familiar with the terrain.

Seen from Native American perspective, however, Red Cloud's War and Custer's Last Stand appear not as historical anomalies, but as the logical culmination of a long history of Indigenous power in North America. They were more expected than extraordinary. From the beginning of colonialism in North America to the Lakotas' final military triumphs, a multitude of Native nations fought fiercely to keep their territories intact and their cultures untainted, frustrating the imperial pretensions of France, Spain, Britain, the Netherlands, and eventually the United States. This Indigenous "infinity of nations" included Iroquois, Catawbas, Odawas, Osages, Wyandots, Cherokees, Comanches, Cheyennes, Apaches, and many others. Although each nation was and is distinct, a cultural crevasse separated the European newcomers from all Indigenous inhabitants of the continent, generating fear, confusion, anger, and violence. That divide fueled one of the longest conflicts in history, while simultaneously inspiring a centuries-long search for mutual understanding and accommodation—a search that continues today.[1]

The great pitfalls in the study of Native Americans are broad generalizations on the one hand and narrow specificity on the other. For a long time, historians tended to see Indians as a human monolith cut from a single—and primordial—cultural cloth, a race defined by its tragic history of dispossession and its epic struggle for survival. This tradition informs many popular books that repackage Native American history into a morality play that is often more concerned with the United States and its character than with the Indians themselves. In these depictions of Native America, Indians appear as one-dimensional stock figures, their complexity and differences pressed flat for dramatic purposes. They are reduced to mere props in the United States' violent transformation into a global power: Indigenous resistance and suffering heighten the drama, enabling people today to glimpse how much was lost and at what cost.

On the other end of the spectrum is a venerable tradition of tribal histories, each focusing on a single Native nation and providing a comprehensive portrait of its traditions, political structures, material culture, and historical experiences. This necessary and often superb scholarship has brought to life hundreds of previously obscured Indigenous peoples as forceful, creative, and resilient historical actors, filling a half-illuminated continent with human texture. The downside of this approach is its particularity. Each nation comes across as unique, embedded in its own microworld. Multiply this by five hundred, and the problem is plain to see. Examining Indigenous America in this way is like looking at a pointillistic painting from mere inches away: it overwhelms; it loses coherence; the larger patterns are impossible to discern.

With the perspective adjusted just slightly, however, a new and sharper image of North America comes into view. *Indigenous Continent* takes a middle course between the general and the specific, uncovering a broad range of Native American worlds that rose and fell across the continent from the early sixteenth century into the late nineteenth century. In numerous realms, Indians and colonists competed for territory, resources, power, and supremacy, with survival often hanging in the balance. Each realm had its own character, reflecting the continent's astounding physical diversity: the stakes and dynamics of warfare, diplomacy, and belonging played out differently along coasts, along river valleys, in woodlands, in grasslands, and in the mountains.

This book is first and foremost a history of Indigenous peoples, but it is also a history of colonialism. The history of North America that emerges is of a place and an era shaped by warfare above all. The contest for the continent was, in essence, a four-centuries-long war that saw almost every Native nation fight encroaching colonial powers—sometimes in alliances, sometimes alone. Although the Indian wars in North America have been written about many times before, this book offers a broad Indigenous view of the conflict. For Native nations, war was often a last resort. In many cases, if not most, they attempted to bring Europeans into their fold, making them useful. These were not the actions of supplicants; the Europeans were the supplicants—their lives, movements, and ambitions determined by Native nations that drew the newcomers into their settlements and kinship networks, seeking trade and allies. Indian men and women alike were sophisticated diplomats, shrewd traders, and forceful leaders. The haughty Europeans assumed that the Indians were weak and uncivilized, only to find themselves forced to agree to humiliating terms—an inversion of common assumptions about White dominance and Indian dispossession that have survived to the present.

When war did come, Indians won as often as not. Older, discredited, and ludicrous notions of "savage" Indians or "noble savages" suggest a certain degree of brutality in battle, but it was the colonists who were responsible for most atrocities. Many colonists, especially the British, Spanish, and Americans, were guilty of ethnic cleansing, genocide, and other crimes, but some adopted more measured approaches to Native peoples. There were colonists who utterly despised Indians and wanted to eradicate them, but there were also colonial regimes that sought to embrace them. There were many types of colonialism—settler, imperial, missionary, extractive, commercial, and legal—and they emerge cumulatively as the story told here progresses. Tracing the evolution of colonialism is vital: the depth and reach of Indigenous power can be truly understood only against the massive colonial challenge from Europe. I have tried to show the full potential of colonialism to destroy lives, nations, and civilizations. It is against that horrific violence that Indigenous power is revealed. Overseas colonialism was a daunting endeavor that required courage and commitment. European intruders were ruthless because they held deep-seated racist ideologies and because the stakes were so high. For most of them there was no going back.

A SINGLE-VOLUME CONTINENTAL HISTORY of North America cannot devote equal attention to all Native nations, regions, and events. Large Indigenous nations and confederacies were able to confront European empires on their own terms, and they drive much of the story through their sheer capacity to keep North America Indigenous. But the smaller nations and their resistance were also essential to the making of the Indigenous continent. Preserving Indigenous power and sovereignty was a total endeavor: every colonial intrusion, however small, could generate a domino effect of Native retreats. Accordingly, this book zooms in frequently to local and intimate scales; it was there, in face-to-face encounters, where the hard work of colonizing and resisting colonization happened. Indigenous Americans were fighting for their land, for their lives, and for future generations. Every inch mattered.

This book covers a vast span of history—four centuries and a continent—but it is given shape, direction, and meaning by a single theme: power. Here, power is defined as the ability of people and their communities to control space and resources, to influence the actions and perceptions of others, to hold enemies at bay, to muster other-worldly beings, and to initiate and resist change. What follows is the story of a long and turbulent epoch when North America was contested by many and dominated by none. This story traces how people gained, lost, and, in rare instances, shared power with strangers, creating many new worlds in the process. The book might be best described as a biography of power in North America. The story follows critical action and key turning points across the contested continent, showing how various parts of it became geopolitical hot spots where rivalries intensified and where history turned violently.

Although the book is inclusive, focusing on both European colonists and Native Americans, the usual actors, events, and turning points of American history retreat to the background. The Stamp and Tea Acts, Boston Massacre, and creation of the U.S. Constitution figure only marginally in this history. Indians controlled most of North America, and often they did not know about the exploits of the Europeans beyond their borders. And if they did, they did not care. Instead, the Indigenous peoples were interested in the ambitions and experiences of other Indigenous peoples—the Iroquois, Cherokees, Lakotas, Comanches, Shawnees, and many others.

A Note on Terminology and Style

I have occasionally modernized direct quotes when spelling makes them hard to understand. Taking a cue from Nancy Shoemaker, I call Native men and women involved in war "soldiers," not "warriors." The settlements of more sedentary Native nations are "towns," whereas the more mobile nomadic settlements are "villages." Rather than "chiefs," I use either Indigenous terms for leaders or simply "officials" or "officers" because they were Indigenous administrators. As for the names of Indian Nations, I have used what they themselves prefer: Odawas rather than Ottawas; Lenapes rather than Delawares; Wyandots rather than Hurons; Illinis rather than Illinois; Meskwakis rather than Foxes; Ho-Chunks rather than Winnebagos; Muscogees rather than Creeks; Ojibwes rather than Ojibwas. The Iroquois are also called Haudenosaunee.[1]

THE DAWN OF
THE INDIGENOUS
CONTINENT

(the first seventy millennia)

Chapter 1

THE WORLD ON
THE TURTLE'S BACK

K ELP WAS THE KEY TO AMERICA.
    During the last ice age, starting 2.5 million years ago, vast
ice sheets locked up so much of the world's water that the sea level
dropped drastically, changing the surface of the Earth. Islands
became isthmuses, and seafloors became meadows. The most consequential exposure in North America took place in the Bering Strait,
where, about seventy thousand years ago, a six-hundred-mile-wide
landmass emerged to connect Asia and America. That swath of new
land—Beringia—was scored by rivers, speckled with small lakes, and
covered with grasses and shrubs that supported thriving animal communities, drawing people into America from the west.

The melting of glaciers started in North America roughly twenty-
one thousand years ago. As the mile-high ice caps slowly melted into
the oceans, a narrow ice-free corridor opened on the eastern flank of
the Rocky Mountains. Groups of people began moving southward
through the passage around 11,000 BCE, eventually arriving in the
great continental grasslands that were swarming with huge mammals:
imperial mammoths, six-ton mastodons, eight-foot-tall bison, giant
ground sloths, short-faced bears, camels, horses, and several species
of antelope. The size and number of the beasts required technological
innovation by the people now in the region, and groups of hunters
began using flint, chert, obsidian, and other malleable stone to craft
sharp-edged, fluted spear points that could penetrate a beast's thick
skin with lethal efficiency. Hunters would travel hundreds of miles
to prime quarry sites to obtain the best stone. Lower-risk subsistence

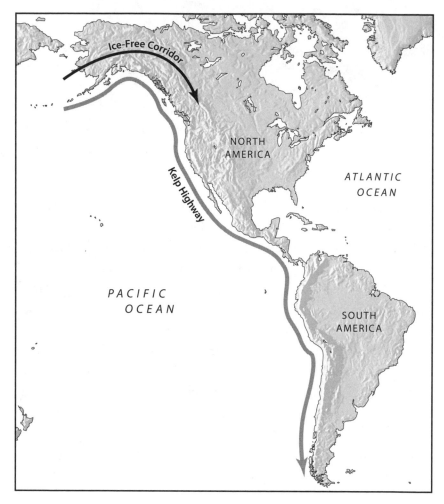

The kelp highway

strategies—foraging, fishing, and hunting small game—rounded out diets, supporting growing and resilient human communities.[1]

Yet the Western Hemisphere was still only patchily inhabited by people. Other migration waves proceeded through an older and quite possibly busier maritime route that traced the Pacific Rim, where people moved in skin boats along the shore, subsisting on the rich marine and estuarine life that flourished in a cool-water offshore zone—a "kelp highway"—that spanned from northeastern Asia to the Andean coast. Nutrient-rich kelp beds supported colonies of fish, shellfish, seabirds, seaweed, and sea otters, enabling people to enjoy rich and balanced diets. For these amphibian people, the quest for food was safer and most likely more efficient than that of the big-game hunters in the interior. They could find a wealth of seafood in the mangrove forests near shore. Shifting from one bounteous habitat to another, splintering when necessary, highly mobile maritime hunter-gatherers may have reached Monte Verde in modern-day southern Chile—ten thousand miles south of the Bering Strait—as early as 16,500 BCE. The earliest traces of people in North America have been found in the Southwest, where human presence dates back twenty-three thousand years.[2]

People who had spread across an entire hemisphere remarkably fast did so against daunting odds. Unlike its eastern counterpart, the Western Hemisphere has a pronounced north–south orientation, and people on the move had to negotiate numerous climatic and ecological circumstances, adapting their food search, tools, clothing, dwellings, social systems, and mindsets to challenging conditions. Many Native American origin stories speak of rising tides and mountains of water that seem to describe melting glaciers releasing themselves over the land. It was already clear, at this early point, that the Americas would be defined by astounding human diversity and resilience.

THERE HAD BEEN ANOTHER world before this one, an island world floating in the sky, happily inhabited by Sky People. But when Sky Woman became inexplicably pregnant, her husband was furious. He ripped up a great tree, creating a hole in the sky and pushed Sky Woman through it toward a watery world far below. Ducks caught Sky Woman with their wings and laid her on the back of the Turtle, who allowed her to rest there. The Turtle declared that her arrival was a good omen. Sky Woman was no longer an outsider. The water animals—the beaver, the loon, and many others—dived deep, trying to bring back mud from the bottom of the sea for Sky Woman to walk on, but they all failed. Only the Muskrat succeeded, delivering a handful of mud. The animals spread it on the Turtle's back and saw that the mud had the power to expand. It became an island, then an enormous expanse of dry land. That was the birthplace and home of the Iroquois people. Sky Woman had a daughter, who in turn had two sons: Tharonhiawagon, who was good, and Tawiskaron, who was evil. Tawiskaron entered the world by tearing a hole in his mother's side, killing her, but Tharonhiawagon made the sun, lakes, rivers, and mountains from her body. Consumed by envy, Tawiskaron tried to undo his brother's creation, and Tharonhiawagon killed him. This was not a sign of dysfunction, but of balance. The world was neither entirely evil nor entirely good. Sky Woman kept it in balance.[3]

The Pawnee people, too, received guidance from above, but they emerged from beneath. In the beginning, Tirawa—Father—was at the center of things below, but the world had no shape, no order, only chaos. Tirawa summoned the powers of the skies. He sent out his thoughts and created celestial gods to bring order: the Evening Star to the west to represent Pawnee men, and the Morning Star to the east to represent Pawnee women. The Morning Star gave birth to the first being on Earth, and through her four helpers—Wind, Cloud, Lightning, and Thunder—guided the Pawnees into the plains, where they discovered corn and buffalo, the foundation of their material and spiritual existence. Rather than cataclysmic change and movement, the Pawnee origin story revolves around a search for social and cosmic order in a very particular place. For Pawnees, the Platte, Republican, and Loup Rivers in the Great Plains were—and are—the center of the world.[4]

An origin story of the Cherokees—who call themselves *Ani-Yun-Wiya*, meaning "real people"—tells of the slow creation of the world. In the beginning, the Earth was a floating island in a sea, suspended by cords attached to Gälûñ'lätï, a sky world of solid rock. The Earth was soft and wet, and the animals sent out the Great Buzzard to prepare the world below for them, but he struggled to find dry land. He grew tired, and his wings began to hit the ground, creating a series of valleys and mountains. That mountainous country became Cherokee land. The Great Buzzard created animals and plants first, humans later. At first there were only a brother and sister. He struck the sister with a fish and told her to multiply. At the start she gave birth every seventh day, and the world was in danger of becoming overcrowded. So, she began having one child every year, thus stabilizing the world.[5]

Like the Cherokees, the Sicangu Lakotas have an origin story that centers on reciprocal relationships between humans and animals and between humans and the Earth. There had been an earlier world, but people did not know how to live in it properly, and *tȟuŋkášila* ("grandfather") decided to create a new one. He cracked the Earth open, and water flowed out, covering everything. All the people and animals died, except for the crow. The crow begged tȟuŋkášila for a place to rest. Tȟuŋkášila covered the world with land and shed tears that became seas, lakes, and rivers. He opened his pipe bag, took out animals and plants, and allowed them to spread over the land. Only then did he form human beings from earth. He promised not to drown the new world if people treated his creation with respect. "Now," he said, "if you have learned how to behave like human beings and how to live in peace with each other and with the other living things—the two-legged, the four-legged, the man-legged, the flicrs, the no-legs, the green plants of this universe—then all will be well. But if you make this world bad and ugly, then I will destroy this world too. It's up to you."[6]

While many origin stories of Indigenous nations in North America explain the creation of the universe along with the creation of a specific people, the Kiowas have a story that explains their distinctive attribute: their small numbers. The Kiowa people—*Ka'igwu*, "principal people"—came to this world through a hollow log, one by one. But then a woman, her body bulky with child, got stuck. Many people were still waiting to emerge from the log, but there was no way out, so the Kiowas never numbered more than three thousand people.[7]

The Navajos emerged from a lower world, but they were still evolving when they did. The First Man and the First Woman were the Mist People who lacked discipline and undermined *hózhó*, "harmony." They moved through several worlds, accruing knowledge and reason in each, and finally arrived in the present world, fully formed and with a gender balance in opportunities and challenges. The First Man and the First Woman now knew how to treat each other, other peoples, and all the living creatures properly. Dinétah, the Navajo homeland, could come into being amid four sacred mountains. The First Man and the First Woman found a baby and raised her. She became Changing Woman, who married the Sun, and together they went to the western ocean, raised four clans, and took them back to Dinétah, making their world complete.[8]

These and many other origin stories explain how a new multi-ethnic world—Indigenous America—took shape. The origin stories are not necessarily in conflict with some scientific theories about the peopling of the Americas. References to lands exposed during the ice age, and to the reemergence of dry land when glaciers began to melt, are not hard to detect in Indigenous origin stories. The ubiquitous floods—sudden, devastating, regenerative—in origin stories tell of the radical changes that humans faced in North America starting about 17,000 BCE. These stories illuminate an Indigenous America that is old, complex, and dynamic. The Pacific coast of Meso- and North America features 143 different Native languages, most likely the result of recurring splintering over thirty-five thousand years from a single original tongue.[9]

THE FIRST AMERICANS DID NOT divide the world into hemispheres and continents. They had not crossed seas or oceans to reach America, and they did not think they had arrived in some kind of new world. They had faced severe ecological upheavals during their travels, and they had prevailed, often by dividing tasks according to gender. Understanding the world and its unpredictability—its dangers and its gifts—was all-important. Forming proper relationships to the land and its life-forms was everything. These people did not think they were occupying new lands, because they had been there always.[10]

By 10,000 BCE, there were people in nearly every part of the Western Hemisphere, from still-glacial Alaska and the Yukon to Monte Verde in South America. North America had become an Indigenous continent. It would remain so for nearly twelve millennia. In 10,000 BCE the people in the Americas were hunter-gatherers, and they were thriving. Their world was filled with megafauna, and they were pioneering new hunting methods, operating in small groups with a range of duties and performing the necessary rituals to establish a proper relationship between hunter and prey: tracking the animals and leading them to a kill site—often near a water hole; felling the gigantic beasts with coordinated spear thrusts; processing the meat, bones, and hides for immediate and future use. The profusion of game persisted for two millennia, but then the continental ice sheets began melting rapidly, and the giant mammals began dying out, debilitated by a warming and increasingly erratic climate. Apparently unaware of how fragile the animal populations had become, humans kept hunting the great beasts, perhaps expanding the use of fire and thereby delivering an unintended final blow. By 8000 BCE, some three dozen species of giant animals had become extinct.[11]

It was at this point that many first Americans in the North American West shifted to bison-hunting. Relatively recent Beringian migrants themselves, bison were aggressive, prolific, and highly adaptive animals that avoided extinction by specializing in shortgrass grazing. They literally shrank—over millennia—to survive the shifting conditions in the arid West, becoming lighter, faster, and more mobile. Hunters, too, had to adapt. A refined, grooved, and extremely thin and therefore powerful spear point announced the rise of a new hunting civilization, whose people operated in highly mobile bands that could follow the herds for hundreds of miles, trap dozens of beasts for a kill, or drive entire herds into a box canyon, down a ravine, or off cliffs.[12]

As the climate warmed, sustaining the growth of grass and other forage, animal populations proliferated, pushing the hunters to continue innovating. The invention of the atlatl around 7500 BCE was a breakthrough. A wooden stick with a shaft on one end and a socket on the other, the atlatl enabled a thrower to propel a light spear faster and farther, with a flipping motion that channeled stored energy in a springlike effect. Essentially an extension of the hunter's arm, the atlatl transformed hunting into a relatively safe and easy affair. Pedestrian hunters could now kill their prey from a distance of up to 150 yards. Maritime foragers found the atlatl highly useful because it left one hand free for steering the vessel. Fluted spear points fell out of use.[13]

Though they slaughtered animals by the thousands, the first Americans treated their quarry with respect and care. To become effective hunters, they had to understand animal behavior intimately and know how to manipulate animal habitats—especially with strategic fires—to ensure predictable herd movements and successful hunts. They needed to approach the animals with correct thoughts and ceremonies to secure their sacrifice, and they had to accept the animals' gifts—skin, flesh, bone, blood—with reverence and compassion. Failing to do so would have alienated animal spirits and shattered the ancient bonds of kinship with human beings. It was this mindset of respect and care that sustained North America as a hunter's world for several millennia. People faced the need to explore other ways of life only from about 4500 BCE on.

ACORNS, THE NUTS OF oak trees, are rich in iron, calcium, potassium, fiber, carbohydrates, monounsaturated fats, and vitamins A, B, and E. They also stabilize the human metabolism and blood sugar levels. The first Americans who made North America's West Coast their home relied heavily on acorns and kelp, founding an entire civilization on them. They fashioned refined stone mortars and grinders to leach the tannic acid out of the precious nuts, and they designed light and capacious baskets to carry and store the nuts. Nomadic peoples built settlements near acorn groves, anchoring themselves to the land, and before long they were practicing small-scale agriculture under local leaders who coordinated fire-fallow cultivation and the allocation of land and crops. So abundant was the acorn yield that West Coast peoples were only marginally interested in corn cultivation.[14]

This Pacific-bound Indigenous world shunned political centralization. Communities consisted of several close-knit kinship groups that enjoyed exclusive rights to wild food patches, hunting ranges, and fisheries. Foodstuffs, tools, medicinal plants, and luxuries circulated through local and long-distance trade networks, creating a vast regional web of reciprocity and sharing, and ocean currents brought resources—flotsam, redwood logs, bamboo—virtually to their homes. What would become known as California was an affluent, politically sophisticated, and safe world. A maritime civilization tethered to an unusually fertile kelp-rich shore and boosted by acorns, it may have been the most densely populated region of North America.

The trajectory of the Indigenous West Coast, though distinctive, points to a broader dynamic: all across the Americas people were recalibrating what was possible; the Western Hemisphere was diversifying into numerous unique worlds. Along the Northwest Coast, the warm

Kuroshio and North Pacific Currents spawned a moderate climate and heavy rainfall. Salmon became the mainstay and the center of the locals' unique culture. They believed salmon were eternal beings who lived in subsurface houses during winter. If summoned with proper prayers, the salmon assumed their form as fish in the spring and filled the rivers, giving themselves up. Seafaring hunters ventured in dugout canoes to track whales, seals, sea otters, and other marine megafauna that flourished in the kelp forests, extending their world—their economies, social networks, and spiritual lives—deep into the Pacific.[15]

Such a dramatic extension of reach and ambition required adaptability, compromise, and creativity. Relatively classless local communities gave way to more hierarchical orders that could mobilize labor on a large scale and enforce social specialization. By the early second millennium CE—around the 1300s—the Northwest Coast was dotted with sumptuous cedar-plank houses that could be five hundred feet long and seventy-five feet wide and accommodate multiple families. These houses were adorned with false-front facades decorated with stylized animal imagery that represented specific clans, and in front of them stood finely carved totem poles, reaching toward the skies. The Northwest Coast people became ranked societies that distinguished individuals by their genealogical distance from elite families. The great houses were the Northwest Coast civilization in microcosm, symbolizing and safeguarding it. Just as the households were founded on a system of social ranking, so, too, were the many nations—the Tlingits, Haidas, Kwakiutls, Bella Coolas, Makahs, Chinooks, and others—that shared the region. The households that together constituted a nation competed openly for prestige and power in sumptuous potlatch ceremonies where wealthy families publicly shared their possessions with poorer ones, reaffirming their preeminence. What worked on the small scale also worked on the large scale. The Northwest Coast people had turned ambition, abundance, and rivalry into a cohesive social force. Much of the land was held in commons as shared resource rather than private property. By 1500 BCE, the Indigenous worlds in North America were flourishing, built on kelp, acorns, hunting, and fishing, and laying the foundation for later civilizations.[16]

Chapter 2

THE EGALITARIAN CONTINENT

CORN IS ONE OF HUMANKIND'S GREATEST FEATS OF genetic engineering. It does not exist in the wild; its kernels are too tightly attached to the cobs to allow self-seeding, so it needs to be sown and tended to survive. It is a cultural artifact, created and perfected by humans through systematic and bold biological manipulation. Its parent plant was teosinte, a weedy inedible mountain grass native to the Mesoamerican highland valleys, but corn looks almost nothing like teosinte. Teosinte had several thin stalks, a small cob, and a hard casing, whereas corn has a single heavy stalk capable of supporting several heavy ears.[1]

Highland peoples domesticated corn between nine and six thousand years ago. They kept refining the plant, inspecting the seeds and breeding numerous local varieties that varied in taste, texture, and color, and that thrived in different climates, soils, and elevations. The size of cobs could range from a few inches to twenty, and they could be covered in multiple rows of kernels. With skilled human help, this highly adaptive species was poised to take over the world. The Tehuacán Valley was an early center of the systematic cultivation of corn, and agriculture-based village life took root there by 1500 BCE. Political centralization followed, giving rise to empires that drew people into their orbit through military might, appealing religious ceremonies, and long-distance trade.[2]

Interlocking webs of local trade networks carried corn seeds south and north from Mesoamerica. Corn cultivation began in the southwestern Amazon rain forest around 4500 BCE, and the crop reached the semiarid highlands of the North American Southwest around 2000

BCE. A true dietary revolution came later, with the arrival of *maiz de ocho* in the first millennium of our era. A major step in the long evolution of corn, the maiz de ocho variety was robust, adaptable, and easy to process. It flowered quickly, requiring less labor, and could withstand harsh weather. When farmers began growing beans and squash along with maiz de ocho some fifteen hundred years ago, they created an ecologically compatible triad of crops—the "three sisters"—that revolutionized food production and diets in North America.[3]

By planting the three crops together, Indigenous farmers created a set of highly beneficial synergies. Corn's tall and sturdy stalks provided a strong structure on which bean vines could climb. Corn's high nutrient requirements could quickly deplete the soil of nitrogen, a vital ingredient in photosynthesis, the process by which light energy is converted into chemical energy that plants can use. Here farmers could rely on beans to help. Nodules on their roots have microbes that pull nitrogen from the air, convert it to a form that corn and squash can use, and return it to the soil as a natural fertilizer. As beans climb up the cornstalks toward the sun, squash provides essential protections: spreading near the ground, it offers shade with its broad leaves, helping the soil to retain moisture and deterring weeds, and its prickly hairs repel rodents and other pests. The outcome of this companion planting was a nearly ideal human diet: corn is rich in carbohydrates, whereas beans, especially when dried, yield plenty of protein, and together the three crops provide most essential vitamins and minerals.[4]

As in earlier eras in Mesoamerica, abundance encouraged ambition and innovation. Towns and cities rose across the vast region, bringing large numbers of people together and incubating new ideas and technologies. Shamans—Indigenous physicians and ritualists—traveled along roads and waterways, seeking and sharing knowledge and rites that helped them to balance the universe. During the second half of the first millennium, the Hohokam and Mogollon peoples turned away from casual farming and embraced large-scale canal irrigation and terrace agriculture in their high-altitude desert homelands along and west of the upper Rio Grande valley, relying on underground water reservoirs, irrigation ducts, and floodwater diversions. They developed bigger strains of corn through hybridization, and soon they could feed several thousand. Men were largely responsible for the intensive agricultural work, although, in line with an ancient tradition, the land and the crops belonged to women, whose kinship networks sustained public order. They constructed multistory adobe-clay buildings with grand courtyards. Grandmothers were the social and moral center of these emerging agricultural communities, and women began to produce crafts and crops for external markets as the origin stories had anticipated.[5]

Around 900 CE, rising global temperatures ushered in a new climate cycle, the Warm Period, which lengthened growing seasons. Hohokam and Mogollon farmers benefited greatly from the new climate regime, but it was the Ancestral Puebloans who made the most of it. By the middle of the eleventh century (around 1050 CE) the ten-mile-long Chaco Canyon in the Colorado Plateau had become a dominant urban center that nearly monopolized the highly lucrative trade in turquoise stones, a luxury item. There, over three centuries, the Ancestral Puebloans built a monumental communal stone building—later known as Pueblo Bonito—that served as the political, commercial, and religious center of the Chacoan world. It is possible that Pueblo Bonito was built by slave labor.[6]

Five stories high, the finely engineered, D-shaped, sandstone structure boasted hundreds of rooms, several stairways, and two large, enclosed courtyard plazas with over thirty *kivas*, underground ceremonial chambers. With high walls on its north, east, and south sides, it sat in the middle of dozens of great houses and countless modest ones. Yet, perhaps only twenty families lived there. Pueblo Bonito may have been an elite-run redistribution center that absorbed goods from the outlying commoners who made regular pilgrimages to the great houses. Four hundred miles of arrow-straight roads linked the magnet-like center to some seventy-five communities, and Pueblo Bonito featured massive storage rooms for corn, beans, squash, and other imported necessities. Long-distance trade networks brought luxuries from Mesoamerica, and an enigmatic forty-mile-long Great North Road may have been built to symbolize Pueblo Bonito's material and spiritual primacy. The settlement was divided into two balanced halves, perhaps to reflect the duality between the sacred and the secular—or a deepening division between elites and commoners. *Kachinas*, spirit beings, moved between the underworld and the Earth, embodying the duality of the Pueblo world as established in origin stories.[7]

THOUSANDS OF YEARS AGO, sometime after 1700 BCE, people started moving earth to a narrow and slightly elevated landform near the lower Mississippi Valley. They persisted in the task from one generation to the next, transporting millions of cubic feet of dirt until, four centuries later, they had what they wanted: a seventy-five-foot-high bird-shaped earthwork, six concentric C-shaped earthen ridges that may have served as dwelling sites, and a large central plaza facing the river—all of it protected against the dramatic annual floods by levees. It was at once a settlement, a ceremonial center, and a commercial hub that welcomed in—and most likely redistributed—large quantities of copper, jasper, quartz, pipestone, shark teeth, and marine shells from all directions. The town's original citizens were egalitarian hunterfisher-gatherers who seem to have established a hierarchical political system in order to mobilize labor on a larger scale.

The architects of this economic regime were pioneers, and their experiment lasted for six centuries, until about 700 BCE. Others picked up where they left off. A new Mound Builder civilization, Adena-Hopewell, emerged in the central Ohio Valley, where people came together to build colossal ceremonial mounds of different shapes—circles, octagons, squares—that publicized the centrality, power, and humility of its inhabitants. They imported obsidian and bear teeth from the Rocky Mountains, mica and quartz from the Appalachians, copper and pipestone from the Great Lakes, and tortoise shells and shark teeth from the Caribbean, and they themselves were artisans who made stunning copper effigies and masks portraying birds, fish, beavers, bears, and human faces. Theirs was a society that depended on connections among peoples. Those linkages disintegrated rapidly when corn and beans became staples in the fifth century; the life-giving plants made kinship networks self-sufficient.

Populations expanded, people moved into walled towns, and face-to-face connections gave way to more formal relations. Towns began to compete for farmlands and political preeminence, and the ancient collective ethos crumbled. By the early sixth century CE the great Adena-Hopewell civilization had dissolved into countless competing groups.[8]

The Indigenous history of North America in the late first and early second millennia CE was characterized by a distinctive pattern of simultaneous centralization and decentralization. Regional centers hoarded power, fueling resentment among subordinate groups that eventually revolted or splintered off, sometimes founding new regimes. The pattern was evident in the sequence from Mogollon to Hohokam to Ancestral Puebloan in the Southwest, and it was particularly pronounced in the shift from Poverty Point to Adena-Hopewellian culture in the Mississippi Valley. Perhaps the most dramatic version of the sequence unfolded in the American Bottom, a sixty-mile-wide floodplain at the junction of the Missouri and Mississippi Rivers, during the eleventh century, at the height of the Warm Period. At an ancient river crossing and transportation hub stood a modest village of hunters and gatherers. But around 1000 CE, newcomers settled in the area. Growers of corn, they razed the existing buildings so that they could build a city.

The newcomers turned the marshy floodplain packed with highly fertile alluvium into fields and started building their new capital city. Their highly driven elites mobilized commoners and slaves to drain marshes, clear rectangular public plazas, and move enormous amounts of soil so that they could build huge earthen mounds and broad causeways to connect them to one another. The great city was laid in a grid pattern, and the newcomers' ultimate achievement would be a colossal central mound—a stately, pyramidal structure that rose in four terraces to one hundred feet above ground. It covered sixteen acres at its base. Centuries later, Europeans named it Monks Mound.[9]

Cahokia, as this new city became known, was built to impress and to embed its inhabitants properly in the cosmos; its geography was sacred geography. Monks Mound was aligned with the cardinal directions, and the principal mounds in the center of the city were aligned with Monks Mound and each other. Monks Mound towered over the

A modern artist's rendering of Cahokia

Grand Plaza, an enormous artificial plain that was created by swales being filled with soil, establishing a literal, vertical distance between elites and commoners. Atop Monks Mound, chiefs and priests connected the worlds above and below and presided over their people, expecting them to show the humility and loyalty that kept their world safe. The city's leaders, and perhaps also the commoners, consumed the caffeine-laced Black Drink to ritually purify themselves.[10]

Cahokia was also an economic experiment. The city's elites—the chiefs and priests—desired luxuries for their own aesthetic pleasure and as status symbols. The city was encircled by satellite townships whose chiefs owed loyalty to Cahokia's paramount chief and made their allegiances tangible through gifts. At the same time, Cahokia was a thriving center of trade. From the city's position near the confluence of the Mississippi, Missouri, and Illinois Rivers, its commercial hinterland extended from the Great Lakes to the Gulf coast and the Appalachians, importing such necessities as salt and sandstone, and such luxuries as copperware, Mill Creek chert, and finely crafted stone knives.

Cahokia may have begun as a collective effort of people who understood themselves as a single kin community, but over time it transformed into an elite-run state. The triggering factor was the colossal building projects that absorbed inordinate amounts of labor. Monks Mound alone consisted of twenty-two million cubic feet of soil, all of it transported in baskets carried by humans to the construction site. Completing that gargantuan project may have taken 370,000 days of labor in total, and although it was the largest, it was but one of some two hundred mounds that would eventually dot the cityscape.

At some point, to get the job done required coercion, giving rise to a ranked society. An aristocracy began to command lesser people and their labor, possibly through violence.

Cahokia had become a theater of power. Whether its elites appealed to spiritual mandates or relied on sheer force, thousands of common people now spent much of their time on the ritual work of transforming the earth into a new shape and on raising food for the nobility. They depended on the generosity of their leaders to access some of the wealth that had suffused the booming metropolis. One elite festival featured nearly four thousand deer, eighteen thousand earthen pots, and a generous offer of potent tobacco. Marine-shell beads, columella pendants, and rattles, as well as figurines of raptors, snakes, and female deities carved of quartz crystals, mica, and galena, flowed from Cahokia into the adjacent rural settlements, publicizing elite power and generosity.

The power of the elite was only superficially political; its true sources and manifestations were sacred. Chiefs and priests knew— or claimed to know—how to communicate with other-than-human beings and to control the sun, the Earth, seasons, rains, crops, and game. The paramount chief needed the city's prodigious wealth in corn and luxuries to flow to him so that he could pass them on to the needy, create bonds of obligation, appease other-than-human creators, forge alliances with outsiders, and proclaim his own prominence. Power in Cahokia became highly personalized, embodied by the paramount chief and his lineage. Cahokians—or a critical number of them—came to believe that a chief's power should extend into the afterlife. In the early eleventh century, approximately 270 people were ritually sacrificed and buried in a series of mass graves to accompany elite persons in death. In another instance, 118 female captives were brought to Cahokia and killed. One mass grave was covered with more than twenty thousand marine-shell beads arranged in the shape of a bird.

Cahokia's theocratic leaders established alliances with the elites of the surrounding Mound Builder villages, creating a fluid network of allegiances that resembled the ambitions of Europe's medieval barons

and other nobility who strove to control scattered castles and contested territories. Games of *chunkey* drew people together into huge
arenas to watch contestants tossing a disc-shaped stone on the ground
and sending spears toward it as it rolled, trying to land them as close
to its stopping point as possible. When Cahokian ambassadors visited the outlying villages, they carried with them both war clubs and
chunkey stones, possibly to emphasize both the competitive and the
cooperative nature of their relationships. The force of their diplomacy
seems to have established a long era of peace and stability—a Pax
Cahokia—in the heart of the continent. At its peak, Cahokia may
have had fifteen thousand residents and thirty thousand people in its
orbit, sustaining the great city.

Cahokia was the zenith of—and perhaps the model for—a widespread Mississippian culture that encompassed much of the Eastern
Woodlands for more than eight centuries in an ever-shifting constellation of regional variations. Large population centers expanded their
food production to near carrying capacity under an unusual weather
regime in which long summers and long growing seasons coincided
with a long wet cycle. But then, in the early fourteenth century, the
climate shifted again, ending the Warm Period. A global cooling
period, the Little Ice Age, brought unpredictable rainfall, droughts,
and cold spells, forcing people to recalibrate their expectations. The
Little Ice Age ushered in a world where almost everything had to be
smaller: harvests, markets, settlements, mounds, alliances, and ambitions. The Mississippian world became more local and equal; having
failed to bring rains and sustain prosperity, the priestly elite lost its
authority. But the world also became more violent as people scattered,
seeking new resources and attachments in new places. A megaflood
may have brought about the final abandonment of Cahokia in the
mid-fourteenth century, but the great city had already been in decline
for several generations. Cahokia's fading was symptomatic: by the
time of its final abandonment, every other major Mississippian city
lay vacant. All across the eastern half of the continent, people seem
to have rejected the domineering priestly class for more collective and
egalitarian social arrangements.[11]

———

A PARALLEL SEQUENCE of instability and adaptation unfolded in the continent's West. A severe drought in the Chaco Canyon region forced the abandonment of Pueblo Bonito around 1130 CE. Facing harvest failures and famine, many Ancestral Puebloans deserted their villages and great houses and moved south, gradually forging new identities as Hopis, Zunis, and Pueblos along the Rio Grande valley. Others migrated north to the Mesa Verde region, where, in a remarkably creative burst, they carved a new civilization out of an unforgiving rocky landscape. Drawing on their long-standing engineering expertise, they constructed multiroom houses and stone palaces featuring dozens of rooms, several underground kivas, and towers on high alcoves beneath protruding cliffs. They refitted their hydrologic technologies to the dry desert conditions and adopted terrace farming, which relied on check dams to capture natural runoff and retain topsoil for corn, beans, and squash. Twenty thousand people may have lived in the Mesa Verde region in the thirteenth century.[12]

As in the East, however, the onset of the Little Ice Age triggered a series of changes that ultimately fractured these early agricultural societies. As the land yielded less and less, and as the traditional systems of authority and hierarchy crumbled, people dispersed. The Hohokam people abandoned most of their adobe villages and irrigation works in the Salt River valley after successive environmental upheavals: a severe, generation-long drought in the late thirteenth century, followed by a protracted period of sparse and erratic rainfall, fueling both internal and external violence. The Hohokams did not disappear; they shifted shape, transforming into a smaller group that would later become the Tohono O'odham people.[13]

Farther south, the Mogollon people seem to have reacted to the changing conditions earlier and more decisively. Sometime in the late twelfth century, a new city, Paquimé, rose south of the Rio Grande in the foothills of the Sierra Madre Occidental range. Surrounded by several wide rivers, Paquimé quickly emerged as a major commercial and political center commanding a hinterland of some ten thousand people living in hundreds of settlements. Its builders were corn farmers, hydrologic engineers, and traders, and they built a new adobe-walled city,

An aerial photograph of Pueblo Bonito

ceremonial mounds, ball courts, and a two-thousand-room apartment complex that bore a resemblance to Ancestral Puebloan architecture.[14]

Paquimé arose in the transitional belt where North America becomes Mesoamerica, embodying one of the greatest turning points in the history of the Americas. North America was diverging from the rest of the Western Hemisphere. Elsewhere the historical momentum was toward greater concentrations of power, monumental ceremonial centers, and cities, and nations of many thousands persisted, reaching apogees in the major Mayan city-state of Chichén Itzá in northern Yucatán, the Inca Empire that extended more than two thousand miles north–south along western South America, and in the fifteenth-century city of Teotihuacán in the Valley of Mexico, home to 150,000 people and ruled by an Aztec emperor and high priests. By then, Cahokia's ruins were already covered by grass.[15]

IF THE LITTLE ICE AGE posed daunting challenges to North America's agricultural societies, it was a boon for the continent's hunters. The cool and wet conditions favored buffalo and grama grasses, the

Paquimé today

bison's preferred forage, and the springs were wet, supporting crucial early growth of grass after the winter's deprivations. Now the sole surviving species of megafauna, the supremely adaptable and prolific bison faced no serious competitors, and the herds expanded their range all the way from the Rocky Mountain foothills to hundreds of miles east of the Mississippi River, and from the subarctic to the Gulf of Mexico. And where bison herds thinned out, thriving deer herds took over, their domain covering much of the eastern half of the continent.

The majority of North American Indians became generalists who farmed, hunted, and gathered to sustain themselves. Instead of striving to maximize agricultural output—an aspiration that had animated Ancestral Puebloans, Cahokians, and other early farming societies—they sought stability, security, and solidarity. Instead of priestly rulers, they preferred leaders whose principal obligation was to maintain consensus and support participatory political systems. Power flowed *through* the leaders, not from them. Most North Americans lived in villages rather than cities. Ancestral Pawnees, Arikaras, Mandans, and Hidatsas were typical. They settled along the upper Missouri Valley, where capillary action drew groundwater to the surface. They lived in dome-shaped earth-lodge villages that housed hundreds rather than thousands. They were horticulturists and built fortifications only rarely. This sweeping retreat from hierarchies, elite dominance, and large-scale urbanization may have turned North America—along with Australia—into the world's most egalitarian continent at the time.[16]

The collective mindset that prevailed, reflecting broad-based and carefully balanced economies, also distinguished North America's Indigenous peoples. The continental grasslands—the Great Plains— were teeming with tens of millions of buffalo. Huge herds blackened the flat plains to the horizon, pulling humans in. The Shoshones moved east from the Great Basin, the Blackfoot came from the northeast, and the Crows, Omahas, Poncas, and Kansas abandoned their villages and fields along the Missouri Valley. The Kiowas migrated south from the upper Yellowstone Valley and forged an alliance with the resident Apaches. Former farmers did not give up tilling, but all of them now hunted bison, surrounding them in large communal hunts and felling them with spears and arrows, chasing them into concealed corrals in riverbeds, or driving them over cliffs to their deaths. In the Black Hills, hunters stampeded bison herds, driving the panicked animals into a corridor marked by stones that channeled the beasts toward a buffalo jump, a steep sinkhole where the high fall did the killing. The Blackfoot called the method of buffalo-jumping *pis'kun*, or "deep blood-kettle," and the Blackfoot word for their main jump site translates to "head smashed in," after an incident in which buffalo falling from sixty feet above had crushed a young hunter. The site had been used for thousands of years, and tens of thousands of bison had been killed, butchered, and processed for food, tools, and clothing. There may have been hundreds of buffalo jumps across the Great Plains.[17]

As the second millennium approached its midpoint, nearly every corner of North America was inhabited or used by humans. People had studied, selected, and perfected seeds, and they had harnessed rivers and streams to carve gardens out of the desert. They had learned how to properly appeal to the spirits, lacing their mastery over the world with humility, and they had imagined new ways to harvest the plant and animal bounty around them. For their labors they had been amply rewarded. Their communities were prosperous and growing in numbers, and they were spreading beyond their core territories, filling in the vacant spaces between them. The continent was home to approximately five million people.[18]

In North America, leaders were not autocrats commanding and coercing subjects. They were instead arbitrators and facilitators striving for consensus. They did not seek to maximize personal power; they sought to maximize the number of their followers. Good leaders were poor. They accepted trade goods and gifts from allies, but to govern effectively they had to redistribute most of the goods among their people. Their reward was loyalty and expansive networks of fictive kinship that could extend to numerous allied nations. With few exceptions, this became the norm in North America. Kinship—an all-pervasive sense of relatedness and mutual obligations—became the central organizing principle for human life. Kinship was the crucial adhesive that kept people and nations linked together. It would be a mistake to see this adaptation as some kind of a failure or aberration of civilization, as European newcomers almost invariably did. North American Indians had experimented with ranked societies and all-powerful spiritual leaders and had found them deficient and dangerous. They had opted for more horizontal, participatory, and egalitarian ways of being in the world—a communal ethos available to everyone who was capable of proper thoughts and deeds and willing to share their possessions. Their ideal society was a boundless commonwealth that could be—at least in theory—extended to outsiders, infinitely.

Chapter 3

BLIND
CONQUESTS

A CROSS AN OCEAN, MIRRORING NORTH AMERICA'S trajectory, peoples and nations had lived through two weather regimes, enjoying startling opportunities during the Warm Period starting in the tenth century and then struggling to adjust to the diminishing prospects of the Little Ice Age from the twelfth century onward. The transitions were particularly acute on the peninsula that formed the western tip of the Eurasian landmass.

Europe, a vaguely defined geographical area, had formed the northern part of the sprawling Roman Empire, which dominated nearly all the lands around the Mediterranean Sea by 117 CE. When the overstretched Romans began to weaken during the third century under pressure by Germanic migrations from the east, Byzantium emerged as the dominant power in the Mediterranean. Power and commerce shifted east, and Europe was relegated to a neglected periphery of little importance.

As Rome shrank back into the small city-state it had once been, the gaping power vacuum it left behind was filled by hundreds of small fiefdoms. Europe languished as an atomistic world until the tenth century, when the climate began to warm up. Western European farmers adopted a three-field system in which two fields were cultivated while only one was left fallow. It was one of the most important developments in European history, catapulting the continent toward increasing wealth and significance. Ruthless warlords built private armies of heavily armed horsemen and staked out vast personal fiefdoms. Land was controlled by the few, and local peasants were reduced to serfs, agricultural laborers bound to a lord's estate. In return, they received the protection of lords and their knights against Vikings, Muslims, and local thugs. War was glorified as a holy affair suffused with notions of duty, honor, and loyalty. As in Cahokia and elsewhere in North America, common people fell under a select cadre of holy men who mobilized them to construct towering structures that glorified the otherworldly—and its servants on Earth.[1]

The parallels between the two continents would not last, however. In the 1330s, the royal houses of France and England clashed over the right to the French throne, the start of a draining on-again, off-again war that seemed to drag on forever. Professional armies replaced feudal armies led by local warlords, and the costs of warfare soared, forcing monarchs and their courts to innovate. The French and English crowns both devised more efficient ways to wage and finance war by levying new taxes, imposing tariffs, and expanding the traditional royal cabinets into nascent state bureaucracies. By the close of the war in 1453—when England relinquished its claims on the continent—both kingdoms were well on their way to becoming fiscal-military states led by powerful rulers, capable of raising vast armies, and animated by religious piety. A new nexus of power developed around monarchs and merchants, as well as among courts, cities, and clergy. Rulers granted trade privileges to cities, and cities pledged loyalty to sovereigns, their protectors. Cities were the great economic engines of the incipient nation-states in western Europe, bustling with business, innovations, unprecedented wealth, and soaring ambitions. By the late fifteenth century, France and England possessed the means and organizational capacity for overseas expansion.[2]

Unexpectedly, however, it was Spain—perhaps the weakest of the western European kingdoms—that planted the first meaningful colonial outposts in the Western Hemisphere. In the early eighth century, Muslims from North Africa had crossed over to the Iberian Peninsula, clashing with the locals and, gradually, over several centuries, shoving them farther and farther to the north. Christendom retreated in the face of people it considered infidels, endangering the entire continent. Iberian Christian kingdoms launched the Reconquista almost immediately after the first Muslim forays, but it progressed slowly. Decisive victories finally came in the thirteenth century, when Christian forces conquered the great Muslim strongholds of Córdoba and Seville. Granada, the last Muslim enclave in the peninsula, became a tributary state of the kingdom of Castile.[3]

Spearheaded by the Iberian kingdoms, Christendom had prevailed against a colossal Islamic challenge—a triumph that quickly transformed into a forceful outward expansion of western Europe beyond its terrestrial confines, with the Spanish leading the way. Their centuries-long Reconquista had refined their fighting skills, instilling their society with a potent martial spirit, and elevating the soldier-gentleman into the higher echelons of social hierarchy. The Spanish conquered the Canary Islands off the coast of West Africa in the fifteenth century, gaining a foothold in the Atlantic, along with an education in overseas colonialism and subjugation of non-European and non-Muslim peoples. The Canaries belonged to the Guanche people from North Africa, who mounted a forceful resistance against Spanish colonization, only to succumb to alien European germs. The few survivors were sold into slavery on the Portuguese island of Madeira and in Spain. The lessons in cruelty and brutality that they learned in the Canaries would serve Spanish adventurers well in the "New World" that was about to appear to them.[4]

In 1474, Paolo dal Pozzo Toscanelli, a Florentine astrologer and cartographer, produced his masterwork: a map that showed the western extremes of Europe and northwestern Africa, a slice of East Asia, and "Oceanus Occidentalis"— the Atlantic Ocean—in between. Like all mapmakers, Toscanelli wanted to show facts and formations, but when facts became scarce, imagination took over. He placed Cipangu, the "land of the rising sun"—Marco Polo's name for Japan—in the northwest corner of Mesoamerica. West of Cipangu, Toscanelli's map showed Cathay (China), also directly reachable across the ocean from Europe. The Western Hemisphere was absent; in its stead Toscanelli planted a cluster of phantom islands that were mere legends.

Toscanelli's remarkable map captured the imagination of an experienced Genoese mariner, emboldening him to propose to the Portuguese court in 1484 an unprecedented exploration voyage: he would sail west—not south around Africa, as others had tried—to reach India, China, Japan, and the fabled gold and Spice Islands of the East

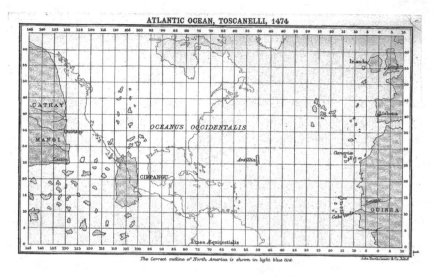

Paolo dal Pozzo Toscanelli's 1474 map of the Atlantic Ocean

Indies. His scheme was promptly rebuffed as absurd. Columbus then tried his luck with Queen Isabel and King Ferdinand of Castile and Aragon, only to be rejected again. But after Granada, the last Muslim city in Iberia, fell to Spain in January 1492, the Spanish monarchs, alarmed by Portuguese advances along the African coast and toward the Canaries, agreed to fund the outlandish enterprise. Christopher Columbus, a self-taught cosmographer of humble origins, had his commission to sail into the unknown, where, in classic Reconquista style, he could claim immense possessions for himself and his sponsors. Led by Spain, western Europe was turning away from the perilous Mediterranean and toward the Atlantic and its untapped riches. But it was an almost blind venture. Expecting very little from the idiosyncratic mariner, Isabel and Fernando promised that he would be admiral and viceroy and governor of any lands he encountered and would hold those titles "from successor to successor forever and always." Not least, and of more immediate interest, Columbus would also receive a tenth of the net yield of the treasures he took.[5]

IN THE FALL OF 1492, the Taínos, an Indigenous people who dominated much of the Caribbean, spotted three curious vessels approaching the coast. As the newcomers landed, the Taínos, a sea-going people and wide-ranging traders, seemed to welcome them as an addition to their hierarchical network. The Taínos were organized into five stratified societies led by paramount caciques (kings), and the strangers could be slotted in as junior allies.

Columbus and his crew of eighty-eight had arrived in what he thought was the East Indies. Although he was relieved to find land—the voyage had taken longer than expected after a stopover in the Canaries—the people he now encountered were disappointing. They welcomed the exhausted Spanish with gifts and food, hoping to turn the strangers into kin, but they lived in seemingly modest villages that contained none of the treasures—gold, silver, spices, silk—that Columbus and his party sought. Appalled, Columbus enslaved the Taínos. He was convinced that the Indians thought the Spanish had descended from the heavens, probably mistaking their awe of the Spanish vessels and metal tools as reverence. He named the land—an island, he soon discovered—San Salvador and claimed it for Spain.[6]

Unknowingly, Columbus had brought together two parts of humankind that had been separated by oceans for several millennia. The Indigenous inhabitants may have appeared utterly alien and inferior to the Spanish, but the two sapiens contingents were genetically identical. All of their meaningful differences were cultural. Columbus may have been disillusioned, but he knew what he, a good European, should do. He came from a society where one's position was determined largely by birth. One found purpose in preaching, fighting, or serving others. For Columbus and his contemporaries, there was little doubt where the Taínos belonged in that order. To Spanish eyes, they were primitive heathens living on an isolated island, and thus familiar: Spanish soldier-mariners had subdued similar people in the Canary Islands only a few decades earlier. The conquest of the Canaries had served as a laboratory of overseas imperialism, educating the Spanish in how to make strangers subjects, even slaves. Obsessed with gold, Columbus spent weeks in the West Indies hunting for it, and along the way he began to distinguish between good Indians and bad Indians. Good Indians were meek and made docile servants; bad Indians resisted Spanish demands and fought back. Good Indians

*Engraving by Theodore de Bry, 1594, depicting Christopher Columbus
receiving gifts from the cacique, or "king," in Hispaniola*

could be converted; bad Indians should be enslaved. Columbus had
given Spain a blueprint for a New World empire. After sailing back
to Spain to secure royal support, he returned to America a year later
with fifteen caravels, two smaller vessels, and fifteen hundred men.
He had identified a new resource, and the Spanish promptly enslaved
sixteen hundred Indians.[7]

Columbus and the Spanish conquistadors who followed in his
wake found the American tropics strangely welcoming. The American tropics were healthy and hospitable—one of the upshots of the
Little Ice Age, and the conquistadors tore through Española, Puerto
Rico, Jamaica, and Cuba within a decade, seeking the ever-elusive
Spice Islands but eventually settling on hoarding gold and slaves.
Extraordinary beasts and technologies—horses, guns, and steel—
coupled with a deep-rooted tradition of violent conquest, brought
galvanizing military victories for the newcomers. Yet it was the diseases the Europeans carried in their bodies—smallpox, measles,
influenza, and others—that made possible the wholesale subjuga-

tion of the Greater Antilles, ripping through unexposed Indigenous populations with lethal efficiency. Military imperialism coupled with biological imperialism caused the first Native American population catastrophe. Hundreds of thousands of people perished, and most of the survivors were enslaved as heathens without rights. Clamoring for quick profits, the Spanish were thorough. On Española's "pearl coast" they forced enslaved Native divers to make life-threatening descents to gather pearls. Soon the Spanish found themselves presiding over islands that were nearly devoid of people. They continued to search for new opportunities, gradually realizing that they faced an unknown landmass that surrounded them on three sides. This was not what Toscanelli's map showed.[8]

An unwavering belief in Spanish superiority over the Indians, combined with a moral crusade to spread Christianity among the heathens, emboldened the Spanish newcomers. Already in 1493, Pope Alexander VI had granted America to Isabel and Ferdinand to rule over and convert Indians. A settlement in the eastern Caribbean that the Spanish called Isabela served as a staging area for inland entradas, and these expeditions soon revealed a new ocean—the Pacific—extending into the eastern horizon. It was becoming clear that there was no direct passage to Asia from the Atlantic; whatever treasures there were to be won would have to be found in this odd new world. Spain changed course. In 1502, Nicolás de Ovando's fleet of thirty vessels and twenty-five hundred settlers launched the colonization of the Americas by landing on an island they called Santo Domingo. As if by fate, exploration and Native informants soon revealed the existence of prosperous Indigenous empires not too far into the interior of the continent. The gold-hungry conquistadors now had their new targets, which turned out to be astoundingly vulnerable. Small groups of Spanish soldiers would be able to carve out a prodigious empire in less than twenty years.[9]

STARTING IN 1519, Spanish conquistadors invaded the fabulously wealthy Mesoamerican Indigenous empires with small but heavily armed forces. Hernán Cortés conquered Tenochtitlán, the seat of the Aztec Empire, with thirteen hundred men, having destroyed his ships after making landfall to ensure that his men would not abandon him. Cortés founded the *encomienda* system, a modified version of European feudalism, which awarded subdued Native communities to individual conquistadors to govern and profit from. His brash incursion, mightily assisted by smallpox and Indigenous allies, had created New Spain, a distinctly Hispanic realm superimposed on a preexisting imperial Indigenous bedrock. Ten years later, inspired by Cortés's feat, Francisco Pizarro marched with a small posse of soldiers into the heart of the Inca Empire, trekking along the steep Inca highways and shocking the empire's foot soldiers with his cavalry. Pizarro captured Atahualpa, the Sapa Inca, ruler of the Inca Empire. By 1550, what the Spanish called Peru had yielded them more than eighty tons of gold and silver and billions of calories drawn from the large, terraced fields of potatoes, quinoa, and corn. Like Cortés, Pizarro had succeeded by placing himself atop a preexisting network of workers, vassals, and wealth.[10]

In the 1550s, roughly half a century after Columbus's landing, Spain seemed primed for hemispheric dominance. A distinctive form of Spanish colonization had emerged, drawn from the experience of the Reconquista and the appropriation of the Canary Islands. Spanish colonization received an enormous boost from what has become known as the Columbian Exchange, the widespread transfer of people, animals, plants, ideas, technology, and diseases among the Americas, Europe, and West Africa. Far more Indians died of European diseases than of European bullets and steel. The Spanish crown held its American colonies in an iron grip, imposing its hierarchical system of government on the colonies and carefully controlling the planning, pace, and practice of colonization. Spain's American empire was to be an empire of towns that each helped oversee political, social, and religious life under the supervision of an *adelantado*, a nobleman serving his sovereign. New Spain would be a stratified multiracial empire of a single language (Castilian), a single faith (Roman Catholicism), and a single ruler (the Spanish monarch), governed from the mother country through a robust bureaucracy of local administrators. A highly effective transportation system of annual and heavily armed fleets transported stolen wealth—silver, gold, pearls, sugar, salt, hides, and slaves—into Spain, fueling further colonial ambitions.[11]

Enjoying nearly complete control of the Caribbean shoreline, Spain began shifting from violent colonial expansion—always an unpredictable enterprise—to bureaucratic colonial governing. Suddenly, at this early stage, there was room for dissenting voices such as that of the Dominican friar Bartolomé de Las Casas, who condemned the Spanish atrocities against Native Americans in the early sixteenth century and advocated a softer form of colonialism, prompting King Charles V of Spain to enact the 1542 *New Laws of the Indies for the Good Treatment of the Indians*, which regulated the encomienda system and outlawed Indian slavery.[12]

As the sixteenth century inched toward its midpoint, Spain had become the world's most powerful nation, the annual silver fleets from America sustaining its might in Europe and beyond. But then its expansionist momentum began to fade. Forging a New World empire had been made remarkably easy by war-horses, steel, gunpowder, and diseases: great Indigenous empires fell like dominoes in the face of small conquistador armies, yielding massive quantities of silver and gold. Spain had won a prodigious New World empire with minimal investments and losses, and a sense of complacency set in. There were smaller, poorer, and harder-to-access Mesoamerican realms to subjugate and plunder, but the Spanish had grown used to quick and huge profits; the more modest and isolated realms did not seem worth the trouble. Increasingly ambitious Spanish began gazing north for new opportunities. They thought they had plenty of time. While the Spanish toppled mighty Indigenous empires, the French and English, preoccupied with each other, were just gearing up to explore the rest of America to the north. They would be disappointed.

PART TWO

APPEAR AT A DISTANCE LIKE GIANTS

(the long sixteenth century)

Chapter 4

TERRA NULLIUS

THEY SPOTTED THE THREE VESSELS APPROACHING from the blue, steadily gliding toward the shoreline. The Calusa Indians had learned about such things, and they knew what to expect. The men on those bulky ships were strangers from the south, where they had killed untold numbers of people and declared themselves masters of the few who survived. Usually their ships skirted Calusa land on their way out to the deep sea, but now they were coming straight toward them.

These were men who wanted everything the Calusas had: their land, their treasure, their labor, their souls. The Calusas knew exactly what to do with them. Despite the lethal epidemics, enslavement, and mass killings, the Caribbean basin was still an Indigenous space thickly webbed by trade and diplomatic networks that disseminated information fast and wide. The Calusas allowed the boats to slip near the coastline before releasing a cascade of arrows. The attack shocked the Spanish; this was not how the Indians were supposed to act in the face of guns, iron weapons, and carracks. The leader of the small fleet was Juan Ponce de León, a veteran of Columbus's second voyage to America in 1493. He had done very well for himself in the New World, having crushed an uprising of Taíno people in the Greater Antilles and claimed Puerto Rico for the Spanish crown, which rewarded him in 1508 with the governorship of the island. Puerto Rico's sugar, gold, and Indian slaves had made Ponce de León stupendously rich. Although the Calusas knew what to expect, Ponce de León knew very little about the land and people he meant to seize through the doctrine of *terra nullius*, "empty land" or "no-man's-land." In reality, Florida was home to some 350,000 Indians.[1]

European nations refused to acknowledge Indigenous sovereignty, because they saw the Native Americans as savages and believed that the Indians did not use the land properly; they did not improve it with intensive farming, leaving it devoid of civilization. Ponce de León did not know that the twenty-thousand-strong Calusas commanded a vast territory and numerous tributary villages that spread out for hundreds of miles, as well as massive watercourts made from shells and sediment to catch fish and other aquatic wealth. Their seat of power was an immense structure that accommodated two thousand people. After the conquest of Mesoamerica, the Spanish considered Florida, the "Land of Flowers," a low-hanging fruit. Taken aback by the determined Indigenous resistance he met, Ponce de León beat a hasty retreat to Puerto Rico in 1514. The Spanish labeled their vanquishers *gente de color quebrado,* "people of broken color."

Nothing if not stubborn, Ponce de León tried again in 1521, leading his second entrada, consisting of two hundred colonists, to the same spot on Florida's Gulf coast. He ordered his men to build houses. They did not finish a single one. The Calusas mobilized immediately, and a fierce battle erupted. Ponce de León was struck by an arrow. He ordered a retreat to Cuba, where he soon died from the wound. In that same year, Alonso Álvarez de Piñeda traced the Gulf coast westward and then southward, discovering the mouth of the Mississippi River and determining that Florida was not an island but a peninsula attached to a landmass of unknown size.[2]

Viewed from the Spanish domains in the Caribbean basin and Mexico, the northern lands appeared promising targets for new colonial ventures. In 1497, Giovanni Caboto, a Venetian mariner in the service of the English crown, landed at a spot on this unknown landform to the north, revealing to Europeans that it was, in fact, a new continent. The Caribbean islands had lost their luster to the conquistadors, who called the Bahamas *las islas inútiles,* "useless islands," because there was no gold or pearls. Spanish ambitions turned north, where untapped reservoirs of minerals, slaves, and converts appeared to await them. Geography itself seemed to invite them in. The breadth of Mesoamerica seemed to offer unrestricted access into the heart of the continent, while the Florida peninsula bulged deep into the Caribbean Sea like an enormous land bridge. By the second decade of the sixteenth century, Spanish slavers were pushing to the north, reaping staggering profits. Native slaves had become scarce on the Caribbean sugar islands, where more than twenty years of enslaving and disease epidemics had brought about a demographic collapse, whereas the Indians to the north were taller, stronger, and seemingly inexhaustible as commodities. Some slavers thought of them as giants.[3]

Geography channeled Spanish colonization northward also in another way: by the early 1520s, exploration had revealed that there was no water passage to Asia from the Caribbean. Impatient conquistadors redirected their ambitions to the northern continent, which appeared to be free of the obstacles they had faced in the tropics: extreme heat, odd maladies, steep mountain ranges, and impenetrable jungles. They began to push in. A generation of exploration and colonization had taught the Spanish that although the coasts might yield few riches, the interior was likely to offer plenty. Florida also seemed to be thinly populated; the Spanish did not know that infectious diseases had cut Florida's Indigenous population by hundreds of thousands within two generations.[4]

In 1528, seven years after Ponce de León's death by a Calusa arrow, Pánfilo de Narváez, who had conquered Cuba in 1511, appeared on the scene. He had lobbied energetically in Seville and succeeded magnificently: the Council of the Indies had authorized him to colonize Florida, the northern Gulf coast, and the lands to the west all the way to the Pacific. If Narváez were successful, his holdings would eclipse Cortés's enormous fiefdom in Mexico. Boasting five ships, eighty horses, some four hundred sailor-soldiers, ten women, several African slaves, and five Franciscan brothers, Narváez's new venture was Spain's most ambitious attempt to occupy, civilize, and purify North America so far.[5]

It also turned out to be one of the most incompetent. Narváez's destination was the Rio de las Palmas on the western Gulf coast, but

Jacques le Moyne's drawing depicting Athore,
son of the Timucuan chief Saturiwa

the Gulf Stream, the world's strongest ocean current, sent the ships hundreds of miles off target: the Spanish landed on Florida's west coast, where they sighted a Native town of the Timucuas. The Indians fled, and Narváez claimed their land for Spain. A reconnaissance party captured four Indians, who told the Spanish of a distant province, controlled by the Apalachee people, where there was much gold. North American Indians had learned what fueled Spanish ambitions. Narváez split his force in two, one contingent following the coast on foot with horses, the other sailing near it, and both heading toward the Rio de las Palmas in Tamaulipas, where they would unite. They never did. The sea party soon lost contact with the overland party and realized that the Rio de las Palmas was hundreds of miles away. They waited a year for the overland party to emerge before giving up and heading to Cuba.[6]

In the meantime, the land-bound contingent had shifted from a colonial venture to a much older Indigenous script. They were only ninety miles away from Cuba, but lacking ships, they might as well have been on the other side of the world. Led by Narváez and his second-in-command, Álvar Núñez Cabeza de Vaca, a nobleman and the royal treasurer of the expedition, some three hundred Spanish and a few Africans marched northwest toward Apalachee country, navigating hot swamps, torrential rivers, and cynical Indians who urged them to move ahead by telling them the riches were that way. Their conquistador fantasies crumbling, the Spanish reached the Apalachees in June and attacked the first village they saw, taking its women and children as hostages. The town leader offered to take the place of the hostages, becoming a hostage himself.[7]

Apalachee country, however, was no Aztec or Inca Empire on top of which the conquistadors could plant themselves as rulers. Instead of hoarding riches, they were reduced to scouring for food while fending off Indians who, according to Cabeza de Vaca, made "continual war upon us, wounding our people and horses at the places where they went to drink water." The captured Native leader portrayed Apalachee country as a poor and sparsely populated realm, while in reality it was a thriving nation of tens of thousands. He urged the newcomers to head to the coast, where, he said, they would find plenty of corn, beans, and fish in a town called Aute. Narváez swallowed the bait.[8]

Apalachee soldiers prepared an ambush in a deep lagoon, where, upon arrival of the Spanish, they released a shower of arrows. Cabeza de Vaca was shocked by the power and accuracy of the Native bowmen, who "appear at a distance like giants" and could send an arrow through an elm tree. Here, in trackless swamps and inlets, the Indians neutralized Spain's technological advantages through superior mobility and creative use of the terrain. The conquistadors made it to the shore, but they had become dangerously weakened. Depleted, they were exposed to viruses, and soon a third of them were sick. They fled on makeshift rafts, desperate to escape the arrows of the local Indians; when they landed on the west coast of Florida, Camone Indians promptly killed them. A gust pushed Narváez's raft into the open sea, leaving him stranded. He died from dehydration, with a panoramic view of his vast paper holdings, which he would never rule.[9]

The surviving conquistadors posed no threat to Native peoples. Now gunless, horseless, and weak, they simply became useful. Cabeza de Vaca became the embodiment of this reduced status. He still had forty men, and they were kindly received by the Capoque and Han

Indians, who fed and healed them. This was the flip side of Indigenous territoriality: outsiders who acted weak and asked to be pitied were likely to be embraced as allies and kin. The surviving castaways became workers. It was a humiliating role reversal, the would-be conquistadors reduced to hauling firewood, carrying water, and digging roots. Cabeza de Vaca reinvented himself as a trader, a role that won him one of the most precious rights an unfree person could have in the Americas: mobility. For the next several years, with three compatriots, including a freed African slave named Estebanico, he operated as a merchant among various Indigenous nations. Cabeza de Vaca assumed the role of a holy man and a healer in an attempt to capitalize on European medical knowledge. For two years the foursome he had assembled traveled along Indigenous roads, visiting Native villages, receiving food, shelter, and escorts from the Indians; they may well have been more entertaining and less extraordinary to their hosts than they liked to believe, however. The four men eventually resolved to move south toward Mexico City, where they arrived in the summer of 1536.[10]

The story of Cabeza de Vaca and his fellow castaways is the story of North America's early colonization in microcosm. The four survivors' improbable journey out of Florida became both a lure and a lesson for prospective colonists. It illuminated a previously obscure continent full of riches and potential subjects, but it also introduced North America as an Indigenous continent thoroughly suffused with human presence—even after many disease outbreaks—and made it clear that newcomers who failed to obey Indigenous rules would have no place in it. Cabeza de Vaca had accepted this reality and was rewarded with kinship and belonging. His pliant immersion offered an alternative, however frail, to the ruthless methods of Cortés, Pizarro, and other European conquerors whose tactics stemmed from the centuries-long Reconquista. When Cabeza de Vaca reported what he had seen, he inadvertently triggered a flurry of invasions into North America. He made only modest claims about northern riches, but a distinctly Spanish idea about the New World, inspired by Cortés and Pizarro's startling coups, had set in. Just beyond the horizon, the Spanish believed, wealthy civilizations awaited discovery.

THE NEW SURGE OF Spanish colonization was a curious blend of the methodical and the fantastical. Within a year of his conquest of the Aztec Empire in 1521, the boundlessly ambitious Cortés was pouring his staggering riches into the construction of a fleet that would scour the North American Pacific coast for golden Indigenous cities and, at the same time, search for the elusive passage through the continent from the Atlantic to the Pacific Ocean. His entradas generated little wealth but plenty of geographical and practical knowledge: the Spanish learned that Baja California was a peninsula and that Asia and North America were two distinct continents. They also learned that the coastal Indians did not take kindly to strangers who intruded into their fisheries and would fight to protect them. There was little gold, and the trope of a poor and primitive continent took root. That false image would embolden and haunt European colonists for centuries.[11]

In 1538, Antonio de Mendoza, the viceroy of New Spain, sent two men—Estebanico, the Black slave who had made his way to Mexico City with Cabeza de Vaca and won his freedom, and Marcos de Niza, a widely traveled Franciscan friar known as Fray Marcos—to explore the lands that Cabeza de Vaca had traversed a few years earlier. The Indians they encountered on this new venture spoke of a place called Cíbola, and of magnificent beasts and riches farther north. Estebanico pushed ahead to Cíbola, which sat in exposed mesa lands near the upper Rio Grande valley. Cíbola's citizens denied the uninvited stranger entry, housing him outside the city without food and water. When Estebanico approached the city's leaders the next day, the Indians killed him. Fray Marcos confronted—from a distance—Cíbola's Zuni leaders, who were indifferent to his pleas. Fray Marcos warned, or so he reported, that "Our Lord would chastise Cibola." He was told that "no one can withstand the power of Cibola." Unmoved, Marcos approached the town himself, but he dared not enter. Unsure what to do, he made a stack of stones and placed a little cross on top of it and left. He returned to Mexico City with stories of beasts whose massive horns forced them to graze sideways and of Cíbola, a city bigger than Mexico City itself, yet merely one of seven of its kind. In March 1540,

Mendoza, now intrigued, dispatched his protégé, Francisco Vázquez de Coronado, to lead an expedition of three hundred Spanish soldiers, more than one thousand Native "allies," six Franciscans, and about fifteen hundred horses and pack animals. Fray Marcos was to lead them to "grander towns" where people "ate out of golden dishes."[12]

The youngest of six brothers, Coronado was highly motivated; his chances of inheriting land in Spain were slim. After traveling on Indian trails for nearly five months, the party finally reached Cíbola. It was a typical Pueblo Indian town. "This distressed the men-at-arms not a little [especially] when they saw that everything the friar had said [to be] the opposite," Coronado reported. He sent Marcos back to Mexico City with a letter that branded him a liar, then sacked the town. The Pueblos, successors of the Anasazi civilization, thought the Spanish were evil *kachinas*, spirits without reason. Desperate for riches and glory, Coronado dispatched search parties in all directions and established a winter camp on the Rio Grande among the Pueblos, who quickly grew disgusted with the greedy strangers. The Indians tried to chase out the interlopers, and the Spanish sacked another thirteen towns in retaliation. Rather than allowing the fleeing Indians to escape, the Spanish tracked them down and burned them at the stake. The war would last into the spring of 1541.[13]

In the winter of 1540, an Indian had approached Coronado at Albuquerque, the largest of the Zuni pueblos near the edge of the bison-filled grasslands, and told him about Quivira, a fabulously rich kingdom deep in the interior of the continent. The story told by the Indian, whom the Spanish called El Turco, bordered on the absurd: "fishes as big as horses, and large numbers of very big canoes, with more than 20 rowers on a side," and a lord who napped "under a great tree on which were hung a great number of little gold bells"—a North American Tenochtitlán. In early July of 1540, the expedition came to Hawikuh, an ordinary Zuni mud and adobe structure on the Little Colorado River, and prepared to seize it. The Zunis sprinkled a line of holy cornmeal between the strangers and their town. Undeterred, the Spanish crossed the line, and the Zunis fired arrows. The Spanish occupied the town. They demanded food and clothing, burned at least thirteen other towns, raped Pueblo women, and set war dogs after resisting Pueblos. By now, El Turco knew the Spanish newcomers for what they were: organized looters obsessed with precious metals and rich Indigenous empires. Most likely knowing what awaited him, he led the Spanish hundreds of miles northeast across immense grasslands into a modest Wichita Indian village. Coronado realized that El Turco had lured them "to a place where our horses would starve to death." Under torture, El Turco confessed that he had brought the Spanish into the deep interior to kill them by thirst. Coronado had him immediately garroted.[14]

Coronado's entrada was Spain's most ambitious expedition into North America so far, and it was a dismal failure. Its ending could hardly have been more emblematic: Coronado fell off his horse, suffering an injury that left him permanently debilitated. He cut his losses and traced his steps back to the Rio Grande valley to winter among the Pueblos. The Pueblos' decentralized political system baffled him. There was no principal leader to capture and replace; he did not know whom to attack. His plan for a New World empire shattered, he returned to Mexico City, but he left behind two Franciscans to minister to the Pueblos. The Pueblos killed them. In Mexico City, Coronado faced an official inquiry into his actions but was exonerated. An ailing and broken man, he may have benefited from the court's pity. In 1542–43, Spain passed "New Laws" to reduce the abuse of Indians.[15]

Indigenous resistance and enormous distances were turning North America into a dead end for the Spanish Empire. Its conquistadors may have still been fearsome, holding a vast technological edge over the Indians. They continued to march into Native settlements, exuding confidence and demanding submission. Yet their conquests were fleeting, failing to create substantial colonial realms like Española or Mexico. Colonial expansion by the Spanish was slow partly because of simple logistics. Spain had become a global power by sending annual fleets of dozens of vessels into the Americas, which tethered the Spanish Empire to its ports, making land expansion a daunting proposition. Distances were vast, even with horses, and too many of the Native Americans were nomads and hard to pin down. Unlike Central and South America, North America was a poor target for Spain's ready-to-rule colonialism. Native misinformation thwarted one expedition after another. A cultural barrier also deterred conquest: most Native nations were at least partly matrilineal, with women heading the households and enjoying institutionalized authority. Such polities perplexed the conquistadors, who sought to fight and supplant male leaders. Decades of pillaging, terrorizing, and converting brought limited results; by the end of the sixteenth century, Spanish claims to the continent were tenuous at best. There would be no Spain-bound treasure fleets from North America.[16]

IT WAS NOT JUST that the Spanish had overstretched. North American Indians possessed numerous practical advantages over the European invaders: deep knowledge of the land and the environment, extensive networks of allies, and flexible political systems that enabled fast mobilizations against approaching threats, whether Indigenous or European. Perhaps most crucially, Native Americans relied on highly successful agriculture that sustained large numbers of people, thriving and well-protected riverside towns, and formidable armies.

Hernando de Soto was one of Spain's most accomplished officers when he landed on the west coast of Florida in the late spring of 1539 with a self-financed expedition of nine ships. Having arrived in America at the age of fourteen, he had amassed a fortune in stolen Inca treasures. Where Narváez had been utterly unprepared for the task of conquering Florida, Soto drew from the accumulated Spanish expertise in subjugating Native Americans in Mesoamerica. Known as an expert hunter of Indians, he brought iron chains and collars to move the human loot he would gather. Even his god seemed to favor him: upon landing, Soto found Juan Ortiz, a survivor of the Narváez expedition, who was living among the Indians, and contracted him as an interpreter.

An encounter at the town of Vitachuco on the Florida peninsula set the tone. The Spanish moved into the town and, meeting with resistance, took its physically imposing leader, Vitachuco, captive. After several days of forced travel, Vitachuco grasped Soto by the neck during a meal and knocked him unconscious. The Spanish killed Vitachuco on the spot. In northern Florida, the Apalachees burned their town before the Spanish could seize it, denying the savage newcomers any loot. Soto's column of more than six hundred soldiers, hundreds of Native porters, and hundreds of horses, mules, cows, hogs, and war dogs then marched north of Florida, adopting a northeasterly course that took them to the capital of the Cofitachequi Nation, which was rumored to be rich in gold, silver, and pearls. The Spanish reported finding twelve horse loads of pearls. They met the nation's leader, the "Lady of Cofitachequi," who arrived carried on a litter. She placed a pearl necklace around Soto's neck; unmoved, Soto took her captive.

Things looked promising for the Spanish adventurers, who believed they were moving toward greater wealth. They crossed the Appalachians—the first Europeans to do so—and followed a wildly meandering route through the continent's southeastern corner, taking hostages, ransacking food caches, torching settlements, and torturing and killing anyone who resisted. There was much to gain: the conquistadors had entered the heart of the still-thriving Mississippian civilization of Mound Builders, who lived in large, walled cities and traded in luxury goods. Influenced by Cortés's methods, Soto announced himself to the Natchez theocracy as "the son of the sun." A Natchez *mico*, "leader," asked him to show his power by drying up the river, silencing the presumptuous stranger. The Spanish moved on. By then, Soto's army was depleted, having been in the field for three years. They were much too far from the coast and effectively doomed. Soto fell ill. He died along the Mississippi River. But his ravages were not over: the disease that killed him may have triggered a pandemic among the southwestern Indians.[17]

Soto and other conquistadors believed they were conquering new lands for the Spanish Empire, but in reality, Indians were carefully steering the Europeans' course, sending them away with fantastical stories of treasures farther ahead. Eventually, the remaining members of Soto's entrada crossed the Mississippi and entered the territory of the Caddo Confederacy at the edge of the continental grasslands. The Caddos lived in multiple domains that featured towns, temple mounds, fields, and hunting grounds—each domain linked to others by closely monitored highways. The Caddos obeyed a ranked social system and built large ceremonial complexes in the tradition of

Cahokia. Their hereditary priests, *xinesi*, were self-consciously elite, but the xinesi's relationship with their people was intimate, and they consulted lesser leaders, *caddis*, seeking consensus. Men broke the soil, women planted the crops, and the xinesi performed the rituals that secured plentiful crops. Fueled by surplus grain, the Caddo trade network extended from the Mississippi Valley to Florida. The nation may have numbered more than a hundred thousand in total. When the Spanish arrived, Caddo border patrols escorted them away from their settlements into areas where they would get lost and die of hunger. Still three hundred strong, Soto's party had to leave Caddo country empty-handed.[18]

Indigenous resistance brought about a long lull in Spain's forays into the interior. A new effort did not get off the ground until the 1580s, when the Franciscan order launched a series of expeditions into what had become grandiosely known as New Mexico, which lay more than eight hundred miles north of the nearest Spanish colony. When they arrived, the Franciscans found that the Pueblos had little patience for Franciscan ideas about how they should conduct the most intimate aspects of their lives; the Pueblos had learned all they needed to know about the world from Corn Mother and Thought Woman, who had shared with them how to make the soil fertile, how to plant the sacred corn, and how to fulfill their purpose on Earth. Corn Mother had taught them how to build *kivas*, underground ceremonial centers that brought them closer to the spiritual underworld, where humans and corn had originated. Corn Mother had been good to them. The Pueblos had prospered, and they numbered more than two hundred thousand in the late sixteenth century.

Confident of their place in the world, both materially and spiritually, the Pueblos were not interested in strange deities. Frustrated Franciscans denounced Corn Mother and Thought Woman, and the disgusted Pueblos started killing the uninvited strangers who carried figures of their slain god everywhere. In response, the viceroy of New Spain sent Don Juan de Oñate, a Mexican-born conquistador whose mother descended from both Cortés and Montezuma, into Pueblo country to build missions at his own expense. Oñate led an entrada of ten Franciscan priests, five hundred colonists, seven hundred horses, and eighty carts up the Rio Grande in 1598. Despite the earlier Span-ish expeditions, he knew very little about the landlocked "New Mex-ico" he was to secure for Spain. His contract allowed him to bring two ships every year to deliver arms and mining tools to the inland colony he was determined to found.

The upriver journey was a protracted display of imperial bravado: Oñate stopped seven times to perform an elaborate ceremony that asserted Spanish dominion over each new region "from the leaves of the trees in the forests to the stones and sands of the river, and from the stones and sands of the river to the leaves in the forests." To dramatize the Indians' submission, he had their emissaries dress like the Span-ish and gave Spanish names to the Native towns he passed through. With the friars positioned around him, Oñate read to each new group of Native leaders the *Requirimiento*, a treatise that explained how omnipotent authority and jurisdiction flowed from God to Jesus to the pope, and to the king of Spain, who had sent Oñate to bring the Indians into the Christian commonwealth. Oñate galloped around his proprietorship for months, inspecting ore samples and drawing pledges of fidelity to Felipe II, king of Spain, from Pueblo leaders. With palpable hubris, Oñate did not codify the appropriation of Pueblo territory through treaties. Spontaneous submission, officially recorded, sufficed to transfer sovereignty in Spanish minds.[19]

ALL OF THESE EVENTS took place far away from the imperial center—a spatial disconnect that turned the Rio Grande valley into a treacherous, mutinous place for the colonizers. Fear of the unknown, Native hostility, and distance from the seats of Spanish authority fueled fear and aggression. When Spanish men demanded sexual services from Pueblo women, the alienation deepened dangerously. In January 1599, Juan de Zaldívar, Oñate's nephew, climbed up to Acoma Pueblo, a town more than five centuries old that sat on a 365-foot-high sandstone mesa, and demanded to be fed and sheltered. A Pueblo interpreter offered Zaldívar terms three times, while Pueblos were denigrated as "Castilian whoremongers." When denied, Zaldí-var's men tore through the town. The Pueblos fought back and killed eleven Spanish, including Zaldívar. Several Spanish soldiers jumped off the mesa to their deaths. Oñate pronounced the battle a rebellion and insisted that "this offence should be punished severely as an example, not only for the said pueblo. . . . but also in order that the other Indians who likewise submitted should know we had sufficient strength and power to punish such transgression and boldness." Oñate ordered an attack that left more than eight hundred Pueblos dead. Every survivor between twelve and twenty-five years of age was enslaved for twenty years, and every man older than twenty-five had one foot cut off. Horrified, the Pueblos allowed Franciscans into their towns, but they never forgot the massacre, the maiming, and the enslavement. These invaders would have to fundamentally change or die.[20]

The ruthless subjugation of Acoma Pueblo faintly echoed the conquests of the Mexica, Inca, and Maya states by small and determined groups of conquistadors, but Acoma was no Cuzco or Tenochtitlán. The savage sacking spread terror among the Pueblos, for whom such flagrant brutality was almost unthinkable. Yet it did not trigger a capitulation. The Spanish thought that the Pueblo people were all part of a single society in the Mesoamerican mold, failing to see that the Pueblos were, in fact, a headless alliance of autonomous towns. Conquering the Pueblo world would have taken several massacres. The conquistadors lacked the will to even try. Oñate wrote, defensively, "If you should want to show lenience after they [the captives] have been arrested, you should seek all possible means to make the Indians believe that you are doing so at the request of the friar with your forces."[21]

Imperial officials in Spain, too, recoiled from Oñate's ruthless methods, although for different reasons. They had come to style themselves as agents of a modern, enlightened empire, and they charged Oñate with excessive cruelty and sent him back to Spain. The Spanish built a string of missions and established Santa Fe as the capital of New Mexico in the upper Rio Grande valley. The king of Spain turned New Mexico into a crown colony and scaled down his empire's ambitions, banning exploration beyond the Rio Grande watershed, which meant that New Mexico would not become a mining colony in the Mexican mold. No missionaries would live among the Indians for twenty years.[22]

Where Oñate's approach had been brutal and outmoded, the official imperial approach was simply naive. The Spanish believed that the North American continent was much narrower than it actually was, so they were tricked into thinking that a single town supported by a garrison could grow into the seat of an empire. In reality, Santa Fe was an isolated hamlet among more than sixty adobe towns that were home to overwhelming numbers of Pueblo Indians. Santa Fe controlled nobody. It survived because the Pueblos allowed it to survive and because the Spanish could be useful to them. Franciscan friars had misguided ideas about the visible and invisible worlds, but they brought in horses, wagons, fabrics, and other valuable things. Their pigs were tasty, and their tools were sharper, lighter, and sturdier than those of the Pueblos.[23]

Spain had a momentous head start in the colonization of the Western Hemisphere, but North American Indians had brought Spanish expansion to a halt: in the late sixteenth century there were no significant Spanish settlements on the continent—only petty plunder regimes. North America was still essentially Indigenous. The contrast to the stunning Spanish successes in Middle and South America was striking: how could relatively small Native groups defy Spanish colonialism in the north when the formidable Aztec, Inca, and Maya Empires had fallen so easily? The answer was right in front of the Spanish—the decentralized, kinship-based, and egalitarian political regimes made poor targets for imperial entradas—but they kept missing it because the Indigenous nations were so different from Europe's hierarchical societies. They also missed a fundamental fact about Indigenous warfare: fighting on their homelands, the Indians did not need to win battles and wars; they just needed not to lose them.

Chapter 5

THE POWHATAN
EMPIRE

WHILE DREAMS OF GOLD, SLAVES, AND INDIGE-nous empires lured one Spanish expedition after another into North America, English and French mariners were probing the eastern face of the continent, making their first attempts at colonization of the New World. They did so more quietly than the Spanish; mostly they sought fish and furs, which stirred fainter but also steadier passions. Whereas Spain relied on a formalized system of conquest forged in the Caribbean and Mesoamerica, the English and French relied on a flexible system rooted in commerce. In 1508, Sebastiano Caboto—Giovanni's son and, like his father, in the service of the English—sailed to the northern tip of Hudson Bay and then down the coast, around Newfoundland, and all the way to the Chesapeake Bay. Along the way he encountered "so great a multitude of certain big fish" that "they sometimes stayed his ships."[1]

Cabot, as the English called Sebastiano and his father, had encountered what would become known as the Great Fishery. For people arriving from northern latitudes, the long, bay-studded coast offered a tantalizing prize: a warm drift current curves across the North Atlantic and generates extraordinary volumes of nutritious phytoplankton, sustaining the world's greatest fisheries off the coasts of Newfoundland, Labrador, and Acadia. The schools of cod and the pods of whales were enormous.[2]

The Great Fishery soon drew fishing and whaling fleets from England, France, Spain, Portugal, and the Netherlands, transforming Bristol, Plymouth, Saint Malo, Cádiz, Lisbon, and Amsterdam into bustling centers of transatlantic commerce. In 1521, when

Cortés conquered the Aztec Empire, Portuguese mariner João Álvares Fagundes established on the southern coast of Newfoundland what might be called the first European colony in North America. The enterprise focused on small-scale farming, soap-making, and fishing, not prospecting or enslaving. Fagundes's settlement lasted approximately five years.[3]

The commercialization of European-Indigenous interactions proceeded rapidly. In 1524, the Narragansetts and Wampanoags on the mid-Atlantic seaboard welcomed Giovanni da Verrazano, an Italian sailing for France. They had little use for gold but were happy to receive his blue and red beads, which they could incorporate into their existing trade in native copper and in small, cylindrical shell beads known as *wampum*. The powerful Wabanaki Confederacy of four Algonquian peoples—Mi'kmaqs, Maliseets, Passamaquoddys, and Penobscots—flatly forbade Verrazano's scouting party from coming ashore; they seemed to be determined to keep their distance from the uninvited newcomers and their diseases.

Jacques Cartier, an experienced Saint Malo mariner who had explored the Newfoundland coast, sailed up the Saint Lawrence River in 1535. Clamoring for wealth, he had recruited an Iroquois village leader, Donnacona, and his two sons as guides. The three Iroquois had an agenda of their own. After traveling far enough, they told Cartier that they were approaching the city of Stadacona. It was a modest Iroquois village. This was to be France's Tenochtitlán, a gateway to America and its riches. The disgusted Cartier seized Donnacona and took him to France, where the Indian died four years later.[4]

England's and France's commitment to overseas colonization seemed weak. They had no articulated method for conquering and governing, and they had to rely on private investors who expected quick returns. The English state was dreadfully frail in comparison to the Spanish Empire, and some of its key figures did not seem to have the stomach for conquest. Henry VII had granted Giovanni Caboto and his sons "all mainlands, islands, towns, cities, castles and other places whatsoever discovered by them," but when Sebastian Cabot landed somewhere in the northeastern corner of North America, he "did not dare advance inland beyond the shooting distance of a crossbow." When John Rut, in 1527, failed to find a northwest passage to China for Henry, the king's interest in America faded. Rather than mounting costly and uncertain explorations, English sea dogs settled for raiding Spanish treasure fleets. England appeared to have resigned itself to a secondary role in the scramble for North America, nibbling at its margins.[5]

English misfortunes and hesitancy emboldened the French, who in turn provoked the Spanish. In 1562, Jean Ribault scouted Florida as a potential "New France," and two years later René Goulaine de Laudonnière led two hundred Huguenots—French Protestants—to Florida, where they built Fort Caroline on the banks of the Saint Johns River in the northeastern corner of the panhandle. The king of Spain, Felipe II, immediately sent a fleet to eliminate the fort from land that he considered his. It would be the first direct clash between European powers in North America. In the fall of 1565, Pedro Menéndez de Avilés landed fifty miles to the south of the fort and claimed possession of the land as his personal fiefdom; from early on, the Europeans considered American land a commodity. The local Saturiba Indians led the soldiers through waterlogged marshlands to the Huguenots—and colonial-on-colonial carnage. Menéndez ordered a frontal attack at dawn, killing more than a hundred members of the "wicked Lutheran sect," who died for "being Lutherans and against our holy Catholic Faith." It was a crippling blow to France's ambitions on the south Atlantic coast, although it did not prevent the French from claiming Florida by the right of discovery.[6]

Fort Caroline was a military establishment, and for a while, Menéndez continued his military buildup in Florida. He founded San Agustín—which later became the town of Saint Augustine—on the Atlantic coast, along with several inland garrisons. Fully aware of Spain's dismal record on the peninsula, which included an account of a Calusa leader who enslaved two hundred Spanish, Menéndez envisioned a softer form of colonialism. As the governor of Florida, he brought in Jesuit missionaries and reached out to the Calusas on the peninsula's western shore.

A Calusa *mico mayor*, "paramount leader," symbolically married his sister to Menéndez to create an alliance. He also accepted baptism.

The mico mayor ruled several confederacies through strategic marriages, and he seemed to consider the Spanish an addition to his vast network of alliances. Recognizing the central role of elite women in the hierarchical and polygamous Calusa society, the Jesuits also baptized the mico mayor's wife, conveniently overlooking the fact that she, like all Calusas, believed that every person has three souls: one in the pupil of the eye, a second in one's shadow, and a third in one's reflection. The core of Calusa religion and society was beyond the Jesuits' reach. One Spanish soldier, Captain Giles de Pysière, marveled at Florida as "the latest discovery in the world" that teemed with "prodigious land and sea monsters" as well as flying lizards "with the head and neck of a serpent" that devoured humans. Half a century after Ponce de León's landing in Florida, the Spanish knew precious little about their colony. Pysière still thought that Florida was an island. Ignorant and exposed, Spanish officials intensely monitored Native behaviors and instituted neighborhood commissioners and frontier justices who relied on whippings to maintain order.[7]

In 1597, appalled by continuing Spanish meddling in their politics and social life, and by the rash execution of the heir to the Guale leadership, the Guales launched a brief war. The war deepened Menéndez's commitment to accommodation. Jesuits built missions that, unlike forts, offered hospitality, food, and shelter to Native Americans. Guale leaders accepted Spanish gifts and Catholic rituals, only to refit them for Guale purposes: they embedded the foreign rituals into Guale religious traditions and redistributed the gifts to boost Guale unity. Spanish colonial pretensions crumbled in the face of Indigenous solidarity. The Spanish could not live in the Spanish way, and Menéndez seemed unable to decide whether to embrace or fight the Indians. *Mestizaje*—racial mixing—became common, spawning a softer brand of colonialism.

Consuming rather than generating funds, Florida had become an embarrassment and a burden to the Spanish, but strategic imperatives compelled them to persevere. The Caribbean basin was infested with pirates who preyed on Spain's homebound silver-laden fleets, denying the Spanish Empire a fortune. For that reason, a base in Florida was critical: it could offer at least a modicum of protection against the pirates. In the late 1590s, Franciscans replaced the ineffective Jesuits in Florida and launched a concentrated missionization program that helped anchor the Spanish to the peninsula through its Indigenous inhabitants. The Guales started a war two years later when a friar tried to interfere in Guale politics and marriage practices by condemning polygyny. Fray Pedro de Corpa had stopped Don Juan, a new mico mayor, from marrying more than one wife, because he had become Christian. When the Guales retaliated, only one friar was allowed to live. The Guales retained their system of female micos and senior wives commanding women's labor.[8]

THE SPANISH AND FRENCH failures in the strategically pivotal Florida created an opening for England. The relatively weak English state had been slow to enter into the contest for the Americas, even though the entire Atlantic coast north of San Agustín seemed wide open to new colonial ventures. Richard Hakluyt the younger, a fanatic promoter of England's overseas colonialism, urged his countrymen to swiftly establish settlements "upon the mouths of the great navigable rivers" from Florida to Cape Breton Island, a sixteen-hundred-mile stretch of seaboard entirely devoid of European presence. Hakluyt's countrymen heeded his call and would name the first colony Virginia in honor of Elizabeth I, the "virgin queen," who authorized her ambitious courtiers from southeastern England, the "West Country men," to lead the settlement of North America. A proficient scholar of Europe's prior American ventures, Hakluyt advocated a robust colonizing scheme backed by military power. His concern, his ideal, and his target was the mighty Spanish Empire, which seemed to be able to mount colonial enterprises all over the hemisphere, while the English still huddled in coastal toeholds. Hakluyt wrote that, rather than mere fisheries and supply bases, England must establish self-sufficient colonies that would "enlarge the glory of the gospel," "plant sincere religion," and prevent "the Spanishe King from flowing over all the face that waste firm of America." The English should build fortified naval bases, missions and trading posts for the Indians, and farms to sustain expansive colonial settlements in the Spanish mode. But, perhaps contradictorily, Hakluyt also thought that colonization could be a leisurely occupation for the elite, if they could persuade poor English people and the Native Americans to do the heavy lifting. With such an agenda, the English leaders were bound to alienate too many people.[9]

In 1584, Roanoke Indians welcomed two ships at one of the sliver-shaped barrier islands along the mid-Atlantic Coast that together stretched for two hundred miles, shielding a yawning bay behind them. Wingina, the principal *weroance*, or leader, of Wingandacoa, the Roanokes' territory, dispatched a small fleet of boats to meet the uninvited strangers. He learned that Walter Raleigh, a staggeringly wealthy courtier, had sent two ships across the Atlantic to establish trade. Wingina faced the strangers with the supreme confidence of an experienced leader: "The manner of his coming," the English reported, "was in this sort: he left his boats altogether as the first man . . . and came along to the place over against the ships, followed with forty men. When he came to the place, his servants spread a long matte upon the ground, on which he sat down." When the English approached Wingina, brandishing their weapons, "hee never mooved from his place." Wingina's quiet authority defined the encounter. The Roanokes would allow the strangers to stay, as long as they adhered to Roanoke customs and were generous with their wares. The English offered various goods, and Wingina accepted a tin plate, which "would defend him against his enemies' arrows." Satisfied with the proceedings, the English sailed home, eager to present a new possession, Wingandacoa, to their queen, whose advisors yearned to thwart Spanish inroads into North America.[10]

By focusing on their European rivals, however, the English picked the wrong target. The land beyond Roanoke belonged to several powerful Algonquian-speaking peoples, one of which, the Ossomocomuck Nation, claimed the island as a part of its territory. Numerous weroances commanded extensive commercial and diplomatic circuits and had traded with European fishermen and explorers for decades. Bloodlines connected people and villages, and intimate words—"uncle," "sister," "brother"—solidified communities and nations through mutual accountability. The Roanoke leaders expected these latest outsiders to obey the established practices of generosity, reciprocity, and civility.

The newcomers had other ideas. The West Country promoters styled themselves as humane colonizers, but the parties they sent over quickly exposed this notion as the fiction it was. Like the Spanish, the English had developed an imperial mindset before embarking on overseas colonization. The Enlightenment philosopher John Locke vaguely mused a century later about "vacant places of America" where Indians could be taught to improve the land and be useful. Just as the Reconquista had prepared the Spanish for conquests in the Americas, so, too, did the English carry into North America an experience of conquest, accrued during the long and violent Tudor conquest of Ireland. Colonists and plantations had been vital in crushing Irish resistance, and colonists and plantations, so the thinking went, would eliminate Indigenous resistance also in America. English policymakers labeled both the Irish and the Indians as lesser people—malicious, devious, barbaric—who did not and could not possess sovereignty over the lands they lived on. Coexistence was possible, but only if the Indians accepted the English or Spanish as their masters.[11]

At first the Indians were impressed by the newcomers. A disease epidemic broke out, and the Indians began dying "very fast, and many in short space," whereas the English seemed invulnerable to the malady, making them appear as powerful people who had access to, but were not necessarily themselves, *montoac* or *manit*, "spiritually powerful." But the English newcomers did not act accordingly. They built a palisaded fortress, isolating themselves from their Native hosts, and they were stingy with their novel tools: brass and iron kettles that could sustain direct flames and seemed unbreakable, and iron knives and axes that cut through skin, bone, wood, and shell with astonishing ease. Their refusal to share their extraordinary technology marked them as uncaring, and then they became outright careless. They expected the Indians to be docile and exploitable, and when the Indians failed to fit the image, the English lashed out. When an Indian stole a silver cup from a colonist, the colony's leader had the offender's town torched. The English thought that any sign of weakness would doom them. When they believed Wingina was plotting to banish them, a colonist beheaded him.[12]

Rather than sapping Indigenous resistance, the murder galvanized it. The colonists conducted no meaningful exploration beyond their coastal foothold. Fearing an uprising, the colonists wanted to be evacuated after just a year; they sailed home on the fleet of Sir Francis Drake, fresh from a circumnavigation. When Raleigh's third batch of colonists—fourteen families, four of them with children—arrived in Roanoke the next year, the Indians were ready. All of the new colonists vanished from the historical record. The only clue to what had unfolded was a single word, "CROATOAN," a reference to a nearby island or settlement, carved into a tree.[13]

Nonetheless, the English persisted with their colonial schemes. In their minds, there was no other option. Emerging mercantilist ideas in Europe postulated that the world's resources were finite and that the wealth of nations hinged on precious metals. Nations that were not amassing gold and silver would inevitably fade, and the key to lasting prosperity was overseas colonies that supplied the mother country with bullion and raw materials. Before transitioning into a rescue operation for the Roanoke colony, Drake's 1586 attacks had razed the ports of Santo Domingo and Cartagena in the West Indies and shattered San Agustín—an audacious double punch that revealed Spain's weakness outside of Mesoamerica and announced England's entry into the contest for North America.[14]

If the southern face of North America appeared a soft target for Spanish conquistadors looking outward from the West Indies, so, too, did its eastern and northern fronts seem to beckon English mariners. Early empire building was as much about water as it was about land. The Atlantic coast was dotted with welcoming estuaries, broadmouthed rivers, sheltering natural harbors, and fertile land.

IN THE LATE SPRING OF 1607, the Powhatan people detected three ships approaching Chesepiooc, a town "at a big river." The vessels anchored close to a small neck of land. The swampy protrusion had no settlements, but it belonged to the Powhatan Empire, which had twenty-four thousand members and dominated a swath of territory from the Atlantic coast to the Appalachians. From the Native perspective, there was little unusual about the event, for stories of similar landings—by Cartier, Menéndez, Ponce de Léon, and many others—had been circulating along the coast for generations. Nor did the new arrivals appear particularly threatening: they numbered a little over a hundred and were all male, suggesting an interest in trade rather than occupation. The English did what they had done for centuries: they demarcated a territory with fences and built a fort, completing a large, triangle-shaped structure with a bulwark at each corner within weeks. They called it Jamestown to honor their king, James I. It was an insult and a violation of Powhatan sovereignty. More menacing still, the strangers approached the Powhatans' satellite villages, trying to draw them into their orbit. The Indians were alarmed but held back, for the time being. Powhatan soldiers painted themselves for war and killed a few colonists, apparently as a warning.[15]

The English did not grasp what they were up against in the lands they now called Virginia. Far more powerful than most of the Indigenous confederacies that Europeans had encountered in North America, the Powhatans were ruled by a paramount leader, Wahunsenacawh, an ambitious and shrewd *mamanatowick*, a title that connoted *manito*, "spiritual power." Wahunsenacawh had subdued numerous local weroánces, extending his authority over more than thirty towns. He was a "keeper of many spirits" and commanded fifteen thousand people across a vast domain called Tsenacommacah, "densely inhabited land." Residing in Werowocomoco—"king's house"—the approximately sixty-year-old leader collected tribute from satellite groups and had about a hundred wives, the foundation of an expansive kinship network that held his empire together. Seventy years earlier, Hernando de Soto had tried to usurp a similar kinship-based empire among the Natchez, with disastrous results.

Wahunsenacawh had subjugated several rival nations and elevated his sons, brothers, and sisters to lead some of them, while allowing obedient foreign leaders to retain their positions, as long as they provided soldiers and paid tribute in furs, copper, pearls, corn, and meat—up to eighty percent of their possessions. In return, Wahunsenacawh

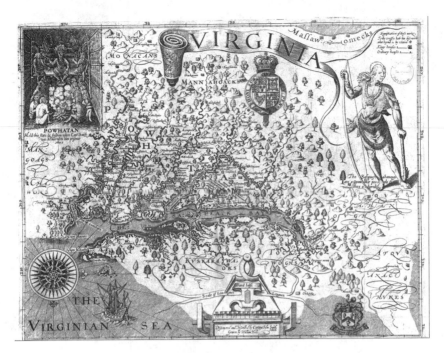

Captain John Smith's 1624 map of Virginia

adopted vanquished leaders and their soldiers, extending his protective embrace over them. He was *quioccosuk*, a "god on Earth," whose spiritual power protected the realm. Now he wanted direct access to the remarkable weapons of the newcomers; the smoke, smell, and noise of the English guns had a deep psychological impact.

Wahunsenacawh received visitors in a 150-foot-long windowless, barrel-shaped palace, sitting on an elevated bench in the back of the wood structure, his wives and counselors on mats below him. This was not a man who would yield to a group of strangers, however impressive were their ships or the weapons they brandished. He was more likely to think of them as a potential addition to his empire, which was founded on far-reaching kinship ties. Impressed by Wahunsenacawh, Captain John Smith marveled at how "the form of their Common-wealth is a Monarchical government, one as Emperor rules over many Kings or Governors. Their chief ruler is called *Powhatan*, and takes his name of his principal place of dwelling called *Powhatan*." His will "is a law and must be obeyed: not only as a King, but as half a God they esteem him.

*Powhatan
(Wahunsenacawh)
in a longhouse at
Werowocomoco
(detail of John Smith's
1624 map)*

His inferior Kings whom they call *Werowances*, are tied to rule by customs, and have power of life and death at their command." It seemed almost as if Smith could join the Powhatans as an inferior king.[16]

In May 1607, however, two hundred Powhatans captured Smith and two other colonists along the Chickahominy River, possibly as a power play: Wahunsenacawh wanted to incorporate the English into his chiefdom and dramatize his power. Only Smith was allowed to live. In December, Smith was brought before Wahunsenacawh, who had the Englishman symbolically clubbed to death and then brought back to life by his ten-year-old daughter, whom the English knew as Pocahontas. As Smith understood the ritual, it established "how well Powhatan [Wahunsenacawh] loved and respected me." Smith and the other surviving colonists had been reborn as kin. Powhatan women raised large crops of corn in 1608 and now shared their bounty. No colonists died of hunger during the colony's second winter. Powhatan women, highly autonomous and public actors, had saved them. Wahunsenacawh had expanded his empire by absorbing the English, though the bond was still a tenuous one. Wahunsenacawh began to capitalize on his ability to leverage the power of exotic and useful goods: colorful cloth, copper kettles, swords, hatchets, beads, and guns in bulk.[17]

The peninsula where the colonists had landed was connected to the continent by a narrow strip of land—a situation they considered a blessing: they thought it made their colony more defensible against attacks, whether Spanish or Indian. In reality, the peninsula isolated the colonists from the mainland, its resources, and its open spaces. Huddling in their fort, they could not hunt and were reduced to drinking the slimy and unusually salty water of the "big river," which ran along an ancient meteor crater that leaked saline to the surface. Even so, they named the river after their king. In the distance, "upon the top of certain red sandy hills in the woods," they could see "three great houses," each "neare sixty foot in length."[18]

Within two months after their arrival, the English had begun dying, succumbing to fevers and fluxes. The hot and humid summer brought millions of mosquitoes, turning Jamestown into a malarial pool. After eight months only thirty-eight colonists were left. The London-based Virginia Company shipped in more people, but the colonists kept dying. "Our drink was water, our lodgings Castles in the ayre"—rocky beach—Smith bemoaned. "With this lodging and diet, our extreme toile in bearing and planting Palisades, so strained and bruised us." These circumstances were simply unacceptable to Englishmen who had expected that their most arduous undertaking in the New World would be to search for a passage to the South Sea, or the Pacific Ocean. In the summer of 1609, their second in America, they offered to crown Wahunsenacawh as a vassal of King James I and lavished him with gifts, hoping to reduce him to a subject. Wahunsenacawh accepted the gifts but refused to kneel, and that was the end of it. The gentlemen-colonists had come to North America to find Hakluyt's supposedly easy riches—gold, copper, and whales— and they were at once unwilling and unable to raise crops. In this, they found a parallel with Powhatan men, who hated "to be seen in any woman-like exercise."[19]

Unlike the Powhatans, however, the English lacked women who

would do most of the farming. During the "starving time" in 1609–
10, they ate dogs, cats, rats, and horses, and some resorted to cannibalism. They died in droves. Desperate to preserve the fiction of
their invincibility, the survivors tried but failed to hide their dead
from the Powhatans. Wahunsenacawh sent food to the wasting colony, apparently aiming to absorb it into his empire as a new tributary
village. But the English proved to be bad relatives. John West De La
Warr, the new governor of Jamestown, set out to rebuild the colony,
but he did not last a year. The colonists tried systematic agriculture
but soon abandoned it for small private lots. They preferred enclosure to commons. Many did not plant crops at all, instead searching
for gold and silver, leaving Smith to despair: "There was no talk, no
hope, no work, but dig gold, wash gold, refine gold, load gold." The
allure of precious metals was also the motivation for a new royal charter that authorized the Virginia Company to colonize all the lands
between the thirty-fourth and fortieth parallels, from the Atlantic to
the Pacific. To capitalize on the gargantuan grant, the company dispatched hundreds of new colonists. Like the others before them, they
were all but useless in the new land. They refused to do manual labor
and were soon starving. Only sixty of them survived the winter. Some
of them ate the dead, and some stormed into Powhatan towns, stealing food and taking hostages. Wahunsenacawh had one of his tributary tribes, the Paspaheghs, monitor and discipline the colonists. The
English launched a surprise attack on a Paspahegh town, killing sixty-
five. The assault meant war.[20]

Jamestown descended even further into crisis. Smith, the settlement's last best hope with the Powhatans, had been wounded in a suspicious gunpowder explosion and had returned home. Two years later,
the colonists had already abandoned Jamestown for land farther from
the shore when, suddenly, three ships from England appeared, carrying still more soldier-colonists—three hundred this time. Jamestown
was reoccupied, and the colonists resumed their project, now with a
desperate urgency that drove them to burn Powhatan cornfields, shoot
Native children for sport, and slaughter entire settlements. Their tactics were altogether hideous, and many Whites recoiled in disgust.
Weary of bloodshed, dozens of colonists joined the Powhatans, sid-

ing with power. Colonial leaders ordered the renegades hunted down and had them burned at the stake or their bones slowly shattered on an execution wheel. Vacillating between despair and viciousness, the colony was devouring itself.[21]

Out of desperation, Captain Samuel Argall captured Pocahontas, Wahunsenacawh's treasured daughter, in 1613 with help from a weroance of the Patawomeck Nation. Pocahontas, also known as Matoaka, had only recently married a Patawomeck soldier and had probably become a mother. Although she was a recognized diplomat, the colonists held her as a hostage to prevent Wahunsenacawh from killing them. She accepted Christian conversion, was renamed Rebecca, and was married to John Rolfe, a Jamestown widower. Wahunsenacawh accepted an English peace offering: secure access to English goods—iron plows, millstones, domesticated animals, and exotic spiritous liquors—which would ratify his standing among the English, as well as with his own people. Rolfe began cultivating a mild and sweet-scented strain of tobacco, which became a sensation in London. In 1616, the Virginia Company decided to bring Pocahontas and about a dozen other Native Americans to England to publicize its commercial and moral successes in the New World. Pocahontas was described, confusingly, as both an Indian princess and a good Christian wife. She had a busy and exhausting social schedule and, after nearly a year in England, fell ill and died. Wahunsenacawh passed on two years later. By then the colonists were planting tobacco in the streets of Jamestown, hoping to maximize their profits. In 1619, English privateers brought the first enslaved Africans to Virginia. Two years later, Virginia produced 370,000 pounds of tobacco.[22]

Still, the colony was far from safe. The title of mamanatowick passed to Wahunsenacawh's younger brother, Opechancanough, who saw how the tobacco boom fueled the colonists' arrogance. Thousands of new colonists poured in, along with cattle and hogs. Opechancanough nurtured outwardly friendly relations with the English while planning a massive assault. On March 21, 1622, large numbers of unarmed Powhatans visited the English in various settlements along the James River and stayed overnight. Some shared breakfast with their English hosts the next morning. Then they made their move,

Engraving of Pocahontas by Simon van de Passe, 1616

snatching weapons from their hosts and joining other Powhatans in a coordinated attack. So sudden was the move that "few or none discerned the weapon or blow that brought them to destruction." The Indians stuffed bread into the mouths of the dead colonists as a warning not to "eat up all the land." The Indians also destroyed the colonists' cows, hogs, and horses. Powhatan women despised the roaming beasts that devastated their meticulously tended gardens and fields. Quick to shift from arrogance to victimhood, the colonists bemoaned how "that fatal Friday morning, there fell under the bloody and barbarous hands of that perfidious and inhumane people, contrary to all laws of God and men, of Nature and Nations, three hundred forty-seven men, women, and children"—nearly one-third of the total colonial population. Opechancanough sent no message to the survivors, allowing silence to do the necessary work. The English concluded of the Powhatans that "conquering them is much more easier than of civilizing them by fair means."[23]

The war became a war of attrition that focused more on the destruction of resources than on killing people. The English timed their attacks with the corn harvest, hoping to send the Indians into winter starving. They succeeded spectacularly in 1624: "We have to our uttermost abilities revenged ourselves upon the Savages having upon this river, Cut down their Corn in all places which was planted in great abundance upon hope of a fraudulent peace with intent to provide themselves, for a future war." The colonists, by contrast, had "a plentiful harvest of Corn," which effectively saved Jamestown. Opechancanough retaliated with guerrilla attacks that terrified the colonists to the point that they stopped planting their crops, whether corn or tobacco. King James I revoked the Virginia Company's charter and turned the failing colony into a royal possession administered by his governor. By 1632, both sides were exhausted and entered into a brief, uneasy peace. A new set of English colonists, now Roman Catholics, founded another tobacco colony, Maryland, far up the Chesapeake Bay and far away from the Powhatans.[24]

All the while, English invasions of Tsenacommacah continued. In 1644, Opechancanough orchestrated multiple coordinated ambushes, a standard Powhatan tactic, to push back the colonists. Powhatan soldiers killed more than four hundred English. A Native captive conveyed that the Powhatans attacked because "the English took up all their lands from them, and would drive them out of the country." Virginians thought differently: "The subtle Indians" knew that the battered colonists were "uneasy and disunited among themselves, and by the direction of Opechancanough, their king, laid the ground work of another massacre." By 1646, both sides were reeling, and the Virginia General Assembly opened peace talks with Necotowance, Opechancanough's successor. Opechancanough, now over ninety years old and so decrepit that he had to be moved around on a litter, was taken to Jamestown and displayed as an oddity. "His eyelids became so heavy," the colonists observed, "that he could not see, but as they were lifted up by his servants." Two weeks later, a disgruntled English guard shot him dead.

Opechancanough's empire was built on kinship ties—based on bloodlines or marriage—backed by military power, and it vanished with his passing. Sir William Berkeley, the governor of Virginia, had wanted to send him to England as a trophy before he was murdered. Opechancanough's wretched death in English captivity was demoralizing for his people, but he left behind a vast legacy. The Powhatans' decades-long resistance to English expansion confined colonial settlements to the tidewater and the eastern shore of the Chesapeake for a long time, inadvertently providing a protective shield for many Indigenous nations in the interior.[25]

Along with Apalachee, Guale, Calusa, and Cofitachequi leaders, Opechancanough may have possessed a deeper understanding of European colonialism than had any other Native person on the continent. He had probably heard stories of strange men appearing out of nowhere since childhood, and he had agonized over the things the invaders had done. He had fought three brutal wars against the English and lived through the rise and fall of the Powhatan Empire. He could have explained what the Indians thought of the newcomers, how they would have wanted them to behave, and what he thought should happen in the future, but no colonists asked. Opechancanough was born a human being and died denigrated as savage.[26]

Virginia survived, but it was curbed, cramped, and unhealthy. The cash-poor English state could send soldiers, colonists, merchants, and diplomats all across the world, but it could not properly support imperial projects. Virginia was a case in point. Tens of thousands of Indians and powerful Native confederacies hemmed it in on three sides, reducing it to a mere foothold at the edge of an Indigenous continent, its sea-to-sea charter now mocking England's imperial pretensions. The colony was also isolated from Florida by a land border that thwarted inter-imperial cooperation. Virginians abandoned nearly all efforts to keep their domesticated animals under control, and they allowed their swine, cows, and horses to roam free and trample Native crops; left to their own devices, domesticated animals were often more effective colonizers than their owners. In 1675, nearly seven decades after the founding of

*Powhatan's
(Wahunsenacawh's)
mantle*

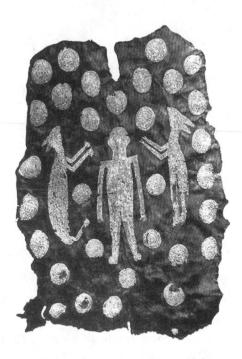

Jamestown, English colonists, numbering more than forty thousand, still hugged the shores of the Chesapeake, feverishly growing tobacco, the colony's lifeline. Tied to their fields, the English still knew precious little about the vast continent and its many peoples, tongues, and riches.[27]

Chapter 6

WARS AT THE WATER'S EDGE

A SMALL GROUP OF WABANAKI FISHERMEN WAS AT work on a little island off the northern Atlantic coast in 1605 when Captain George Weymouth, an English shipbuilder-sailor, landed with his crew near them. He and his men hoped to find potable water and food. They found both, but they also spotted the Wabanakis and promptly captured four of their members and took them to London. Six years later, at Cape Cod Bay, another English adventurer, Captain Edward Harlow, seized several local Indians, who seemed to know precisely how to navigate the situation, having traded with the Europeans and having fought them when necessary. They told their captors that their home island, Noepe, "Dry Land amid the Waters"—now Martha's Vineyard—was rich in superb corn. When the ship landed, they immediately escaped. Stories of Verrazano, Cartier, and other European slave hunters were fresh in the Native communities along the water's edge. Fishing, slavery, and greed were generating an explosive mix on the Atlantic coast.

In 1614, the Wabanakis, an amphibious people, welcomed an Englishman who knew exactly how to act and what to say; he approached them humbly and with the right words. John Smith was back in America, now bartering fish for furs with coastal Indians from Maine to the Massachusetts Bay. He was still operating in a colonial mode. He visited the Abenakis and Wampanoags and claimed their lands for the colony of "New England." His work finished, he returned to England and left the commander of his second ship in charge of negotiating trade deals with the local Nausets and Patuxets. Instead of trading with them, the man took about two

*Map of southern
New England in 1634*

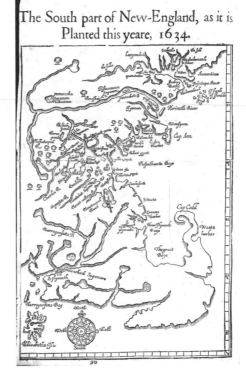

The South part of New-England, as it is
Planted this yeare, 1634.

dozen of them captive and sailed to Malaga, in Spain, where he sold
them into slavery.[1]

Along the mid-Atlantic coast, the contest for dominance began
on water. Two maritime giants—England and the Dutch Republic—sent ships to probe the shore for ports, forelands, and fisheries,
while Algonquian mariners monitored and, if needed, boarded and
attacked them as defensive measures. So overwhelming was Indigenous sea power that it kept much of the Atlantic coast free of colonial
bases for decades. An early colonizing attempt at Sagadahoc River
in the Gulf of Saint Lawrence by English Puritans and West Country promoters failed miserably under the leadership of the headstrong
Raleigh Gilbert. Algonquian vessels commanded the coast, leaving
the uninvited strangers isolated and starving. The dejected colonists
sailed home at the first opportunity.[2]

A new effort in 1620, consisting of a single ship, the *Mayflower*,
brought 102 colonists who landed on a widowed coast; a recent disease
outbreak had killed almost ninety percent of the Wampanoags. The

*Ousamequin smoking a calumet with John Carver, the governor
of Plymouth Colony, 1621 (artist unknown)*

malady may have been leptospirosis, which had been spread by the urine of European rats. The colonists swiftly occupied a vacant Native village. They were overjoyed: in front of them was "a great deal of land cleared," a reward after their biblical exodus. "Our land is full," one colonist wrote, whereas "their land is empty." Thirty-seven of the strangers were militant separatists who wanted to purify the Protestant faith and European society overall from Catholic residue—the pomp, the hierarchy, the corruption, the formulaic liturgy—and create a new order that balanced reason and faith, the intellectual and the emotional. Some forty of the newcomers were "Strangers" with no connection to the church. When the captain missed the landing site, the Strangers became mutinous. The two contingents negotiated a compact, and the *Mayflower* was able to anchor at the tip of what the newcomers called Cape Cod.

The horribly reduced Wampanoags were desperate to secure new allies, and they took in the serious and zealous newcomers. The first winter was brutal, and roughly half of the Europeans died. Samoset, an Eastern Abenaki sachem, and Squanto, a Patuxet Indian, helped mediate a mutual defense pact between Ousamequin—*Massasoit,* "great sachem," of the Wampanoag Confederacy—and the colonists. Ousamequin believed that the pact entitled him to collect tribute from the newcomers, and he soon recruited them into a fight against a rival sachem. He allowed the English to build a colony—Plymouth— because they were useful. It was clear that the English could do very little without the Indians, and although poor, the colonists were willing to engage in small-scale barter. Mostly they wanted to farm their small plots and pray according to their convictions. In the fall of 1621, the English rejoiced in their first successful harvest. Ninety Wampanoag men led by Massasoit were invited to celebrate the achievement with the colonists. The highlight of the feast was *nasaup*, a mixture of boiled cornmeal, vegetables, fruits, and meats.[3]

Perhaps mistaking Ousamequin's generosity for submissiveness, the colonists thought that the sachem could be reduced to a subject of the king of England. Ousamequin openly denounced Christianity, and William Bradford, the governor of the Plymouth Colony, branded the Wampanoags as malevolent savages. Like the Spanish before them, the English thought that the Indians did not use the land properly because they did not improve it, echoing the Lockean view of the New World. "The country is yet raw; the land untilled; the cities not built; the cattle not settled," one planter complained. "We are compassed about with a helpless and idle people, the natives of this country, which cannot, in any comely or comfortable manner, help themselves, much less us." The colonists missed the obvious alternative explanation: the Indians simply chose not to help the uninvited strangers. "God did once so train up his people," Bradford wrote, "but now he doth not, but speaks in another manner, and so we must apply ourselves to God's present dealing, and not to his wonted dealing." The English asked Indians' help with growing corn. Like the Virginians fourteen years earlier, the Pilgrims built a guarded palisade around their vulnerable settlement.[4]

Deterred by Algonquian prowess on both water and land, Plymouth remained the sole New England colony until 1629, when the Massachusetts Bay Company established Boston fifty miles to the north at a spot where a superior natural harbor promised centrality and wealth. Native fears of colonial invasion became real when what would become known as the Great Migration brought three thousand Puritans to Massachusetts between 1630 and 1633. The Puritan influx broke the pattern. The colony received a stream of ships that brought in more supplies and more people. Alarming to the Indians, many of them were women; these new arrivals had come to stay. More alarming still, English families began to spread in all directions, clearing forests, marking out farms, and building roads without consulting the Indians. When the colonists imported large numbers of hogs, cattle, sheep, and horses, the Indians saw it as an invasion by alien species that threatened their fields, crops, and livelihoods. The Massachusetts project was fraught with ambiguity from the start. The English claimed land for a colony without Indigenous consent, while the colony's seal depicted an Indian uttering a biblical quotation, "Come Over and Help Us," announcing a Christian commonwealth that would embrace Native Americans. It was a sham that was aimed at securing funding for a colonial project. Unlike the Spanish and French, who justified colonization with the gift of European civilization and religion, the English had few qualms about the word "colony." They simply projected fictional property rights over Indigenous territories, hiding the emptiness of such claims with elaborate charters.[5]

IMPERIAL RIVALRIES among the European powers exacerbated the tense situation in New England. More quietly than the Spanish, French, and English, the Dutch had entered the contest for North America in 1609, when Henry Hudson, having failed to find a sea route to China through North America, came to a river that still bears his name. When Dutch merchants arrived in the Hudson Valley in the 1610s, they realized it was a place of vast advantages. The Hudson was navigable for 160 miles into the interior, allowing access to bustling Native markets along the Saint Lawrence Valley and in the Great Lakes. Uninterested in converting and "civilizing" the Indians, the business-minded Dutch treated Indians as customers and trading partners.

The Dutch Indian policy was persistently practical. Dutch merchants quickly determined where the power lay and acted accordingly, forging close ties with the Mahican Nation, which dominated the interior trade. The Dutch built Fort Nassau in 1614 on the Hudson and, through the Mahicans, sold guns, powder, and iron tools across an enormous hinterland. In return, Fort Nassau was flooded with beaver pelts, North America's most coveted commodity, making a fortune for the Dutch. The fort had only about four dozen employees, half of them traders and the other half soldiers. This kind of light colonialism was not exactly by design—Dutch imperial ambitions in Asia drew most of the available resources—but the relative modesty of their operations in North America would serve the Dutch well.[6]

Dutch commercial prowess alarmed the English, triggering an unexpected imperial contest centered on processed clamshells. Clamshells were the raw material for wampum beads, which were sacred to many eastern Indians. They painted them with various colors and strung them into belts that were used in religious ceremonies, to proclaim social status, to stabilize border relations, and as mnemonic devices in relating traditional stories. Wampum also served as currency, and there the entrepreneurial Dutch merchants spotted an opportunity. They began to supply the coastal Indians with metal lathes that enabled them to manufacture wampum on an industrial scale. Native women could produce five to ten feet of wampum belt a day, and soon some three million monetized wampum beads were circulating in the Northeast, fueling an expanding exchange economy. Europeans had accepted a currency that a moment earlier meant next to nothing to them.

Struggling to enter into the lucrative wampum trade and to pay their European debts—building colonies was extremely expensive—the still fragile Puritan colonies approached the Wabanakis, who were expert mariners and trappers equally capable of producing great quantities of prime beaver pelts, swordfish, cod, or right whales. Living far to the north of the main clamshell-farming area, Wabanakis were eager for access to wampum; the Puritans began to demand it from their Native neighbors to buy Wabanaki furs. Their methods were harsh, ranging from naked extortion to thinly disguised tribute payments. New Englanders and the Dutch began using wampum belts as currency in their internal trade. In 1637, the Massachusetts General Court declared wampum legal tender, exchangeable for shillings and pennies. Weetamoo, a *saunkskwa*—female sachem—of the Pocasset people of the Wampanoag Confederacy, relied almost exclusively on wampum in her expansive diplomacy with colonists. It was a precarious dynamic, and the Wabanakis began to carefully consider the extent to which they should engage with the Indians in the interior. For them the interior was a terrifying place where the contest over territory unbalanced the world. The amphibious Mi'kmaqs, not the English, were their most dangerous neighbors. Mi'kmaqs traded with Europeans, accumulating guns and powder and projecting their power deep into the interior and far out into the sea, securing a near monopoly on fisheries and other maritime resources around the Saint Lawrence Bay. They became the foremost maritime power along the Northeast Coast. In their slipstream, the Wabanakis extended their operations in the Saint Lawrence Valley and New France, unnerving New England traders and officials.[7]

SUDDENLY, THE WABANAKIS on the sea and the powerful Pequots on land surrounded the New Englanders. Like the Powhatans, the Pequot Confederacy had expanded rapidly in the early seventeenth century, drawing several neighboring groups into their orbit. Pequots called the Narragansetts, powerful in their own right, "women-like men." Highly organized under a great sachem and a confederacy-wide council and numbering about thirty thousand, the Pequots dominated the fur and wampum trades in the Connecticut Valley. Their authority extended from the coastal plains to offshore islands through reciprocal attachments, and they categorically refused to pay tribute to the English. The English struggled with this reality. What did the persistence of Pequot supremacy reveal about the colonists' quest for the perfect Christian commonwealth and about their worth in the eyes of their god? They saw Indians as ungrateful and ungovernable savage sinners, yet they failed to subjugate them. The Virginians were aspiring settler-colonists who wanted to repress and control the Indians, but they were beset by a number of deficiencies:

they lacked profitable cash crops such as tobacco, they were too poor to buy African slaves, and they relied heavily on farm animals—oxen, cattle, hogs, and horses—because they did not want or dare to hunt in the woods. Their domesticates needed large pastures and hayfields, but the colonists failed to secure enough land. Were they not worthy after all?[8]

At long last they had a breakthrough. Seventeenth-century Europeans lived in a mysterious and frightening world where omens were commonplace, witches could control a person's fate, swallows wintered at the bottom of lakes, and God seemed to have intervened on behalf of the righteous, striking down their enemies. In 1633, as if God wanted the English to persevere, an unusually virulent smallpox epidemic devastated the immunologically defenseless Indians around New England. More than eighty percent of the Native Americans in the region died. The powerful Pequots lost four thousand people. Traditional healing practices were ineffective, spirits angry. To the English, too, this was a divine intervention; emboldened, they pressured the diminished Pequots to acknowledge English supremacy, pay tribute in wampum, and allow English settlements in the Mystic River valley, a vital commercial artery. The Pequots refused; if anything, they expected the English to appease them with gifts and goods and assume their proper place as a tributary group under Pequot suzerainty. The two peoples were deadlocked, struggling to coexist because neither would yield.[9]

The long descent into a sprawling, apocalyptic violence began in the spring of 1634 when John Stone, a rowdy, hard-drinking Virginia trader, took two Pequot hostages and forced them to guide his ship up the Connecticut River. Pequots and their Niantic allies seized the vessel and killed Stone and his crew. Stone was widely despised among the colonists—he had been fined for sexually assaulting a married woman—but his killing strained relations between the colonists and the Pequots nonetheless; the English could not have "savages" murdering any of their members. Two years later, in July 1636, a party of Manisses people of the Narragansett Confederacy captured the vessel of John Oldham, who, they believed, was trading with their Pequot enemies. They executed the captain, cut off his hands and feet, and

Engraving by A. R. Waud, ca. 1876–1881, depicting
Endicott's landing on Block Island

took his cargo. The colonists insisted that "the blood of the innocent called for vengeance."[10]

In late August, Colonel John Endicott, a man known for his religious zealousness, launched a punitive raid on the Manisses living on Block Island. His force of ninety soldiers made a successful landing but failed to engage with the Indians, who executed a swift retreat into the island's swamps. Endicott then sailed to the mainland to punish the Pequots for the killing of an English trader. The English disembarked near a large town by a short river. In the morning the Indians sent an envoy; the English said they needed the heads of the soldiers who had killed their countrymen. The Pequot ambassador admitted to having killed treacherous English sailors himself before, but he denied this latest charge. The English attacked the town and "gave fire to as many as we could come near, firing their Wigwams, spoiling their corn, and many other necessaries that they had buried in the ground we raked up, which the soldiers had for bootie." Soon after, the Pequots "made many proud challenges" against Saybrook Fort at the mouth of the Connecticut River, destroying "all they found

in their way." The distressed John Winthrop, governor of the Massachusetts Bay Colony, begged the Plymouth Colony to "join against the
common enemy, who, if he were not subdued, would prove as dangerous to them as to us, and, he prevailing, would cause all the Indians
in the country to join to root out all the English." Puritan minister
Roger Williams wrote later, apparently as a justification, that "the
Pequots now commenced more serious depredations, so that the Connecticut government determined to send a force against them." Uncas,
a Mohegan sachem, had allied with the English against the powerful Pequots. After generations of colonial expansion, many Native
nations still considered other Indians to be their main rivals.[11]

Facing viral Indigenous resistance, the overstretched English
thought they had only two options: go to war against either the
Pequots or the Narragansetts. They chose the Pequots, who seemed at
once more powerful and more vulnerable. It turned out to be the right
choice. Spotting an opportunity in the commotion, several tributary
groups abandoned their Pequot overlords for the Narragansetts, who
informed the English of the sudden Pequot vulnerability. The Narragansetts would weaken their rivals by having the English do their
bidding: kill and diminish the Pequots.[12]

What became known as the Pequot War marked a shift from pre-
dominantly maritime English colonialism to more intrusive territorial colonialism, in which property—farms, food stores, houses, and
noncombatants were targets. The English realized that they could
not match the Pequots' prowess on water, which was based on light
canoes capable of navigating shallow coastal areas. They planned an
overland attack to stop the Pequots who kept harassing Fort Saybrook
and other English bases, destroying warehouses, interrupting river
traffic, and killing colonists. More than three hundred Narragansett,
Mohegan, and Wangunk soldiers fought alongside the English. Like
the colonists, these Native peoples wanted to redefine their relationship with the Pequots, who dominated trade with the English. Unlike
the colonists, however, they thought that coexistence with both the
Pequots and the English could still be possible. They joined the campaign to create a safer Indigenous world.[13]

The Pequots knew to expect an attack and gathered at Mistick, a fortified hilltop village half a mile from what the colonists called the Mystic River. What the Pequots did not expect was that the English would employ new tactics. The English came upon "two Forts almost impregnable" and decided to attack the nearest. Shockingly, the assault came before dawn. When the Pequots realized what was unfolding, the English and their Native allies already had them trapped. The English shot volleys through gaps in the palisade, killing people in their sleep. Pequot soldiers mounted a stiff resistance, their arrows and bullets finding flesh in the heavily armored bodies of the English, killing and wounding twenty soldiers within minutes. The attackers seemed to lose heart. But then the Pequots saw the fire: the roofs of their homes were burning, flames jumping from building to building, working their way toward the center. The English soldiers sealed off the town's two exits, shooting all who managed to escape. The trapped Pequots "fought most desperately through the palisades," but the densely built wooden town was in ashes within half an hour. Three to four hundred Pequots, most of them women, children, and elderly, had died. The horror of the slaughter was such that the colonists seemed to want to detach themselves from it: "Such a dreadful Terror did the ALMIGHTY let fall upon their Spirits, that they would fly from us and run into the very Flames, where many of them perished."[14]

The brutality of the attack also shocked the colonists' Indian allies: it was entirely outside of the proper conduct of war. "Our *Indians* came to us, and much rejoiced at our victories," wrote Captain John Underhill, a New England mercenary, but the Narragansetts, Mohegans, and Wangunks "cried *mach it, mach it*; that is, it is naught, it is naught, because it is too furious, and slains too many men." Underhill himself conceded that "it may be demanded, why should you be so furious (as some have said) should not Christians have more mercy and compassion?" He found a strained justification in the Bible: "Sometimes the Scripture declareth women and children must perish with their parents; some-time the case alters: but we will not dispute it now. We had sufficient light from the word of God for our proceedings." For Underhill, genocidal violence was not only justifiable but necessary, because the Pequots were "insolent and barbarous,"

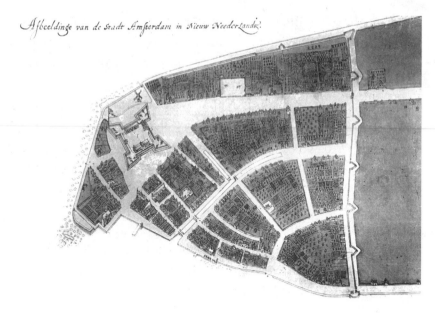

Afbeeldinge van de Stadt Amsterdam in Nieuw Neederlandt.

Map of the city of New Amsterdam in New Netherland, 1660

lesser people who needed to be destroyed to make room for a better world. When peace came, the English and Indians began to exchange body parts—heads, scalps, hands, feet. These were not trophies but cultural cognates—a means to atone and restore order to shattered worlds. Graphic symbols of death and suffering, the body parts were tokens of renewed reciprocity, loyalty, and connections.[15]

THE JUNCTION OF the Hudson and Mohawk Rivers was one of the most coveted places in early-seventeenth-century North America, and it belonged to the formidable Iroquois, the peoples of the long-house, who had lived in the region for centuries. As colonial ambitions expanded, the Iroquois sought ways to contain them. The most effective means was trade. The Iroquois allowed the Dutch West India Company to build Fort Orange at the Hudson-Mohawk confluence in 1624 and ship in a batch of colonists. With that, the Netherlands committed to North American colonization, but the Dutch methods were different from those of the Spanish, English, and French. Because the Dutch sought profits, not dominance, and were generous with their wares, the Iroquois allowed them to stay. The Indians authorized Fort Orange and began calling the Dutch *Kristoni*, "I am a metal maker." It was a major coup for the Dutch. Roughly twenty thousand strong, the Iroquois lived in thirteen heavily fortified and nearly impregnable towns that the Europeans appropriately called "castles." The Dutch saw in the Iroquois a large pool of potential fur producers and clients who could prop up a new colony. A year later, in 1625, the Dutch West India Company erected a fortified settlement, New Amsterdam, on Manhattan Island at the mouth of the Hudson. Peter Minuit, the future governor of New Netherland, had bought the island in 1621— the exact sum is debated—but it was the gesture, the mutual transaction, that mattered. Minuit secured Indigenous consent for the Dutch base that was mostly symbolic: the Dutch marveled how the local Indians "are not aware of any end, limit, or boundary, and appear amazed when questioned concerning it."[16]

Capitalizing on the Iroquois connection proved frustrating, though. The Mohawks of the Iroquois League attacked their Mahican rivals until they won a near monopoly on trade with Fort Orange. Dutch and Mohawk interests began to diverge, rendering the Dutch position unstable. The Mohawks allowed the Mahicans into Fort Orange only if they paid tribute to them, effectively turning the fort into a private Mohawk possession. Mohawk soldiers guarded the roads to the fort and decided who could enter. The role of Dutch traders was simply to make goods available—a task that the Mohawks monitored diligently. When the Dutch sought to open trade with the Mahicans, the Mohawks punished them. Soon there were killings on both sides. Mohawk soldiers vandalized the homes of wealthy Dutch landholders, killed Dutch cattle, and burned a Dutch ship in the harbor. In Dutch eyes, the Mohawks had transformed from customers into overlords. Humiliated Dutch colonists beat and kidnapped Mohawk leaders, only to further antagonize the Indian nation. When six Dutch traders joined a Mahican war party in 1626, Mohawks killed three of them and, as a warning, burned one of the bodies.

The Dutch were desperate to untangle New Netherland from the Mohawk grip—a draining state of affairs that rendered them vulnerable in their rivalries with the bordering English colonies. To boost the battered colony, the Dutch West India Company offered cheap land to Protestant immigrants and aristocratic titles to wealthy Dutch investors, drastically changing the colony's character: most of the original colonists had been company workers who served for six years during which they could not take up tenancies. Unsettled by Mohawk assertiveness, the Dutch began to pay the Indians for land. When the Dutch West India Company built Fort New Amsterdam at the mouth of the Connecticut River in 1633, it agreed to pay tribute to the resident Pequots, even though the fort boasted a garrison of more than 150 soldiers and combat mariners. By the end of the decade, New Netherland was a sprawling mesh of farms, orchards, towns, and small forts spreading along the Long Island Sound. Fruit trees were a particularly significant symbol of belonging. Yet New Netherland was a colony with a difference. Unlike the English, Spanish, and French, the Dutch thought they could claim ownership of land as long as it was home to Indians with whom they could trade. They claimed the land through, not over, the Indians. They knew they needed to embed their colony in alliances with their Native customers.

However, New Netherland was still a modest enterprise and susceptible to the whims of the mother country. In 1640, the Dutch West India Company lost its monopoly on trade and became an administrative body. Commerce was no longer the central focus of Dutch ventures in North America, and New Netherland transitioned from a trading outpost into an aspiring colony. Deeply uneasy over being a minority group among the far more numerous Native nations, the governor of New Netherland, Willem Kieft, an exacting and prickly man, asserted Dutch authority by ordering the neighboring Algonquians to pay an annual tribute in corn, pelts, and wampum. Almost overnight, the Dutch trader had been replaced by the Dutch colonist. The Algonquians, who valued hospitality, were aghast.[17]

The Dutch had begun to develop an imperial mindset—a toxic blend of ambition and arrogance, all fueled by fear. Like the English, the Dutch colonists wantonly allowed their hogs and cattle to graze on Native cornfields, and when the Raritan Indians of the Lenape Nation killed the invading beasts, the Dutch lashed out. Trying to assert his authority, Kieft ordered a disproportionate attack in February 1643, sending fifty soldiers and twenty sailors to destroy the Raritans' harvest and seize as many captives as possible. An intense fight erupted, leaving three Raritans dead. With the Dutch heading back to their base, one colonist mutilated the genitals of a Raritan captive. The response came a year later when Raritans killed four colonists on Staten Island. Kieft demanded the heads of the killers and began to offer bounties for Raritan scalps—ten fathoms of wampum for each. The bounties only caused more violence, pulling the colony into a draining on-again, off-again conflict. Kieft demanded that the Raritans who had been involved in the violence be brought to justice under Dutch law. The Raritan Nation refused.[18]

Not long after, a Dutch trade ship anchored near Raritan towns south of Staten Island. A few Raritans boarded the vessel, but "instead of showing the customary friendship and disposition to trade," they "began to scoff." They slapped a trader across the face with squirrel skins, and more Raritans stormed in, "all armed with tomahawks, rapier blades and other weapons." When the Raritans brought their heavy canoes around the ship, ordering the traders to go ashore, the Dutch organized a hasty retreat. Killings and insults continued, but Dutch colonists kept rejecting Kieft's demands for war. On February 23, the infuriated governor dissolved the colony's popularly elected governing body and announced that an attack would take place two days later, at night near a Dutch fort on Manhattan Island. As many as a thousand people ended up dying in what became known as Kieft's War.[19]

The Raritans woke up on February 25 to gunshots; there would be no battle, just butchery. "A great shrieking" filled the air as the soldiers began their work. "Infants were torn from their mother's breasts, and hacked to pieces in the presence of the parents, and the pieces thrown into the fire and in the water, and other sucklings, being bound to small boards, were cut, stuck, and pierced." The few Indians who survived carnage approached the colonists, "some with their legs cut off, and some holding their entrails in their arms." At least eighty Raritans were murdered. Nearby, forty more had been "in the same manner attacked in their sleep, and massacred in the same manner."[20]

The Raritans and their allies retaliated by raiding farms and killing colonists, and they took the war to the outskirts of New Amsterdam. The rattled Kieft recruited John Underhill, the New England mercenary whose main qualification was the orchestration of the slaughter of hundreds of Pequots six years earlier, to finish the task of subduing the Indians. In March, Underhill led a mixed force of 130 Dutch and English soldiers to a Native town on a hill near the Hudson Valley and had it surrounded. As at Mystic, he ordered a night attack. Soldiers set the town on fire and waited for the occupants to flee. They then shot down between five hundred and seven hundred people.[21]

The leading Dutch colonists had seen enough. They complained about how "the poor inhabitants of New Netherland have been persecuted" by "evil heathens and barbaric Indians." They informed the Dutch West India Company that New Netherland had been "all together through a thoughtless bellicosity laid in ashes." The countdown for the dissolution of New Netherland had started. In 1648, Peter Stuyvesant, the new governor, claimed territory "within a cannon shot" from Fort Orange—his feeble effort to reassert Dutch power.[22]

The Pequot and Raritan massacres, taking place six years apart, seemed to mark the sweeping collapse of Indigenous power in the Northeast. In truth, the massacres exposed a deep-rooted European anxiety over enduring Indigenous power: the attacks were so vicious because the colonists feared the Indians who refused to submit to their rule. The wars with the far more numerous and larger Native nations stretched the colonists near their breaking point. Native men were superior soldiers, having trained and prepared for war from a young age, internalizing an exacting warrior code that was drilled in by military societies. War was to them normal and suffused with spiritualism, whereas the European intruders struggled with the environment and the fluid nature of Indigenous warfare. Their farms and fields abutted Native homelands and hunting grounds, infusing everyday life with fears of reprisal. The Europeans also started losing their technological edge when independent traders violated colonial laws and began selling guns and munitions to their Native customers. In 1629, the Massachusetts Bay Company had decreed that all men must be "exercised in the use of arms" and forbade Indians from entering the colony "except at specified times." That decree no longer held sway.[23]

Chapter 7

THE PEQUOTS SHALL
NO MORE BE
CALLED PEQUOTS

THE MOHEGAN SACHEM UNCAS SEEMED TO BE everywhere, shaping every major development in the borderlands between the colonists and the Indians. In 1626, at the age of thirty-six, he had forged a Mohegan-Pequot alliance by marrying the daughter of Tatobem, the great sachem of the Pequots. Uncas accepted a subordinate role under the senior sachem, only to immediately challenge Pequot authority when Tatobem died in 1633. Uncas persuaded the Narragansetts to join him but struggled to challenge the supremacy of the Pequots, who had drawn the Dutch into their orbit. The Pequots banished Uncas to live among the Narragansetts. Stripped of followers, Uncas seemed to have exhausted his options. The Mohegan territory was shrinking rapidly, and he had but a handful of followers.[1]

But then Uncas spotted an opening in the form of the new English colony of Connecticut. He approached the newcomers and established ties with the leading Puritans. He warned the colonists of an imminent Mohegan attack and earned their trust. When the English moved against the Pequots, Uncas supported the colonists, having become alienated from the haughty Pequots. When the Pequots were crushed, he adopted several survivors as newly born Mohegans. He was one of the crucial signers of the 1638 Treaty of Hartford, which dispossessed all the Indians who were not party to it. He promised to live in peace with the English; in return, the remaining Pequots would be divided between the Mohegans and the Narragansetts. It was at once revenge and an attempt at ethnic erasure. The treaty's clause that the Pequots "shall no more be called Pequots but Narragansetts and Mohegans" was as much Uncas's doing as it was that of the colonists. Acutely aware of their weakness in the midst of powerful Indigenous confederacies, the English expected the Mohegans and Narragansetts to punish the Pequots and "as soon as they can either bring the Chief Sachem of our late Enemies the Pequots that had the chief hand in killing the English to the said English or take off their heads." When peace came, the English held more than three hundred Pequots captives. They carried many of them to the colony of Providence Island, near the Spanish-controlled Mosquito Island, trading them for African slaves. New Englanders did not want Pequots nearby.[2]

With the Pequots utterly defeated, the Mohegans emerged as a major regional power. While maneuvering to marginalize the leading Narragansett sachem, Miantonomi, Uncas directed the English—apparently through misinformation—to move against the Narragansetts. In the mid-1640s, the English began to encroach on Narragansett lands. Uncas captured Miantonomi and turned him over to the English. The colonists sentenced the sachem to death and asked Uncas to execute the order. With a Puritan delegation witnessing, Uncas's brother Wawequa sank a tomahawk in the sachem's skull. The Narragansetts soon signed a peace treaty with the Connecticut Colony.[3]

Uncas's opportunistic diplomatic maneuvering and his ability to create and break alliances placed the colonists at a significant disadvantage in the contest for position and power. Uncas and his Mohegans endured endless colonial challenges, large and small—not just surviving as a people but controlling the world around them. Huddling in their small colonial enclaves, the English and Dutch were insular and powerless in comparison, managing little more than glimpses of the Indigenous politics that determined events and outcomes. The English thought they could regulate matters of war and peace in the New World, but more often than not, Indians steered them into fighting and financing Indian wars and facilitating truces and treaties with goods and gifts when the fighting stopped. The colonists—whether Spanish, French, English, or Dutch—could be arrogant and brutal, but the Indians had learned how to exploit them for their own purposes. Properly managed and manipulated, they could be useful.

THE INFAMOUS MASSACRES of Pequots and Raritans distort the historical reality in a more elemental way: they make the colonies seem more powerful than they actually were. At midcentury, colonial settlements in North America consisted of some two dozen seaside towns and a handful of forts of little consequence on the coastal plains, secured only through massive loss of life. Forts, the European thinking went, made empires, and the English were failing in that quest. Curbed by Indigenous power, the English colonists had spread up and down along the Atlantic coast, latching onto its sheltering estuaries and managing only fleeting inroads into the continent's interior. The Appalachians and the lands west of them remained largely unknown to White people. Plymouth, Massachusetts, Connecticut, and Rhode Island were modest ventures, their combined population barely reaching thirty thousand, and New Netherland was a fragile enterprise, neglected by its mother country and undercut by reckless leadership. Only the wealthy tobacco colonies—Virginia and Maryland—managed to dispossess Native Americans on a large scale; everywhere else the Indians held the line. When Virginia planters grew wealthier, they began to sell guns to the Westos, a diasporic people displaced by the Iroquois, in exchange for Indian slaves. Westos became professional slave hunters and traders. They built a town at the falls of the James River, from where they could move captives in canoes to Virginia's tobacco fields. They also targeted the Spanish Indian missions in Georgia and Florida, bringing back thousands of slaves.[4]

If there was an exception among the major European colonial projects in the seventeenth century, it was the second phase of French colonialism. Since their humiliating expulsion from Florida in the mid-1560s, the French had observed their rivals' colonial efforts in North America from a distance, limiting their ambitions to the northeastern corner of the continent. They established a colony of convicts on Sable Island and a small trading post, Tadoussac, in the lower Saint Lawrence Valley. The local Indians did not allow Europeans to travel west of the post; they wanted to monopolize the fur trade. France's most lucrative venture in North America was reflected in the now-traditional Norman, Basque, and Breton fishing forays in the Grand Banks of Newfoundland. Some three hundred French fishing and whaling boats sailed to the area annually, mingling with hundreds of Dutch, English, and Portuguese vessels and reaping massive profits.[5]

After a hiatus of nearly four decades, France made a new effort at colonizing, now in the colder latitudes and with a different mindset: they vigorously pursued alliances with Native nations. Leading the renewed effort was Samuel de Champlain, who came from an ordinary family of seafarers. He was part of an expedition that established Port Royal in Acadia in 1605, and three years later he spearheaded an expedition along the Saint Lawrence River to take over the fur trade in the region. He built a trading post, Quebec, on a strategically significant site where the great river suddenly narrows. Like the zealous early French conquistadors in Florida, Champlain was a dreamer who sought personal and national fulfillment in the New World. But unlike his predecessors, Champlain was also a realist and fully aware of the limitations of French power in the Americas. French immigration to North America was much more limited than that of the English and Spanish, rendered so by the French court and powerful trade guilds that focused on launching colonial ventures in Asia. Now at a serious disadvantage with their European and Native rivals in the Americas, the French were forced to innovate. Champlain, a devout Catholic who believed that all people were God's children, knew that the Native peoples would be the key to any success the French might enjoy in America. Mirroring John Smith's endeavors farther south, Champlain envisioned Quebec as the heart of New France, an unprecedented colonial venture that would be grounded not in French supremacy over the Indians, but in trade, sharing, and bonds of kinship.[6]

Champlain cultivated ties with powerful French patrons, investors, and clergymen with unusual energy—he would end up crossing the Atlantic twenty-seven times—and he took similar care in nurturing relationships with Indians. Already in 1603, he had advocated for building a fort at Trois-Rivières to "secure the freedom of some tribes who dare not come that way for fear of their enemies of the said Iroquois, who

Sketch (an 1885 reproduction of a 1609 work)
depicting Samuel de Champlain in battle with Iroquois

infest the bank all along the said River of Canada." Champlain wanted
to envelop Quebec with Native allies, and he personally adopted three
Montagnais girls, whom he named Faith, Hope, and Charity—his
design for a New France as a shared domain in microcosm. Crucially,
he was willing to fight alongside his Native allies, the Wyandots, Algonquians, and Montagnais, all of whom shared his fear of the powerful,
forty-five-hundred-strong Mohawks. The muzzle-loading harquebuses
that Champlain and his soldiers brought to battle may have been cumbersome, but their shock value was overwhelming. In 1609, near the
lake that would be named after him, Champlain loaded his harquebus
with four bullets and, steered by his Native allies, walked alone toward
the enemy line. He "shot straight at one of the three chiefs, and with this
shot two fell to the ground." Another shot by one of his soldiers from
the woods "astonished them again so much that, seeing their chiefs
dead, they lost courage and took to flight." Traditional Native armor
and shields were suddenly obsolete. French missionaries converted the
first Native leader, Membertou of the Mi'kmaqs, a year later.[7]

Inspired by Champlain's vision of coexistence, French traders
forged a close partnership with the thirty- to forty-thousand-strong
Wyandot Confederacy, whose twenty-eight towns were huddled close

Siege of an Iroquois village

together around the centrally located Georgian Bay. From there, supremely mobile Wyandot hunter-traders scoured rivers and streams for thick winter beaver pelts and then took the processed furs to Quebec for spring fairs, filling their canoes with guns, lead, powder, and metal tools for homebound journeys. The Wyandots informed the French that they would not accept haggling, and still their trading empire stretched from the lower Saint Lawrence Valley to the western Great Lakes. The vastness of their domain posed an existential threat to the Iroquois, who had traded with Europeans in the Grand Banks and in the Saint Lawrence Valley for generations and had come to rely on European metal knives, axes, kettles, pans, and needles. The Mohawks, acting alone, set out to extinguish New France's Indian trade along the Saint Lawrence River and monopolize the beaver-hunting grounds around the valley and in the west. The French, Dutch, Wyandots, and anyone else who stood in their way, would have to yield in the face of Mohawk war expeditions. Champlain, the de facto governor of New France, was one of them.[8]

In 1622, desperate to put an end to the violence that disrupted the fur trade, the raison d'être of New France, Champlain yielded to Mohawk demands. The Dutch came to their own conclusions about Mohawk power around the same time, retreating from closer inter-actions; and Champlain, spotting an opening, extended a peace pro-posal to the Indian nation. The Mohawks accepted a treaty, which freed them to focus on their Native rivals. They attacked Montagnais towns in the Saint Lawrence Valley, securing the northern and west-ern flanks of Iroquoia, the Iroquois homeland. In the south and east, Mohawks, the "Keepers of the Eastern Door," moved to discipline the Dutch, who, placing profits before politics, had opened Fort Orange to Mahicans. By 1628, the Mahicans and the Dutch had seen enough. The Mahicans agreed to pay the Mohawks an annual tribute in wam-pum, and the Dutch resigned to placate the Iroquois League with goods. Mohawk sachems now controlled who was allowed to trade at the fort—whose guns, lead, and powder could make and unmake Indigenous regimes in the Northeast.[9]

France's support for its Native allies was not altruism; it was secured by a generous trade in beaver pelts and through the social alchemy of sharing. "The Beaver does everything perfectly well," a Montagnais hunter declared, "making sport" of French traders. "It makes kettles, hatchets, swords, knives, bread; and, in short, it makes everything." It is only a slight exaggeration to say that the beaver also made New France itself. In 1627 the colony was home to mere eighty-five people, yet its charter granted it all of North America, from Flor-ida to the Arctic Circle. To prop up the colony, Cardinal Richelieu, the chief minister of King Louis XIII, established the Company of One Hundred Associates to facilitate immigration. Expectations were still modest. The company had to bring in fifteen hundred French "of both sexes" during the first ten years, or face heavy sanctions. It was clear that collaboration with the Indians through the beaver pelt trade would remain New France's lifeline.[10]

However, New France was also a religious and moral project that mobilized French officials, missionaries, and soldiers to make a con-certed effort to enforce acceptable behavior. Marriage customs, espe-cially polygyny, became a source of contention between Jesuits and

Indians. For Native men, having multiple wives was essential as a mark of status, as well as insurance that they would produce more children who would contribute to the household's prosperity and reputation. When French missionaries challenged Indigenous marriage arrangements, both Native women and men fought back fiercely. But large numbers of women—especially captured secondary wives—also sought relief from the grueling labor and lack of autonomy under authoritative and abusive husbands. For them and others, missionaries and Christianity could be useful: they could offer a different life.[11]

In the early 1630s, New France, already inseparable from its network of Indian allies, encompassed an expanding domain around the Saint Lawrence Valley. French traders were reaching out to the Indians for their furs, and Jesuit friars were reaching out for their souls, entrenching the French in North America. In 1631, Champlain wrote a booklet on French and English colonization in the New World, stating that the English "do not deny us all New France and cannot question what the whole world has admitted."[12]

In 1636, Tessouat, an Algonquian leader, tried to shame reluctant Wyandot sachems into joining him on a campaign against the Iroquois. According to a Jesuit priest, he declared that "his body was hatchets; he meant that the preservation of his person and of his Nation was the preservation of the hatchets, the kettles, and all the trade of the French, for the Hurons," capturing the enormity of the technological change that had swept over his world and those of many others. That did not make him a subordinate of the French, however. On the contrary, Tessouat declared himself the "master of the French," and proclaimed that "he would lead us [the French] back to Kébec and make us all recross the sea." New France survived because he chose not to do that. The Indians had quickly learned how to manage the aggressive newcomers: when negotiations failed, they had to rely on in-your-face self-assurance.[13]

By the mid-seventeenth century, the colonies in Maine that had been founded by European powers were confined to the Atlantic coast below the Penobscot River, and most of those colonies were small and vulnerable. European maps were remarkably accurate when depicting coasts and rivers, but the rest of the continent remained terra incognita. The English, French, and Dutch colonies had not become launchpads for territorial expansion, and only the French had a plan for colonization—a plan that emphasized coexistence. All colonial powers simply struggled to survive. Rather than looking to the west for conquests, they looked to the east, toward their mother countries, for goods, weapons, and soldiers to keep them safe. The settlements were more footholds than full-fledged colonies. It is telling that the out-of-the-way Great Fishery was still the most lucrative of the European schemes, and it was a business venture, not a colony.

The Spanish Empire had instigated an early European surge consisting largely of ruthless pillaging, which was lucrative but not sustainable. It had not led to permanent possessions in North America. By 1600, the Spanish were seriously questioning their methods. More than a century of colonialism had merely scratched the surface of the Indigenous continent.[14]

PART THREE

THE CONTEST FOR THE GREAT AMERICAN INTERIOR

(early and mid-seventeenth century)

Chapter 8

THE RISE OF THE FIVE NATIONS LEAGUE

I ROQUOIA, THE BIRTHPLACE AND HOMELAND OF THE
Iroquois, emerged from beneath receding ice sheets in the eighth
millennium BCE, the dry land spreading in all directions on the Turtle's back with the help of Sky Woman and her son Tharonhiawagon.
But not all the water had vanished. Deep gashes carved by ice became
rivers that scored Iroquoia from north to south and would later be
known as the Connecticut, Hudson, Delaware, Susquehanna, Allegheny, and Ohio, together demarcating a massive rectangle-shaped
domain that extended nearly four hundred miles from the Connecticut River to Lake Erie.

Another set of rivers—the Mohawk, Saint Lawrence, and
Ottawa—facilitated mobility along an east–west axis, opening access
to the great interior through Lakes Ontario and Erie. It was via these
waterways that corn, beans, and squash arrived in Iroquoia, sparking population growth that brought the Iroquois numbers to between
twenty and thirty thousand in the fifteenth century. From the very
beginning, the Iroquois were primed for centrality. Accruing power
required more than geographical luck, though; it also demanded
political creativity and flexibility. Land was essential for belonging
and survival, but to secure land, people first needed to secure access
to rivers, which made possible farming, mobility, trade, warfare, and
alliances. "Dish with One Spoon," an ancient Indigenous law, helped
to facilitate the sharing of territory and resources.

The Iroquoian nations had fought one another for generations, but
in the late fifteenth century the Great League of Peace and Power, a
ritual and spiritual compact, put an end to the bloodshed. The Great

An Iroquois longhouse

League's foundation was the Great Law of Peace, an oral narrative that traces the formation of the Great League of Peace and Power, a layered alliance of five nations, or council fires, that clustered along the Finger Lakes south and east of Lake Ontario. The Iroquois call themselves Haudenosaunee, which means "the whole house." Within that metaphorical longhouse, each nation had a specific role. The Mohawks, "the people of the flint," served as the Keepers of the Eastern Door, and the Senecas, "the people of the great hill," served as the Keepers of the Western Door, enclosing the other three nations: the Oneidas, "the people of the standing stone"; the Onondagas, "the people of the mountain"; and the Cayugas, "the people at the landing," in the middle.[1]

The Five Nations League was the collective, outward-facing front of the Great League of Peace and Power, conducting trade, diplomacy, and war with outsiders. The Five Nations convened among the Onondagas, the Firekeepers, at the symbolic center of Iroquoia to the south and east of Lake Ontario, where the Grand Council of fifty sachems—clan leaders—gathered to deliberate league-wide matters. The sachems were to follow the lessons of the mythological Peacemaker who had delivered the Good News of Peace and Power to Hiawatha—"he who combs"—a cultural hero who cured a misanthropic Onondaga sachem Tadadaho, a man so full of hate that his hair had become a wild mesh of snakes. Hiawatha untangled Tadadaho's hair, giving him and, by extension, the Iroquois, reason. Each nation voted in unison, and all Grand Council decisions had to be unanimous. A Jesuit missionary who visited the Onondaga Nation during a council meeting was surprised and impressed by the proceedings. "Their policy in this is very wise, and has nothing Barbarous in it. . . . There all the Deputies from the different Nations are present, to make their complaints and receive the necessary satisfaction in mutual gifts—by means of which they maintain a good understanding with one another."

By long-standing tradition, senior women served as heads of Iroquois clans and appointed the sachems to their roles, selecting suitable candidates from among the adult men who met the key criteria: eloquence, the ability to listen, and the necessary gravitas to build consensus. The clan mothers could also dismiss council sachems, and they decided the fate of captives—a critical responsibility in Iroquois politics. A French captive was struck by the women's central role in Five Nations politics: "He then, or she, who has some propositions to make begins by assembling the elders of his or her family, and if it is something that concerns the warriors, one or two captains of this same family are summoned to be as witnesses to the thing being proposed. Each one there gives his opinion in a very serious manner, after which they agree upon the procedure. That being finished, an elder appointed by them goes to invite the other families, I mean the elders and war chiefs, supposing the thing requires it." As in many other Native nations in the East, women did all the farming, and Iroquois women's contributions to the wealth and security of their confederacy were overwhelming, solidifying the clan mothers' role as decision-makers: they introduced political initiatives that did not require men's endorsement to be adopted. Female rule had a practical dimension: men were hunters and traders who ranged widely and were often absent for long periods. Longhouses, multifamily dwellings, belonged to women. Among all Indigenous nations, the Iroquois came the closest to a matriarchate. A Jesuit priest thought that "nothing . . . is more real than this superiority of the women. It is of them that the nation really consists." Jesuit missionary Joseph-François Lafitau concurred, calling the Iroquois government gynococracy.[2]

Led by clan mothers, the Iroquois were committed to a vision of peace and belonging under the Tree of the Great Peace, which could be extended beyond Iroquoia like a sheltering roof to embrace strangers who demonstrated that they were able to adopt the proper mindset. The Five Nations League was both a political and a spiritual body committed to peace, unity, and cooperation. The early-seventeenth-century European invasions instilled that ideal with new urgency and then militarized it. The result was war and an unprecedented burst of Indigenous power.[3]

IN THE LATE 1620S the Mohawks negotiated trade relations with the Dutch at Fort Orange. After establishing commerce with the Dutch, the Mohawks joined the other Iroquois nations to end the French-Indian trade in the Saint Lawrence Valley once and for all. They harassed and killed Wyandots, Algonquians, and other Indians allied with the French, forcing them to retreat. As their power and ambitions swelled, the Iroquois made a concerted effort to reshape the geopolitical makeup of the Northwest to serve their needs: they wanted to redirect the flow of furs, guns, metal, people, and power southward into their villages. In 1633, the Iroquois solicited English traders who had anchored at Tadoussac in the lower Saint Lawrence River. Terrified by that move, Champlain pleaded with the Iroquois not to abandon the French, who "had always loved them and defended them." He wanted them to remember that he "had assisted them in person in their wars," in which "he himself was wounded by an arrow."[4]

Not long after, in Boston, John Winthrop sat down to write a letter to his friend Simonds D'Ewes. Winthrop mused about Massachusetts politics and his plans, and assured his friend that "I am still as full of Company and business as before. But for the natives in these parts, God hath so pursued them, as for 300 miles space, the greatest part of them swept away by the small pox, which still continues among them: So as God had hereby cleared our title to this place, and those who remain in these parts, being in all not 50, have put themselves under our protection, and freely confined themselves and their interest within certain limits." The jarring juxtaposition of his own robust health and the mass death of Native Americans was more than a cognitive slippage: Winthrop saw destiny in the carnage.[5]

According to Winthrop, God had cleared the land of savages, securing America for a worthier race. Winthrop was half-right; there might have been no New England—indeed no English colonies—in North America without this biological catastrophe. The death zone extended from the Atlantic coast to the Appalachians and from the Chesapeake Bay to the Saint Lawrence Valley, destroying countless Native communities. Yet regardless of Winthrop's conviction of divine partiality, nothing in North America was preordained. The same epidemic that seemed to offer the English an entire new world also triggered the most explosive Indigenous expansion since the first migrations across the length of the hemisphere. The Iroquois League, having lost nearly half of its members, went to war to repopulate itself by making Iroquois out of others. An old Wyandot sachem told the Jesuits that he did not "yet know whether we shall escape the fury of this Demon. I have seen maladies in the country before, but never have I seen anything like this." After the pox had run its course, the league's central location amid Dutch, French, and English colonies and several Native nations suddenly turned into a liability. The Five Nations League was horribly exposed, and it needed new people to survive. That meant attacking the Native settlements around it and taking captives. Mass death and grief demanded war.[6]

It was a specific kind of war—a distinct military-cultural dynamic known as "mourning wars." Traveling along rivers and over lakes in canoe fleets, the Iroquois conducted a measured tactical war aimed at making themselves untraceable, holding their enemies at bay, keeping market outlets open, and restoring spiritual balance to their world by transforming others into Iroquois. Their logistical and spiritual prowess was overwhelming. Every return of a war party was an occasion for communal celebration, as one Jesuit observed: "All the people came out to witness this Triumph of the Savages. Joy animated the souls of the victors, while sorrow afflicted those of the vanquished.

When all had landed, they were taken to the cabins of the Algonquins. Some threw themselves on him who had been given to them, tore out his nails, cut off several of his fingers, and burned his feet with heated stones." The political spectacle—the assertion of Iroquois suprem-acy—sustained Iroquois unity and spiritual primacy.[7]

Mass death also demanded bold and creative diplomacy. While relying on war and captive raiding to stabilize their world, the Five Nations also approached the Dutch, French, Wyandots, Mahi-cans, Munsees, Montagnais, and other Native nations, hoping to bring peace and remove barriers to trade. For years, Dutch agents in Manhattan had lavished the Mohawks with gifts, eager to estab-lish a tighter relationship with the most powerful Native nation in the Northeast. In August 1645, a Mohawk headman, Agheroense, entered the colony, offering, in fluent Dutch, an alliance with New Netherland. He had "streaked his face with a glittering yellow paint," apparently impressing Governor Willem Kieft, who entered into a treaty with the Mohawk Nation. Unlike the Spanish in New Mexico, the Dutch did not live among the local Indians, the Iroquois, and this separation created a more stable relationship.[8]

Just a few weeks later, Kiotsaeton, a Mohawk ambassador, arrived in Trois-Rivières, a French fort in the lower Saint Lawrence Valley, to make a plea to *Onontio*, "Great Mountain," the name the Indians used for the governor of New France, who at the time was Charles de Montmagny. Onontio welcomed Kiotsaeton and his two companions, who sat down at his feet in the courtyard "as a mark of the affec-tion that they bore to the French." Opposite them were Algonquian, Montagnais, and Wyandot envoys. The fort may have been French, but the Iroquois were in charge of the proceedings. Collars—sumptu-ous wampum necklaces—symbolized good feelings, and Kiotsaeton made his plea: "We have a multitude of war songs in our country; we have cast them all on the ground; we have no longer anything but songs of rejoicing."[9]

Having temporarily buried war, Kiotsaeton focused on the most urgent matter: trade. " 'There,' said he, 'is the road, quite smooth and quite straight.' He bent toward the ground, looking to see whether there were any more thorns or bushes, and whether there were any mounds over which one might stumble in walking. 'It is all finished. We can see the smoke of our villages, from Quebec to the extremity of our country. All obstacles are removed.'" Kiotsaeton's vision of belonging was expansive. He wanted the French, Algonquians, Montagnais, Wyandots, and Iroquois to "be but one Nation, and I would be one of you."[10]

Kiotsaeton's efforts did not stop the canoe-borne Iroquois from attacking the annual trade fleets of French canoes along the Saint Lawrence or from blocking French trade routes in the interior. New France consisted of a mere three hundred colonists, and the recently established Montreal was but a hamlet. Fearing the neighboring Mohawks, colonists struggled to muster the courage to urinate outside of the town walls. The Indian attacks were more than simple looting. In 1648, while Quebec, Trois-Rivières, Tadoussac, and Montreal were enjoying a rare lull in Native assaults, the Iroquois launched a carefully organized campaign to disrupt the French fur trade in the Great Lakes region. Their war parties seized prime trapping grounds and captives, pushing west and north of Lake Ontario in summer-long campaigns. The result was a massive diaspora: Wyandots, Wenros, Nipissings, Eries, Neutrals, and Petuns all abandoned their ancient homelands and retreated deep into the west, eventually clustering along the southern shore of Lake Superior and the western shore of Lake Michigan. At least a dozen nations fled "the fury of the Iroquois," dispersing across the Great Lakes to places that seemed "the very end of the world." By the late seventeenth century, the Iroquois may have absorbed nearly three thousand Wendats into Iroquoia.

The lands west of Lake Michigan, however, were not empty. They belonged to the Algonquian-speaking Anishinaabeg peoples— Odawas, Potawatomis, Sauteurs, and Ojibwes—who had lived around the Great Lakes since the fifteenth century and whose kinship networks, *nindoodemag*, covered much of the region, facilitating mobility, alliance-making, and trade. The refugees clashed with the Great Lakes peoples at first, but relentless Iroquois pressure soon pushed them together. The resident Indians opened their villages to the emigrant Indians and, through countless reconciliation ceremonies, incorporated them into their homeland, Anishinaabewaki,

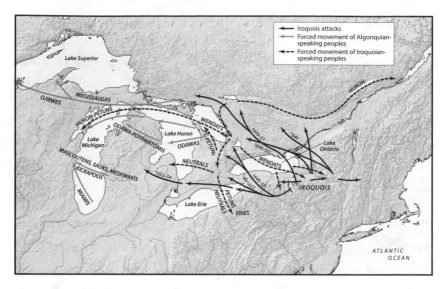

The Iroquois mourning wars

which enveloped Lakes Huron and Superior and the northern half of Lake Michigan. Local villages swelled into large, mixed settlements where people sought to restore normalcy to a suddenly destabilized world. Soon, some two dozen hybrid villages dotted a triangle-shaped area stretching from the Illinois River to both ends of Lake Superior— a region the French knew as *pays d'en haut*, "upper country." At its center sat *La Baye des Puants*—Green Bay—now home to some ten thousand people.[11]

The Iroquois had driven thousands of people into the west, gaining a vast domain in their wake. It was the first large-scale westward expansion in early American history. But this did not put an end to the warfare, which only seemed to escalate as the Iroquois's enemies dispersed. The explanation was at once simple and unique: the Iroquois needed people more than they needed territory. They needed captives to replenish disease-ravaged populations, mend fractured lineages, alleviate pain through vengeance, and restore the spiritual vitality of their communities. The intense Five Nations violence was a strategic, emotional, and spiritual response to catastrophic losses. The Iroquois mourning wars were changing the face of the North American interior almost beyond recognition.[12]

The mourning wars reinforced the influence of the clan mothers.

When Iroquois armies mobilized to attack their enemies, clan mothers escorted the soldiers out of their villages to the edge of the woods, where the men put on their war uniforms. With the clan mothers observing them, the soldiers carved pictographs into trees to note the strength of the expedition—a public record of the battles that were about to take place. When the soldiers returned, almost invariably with prisoners—women, men, children—the clan mothers decided whether the captives would be literally or ritually adopted into their households. Those chosen for literal adoption went through a "quickening" ceremony in which they received the name and the social role of a deceased Iroquois. These people—known as *we-hait-wat-sha*— or "a body cut into parts and scattered around"—were adopted into clans, became full-fledged members of the Iroquois League, and were obliged to defend it in battle, even against former kin. The ritual adoptees were slotted into Iroquois families as "uncles" or "nephews." Their faces were painted red and black, and they were allowed to give a feast and recite their war honors before being executed. Condemned captives were tied to a stake, and their new relatives took turns to "caress" them with firebrands. Women cut up the corpses and boiled the pieces in kettles so that the Iroquois could absorb the prisoners' spiritual power. The Iroquois aimed to dismantle "their nationality," to prop up their own.

The Iroquois conducted these ceremonies not because they clamored for war but because they wanted peace. Ritual absorption of enemy bodies and souls—whether real or imagined—eased the Iroquois's pain and helped them regain reason; it restored normalcy. An epic tale reminded them of how Deganawidah, the Peacemaker, revealed to Hiawatha, who had lost all his daughters, the Good News of Peace and Power. Deganawidah showed to Hiawatha the condolence ceremonies that helped remove his grief and regain his sense. The Good News of Peace and Power would make war and bloodshed unnecessary. But it could not assuage the enormous pain that smallpox had brought. Hundreds of grieving families demanded war that would produce captives to replace lost relatives, and clan matrons authorized massive war parties that could deliver consolation.

By midcentury, the Iroquois were superbly equipped to wage war.

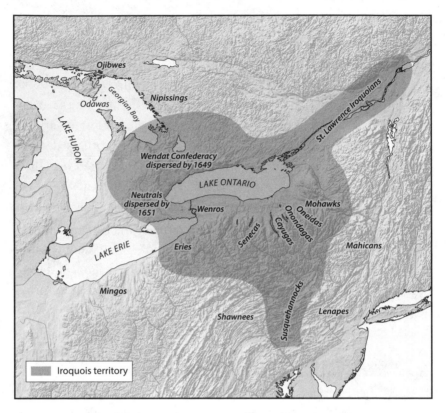

Iroquois dominance in the interior in the mid-seventeenth century

Their roughly two thousand soldiers possessed three hundred har-quebuses and were "skilled in handling" the heavy flintlock guns in close-range attacks and ambushes, both on land and along rivers and streams. A typical fight began with a single volley—loading the guns took nearly half a minute—immediately followed by a charge with iron axes and knives. French officials in Quebec concluded that they "must not take the initiative in irritating the Iroquois." They also agreed that they "must prevent the Iroquois, whether upper or lower," from attacking their Indian allies "in sight of our settlements."[13]

In 1648 the Mohawks and Senecas overpowered the Attignee-nongnahac Wyandots, killing and capturing seven hundred people. The next year a thousand-strong Iroquois army broke the back of the Wyandot Confederacy but lost some three hundred soldiers—a disaster that demanded retribution and still more captives. The Iroquois told the Jesuits that "all the four Nations of the upper Iroquois were on fire; that they were leaguing together, and arming to repulse" their enemies. The Great Lakes nations learned to expect Five Nations invasions every year. Launching campaigns from their core area between the Hudson Valley and Lake Ontario, Five Nations soldiers pushed west across the Oswego River and Lake Ontario and deep into the region in search of captives and spiritual balance. By 1660, the Iroquois had fought every nation in the Great Lakes, creating a vast shatter zone of destruction. Ancient Indigenous confederacies collapsed, and the Wyandots' homeland, Wendake, disintegrated. People scattered in all directions, seeking refuge. The Iroquois moved to absorb—not to kill—the survivors of the broken nations, we-hait-wat-sha, devastating other nationalities to build up their own. Navigating this new world could be disorienting. In 1655, a Five Nations envoy proposed peace to the Wyandots and French, announcing, "My brothers, I have not changed my soul, despite my change of country; nor has my blood become Iroquois, although I dwell among them. My heart is all Huron, as well as my tongue." War captives now made up more than half of the Iroquois population, generating both protection and dissonance.[14]

THE FIVE NATIONS LEAGUE had become the dominant power in the Eastern Woodlands, its movable settlements covering a domain that dwarfed the French, English, and Dutch colonies clustered on the Atlantic coast. Yet French policymakers were slow to adjust to an order in which Iroquoia, not New France, was the dominant power. "Were one to believe them," a Jesuit missionary wrote, "either New France would be almost entirely Iroquois, or we would no longer have any French except among the Iroquois." The French recoiled. They did little to appease the Five Nations, ignoring the Indians' requests for accommodation, coexistence, and equitable trade almost as an imperial reflex. In a grave violation of Indigenous protocols, they imprisoned Iroquois ambassadors, keeping them as hostages in Montreal and Quebec. Revealing the French mindset, a Jesuit priest concluded that "it is beyond doubt that, if the Agnieronnnons [Mohawks] were defeated by the French, the other Iroquois nations would be glad to compromise with us, and give us their Children as hostages of their good faith." French colonialism operated on the same moral key as English and Spanish colonialism; the differences in the three powers were a matter of capacity, not of choice.[15]

The Iroquois moved to educate and punish the arrogant French. "Everywhere," a Jesuit priest deplored, "we find the Iroquois, who, like an obtrusive phantom, besets us in all places. If he finds us among our new Christians, he slaughters them in our arms; if he meets us on the River, he slays us; and if he takes us in the cabins of our Savages, he burns us with them." In 1660 the Jesuits lamented, "If they last year made us cry out loudly enough to be heard in France, they now leave us naught but tears to shed for our dead." Onondaga and Mohawk armies "filled with fire and bloodshed the neighborhood of Kebec, . . . made a desert of Tadoussac, . . . [and] left their taint in the entire island of Orleans, having massacred there, in particular, Monsieur the Seneschal Delauson and his Brave Companions, . . . [and] made Three Rivers mourn." In 1663, when a royal commissioner of New France, anticipating massacres, ordered "all the French colonists to live together in Villages and not a great distance the one from the other," the king of France took over direct control of New France. To save the reeling colony, he launched a program that brought single women, *filles du roi*, to the colony. The women started families, which helped stabilize New France.[16]

Overwhelming Iroquois military dominance quickly translated into economic, political, and cultural power. Their place in the world secure, the Iroquois made a concerted effort to stabilize their borderlands through trade, diplomacy, and alliances. They did so on their own terms. The Dutch had long ago accepted their subordinate role in the shadow of the Iroquois, especially the Mohawks. A Dutch pastor wrote that "the Principal nation of all the savages and Indians hereabouts with which we have the most intercourse is the Mahakuaas [Mohawks], who have laid all the other Indians near us under contribution." The Iroquois refused to accept English and Dutch currencies in commercial transactions and insisted on the use of wampum beads instead. Wampum beads had been a major trade item since the

1620s, and by midcentury the Dutch had developed new techniques to produce shell beads. The result was a lucrative trade triangle that saw the Dutch buying beads from New England Algonquians with manufactured goods, then using those beads to buy pelts from the Five Nations, and finally shipping the pelts to Europe to buy goods for North American markets. Much of New England's prosperity was built on wampum, a classic Iroquois product.

Iroquois expansion was driven by a desire for stability and power, and by the middle of the seventeenth century the Five Nations had made themselves indispensable. No one could ignore them. New France established a fund to rescue Iroquois captives from their enemies and provided the Iroquois with pensions. In 1659, Mohawk sachems met with Dutch representatives at Fort Orange and made a series of demands, handing out strings of wampum after each stipulation. They said that "it is very wrong, that the *Dutch* scold [the Indians] so much without regard to tribe," and they reprimanded the Dutch for calling Indians "dogs" and "rascals." The sachems demanded that the Dutch treat their Lenape, Mahican, and Catskill allies with respect and "live with them as brothers." Certain of their authority and position in the world, the Mohawks had moved beyond mere containment of the Europeans. They now expected compliance.[17]

Chapter 9

ENEMIES OF
THE FAITH

I**N MID-MARCH 1649, TWO JESUIT PRIESTS WENT** missing when an Iroquois party attacked a Wyandot village near Sault Sainte Marie at the Straits of Mackinac between Lake Huron and Lake Michigan. As Father Paul Ragueneau prepared to dispatch a search party, the Jesuits "perceived several savages on the road, coming straight toward us. We all thought it was the Iroquois who were coming to attack us; but, having considered them more closely, we perceived that they were Wyandots who were fleeing from the fight, and who escaped from the combat. These poor savages caused a great pity in us. They were all covered with wounds. One had his head fractured; another his arm broken; another had an arrow in his eye."[1]

The Jesuits' error was understandable. The Iroquois had harassed them for decades for having ministered to their rivals and enemies, especially Wyandots, Illinis, Odawas, Ojibwes, Montagnais, Naskapis, and Nipissings. The Jesuits focused their efforts so heavily on the enemies of the Five Nations precisely because they had rendered neighboring Indian nations weak, needy, and desperate—perfect targets for the Jesuit gospel of a better life in the hereafter. Eager to reap the souls of Iroquois victims, the Jesuits, with their untiring leader Claude-Jean Allouez, established several missions and smaller stations in the Great Lakes region. The Iroquois could tolerate this small footprint, but when French traders began to follow the Jesuits to the west in nimble and sturdy birchbark canoes, seeking out the large Native communities near the missions and selling guns to their rivals, the Five Nations had had their fill. Killing Jesuits became as valuable as killing Native enemies.

The Wyandots told the Jesuits what had happened to the two priests: "The Iroquois came, to the number of twelve hundred men; took our village, and seized Father [Jean de] Brebœuf and his companion; and set fire to all the huts. They proceeded to vent their rage on those two Fathers; for they took them both and stripped them entirely naked, and fastened each to a post. They tied both their hands together. They tore the nails from their fingers. They beat them with a shower of blows from cudgels, on the shoulders, the loins, the belly, the legs, and the face—there being no part of their body which did not endure this torment." Brebœuf suffered the torture stoically, impressing his Jesuit brothers. "Overwhelmed under the weight of these blows, he did not cease continually to speak of God, and to encourage all the new Christians who were captives like himself to suffer well, that they might die well, in order to go in company with him to Paradise."[2]

The thoroughness of the description captures the horror and confusion that the Jesuits faced when the Iroquois descended on them. The violence was both methodical and spectacular—a form of cross-cultural communication designed to shock. The Iroquois wanted to banish the Jesuits from the interior, where they interfered with Iroquois operations and ambitions; the violence served political, economic, and spiritual ends, restoring order where European expansion had disrupted it. But the exhaustive nature of the account also served another goal. As terrifying as the torture was to the Jesuits, many of them welcomed and even sought it out: the greater the suffering, the greater the sacrifice in God's eyes. Brebœuf, facing imminent death, spoke to his baptized Native proteges: "My children, let us lift our eyes to Heaven at the height of our afflictions; let us remember that God is the witness to our sufferings, and will soon be our exceeding great reward."[3]

Jesuits were seeking martyrdom in what to them was a heathenish wilderness, but in the long run, mass martyrdom was not sustainable. The Jesuit order, the Society of Jesus, was a relatively modest enterprise in North America, with between thirty and forty active missionaries in the field at any given time. Yet they represented a major investment, having been thoroughly trained in classical studies and theology in seminaries in France, while also learning Indigenous languages, studying Native customs, and familiarizing themselves with the geography of their destinations. Once in North America, they lived in Native communities, conforming to Native ways. Each responsible for hundreds of souls, the priests were a crucial asset for the order. The problem was that, as individuals, most Jesuits put little value on their earthly existence. Steeped in mystical Catholicism, they strove for "indifference," the annihilation of the self, which they saw as an entity detached from God. The Jesuits were an endangered resource for the French Empire in the New World.[4]

Between 1642 and 1649, eight Jesuits died violently, and the missionaries branded the Iroquois as "enemies of the faith." The Jesuits at the mission of Saint Ignace on Mackinac Island remembered that March 16, 1649, "marked the beginning of our misfortunes—if, however, that be a misfortune which no doubt has been the salvation of many God's elect." The Iroquois, "enemies of the Hurons, to the number of about a thousand men, well furnished with weapons—and mostly with firearms which they obtain from the Dutch, their allies—arrived by night at the frontier of this country, without our having any knowledge of their approach." Having studied the lay of the land during the night, the Iroquois attacked at dawn. As with most Iroquois-Wyandot battles during the mourning wars, it was a rout: "This village was taken, almost without striking a blow," a Jesuit priest reported, "there having been only ten Iroquois killed. Part of the Wyandots—men, women, and children—were massacred then and there; the others were made captives, and reserved for cruelties more terrible than death."[5]

The *Jesuit Relations*, the annual report of Jesuit priests in North America, became a litany of Iroquois atrocities: torched towns; men burned at the stake; the Saint Lawrence Valley "infested with the Iroquois Enemies"; mission Indians burning their own settlements, "lest they should serve as retreat and fortresses to the Iroquois"; Wyandots abandoning their towns, "scattering where they could"; Iroquois capturing Wyandots "in the sight of Montreal," at the doorstep of New France. The Wyandots were constantly in retreat, trying to put distance between themselves and the Iroquois. Some "flung themselves into the deepest recesses of the forest," while others chose "to find death in the waters, or from the cliffs, [rather] than by the fires of the Iroquois." In 1649, a force of three hundred Iroquois sacked Saint Jean, a Tionontati Indian mission in Georgian Bay.[6]

The master plan of the Society of Jesus had focused on building permanent missions in North America in order to monitor, control, and educate the Indians, replacing Native religions with biblical dogma. Their ideal landscape was a multitude of strategically located missions, near large Indigenous settlements and surrounded by fields, gardens, and workshops. The Jesuits wanted their wards bound to the soil. The Iroquois had made that all but impossible, and the Jesuits started styling themselves as victims. They complained about having "to make some itinerant Missions," while others moved into the "more distant islands of the great Lake, at sixty, eighty, and a hundred leagues from us; others to journey by land, making their way through forest-depths, and scaling mountains." The Jesuits were scattering, and their divine plan for North America was unraveling. Fearing that the mother country's commitment to New World missions might fade, one missionary insisted that "the spirit of the Faith is not less divine [in America] than in the Louvres and most superb Palaces of Europe." "My pen can no longer express the fury of the Iroquois in these encounters," despaired another. Short on neophytes, other missionaries mobilized apocalyptic images of the Devil and hell to force conversions.[7]

In the summer of 1650, after a winter of starving, the Jesuits, together with dozens of Wyandot families, retreated to Quebec. They found no respite: the Iroquois now targeted New France. Iroquois soldiers traveled in fleets of forty-foot-long canoes that could hold eighteen people and began to appear in Trois-Rivières, seizing and killing Wyandot refugees and putting fear into the colonists. When thirty-six Wyandot canoes arrived in Quebec, the French rejoiced, thinking that they were "coming to swell our Colony." In Montreal, the colonists were more realistic. The settlement "would be an earthly Paradise for both the Savages and the French, were it not for the terror of the Iroquois, who make their appearance there almost continually and nearly render the place uninhabitable."[8]

The Iroquois reshaped geopolitics to serve their needs. In the summer of 1652, a thousand-strong Iroquois army captured between five and six hundred Wyandots in a single campaign, delivering a paralyzing blow to New France's most important ally and leaving the colonists exposed. France's colonial enterprise in North America seemed to be failing. The double purpose of French colonialism—the fur trade and saving souls—was sputtering under Iroquois pressure. The Five Nations now had the French exactly where they wanted them: diminished, terrified, confused, and pliable. In the summer of 1653, Iroquois ambassadors made a peace offer to New France.[9]

The French could hardly believe it. "At last we have peace," one Jesuit rejoiced. "Would to God that these words were as true in the mouths of the French as they are sweet and agreeable to the Inhabitants of New France!" For others, the surprising development only fed existing fear and paranoia. Many believed that "the Iroquois are treacherous, making peace only in order to betray us to better advantage in fresh war." Still, the same Jesuit thought "this change so unexpected, these tendencies in Barbarian minds so surprising, that, it must be admitted, a genius more exalted than that of man has guided this work." In the earthly realm, that genius could be found in the political organization of the Five Nations League. Its coordinated and deliberative decision-making tradition, which the clan mothers guided through their moral authority, allowed for nuanced and, when necessary, speedy foreign policy turns. The Mohawks had objected to the peace with the French, dreading that it would benefit the Onondagas disproportionately, yet they joined the consensus. New France had been swept into an Iroquois orbit through resolute and supple Five Nations diplomacy.[10]

The Five Nations made peace with New France because they thought that the colony, beaten down as it was, could still be useful as a source of arms and trade goods. The Iroquois had always prioritized relations with other Indigenous nations over relations with European colonies, which they saw mainly as market outlets and providers of weapons and metalware. In the early 1650s, the Iroquois, especially Onondagas, faced growing challenges from the Erie Nation, which controlled much of the southern shore of Lake Erie. The Onondagas and Mohawks approached New France in early 1654, asking for guns and soldiers. The French delivered both. The Indians also approached the Dutch, securing weapons. An Onondaga leader then proposed, as one Frenchman put it, "to separate the Huron Colony from us, and induce the families to go in a body—men, women, and children— into" Onondaga country, in a peaceful reiteration of the mourning wars. The French found themselves "in as great perplexity as Hurons themselves. . . . 'We see plainly,' these Huron Captains said to us, 'that those two Iroquois Nations, in a spirit of mutual envy, wish to win us each to its own side. Whatever plan we adopt, we are equally confronted with misfortune.'" They were right. In the summer of 1654, the Iroquois reintroduced the violent version of the mourning wars when they attacked the Eries with an army of some fifteen hundred soldiers. Two years later, more than fifty French priests, laborers, and soldiers settled in a new mission, Sainte-Marie de Gannentaha, next to the principal Onondaga town.[11]

New France was a crippled colony. The fur trade, its economic backbone, was disrupted by war, and the Jesuit order, its spiritual backbone, had weakened dangerously. The fur trade would recover over time, but the Jesuit enterprise, facing abandoned missions, murdered friars, and a growing number of apostates, went into survival mode. In 1658, the acting governor of New France received Five Nations envoys, who informed him that "the Iroquois and the Dutch are united by a chain of iron, and their friendship cannot be broken." Mohawks boasted that the French "were not able to goe over a door to pisse" without being shot. By then the Great League of Peace and Power had absorbed nearly all Iroquoians.

In 1663, when the Iroquois pressure forced King Louis XIV to assume direct control of New France, he assigned the running of the colony to Jean-Baptiste Colbert, his minister of finance. One of the most talented administrators in history, Colbert set out to transform New France into a centralized colony and a continental powerhouse through exploration, economic reforms, and emigration, including also people beyond the *filles du roi*. He turned the colony into a royal fiefdom and moved to replace the sprawling French system of forts and missions with a compact, agriculture-based colony in the Saint Lawrence Valley. Colbert wanted the colonists to focus on prospecting, fishing, and farming rather than war. He had the charter of the

Company of One Hundred Associates revoked and appointed Jean Talon as the colony's intendant. Talon promoted measured exploration, the fur trade, and new alliances with Indians to contain the Five Nations. Pierre-Esprit Radisson, an Englishman serving the French, established a trading post in James Bay, extending the French reach by hundreds of miles to the northeast—hundreds of miles in the wrong direction, from the Five Nations' viewpoint.[12]

IF THE FRENCH WERE struggling on the Indigenous continent, the Dutch were unraveling. In 1664, New Netherland vanished when England absorbed it bloodlessly in the sprawling English-Dutch trade wars, depriving the Five Nations of yet another essential trading partner. With the stroke of a pen, the metal makers were gone. New Netherland had lasted only six decades, dwarfed by neighboring Indigenous powers. The loss of the major trading outlet was disastrous for the Iroquois, who were reeling from another smallpox outbreak and a war with the Susquehannocks, whom the Jesuits dubbed the "Savages of new Sweden, very warlike, and better than any others to exterminate the Iroquois." Realizing that "the Iroquois are more crafty than is imagined," Jesuit friars reported that the Onondagas had dispatched an embassy to Montreal and proposed peace. Having read a dramatic shift in colonial power dynamics correctly, the Iroquois sided with the French.[13]

In 1665, exhausted by the wars and their ranks filled with adoptees, the Senecas, Cayugas, Onondagas, and Oneidas agreed to a treaty with the French in Quebec, but the Mohawks held out. A year later, the governor of New France, Alexandre de Prouville de Tracy, led an army of thirteen hundred regular troops, militiamen, and Wyandot and Algonquian allies into Mohawk country to cut the unruly nation down to size. The Mohawks fled, and the colonial army burned their towns and crops. The Five Nations had to make a comprehensive peace with the French and open their villages to Jesuits, who had clamored for their souls for decades. The diminishment of Iroquois power would be only temporary.[14]

After three generations of contending with Europeans, the Iroquois knew to expect drastic changes from them, and they adjusted quickly. Under the cloak of peace, they began to resettle the Saint Lawrence Valley and extended their domain to the north shore of Lake Ontario, where they built several new towns that enveloped the vast body of water, turning it into an Iroquois lake. Having positioned themselves securely in the east, the Iroquois launched a new campaign that took their armies west, south, and north. They banished the Shawnees from the fertile Ohio River valley to the south, and launched a devastating attack on a Mahican village in the east, finally putting an end to the decades-long war with the Mahican people. They pushed the Atikamekws far to the north and sent a flurry of war expeditions into Susquehannock villages in the south, bringing back scores of captives. In the spring of 1670, the Cayugas executed a Susquehannock emissary and, joining forces with the Senecas, raised a six-hundred-strong army to attack the Odawas. Ranging from New England to the Great Lakes and from the Saint Lawrence Valley to Virginia, the Iroquois seemed to be everywhere at once, keeping a huge portion of the continent in a state of terror.[15]

Despite appearances to the contrary, the Five Nations League was not a blind conquering machine. Far in the north, the Saint Lawrence Valley was becoming speckled with Iroquois settlements. Drawn there not by captives and loot, but by fish, game, trade, medicine, and Jesuits, the Iroquois sought solace from and explanations for the diseases and mass death, and for the failure of traditional rituals to restore order to the universe. In fact, the new settlements signaled a homecoming: a century earlier the Saint Lawrence Valley had been the heart of Iroquoia, but a combination of cold weather and famine in the late sixteenth century had forced the Five Nations to disperse. Now, peace and a warm climate cycle drew them back. The Saint Lawrence Valley had enjoyed a period of relative quiet since the mourning wars pulled the Iroquois to the west, turning the valley into a safe haven.

The Jesuits were overjoyed. "It is a stroke from Heaven—the change that is becoming manifest in New France," one wrote. "Formerly, there came out of the Country of the Iroquois only monsters of cruelty, who filled our forests and fields with terror, and laid waste all our settlements. But now that peace prevails everywhere . . . there is no cabin among these barbarous Nations whose door is not open to the Preachers of the gospel." Jesuits also reported with satisfaction the beginnings of a "little Church" around which a multiethnic community, Kahnawake, had emerged in a place that the Iroquois considered theirs. The Indians showed an "admirable respect for their Pastors, and among themselves a charity and union exceeding all power of conception, especially in view of the fact that they are people gathered from different countries"—Wyandots, Neutrals, Susquehannocks, and Five Nations. Kahnawake and the other new Saint Lawrence settlements were Indigenous places in the heart of what colonial maps labeled as New France. French soldiers avoided them, and Jesuits, though welcome, trod carefully in them—too timid to condemn the ritual torturing of captives, but not above baptizing them at the moment of their deaths. The Saint Lawrence Valley was not a French possession. It was the northern edge of the Iroquois territory.[16]

The genius of Iroquois foreign policy was its principled plasticity, which enabled the Iroquois to forge alliances with European powers that were locked into intense rivalries over territory, trade, and Indian allies. In 1675, just as Kahnawake and the other Saint Lawrence settlements seemed to be delivering the Five Nations into the French orbit, the Mohawks sought an alliance with the English in New York. Their timing was not accidental. Eager to expand their commercial networks, the Mohawks had approached New York numerous times with little success. But now the English had been chastened by the Dutch, who had briefly taken the colony in 1673–74, and in 1675, in a highly symbolic gesture, the new governor of New York, Edmund Andros, traveled among the Mohawks, the League's eastern door; visited all the Mohawk castles; and entered into Tionnontogen, the Mohawk capital, to deliver New York into an alliance, tacitly accepting Iroquois primacy. The result was the Covenant Chain, a coalition between the Mohawk Nation and New York, which would be later extended to include all the Five Nations and the colonies of Massachusetts, Connecticut, Rhode Island, Maryland, and Virginia. In a crucial act of self-serving generosity, Andros opened Albany's fur and gun markets to the Iroquois, pulling them away from French trade and

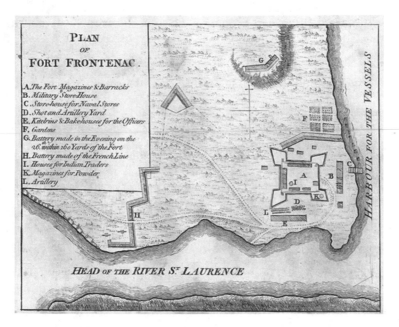

Plan of Fort Frontenac

influence. Suddenly, by comparison, the French seemed stingy and uncaring, and long-sidelined Anglophile Iroquois assumed a more prominent role in Five Nations foreign policy. Andros urged the Iroquois to banish French traders from the lower Great Lakes, and soon violence washed over Iroquois-French borderlands. The Five Nations attacked Fort Frontenac, New France's largest inland bastion, and French resolve crumbled. The Five Nations forced New France to stop protecting its Illini and Miami allies. Those two peoples, the Five Nations demanded, now belonged to them.[17]

The members of the Iroquois-English alliance recognized their mutual dependency, traded in essential goods, and conceived new ways to resolve conflicts, but the compact was fundamentally embedded in Iroquois political ideology and symbolism. The Five Nations expected the English colonies to periodically placate them with gifts—to symbolically polish the silver chain—in order to keep the bond pure and strong. They insisted on calling the English "brethren," which denoted equality and mutual respect. Andros hated the moniker and insisted on using "children," but the Iroquois would not allow it.[18]

Rising amid the beleaguered French and the comparatively more stable English colonies, the Five Nations became the dominant power in the Northeast. Buoyed by their strong connection with New York, they commanded, as the first among equals, an expanding Indigenous network of alliances. In 1677 a Mohawk sachem announced in Albany, "We are one, and one heart and one head, for the Covenant that is betwixt" the governor-general of New York "and us is Inviolable." The Iroquois accepted Andros and Albany's symbolic leadership within the Covenant Chain, which facilitated its extension to include Maryland and Virginia. In 1679 an Onondaga sachem announced that the Virginians were always welcome in "our Castles." That any leadership by the English was, indeed, merely symbolic was made clear by Iroquois leaders, who insisted on being treated as equals. The peace extended "unto the utmost limit of our great Kings Dominion of this Continent of America."[19]

The Covenant Chain confirmed the Five Nations' privileged access to English markets and diplomatic support—a position of unprecedented political clout that they leveraged on multiple fronts. The Five Nations protected their core territory by allowing weaker groups to settle on their borders as tributary allies, who also served as buffers against enemies. They embraced subjugated enemies—Odawas, Wenros, Lenapes, Shawnees, Meskwakis, and Wendats—as "women" and "nephews," guiding and commanding them as "uncles," and expecting them to offer soldiers for their campaigns. The seemingly insulting gendered metaphors tied nations together as allies. The mourning wars—the greatest display of military power in seventeenth-century North America—had brought peace in the interior. The Odawas emerged as the leading traders in the western pays d'en haut.

PEACE IN THE EAST fueled expansion in the West. Once again, after two decades of relative calm, Iroquois hunting and war parties pushed deep into the interior, seeking beavers and captives. Most of their pelts now flowed into Albany, where they fetched prices that could be twice as high as those that French merchants had offered.

Andros was eager to see the Five Nations interrupt France's interior trade, and he generously sponsored their operations, but the Iroquois were careful not to provoke a war with the French, who in 1673 had turned Forts Frontenac and Niagara on Lake Ontario into bulwarks against their western forays. The Five Nations depended on unhindered movement to secure vital resources and to keep themselves safe. In 1676, French missionary Louis Hennepin invited a larger number of Iroquois to settle near Fort Frontenac. A "Village of about Forty Cottages" materialized almost immediately, "lying betwixt the Fort and our House of Mission." Soon, fields of "*Indian* Corn and Pulse" stretched out around the fort. The Iroquois had made Fort Frontenac theirs—at least momentarily.[20]

The Iroquois were becoming an empire. They now posed an existential crisis for New France, which relied on furs and Native allies to survive. The Iroquois onslaught had exposed the Illini country—which was thought to extend from the middle Mississippi Valley to the Ohio Valley and the lower end of Lake Michigan—as the soft underbelly of the French Empire, causing panic among New France's Indian allies. Making matters worse, the French colony was also under threat in the north: English merchants had entrenched themselves in Hudson Bay in the 1670s and were now expanding their operations through Native trappers and a complex fan-shaped river system that extended deep into the interior. New France was losing people to Indian wars, and Colbert, realizing that his vision of a Saint Lawrence–based empire no longer sufficed in an intensifying imperial milieu, imagined a new kind of French empire in North America—one whose tentacles extended into the heart of the continent. To thwart the Five Nations and the English, Colbert established a permit system that enabled French traders to push inland and buy pelts directly from Native trappers. Reluctantly, he also allowed the wide-ranging *coureurs de bois*—runners of the woods—highly mobile independent traders, to move into the western forests, hoping to regain control of the interior fur trade. Soon, several hundred coureurs de bois and *voyageurs*, rugged long-distance carriers who canoed the pelts to colonial outposts, were operating in the pays d'en haut.[21]

Colbert miscalculated. By focusing on the English threat and by

The highly mobile French voyageurs
cooperated closely with Native Americans.

unleashing the coureurs de bois among the Indians, he alienated the Iroquois, who thought that much of the interior and its resources now belonged to them. The Iroquois made a concentrated bid to open trade with several nations around Lake Michigan but were denied. Led by the Senecas, the Five Nations launched a major offensive—their third in four decades—to seize furs and captives. They attacked the French-allied Illinis, Miamis, Odawas, Otoes, Wyandots, and Meskwakis across the pays d'en haut and beyond, nearly paralyzing interior trade. The French agonized over how the Iroquois had "obtained so great an advantage over" the Illinis "that, besides three or four hundred dead, they took from them nine hundred prisoners." In a particularly gloomy assembly in Quebec, Governor Joseph-Antoine Le Febvre de La Barre reported that the Iroquois's "undertaking is, to destroy, one after the other, all the nations allied to us, while they keep us in uncertainty, with folded arms." This, he warned, spelled disaster for New France: "After they have taken from us all the trade in peltries, which they wish to carry on alone with the English and Dutch settled at Manatte and Orange, they may attack us alone. Then they will ruin the Colony by obliging it to concentrate its people and forsake all the outlying settlements, thus putting a stop to the cultivation of the soil." The English, La Barre lamented, had the Five Nations League on their side, which made all the difference. They were reported to be thinking of little else "than putting Onontio in a kettle," possibly to symbolically diminish him. "The terror that they have inspired in all the others [has] rendered them so haughty that they consider themselves the masters of the earth," wrote Father Thierry Beschefer. "They are at the same time very maliciously disposed toward the French, which causes us to feel great apprehensions of war."[22]

What the missionary thought was simple maliciousness was, in fact, policy. In 1674 the Five Nations met with Governor La Barre in Montreal. The French were eager to put an end to escalating violence that was ruining the fur trade in the Great Lakes, but the summit turned into a kind of conciliation ceremony that saw the French governor do his utmost to appease the people who had waged relentless war for decades against the French and their Indian allies. New to the post, La Barre had taken stock of Five Nations foreign policy and was both alarmed and impressed. The Five Nations had methodically weakened or sidelined their Native rivals while preserving access to colonial markets. Battle by battle, war by war, they had shaped the interior to meet their needs.

At the summit, La Barre apologized to the Five Nations ambassadors for arming their Illini enemies, and he lavished more than forty Iroquois with gifts. He professed that the Five Nations were "the bravest, strongest, and shrewdest [nation] in all North America, having twenty years ago subjugated all their neighbors." He certainly did not want a war with them. Where the Iroquois could muster hundreds of highly skilled soldiers, he had five fit officers. "Advanced years, or corpulency, render the others incapable of supporting fatigue of that sort," he would later complain. Fighting the Five Nations, La Barre accepted, was folly. "They will not fail to seize on the most trifling occasions to endeavor to render themselves masters of those people and those posts [in the Great Lakes], and, by robbing us, destroy the Colony of the King of France in Canada."[23]

AROUND 1680, ABOUT FIFTY YEARS after the terrible smallpox epidemic that cut their numbers by half, the Five Nations were at the height of their power; they were now the domineering nation in the great interior. The French feared them, the English respected them as allies, and the Dutch no longer had a colony in North America. The Iroquois seemed to be everywhere. Their fleet-footed war parties ranged across the Great Lakes, seeking captives, pelts, and spiritual and emotional healing. Their world had expanded explosively, covering a massive domain. They seized pelts and captives from the Ottawa Valley to the western limits of the pays d'en haut, which the French still claimed—feebly now—as part of their empire.

With most English colonies now in their orbit, the Five Nations moved to draw their Native neighbors within their sphere of influence. Weakened Susquehannocks, Piscataways, and others sought refuge in Iroquoia against Maryland and Virginia, and soon Iroquois-Susquehannock war parties set out to "scour the heads" of the Potomac, James, and Roanoke Rivers to bring their Native tributaries into Iroquoia. The Iroquois also took in "Christian Indians" from Massachusetts and refused to return them—now their "flesh and blood"—to New England when asked. In the West, the Iroquois raided the French-allied Illinis, Miamis, and Odawas, taking hundreds of captives and shattering France's commercial networks in the interior. When the Miamis offered three thousand beaver pelts in exchange for their relatives, the Iroquois took the furs but refused to release the captives. Iroquois sachems thought it politic to inform the governor of New France—Louis de Buade, comte de Frontenac—that "they would not eat his children."[24]

As Iroquois ambitions swelled, the confederacy became entangled in complex foreign political arrangements with the surrounding colonial powers. Since the mid-seventeenth century, New France had posed the most serious challenge to the Five Nations' ambitions and sovereignty. Tracy's invasion of Iroquoia in 1666 appeared to have locked the Iroquois into the French orbit by opening their towns to Jesuit black robes. The Five Nations had suffered enormous losses in their relentless beaver and mourning wars, leaving them uncertain of their spiritual virtue and political primacy. Many seemed to have become stout Francophiles who embraced the Christian god, accepted Onontio as their father, and opened their settlements to French merchants.

Against this backdrop, the Five Nations' Covenant Chain with New York in the 1670s might appear to signal a splintering of the Iroquois League into rival factions. The sudden Jesuit ascendancy among the Saint Lawrence Iroquois seemed like a capitulation to a colonial power, and it fueled virulent anti-French sentiments within the league. The pro-English bloc of the Iroquois was emboldened to steer the league into a tighter alliance with the increasingly powerful New York. All this did not mean, however, that the Five Nations were divided or in conflict. On the contrary, the Francophile and Anglophile blocs together enabled the Iroquois League to keep North America's two most powerful empires in a state of uncertainty, nurture commercial and political relations with both, and draw major concessions from each.[25]

Suddenly, New France was besieged by a newly ascending Five Nations. France's North American empire did not exist outside of its web of Indian alliances, and the Five Nations were at once usurping that web and tearing it apart. Captives poured into Iroquoia—a single raid yielded eight hundred Illini captives—and the number of Iroquois villages increased from fifteen in 1666 to twenty-four in 1680, while the area covered by their settlements increased from roughly seven thousand square miles to forty-five thousand. Iroquois war parties looted French vessels and demanded tributary goods at Fort Frontenac, while selling the bulk of their pelts to Albany. New France suffered a twenty-five percent drop in its fur revenue. Governor Frontenac kept postponing direct talks with the Iroquois. He had a good reason: they had threatened to boil and eat him.[26]

There had never been anything like the Five Nations League in North America. No other Indigenous nation or confederacy had ever reached so far, conducted such an ambitious foreign policy, or commanded such fear and respect. The Five Nations blended diplomacy, intimidation, and violence as the circumstances dictated, creating a measured instability that only they could navigate. Their guiding principle was to avoid becoming attached to any single colony, which would restrict their options and risk exposure to external manipulation.

French officials believed that the Iroquois strove to become "the sole masters of commerce." Such an idea was not far-fetched. Having observed how the Five Nations "completely ruined" several Native nations, the French knew they were defenseless. An Iroquois empire was consolidating in the interior.[27]

A thousand miles to the east, in the Saint Lawrence Valley, stood Kahnawake, facing Montreal across the river. The mixed settlement now boasted sixty longhouses, a result of sustained incorporation of adopted captives into the Iroquois League. Not far upriver, the mission towns La Montagne, La Prairie, Lorette, and Notre-Dame-de-Foy served similar functions as the foundation of the Iroquois presence and power along the great river. All the settlements received generous support from their French neighbors, whom they considered kin and who facilitated negotiations between the Five Nations League and New France. The Iroquois had been drawn to Kahnawake by a woman whose mother was a Christian Algonquian captive and whose father was a Mohawk. Her entire immediate family had died of smallpox. She had a "reputation of sanctity," wrote Father Claude Chauchetière, who thought that her spirituality surpassed his. The woman asked to be baptized, alienating her Mohawk kin, who detested Christianity, and became Kateri Tekakwitha. She died of smallpox at age twenty-four, her body weakened by rigorous self-mortification. "Journeys are continually made to her tomb," wrote Father Chauchetière, "and the savages, following her example, have become better Christians than they were."[28]

Living in mission towns and accepting Christian rites did not mean submission to French ways, nor did it signal French control over the Five Nations. They had embraced the French and their resources, but they were not under their influence. The Iroquois welcomed the Jesuits because they were useful as intermediaries, sources of information, and hostages against French aggression. Many women actively flocked to Christianity and used their faith to assert their power against the Jesuit friars.[29]

Hundreds of miles to the south of Kahnawake, the Iroquois routinely entered Virginia and Maryland under the Covenant Chain to hunt, trade, and recruit soldiers among their Susquehannock, Lenape, and Erie adoptees. They saw the English as kin and refused to accept New France's enmities with the English as theirs. Governor La Barre came close to the truth when he reported that the "lack of any aid from France had begun to inspire these Iroquois with contempt for us, as they believed us destitute." The Iroquois demanded Onontio's affection and goods. "They are now treating with the English at Orange," La Barre warned, but "with a slight assistance from His Majesty, we might prevent war and subdue these proud and fiery spirits, which would be the greatest good that can be procured for the country." It was posturing; the imperial Iroquois were now in charge.[30]

Chapter 10

THE POWER OF
WEAKNESS

T HE FIVE NATIONS' RISE TO POWER WAS COUNTER-
intuitive. Their expansion was triggered by a population catastrophe caused by smallpox, a European import, and they grew stronger
by pushing toward, not away from, European colonies whose leaders
denounced them as savages, as obstacles, and, ultimately, as expendable. The Five Nations were surrounded by three global empires—
French, Dutch, and English—but they managed to turn the apparent
death trap into a position of advantage. There were moments when
they seemed to unravel under the pressure of multiple rivals. Yet they
not only prevailed but dominated. No nation, European or Indigenous, could match their geographical reach and political power in
North America over the course of the seventeenth century.

Boosted by English munitions, the Five Nations were poised to
absorb or destroy all their Native enemies and "render themselves
masters of Massilimakina [Michilimackinac], Lakes Hérié [Erie] and
Huron, and the Bay des Puans." Their control of interior waterways,
La Barre wrote to his superiors in France, would deprive the French
of "all the trade" in the pays d'en haut, "destroying, at the same time,
all the Christian Missions." New France faced annihilation. "This
is a war which must not be begun to be left incomplete," La Barre
insisted. "If it were undertaken and not finished[,] there was no hope
left of preserving the Colony." But when the Iroquois ransacked the
stores of Fort Frontenac, La Barre's army managed to mount only a
feeble response. The Five Nations made the governor accept a humiliating peace in 1684, forcing him to withdraw French support from the
Illinis and Miamis. This abasement was ruinous to the reputation of

New France, whose governor was a father to his Native allies—loving, generous, and powerful.[1]

Greater resources are not what gave the Five Nations their advantage; rather, they overpowered New France by being more creative and more nimble. Born of chaos and terror, the Great League of Peace and Power was both conciliatory and inclusive. All league-wide decisions were based on consensus, but at the local level the league was nearly a pure meritocracy. A skillful and powerful local leader with many supporters could launch attacks, wage war, and make and break truces virtually at will. He could take war parties into enemy settlements to seize captives, force hunting privileges, and protect trade outlets. The Iroquois showed two faces to colonial powers. One was that of a sophisticated league with whom one could negotiate, conduct trade, and coexist. The other was that of a military power—forceful, decentralized, unpredictable, uncontainable.

The Five Nations League profoundly shaped American history by bolstering certain colonial projects—New Netherland, New York, and the other middle colonies—while thwarting others, most notably New France, whose commercial and territorial ambitions in the interior were severely reduced by Iroquois power. Officials in Quebec were required to compile maps of North America and send them to the Ministry of the Navy in Paris. They could not deliver much: their maps went blank roughly a hundred miles west of Lake Superior. Beyond that, their imaginations took over. A number of French scholars and cartographers believed that there was a "Sea of the West" not far west of the Mississippi Valley—an enormous Mediterranean-like extension of the Pacific into the heart of the continent that offered the long-sought sea route to China.[2]

One explanation for the Five Nations' success was geography: Iroquoia was not so close to colonial settlements that it would fall under their shadow, nor was it too far from European settlements to reap the technological and material benefits that they offered. During the Five Nations' ascendancy, their soldiers were consistently the best-armed Indigenous power on the continent. By the 1680s, French imperial officials, unable to match Iroquois firepower, mobility, and reach, seemed to have resigned themselves to the Indians' dominance over New

France and Illini country. In the spring of 1687, the French fretted that the Five Nations "spread themselves on all sides in those directions [west and south]." The French officials were particularly horrified by the maneuvers of the Five Nations leader La Grande Gaule and his soldiers. "The facility with which they could exterminate our people, in consequence of the knowledge he possessed of our weakness," stopped France's empire-building in its tracks.[3]

The world was as it should be. Iroquoia was in the center, hugged by European colonies whose leaders and inhabitants feared and respected the Iroquois and wanted to be their allies. They wanted to trade with them, arm them, protect them against diseases, and rescue their souls. Europeans did all of those things because they needed the Five Nations, whose power propped up theirs. They knew that, without the Iroquois, there might not be any colonies in the New World. A budding Iroquois Empire was now the domineering power in the great interior.

FOR THE FRENCH, HOWEVER, the world was out of joint. The Five Nations had eclipsed New France. When Governor-General Daniel de Rémy de Courcelle confronted Seneca leaders in 1670 over their military operations in the interior, a Seneca spokesman retorted, "For whom does Onnontio take us? . . . He is vexed because we go to war, and wishes us to lower our hatchets and leave his allies undisturbed. Who are his allies? How would he have us recognize them when he claims to take under his protection all the peoples discovered by the bearers of God's Word through all these regions." The Iroquois were at war with those nations, and they would not simply lay down their arms at Courcelle's demand. "Let Onnontio check their hatchet if he wishes us to stay our own. He threatens to bring desolation on our Land; let us see whether his arms be long enough to remove the scalps from our heads." Courcelle flinched, refusing to test the Senecas' resolve. That submissiveness is what kept the Five Nations peaceful and New France safe.[4]

Iroquois dominance had dramatically curtailed French access to furs, wealth, and souls in the deep interior, and some believed that the Iroquois had denied France's passage to Asia. Yet that was only half the story. Iroquois power extended far beyond France's territorial control, which in the late seventeenth century was still limited to the western shore of Lake Ontario. The sprawling beaver and mourning wars had transformed huge sections of the Great Lakes region into an extractive hinterland where mobile Five Nations war expeditions kept numerous Native nations in a state of terror. Under this unremitting pressure, an extraordinary new world began to form in the pays d'en haut. It was neither an Indigenous realm nor a European realm; it was instead a mixture of the two. The new world that took shape in the West had its roots in world-changing violence, and its most important binding agent was mutual weakness.

In the mid-seventeenth century, the Great Lakes region had become a hodgepodge of languages, customs, sensibilities, and ambitions. Common-law marriages *á la façon du pays*, "according to the custom of the country," soothed some of the differences between groups by creating new bonds of kinship, while the calumet ceremony encouraged reflection, stilled vengeful minds, and created ties of symbolic kinship. Each cross-cultural bond required painstaking effort because this was a world of villages, a world assembled from diasporic fragments; it had no overarching governing mechanisms. All negotiations—whether over hunting grounds, trade privileges, murders, or cooperation— took place at the village level, face-to-face. Often, the methods of conflict resolution had to be improvised and reinvented because traditions varied so widely: some nations wanted to eat their enemies and some did not; many venerated the calumet and some did not; many thought that the pain caused by the death of a relative could be assuaged with gifts and others did not. The fact that game was becoming scarce in the Great Lakes under the refugee influx intensified every dispute. Yet remarkably, this refugee world survived.

It survived because the Indians found ways to make the French valuable—much as the Iroquois had. The refugee communities approached Onontio directly in Quebec. In 1665, an old Wyandot spokesman addressed Tracy, now the lieutenant-general of New France. " 'Great Onnontio,' he said, 'thou see at thy feet the wreck of a great country, and the pitiful remnant of a whole world, that was formerly peopled by countless inhabitants. But now thou art addressed by mere carcasses, only the bones of which have been left by the Iroquois, who have devoured the flesh after broiling it on their scaffolds.'" The spokesman laid down a moose skin and asked "the greatest of all Onnontios on earth" to accept "this little present from the emptiness of our land." He then explained, with succinct clarity, his people's misfortune. He was asking for Onontio's protection.[5]

During periodic truces with the Iroquois, independent French traders moved into the refuge zone, whose crowded villages drew them in like magnets. They brought iron weapons and guns, which enabled the Lakes Indians to give up the dangerous trading expeditions to Montreal and New York. The French were people with extraordinary powers. So, too, were the Jesuit missionaries who arrived soon after, animated by quixotic dreams of "La Nouvelle Jérusalem" in the backwoods. In 1668, Jacques Marquette established a mission, Sault Sainte Marie, on an ancient Indigenous domain at the Straits of Mackinac between Lakes Huron and Michigan. The mission served the Indians less as a place of spiritual salvation than as a base for fishing operations—something that the Jesuits readily acknowledged. It was French protection and fish, not gospel, that attracted about two thousand Indians to the site. Some refugee groups, most notably the Wyandots, reconsolidated at the mission, reviving their ancient confederacies.[6]

The refugee Indians wanted the French as allies not only against the Iroquois but against another foe as well: the great Sioux Confederacy, the Očhéthi Šakówiŋ, the "Seven Council Fires," which controlled the lands west of the Great Lakes, commanding a roughly sixty-thousand-square-mile core territory that stretched out on both sides of the upper Mississippi Valley and was anchored at Mde Wakan, their sacred lake and the center of the world. The Seven Council Fires had maneuvered for decades to gain access to the fur trade that delivered crucial technology and allies to other Native nations, but their efforts had yielded little beyond a tenuous connection with the Sauteurs who occupied a resource-rich peninsula at the southwestern corner of Lake Superior, a strip of land the French called La Pointe du Chequamegon. "Their manners and customs are quite extraordinary: they chiefly adore the Calumet," the Jesuits observed, and they spoke "a language that is utterly foreign, the savages here not understanding it at all." When a visitor arrived, the Sioux fed "him with a wooden fork, as one would a child." The Sioux were strangers to the Lakes Indians, and their ceremonies and diplomatic protocols were drastically different. Ignored and excluded from commercial and diplomatic circles, the Sioux retaliated, attacking and killing Meskwakis, Odawas, and other Lakes peoples. "A general League" formed "against a common foe," and when Sioux ambassadors visited the village of Chequamegon at Lake Superior's Chequamegon Bay in 1670, Wyandots ritually boiled and ate them.[7]

The Jesuits labeled the Sioux "the Iroquois of this country, beyond la Pointe." In the 1650s and 1660s, Iroquois war parties had functioned as a hammer that pinned the westward-fleeing refugees against the Sioux anvil, but in the 1670s the positions were reversed: the Sioux became the hammer, while the Iroquois presence in the East kept the refugees in place. The Sioux themselves were soon in an untenable position, for each strike only created more enemies. The Jesuits depicted the Seven Council Fires as "a nation exceedingly numerous and warlike," and "the common enemies of all the savages Included under the name outacoac, or upper algonquines." Their soldiers "even pushed forward their arms vigorously toward to the north; and, making war on Kilistinons [Crees] who dwell there, rendered themselves everywhere terrible by their daring, their numbers, and their skill in Battle." In 1674 the Anishinaabeg surprised the overstretched Sioux in their own country and took eighty prisoners. The Sioux dispatched "ten of the most daring among them" to Sault Sainte Marie to negotiate for the captives' release. But the Crees and Anishinaabeg Mississaugas moved to derail the conciliation and resolved to "massacre the ten ambassadors." They managed to kill only one before the Sioux, "stirred up to vengeance[,] . . . struck their Knives at all the assembled savages, without making any distinction between Kilistinons and Sauteurs, believing that they had all equally Conspired in the design to assassinate them."[8]

Indigenous ambitions, rivalries, murders, wars, and hatreds—all magnified by colonial rivalries—were stretching the interior nations to their limits. But the colonists could also be valuable. Because there were not many colonists in the West, they had to adhere to Indigenous practices. They were too weak to exercise control and dictate terms. On the contrary, to justify their presence in the Indigenous West, they would have to help the Indians restore order to the world. Then they might have a place in it too.

NICHOLAS PERROT WAS SOMEONE who could help. He seems to have come to New France as a lay Jesuit missionary, and he had met with several Native nations and learned their languages. He soon left the order to become a trader, visiting the refugee Indians in La Baye des Puants—Green Bay—and earning their trust. In 1670, Jean Talon, the intendant of New France, asked Perrot and Simon-François Daumont de Saint-Lusson, a military officer, to search for copper mines and explore the West toward Lake Superior and all the way to a "Freshwater Sea"—the Pacific. They were to "take possession, in the name of the king, of all the country" of the Odawas. Perrot invited several Lakes nations to La Baye des Puants. There he distributed gifts and asked the assembled Indians "if they would acknowledge, as his subjects, the great Onontio of the French, our sovereign and our king, who offered them his protection." The envoys embraced the offer, and Perrot pledged that Onontio would protect them "as his own children": "If any enemies rise up against them, he will destroy them; if his children have any disputes among themselves, he desires to be the judge in these." In return, Onontio expected loyalty.[9]

More concretely, Onontio was also the head of an empire, and in that role he was tasked with arbitrating grievances among France's Indian allies. Governor La Barre dispatched Perrot into the interior to manage the fur trade and preserve peace as a go-between. French traders were already pushing west of Lake Superior and into Sioux country, which was now known as "a nursery for beaver"—an upshot of the Seven Council Fires' isolation from the French fur markets. The Lakes Indians were appalled; Onontio seemed to have turned his back on them. The Sioux and their Sauteur allies attacked the powerful Meskwakis, hoping to marginalize them and lure in French traders. The Meskwakis—"Foxes" to the French—killed Sioux in retalia-tion. The disorder did not deter the French traders who now trekked eagerly into the West, bringing guns into Sioux country. The interior exploded into violence.[10]

Paradoxically, that violence drew the Great Lakes Indians and the French closer together. The French in the region were isolated from the core of their empire in the Saint Lawrence Valley, and the Indians were reeling from Iroquois violence and internal discord. Unable to dominate each other, the French and the Lakes Indians both had to make concessions that could become mutually beneficial. Gradually, one encounter at a time, they forged an extraordinary common world, a middle ground, where they could coexist as allies and equals. Born of weakness, the middle ground was a social space where people accepted their mutual dependency. Too weak to dictate, they had to accommodate one another. Much of the accommodation required appealing to the cultural norms and customs of the other—customs that often seemed absurd and outright repulsive. It could be more useful to be creatively misunderstood than to be perfectly understood: from those misunderstandings arose new meanings and practices, the sinews of the middle ground. The apogee of the French-Indian accommodation was the Feast of the Dead, an ancient ceremony in which a host nation sponsored a mass reburial of the bones of the departed and distributed massive amounts of gifts to ease the pain and create new relatives and allies.[11]

Perrot was at the center of this emerging world. In 1683, during a conference at a Meskwaki village west of La Baye des Puants, he assumed Onontio's role, reprimanding his hosts for their attacks. Now fluent in Indigenous idioms, Perrot challenged them: "Listen, Outagamis [Meskwakis], to what I am going to tell you. I have learned that you are very desirous to eat the flesh of Frenchmen. I have come, with these young men whom you see, to satisfy you; put us into your kettles, and gorge yourselves with the meat you have been wanting." The "foremost" Meskwaki war leader promptly objected: "What child is there who would eat his father, from whom he has received life?" Perrot understood this as an acknowledgment of the debt the man owed to the French, who brought guns and iron to his people and mediated their conflicts. Speaking once more on behalf of Onontio, Perrot demanded, "Vomit up your prey; give me back my body, which you

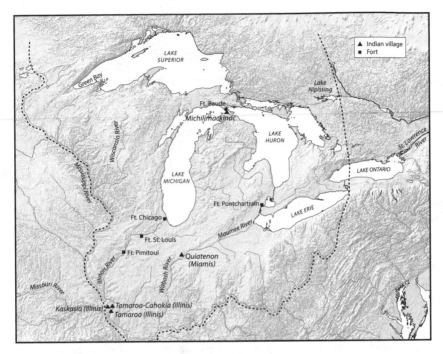

The middle ground

wish to put into your kettles . . . if you cook it, [it] will stir up vapors that will form stormy clouds which will extend over your village—which will be in a moment consumed by the flames and lightnings that will issue from them." Perrot exhorted the Meskwakis to "believe your father, who will not abandon you until you compel him to do so."[12]

That summit at the Meskwaki village was the French-Indian middle ground in microcosm. It was a shattered world made up of exiled Native villages, mixed refugee settlements, and a few French forts at the margins. The French had entered this atomistic and seemingly disjointed realm with trepidation, struggling to understand the Native efforts to restore order through good words and gifts. The French saw only chaos, recoiled at it, and dismissed the pays d'en haut as defunct. To that point it had been a typical early-American story. Different people came together, saw one another as alien, and were overcome by frustration and contempt. In the pays d'en haut, however, a different kind of trajectory took root. The Indians, Perrot reported, insisted on the "arrogant notion that the French cannot get along without them and that we could not maintain ourselves in the colony without the assistance that they give us." Crucially, Perrot did not protest. He acknowledged that the French were weak and needed the Indians to survive. It was telling that Perrot was building an alliance alone, without colonial infrastructure; France and the other colonial powers had reached their logistical capacity in the distant Great Lakes.[13]

In the middle ground, Perrot and other French officials arbitrated quarrels and sponsored Indigenous rituals that kept the world in balance, and soon new ways of coexisting emerged. Rather than imposing their own norms and values, they had to find something in an alien culture that could be used, appropriated, and repurposed, however odd or abhorrent it might be. One concession and one expedient misreading at a time, Native Americans and newcomers began shading into one another—a prime manifestation of Indigenous pragmatism.[14]

The Illinis and Mascoutens wanted the French to join them against their enemies and mobilize French spiritual and military power on their behalf. These Indians nudged the Jesuits, and by extension the French Empire, to join them against the *Nadouessi*—the French name for the Sioux—and offered the priests "free access to the cabins." But Claude-Jean Allouez, the leading Jesuit in North America, and his fellow friars had other priorities. "We availed ourselves of this advantage to instruct the people everywhere, and to seek out sick persons in all the cabins"; deathbed conversions had become a standard Jesuit practice. The entire episode was a series of misunderstandings, both accidental and intentional, but it yielded tangible results. People came together, ideas percolated, bonds emerged, and both sides could claim success, and even supremacy. The Illinis and Mascoutens had been able to appeal to Onontio himself through the Jesuits and ask for his pity and support. The Jesuits had managed to instruct Native Americans about the mysteries of the Christian god, planting seeds that might someday yield souls.[15]

The most delicate maneuvering and the hardest compromises involved cross-cultural murders. Murder posed a grave danger to the social order, but if properly atoned for, it could strengthen the shared world. In 1683 a joint Ojibwe-Menominee expedition ambushed and killed two French voyageurs on the Keweenaw Peninsula off the southern shore of Lake Michigan, possibly to stop them from trading with the Sioux, who were rivals of the Ojibwes and Menominees. Achiganaga, an Ojibwe *ogimaag*—leader—at Keweenaw, had recently launched an attack on the Sioux and was planning to organize more. Not long after, Achiganaga's two sons joined with at least one Menominee to attack the French again. The western Great Lakes had been a tinderbox for years, and the murders of the Frenchmen threatened to throw the region into turmoil. Daniel Greysolon Dulhut, a former coureur de bois and now one of Governor La Barre's most trusted officers, took over. He arrested the Menominee man at the Jesuit mission Sault Sainte Marie and sent out Jean Péré, an experienced coureur de bois, to detain Achiganaga and his two sons and bring them to the mission for a trial. Péré came back with four of Achiganaga's sons.

The trial started as a distinctly French affair. With several Chippewa, Odawa, Ojibwe, and Wyandot-Petun elders in the audience, Dulhut interrogated Achiganaga's sons and the Menominee man, who "made accusations without denying the murder." Achiganaga, however, denied any wrongdoing. "This confrontation, which the savages did not expect, surprised them," Dulhut observed. "Seeing that they were convicted of the murder," the elders in the audience intervened: "It is enough; you accuse one another. The Frenchman is now master of your bodies." From the Indigenous perspective, the matter was now resolved. Dulhut was to act like a benevolent father and pardon the killers, thereby repairing the familial bond between the French and the Chippewas. Instead, he assembled a few fellow Frenchmen at the fort to review the case. They called for blood revenge and decided "to put them all three to death."

By clinging to European legal conventions, Dulhut had pushed the trial into a dangerous deadlock. More experienced local Frenchmen sent Dulhut a message, pleading with him "to treat this affair with all the mildness possible—because the savages murmured that, if all the accused were put to death, they would revenge themselves upon the French." Dulhut pulled back. He later reported, "I believed it was expedient, for the safety of all their companions who were wintering at Lake Superior, to put to death only two": a Menominee and one of Achiganaga's sons. Dulhut had conformed to an alien cultural practice that he understood only vaguely, and it made him uneasy. He explained to his superior, "If I were not relaxing the rigor of our laws, I would put to death all six of them as being guilty of participating in the robbery."[16]

Fearing a last-minute Native attack to stop the executions, Dulhut moved quickly. He asked the Jesuits to "baptize those two wretched men, which they did. An hour afterward, I put myself in sight of more than 400 men, and 200 steps from their fort, I had their heads broken." Achiganaga had overestimated the French capacity for forgiveness and underestimated their capacity for violence, and he had lost a son for it. Yet only two days later, three Odawa ambassadors gave Achiganaga "six collars" to "cover" the killed Frenchmen and "efface their blood, in order that the earth might be clean in the future." They did so because they needed French goods and guns to survive. Dulhut covered the dead with guns, powder, lead, blankets, axes, and knives, easing the Odawas' pain and restoring the alliance. Dulhut craved authority over the Indians, but he had accepted that he would need to meet the Indians halfway. Reluctantly, unknowingly, he was entering a middle ground.[17]

The middle ground was, in the first and last instance, a diplomatic innovation, a perpetually shifting set of alliances that revolved around patriarchal metaphors and specific mutual obligations. In Quebec, the French governor commanded an empire with an iron grip, but on the middle ground he was Onontio—generous, forgiving, and loving. He was expected to care for his Native allies—his symbolic children—and give gifts, not orders. The most elemental human desires—sex, procreation, and the need for companionship—gave the middle ground depth and staying power. Those needs were dramatically intensified in the pays d'en haut by the fact that very few Frenchwomen accompanied their husbands into what the French thought was a wilderness. Apart from the Jesuits, most Frenchmen sought sexual relations and marriages with Native women, who had their own reasons to favorably respond to being courted by the French: marriages with traders opened access to crucial goods and could dramatically enhance the standing of the women's families. Native women who married fur traders often became mediators between the French and Indians and built extensive kinship networks through the Catholic institution of godparenting, expanding and solidifying the middle ground. Some women who married traders assumed important roles in their communities as religious educators. Marie Rouensa-8cate8a, who was from a prominent Illini family, married a French fur trader, converted to Catholicism, and moved into the grand village of Kaskaskia, where she translated a Jesuit tract into the Kaskaskia language, becoming a leader in her community.[18]

Underneath all the artful accommodations, however, the Great Lakes region remained a distinctly Indigenous space: French priests, French traders, and French forts thrived there because Indians wanted them to thrive. The middle ground was a negation of colonialism in the vast North American interior. The Anishinaabeg people brought the sacred power of *manidoo* in the middle ground, which enabled strangers to become kin, trade, hunt, and travel together. The French were allowed to stay because they respected Native rituals and because they were useful and sufficiently meek. When they were not, the Indians found ways to make them pliable. When the Sauteurs moved, after several false starts, to bring the French traders among them and their Sioux allies, a Sauteur leader named Oumamens reached out to Dulhut. The Frenchman saw an opportunity to elevate his own reputation and followed Oumamens to the western end of Lake Superior, where the Sauteurs and Sioux had made peace. Dulhut's role was to report back to Quebec and extend French gun trade among the Sauteurs and Sioux and expand the Indigenous peace process. A year later, Dulhut brought Crees and Assiniboines to a meeting near the western tip of Lake Superior to "make peace with the Nadouesioux, their common enemy." Dulhut imagined himself as a New World adventurer who had single-handedly directed the interior fur trade in the French orbit. But his endeavors did not bring a single Sioux to Quebec. The Sioux expected the French traders to come to them.[19]

Unlike most of the Lakes Indians, the Sioux were neither refugees nor weak. They lived in their ancestral lands and possessed a strong communal ethos as the Očhéthi Šakówiŋ, the alliance of Seven Council Fires. Their population may have reached thirty thousand, which meant that they outnumbered any of their enemies many times over. They also dwarfed New France and its population of ten thousand. The Sioux did not want to travel east to get guns and iron; they expected French traders to bring weapons and goods to them. Realizing where the real power lay, Dulhut did just that. He began sending traders among the Seven Council Fires and built a fort for them near Mde Wakan, the heart of Sioux country. In a world where a single trading fort could launch an Indigenous empire, the Seven Council Fires were now a domineering power.

The Lakes Indians were terrified and aghast. The Sioux were their archenemies, and Dulhut had abandoned Onontio's loyal children for them. The Lakes Indians appealed to Nicholas Perrot, who had once offered to give his body away to save the French-Indian alliance. They handed the calumet to Perrot in the transitional zone where the Great Lakes give way to grasslands and carried him on a bison robe to the cabin of the sachem, who wept over Perrot's head, "bathing it with his tears," and placed a piece of boiled bison tongue in Perrot's mouth. Just as the sachem now fed Perrot, keeping him alive, Perrot should keep Onontio's children alive with iron and guns. But Perrot's efforts were to no avail. The Sioux were too powerful to be denied. Perrot offered Onontio's children the calumet and told them that "this was his breast which he had always presented to them to give them nourishment." Now, however, he had to "give suck to the Nadoüaissioux," offering Onontio's "milk"—the iron, guns, and other trade goods that kept them safe and alive. Perrot sent a few of his men to alert the Sioux of his visit. "They found on the ice twenty-four canoes of Nadoüaissioux, delighted to see these Frenchmen." The French had turned their back on their oldest allies and brought their traders and their empire into Sioux country simply because the Sioux willed it so.[20]

The Očhéthi Šakówiŋ wanted more than goods. The Sioux wanted the French to limit all their commercial operations to within their domain. When a Miami sachem approached Perrot, hoping to "settle near the Frenchman's fire"—a scene that had been acted out in the pays d'en haut a thousand times—Perrot turned him down. The Očhéthi Šakówiŋ would not allow the French-Indian alliance to expand among their rivals. Perrot sent the dejected sachem away. "He was going to establish himself on the upper Mississippi, this side of the Nadouaissious."[21]

Perrot's siding with the Sioux marked the consolidation of the Očhéthi Šakówiŋ's dominion between the western Great Lakes and the Mississippi Valley. They now controlled Jean-Baptiste Colbert's "nursery for beaver." Perrot built two new trading posts for them—Nadouessioux and Fort Bonsecours—near the Mississippi–Saint Croix junction. The Očhéthi Šakówiŋ became a gravitational center in the heart of the continent. Sauteurs and Cheyennes moved to live with them and tightened their bonds through intermarriage, military collaboration, and the sharing of wealth. A little farther to the west, near the transition zone where forest gave way to prairie, dwelled the Lakotas, the sharp defensive edge of the Očhéthi Šakówiŋ. Even the domineering Five Nations would not challenge the Očhéthi Šakówiŋ.

There is no record of these two powerful Indigenous confederacies ever clashing. The Sioux and the Iroquois were compatible. The Iroquois pushed westward seasonally in large canoe fleets from their eastern bases, whereas the Sioux were about to make a concentrated push into the bison-rich continental grasslands beyond the Mississippi River. They did not compete for resources: the Iroquois sought pelts and captives; the Sioux sought bison and, increasingly, horses. Expanding simultaneously to the west, the two powers always had space between them. There was little incentive for them to trade or fight.

In contrast, the colonial powers had become locked in chronic conflicts. The English, French, Spanish, and Dutch fought over territory, river valleys, power, wealth, precious metals, converts, slaves, and trading privileges with Native Americans. From the late eighteenth century on, increasingly imperial clashes between England and France spilled over into North America, presenting both challenges and dangers to Native nations.

PART FOUR

THE INDIGENOUS BACKLASH

(late seventeenth century)

Chapter 11

THE ENGLISH
AS A LITTLE CHILD

NATIVE AMERICANS AND SATAN NEARLY DESTROYED
New England in 1675. Indians attacked fifty-two colonial settlements and ruined twelve of them in an exercise of total war, targeting women, children, men, cows, hogs, horses, houses, and Bibles.
The colonists had anticipated a war, but when it came, its intensity
was shocking. The English realized how very little they knew about
the surrounding Indians and their plans and ambitions.

After more than a century and a half of European colonization on
the continent, there still was no complete European map of North
America. Each colonial power perceived the continent from its specific vantage point, focusing on a particular slice or slices of it and
leaving the would-be colonists exposed. The English knew the Atlantic coast and Hudson Bay, the Spanish knew New Mexico and Florida, and the French knew the Saint Lawrence Valley. Only the French,
owing to their alliance with interior Native nations, had an inkling of
the vast Indigenous continent that stretched out to the horizon from
their colonial enclaves. Nowhere were Europeans able to dictate to the
Native Americans.

A precise map of North America in 1675 would have shocked those
White interlopers who had claimed the land for themselves. The map
would have shown a patchy belt of English colonies on the coastal
plains, extending from the contested Acadia—the French claimed it
too—to the Chesapeake Bay in the south. It would have shown the
tiny, recently established Charles Town, two English posts in the James
Bay, and an Indian village only fifteen miles from Boston. It would also
have shown thirty-five Spanish missions in Florida, reaching from the

Atlantic seaboard two hundred miles into the interior, run by a mere forty Franciscan priests who ministered to thousands of Native Americans. There was only one Spanish settlement of any consequence: San Agustín. The accurate map would have shown three French villages and four French forts in the Saint Lawrence Valley and two inland forts, Frontenac and Niagara, at Lake Ontario. It would have depicted dozens of French forts, trading posts, and temporary trading huts dotting the Great Lakes region in an ever-changing constellation. English America may have dwarfed both the French and Spanish Americas demographically—more than four hundred thousand English migrated to North America and the West Indies during the seventeenth century—but the French and Spanish could still feel relatively safe in the New World, because they had entered into alliances with Indians. Forging marriages á la façon du pays, the French won access to a vast number of Indigenous communities, securing their position from the Great Lakes region to the Hudson Bay. There, a thick lattice of kinship ties created an uncommonly stable world.[1]

But then, between 1675 and 1690, every colonial project on the Indigenous continent seemed to either wobble or expire altogether. New England exploded into violence over hogs, cows, fences, game, and deeds. The borderlands between Susquehannock country and Virginia became the site of a war no one wanted. The Pueblo Indians attacked their self-styled Spanish masters in a carefully planned uprising. The Five Nations began killing French traders and New France's Indian allies in the interior, taking their war all the way to Montreal. The Dutch departed the continent after only twelve years, leaving behind a mixed colonial record. Suddenly, the New World seemed to have become a graveyard for Old World empires as Native Americans mounted a concentrated counterattack against generations of colonial aggression.

THE FIRST SIGNS OF TROUBLE appeared in New England, the site of several brutal wars that left thousands of Native Americans dead by the 1670s. Ousamequin, the powerful Wampanoag sachem, had maintained an alliance with the Pilgrims since the 1620s, but the relationship had become strained. The Pequot War in 1637 had exposed Native Americans within and around New England to genocidal violence, shocking and alienating them. In 1642, the outbreak of civil war in England between Royalists and Parliamentarians all but stopped migration to America, leaving the New Englanders to fend for themselves. A year later, the colonies of Plymouth, Connecticut, New Haven, and Massachusetts Bay formed a military alliance, the New England Confederation, against the Indians. The English colonies were becoming full-fledged settler societies: self-contained, land-hungry, and impatient with the Native presence on their borders. As a minority group surrounded by Indians, the colonists were obsessed with control at every level of their society. Connecticut adopted a law that imposed a death penalty on boys over sixteen years of age who refused to obey their parents and, on any child, over sixteen, regardless of gender, who cursed or hit a parent.[2]

The New England Confederation nurtured ties with the Mohegans who had delivered Pequot heads to the English during the Pequot War, and in 1644, Massachusetts Bay colonists and Wampanoags entered into a covenant, which the English chose to understand as Native submission to their rule. Economic instability made the already fraught situation worse. By midcentury, the New England colonies had accumulated enough coinage to discard wampum as a currency, leaving their Native trade partners reeling. The English began pushing their settlements inland, hoping to find silver and iron. The Wampanoags were reduced from partners to dependents.[3]

The Wampanoags challenged the demotion in 1662 when half brothers Wamsutta and Metacom addressed the Plymouth General Court about the "damage done by the swine of some of the inhabitants of Rehoboth in their corn." The court authorized them to impound stray hogs and ordered colonists to keep their animals at sufficient distance from Wampanoag fields. Seeking English recognition of becoming chief sachem, Wamsutta announced that he wanted, "according to the custom of the natives," to change his name. He would be known as Alexander Pokanoket. Metacom, too, wanted to change his name. He was to be known to the English simply as Philip. The new moniker did little to improve his status among the English.[4]

KING PHILIP.

Metacom,
or King Philip

The New Englanders, still overwhelmingly Puritan, had long suffered persecution for their faith—an experience that had instilled in them a potent mix of paranoia and martial spirit. Many things offended them, and few things offended them more than Native peoples coming into their villages and homes. Indians could be unacceptably sociable—entering houses uninvited and expecting hospitality. They could also seem arrogant—stealing food, killing farm animals, and torching fields. Indians loomed, skulked, and sinned, threatening the Puritans' most precious and brittle possession: their souls. Hatred was born of proximity, not distance, between two peoples. The Puritan dilemma was at once religious, demographic, and generational. If Puritans became a minority group in Massachusetts, their dream of a godly society would be in danger. Their ministers could adjust the community's exacting religious standards through the Half-Way Covenant, or partial church membership, but the Indians could not be managed with semantics. Leading Puritans thought that they had to distance themselves from Native ways and bodies.[5]

Some English colonists embraced the Indians, convinced that a perfect Christian community in the New World could not deny God's grace to pagans. Members of this rump group believed that they needed to protect the Indians from other colonists, purge the Indians' souls of evil and heathenism, and isolate them from the corrupting influence of their sachems and *powwaws*, spiritual leaders. John Eliot, the Cambridge-educated Puritan minister, began preaching to the Indians at Natick and other villages. He translated the catechism and the Bible into Massachusetts, a dialect close to Wampanoag, and delivered sermons in that tongue. He also built a large Indian Library that boasted some seven thousand volumes of Christian literature in 1665. Eliot's was a civilizing mission aimed at reforming the Indians according to Puritan ideals. He wanted the Indians to adopt a European work ethic, raise livestock, become sedentary, and earn the grace of God. He hoped to extend God's unique covenant to them, which required co-opting local Native leaders. He expected Indians to move into secluded settlements where they would trade bows for plows, learn to read and write, accept "proper" gender roles by freeing women from farming, and learn to dress, speak, and worship like the English. Some were to be trained to become preachers and teachers who could deliver their brethren to English civility. The underlying, unspoken impulse was to turn the Native Americans into productive laborers for colonial markets. Eliot was trying to peacefully eliminate Indigeneity. Yet, defiantly, the mission Indians mixed Christianity with their traditional beliefs, ceremonies, and celebrations. Many refused to cut their hair. Women put Indigenous beliefs in a dialogue with Christianity, carving out a space for Indigenous spirituality.

By 1674, fourteen mission communities, or "praying towns," dotted the New England landscape—home to nearly twenty-five hundred Indians in different stages of conversion. In the isolation of the island of Noepe, ministers Thomas Mayhew Sr. and Jr. relied on more measured methods than Eliot's to win the Indians over. The Mayhews consulted sachems on proper goals and methods, protected Native property and lives against colonial mobs, and incorporated Indigenous religious traditions into Christian doctrines. Many Native women welcomed missionaries who taught them to read and write— a crucial advantage in dealing with the colonists—while the Wampanoags introduced Puritan ministers to the art of whale-hunting. The missionaries began using the Native term *Manitoo* for God, and many Indians seem to have embraced the missions and Christianity as a way to disentangle themselves from the tributary relationships with the powerful Indigenous confederacies on the mainland. Others found the missionaries' interference with their domestic and sex lives deeply disturbing. Many Indians distanced themselves from the English, keeping their Indigenous names and refitting Christian teachings to meet their spiritual needs, stymieing their ministers.[6]

Still, the ministers kept at it. Disease facilitated their efforts. While the Iroquois had launched mourning wars after being struck by small-pox, the mission Indians, when rocked by mass death, embraced the Mayhews' and Eliot's message of God's punishment and mercy. Several Nipmuc leaders on Noepe sent their sons to English schools and households to learn English ways, and some Native pupils attended Harvard Indian College, where they mastered English, Latin, and Greek. Nipmuc scholar James Printer set the type on the first Bible published in North America, and Caleb Cheeshateaumuck, a Wampanoag literary scholar, drew from classical literature to compose a missive celebrating education. On Noepe, many Wampanoags strove to be good Christians and not sin. They pledged loyalty to the king of England and seemed to have accepted the supremacy of the English court system and laws. But on the mainland, the Wampanoag sachem Metacom insisted that Noepe's people belonged to him. In the leading role of fighting English expansion in the East, the Wampanoags were about to supplant the weakened Powhatans.[7]

METACOM'S CHALLENGE to the allegiance of the Noepe people had deep roots. Most New England colonists had arrived uninvited on Indigenous lands, and their population exceeded fifty thousand in 1670, outnumbering local Indians three to one. John Winthrop's vision of New England as "a city upon a hill," a call for cooperation and a godly society, was still a fragile proposition, but the colonists had certainly prospered. In terms of status, most New Englanders were "middling sorts," tied to the world of commerce. Boston, Salem, and Newport were home to an expanding elite of lawyers and land speculators. By 1674, Harvard College had produced two hundred graduates. Boston, the largest of the New England settlements, had become a nearly autonomous city-state, modeled on classical ideals of a sovereign republic. It competed with the mother country's fisheries, shipbuilding industry, and carrying trade, which in New England rested heavily on slave labor. Countless Indians were shipped into slavery in the West Indies, while African slaves were brought to New England to clear forests and improve the land. Massachusetts Bay had approved the first slave law in the English Atlantic in 1641, partly to clarify the status of hundreds of Pequot captives in colonial households. In 1670 the colony decreed that enslaved status would be inherited through the mother.[8]

Led by Boston, New Englanders were reimagining themselves as empire builders, a transformation that had been anticipated by the Massachusetts Bay Company's original charter, which did not specify a boundary between English and Indigenous lands. Instead, the king's charter granted the company all the lands between 40° and 48° north from "sea to sea"—a blueprint for a continent-spanning empire for people who, decades later, still had little idea of the shape and scope of the continent. A long list of specific geographical realms and resource domains revealed the underlying logic of conquest. The colonists thought that Indians did not use the land properly, because they did not try to improve it and maximize its yield. The colonists argued that the land was underused and therefore free for the taking. The king of England personified a collective sovereignty that endorsed a system of property rights that allowed easy transfer of land from the crown to colonial villages and from the villages into private hands as a commodity, in perpetuity—an utterly alien concept to Native Americans. The English were appropriating Indigenous territory one deed at a time.

The Indians moved to confront the arrogant colonists. Few things vexed the neighboring Indians as much as fences, livestock, and trees. The English cut down trees in massive quantities to build ships and houses and to clear the land for crops and for fences to keep livestock out of their fields and farms. The fences posed a grave threat to the Native inhabitants, disrupting traditional migration routes of deer and other game, while also compromising the animals' reproduction patterns and the Indians' hunting routines. The absence of fences allowed colonial livestock—cows, hogs, horses—to wander into Native cornfields, devour crops, and ruin hunting grounds. Cows and hogs could destroy a carefully cultivated field in a matter of hours, invalidating weeks of Native women's work. Contrasting understandings of what counted as property exacerbated the conflict: the English insisted that they owned their farm animals even when they strayed and ravaged Native fields, but the Indians argued that such animals were fair game and could be killed and consumed at will. The Indians insisted that only dead animals could be owned, and they kept killing the invading strays. The Indians also sought compensation for the damages to their crops in colonial courts, but they received restitution only rarely. In the end, they had no choice but to accept fences and private ownership of the land and of animals as facts. Fences had ushered in a new order. The Indians were in danger of becoming strangers in their own land. The colonists, too, were angry and concerned: in their minds, there could not be colonialism without domestic animals. Indians, for their part, made no rigid distinction between human and animal beings, which could be *manitous*, or spiritous.[9]

By early 1675, Metacom and the Wampanoags had seen enough. The colonists refused to recognize the Wampanoags and their allies as sovereign nations, and they allowed their beasts to graze on Indigenous lands. The English had also denounced Weetamoo, the saunkskwa of the Pocasset Nation, as their inferior because of her gender, overlooking that they had recently been governed by Queen Elizabeth I. The English had filled their record books with so many property deeds that Plymouth, Rhode Island, Massachusetts Bay, and Connecticut felt entitled to claim much of the Wampanoags' territory. Metacom had also lost many tribute-paying Indians to missions and Christianity. The English had captured and enslaved hundreds of Native women and men, fracturing life-sustaining kinship networks and denying Indigenous humanity. There were hundreds of Indian slaves in New England households, living in fear of being sold, raped, killed, or sent somewhere faraway—the West Indies, Europe, or "in any part of the king's dominions." This was not how it was supposed to be. The colonists had seen the Indians as useful, a potential source of labor, but they were now destroying the Indians. New England's colonialism was reaching its destructive zenith.[10]

Two years later, Alexander Pokanoket died in Plymouth under suspicious circumstances. It was not clear whether he had been inciting Wampanoags to rise up against the English; he may have died of a disease, or he may have been poisoned by Plymouth agents. What was clear was that he had been selling Indian land to Quakers and other nonseparatists from Rhode Island and other colonies, ignoring Plymouth's claims to the land. Metacom inherited the Wampanoag sachemship and pledged not to sell land to strangers—that is, to any New England colonies other than Plymouth. He received a collective promise that Wampanoags would not be asked to sell any land for seven years. He insisted on having that covenant in writing. He also believed that the English had killed his brother.[11]

The road to war was paved with greed, rumors, fear, misunderstandings, and frustration. The colonists clamored for more and more land, and war could make Indian land theirs far faster than written deeds could. The major hindrance with the deed-based land grab was Weetamoo, who had fought the deed system for years. She had succeeded in turning the colonial instrument of Indigenous dispossession into a weapon to protect Indigenous landholdings: in a brilliantly simple move, she had both Native and English men—whose property rights were far stronger than women's under English law—sign deeds on her behalf. The road to war was also paved by sheer arrogance. Unlike the earlier Indian wars in the region, the coming one seemed unlosable to the English, who vastly outnumbered the Indians. English traders and ministers openly urged the Indians to abandon their sachems, and growing numbers of Christian Indians renounced their loyalty to Metacom. In April 1671, Metacom was summoned to Taunton in the heart of the Plymouth Colony. He signed a peace treaty that ostensibly reduced his followers to subjects of the colony. But Metacom made only faint gestures to honor the treaty, and in September he was in Boston, facing the leaders of Plymouth, Massachusetts Bay, and Connecticut, who demanded an explanation for why the Indian disarmament was proceeding so slowly. They fined him £100. One of Metacom's mentors reprimanded him for not going to war, calling him a coward. In reality, Metacom was stalling deliberately, hoping to buy enough time to secure weapons for his anticolonial coalition.[12]

INTRIGUE AND UNCERTAINTY on both sides fueled animosity, which centered to a remarkable degree on a single individual, John Sassamon, a bilingual Indigenous scholar and a Christian minister of the Massachusett Nation. Orphaned by disease outbreaks, Sassamon had been raised in English households. He had been expelled from Harvard for drunkenness, but he could move lucidly between colonial and Indigenous worlds. John Eliot had instructed him on Christianity, and Sassamon had helped Eliot in translating Christian tracts. Sassamon became Metacom's aide, scribe, and confidant. He also assisted the English with several land transfers, many of them controversial. In the spring of 1674, he arranged deeds that made him, his daughter, and her husband the new owners of land around a pond at Assawompset Neck. In late January 1675, he traveled to Plymouth and warned the governor that Metacom was plotting an uprising. A week later, Sassamon's bloated body was found under the ice in Assawompset Pond. Increase Mather, the learned Boston minister, wrote that there was "but one reason why the Indians murthered John Sausaman": his faith. "He was Christianized and baptized, and was a Preacher amongst the Indians." Soon after, Mather wrote, "Thus did the *War* begin, this being the first english blood which was spilt by the Indians in an hostile way."[13]

A mission Indian named Patuckson emerged to announce that he had witnessed three of Metacom's men killing Sassamon. Harboring few illusions about the impartiality of English courts, Metacom kept his soldiers in the field, but he informed Josiah Winslow, the governor of Plymouth Colony, that he "would do no harm." In March 1675, the Plymouth General Court, composed of twelve Englishmen and six nonvoting mission Indians, convicted the three Wampanoag men that Patuckson had identified for the murder; they were executed on June 8. John Easton, the deputy governor of Rhode Island, met with Metacom, who came to him with unarmed soldiers. Metacom seized the initiative by announcing that "they had done no wrong, the English wronged them." "All English," he continued, "agreed against them, and so by arbitration they had had much wrong, many miles square of land so taken from them." Easton, who was a Quaker, and his magistrates agreed with Metacom's account. The Wampanoags reminded them that "they had been the first in doing good to the English, and the English the first in doing wrong; they said when the English first came, their king's father was as a great man and the English as a little child" and "had let them have a 100 times more land than now the king had for his own people." The Wampanoags were referring to the generosity shown to the Pilgrims. The English were startled. Easton wrote that "for 40 years time reports and jealousies of war had been so very frequent that we did not think that now a war was breaking forth."[14]

On June 19, Governor Winslow sent a message to Metacom, demanding that the Wampanoag soldiers lay down their weapons. It would have meant unconditional surrender. The next day, Metacom's men, outfitted with rifles and body armor, killed dozens of colonists in the isolated town of Swansea. Wampanoag and Narragansett sachems met with emissaries from Rhode Island and Massachusetts Bay at a large pond near their villages, hoping to prevent a general war. When the English urged the Narragansetts to isolate themselves from Metacom, the Narragansett sachems retorted by asking why Rhode Island and Massachusetts Bay would join Plymouth Colony in fighting Metacom. The response gave the Indians pause: the English said that all New England colonies were subjects of the king of England, their sovereign, and were duty bound to fight together. The sachems appealed to their long-standing alliance with the two colonies and asked the emissaries to detach themselves from Plymouth. Soon after, Wampanoag soldiers killed five English colonists and brought their heads to Metacom.[15]

English troops sacked Montaup, Metacom's seat of power, in late June, forcing a hasty retreat in canoes. The English hunted Metacom "from all the sea shores" but "could not tell what was become of him." The survivors seemed to have fled the region. In reality, many of them had gathered at Menimesit, a protected island on the Ware

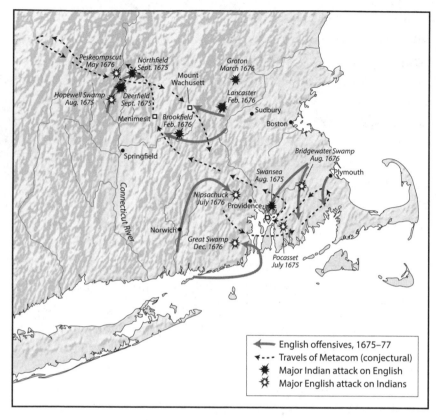

The battles and maneuvers of Metacom's War

River, where they fished and, as the summer advanced, ate berries and plants. They also prepared for war. As summer turned to fall, Metacom organized a strategic retreat along ancient riverside trails to a winter camp north of Albany in Mohawk country. The hope was to forge an alliance with the Mohawks and Mohegans, who, through the Covenant Chain, might be able to secure the Duke of York's royal protection for Metacom's two thousand followers.

Wampanoag soldiers monitored English operations from a distance, launching surprise attacks and raids that aimed to wound and disorient, not kill. Massachusetts Bay troops focused on defending the exposed Swansea settlements near Wampanoag country and on capturing Metacom. Violence washed over the land like a contagion. The fighting centered on Narragansett Bay and the village of Pocasset for weeks and then began to spread into the interior, leaving behind dead colonists and livestock. Dozens of New England towns lay in ruins. Even the Christian Indians now appeared dangerous, as the war took on racial undertones. The colonists locked up the mission Indians on an island in Boston Harbor. Some Pequots and Massachusetts joined the English, hoping to find some relief.[16]

For his part, Metacom sought an alliance with the Nipmucs to the northwest, while Weetamoo capitalized on her expansive kinship networks and her deep knowledge of the landscape to secure shelter, food, and protection for her people. She found refuge among the Narragansetts near a sheltering wetland known as Great Swamp. Having left her husband, who seemed to have sided with the English, Weetamoo married Quinnapin, who, together with his cousin Canonchet, led the Narragansett Nation, thereby creating a transnational confederation of mutual support. The Wampanoag struggle became the Narragansett struggle. A Narragansett mason named Stonewall John organized the construction of a massive earth-and-stone fort covering five acres to protect the allied Indians. Canonchet visited Boston to open talks, hoping to buy time for the allied Wampanoags and Narragansetts. The Narragansetts brought to the alliance a highly mobile style of warfare that was captured by the word *Nqussutam*, which means "I remove house." The Wabanakis and Nashaways soon joined the alliance.[17]

The English, though, were already on the move. Plymouth, Connecticut, and Massachusetts Bay militias had combined forces and recruited some 150 Pequot and Mohegan soldiers to join them, bringing their collective strength to approximately fifteen hundred. They had captured a Narragansett Indian named Peter and threatened to hang him unless he guided them to the new Narragansett and Wampanoag fort. Peter yielded. On their way, the English troops burned two Indian villages, readying themselves for battle. But when they reached Great Swamp, the size of the fort gave them pause, as did the hundreds of wigwams around it. On December 19, an exceptionally cold day, English militias attacked the boggy stronghold and the fort, which housed roughly thirteen hundred people.

The war did not start promisingly for the English. Town elites throughout New England avoided drafting men from their own class,

Sketch depicting the Great Swamp Fight

and an overwhelming majority of the impressed men were criminals and other undesirables, whereas the Indians fought as tight communities of men, women, and children, all contributing to the war effort. The Indians also knew the land far better than the English and used difficult terrain to dull the invaders' technological advantage. The English attackers failed to penetrate the wigwams around the swamp, because the Indians had reinforced their lodges with bags of grain, rendering them bulletproof. Stymied, the English turned to proven tactics: they invaded the fort and torched houses, keeping people inside with gunfire, and burning five hundred homes.

Approximately six hundred women, men, and children were killed. It was a near repeat of the Pequot massacre on the Mystic River thirty-eight years earlier. The English also took almost seven hundred prisoners; they would sell many of them into slavery in the West Indies. The colonists had suffered approximately seventy dead. The overall toll on the Native side would have been higher, had not "a strange sudden Thaw happened in the midst of January," allowing the allied Indians to seek sanctuary in Narragansett country.[18]

Soon after, Uncas, the Mohegan sachem, mobilized three hundred soldiers and razed Metacom's winter camp forty miles northeast of Albany in Mohawk country, forcing Metacom and his followers to recross the Hudson and return to the north. Rejected by the Puritans, by New York governor Edmund Andros, and, shockingly, by their Christian kin, the Wampanoags and Narragansetts had to reconsider their options. The Narragansetts took the initiative. Canonchet, their sachem, organized an army of nearly two thousand soldiers and practically emptied central Massachusetts of colonists. Experts in mobile battle, the Narragansetts burned villages and destroyed almost all the farms west of the Narragansett Bay. Their path could be traced by dead farm animals, torn books, strewn church bells, bodies, and body parts.[19]

Chapter 12

METACOM'S
CHALLENGE

THE REPERCUSSIONS OF METACOM'S WAR EXTENDED far beyond New England, triggering an array of moves and stratagems by both colonists and Indians. While Metacom and his followers struggled through the cold and snow toward more violence and bloodshed, Edmund Andros, the governor of New York, hosted Mohawk clan mothers and sachems in Albany, branding himself as the savior of the Puritan planters, while simultaneously working to shield the colony from the virulent Indian war. All along, he had stockpiled arms and gunpowder, fearing that the war would reach his colony. He had also arranged "row boats all along the shore." The savior of New England seemed to be preparing to abandon New York at a moment's notice.[1]

Defending New York was challenging because of its disunity: it was home to a jumble of English, Scots, Dutch, Germans, French Huguenots, and free Africans, each group forming its own enclave, whereas Indians were unified through kinship ties. New York was also difficult to defend because of its topography. The Five Nations and the French could launch swift, river-based attacks from three directions. Andros was desperate for a treaty with the Mohawks, who had announced that they had "always been one flesh" with the Dutch who, even after New York's transfer to England, posed a chronic threat to English America. Recognizing the weakness of his position, Andros proposed a treaty that merely "encouraged" the Mohawks' loyalty toward the English and asked them "not to molest them without Cause."

In a desperate move, New Englanders recruited Christian Indians to join them in fighting their relatives "as Spies," spawning an Indigenous civil war within the larger war between Indians and colonists. Soon after, Metacom's Wampanoags attacked the town of Northampton, prompting the Massachusetts Council to consider building an eight-foot-high wall around Boston. Metacom and his soldiers were within striking distance of the city. Although removed more than four hundred miles from the active war zone, Sir William Berkeley, the governor of Virginia, fretted about how "the infection of the Indians in New-England has dilated itself to the Marylanders and the Northern parts of Virginia." The Indians, he believed, "would be rid of us if they Could but I thank god they have not dared to shew themselves our Enemies yet."[2]

The war was expanding into the religious realm. The Puritan Bible commonwealth was collapsing under Indian attacks that were already spreading east toward New York, filling the English with fear that Satan and the Indians whom they had abused would now retaliate. God was punishing them for their sins. To prove their worthiness in their God's eyes, they had to destroy the heathens. A story of an Englishman facing an Indian war party in front of his house with a Bible in hand, as if he were invincible, set the tone. Native soldiers killed him on the spot, "deriding his groundless Apprehension, or Folly therein, ripped him open, and put his Bible in his Belly." In the spring of 1676, Narragansetts ambushed and killed nearly eighty Plymouth troops and Christian Wampanoags, and soon after, a Narragansett expedition attacked Providence and burned several houses. One belonged to the Puritan minister Roger Williams, who had previously welcomed Indians into his home and learned their language. The Narragansetts told him that God was now with them and had abandoned the English because they had killed so many Indians. Yet they allowed Williams to live. Not long after, the minister began promoting the sale of Providence's Indian captives into slavery. The shaken colonists thought that only massive bloodshed would save their souls.[3]

The brutal and graphic Indigenous violence was fueled by accumulated grievances over several generations, and its unleashing was aimed at purging the arrogant and genocidal colonists from their world. For a moment, it seemed as if the Indians might drive the colonists into the sea. They were tearing through towns, villages, and forts with ease. The allied Indians invited Puritan representatives to Nipmuc country, believing that they could now negotiate from a position of strength. Monoco, a Nashaway sachem, warned the colonists that if they did not agree to the Indians' terms, the Indigenous alliance would sack every English town on the way to Boston. Metacom's forces were poised to rearrange the colonial-Native power dynamics around colonial-Indigenous equality, which the Puritans saw as equivalent to apocalypse.

But then the tide turned. The New England Confederation launched a joint campaign against the Indigenous armies, mobilizing their citizens, their god, and, most important, their Indian allies for a holy war that would see the righteous prevail over the Native "marauders" and "beasts." The colonists convinced loyal mission Indians and Mohawks to join them with lavish gift-giving, and they abandoned the rigid European ways of waging war in favor of fluid Indigenous tactics that relied on ambushes, tactical retreats, dispersions, and individual marksmanship. When the Mohawks organized a winter campaign in 1676–77 against Metacom's coalition, they were fighting for themselves. The New England Confederation was the most formidable colonial project in the East, and the Mohawks wanted it on their side.

Metacom's position deteriorated. His reserves of food and munitions were running low, leaving this coalition vulnerable to the wrath of the colonists, who could draw from deeper pools of weapons, necessities, and people. On May 9, 1677, Mather learned that "God had let loose the Mohawks upon our Enemies, and that they were sick of Fluxes, and Fevers, which proved mortal to multitudes of them." It was the turning point. On May 19, Captain William Turner led more than a hundred troops and volunteers to an Indian fishing village at Peskeompscut. He ordered a night attack that left two hundred women, men, and children dead. The Indians retaliated, triggering another massacre. Unable to find Metacom, the Mohegans, Pequots, and their Connecticut auxiliaries located a group of Narragansetts at Nipsagchuck Swamp. The Mohegans and Pequots advanced in the middle, while the English launched a mounted charge on the flanks. The Narragansett death toll of 126 would have been higher, had the

Mohegans and Pequots not insisted on restraint. The war had become genocidal and, for Metacom's followers, unsustainable.[4]

Across New England, colonists began hunting down Indians who had killed English soldiers under the laws of war, putting them on trial and then hanging them. Mather wrote, "The Heathen are sunk down into the pit that they made, in the net which they had hid, is their own foot taken." The colonists captured more than a hundred Wampanoags—a crippling loss to Metacom. Forces from Plymouth and Rhode Island converged around Weetamoo and Metacom and their diminished body of followers. Metacom cut his hair short and retreated to his ancestral home and stronghold at Montaup. On August 6, Weetamoo drowned in a river while trying to flee colonial troops. The English left her uncovered body on the ground, demonstrating their dominance over her and her gender. Six days later, a mission Indian named John Alderman, who had joined the English, shot Metacom. The colonists cut off his head, took it to Plymouth, and mounted it on a pole atop a watchtower. They kept his skull there for twenty-five years. At least three thousand Native men, women, and children had been killed, nearly seventy percent of Metacom's and Weetamoo's peoples, and perhaps two thousand left the region. On October 19, 1677, Wampanoag soldiers lit a bonfire in the woods near the town of Hatfield. When the locals came to inspect, Wampanoags killed nine of them.[5]

THE VIOLENT CLASHES BETWEEN Native Americans and colonists during the late 1670s, which later came to be known as Metacom's War, or King Philip's War to the English, were a shocking calamity to the colonists, even in apparent victory. New England had lost six hundred soldiers, roughly ten percent of the total number, and at least a thousand colonists had died facing Indian soldiers, whom the English branded savages. The colony suffered the loss of a staggering £150,000 in property at a time when £100 was a very comfortable yearly salary. More than a thousand colonial homes had been burned, and some two dozen towns had been either destroyed or severely damaged. The English would not reoccupy their prewar borders until

1700, and the New Englanders faced the imminent collapse of their Bible commonwealth. Metacom had been killed, but Indian wars raged on in the north along the New England–Acadia border, where Western Abenakis raided encroaching English settlements, destroying nearly all of them. Increase Mather condemned his fellow colonists' land hunger: "Farms and merchandising have been preferred before the things of God."[6]

The carnage that the English exacted on the Native Americans was a sign of weakness, not strength. The Puritans had lived in fear of the Indians, conscious of the fact that the Indians knew the landscape better and could outfight them everywhere, whether in swamps, the woods, and even their own towns. Long before the shocking war, the Puritans had been obsessively concerned with the state of their souls, and their anxiety only intensified at war's end. Their slaughter of Native women and children, mutilation of Indian bodies, and sheer hatred and rage shook the colonists' view of themselves as civilized people. New England as a whole seemed to be slipping into savagery, its moral rot confirmed by the heathens' victories on the battlefield.

To make sense of it all, the colonists relied on ink. Between 1675 and 1682, twenty-nine narratives were written about the war. The most famous of them was Mary Rowlandson's account of her captivity. In February 1676, Rowlandson had been taken in the town of Lancaster by Nipmuck Indians, and she spent three months among them. She was "redeemed" for £20, and she moved to Boston with her Puritan minister husband. While there, she finished *The Soveraignty and Goodness of God . . . : Being a Narrative of the Captivity and Restauration of Mrs. Mary Rowlandson*, which became an instant best seller—America's first. Her theme was redemption, the deliverance of the soul from captivity in the wilderness, and it resonated powerfully with the battered colonists. Rowlandson wrote herself out of bondage and back into civilization, delivering herself and her thousands of readers from perdition. But her stunningly popular account also kept the war and its horrors fresh in New Englanders' minds. When people read, again and again, her reprimand that "our perverse and evil carriages in the sight of the Lord, have so offended him, that instead of turning his hand against them [the Indians], the Lord feeds and nourishes them up to be a scourge to the whole Land," the effect was profound. The shared calamity and suffering became a possibility for future coexistence.[7]

While some colonists read to understand their new world, others tried to heal themselves by purging the Devil from their souls, with varying degrees of success. Mather saw the war as God's punishment for New England's sins and moral failures. The pacifist Quakers agreed, arguing that Puritans had invited God's wrath by persecuting them. The English colonists were becoming divided, and they had to adopt drastic measures to protect themselves against the Devil, the Indians, and the French. In 1686, King James II decreed the merging of the mosaic of small mid-Atlantic colonies—Massachusetts, Connecticut, Plymouth, Rhode Island, and the nebulous territories of Maine and New Hampshire—into a single megacolony, the Dominion of New England. This new entity would protect the colonists and enable them to focus on the one truly essential task: to make the mother country rich through trade, taxes, and imported slaves. The king placed the capable and autocratic Edmund Andros in charge of the massive colony. Andros was to govern the dominion with an iron fist, without the interference of elected assemblies. The formation of the dominion was a heavy blow to the individual colonies, limiting their economic options, increasing their tax burden, and threatening their religious freedom. In 1688 the dominion was expanded to include New York and New Jersey, only to be terminated a year later when William of Orange, the stadtholder of Holland and self-proclaimed protector of the Protestant faith in Europe, crossed the English Channel with a massive fleet and forced James II to flee.[8]

In early August, Wabanaki sachems Madockawando and Moxis announced that Andros was a rogue and that they meant to push into New England and "have all their Countrey by and by." Crises were multiplying, overwhelming the colonists. The year 1689 became an annus horribilis. The rebellion against Andros had been bloodless, but violence followed soon after. Militiamen deserted forts and garrisons in droves, exposing the length of the New England frontier to joint Wabanaki-French attacks. English towns began to fall like dominoes as violence spread over the land. In late May of 1689, militia captain

Jacob Leisler staged a revolt against the Indians, but the rolling crisis persisted. Leisler held the southern part of New York for two years, hoarding power. He was executed in 1691 as a traitor. In midsummer of 1692, Reverend Ebenezer Babson insisted that a "Molestation" that befell the town of Gloucester in Massachusetts was not the work of "real French and Indians, but that of the Devil and his Agents."[9]

BETWEEN JUNE AND SEPTEMBER OF 1692, the Massachusetts Bay Colony hanged fourteen women and five men for witchcraft in the village of Salem. One man was pressed to death by heavy stones. Two dogs were found guilty as well. The Devil seemed to have entered the village, and a number of children, young women, and orphaned female servants had accused older women of tormenting them in the spectral form of the Devil. A local magistrate interrogated Dorothy Good, aged five, for conversing with the Devil and crippling people by simply looking at them. She announced that she nursed a snake at the lowest joint of her index finger. She was sent to prison, where she spent nine months in heavy irons. Others soared in their minds, surging through the sky, high above the American woods where stealthy shape-shifting creatures prowled, plundered, and took lives. According to the possessed, these were Indians, and they not only plundered and killed; some of them had joined the abominable French to assault English settlements. It was no coincidence that in 1692 the Indian frontier was within fifty miles of Salem: the proximity fueled terror, supercharging an already-established tradition of witch hunts in the New World. As much as the colonists tried to be pure and virtuous, they felt the Devil's tentacles creeping around them.

Among them was Tituba, a Carib Indian slave, who became the first woman accused of practicing witchcraft. She defended herself shrewdly and methodically, repenting piously. She knew her catechism and Bible and—apparently to mollify the colonists—admitted to having ridden upon a stick in the sky with two colonists, Sarah Good and Sarah Osborne. The three of them were carted to Boston for trial. Tituba calmly explained that she had refused to torture children when a white-haired man ordered her to do so in the hysterical village. She then identified Good and Osborne as witches. She seemed to know exactly how to survive in the unraveling colonial settlement.

Such crises had occurred before, serving as a warning against fear-induced witch hunts, but the people of Salem pushed ahead with accusations. In all, 144 persons—38 men and 106 women—were indicted. Witchcraft was seen mainly as women's crime; their weaker bodies, the theory went, rendered them more susceptible to sin. But there was an earthlier dimension to the women's overrepresentation among the accused: many of them were unhappy with their circumstances, especially chronic overwork involving clearing fields and hauling wood, and had complained about it, violating existing gender roles.

The accusers and judges included people who were familiar with Isaac Newton's writings and who embraced the incipient scientific revolution, yet somehow they were led to execute people on the basis of dreams and visions. Abnormal body parts, unusual physical strength, and insensitive skin could lead to a conviction, as could successful fortune-telling. The colonists struggled to understand what was real, what was not real, and what was happening to them. They questioned their very autonomy as human beings, having been outdone by the Devil, who was also God's creation. Disputes between neighbors and envy of well-to-do fellow colonists instigated accusations, and many believed that their sufferings and losses in the continuing Indian wars were signs of their unworthiness in God's eyes. North America—its persisting Indigeneity, its stubborn imperviousness in the face of the one true God, its strange codes of violence and war—had turned New Englanders against one another.[10]

Chapter 13

VIRGINIA'S CIVIL AND UNCIVIL WARS

WHEN NEW ENGLAND PLUNGED INTO KING PHILIP'S War in the 1670s, Virginians lost little time in arguing that God was punishing the Puritans for their sins. The Puritans had been an unpopular minority group in England, and they were an unpopular minority group in America. Governor William Berkeley and other Virginians had little tolerance for the stubborn dissenters, who did not seem to realize that English institutions and traditions needed to be adapted to New World conditions. Berkeley denounced them as fantasists, detached from reality, who failed to grasp how serious the Indigenous challenge to English America was. "The New England men might as soon and as well have expected to have been invaded by the Persian or Mogul as from their Indians," he wrote. The Indian question was exposing dangerous fault lines among the English, within and between colonies.[1]

Virginia was afflicted by distinctive and potentially explosive problems of its own. In the early 1630s, tobacco prices had bottomed out and remained low, making it almost impossible to turn a profit. Only the wealthiest persevered, while many poor Virginians struggled to make ends meet. A steady trickle of African slaves pushed the colony toward a dangerous pathology: poor Whites and Black slaves had begun to form a single pool of exploited people who worked for the wealthy White aristocrats and shared a resentment for the White elite.

It was an exceptionally shaky foundation for a New World colony. While more than ten million pounds of tobacco flowed from Virginia to London each year, tens of thousands of immigrants poured into the colony, drawn by the prospect of becoming landowners: each male

immigrant, however lowly in England, received fifty acres—a dizzying opening for social ascent. But there was a catch. Few among the
poor could afford the cost of a transatlantic crossing, forcing them
to mortgage themselves to a ship captain or a Virginia planter for
years by signing an indenture, a contract that effectively turned them
into unfree laborers serving a master class. An individual's passage
to Virginia may have been filled with hope, but in the short run, emigration meant grueling work in tobacco fields and subservient status
under a master who could whip them, extend their contracts by years
for minor misdemeanors, and even sell them to settle gambling debts.
The colonists were in danger of losing their most precious commodity
in the New World: their meticulously constructed manhood.[2]

Eager to appease the disillusioned servants, Berkeley curbed settler expansion to prevent the production of too much tobacco, which
would cut prices. Yet elite planters pushed into the interior, defrauding
poor colonists and Indians of land. Tensions mounted between colonists and Indians, as well as between servants and Indians, who saw
one another as rivals and enemies. Since the collapse of the Powhatan
Confederacy in 1644, Indian-hating had only intensified in Virginia.
By the 1670s, Virginia had become a self-conscious settler colony—
arguably North America's first—driven by fear and land hunger and
determined to eliminate Indigenous peoples from its claimed borders.
Berkeley advocated an all-out war against the Susquehannocks, the
hunter-fisher-farmer Doegs, and other Indians who had not yet been
reduced to tributary status. He thought that even enslaved Indians
should be sold elsewhere to keep the colony pure.[3]

Under such conditions, it took only a single clash to trigger an all-out
war. In July 1675, a Doeg party approached Thomas Mathews, a Potomac River valley planter, and asked him to pay an old debt. Mathews
refused, and the Doegs stole some of his hogs. Mathews's overseer
chased the Indians and killed one of them. The Doegs retreated, only
to return to kill the overseer. The Virginia militia pursued the Indians
into Maryland. They came upon two quiet cabins and launched an
attack. It was only when a man materialized from the shower of bullets
to face Captain George Mason, grabbing his hand, that the Virginians realized they had killed friendly Susquehannocks. In August, the

Susquehannocks killed a number of colonists in retaliation, prompting Berkeley to summon up 750 militiamen. As rumors of imminent attacks spread, the Maryland government mobilized 250 militiamen and a hundred tributary Indians. No colonist offered to cover the dead, to assuage the Iroquoian Susquehannocks. Instead, militia captains had the skulls of five Susquehannock sachems cracked. The Susquehannocks went to war, just weeks after Metacom's War erupted. Suddenly, almost all the English colonies were fighting for survival.[4]

ALTHOUGH A SMALLISH NATION, the Susquehannocks turned themselves into a major regional power with wide-reaching connections. In the mid-seventeenth century they had dominated the lands around the Susquehanna Valley watershed from a central town that relocated roughly every generation from group to group. But over the course of the 1660s, their centrality backfired. They were hit repeatedly by epidemics, and their numbers collapsed from roughly five thousand to a mere four hundred in 1675. The Susquehannocks had become badly outnumbered by all surrounding groups. Their war parties were now composed of teenage boys and young men carrying axes, bows, and flintlocks. Overwhelmed by grief and driven by distress, these youth armies did not take captives, preferring to torture their enemies rather than killing them swiftly. The Iroquois, too, inflicted heavy losses, forcing the remaining Susquehannocks to resettle in a new base on Piscataway Creek in the south.

It was there, in the summer of 1675, that the Susquehannocks faced a thousand-strong Virginia and Maryland army. The Susquehannocks held off the colonists for six weeks and then began raiding Virginia's northern frontier in the dead of winter, unnerving the colonists, who had grown to expect Indian attacks during warmer months. Susquehannocks, it seemed, had held the Midwinter Ceremony, during which they interpreted dreams. They appeared to have dreamt of war. They killed three dozen colonists and left behind bodies that had been mutilated in a telltale manner. Colonists fled in panic, abandoning their plantations. By March 1676, dozens of Virginians lay dead, and sixty plantations along the Rappahannock River stood deserted. An "approaching calamity," some believed, "made the giddy-headed multitude mad."[5]

That blend of fear and anxiety pushed Virginia toward civil war. Governor Berkeley preferred a defensive strategy and wanted to build a chain of frontier forts along major rivers above the fall line on the western edge of the coastal plain to keep the Native Americans out. He also wanted to focus the coming war against the hostile Susquehannocks, and thus angered the small planters whose lands abutted other Indigenous domains, blocking their access to new landholdings. The colonists clamored for an indiscriminate war against all the Indians.[6]

Enter Nathaniel Bacon, a newcomer to Virginia and a cousin of Berkeley by marriage, crackling with ambition. Bacon had been educated at Cambridge, but he had arrived in the New World with a whiff of shadiness and plenty of silver, and he moved quickly into both elite and lower-class circles. He traded with Indians, became a leader among Virginia's frontiersmen, and used his connection to Berkeley to win a seat on the governor's council. He owned a plantation at Curles Neck on the James River near the fall line, where he lived with his pregnant wife, Elizabeth, and their infant daughter, unprotected against Indian attacks. Bacon began to advocate for a genocidal war against the Indians, and he wanted to take the war to the south and away from his family plantation. His view of himself as a patriarchal master was at stake, and he was not alone; many Virginia men shared his anxiety. The line between the household and the colony was becoming blurred when the colonists faced Indians who attacked and taunted them, calling them cowards. Bacon thought that his cause, however subversive it might seem, should be Virginia's cause. In his own mind, he remained a self-professed loyal subject of the king.[7]

Bacon delivered a six-point critique of Berkeley and his policies, accusing the governor of imposing unjust taxes and monopolizing the beaver trade. But it was the Indian question that truly divided Virginia. Bacon denounced Berkeley for "having protected, favored, and emboldened the Indians against His Majesties loyal subjects, never contravening, requiring, or appointing any due or proper means of satisfaction for their many Invasions, robberies, and murders committed upon us." Virginia's Indian policy was a matter of its very survival, Bacon seethed, and Berkeley had botched it, endangering the entire colony. Making matters worse, there was danger of a Catholic insurgency: Lord Baltimore, the Catholic proprietor of Maryland, was rumored to have assembled an alliance with Indians and "papists" to destroy Protestantism in North America.

Defying Virginia's governor, and effectively hijacking the colony's Indian policy, Bacon led a private army of colonists and indentured servants south to find Susquehannocks to kill. These men, known as the "Volunteers," were aware that many Susquehannocks had approached the well-connected Occaneechis on Roanoke Island, hoping to form an anti-Virginia alliance with them. But the Volunteers reached the Occaneechis first, and Bacon persuaded them to attack the Susquehannocks. When the Occaneechis returned with Susquehannock captives, Bacon insisted that the prisoners be handed over to him. In the ensuing commotion a shot was fired, and the Volunteers stormed the Occaneechi stronghold. The fight continued through the night and into the next afternoon. Bacon reported that "wee destroyed about 100 men and 2 of their kings, besides women & children," giving "satisfaction to the people." But the victory "soe enraged" Berkeley, said Bacon, that he "came home with greater danger."[8]

The governor branded Bacon an outlaw and called a general election for the House of Burgesses, the first since 1661. To Berkeley's disgust, Bacon was elected. Bacon traveled to Jamestown with his followers, and Berkeley had him detained and made Bacon kneel in front of him. Bacon fled, only to return with an army of five hundred. He forced Berkeley to appoint him as general of the Volunteers and made the legislature authorize another Indian campaign. The war against the Susquehannocks expanded into a civil war among Virginians. In late June 1676, Elizabeth Bacon wrote, "I am sure if the Indians were not cowards, they might have destroyed all the upper plantations, and killed all the people in them; the Governour so much their friend, that he would not suffer any body hurt one of the Indians." Such was the power of Indian-fearing and Indian-hating in Virginia that the quarreling English colonists failed to find any common ground.[9]

It may have been the most confusing and malicious of North America's Indian wars to that point. Having failed to locate the elusive Occaneechis and Susquehannocks, Bacon and his soldiers began killing the peaceful Pamunkeys, Nanzaticos, Rappahannocks, Portobaccos, Wicocomocos, and Appomattucks. Emboldened, Bacon's followers pushed through laws that legalized the enslaving of all Virginia Native Americans, whether tributary Indians or foreign ones, and they systematically banished friendly Indians from their homelands to make room for tobacco. Berkeley, for his part, assembled a small fleet and retook Jamestown, only to lose it again to the rebels, who burned it to the ground. After Bacon died of dysentery in late October, his movement collapsed. Berkeley ordered twenty-three rebels summarily hanged.

To Britain's King Charles II, Virginia appeared thoroughly dysfunctional. He dismissed Berkeley as an "old fool" who "has slain more men in that naked country than I did for the murder of my father," and he dispatched Colonel Herbert Jeffreys to Jamestown with more than a thousand troops to restore order. Jeffreys placed the colony under military occupation. He sent Berkeley to England, where he died before having an opportunity to explain himself to the king. Many thought that Virginia's independent status as a colony was compromised. The crown had been forced to rescue two major colonies within twelve years. Marylanders now denounced their proprietors and demanded a fundamental reform of the empire. They wrote the king in England and asked to be governed by a powerful viceroy.[10]

In the end, it was the Iroquois who restored order in the region. Edmund Andros offered the Susquehannocks asylum in New York, but their leaders refused, opening the way for the Senecas, who "utterly defeated" the Susquehannocks, "their ancient and most redoubtable foes." The Onondagas and Cayugas adopted numerous Susquehannock refugees, boosting their own demographic and military might. By this point, the Iroquois League had become the central power in the Northeast, monitoring behaviors, enforcing policies, and conducting wide-ranging "forest diplomacy." A Jesuit priest thought they had become indomitable: "Their insolence knows no bounds." Operating in the slipstream of the Iroquois, the fragile English colonies tried to claim imperial control over the mid-Atlantic by proxy.[11]

In the late spring of 1677, Jeffreys, now the lieutenant general of

Virginia, arranged a large treaty council with the Pamunkeys, Appomattucks, and other remnants of the Powhatan Confederacy. Cockacoeske, the "Queen of Pamunkey[s]," strongly shaped the Treaty of Middle Plantation, which demarcated a three-mile buffer zone around each Indigenous settlement that was off limits to colonists. The colonists were now obliged to respect Native land and property rights by law. The "Indian Kings and Queens" acknowledged their dependency on the king of England—a token concession that was balanced by a stipulation that "each Indian King, and Queen have equal power to Govern their own people and none to have greater Power then [*sic*] other, except the Queen of Pamunkeys to whom several scattered Nations do now again own their ancient Subjection." Cockacoeske retained the title of mamanatowick, or "paramount weroance," over the tributary tribes of the Powhatan Confederacy. Virginia's recognition of her power created a paper empire of loyal Native subjects, but it also acknowledged Indigenous perseverance against terrible odds. Virginia, the continent's most racist and anti-Indian colony, had made space for Native Americans. The Virginians pledged to abolish the trade in Indian slaves, and they expected that "every Indian King and Queen in the month of March every year with some of their great men tender their obedience to . . . his Majesties Government the place of his residence and there pay the accustomed rent of twenty beaver skins"—a clause that adhered as much to Indigenous practices of gift exchanges as it did to colonial posturing.[12]

IN 1683, THE FIVE NATIONS confronted a peculiar and presumptuous new arrival who, in the previous year, had brought twenty-three ships from England to the Delaware Valley and concluded a treaty with the Lenape Nation, hoping to build a new colony. He then moved to buy land from the depleted Susquehannocks for the enormous proprietary grant, his "Holy Experiment," bestowed on him by the king of England as payment of a debt to his father. Charles II had cavalierly bestowed on this man a domain of forty-five hundred square miles, and allowed him to call it Pennsylvania. The Iroquois moved immediately to block the attempt to establish a new colony; they wanted the lands for themselves. Yet William Penn entered American history as the good colonist who respected Indigenous sovereignty: thousands of Indians moved to Pennsylvania over the following decades. But Penn's conciliatory approach was not pure altruism; he was reacting to Native-driven geopolitics and power. Penn's choices had a lot to do with Metacom's War and the Susquehannock-Virginia conflict, which had shaken the colonists. Now, the Five Nations had given him pause and taught him a lesson: Indigenous soil was not free for the taking. After the Iroquois encounter, Penn would negotiate land transfers with the Native Americans from the outset. The deeper irony was that the Iroquois did not want to occupy the contested stretch of land; they aimed to use it as a bargaining chip with New York.[13]

In the fall of 1684, amid New York's intense meddling with Iroquois-French relations, Governor La Barre set off for Fort Frontenac, France's largest inland bastion, with five hundred soldiers, determined to prevent any land transactions. It was to be a campaign of intimidation that would deliver the Iroquois into the French fold once and for all. The operation did not go as planned. "The Warriors of these five Nations have introduced the English to the Lake, belonging to the King my Master," La Barre reprimanded the Iroquois leaders he had summoned to the fort. Their intention, he feared, "was to ruin the Commerce of his Subjects, and to oblige these Nations to depart from their due Allegiance." The Iroquois maneuvering, the governor dreaded, destabilized the French Empire in North America. "French who are Brethren and Friends of the five nations," he promised, "will never disturb their Repose; provided they make satisfaction I now demand, and prove religious observers of their Treaties." If they failed to do so, La Barre warned, "I have express orders to declare War."

The Onondaga sachem Otreouti listened to La Barre's harangue, looking "upon the end of his Pipe." He must have noticed how the French governor relied on Five Nations words and metaphors; Iroquois diplomatic culture had saturated the eastern half of the continent, providing the lingua franca for nation-to-nation diplomacy. Then he spoke. "Onontio, in setting out from Quebec, you must have fancied that the scorching Beams of the Sun had burnt down the Forests which render our Country inaccessible to the French." La

Barre seemed to be the least informed person at the fort. Unaware of the Five Nations' expansive diplomacy, and not knowing that the Five Nations had already placed some of their land under New York's protection, he warned the Indians that, if defied, he would "joyn the Governor of New-York, who has orders from the King his Master, to assist me to burn the five Villages, and cut you off." Otreouti bluntly ignored La Barre's threats, saying, "I must tell you, Onontio, I am not asleep, my Eyes are open." Asserting Five Nations' autonomy and sovereignty, Otreouti told La Barre that "we are born Freemen, and have no dependence either upon the Onontio or the Corlar," the governor of New York. The Iroquois had decided to relinquish their claims to the upper Susquehanna Valley in order to secure New York's protection against French incursions. The Onondagas expected New York to "protect them from the French otherwise they shall lose all the Beaver and hunting," but they were not attaching themselves to the English in a subservient role. They demanded that "Penn's people may not settle under the Susquehanna River." Protected by compliant English, the Onondagas would continue to capture and kill New France's Indian allies as circumstances dictated.[14]

Humiliated, New France's governor Jacques-René de Brisay de Denonville sent an apology from Montreal to Secretary of State Jean-Baptiste Colbert in France. "I am very sorry, My Lord," he wrote, "to find the affairs of this country in so deplorable a state. I am still more sorry to see myself constrained, if I would avoid the loss of all by too much precipitation, to temporize and to incur the danger of being overpowered by the Iroquois." Denonville mobilized five hundred men to enclose Montreal with fifteen-foot stakes, but he found little reassurance behind the newly erected walls. "The Iroquois destroy our allies on all sides," he complained, and he warned that if their attacks were not stopped, "the Colony must be put down as lost." Denonville's despair was widely shared: diminished by the Five Nations, both English and French colonial projects seemed to be petering out.[15]

Chapter 14

THE GREAT SOUTHWESTERN REBELLION

THE CAMPAIGN HAD BEEN PLANNED CAREFULLY behind a thick curtain of secrecy. Its architect, Po'pay, a religious leader of the Pueblos of Ohkay Owingeh—fearing that the secret plan might be revealed to the Spanish—had killed his own son-in-law to protect the operation. On August 10, 1680, knotted cords of yucca fiber began to appear among the Pueblo Indians across New Mexico, officially a kingdom of the Spanish Empire. The cords were carried by trained runners, each of whom covered hundreds of miles. In every town the runners delivered the same message from Po'pay: untie one knot each day, and on the morning of the last knot, kill the Spanish in your town. The Spanish learned the meaning of the knots when they detained two runners, but by then it was too late. The Pueblos had already launched a war against New Mexico. Word reached Governor Antonio de Otermín in Santa Fe that "all the nations of this kingdom were now implicated in it, forming a confederation with the heathen Apaches so that, on the night of the thirteenth of the current month, they might carry out their disobedience, perfidious treason, and atrocities." It was not a revolt of a subjugated nation. It was a carefully orchestrated war launched by the sovereign Pueblo people against Spain's imperial pretensions.[1]

The grievances and resentments that pushed the Pueblos to rise up against the Spanish had been brewing ever since the Acoma Massacre in 1599, when the Spanish killed eight hundred Pueblos under Juan de Oñate's leadership, roughly a century earlier than the wars between Native Americans and the English, which gave them a different tone. The Spanish crown had tried to institute softer rule in New Mexico after Oñate's removal by putting Franciscan friars in charge of the colony, but that only brought a different kind of violence. In 1629, Fray Estevan Perea, thirty Spanish friars, a cadre of soldiers, and thirty-six oxcarts arrived in Santa Fe, the final destination of their fifteen-hundred-mile march from Mexico City. Presenting themselves as magicians with supernatural powers, the Franciscans tried to appropriate the roles of Pueblo medicine men and impose a Christian theocracy on the Pueblo world. The Franciscans planted themselves in Pueblo towns, while leaving the soldiers beyond the town limits— yet close enough to lend a disciplining hand if needed. The mounted Spanish soldiers possessed an immense technological edge over the Pueblo soldiers. The friars established themselves as the masters of nature, souls, and sacred spaces in the Pueblo world. By the 1630s, the "land was filled with churches," some fifty missions, churches, and friaries that, as a collective, were arranged in the shape of a cross over the region. The configuration kept as many as eighty thousand neophytes under Franciscan watch—a new geography of power, based on religious imperialism, that seemed to the friars nothing if not providential. Their perception of their own dominance entered international discourse in the late seventeenth century when New Mexico appeared on European maps as a compact urban colony anchoring vast Spanish claims in interior North America. The maps concealed how tenuous Spanish authority was in the Americas. The Chichimeca War in the Central Mexican Plateau, arguably the longest frontier war in the history of the Western Hemisphere, had already raged for generations and would continue to rage decades longer.[2]

The Spanish missions, churches, and friaries along the Rio Grande constituted a network of power and surveillance, unveiling the anxiety of the Franciscans and Spanish soldiers, who knew painfully well how much the Pueblos and other Native Americans resented their demands and interfering. The Hopis called the Spanish priests *tutáachi*, "dictator and demanding person." The colonists coerced Pueblos to work for them through a forced labor system whereby individuals and sometimes entire communities were entrusted to privileged Spanish as encomiendas. Empowered by Spanish law, the colonists

could order Indians to tend their herds, till their fields, produce animal hides, and provide domestic service. Franciscan friars, however,
insisted on the primacy of ecclesial rule in New Mexico and claimed
final authority over governors and colonists in Indian affairs. Pos-
sessing charismatic sway and equipped with the prerogatives of the
church—censures, interdicts, and excommunications—Franciscans
held the upper hand over the colonists until the mid-seventeenth
century. They never abandoned their dream of saving Pueblo souls,
which often pitted them against lay Spanish.[3]

In 1630, Fray Alonso de Benavides denounced the Spanish governors
of New Mexico for issuing permits "to take Indian boys and girls from
the pueblos on the pretext that they are orphans, and take them to
serve permanently in houses of Spaniards where they remain as slaves."
Governor Luís de Rosas turned a deaf ear to complaints and moved to
systemize slave-raiding in the late 1630s by sponsoring frequent forays
into the surrounding mountains and plains and by inducing Indians
to raid other Indians for captives. The raids were a boon to the governor and his supporters. By the late seventeenth century, the colony
held some five hundred non-Pueblo slaves, a significant pool of labor
for the approximately eighteen hundred colonists. Slaves were wealth,
and wealth gave governors more control over New Mexico's Indian
affairs—and by extension its economy and politics—enabling them to
develop crucial patronage connections and challenge the Franciscans'
iron grip on the colony's relations with Spanish imperial centers. The
Franciscans' hold over New Mexico was giving way to a secular elite.[4]

The fault lines within the Spanish imperial system created blind
spots in Spanish rule, offering openings for the beleaguered Pueblos.
The Spanish condemned Pueblo religion as devilish, and tradition-
alist Pueblo medicine men—who had cured ailing Spanish—evaded
Spanish surveillance by literally going underground: they moved
their religious ceremonies into subterranean kivas, where Pueblo sovereignty and religion survived. They were guided by Iatiku—Corn
Mother—and kachinas, ancestral Cloud Spirits who visited them,
keeping the world in balance. At the same time, many Pueblo farmers fled uphill to flat mesa tops where, insulated from the river-bound
Spanish settlements by rugged terrain, they built small farms and

work stations, keeping the fruits of their labor for themselves. When Governor Bernardo López de Mendizábal banned labor drafts in New Mexico in 1659—mainly to spoil Franciscan attempts to hoard Pueblo workers—so many Indians stopped working altogether that Franciscans feared they might lose their animal herds. To undercut Franciscan authority, López de Mendizábal outlawed corporal punishment at missions and allowed the Indians to perform ceremonial katsina dances, which the Franciscans had banned. Suddenly, Indians were again dancing in plazas, reaffirming their religious authority and reclaiming a public social space for themselves. And then, in the early 1660s, unnerved by spreading slave revolts in Chile, Philip IV, the dying king of Spain, moved to outlaw trafficking in Indian slaves—a reform that fell to his widow, Queen Mariana, to carry out. She completed his antislavery crusade with pious determination. Slave-trafficking shrank dramatically, not only in Chile but also in New Mexico, from where Spanish slavers had exported Pueblo Indians to South American silver mines. The Pueblos understood life as a series of transitions and as an incorporation of others—a spiritual foundation that carried them through ordeals and suffering.[5]

Spain's efforts to accommodate, even if tentatively, the Pueblos and other Indigenous peoples in the region might have spawned something similar to the Great Lakes middle ground in the Southwest, had disease and starvation not interfered. A smallpox epidemic broke out along the Rio Grande in 1636, killing some twenty thousand Pueblos. A severe drought three decades later brought starvation, weakening the Franciscans' already shaky moral authority. Local uprisings erupted at Taos, Jémez, and several Tewa towns between 1639 and 1650, and in 1668 another drought brought famine and devastation. One Franciscan reported that "a great many Indians perished of hunger, lying dead along the roads, in the ravines, and in their huts. There were pueblos (as instance[,] Humanas) where more than four hundred and fifty died of hunger."[6]

IF NEW MEXICO was not quite as solid and secure internally as Spanish leaders imagined, neither was it as outwardly imposing as

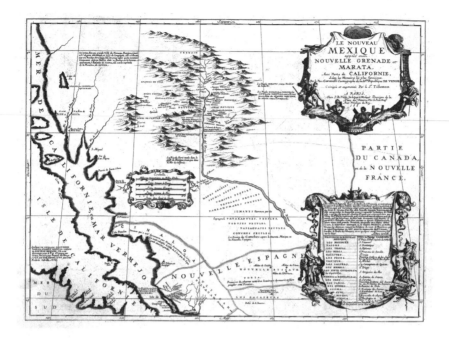

*Map of New Mexico by Jean-Nicolas du Tralage
and Vincenzo Maria Coronelli, 1687*

they wished it to be. The number of Spanish colonists may not have reached twenty-five hundred, but still Spanish maps portrayed the colony as an extension of New Mexico. In reality, New Mexico was an isolated archipelago in a vast Indigenous sea; it was hemmed in by powerful Indigenous nations whose domains converged around the upper Rio Grande valley. That convergence was ancient. The Pueblo world had been linked to outlying regions for centuries, but the linkages intensified with Spanish colonization. Rather than distancing themselves from the colony, many Native people—Apaches, Navajos, Jumanos, Utes, Shoshones, and others—gravitated toward it, enticed by its manufactured goods, political clout, and especially horses.[7]

For the neighboring independent Indians, the prosperous but confined New Mexico was both a commercial outlet and a magnet. Moving toward it, they competed and clashed with one another, becoming entangled in prolonged wars. Mounted Apache soldiers pushed from the north and west into the plains bordering New Mexico, colliding with the Jumanos, a multiethnic coalition of hunters, farmers, and traders that commanded a sprawling commercial network extending from the Gulf coast to the upper Rio Grande valley. The Apache-Jumano collision, a mixture of violence and assimilation, brought a new order to the Southwest. The Jumano coalition disintegrated, the equestrian Apaches took over the trade in New Mexico's border towns, and the southern plains started to became a new geopolitical entity, Apachería. Spanish leaders seemed to be more concerned about the safety of their supply lines than about the safety of their putative Pueblo wards. El Cuartelejo, "fortified village," an Apache stronghold northeast of New Mexico, became a safe haven for disgruntled Pueblos. The kingdom of New Mexico was bleeding subjects, signaling the collapse of Spanish colonial ambitions.[8]

The demise of their colony confounded the Spanish. As in New England and Virginia, the colonists struggled to establish tight colonial rule. The Spanish colonists imagined themselves as the masters of an inviolate New Mexico that projected Spanish power over the Native Americans, and that vision was crumbling rapidly. The Apache Nation surrounded New Mexico, but the Apaches remained aloof, restricting trade interactions and pushing deep into Mexico to raid horses and captives as they pleased. The people of La Junta de los Ríos, a fertile region of floodplains and hills in the northeastern corner of the Chihuahuan desert, challenged Spanish aspirations more directly, attacking ranches and villages from their mountain bases and retreating quickly to escape retaliation. The Spanish were soon running out of Indians to rule over. Where Apaches and Jumanos had undermined Spanish designs through horse-powered mobility, the Pueblos were simply dying. Repeated epidemics and famine had reduced Pueblo numbers from eighty thousand to forty thousand by midcentury, thereby heightening the jurisdictional rivalries between Franciscans and colonists over Pueblo labor, the principal source of wealth in the mineral-poor kingdom. The friars tried to attach the Indians to missions, and the colonists wanted to tie them to encomiendas, which made their goals incompatible.[9]

Spain's rescue plan for the reeling colony was drastic: it revived slave-trafficking in the province. From midcentury on, slave caravans were again carrying Pueblo and Apache captives into the unknown, breaking up families and inciting hatred. The hatred centered overwhelmingly on the Franciscans, who professed to love and care for the Pueblos but did nothing to stop the trafficking. In New Mexico, "Apache" and "slave" became nearly synonymous, and grievances mounted. The decades-long record of famines, plagues, and deaths had made it plain that the friars could not stabilize the world. Yet they felt entitled to interfere with the most intimate aspects of Pueblo life, probing Pueblo customs and traditions with zealous urgency because they found them disturbing. Pueblo marriages were not monogamous, polygamy was common, and divorce was normal. Women and men had their distinct possessions, but amassing wealth was linked with witchcraft. Women oversaw the construction of houses, and households themselves belonged to women. Sexuality, equated with fertility, was publicly celebrated, and people could become increasingly godlike with age. All of this was sacrilegious to the Franciscans, who feared that things were only getting worse. In 1675, Spanish officers panicked. They organized an investigation that concluded New Mexico was in danger. The officials hanged three Pueblo priests in a public execution and lashed forty-three others at a whipping post. One of the whipped was Po'pay. Such cruelty was unthinkable to the Pueblos.[10]

After that, and for the next five years, Pueblo leaders visited one another, tightening their bonds, pooling information, and debating how to best rid their world of the Spanish and their hateful beasts and institutions. They sought distance from the Spanish at El Cuartelejo, where they could strategize in secret. Mobilizing soldiers from more than two dozen independent towns demanded a new kind of strategic thinking. Five years later, Po'pay retreated north to a kiva in Taos, the most isolated of the Pueblo towns, where the old priesthood endured. That sacred room would serve as the headquarters of his campaign.[11]

The Spanish officers had discovered the meaning of the knotted cords, but that knowledge mattered little. When the time came, in each location Pueblos brought overwhelming numbers against the Spanish and forced them to fight for survival in many separate battles, thus preventing any attempts at a colony-wide military response. The fighting was intimate and sprawling because the Pueblos willed it so. Most colonists lived outside of the Pueblo towns and next to their

Taos Pueblo today

fields along the Rio Grande, which meant that they were extremely isolated, and easy prey. From there the violence spread, tellingly, through two slave-trafficking corridors—one extending from New Mexico to Parral in Chihuahua, the other to the west toward the silver mines in San Juan Bautista, Opodepe, and Teuricache. Since the early seventeenth century, large numbers of Pueblos and Apaches had been sold to mining towns far to the south. The area covered by the slave corridors was almost identical to the radius of the rebellion. Governor Otermín managed to have one Pueblo Indian apprehended so that he could ask, "How could he have gone so crazy?"

Most of the surviving Spanish fled to Santa Fe and Isleta Pueblo, one of the few towns that had not joined the rebellion. Fifteen hundred colonists huddled at Isleta for a few days before retreating toward El Paso del Norte, three hundred miles to the south. The remaining colonists in New Mexico could do little to quell the uprising: the geographically dispersed and politically decentralized Pueblo Nation offered no major center to strike and conquer. The Spanish, however, did. The retreat to El Paso allowed two thousand Pueblos to fall on Santa Fe, where Governor Otermín and roughly a thousand soldiers struggled to fend off their attacks. Only one in ten soldiers carried a gun, whereas the Pueblos, having killed and disarmed more than four hundred colonists, now carried flintlocks, lances, and swords. They set buildings on fire to force the colonists out, and Otermín and his soldiers retreated into the Palace of the Governors in Santa Fe. They held out for days, Otermín weakened by two arrow wounds in his face and by a gunshot wound in the chest. The Pueblos cut off the town's water supply and then waited. Otermín announced that the Spanish would retreat on August 21, "to the greater service of the two majesties." On the eleventh day of the uprising, Otermín and his soldiers were allowed to march out of the scorched Santa Fe.[12]

Like the wars waged by the Powhatans and Wampanoags in the East, the 1680 Pueblo insurrection was at once an act of self-preservation, cultural revitalization, and spatial reimagination. Attesting to strong intergroup attachments that transcended Spanish-imposed boundaries, many Apaches and Navajos fought alongside the Pueblos. The allied Indians killed nearly four hundred colonists and twenty-one friars, and they routed a thousand Spanish soldiers, sending them to El Paso, the colony's southernmost town. The leaders of the rebellion set out to restore the physical and sacral landscape of the pre-Spanish era. Churches were to be demolished, their bells were to be shattered, and images of Jesus Christ and the Virgin Mary were to be destroyed. Alien crops were to be torched, and corn and beans planted in their stead. Not one Spanish word would violate the restored Indigenous soundscape. Even horses began to vanish from the Rio Grande valley. Repulsed by horses' tendency to trample cornfields and by their elevated power, which symbolized Spanish might, the Pueblos embarked on vigorous horse trade with the outlying nomads and pastoralists. It had to be as though Spanish colonialism had never happened.[13]

DESPITE THE PUEBLOS' DESIRE to erase Spanish colonialism from their memory, it had, of course, happened, and its legacy proved sticky. As frail as Spanish dominance over the Pueblo world had been, Spanish colonists had profoundly altered Indigenous life in the Rio Grande valley. To reinstate the old cultural order—to turn back time—the Pueblo leaders issued sweeping decrees that bound all Pueblos. In order to purge Spanish influences, the Native leaders claimed all-encompassing dominion over the Pueblo world. But a single Pueblo world was a foreign fiction. Before the Spanish invasion, the Pueblos had lived in more than 150 communities that shared a general cultural outlook but possessed no central governing structures. When the colonial edifice dissolved, local identities resurfaced. In the 1680s, the Spanish built a buffer region of presidios and missions to keep European rivals away from the abandoned colony. They called it Tejas, a Spanish spelling of the Caddo word *taysha*, meaning "friend."

Four generations of colonial presence had left a deep imprint on Pueblo life, and many had grown to see certain Spanish imports as natural. Renouncing the Franciscans and colonists roused little controversy; pigs, sheep, woolen textiles, metal tools, and spouses taken in matrimony were another matter. When droughts spoiled harvests, the already delicate Pueblo coalition began to disintegrate. Civic leaders, medicine men, and soldiers competed for authority within communities that soon descended into civil wars. Towns fought over diminishing resources and raided one another for grain. The Apaches, incensed by the collapse of trade relations, took what they needed through force.[14]

While the Pueblo people struggled with lingering colonial legacies, the Spanish struggled with the legacy of Pueblo resistance. The Pueblo uprising had proved contagious, triggering a series of rebellions against Spanish rule from Coahuila to Sonora and Nueva Vizcaya. Janos, Sumas, Conchos, Tobosos, Julimes, and Pimas attacked colonists and destroyed missions, towns, and farms, rolling back Spanish colonialism across a vast area. The Spanish seemed paralyzed in the face of this explosion of Indigenous hatred and power. Colonial officials sentenced four hundred Native rebels to ten years of forced labor.[15]

It took a poor nobleman, desperate to boost his family fortune, to break the Spanish inertia. Diego de Vargas had left his family in Madrid, hoping to find prosperity in the New World, come what may. After two decades, he had little to show for himself, but he saw that winning New Mexico back could change everything for him. In 1692, Vargas launched a reconnaissance expedition that soon morphed into a reconquest. The Pueblos allowed the stern Spanish into Santa Fe only when the colonists left their weapons behind. On September 14—the feast day of the Exaltation of the Holy Cross—Vargas entered the city, trailed by several friars. The Indians erected a large cross in the plaza, and Vargas kissed it. He then pardoned all Indians who praised the Spanish king. When the news of Vargas's successful entry into the Pueblo-controlled Santa Fe reached Mexico City, cathedral bells were rung in his honor.[16]

Yet when Vargas returned to Santa Fe a year later—in cold December with a caravan of seventy Spanish families, one hundred soldiers, eighteen friars, numerous Indian auxiliaries, and three thousand horses and mules—the Pueblos refused to let him in. Rumors of executions had preceded the new expedition, and the signs of reconquest were palpable—something that had not occurred in the aftermath of Metacom's War. Vargas and his retinue spent a week outside Santa Fe' s walls, freezing in deep snow. They approached the Pueblos carefully, carrying the wooden statue of *La Conquistadora*, the Virgin of the Conquest, which had been whisked away from Santa Fe thirteen years earlier during the rebellion and retreat. Vargas appealed to the Pueblos through La Conquistadora, but the Indians retorted that the Devil was more powerful than the Virgin Mary.

A fierce battle broke out. Vargas's men fired volleys, and the Indians dropped stones and boiling water from the walls. The Pueblos, running out of supplies, surrendered after three days. The Spanish punishment, betraying their uneasiness, was vicious: they executed seventy men and condemned four hundred women and children to slavery. Vargas then moved to subdue the colony's other villages. He ordered a presidio and an armed garrison to be constructed in Santa Fe, where the Indians had built a pueblo "over the dwelling of the governors of this kingdom." Yet Vargas had not achieved an easy victory. He spent much of 1694 in the field, putting down local uprisings and squelching pockets of Pueblo resistance. That resistance proved enduring. Juan de Ye, the Spanish governor of Pecos Pueblo, rode to Taos to reprimand Pacheco, the town's Indigenous governor. The Spaniard was never seen again. Rumors of another impending rebellion kept circulating in New Mexico, and in 1696 the Pueblos rose up again, killing five friars and razing several churches and convents.[17]

Vargas extinguished the second rebellion with a focused war of attrition, but the rebellion proved crucial for the future prospects of the Pueblo people. Vargas reinstated colonial rule in New Mexico, but it was not the colonial rule of old. Traumatized and exhausted by the latest rebellion, the Spanish accepted smaller landholdings than before, and they replaced the slavery-like encomienda labor system with the *repartimiento* system, under which the amount of required work was regulated. They appointed a public defender to protect the Pueblos against Spanish abuse, and Franciscans turned a blind eye to the previously banned Pueblo ceremonies—a concession that was made easier by the Pueblos' token acceptance of Catholic sacraments. The colony had shrunk conspicuously.[18]

The administrative apparatus of the Spanish colonial state remained in place, but the social distance between the Spanish and the Pueblos narrowed through intermarriages, quasi-kinship institutions such as *compadrazgo*—co-godparenthood—and multiethnic towns. The Spanish and the Pueblos remained distinct people separated by sharp disparities in power and privilege, but unwavering Pueblo resistance had forced the Spanish to enter a shared world where the colonists were allowed to reestablish only a drastically reduced version of their grandiose imperial project. Like Juan de Oñate a century earlier, Vargas had tried to create a bounded colonial state with carefully regulated commercial channels, and like his predecessors, he had encountered an Indigenous world that refused to bend to a rigid imperial logic. The Pueblo resistance proved contagious, igniting a series of rebellions that spread across northern New Spain. The terrified governor of Nueva Vizcaya insisted that all captured Indian rebels should be sentenced to ten years of enslavement.[19]

The Pueblo Revolt—also known as the Great Southwestern Rebellion for its virulence and scale—changed the history of the region irrevocably. It cut the Spanish colonists down to size and emboldened the Indians—not just the Pueblos but also many other Indigenous nations—to challenge Spain's imperial claims. During the decade after the rebellion, numerous uprisings and wars broke out between the Spanish and the Indians: Tarahumaras, Conchos, Pimas, Sobaipuris, Sumas, Jocomes, Janos, Opatas, Apaches, and many others fought to contain, punish, and kill the Spanish, and keep their territories inviolate. Their systematic mobile guerrilla war had confined the Spanish to their northwestern frontier.[20]

By shaking up ancient traditions and practices, the war changed the Pueblo world from within by giving Pueblo women new avenues to express their religious ideas and spirituality; they began to explore Catholicism more deeply and to question ancient traditions. The most important geopolitical change came when the Pueblos started selling Spanish horses to neighboring nomads in the plains and the surrounding mountains. The horse trade ignited a technological revolution that reconfigured several Indigenous worlds within a generation. An ancient trade corridor in the Rocky Mountains became a conduit for the spread of horses far to the north. The Shoshones acquired horses in about 1690 and, emboldened by their suddenly supercharged capacity to move about, hunt, and fight, they pushed into the bison-rich northern plains. Others even farther away traced the flow of horses back to the source in the upper Rio Grande valley. In 1706 the residents of Taos Pueblo in the northeastern corner of New Mexico reported the arrival of strange people from the north. These newcomers, *Nʉmʉnʉʉ*—"the people"—were rumored to be preparing an attack on the town. The Comanches had entered the Spanish consciousness as a shadowy frontier menace.[21]

THE NEARLY SIMULTANEOUS Indigenous rebellions against European imperial ambitions in all regions of North America at the end of the seventeenth century brought English, French, and Spanish colonists near their breaking points. Shockingly, Native Americans had rolled colonialism back in different corners of the continent, forcing colonists to retreat, recalibrate their ambitions, and reconsider their ingrained ideas about Native peoples. The Europeans suffered a crisis of self-confidence. Traumatized New Englanders, consumed by Indian wars, believed that their god was displeased with them. They turned against one other, denouncing neighbors, relatives, and those who were generally suspect as witches. Virginians, unable to decide what to do or how to live with their Native neighbors, fell into a civil war that nearly pulled the colony to pieces. New France, once the most promising of the colonial ventures, found its expansive sphere of influence in the interior dramatically reduced in the shadow of the ascending Five Nations League. In New Mexico, Spanish colonists entered into a tense, postrebellion accommodation with the Pueblos—an imperial retreat that instilled a softer edge on Spanish colonial rule.

What explains this simultaneity? It may have been pure coincidence, but perhaps something more structural was at play. By the time the rebellions erupted, the Wampanoags, Nipmucs, Susquehannocks, and Pueblos had withstood colonial abuse for two to three generations. Among them were Indians who had seen the beginning of colonial conquest, the seizure of Indigenous lands, and the marginalization of their people in their homelands. They had lived with colonialism most of their lives, and they could see that things were getting worse, not better, with time. As Indigenous elders recounted their nations' histories, a subversive undercurrent may have crept into their stories, finding expression in disgust, hatred, and, eventually, cleansing violence. The elders may have warned that the opportunity to reverse the historical momentum was closing rapidly.

PART FIVE

THE ENDURING INDIGENOUS CONTINENT

(early eighteenth century)

Chapter 15

HOLDING THE
LINE

THE LEADERS OF THE NASAWS, MEMBERS OF THE
Catawba Confederacy, were happy to welcome Francis Nichol-
son, the newly appointed governor of South Carolina, to their town.
They handed the governor a gift, a deerskin map of their world.
Drawn by a Nasaw cartographer, it depicted eleven Catawba towns,
as well as one Cherokee and one Chickasaw town to the west of the
Catawba territory, Kadapau. The year was 1721, and the map also
showed two colonial entities: Virginia, depicted as a square, and
Charles Town, the capital of South Carolina, with its grid layout and
harbor. Perusing the map must have been a perplexing experience for
Nicholson, since it did not conform to European cartographic rules.
It recognized neither cardinal directions nor geographical features.
Rather than detailing the spatial coordinates of the various societies
in the region, the map focused on the relations among them. It was an
intensely political map made by an intensely political people.

The unnamed Nasaw mapmaker placed his town in the center of
the map and drew seven pathways that connected it to the surrounding
towns and colonies, including Virginia. There was also "the English
Path to Nasaw." The seminomadic Catawbas were the primary people who dominated the southern Piedmont, having lived there since
the mid-sixteenth century. Native Americans and English colonists
shared the map, but they were fundamentally different: Virginia was
represented as a square, while the Indigenous groups were shown as
circles. The largest circle belonged to the Nasaws, even though the
Cherokees and Choctaws overpowered them demographically and
geographically, commanding a territory that stretched from the south

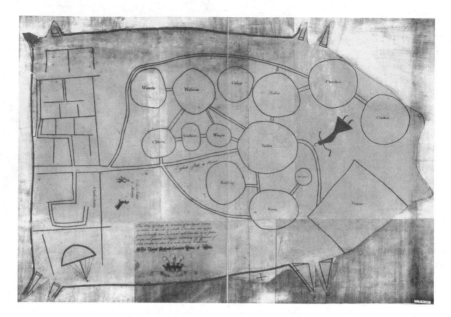

Catawba map, 1721

of the Ohio Valley to the Gulf coast. Two human figures—one of them a hunter—and a deer signaled that the Piedmont was actively used and occupied by the Catawbas, *Ye Iswa*, "the people of the river." The map was a graphical social manual aimed at instructing the colonists how to behave in Native-colonial borderlands, how to treat Indians with respect, and how to survive in a world that was intensely Indigenous. European traders were welcome at Catawba villages, but they had to be summoned and allowed in. They had to be generous with their goods and honor Catawba customs. Nearly four hundred miles to the southwest, Chickasaw cartographers relied on almost identical representational techniques to demonstrate their supremacy and authority. In their maps, hierarchy took precedence: the circles assigned to different nations varied in size and possibly status.

There were many such maps in the Piedmont and elsewhere in North America—maps that kept the invaders out and taught newcomers how to behave. Colonies had to bend around Indigenous borders, rather than vice versa. Although Europeans had planted themselves on the Eastern Seaboard and along several major rivers from the Saint Lawrence to the Rio Grande, Native Americans controlled ninety percent of the continent, including most of the lands claimed by the British, French, and Spanish Empires, having fought several wars to keep them at arm's length. Heirs to the fabled Cofitachequi Confederacy, the well-connected Catawbas called Europeans "Nothings," pitiful people who lacked kin ties and did not belong. They made their opinion clear to the colonists through carefully planned pomp. One European traveler reported that "our Landlord was King of the Kadapau Indians, and always kept two or three trading Girls in his Cabin. Offering one of these to some of our Company, who refused his Kindness, his Majesty flew into a violent Passion, to be thus slighted, telling the Englishmen that they were good for nothing." The Europeans missed the crucial element of the practice: the creation of all-important kinship ties through intimacy. Around the same time, the great southeastern Indigenous confederacies—the Cherokees, Choctaws, and Muscogees—began to self-identify as people separate from the Whites. To distance themselves from the colonists geographically, the Catawbas denied them kinship. Continuing a centuries-long process, Cherokees, Choctaws, Chickasaws, Muscogees, and Catawbas were teaching the European newcomers how to treat the continent's Native inhabitants and educating them about proper behavior, boundaries, and how to think and speak properly—a process that had begun with Cabeza de Vaca nearly three centuries before.[1]

In the early eighteenth century, in the aftermath of Metacom's War and the Great Southwestern Rebellion, colonial control in North America was limited to small coastal and riverine settlements. Curbed by Indigenous presence and territoriality, English colonists had expanded south- and northward on the coastal lowlands, huddling close to the coast and rivers. Their towns, plantations, and forts had become pockets of concentrated colonial power, but their influence remained conspicuously constrained. As the Catawba leaders had informed Governor Nicholson, there was a narrow colonial rim and a vast Native-dominated interior. It was clear where the power lay. When Hoyter, the headman of the Chowans, a tributary Indian nation of the Province of North Carolina, a recently established British colony, dined with the governor and had his soldiers performing war dances in the streets, it was plain that Indigenous subjecthood was a fiction. The tributary relationship was more alliance than subordination. By the 1710s, the English had spent a staggering 100,000 crowns on Indian diplomacy and trade, adopting the French model of embracing the Indians as trading partners, military allies, and kin. They had withdrawn from dispossessive settler colonialism.[2]

Effective Indigenous resistance had forced the Europeans to radically reevaluate their methods. The populous English colonies still relied on raw military power, fighting, dispossessing, and killing Indians on their borders, but they had also embraced softer tactics. Like the French, the English sought to expand their reach *through* Indians. The Spanish, too, adopted facets of the French approach, relying on trade, accommodation, and military cooperation. The three colonial powers were still committed to the expansion of their respective empires, but they would be negotiated empires that offered distinctive places for Native peoples and depended on Native assent for their survival.

THE LURE OF THE WEST INDIES, which had been the most lucrative region in the New World for generations, had drawn massive numbers of European colonists, inadvertently shielding the Indigenous nations in North America from colonial aggression. But in the 1660s, the West Indies were in steep decline. Almost all of the land was either claimed or exhausted by sugar plantations, discouraging further immigration from Europe. The next generation would do worse than the previous one—a circumstance that was unacceptable to the growth-obsessed Europeans. To rectify the situation, a group of West Indies planters approached the wealthiest men in England and secured funding for an enormous new colony on the East Coast of North America between Spanish Florida and Virginia. The richest of these proprietors had made possible the restoration of King Charles II after the collapse of Cromwell's commonwealth in 1660, and the king now awarded those in this small, elite group their own colony, Carolina.

The "absolute Lords and Proprietors" imported both colonists and slaves from the overcrowded Indies and soon grew rich from indigo, hemp, flax, mulberry, wine, ginger, wax, olives, and—most tantalizingly—silk, earning for their colony the moniker "Carolina in the

West Indies." The summers were hot, humid, mosquito infested, and potentially deadly, but the coast was inviting, its expansive plain and wide, muddy rivers promising an agricultural boon. The planters fancied themselves independent pioneers, but in reality, they relied heavily on Indigenous products and trade. An early observer was skeptical of Carolina's prospects "in so remote a Country" and surrounded "among so many Barbarous Nations." "Savages as other Enemies, Pirates, and Robbers," he predicted, "may probably be feared"—the absurdly racist language betraying both ignorance and fear. The Tuscarora Nation of eight thousand people, which was loosely attached to the Iroquois League, reached an accommodation with the English newcomers in the nascent colony of Carolina, which had been founded by slave owners from Barbados. The first English settlements arose near the Chesapeake Bay, but the province soon collapsed into a reservation for White people.[3]

The prediction of fearsome Indians had proved accurate. One of the first moves the colonists made was to establish a six-company-strong militia and build a wall around Charles Town. Meanwhile, the region's Indigenous nations positioned themselves on Carolina's borderlands to make the most of the new trading opportunities in staples, especially deerskins. By the early 1700s, as many as fifty thousand skins were being shipped out of Charles Town harbor each year, creating unprecedented wealth for the colonists. Their governor boasted that "Charles-Town Trades near 1000 Miles into the Continent." Wealth on such a scale fueled fierce rivalries. Jockeying for position, the Muscogees spread out along the main river valleys and soon cornered the English markets. They centralized their confederacy around a national council to bolster their bargaining power with the Europeans. Numbering approximately fifteen thousand and dwelling in sixty distinct towns, the Muscogees emerged as the domineering nation in the Deep South.

In the matrilineal Cherokee, Chickasaw, Choctaw, and Muscogee societies, women were powerful political and economic actors who decided the fate of captives—a major source of labor—and enjoyed substantial personal freedom, which multiplied the pool of gifted leaders. Land was used rather than owned, allowing a flexible property regime. Matriarchs owned their families' houses, and women controlled the crops they grew; wealth and power resided in the maternal line. Unmarried women possessed complete autonomy, and many chose to enter into marriages with Carolina traders to secure steady access to goods for their families. By doing so, they stabilized potentially fraught commercial transactions between Indians and Whites through kinship, while shrewdly challenging European gender roles: Cherokee women could become "war women" who went to battle. When Muscogee soldiers planned to attack a group of colonists around 1700, Sophia Durant, a member of the authoritative Wind Clan, rode to the Muscogee town of Otciapofa and summoned its leaders. When the soldiers arrived, she chastised them and sent them away. She was nine months pregnant.[4]

ENGLISH AMBITIONS WERE SWELLING TOO. Unlike in the French and Spanish Americas, in English America colonial households, not imperial governments and their officers, were the main agents of expansion. By the late seventeenth century, there were nearly 250,000 English colonists in North America, and the population growth showed no signs of abating. English America was now an integral part of a vast and tightly run transatlantic empire of commerce based in London, but the North American colonies themselves constituted a sprawling empire of colonists—farmers, planters, traders, and self-styled pioneers. Colonists now lived longer, had larger families, and became more mobile. They also became more aggressive, clamoring for Indigenous lands and Native slaves, but they lacked the necessary military muscle to seize them.[5]

A smallpox outbreak in Virginia in 1696 helped the colonists. The scourge was unusual in its virulence, comparable perhaps only to the 1633–34 epidemic that had devastated the Pequots and other Native nations around New England. The pox moved from Virginia to the Carolina Piedmont and then along trade routes and slave-raiding paths across the Southeast and, disastrously, to the Mississippi Valley, which became a disease corridor. The pox killed tens of thousands of Indians. The population catastrophe was human induced: Vir-

ginia and South Carolina had integrated the Southeast into a larger
Atlantic world, which allowed an unprecedented volume of goods and
germs to infiltrate Native settlements.[6]

The mass death was the kind of upheaval the colonists had hoped
for. Colonel James Moore, the opportunistic and avaricious governor of Carolina, leveraged it to launch a private war of his own in
the shadow of the War of Spanish Succession over dynastic rights.
Between 1702 and 1704, he repeatedly invaded Florida with armies
of Indian allies—Muscogees, Yamasees, Savannahs, Alabamas, and
Coushattas—who sought to replenish their numbers after the smallpox outbreak. Controversially, Moore sold large numbers of guns to
his Indigenous allies, who then razed fourteen Spanish missions, forcing thirteen hundred Apalachees into slavery. Moore's was but one of
many slave-hunting armies. Carolina's original 1665 charter encompassed all of the surviving Spanish missions and San Augustín; Moore
and other Carolinians were making the charter real by cleansing Florida of Indians, Spanish, and the Papacy.

English colonists saw the Indians as an exploitable and expendable
resource, as a mass of bodies that could be either shoved aside or put
to use. This was the origin of systematic Indian slavery and slave trade
in the English colonies, which turned the North American Southeast
into a war zone. Colonists hunted Native captives, and Indians raided
Indians to secure slaves, the continent's most precious commodity.
By the late seventeenth century, numerous "warrior paths" extended
from the Onondaga territory near Lake Ontario to Catawba towns in
the southern Appalachians.[7]

The shift in English treatment of Native Americans had been
unusually harsh, and it drew a dramatic response. In 1710 the Iroquois League sent four envoys—Tejonihokawara, Sagayenkwaraton,
Onioheriago, and Etowaucum—to London. Queen Anne received
them at St. James's Palace, where they shared their grievances with
the British sovereign. Dubbed as "The Four Kings," they dined with
William Penn and other London elite and were received by the arch-
bishop of Canterbury. They visited the queen's private yacht and the
docks along the Thames, and they took in the vastness of London
from the top of St. Paul's Cathedral. The Four Kings may have been

entertainment for the English elite, but the British leaders clearly understood the centrality of the Iroquois in North America. The British traders and smiths were careful to offer satisfactory terms to the Iroquois.[8]

THE ONCE MIGHTY TUSCARORA NATION had been gravely weakened by slave raids in 1711. Fighting back, the Tuscaroras mobilized five hundred soldiers, who destroyed several Carolina plantations and killed more than a hundred colonists, creating terror across the British colonies. Carolinians enlisted allies among the Catawbas, Yamasees, and Apalachees to mount a campaign that quickly morphed into yet another slave-raiding expedition. But the violence only escalated. Euchee Indians burned an English trader for his misdeeds. The following year, Carolina was split into two colonies: South Carolina and North Carolina.[9]

Edward Hyde—North Carolina's first governor—and his followers seized hundreds of Indians, and Hyde's successor, Thomas Pollock, one of North Carolina's wealthiest landowners, captured between one and two thousand Tuscaroras in a single raiding expedition. James Moore, still hunting slaves, killed or captured nearly a thousand Indians in 1713. In that year the Yamasee matrilineal clan sent the seventeen-year-old Yamasee "prince" to London to establish diplomatic ties in the hope of mitigating the escalating violence. The mission failed, and the slave raids continued. The Yamasees engaged in "skulking" warfare, which relied on the systematic use of swamps, throwing the leaders of South Carolina off balance. As many as fifty thousand southern Indians may have been enslaved. Many of them were shipped to Caribbean slave islands, while others were sold to planters on the Eastern Seaboard, where they labored in rice and tobacco fields alongside African slaves. Florida's Indigenous population had collapsed from roughly sixteen thousand to less than four thousand. The few remaining missions were empty shells, serving slowly-collapsing nations.[10]

The southern Indians, however, were far from being defeated. In the spring of 1715, South Carolina dispatched agents to conduct a census of the Native towns surrounding the colony, which the Indians saw as a preamble to more slave raids. The Yamasees, Muscogees, Choctaws, and Apalachees went to war. Separately, Charles Craven, the governor of South Carolina, sent agents to the town of Pocotaligo to scold the Yamasees for unpaid debts—accrued mostly in the rum trade—amounting to a staggering one hundred thousand deerskins. The Yamasees were appalled. If anything, they expected the Carolinians to compromise; South Carolina was weak, and North Carolina was simply wretched—a collection of abandoned plantations, makeshift houses, and starving people. At dawn, an Indian woman, the wife of a trader, warned the Yamasees that English agents had come to spy on them. Yamasee leaders brought Thomas Nairne, the colony's Indian agent, to Charles Town's central square and burned him alive. They then joined with the Muscogees, Choctaws, and Apalachees in killing traders and destroying English settlements, plantations, and garrisons. It was the most coordinated Indigenous war since the Pueblo Revolt of 1680. More than four hundred colonists were killed, and the slave raids—a terror-inducing brand of settler colonialism—effectively stopped. Two Yamasee and two Muscogee leaders approached the Spanish in Florida, seeking an alliance with the Spanish Empire against the English. They seemed to be aware of the Spanish weakness. Indigenous intelligence networks were operated by go-betweens, trained runners, translators, and leaders fluent in metaphorical language.

The Yamasee rebellion was followed by a Muscogee rebellion. Both confederacies were communicating through war, telling the English how to behave. They wanted the English to adopt a new mindset and conform to Indigenous ways by negotiating, compromising, and sharing. The Muscogees knew that such a direct denouncement of English ways demanded a stronger strategic position. Guided by Brims, a shrewd *mico*—"leader"—they widened their diplomatic network across the Southeast, forging ties with the Spanish in San Augustín and the French in one of their settlements, Mobile. In late 1716, the Muscogee national council sent ambassadors to New York to ask the Iroquois to intervene. With calculated bravado, the ambassadors announced that they represented "50 Nations of Indians." Impressed,

the Iroquois dispatched twenty ambassadors to accompany the delegation home. A year later, Muscogee ambassadors traveled on a Spanish ship from Pensacola in Florida to Veracruz in Mexico, and then to
Mexico City, where they won an audience with Baltasar de Zúñiga y
Guzmán, the viceroy of New Spain. Indigenous diplomacy was wide-
ranging, forceful, and sophisticated all at once.[11]

Shocked and deterred by Indigenous armies and their expansive
diplomacy, South Carolinians failed to mount an effective counterattack. Spotting an opening, the Cherokees forged an alliance with
the Carolinians and duped the colonists into attacking their Muscogee rivals, thereby making it impossible for the English to win the
war. South Carolina effectively stopped buying Indian captives. The
remaining Yamasees moved to Florida and staged attacks to keep the
English at bay. South Carolina had become a fiasco. Almost all its
citizens were hiding in Charles Town, and it lost its status as a proprietary colony. Not since the Spanish-Pueblo war had any European
colony come so close to being wiped out by Indians. This was also the
moment when Catawba leaders gave the governor of South Carolina
the maps that put the British in their place. The Iroquois believed that
evil spirits resided in the settlements; if asked, the British would have
probably concurred. The colonists shifted, with ruthless efficiency,
into rice cultivation and African slavery. By the 1720s the colony was
dotted with sprawling rice plantations, where some twenty thousand
West African slaves worked under a brutal regime.[12]

WHEN THE MUSCOGEES SPOTTED the vessels, in early 1733, they
moved to welcome the strangers. The newcomers were not too numerous, they came with families, and they did not brandish weapons.
But almost immediately after they landed, they began to cut trees
and build a structure along the river that linked the Muscogee settlements. James Oglethorpe had landed, boldly and arrogantly, on the
Atlantic coast below South Carolina. The would-be colonists named
the region Georgia Colony after their king, ignoring Spanish claims
and Indigenous rights: the land belonged to the Muscogee Confederacy. Muscogee matriarchs were powerful political actors, and Mary

Musgrove, the daughter of a Muscogee mother and an English father, operated as a go-between, fostering peaceful relations with outsiders.

Patrick Gordon, the deputy governor of the Province of Pennsylvania, thought it prudent, however, to inform Oglethorpe, a member of parliament and a passionate and controversial social reformer, of the colony's tricky strategic position: "I doubt not but you are sensible that the French being possessed of Canada and that vast Country they call Louisiana, on the River and Branches of Mississippi, enclose all these English Colonies on the Main on the North and West." Worse still, the French "constantly endeavour to debauch our Indians from us and lay Schemes for their Encroachments."[13]

The advice was necessary. An anomaly among the British colonies, Georgia may have been the most utopian of North American colonial schemes. It was designed to turn a profit and provide defense against rival empires, but it was also a philanthropic and self-consciously idealistic project. There were to be no wars, no dispossession of Native Americans, no slavery, no lawyers, and no hard liquor—just a better life for common White people than was possible in Europe. Georgia was conceived as an experiment in social uplift that would alleviate urban poverty in England by offering the destitute a home in North America. The colony was managed by the Georgia Trustees, a group of London reformers and humanitarians that envisioned a model colony where yeoman farmers would be the backbone of the society and where they could find material and moral fulfillment. The trustees framed the endeavor as a part of a centuries-long mission, the latest instance of "the ancient custom of sending forth colonies, for the improvement of any distant territory." Yet there was a hint of doubt. Oglethorpe had written that occupancy "must at all Times be accompanied with a sufficient Force to defend it from Invaders."[14]

Georgia was a loaded project. It was to be a White utopia and a buffer colony that confined the Spanish to Florida, while also producing staples and luxuries for Atlantic trade. Revealing their colonial mindset, the trustees sought to turn the region's Native inhabitants into laborers to alleviate the colony's great dilemma: the trustees had banned slavery. They did so out of professed idealism, as well as for strategic reasons: they wanted to avoid the problem of runaway slaves. Spanish Florida had offered freedom to runaway slaves from other colonies in return for military service, creating a dynamic that could turn every potential Georgia slave into an anti-English Spanish auxiliary. Oglethorpe branded the runaways "secret enemies." Unsettled, Georgians reached out to their Indigenous neighbors, paying the Muscogees handsome bounties for capturing runaway slaves from other English colonies. In 1734, the Georgia Trustees brought a delegation of Lower Muscogees to London to meet King George II and Queen Caroline. The Muscogees demanded fair trade. When George Galphin, an ambitious Irish immigrant, arrived in South Carolina in 1737, he created an intimate empire by embracing Indians and facilitating intermarriages in the search of belonging and profit. He married Metawney, a Muscogee woman, which gave him access to Muscogee trade.[15]

Indians may have welcomed the ransoms, but they were not particularly keen on the new arrivals, who had built a town, Savannah, without securing permission from the Muscogee Confederacy. The Cherokees, Muscogees, and Choctaws loomed over the puny colony, which struggled to survive with its three thousand colonists and six hundred African slaves. The Cherokees occupied a strategically central realm that resembled the Iroquois position in the north. The Indians, moreover, were united in ways the colonists could only dream of. The Cherokees lived in a vast collection of towns. Each town had its leader and a council, which were inclusive: women, men, and children participated and voiced their views. Women routinely advised male council members, and matrilineal clans served as arbiters of justice. A strong communitarian ethos—*gadugi*—pervaded the Cherokee world. Men and women cleared fields, burned underbrush to create fertile ash, and harvested crops. Most Indigenous nations had broadly similar governing systems. As elsewhere, kinship ties were all-important; Cherokees considered an individual without kin less than a person. Most Europeans seemed to fall into that category.

To Europeans, the southern Indian nations were formidable. Georgians lived in constant fear that their African and Native slaves would launch a rebellion, and an alarming number of settlers left the colony. Nonetheless, a sufficient number of colonists stayed and survived to

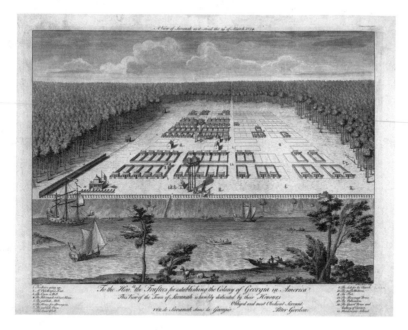

The Georgia Colony

keep the colony going. It was only in 1738 that Georgia could be declared "past Danger." Oglethorpe bragged that "this Province bridles the Spaniards in America, and covers the English frontiers." He expected that "the Parliament will give the necessary Supplies to the Trustees for the carrying on the Civil Government and the Improvement of the Countrey."[16]

Improve it they did, although the undertaking required a more appeasing Indian policy. In 1739, Oglethorpe began cajoling the Muscogee Confederacy, the dominant regional power. He traveled to the Muscogee town of Coweta—an extraordinary thing for a governor of an English colony to do—and signed a treaty with the confederacy that controlled trade along the Apalachicola and Chattahoochee Rivers, relying on an interclan police force. The Muscogees granted Oglethorpe a corridor-like realm between the Savannah and Ogeechee Rivers. In return, Oglethorpe acknowledged Muscogee sovereignty by accepting Georgia's limited territorial presence in the Southeast: "The English shall not enlarge or take any other Lands except those granted as above by the Creek [Muscogee] Nation to the Trustees." The Georgians had been put in their place by an imposing Indigenous regime of *Malatchi Opeya Micco*, the "Rightful and Natural Prince of the said Nations." The Muscogee towns would continue to safeguard the Muscogee nationhood.[17]

But Georgia would prove to be no exception among the New World colonies. Its inhabitants were in a desperate rush to entrench their colony. A year before the treaty talks, they had already ordered thousands of grape trees from Europe to plant vineyards and were becoming uneasy over the bordering Indians, especially the Choctaws, who seemed to have "10,000 Fighting men settled in near fifty Towns." They worried about French stratagems and Spanish invasions; they desperately wanted to be safe and in control. The generally buoyant Oglethorpe admitted that the colony was far from safe, regardless of the treaty with the Muscogees. "The poor People that are here have been so harassed by their Threats and so constantly under Arms that they have not been able to make that Provision for their Subsistence which was necessary." Without immediate emergency measures, Oglethorpe warned, "the Misery will be too great for Description."[18]

The colonists became scared and then spiteful; utopias tend to crash hard. A man named Patrick Tailfer emerged to lead a group calling itself the Malcontents, consisting of colonists who resented the trustee control, in particular the ban on slavery. In 1741, Tailfer published *A True and Historical Narrative of the Colony of Georgia*, a cutting denouncement of the trustees, who, he argued, were denying the colonists a fortune. As increasing numbers of colonists left the colony, the Indians seemed to be filling the gaps, taking over land and fields. This situation was Oglethorpe's fault, Tailfer argued: "The First Thing he did after he arrived Georgia, was to make a kind of solemn Treaty with a Parcel of fugitive Indians, who had been formerly banished [from] their own Nation for some Crimes and Misdemeanours." While the Trustees failed to rectify things, the colonists began to seize Indian lands. By the mid-1700s, the Muscogees were calling the English "Ecunnaunuxulgee," "people greedily grasping after the lands of the red man."[19]

FROM AN INDIGENOUS PERSPECTIVE, Georgia was part of a much larger dynamic. In the late seventeenth century, Native Americans had rolled back imperial advances across the continent. But in the early eighteenth century, colonial pressure brought by land-hungry colonists was becoming uncontainable along the Eastern Seaboard; by the 1730s, due to immigration and improved farming methods, the number of English colonists reached nearly six hundred thousand. There were still many Native communities on the coastal plains, but the English colonies now dwarfed them. Indians were forced to scrape by at the margins of what had been their homelands only years earlier. The colonists expected them to shed all things Indigenous and assimilate. Most Indians who stayed in place blended in selectively, hoping to preserve their Indigeneity behind a facade of compliance. They dressed, drank, cursed, and worshipped like the English, trying to make themselves inconspicuous. It was a survival strategy that often brought them more disdain than acceptance: imitating alien behaviors was a subtle hit-or-miss endeavor in which every slip in style, pitch, or idiom could set them back. Many chose to live in English-style houses, practice plow farming, raise livestock, and build fences. Others resigned themselves to selling their labor as farmhands, woodcutters, tanners, potters, sailors, soldiers, and slave catchers. Some relied on charity, and others became vagrants to preserve a measure of personal autonomy. Some Native women took African husbands—there were no longer enough Native men—to rebuild families. Some became indentured servants.

Perhaps the most difficult challenge facing the Indians was gauging how much success they could safely enjoy. The colonists wanted the Indians to accept their god, customs, and values, but too much adaptive acuity could be dangerous, provoking the English to see the Indians as competitors. If Indians managed to register their landholdings, they faced the threat of being labeled "Blacks" and having their claims abolished; if they thrived as farmers or livestock breeders, they risked incurring the wrath of their less capable English neighbors. For each Indian who managed to carve out a niche among the English, there were many more who were reduced to bound servitude or outright slavery. In 1708, South Carolina planters held fourteen hundred Native Americans in bondage, and the South Carolina assembly supplied Catawbas with "fifty guns a Thousand flints and

200 tw of powder 400 tw of Bulletts" in the hope of securing more Indian slaves. This is when Native Americans began to profoundly question their foreign political strategies in the face of colonial aggression, spawning "modern Indian politics," which recognized that Native people would have to accept a larger presence of White colonists in their world. Everything from trade and diplomacy to war and hunting and hospitality had to be recalibrated when the social space shrank between the two people, who now needed to coexist in order to survive.

Over the course of the eighteenth century, many of the rights and privileges that the Indians in English colonies had enjoyed earlier— advising juries, giving testimony, becoming constables, carrying fire-arms, moving about freely—disappeared. Indians could no longer expect impartial rulings by courts, nor could they take for granted such basic pleasures of life as enjoying a drink in public or dressing as they pleased. A legal and physical color line—spawned by fear and a sense of weakness—came to separate the English from their Indige-nous neighbors, who no longer could own real estate, marry a White person, have multiple wives, or take a walk at night without a pass-port and a lantern.

Native languages were sidelined in diplomatic meetings because the colonists expected the Indians to learn English and refused to provide translators. Medals and written documents replaced wampum, picto-graphs, and tattoos as means of cross-cultural diplomacy. But the laws against Native property ownership, intermarriage, and mobility applied only within the borders of English colonies, and the vast majority of Native Americans lived outside those borders by choice. Dependent on European wares, the eastern Indians began killing deer solely for hides, leaving the meat to rot, while wampum, now mass-produced, lost much of its diplomatic value. But much survived too—from Cherokee bas-ketry to Catawba pottery. Refusing to relocate and vanish, the Indians preserved the connection to ancient Indigenous territories, challenging the racist and genocidal policies of the English colonies. The small foot-holds they retained were at once fragile and vital.[20]

Chapter 16

THEY SMELLED LIKE ALLIGATORS

WHILE ENGLISH COLONISTS WERE CARVING THE Atlantic coastal plains into distinct colonies, the French were focusing on trade and diplomacy with Native Americans. In a striking contrast to most English colonies, New France was built on close collaboration with the Indians, who became trading partners, military allies, and kin over the course of the seventeenth century. But as their rivalry with the English intensified, largely over religious differences, the Bourbon kings awakened to the reality that most of their North American territories were paper claims. The French started to expand their domains in ways that would shape the Indigenous continent well into the eighteenth century. While French ambitions had previously centered on the Saint Lawrence Valley and the Great Lakes, they now turned increasingly to the West and South.

Exploration was the vanguard of expansion. Already in the 1670s, French explorers had confirmed that the Mississippi flowed not to the Pacific but to the south, and in 1682 René-Robert Cavelier, Sieur de La Salle, sailed down the river with twenty-three Frenchmen and eighteen Native men, women, and children; when he arrived at the Gulf of Mexico, he claimed the whole region from there to the Great Lakes for France. At the beginning of his journey south, La Salle had built a series of outposts for the ten-thousand-strong Illini Confederacy—roughly the same population size as that of New France—near the confluence of the Mississippi, Missouri, and Ohio Rivers, striving to thrust the French Empire into the south with Illini support. He had traded for years with Great Lakes Indians, and he knew that the Native Americans expected trade and generosity. He understood the artful accommodations of the middle ground. Sailing south, La Salle offered alliances to Quapaws, Taensas, and Natchez to secure access to the Gulf and extend the middle ground deep into the south. While among the Quapaws, he claimed the entire Mississippi watershed for his king and named it Louisiana—a thoroughly hollow gesture, and he knew it. On his return trip upriver, La Salle founded Fort Saint Louis on land that belonged to the Illini Confederacy, near the grass-covered ruins of Cahokia. The fort was to be the nucleus of a new French domain, *Pays des Illinois*, the Illinois Country. The stiffest resistance to this colonial extension came from neither the Spanish nor the English, but from the Iroquois, who had raided the Illinis for years and claimed them as vassals. Wherever the French moved to expand their empire, it seemed, they ran into the Five Nations, their on again, off again allies. France's empire-building in the lower midcontinent would be experimental, halting, and risky.[1]

The Illini Confederacy became France's most important ally in North America, and the alliance posed a threat to the Five Nations, who were suffering through yet another vicious smallpox epidemic that had killed "immense" numbers. Strategic concerns blended seamlessly into a mourning war, generating what became the single most explosive moment of Five Nations expansion. The Illinis were conducting their own mourning wars, guided by the idea of *nirapakerima*, "I adopt him in place of the dead." In 1680, eight hundred Iroquois soldiers launched a coordinated attack on the grand village of Kaskaskia, an Illini stronghold. According to a distraught Jesuit priest, they "killed and ate over 600 on the spot, without counting those whom they burned along the road. They saved the children who could live without the Milk of their mothers whom they had killed; but the others were cruelly roasted and devoured." The survivors fled, and the Iroquois "took no more trouble with them." Extending their raids in all directions, they attacked the Andostagués, "who were very numerous, and whom they entirely destroyed." The middle Mississippi Valley had become a new and secure base for Iroquois mourning wars; there was not a single French fort between the Five Nations and the western Great Lakes.[2]

By symbolically and literally absorbing other Native peoples, the Iroquois created a massive colonial vacuum in the interior. Euro-

*This European map captures the centrality of the Illini
Confederacy in the heart of the continent.*

pean colonialism in the heart of the continent could not exist without
Indian allies. The governor of New France, Louis de Buade, comte
de Frontenac, openly admitted that he could not stop their expansion. He did not even dare try, fearing that the Iroquois might realize
"that we do not offer any succor to our allies." He dreaded "a want of
power that may create in them a desire to come and attack us."[3]

Two years after his trip down the Mississippi, La Salle embarked
on another mission, this time from France: a reconnaissance expedition of four vessels and three hundred people to pinpoint the mouth
of the Mississippi from the sea and establish a colony on the Gulf
coast. But La Salle missed the landing site. The French built a small
base on Lavaca Bay, and La Salle departed on a meandering adven-
ture to the northeast. He entered Caddo territory, where he was killed
by a disgruntled follower. The French at the tiny colony did not fare
much better. They struggled to grow crops and exploited their Native
hosts, stealing food and canoes. And after three years, in 1688, the
Karankawas, who dominated the Gulf coast from the Brazos River to
Galveston Island, destroyed the settlement in a surprise attack.[4]

Although a failure, La Salle's expedition rekindled an old French ambition of linking the Saint Lawrence basin, the pays d'en haut, and the Mississippi Valley into a vast inland empire stretching from an eastern sea to a southern one. France's empire in North America had never been more than a collection of dispersed forts, villages, and ports, and the more populous and more entrenched English drove the French to reexamine their goals and methods. They needed a centralized New World empire that could implement a continental strategy, contain the English east of the Appalachians, and execute a leap to the Pacific. That imperial ambition had to start in the East with the Five Nations, who had diminished and humiliated New France in the early 1680s, allying with New York and trading with the English against French objections. The future of New France would hang in the balance as long as the Iroquois were not suppressed. Only then could the French do what they did best: build Indian alliances that gave them access to the continent's staggering wealth.[5]

In 1685, Governor Jacques-René de Brisay de Denonville arrived in Montreal with five hundred marine troops, determined to restore France's battered reputation in North America. Realizing that he did not have enough soldiers to face the Five Nations in battle, he decided to attack the new—and in the French view, illegal—English posts on James Bay. The French troops captured several fur trade centers—a stinging blow to English designs on the far north. Denonville then moved against the Five Nations with a seventeen-hundred-strong French-Native army and burned several Seneca villages and their food stores. The Iroquois retaliated by raiding frontier villages near Montreal, and the French, recoiling, took the fight to the English, starting what became known as King William's War. Allied French and Indians wrecked coastal Maine and parts of New Hampshire, and sacked several Mohawk "castles" in an unexpected midwinter attack in 1693. Three years later the French mobilized more than two thousand soldiers to raze Onondaga and Oneida settlements. The Iroquois, now numbering only some eight thousand people, realized that they needed to disentangle themselves from imperial rivalries and wars once and for all.

The Five Nations met this colonial aggression with restraint and bold diplomacy—an extraordinarily difficult thing to do for a nation that had dominated European intruders for generations. They adopted a neutral stance, which enabled them to approach the English in New York and play them against the French—a maneuver that forced the French to open negotiations. The Five Nations made peace with the Wyandots, Odawas, Illinis, and Miamis, freeing their soldiers to confront the French army in the east. The talks with New France and its Native allies came at the last minute for the Five Nations, which had lost nearly half of their soldiers and had seen their armies reduced to only twelve hundred men. The Five Nations had also become dependent on European markets and technology to the point that they could not wage war without them. The Iroquois had faced numerous existential threats before and knew that perceptions mattered. Before long, the French could observe how Mohawks "are left at perfect liberty, and walk daily in the streets of Montreal with as much confidence as if Peace were perfectly ratified. . . . We do not wish to alarm them," the French concluded.[6]

The shrewd Five Nations diplomacy paved the way for a massive summit in Montreal in the summer of 1701. More than a thousand delegates representing some forty Indigenous nations arrived and stayed for months, restoring order to their world one encounter, one ceremony, and one bargain at a time. They planted a tree so that a general peace could grow from its root and concluded with the French what became known as the Grand Settlement, the crowning achievement of French-Indigenous diplomacy. The Iroquois, whose territory still covered more than thirty-five thousand square miles, pledged to remain neutral in any future conflicts between England and France. Their Feast of the Dead would allow people to adopt a new mindset and end the violence. This was a strategic ploy: the seemingly endless colonial conflicts were draining, offering diminishing returns. The Iroquois agreed to cease their operations in the pays d'en haut, and the French granted the Indians privileged access to their new trading post, Fort Pontchartrain, near the strait joining Lakes Huron and Erie. The French thought they had, at long last, pacified the Iroquois, but they were mistaking diplomatic suppleness for submissiveness.

The beginning of the eighteenth century was a critical moment for France's imperial ambitions on the continent. With the Iroquois conciliated, the French could move to realize their thwarted imperial ambitions. The Five Nations soon began sending their armies to the south, targeting Catawbas, Sugarees, Saponis, Tutelos, Keyauwees, and other small Native nations in the Piedmont. For the Five Nations, the peace with New France was neither a concession nor a constraint. It was, instead, yet another strategic maneuver that took advantage of their confederacy's Francophile and Anglophile factions, an intentional partition that gave them options and allowed radical foreign policy maneuvers without causing internal strife. Alarmed, the governor of Quebec declared that "the five Iroquois [nations] are more to be feared than the English colonies." "Peace," an Iroquois leader announced, was "to live out of their Element." Spiritually infused war, embodied by the mourning wars, was normal. The Iroquois waged an on-again, off-again war against the Catawbas that lasted a half century. In the end, the Five Nations would make peace on their own terms.[7]

In the winter of 1704, a multiethnic party of two hundred French, Mohawk, Wyandot, and Wabanaki soldiers attacked the town of Deerfield in Massachusetts. The soldiers entered the town from three separate points before dawn, surprising the sleeping inhabitants. The attackers knew exactly what to do. They captured Eunice Mather Williams; her husband, pastor John Williams; and their five children—confident that they could expect a healthy ransom for their redemption. Overall, forty-one English colonists were killed, and more than a hundred women, men, and children were taken captive. The Williams's daughter Eunice, seven years old, spent seven years in captivity, her story becoming a sensation in the English colonies and New France. She was adopted into a Mohawk family, converted to Catholicism, married a Mohawk man, had three children, lost her English, and became known as Kanenstenhawi. She did not want to be redeemed. She died in Kahnawake, near the Saint Lawrence Valley, at the age of eighty-five.[8]

The attack on Deerfield announced the revival of French confidence and expansionism in North America. Emerging from the shadow of the Five Nations, French colonists, traders, and officials slowly picked up where they had been forced to stop in the 1680s. The outbreak of the War of Spanish Succession—which involved France, Spain, and Great Britain—instilled further urgency in French maneuvers, and the early decades of the new century saw the Saint Lawrence Valley quickly become safer, richer, and more crowded: its population of fifteen thousand in 1700 would more than triple by 1750. Fantasies of a New Jerusalem drew in colonists and soldiers from France, and a continuous strip of riverfront farms stretched for more than two hundred miles on both sides of the river. Native peoples from the interior trekked with their goods to Montreal, Trois-Rivières, and Quebec, and many of them were willing to fight with the French to keep the English at bay.

New France was becoming a realm of hard colonial power. The most obvious manifestation of its aggressive stance toward Native Americans was Indian slavery. The French began purchasing captives, mostly children, from Odawas, Ojibwes, Potawatomis, Miamis, Meskwakis, and Wyandots in the interior. Code Noir, established to regulate slavery in France's Caribbean colonies, was now applied in New France. Soon the colony had hundreds of Indian slaves working as millers, field hands, dock loaders, launderers, and domestics. Some were forced to labor as ship crewmen, and Indians with more skills were assigned to shops and factories. The French called the enslaved Indians *Panis*, a label of obscure origins that connoted loss of freedom, as well as slave status, that erased all ethnic identities. Some female slaves became concubines, and some married French men. Almost all were subjected to intense religious indoctrination and struggled under the demands made by their owners. The average slave entering the colony was just ten years old and died by the age of eighteen.[9]

IN THE FALL OF 1698, a group of colonists led by the Canadian-born Pierre Le Moyne, Sieur d'Iberville, and his brother, Jean-Baptiste Le Moyne de Bienville, sailed from the port city of Brest in France with two frigates and two freighters. Fifty-eight days later, the ships arrived in the Gulf of Mexico. Iberville traced the northern shore of the Gulf coast toward his main target, the ever-elusive mouth of the

Mississippi River, in a labyrinthine delta. The brothers were seeking to revive the old expansionary dream pursued by La Salle in 1682 and extinguished by the Karankawas in 1688: the conquest of the Mississippi Valley. Iberville's mandate from Louis XIV directed him to build forts to keep the Carolinians away from the Mississippi River and to challenge Spain's exclusive claims to the Gulf coast. Yet he was going at it all but blindly. The existing maps were rough drafts, and the Native Americans living along the coast were mostly unknown.

As the expedition slowly drew near its destination, the discovery of more than sixty fresh corpses on a small island gave the French pause. So, too, did the first living Indians they encountered: the Native Americans showed them a coat of mail that had allegedly belonged to Hernando de Soto, who had died on the western bank of the Mississippi during a slave-raiding rampage 156 years earlier. Grasping the message, Iberville smoked the calumet with the Indians and handed out gifts that amounted to toll fees. It was only when a group of Indians told him they remembered La Salle's expedition that Iberville realized he had arrived. The Bayagoula and Mongoulacha nations took pity on the decrepit strangers and fed them corn and chickens. Relieved and revitalized, the French built a new fort on a bay that Iberville named Biloxi. Complete with four bastions and twelve cannons, Fort Maurepas was to be the foundation of a new American colony. Bienville, meanwhile, approached the Yatasi Nation of the powerful Caddo Confederacy in the Red River valley.

Not long after, a sixteen-gun English man-of-war anchored near the French camp at Biloxi. Aboard the vessel was a French engineer, M. Secon, carrying a petition to the king of France: if Louis XIV granted religious liberty to a new American colony, Secon would ship in four hundred French Huguenot families who would help contain Spanish and English colonial ambitions. New World colonialism was still in adventurer mode: the home nations were mere abstractions, and a single person could establish a personal fiefdom. Secon's far-fetched scheme prompted Iberville to sail back to France to seek crown support for a full-fledged colony of his own. He prevailed and returned in 1701 with a fleet and as the governor of a new province, Louisiana. Convinced that the exposed domain had to be secured with satellite

colonies, Iberville made rounds among the bordering Indigenous confederacies to explain the French aims.[10]

Iberville knew that an enduring French presence in Louisiana had
to be entrenched through trade and alliances. He established a new
colonial headquarters in Mobile Bay, close to the twenty-thousand-
strong Choctaw Confederacy, which boasted some fifty towns and six
thousand soldiers and had "an air of Iroquois in their ways of waging
war." He also approached the Chickasaws, the region's leading military might. The Chickasaw Confederacy may have been less than
half the size of the Choctaw Nation, but a stunning forty percent of
Chickasaw men owned guns, procured from English slave traders. At
the time Iberville was coaxing the Choctaws, the Chickasaws held
hundreds of Choctaws in captivity. The impressed French labeled the
Chickasaw towns as "forts."[11]

Louisiana's founding marked a new phase in the contest over North
America. French strategists began to think in continental terms,
imagining a vast crescent-shaped empire stretching from sea to sea.
Anchored in the Saint Lawrence Valley in the northeast and in Louisiana in the south, with a budding Illinois Country in the center that
cemented French claims to the Mississippi, such an empire could hem
in the Spanish in the Southwest and the English on the Eastern Seaboard, ending all foreign threats once and for all. As in the pays d'en
haut decades before, the French had to appease the Indians to realize their grand ambitions. In an astute move that drew from the long
French tradition of appealing to Indigenous mores and sensibilities,
Iberville told the Choctaws and Chickasaws that the French, unlike
the English, did not want to enslave them.[12]

With Indigenous consent to enter secured, the lower Mississippi
Valley became a magnet for the itinerant coureurs de bois and the
backbone of the reinvigorated French Empire in the New World.
Around 1700, disgruntled Quebec Catholics established a base—
which they named after the ancient city of Cahokia, near Kaskaskia—that occupied a strategically vital location where woodlands
and grasslands overlapped, offering a range of resources, from bison
to wild plants to slaves. The Illini Confederacy dominated the middle
stretch of the Mississippi River around its confluence with the Ohio,

holding several Native groups—Peorias, Tamaroas, Chepoussas, Quapaws, and others—in its orbit. The Illinis were willing to extend their inclusivist policy to the French as long as the French respected Native customs. Still few in number—only three hundred colonists lived along the Mississippi—the French shared their wealth and won access to the valley. By the early eighteenth century, Kaskaskia was in decline—a victim of overpopulation and ecological degradation—and the Illinis may have considered the French merchants a resource. Jesuits established missions at Kaskaskia and Cahokia, while the French built a string of trading posts that linked the Gulf coast to the Great Lakes. In 1719, the French constructed Fort Chartres to protect the Illinois Country. Once again, the French were propping up their empire on an Indigenous bedrock.[13]

The strategy involved profound challenges. French colonists may have been more fluent in Native diplomacy than their Spanish and English rivals were, but the sheer complexity of Indigenous politics could overwhelm even the most experienced French officers. Fort Detroit, established in 1701, was a case in point. The French had encouraged Indians to move near to the fort, where, alongside French soldiers, the French thought they could stave off the English in the East. But the concentration of multiple nations created a powder keg. France's old allies—the Illinis, Miamis, Odawas, Ojibwes, Potawatomis, and Wyandots—clashed with its new ones, the Iroquois, who resented the other nations' presence in the region. French agents failed to mediate, and the aggrieved Iroquois made a bid to shift the center of the fur trade from French Montreal to British Albany, which, after the Grand Settlement, had become a flourishing marketplace. The Iroquois now strove to dominate all of the middleman trade between the interior hunters and the English. Another storm started with Le Pesant, a chameleonic Odawa ogimaag who demanded a privileged position in French trade and diplomacy, yet seemed ready to drop the French if the Iroquois and the English bought Odawa pelts. The Miamis urged the French to kill and boil Le Pesant.

In 1712, more than a thousand Meskwakis relocated next to Fort Detroit—and announced that the fort belonged to them. They had rejected the middle ground. It was a bold move, targeting more their

Native rivals than the French, and it brought an instant backlash. When Meskwakis laid siege to the fort, their Illini, Miami, Odawa, Ojibwe, and Wyandot enemies retaliated. Fort Detroit and the lower Great Lakes became a war zone, which endangered the entire French imperial system: if Detroit fell, New France stood to lose the critical pivot that linked Louisiana and Canada and kept the tenuous French imperial dream alive. Governor Charles de La Boische, Marquis de Beauharnois, contrived a genocidal war on the Meskwakis by generously arming their enemies. Soon on the defensive, the Meskwakis retreated into the western Great Lakes, seeking refuge among the Dakota Sioux, their rivals. In 1716, an eight-hundred-strong French-Indigenous army attacked fortified Meskwaki villages in the region, forcing a truce. By then, France's Indian alliance, its bedrock in North America, was already disintegrating. The Meskwaki power politics had made the French Empire fragile at its strategic center, in a bridge area where the Mississippi Valley and the Great Lakes come together. French strategists reported "great damage upon the mutual Commerce between the two Colonies": the Illinois Country and Louisiana.[14]

The 1716 truce saved Fort Detroit and France's Indian alliance in the pays d'en haut. In a roundabout way, it also saved Louisiana. With New France at least momentarily secured, the building of the fragile colony could proceed. Since 1712 it had been a proprietary colony of the fantastically wealthy Antoine Crozat, Marquis du Châtel, who preferred to manage things from the safety of Versailles, and Louisiana had languished: it had only 215 French inhabitants. Bienville believed that not a single French soldier had fired a musket. Yet, inexplicably, in 1719 in a misguided and mistimed policy scheme, French officers began to remove Indians who were not spouses or offspring of slaves from the Illinois Country, alienating the Indians. French colonialism, based on alliances with Native Americans, seemed to have turned against itself.

In that same year, more tension came when John Law, a brash Scottish adventurer-economist who had once killed a rival suitor in a duel, established a transshipment center in Louisiana in anticipation of flourishing upriver trade with Indians. Rashly, the French crown had leased the Mississippi watershed—essentially the entire midcontinent—to Law's Company of the West, hoping to attract investors and colonists to the fledgling and exposed Louisiana. In a singular colonial move, Law shipped in more than seven thousand colonists and two thousand African slaves over four years, creating a solid demographic foundation for Louisiana. Over the objections of the commandant of the Illinois Country, Law had the colony transferred under Louisiana's jurisdiction. An economist with no military or diplomatic background and little understanding of or interest in Native Americans was running France's newest, largest, and most precarious colony. No one with proper experience wanted the job.[15]

As so often happened, the French relied on their Native allies to restore order. Iroquois, Sioux, and Wyandot soldiers joined the French in punishing the troublesome Meskwakis, who kept the interior of Louisiana in a state of flux, hurting commerce. In the end, it was the powerful Natchez who stabilized the region. The Natchez had an agenda of their own. They knew that the French possessed an essential skill—the ability to assemble alliances with Indians through generosity—and the Natchez brought their considerable military might to a war that neutralized the Meskwakis. The Natchez were awarded a trading post for their confederacy—a windfall that gave them a crucial edge over their rivals. Occupying uncommonly fertile land on the eastern side of the Mississippi, the Natchez lived in nine towns that housed six thousand people who were arranged into a strict caste system of Suns, Nobles, Honored People, and commoners. In the ancient Mississippian tradition, the Natchez had built a theocratic state, venerating the sun. Each town had a sacred mound, serving as a spiritual and ceremonial center for its citizens. French travelers marveled at how the Mississippi River had "a large number of tribes on both its banks," but thought that the Natchez Confederacy "deserves to be distinguished from the rest, since this tribe is governed by a sovereign whom they obey with great respect and submission. He has a very comfortable dwelling, which, as far as the resources of the country permit, has various apartments. No one enters his presence until he has been informed of their coming." The French were particularly enthralled to learn that this paramount leader, the Great Sun, "alone decides questions of peace or war, and all the important business which concerns the public." This was a polity the French could understand and, perhaps, win over, potentially saving their unraveling empire.[16]

In 1715, Natchez micos offered the calumet to Antoine de La Mothe Cadillac, the governor of Louisiana, but he refused to smoke it. It was a major faux pas. Sharing the calumet reaffirmed amity, alliances, and coexistence. Cadillac's rejection amounted to a rejection of the nascent alliance: by mutual understanding, the king of France was obliged to protect the Indians, who retained their autonomy and sovereignty. Natchez soldiers killed four French traders, and Cadillac retaliated by sending an army to punish them. A mico delivered three severed Natchez heads to the French as a peace offering, but the Natchez had already begun to question the wisdom of allowing a French presence in their world.[17]

At least momentarily safe, the French resumed the expansion of their colony. In 1718, Bienville founded New Orleans at a sharp bend of the Mississippi on the lands of the Chitimacha Indians. Soon a belt of riverfront settlements stretched dozens of miles south and north of the initial site. To protect the growth around New Orleans, Law's company built the Arkansas Post at the confluence of the Mississippi and Arkansas Rivers, where it survived in the sheltering shadow of the Quapaw town of Kappa. The post was poised to become a major regional center when Law's company dispatched nearly a hundred African slaves and White indentured servants to it; they were to turn it into an agricultural powerhouse managed by imported German colonists. But the Germans, unsettled by rumors of germs and disease, never came. Law fled, leaving behind dozens of French men, women, and children.

Those abandoned French became slaves. The Quapaws took them in and put them to work in their fields around Osotouy, one of their four principal towns. Some of the French became hunters, blending into the Quapaw population. Scores of French deserters escaping military and indentured service also sought refuge among the Quapaws, as did a number of runaway African slaves. Only rarely did French colonial officials dare pressure the Quapaws to return their subjects.

A newcomer might have taken Osotouy, not New Orleans, as the capital of the colony.[18]

The Quapaws seemed to be one of the most isolated people on the continent: their lands sat over a thousand miles from the English and French colonies in the East, and travel to New Orleans along the Mississippi was becoming dangerous. Yet they managed to build a dense network of commercial and diplomatic ties by forging relationships with French missionaries and traders in the Illinois Country. They become a gravitational center in the heart of the continent, pulling people into their world and accruing considerable moral and political power. In their many borderlands, the Quapaws determined what counted as crime and who deserved to be punished. They saw the French soldiers at Arkansas Post as children who needed their protection; the French had fallen under Quapaw jurisdiction and were expected to behave accordingly. Determined to keep the market economy at arm's length, Quapaws produced very little for the French—roughly a thousand deerskins per year. Yet they expected the French to be generous with their wares and to embrace the Quapaws as preferred allies, even when they themselves forged commercial ties with Carolina traders. When the French needed the Quapaws' assistance in diplomacy or war, they had to secure it through tribute payments. This arrangement was worthwhile for the French: the Quapaws remained loyal and helped keep Louisiana alive. The French also built a trading post for the mighty Osages, or *Ni-u-kon-ska*, "People of the Middle Waters," in the middle Arkansas Valley. The Osages numbered ten thousand, making them one of the largest nations in the interior. French traders cajoled them with gifts—including horses—but the Osages did not hesitate to kill French traders who sold weapons to Osage enemies.[19]

Overwhelmed on all sides by Indigenous maneuvers, the French relied on subterfuge. In 1723, Bienville, now the governor of Louisiana, moved "to put these barbarians into play against each other, the sole and only way to establish any security in the colony because they will destroy themselves by their own efforts eventually." It was wishful thinking: Native Americans had learned to spot such tactics and now turned them against the colonists. The Muscogees, living between

British and French settlements, played the two colonial powers off each other. James Adair, a veteran English fur trader, explained the system: "The Old men, being long informed by the opposite parties, of the different views, and intrigues of those European powers, who paid them annual tribute under vague appellation of presents, were becoming surprisingly crafty in every turn of low politics. They held it as an invariable maxim, that their security and welfare required a perpetual friendly intercourse with us and the French; as our political state of war with each other, would always secure their liberties."[20]

Operating on the margins of forceful Indigenous polities, the French relied on over-the-top gestures to conceal their weakness. In 1725, Étienne de Bourgmont—a deserter, a criminal, and a coureur de bois—lived with a group of illegal traders among Indians in the lower Missouri Valley. In exchange for expanding French trade along the strategically vital river, he was granted letters of nobility and the title of "commandant of the Missouri River," an empty title if there ever was one: the lower Missouri Valley was a thoroughly Indigenous world, ruled by the Osages, whose territory covered much of the midcontinent between the Arkansas and Osage Rivers. The Osages had become power brokers between French Louisiana and the Native nations to the west and north, regulating the upriver trade from New Orleans just up to the point where it did not stop altogether. Apparently at a loss over what to do with his title and the Indians, Bourgmont took a delegation of Osage, Otoe, Missouria, and Illini leaders to France, where they saw Versailles, the Paris opera house, the Hôtel des Invalides, and the fifteen-year-old king Louis XV. The Indigenous visitors were not impressed. One of them was taken aback by men "who were half women, with curled hair, earrings, and corsages on their chest." He said they "smelled like alligators."[21]

Osage dominance in the lower midcontinent only grew. Surrounded by nations that relied on hunting for subsistence and trade, the Osages, as another hunting people, had little to offer their neighbors. Similarity bred rivalries and resentment, and soon the Osages were at war with most of the bordering nations. The French, recognizing their power, built the Osages their own fort, generously stocked with weapons. Instead of siding with the French, the Osages

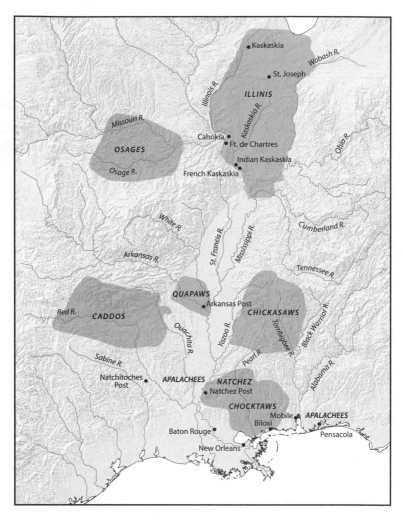

*Map depicting Indigenous dominance in the contested lower
midcontinent in the early eighteenth century*

used the guns to expel their Native rivals—Taovayas, Tawakonis,
Iscanis, Guichitas, and Panis Noirs—from the Arkansas Valley in the
early eighteenth century. The ambitions of the Osages swelled; they
sought to control all trade in the vast region, whether in furs, hides,
humans, or horses, and they monopolized Arkansas Valley commerce
with strategic blockages. They created the position of Protector of the
Land, who was responsible for keeping uninvited strangers out. By
the 1730s, the Osages controlled five hundred miles of the Arkansas

Valley as a river empire. They traded with the mobile French and controlled the flow of goods to the south and west, and they fought the Wichitas, Pawnees, and Caddos, monitoring the goods that reached the Great Plains. Failing to exercise any sway over the Osages, the French became their staunch allies and granted them a highly privileged position at the expense of their Native rivals. Yet the Osages routinely punished French traders and voyageurs—long-distance fur traders—for crimes, ignoring European laws. French authorities rarely protested, although a Spanish officer complained in 1790 that "the Osages [and Lakotas] are the worst two tribes that we have on the Missouri." Instead of trying to rule over the Osages, the French smoked the calumet with them and placated them with gifts. The Osages had war leaders, civil leaders, and a council of priests to facilitate their multilayered foreign policy. Osage women were highly skilled farmers, and their work was the foundation of Osage hegemony in the midcontinent. They enjoyed considerable autonomy. If an Osage woman was dissatisfied with her husband, she divorced him by throwing his possessions out of their lodge.[22]

Farther south in Louisiana, the French faced a more pointed Indigenous challenge: the Natchez staged a rebellion in late 1729. The French leaders, preoccupied with commercial maneuvers in the interior, had failed to protect their Indian allies, who had sought safety among them against slave raids. The Natchez severed ties with the French, who, alarmed, acted rashly: they recruited Choctaws to hunt Natchez scalps, triggering an on-again, off-again war that lasted for years. The commandant of Fort Rosalie, Sieur de Chépart, a ferocious, megalomaniac drunkard, stoked virulent anti-French sentiments among the local Indigenous people. When Chépart pressed the Natchez to vacate a town that was the site of a sacred mound to make room for French livestock and plantations, Natchez soldiers painted their faces red, drank kettles of "war medicine," and moved to eliminate the French from their world once and for all. Approaching Fort Rosalie, they offered gifts to the French, distracting the soldiers just long enough.

The carefully planned attack left more than two hundred French dead. Étienne Périer, who governed Louisiana as commandant-general for the Company of the West, panicked. He did not seem to know what to do. Eventually, he lashed out by ordering soldiers to destroy the peaceful and long-beleaguered Chaoucha Indians.[23]

"The colony is two fingers away from being lost," a French officer wrote in June 1730. Beset by disgruntled Native residents and by maroon communities, Louisiana was gripped by fear. Colonists hunkered down and left their fields untended. The next summer, French officials sent several regiments to punish the Natchez, but the operation was aborted when a slave rebellion erupted in the colony, petrifying the French: a staggering sixty percent of Louisiana's population were slaves, both Native and African. The humiliated Périer portrayed the two uprisings—the first by an Indigenous nation, the second by African slaves—as a conspiracy, but few listened. Along with the Company of the West, he had failed miserably. To redeem himself, Périer mounted yet another punitive campaign against the Natchez and took some five hundred—mostly women and children—as slaves. In one of its final acts, the Company of the Indies shipped the captives to Caribbean sugar islands.

The Meskwakis, too, had lost hundreds of their members to French slavery, and in late 1727 they went to war, attacking the French and their Illini and Odawa allies. In 1731, the collapsing Louisiana colony was put under royal control. In a desperate attempt to redeem himself, Beauharnois, the governor of New France, mobilized French troops and Indian allies to exterminate the Meskwakis. Their aim was the "total destruction of that nation." Yet the French had to rely on their Iroquois allies to deliver "the last blow." The French and Iroquois nearly succeeded. Only five hundred Meskwakis survived.[24]

THE DUAL THREAT of Indigenous power and English expansion from the east terrified the French inhabitants in Louisiana to their core. The Natchez war had shown, with graphic immediacy, what disregard for Indigenous sovereignty, traditions, and needs could bring: cataclysmic violence, massive loss of life and property, the utter collapse of colonial institutions. The violence discouraged French investments in the colony and impeded France's empire-building in the lower Mississippi Valley. It also taught the colonists how little they could do without Native approval. In Louisiana, Indigenous customs prevailed, turning a colonial space into a hybrid one. Choctaw, Illini, Quapaw, and Apalachee societies were all intact, and they expected the French to comply with their traditions. The consequences for Louisiana were far-reaching. *Métissage*—cultural mixing—became the norm, shaping the most intimate aspects of the colonists' lives: sexual practices, gender roles, and child-rearing. The French in Louisiana came to realize that to survive in North America, newcomers needed to embrace its Indigenous inhabitants and convince them to become allies. The French had been doing so elsewhere, and by the early eighteenth century, all the European empires had grasped, if not necessarily accepted, that reality. They had also learned that the most effective way of building alliances was generosity and trade, which could turn enemies into kin.[25]

In the wake of the war and loss, French officers set out to appease the Indians with gifts and goods, creating a robust frontier exchange economy that stabilized French relations with the Indians. A new and improved French-Indian alliance centered on the Choctaw Confederacy, which, even after losing hundreds of its members to South Carolina slave raiders, numbered more than twelve thousand people and could mobilize five thousand soldiers. The Choctaws commanded more than twenty-five thousand square miles, overshadowing the neighboring Quapaws, Alabamas, Chickasaws, Taensas, Tunicas, Natchez, and Houmas. Their own slave-catching and -trading had garnered for the Choctaws a sizable arsenal of guns, turning them into a domineering military power in the lands between the lower Mississippi and Yazoo Rivers. They also welcomed a regular flow of English trading parties from the east. Weakened Native groups on Choctaw borderlands found shelter in their fortified towns, and the French asked the Choctaws to help restore order to Louisiana. The

Choctaws punished the Chickasaws and Natchez, whose raiding operations destabilized the colony and disrupted trade; the Choctaws wanted an economically viable French Louisiana that could continue to supply them with guns, powder, lead, tools, and other goods.

The Choctaws were fighting for themselves. As much as the French officials wanted and needed to claim suzerainty over them, they could not deny that the Choctaws were the masters of the lower Mississippi Valley. When traders from the newly established colony of Georgia visited, the Choctaws welcomed them and their goods—to the dread and embarrassment of French officials. The Choctaw Confederacy had become Louisiana's last best hope—a humiliating role reversal that the commandant of the New Orleans troops was forced to accept. He called the confederacy "the bulwark and security" of the colony and admitted that "none of those who have come to the country fail to be aware of the impossibility of keeping a country as vast as the one we occupy with the few troops and colonists who are there and who would soon be obliged to depart from it if the Choctaws refused us their assistance and decided to act against us."[26]

Far to the west, another Indigenous confederacy was about to enter into the struggle over the interior and its resources: the Očhéthi Šakówiŋ, the Great Sioux alliance of the Seven Council Fires. A French official confronted Sacred Born, a Dakota Mdewakanton ithą́nčhaŋ—leader—whose soldiers had harassed French traders over proper treatment and fair trade. Sacred Born informed the official that the abuse was inflicted "with reflection and design." The French officials envisaged the pivotal Fort Beauharnois in the upper Mississippi Valley, on the shores of Lake Pepin, as the anchor of an enormous western fur-trading domain in the trans-Mississippi West. The Dakotas now claimed the region as theirs and resumed the fight against colonial arrogance and aggression where the Meskwakis had left off. In the winter of 1731, a French-Iroquois-Wyandot army "caused the destruction of the majority" of the Meskwakis. Soon after, ninety-nine Dakota lodges and three hundred Lakotas materialized at Lake Pepin, monitoring French trade policies and French behavior. Unable to dislodge the Dakotas and Lakotas, the French were forced to close

Fort Beauharnois for business. It was reopened in 1731, now serving the Dakotas and Lakotas. The Očhéthi Šakówiŋ had forced the French Empire to embrace the Sioux as preferred allies. In 1742, in a grandiose intervention, Governor Beauharnois invited almost all western Native nations to talks in Montreal. Sacred Born and other Dakota leaders met with Beauharnois, who was ready to embrace the Sioux as preferred allies. "My Children, as I see you naked, I give you what you need to cover yourselves," he pledged, and he authorized regulated and nearly unrestricted trade with the Očhéthi Šakówiŋ, hoping to extend New France's commercial reach deep into the West through the increasingly powerful confederacy. But then the French committed a faux pas that nearly ruined the nascent peace process: they had very young Sioux slaves serve the Sioux delegates at a celebratory dinner. Beauharnois freed the slaves, meeting the Sioux in the middle ground—a concession that bought France's troubled North American empire a little more time. Battered as they were, the French could still be useful. The Dakotas and Lakotas engaged in a lucrative trade with the French, who now frequented almost all Sioux villages along the Mississippi and Minnesota Rivers. The Očhéthi Šakówiŋ was emerging as the most powerful Native confederacy in North America.[27]

The Sioux nations, however, did not press the advantage; they were comfortable in their place in the world, and they knew that time was on their side. Their power and dominance did not translate into an aggressive expansion, which challenged the Europeans' entrenched and misguided views of Native American perfidy and savagery. It was the French officials who seemed to be unraveling on the Indigenous continent. The great ambition of the French policymakers was to find a water route from the "Sea of the West," the imaginary body of water that would offer access to the Pacific Ocean and, beyond that, China's fabled riches. French traders kept sending boatloads of guns, powder, and lead to the Sioux, confident that the Očhéthi Šakówiŋ's authority would secure the interior North America and China's riches for France. In an extraordinarily generous and misguided move, the French built three forts: Fort Vaudreuil below the mouth of the Wisconsin River, Fort Duquesne in the upper reaches of Wisconsin, and

Fort La Jonquière on the western shore of Lake Pepin. French policies had become utterly detached from reality. A single fort could give a Native nation a decisive edge in the contest for dominance, and the Sioux suddenly had three. Instead of pacifying the Očhéthi Šakówiŋ, the French had created an instant Indigenous superpower that would change American history irrevocably.[28]

Chapter 17

AN INFINITY OF RANCHERÍAS

F OR MORE THAN A THOUSAND YEARS, THE FORMIDABLE
Hasinai Confederacy had dominated a vast domain of roughly
one hundred thousand square miles between rivers, its largest towns
spreading for dozens of miles along the Neches, Angelina, Sabine,
and Red Rivers. The confederacy dwarfed all other powers nearby,
whether Indigenous or European. Over generations, the Hasinais had
become expert traders, their houses abounding with metal knives,
rifles, gunpowder, balls, cloth, kettles, beads, and tobacco. This was
the kind of Indigenous regime that all European colonists dreamt of
winning over.

Louisiana's unlikely perseverance and, over time, growth terrified
Spanish officials in New Mexico, who had for decades monitored how
the French enlarged their presence along the northern coast of the
Gulf of Mexico, posing a threat to Spanish shipping lines and silver
mines in Mexico. Spanish leaders had strived to contain Louisiana,
but their efforts had been more symbolic than effective: a few missionaries dispatched among the Indians occupying the lands between
the two colonies; a garrison stationed in Pensacola Bay to establish
a foothold on the coast; a proposed line of forts to block the French
advance. In 1716, terrified that French traders, with their renowned
fluency in Indigenous customs, might bring the Indians who were in
or near New Mexico under Louisiana's patronage, the Spanish made
another bid to expand their modest network of Indian alliances into
the east by winning over the awe-inspiring Hasinais and extending
the middle ground between them.

Astoundingly and clumsily, Francisco Hidalgo, a volatile Spanish

Franciscan priest, sent a letter to Louisiana's governor Cadillac, sharing an idea: the Spanish and the French should collaborate in establishing missions for the thousands of Indians living between New Mexico and Louisiana. Equally astoundingly, Cadillac accepted the offer. France's North American empire was still far from a tightly organized bureaucratic entity, and Cadillac hoped to launch a personal contraband trade with New Mexico. He dispatched Louis Juchereau de Saint-Denis, a flamboyant Quebecois trader, to prepare the ground for the joint operation. Following the Mississippi and Red Rivers, Saint-Denis entered the heart of the larger Caddo Confederacy and, led by Caddo guides, traveled more than a thousand miles to Mission San Juan Bautista on the Sabinas River.[1]

Spanish officers were baffled. They were also distressed, and quickly sent an expedition of seventy-five colonists, friars, and children to build a colony far to the east to stop any French encroachments. Remarkably, with them was Saint-Denis, officially under arrest but, for all intents and purposes, a member of a Spanish expedition that aimed to curb Louisiana. Led by Captain Domingo Ramón, the expedition traveled the region for nearly half a year, displaying crosses and performing masses for the Indians they encountered, naming places, and identifying natural resources along the way, until they finally reached their destination: the Hasinai territory, where they found "an infinity of rancherias with corn stalks, watermelons, beans, cantaloupes, tobacco, and a buffcolored flower, of which they eat a lot, but we do not know the name." Captain Ramón was overjoyed. "I named a chaplain," he reported, and "a church and a dwelling place were built."[2]

With those ceremonial gestures the Spanish launched a colonial project among the formidable Caddos, who controlled the balance of power in the borderlands. They constructed four wooden churches near Caddo settlements and a presidio on the Neches River. With their domain seemingly secure behind the Caddo barrier, Spanish leaders moved to confront the French directly. By 1718, the presidio of San Antonio de Béjar and the mission of San Antonio de Valero faced French Louisiana. Three years later the Spanish added the wooden presidio of Los Adaes to the buffer zone to defy Natchitoches, the westernmost French settlement, only seven miles away. In 1729, Los Adaes was made the capital of the new Spanish province of Texas, but its status was almost entirely symbolic. It had a mere 250 Hispanic residents and was utterly isolated from the Spanish centers of power. The closest supply depot, Saltillo, was eight hundred miles away, and the fabled royal highway, El Camino Real, was but a dirt path in Texas. Indigenous roads and paths, in contrast, enabled Native soldiers, traders, and diplomats to reach nearly every group and nation in the Southwest.

As a colony, Texas was miserable. For dozens of miles in every direction around it, the only inhabitants were Native Americans. The local Adaes Indians kept the capital alive because for them, too, it served as a buffer against their rivals. The Caddos expected the Spanish to provide them with guns, tools, cloth, and other goods, but the isolated Spanish in Texas simply could not deliver. They were desperately poor—so poor that they had to rely on Natchitoches, a settlement the Spanish considered illegal, for essentials. What the Spanish lacked in terms of military power, they tried to compensate for with bureaucratic prowess. A 1729 *Reglamento* included 196 articles that defined the duties of presidio commanders. The tiny contingent of Spanish soldiers was now responsible for keeping the French Empire out of Texas.[3]

Spanish and French strategists had envisioned their colonies as imperial launchpads that would facilitate further expansion, but that goal proved elusive for both empires. Colonists could do very little in North America without Native support and consent—a constraint that drove them to radically recalibrate their ambitions. The early-eighteenth-century low midcontinent became a world of flexible alliances, malleable identities, and imperial failures. Colonies founded as imperial power centers morphed into Indigenous resource domains. As in the pays d'en haut decades earlier, imperial ambitions were diverging from reality in the lower Mississippi Valley.

Following the pattern established earlier in the Northeast, the two empires would collide, even as they were at the mercy of powerful Indigenous nations. In the 1720s, just as the Spanish began to feel threatened by the French, the French came to see the Spanish threat from the west as a serious concern. It was not that the French were anxious about Spanish accomplishments; the official French view was that Spain had "neither established posts, planted colonies, nor acquired rights superior to the French, who were first to make explorations, build forts, and plant colonies in all that part of Florida afterwards called Louisiana." The French were worried because the Spanish had won access to the Caddo Confederacy by bowing to Caddo sovereignty. Acutely aware of their inability to dictate terms, the Spanish—missionaries, soldiers, would-be colonists—submitted to rigorous border control procedures, which included traveling only along designated roads with Caddo escorts and days-long stops under close surveillance; the Caddos, it seems, were ensuring that the visitors did not carry lethal diseases. When visitors approached their towns, Caddo leaders, together with women and children, came out to greet them. They formed columns and escorted the visitors in. A French colonist marveled that the Caddo roads were "as well beaten a road as that from Orleans to Paris." Outsiders could enter the Caddo territory, but they had to be healthy, humble, and generous. The Spanish needed to conform to Caddo rituals and distribute gifts and goods that served as symbols of a political alliance.[4]

Indians kept Louisiana small, isolated, cramped, and accommodating through a threat of violence. The Chickasaws and Natchez raided the annual supply convoys between New Orleans and the Illinois Country, attacking both French traders and their Native allies, while the Choctaws opened their towns to South Carolina merchants, who coveted the lucrative deerskin trade and had few qualms about selling guns to Indians. All of this pushed French officials to appease the Choctaws with gifts. Led by the controversial war leader Red Shoes, the Choctaws traded with both the English and the French, pitting them against each other and drawing concessions from both. The French, hoping to create a centralized Choctaw polity that could be absorbed into the French colonial hierarchy under French "fathers," tried to gain the upper hand by offering the Choctaw leaders lavish gifts. The gambit backfired; for the matrilineal Choctaws, the role of a "father" carried little authority. Although they handed gifts to more than a hundred Choctaw men, the French had little to show for the gesture. Keeping their options open, the Choctaws continued to trade with both the English and the French.[5]

Managed and diminished by Indians, Louisiana was in danger of becoming a pawn in complex struggles among more powerful protagonists: the Choctaws, Chickasaws, Spanish, and English. French officials had to act. In 1736, the Ministry of the Navy sent orders to eliminate the Chickasaw and Natchez nations. The French mobilized two armies. One pushed south from the Illinois Country under Pierre d'Artaguiette, and the other moved north from Mobile Bay under Louisiana governor Bienville, who had argued for years that the Chickasaws had to be eliminated. Bienville's force, composed of nearly five hundred French troops and hundreds of Indian auxiliaries—mostly Choctaws—converged on the Chickasaws and Natchez to destroy them. But six hundred Chickasaw soldiers ambushed the approaching army, firing on it from the hills around their own towns and killing more than a hundred. Bienville ordered a hasty retreat to New Orleans, where he learned that the Chickasaws had ambushed d'Artaguiette's Illinois army too.

Bienville insisted again that only the "entire destruction" of the Chickasaws could save Louisiana. He was posturing. His campaign had left Louisiana destitute, having cost a staggering 120,000 livres. Rival empires were inching in, coveting Louisiana's greatest asset, the Indian trade, as well as the Illinois Country itself. Hugging the Mississippi, Ohio, and Missouri Rivers, the Illinois Country was France's key to an empire in North America. Bienville put his troops to work building a road to bring in artillery for use against the Chickasaws. Even he did not seem to think it could work. His dream of an empire— which he had shared with his brother, Iberville—was over. Defending his actions to the king, Bienville complained that the French troops were not only cowardly but also too short, almost invariably under four feet ten inches. In 1740, Bienville announced that he could not continue the war.[6]

Native Americans had been Louisiana's masters and tormentors, but they could also be its deliverance. Gradually, French agents began placating their Native neighbors with regular gifts, trade, and mediation of Native-French and Native-Native grievances. France effectively gave up its imperial ambitions in the lower midcontinent. Like the French in the pays d'en haut, the Louisianans embedded a colony in an ancient Indigenous substratum. They accepted their weakness in the face of an Indigenous multitude, creating a version of the Great Lakes middle ground. The French and Indians remained distinct people separated by a yawning cultural gap, but they soon found common causes. Sustained by a blend of Indigenous resilience and restrained colonialism, Louisiana survived. By 1740, New Orleans had a populous and vibrant local civic district, and settlements and levees extended on both sides of the Mississippi for forty-two miles.

THE EXPANDING MIDDLE GROUND posed a direct threat to British colonists, who struggled to create trading networks with Native Americans. To rectify the situation, British traders at Hudson Bay started in the 1730s to arm the Crees and Assiniboines with muskets, spurring them to expand their hunting and trapping operations around the bay. The French reacted immediately. The Vérendrye dynasty of explorer-traders, led by two brothers, pushed deep into the heart of the continent to establish trade with the Indians, while simultaneously charting its waterways, mountain ranges, and human geography. The Vérendryes were superior explorers among the Europeans and established Fort Maurepas on the southern tip of Lake Winnipeg. Yet they, too, were soon overwhelmed by the complexity of Indigenous politics. When they sought trade relations with the powerful Cree Confederacy, Onontio's old allies—Dakotas and Lakotas—were taken aback. Both nations had enjoyed a privileged position in French trade since the late seventeenth century, and the Vérendryes' maneuverings threatened that position. The Indians killed Jean-Baptiste Vérendrye and twenty of his compatriots in an attack aimed at preserving their privileged status in French trade and diplomacy. They decapitated the bodies, wrapped the severed heads in beaver skins, and arranged the corpses in a circle. It was a warning; they were communicating through violence.[7]

The Vérendrye catastrophe in the deep continental interior was revealing. In 1732, when the thirteenth colony, Georgia, was added to

British America, most of the western part of the continent remained unknown to Europeans. It was still an article of faith to many Europeans that much of the western interior was covered by a "Sea of the West," offering an extraordinary shortcut to China and its markets. Four-fifths of the continent remained under Indigenous control—a striking display of Native American resilience and power. Indians had held the colonists at bay through diplomacy, war, and sheer numbers. Recurring disease outbreaks had ravaged their communities, but Native Americans still outnumbered the roughly seven hundred thousand English, French, and Spanish Americans. The French had given up on western exploration and their dream of a continental empire.[8]

Through diplomatic and commercial reach, intimate knowledge of the terrain, and military power, the largest Indigenous nations and confederacies had played a key role in curbing European expansion. They confronted colonialism on their own terms. Other Native nations coped by making themselves small. In the lower Mississippi Valley, remnants of disintegrated Indigenous societies gathered together to form what the French called *petites nations*, small polities whose numbers ranged from fifty people to a few hundred. By the 1720s, there were nearly forty groups around Biloxi, Mobile, New Orleans, and other French settlements. Politically nimble and mobile, the petites nations forged extensive diplomatic, commercial, and military networks with one another, with the French, and with the powerful Indigenous confederacies. Where Choctaws, Chickasaws, and Natchez thrust themselves into the very center of midcontinent geopolitics, the petites nations did the opposite: they remained neutral, keeping their options open, capturing runaway slaves for rewards, raiding captives, and forcing boundaries. They survived into the tumultuous 1760s, when the British and the Spanish moved to build defensive alliances with Native Americans, including these small nations. After a half century of struggle, the petites nations began to recover, and their populations began to grow.[9]

Becoming small functioned as a camouflage, enabling Native Americans to hide in plain sight. Mobility served the same purpose. Tethered to villages, cities, plantations, fields, and harbors, the colonists struggled to cope with itinerant people whose very way of being was the antithesis of the spatial fixity of colonial rule. Many Native Americans relied on mobility as a survival strategy, but no other nation committed to a kinetic existence as completely as the Shawnees. Having descended from the Upper World above the Sky to the center of the Earth, the ancestors of the Shawnee people launched a series of epic migrations, which took them in different directions and across rivers and huge bodies of water. Meteelemelakwe, the Creator, came to them and told them they should be called *Shāūwonoa*. They were organized into five divisions—Chalaakaathas, Mekoches, Pekowis, Kishpokos, and Thawikilas—which had coalesced during the fifteenth century into a confederacy in the middle Ohio Valley, one of North America's great hubs where people, goods, and civilizations came together. The increased rainfall and agricultural productivity brought by the Little Ice Age encouraged the concentration of people and power to protect prime farming lands. The name Shawnee became fixed in the late seventeenth century. By then, corn had been one of their staples for ages.[10]

Over decades, the Shawnees had escaped the Five Nations by retreating west into the Great Lakes region and dispersing across a vast area. In 1686, La Salle, searching for the ever-elusive mouth of the Mississippi, had encountered three Shawnee captives among the French in Kaskaskia. He caught a glimpse of the kinds of calculations the Shawnees had to make when leaving old lives behind. La Salle offered to pay the ransom to free them, but they declined. They said they had married and "were not unnatural enough to abandon their wives and children." They now lived "in the most fertile, healthy and peaceful country in the world," and it "would be devoid of sense to leave it and expose themselves to be tomahawked by the Illinois or burnt by the Iroquois." By the early eighteenth century there were Shawnees in the mid-Atlantic, in the Illinois Valley near the newly established Fort Saint Louis, and deep in the south near Spanish Florida. They had become a diasporic people.[11]

Many Europeans believed that the Shawnees had withdrawn from all things colonial to save themselves. They were wrong. The Shawnees had redefined the relationship, opting for more selective and fleeting interactions that they could control. Instead of retreating, they moved closer to colonists to trade and forge alliances with them. The Shawnee Confederacy shifted shape, loosening at its seams and becoming suppler in the process. Like the Iroquois and Caddos, the Shawnees built settlements quickly, only to abandon them for new strategic possibilities. Such maneuvering made them almost impossible to control. The Shawnees had become even more decentralized and mobile, but it did not mean that they were a failed nation. The more institutionalized elements of their confederacy may have dissolved, but deep ties of kinship through clans kept the people on a common plane. Clan divisions made the allocation of duties clear. The Thawikilas and Chalaakaathas provided sachems, the Pekowis appointed the head of soldiers, the Kishpokos oversaw the conduct of war, and the Mekoches nurtured Shawnee cohesion. A headless confederacy built on mobility, the Shawnees surprised, outmaneuvered, and eluded the colonists over and over. Their confederacy may have had no more than two thousand people.[12]

The Shawnees reimagined their relationship with the land, adopting a flexible attachment to place, but they were not rudderless. In all their new destinations, they reached out to locals, creating new political, economic, and spiritual attachments. Patiently, one encounter at a time, they built an expansive web of kinship that covered much of the Southeast—their version of the middle ground. They turned safe havens into homelands by re-creating their old political order of villages and clan networks, often in miniature form, with new partners. The Pekowis, having settled in the lower Susquehanna Valley, entered into alliances with the Lenapes, Piscataways, and Susquehannocks that confronted Pennsylvania and Maryland as a single body. More precariously, the Pekowi sachem Opessa approached the Iroquois, who had extended their hunting operations to the Susquehanna Valley in the south. He joined the Senecas to negotiate peace with Pennsylvania in 1710. The English, struggling with Indigenous idioms, reported that the Shawnee "king" joined a Seneca "king" in handing out wampum belts, demanding the "liberty to visit their neighbors" and freedom of movement "without fear of death or slavery." Many Shawnees settled at the fall line, the divide that marked the point where the coastal plains met the Piedmont and that separated Spanish and English colonists. It was a position of great power. In 1710, Opessa met with Pennsylvania governor Charles Gookin about reported killings of English colonists. Gookin demanded that the offenders be executed, only to back off, opting to show mercy. Fluent in Indigenous-colonial discourse that revolved around carefully balanced mutual compromises, Opessa assured the English that "if hereafter any such thing should happen, he himself would be the Executioner, and Burn them that should dare to Do it." Appeasing the colonists while reasserting Shawnee sovereignty and his personal power in the face of English law, Opessa defused the situation with a few carefully chosen words. John Lawson, the surveyor-general of North Carolina, praised the Shawnees as a "famous, warlike, friendly Nation of *Indians*." Like many Native peoples in the South, Opessa and the Pekowis resisted racial reclassification as "colored," which would have marginalized them.[13]

While Opessa's Pekowis relied on words and diplomacy, other Shawnee groups joined with the Munsees, Tallapoosas, and Alabamas to thwart colonial expansion in the Southeast. The task demanded both assertiveness and sensitively calibrated diplomacy because most of their places of refuge were entangled in chronic wars. Much of the Southeast below the Savannah and Tallapoosa Rivers had become an unstable world where English mercenaries raided for Indian slaves, fueling violence, destruction, and hatred. The Shawnees maneuvered shrewdly through the deadly shatter zone, shifting from one safe spot to another and using the rivers to reach markets, allies, and shelter. They had to be nearly constantly in motion to survive, because the bordering colonies were growing fast and recalibrating their ambitions.

IN THE EARLY EIGHTEENTH CENTURY, Pennsylvania, New York, and Virginia embraced the Five Nations as preferred allies, siding with the dominant power in the interior, and leaving the smaller nations exposed. In 1720, a Susquehannock sachem faced the governor of Pennsylvania, reminding him of Penn's vision of coexistence: "William Penn made a League with them to last for three or four Generations. . . . he is now dead, and most of their ancients are also dead, but the League still remains." The sachem wanted to renew the league "with their friend, who has always represented William Penn to them since he left them." But Pennsylvania had already adopted commercial agriculture and was becoming increasingly intolerant of the Indigenous presence on its borders. The colony's population swelled to forty-nine thousand, and the Shawnees were swept into a colonial vortex where squatters, coerced land sales, treaty violations, and removals were normal. The Pennsylvanians argued that the Shawnees had never held territorial rights; they were mere visitors who had now overstayed their welcome.

Two years later, the Tuscaroras drew their own conclusions from the situation. They "abandoned their Castles" and sought shelter under the Great League of Peace and Power. The Five Nations took them in "as our Children who shall obey our commands," and together they became the Six Nations. The expansion of the confederacy sent the colonists into a panic. The New York commissioners for Indian affairs issued a warning that the Iroquois "are the balance of the continent of America, who if the French bring over to their interest will prove the ruin of many thousand families." It would be "the ruin and destruction of the greatest part of this continent," they said.[14]

To bring clarity to the treacherous situation, in 1722 the governors of Pennsylvania, New York, and Virginia invited Iroquois sachems to Albany to hear the colonists' new vision for a reconstructed East. The governors wanted to remove all Indians south of the Potomac to west of the Appalachians, and they asked the Iroquois to execute the scheme, which amounted to ethnic cleansing. Spotting an opening, Mahican envoys rooted the arrangement in Indigenous politics. "We now renewed and brightened the Covenant Chain," the sachems announced, "but since a Chain is apt to rust, if it be not oiled or greased we will grease it with Beavers grease or Fat [and] the smell thereof will endure for a whole year." The resulting treaty did not include a word on Shawnee rights; they were too small to matter in the new era of intensifying imperialism in North America. Only the Six Nations possessed the kind of presence that won the respect of English authorities. Almost as an afterthought, the governors demanded that the Six Nations "would never molest Virginia nor any other of the Kings Provinces." By 1730, most of the Shawnees had moved back to the Ohio Country, joining other migrants, including Lenapes, Wyandots, and Miamis. The Shawnees came to specialize in face-to-face borderland trading, operating on the margins of larger nations, and they prospered. Native women's technological expertise had made the region a flourishing agrarian realm. There were also great quantities of wild berries and fruit, ensuring balanced diets.[15]

THE SHAWNEES EMBODIED the strategies and accommodations that smaller nations had to accept in North America when the pace of colonial expansion began to pick up. They relied on mobility not only to make themselves seem more powerful than they actually were, but also to make themselves undetectable. Looking back in 1755, Edmond Atkin, the superintendent of Indian affairs, dubbed the Shawnees, not without admiration, as "Stout, Bold, Cunning and the greatest Travellers in America." These adaptable people, he reported, "lived heretofore on the River Savanoe [Savannah]" before moving west with the Lower Muscogees during the Yamasee War, a conflict between South Carolina and the Yamasee Nation, after which they "withdrew to the Mississippi. . . . From thence it was not known for many Years where they were gone." In 1744, some of the Shawnees returned and "settled in a Town by themselves." They were a piece of a larger pattern. In the aftermath of the devastating 1696 smallpox epidemic, much of the Southeast had become a world of small polities. As colonial rivalries intensified, evasion and dispersal became essential survival strategies across the eastern half of the continent.[16]

In northwestern Florida the Apalachees, the once formidable Mississippian nation of tens of thousands of members, had been struck hard by English and Muscogee slave raiders and outbreaks of disease, suffering an appalling demise. By 1704, most Apalachees were clustered in small towns next to Spanish missions in the Florida panhandle, but their world was all but destroyed in a two-year torrent of slave raids and epidemics: uncounted numbers of Apalachees succumbed to diseases, and between two and four thousand were captured and sold into slavery. The survivors scattered, fleeing to Spanish Pensacola and the Spanish mission San Agustín. One contingent of some four hundred Apalachees walked three hundred miles to French Mobile, where they came upon several petite nations. Like these small groups, the multilingual Apalachees won French trust by offering their labor, military support, and expertise in Indigenous politics. They studied French customs from gender roles to religion, and adopted what they thought was necessary. They endured by blending in.[17]

The Catawba Confederacy in the southern Piedmont, too, relied on a range of strategies to fend off colonial intrusions, asserting territorial sovereignty through maps and words. As colonial pressure increased in the early eighteenth century, the Catawbas broadened their tactical repertoire, relying more and more on difficult terrain as a bulwark against colonial intrusions. English colonists were anchored to their plantations, farms, harbors, and rivers, which fulfilled their material needs and cultural ambitions. They were lowland agrarian people comfortable only on flat land and were unwilling to move vertically; they struggled with hills and mountains. Mountains functioned as natural filters that separated the aggressive and unwelcome colonists from the generally welcome traders who respected Indigenous customs. Higher elevations also hindered the spread of infectious diseases, helping the Catawbas to stay safe.[18]

The Catawbas became collectors of people. Elevation and rough terrain could protect them only to a point. Slave-raiding and land greed had turned much of the Southeast into a battleground, threatening to overwhelm the Catawbas in their up-country sanctuary. Over time they incorporated many refugee groups—Cheraws, Esaws, Peedees, Sugarees, Waterees, and others—into their confederacy as tributary allies, offering them restored power, safety, trade, and normalcy. European visitors could sometimes catch more than twenty Native languages spoken among the Catawbas, and John Lawson, described the Catawbas as a "great" and "very large nation, containing many thousand people." It was a gross overestimation, but his error captured how powerful the Catawbas appeared in a world destabilized by disease and war. In 1715 the Catawbas defeated their most persistent enemies, the Waxhaws, while also fending off Iroquois armies traveling along the nearby Great Trading Path, the gateway to the Atlantic Southeast. In the 1730s, when colonial expansion accelerated across the East, the Catawbas were comparatively secure.[19]

Like the Catawbas, the Lumbees found safety and sovereignty in the rolling hills and high altitudes of the Piedmont. Originally a coastal people living on Roanoke Island and along the swampy lands around the Lumber River, the Lumbees had withstood colonial encroachments from the sixteenth century onward. Unlike the Catawbas, however, the Lumbees relied on sheer numbers, welcoming scores of English newcomers into their family and kinship. Beginning in the 1660s, the Lumbees had faced growing colonial pressure, brought by wars, enslavement, and dispossession. They sought sanctuary in swamps, hard terrain, and the Appalachian foothills, where colonial tentacles could not reach them. In the early eighteenth century, Scottish Highland refugees built settlements near Lumbee country, and the two groups formed an expedient alliance. The Scottish were astounded to find English-speaking Indigenous people living in small houses surrounded by farms. The Lumbees had subsumed English words, foods, ideas, beliefs, and technologies into their lives while remaining distinctly Indigenous.[20]

In the early eighteenth century, Virginians pushed aggressively into the Piedmont along the Rappahannock, James, South Anna, Nottaway, and Roanoke Rivers, forcing resident Indians to flee west. The refugees blended into the Catawba social fabric through marriages and fictive kinship ties. Orbiting around tightly clustered Catawba towns, the two groups kept their distance from each other. They built their towns a day's walk apart—close enough for effective cooperation and dispersed enough to avoid drawing colonial aggression. There was no obvious center to attack and conquer—just a collection of towns that seemed to pose no threat to English ambitions. By making themselves inconspicuous, the Catawbas and their allies endured in the Piedmont. They could not stop the colonial advance, but they could slow it down.

In the late 1710s, Virginians demanded that Catawba leaders send them a number of children to be educated in their schools. Betraying their uneasiness about the indomitable nation, the colonists used the children as hostages to negotiate peace. English settlement of the Carolina uplands did not begin until the start of the 1720s, just as the Natchez, Chickasaws, and Choctaws were punishing Louisiana for its transgressions. Even as colonial holdings were expanding across the eastern half of the continent, the European empires were facing fierce resistance in their borderlands.[21]

PART SIX

THE HEART
OF THE
CONTINENT

(mid- and late eighteenth century)

Chapter 18

MAGIC
DOGS

THE CREATURE HAD MANY NAMES, EACH REVEALING the awe it elicited among the people who encountered it. For the Lakotas it was *šúŋka wakȟáŋ*, sacred dog; for the Blackfoot, elk dog; for the Comanches, magic dog; for the Assiniboines, great dog; and for the Sarcees, seven dogs. The arrival of the horse was a galvanizing moment for numerous Indigenous peoples in the North American West, and a turning point for the continent as a whole. Comparisons to the dog, the Native Americans' first domesticated animal, captured the scope of the transformation.

In the aftermath of the Great Southwestern Rebellion, the horse frontier moved rapidly outward from New Mexico along the ancient Indigenous trade routes that webbed the Colorado Plateau, the Rocky Mountains, and the Great Plains. A Rocky Mountain trade chain had carried horses to the northwestern plains by the 1730s, moving them across several climatic belts, which required careful modifications in the ways of tending, feeding, and using the animals. East-to-west spread was even faster, posing fewer climatic challenges. The Sicangu Lakotas had received their first horses from Omaha Indian traders already in 1708.[1]

The modern horse, *Equus ferus caballus*, had returned to its birthplace after nearly a million years of absence, and its arrival triggered a revolution. Wherever horses became available, they spawned profound economic, military, and political changes. The Blackfoot had lived in the northwestern corner of the Great Plains for a thousand years and had developed deep attachments to the land and to countless cultural traditions, from tools and weapons to prayers and deities.

They lived in the shelter of the Backbone of the World, a series of mountains that Náápi, "Old Man," had created for them. Yet horses upended Blackfoot life. Saahkómaapi, an elderly Cree Indian who lived among the Piikanis, one of the three Blackfoot groups, remembered vividly how the arrival of horses changed the Blackfoot world forever. Before horses, the Blackfoot had been exposed to enemy attacks. "The Peegans [Piikanis] were always the frontier Tribe," Saahkómaapi recounted, "upon whom the Snake Indians [the Shoshones to the south] made their attacks." Around 1730, approximately 350 Piikani soldiers moved to punish the Shoshones. "By this time the affairs of both parties had much changed," Saahkómaapi related. "We had more guns and iron headed arrows than before; but our enemies the Snake Indians and their allies had Misstutim (Big Dogs, that is Horses), on which they rode, swift as the Deer, on which they dashed the Peegans, and with stone Pukamoggan [a club with knobbed head] knocked them on the head, and they had thus lost several of their best men. This news we did not well comprehend and it alarmed us, for we had no idea of Horses and could not make out what they were."[2]

They set off to find out. "We pitched away in large camps with the women and children on the frontier of the Snake Indian country," Saahkómaapi remembered, "hunting the Bison and Red Deer which were numerous, and we were anxious to see a horse of which we had heard so much." Finding the mounted Shoshones proved difficult for the pedestrian Blackfoot, but finally, "as the leaves were falling," they heard of a horse that "was killed by an arrow shot into his belly." The Blackfoot gathered around the dead animal, trying to make sense of the extraordinary encounter: "We all admired him, he put us in mind of a Stag that had lost his horns; and we did not know what name to give him. But as he was a slave to Man, like the dog, which carried our things; he was named the Big Dog." The geopolitics of the northern plains had shifted drastically and irrevocably: an Indigenous arms race had begun. "The terror of that battle and of our guns has prevented any more general battles," Saahkómaapi said, "and our wars have since been carried by ambuscade and surprise, of small camps."[3]

Horses brought a revolution. Not since the spread of corn across the continent had Native Americans experienced such an increase in power. Equestrian nomads could do almost everything—move, hunt, trade, fight, kill, evade, and protect themselves—faster and more efficiently. There was the time before horses, and there was the time after them. The Blackfoot became more mobile, more powerful, more ambitious, and, potentially, more vulnerable: a single mounted attack could exact far more damage than the on-foot war parties of old. Native peoples had entered a new technological age from which they benefited, but from which there was also no escape.[4]

Horses also overturned the power dynamics between the nomadic Indigenous nations and European colonists in the West. At its most basic level, this shift was a matter of harnessing energy. Dogs, Native Americans' only domesticates before horses, were omnivorous and could use the West's greatest resource—grass—only indirectly. They relied on their masters to provide them with the flesh of herbivorous animals, whereas horses, with their large and finely tuned intestines, could process vast quantities of cellulose-rich grass. The horse was a bigger and stronger dog, but, more profoundly, it was an energy converter. By transforming inaccessible plant energy into tangible and immediately available muscle power, horses opened up an astonishing shortcut to the sun, the source of all energy on Earth. For the Comanches the sun was "the primary cause of all living things," and horses brought them closer to it, redefining what was possible: the biomass of the continental grasslands may have been a thousand times greater than that of the region's animals. The Comanches plugged themselves into a seemingly inexhaustible energy stream of grass, flesh, and sunlight.[5]

It took time to build substantial herds—the would-be equestrians had to learn how to use the animals and how to train, breed, and protect the precious creatures—but once they did, the world appeared dramatically different. Distances became shorter, hunting became easier, trading became more lucrative, and inflicting harm on enemies became more efficient. The nations that mastered equestrianism the quickest would enjoy enormous advantages over others.

Having shifted westward over generations, the Blackfoot occupied in the early eighteenth century a large territory near the eastern base of the Rocky Mountains, between the upper North Saskatchewan and

Missouri Rivers. Although they lived deep in the northwestern plains, where cold winters were taxing for horses, the Blackfoot forged a flourishing equestrian regime, capitalizing on two more auspicious features of the local ecological boons: their domain was in the chinook belt, where warm, dry winds descended the eastern slopes of the Rockies and where they had access to the Marias River, whose steep banks sheltered their horses during the harsh winters. An average Piikani family owned ten horses, enough for effective equestrian hunting, transportation, and warfare. The Blackfoot now occupied a place of vast advantage.

They also faced far too many rivals and enemies: Shoshones, Crows, Flatheads, and Pend d'Oreilles—all mounted now and determined to pilfer the growing Piikani horse herds. Raids, retaliations, retreats, and expansions settled into a brutal and draining cycle. To break free from it, the Blackfoot made a concerted effort to win access to European weaponry—iron knives, iron arrowheads, iron axes, and guns. Far removed from the westernmost colonial markets along the Mississippi Valley, in the Great Lakes, and in New Mexico, they worked through Indigenous traders. The Crees and Assiniboines specialized in long-distance middleman trading, moving guns and goods westward from the English trading posts at Hudson Bay—in 1713 the Treaty of Utrecht had assigned the lands around the bay to Britain—and from the French traders in the pays d'en haut. In the 1730s, French traders themselves arrived in the far West and constructed forts in the Assiniboine and Saskatchewan Valleys. Their wares, especially guns, gave the Blackfoot a stunning military and psychological advantage over their enemies, who now had to face lead with stone and flesh. The Blackfoot called the French "Real Old Man People." The world was wide open.[6]

While the Blackfoot were acquiring and becoming proficient with horses and guns in the northern Great Plains, the newly mounted Lakotas were staging hunting expeditions deep into the western grasslands. Geography itself seemed to invite them in: a series of north-to-south-flowing rivers—which would later become known as the Des Moines, Little Sioux, Floyd, Big Sioux, Red River of the North, Sheyenne, James, and Missouri—enabled them to carve out an enormous hunting range one valley at a time.

Bison herds were more massive as the Lakotas pushed farther west, and they could purchase and steal horses from Native nations that had already built substantial herds. Unlike the Blackfoot, the Lakotas were newcomers from the East, and they had to force their way to the West and its bison, horses, and grassland that sustained the animal bounty. By the early eighteenth century, the Lakotas had fought Otoes, Omahas, Poncas, and Iowas over the control of the valleys, forcing all of them to retreat. The Lakotas had expanded the dominion of the Očhéthi Šakówiŋ, the Seven Council Fires, nearly two hundred miles to the west. It was North America's first sustained westward expansion beyond the Appalachian Mountains. They were only a few steps away from the Missouri River, one of the continent's greatest transportation and trade arteries.

The Missouri Valley, however—especially its fertile middle section—was already occupied by Pawnees, Otoes, Omahas, Poncas, Iowas, Arikaras, Hidatsas, and Mandans, many of them jammed together in the area by the early stages of Lakota expansion. Some fifty thousand people dwelled in the valley, combining hunting with agriculture, raising crops of corn, squash, and beans, their fields and villages dominating the banks of the river for hundreds of miles. The Missouri was home to the greatest concentration of humans and wealth in the heart of the continent, and it exerted an irresistible pull on the Lakotas, who, over generations, had moved away from the agricultural centers in the Great Lakes and along the Mississippi. As a result, they now faced dangerously limited diets that exposed them to protein poisoning, a metabolic condition caused by oversupply of protein and undersupply of carbohydrates and fats.

The Missouri Valley nations viewed the Lakotas as aggressive invaders and strangers and tried to keep them out. Lakota winter counts, *waníyetu iyáwapi*—pictographic calendars that mark each year with a single event—depict attacks by Indians who had more horses, more guns, and more allies. The early-eighteenth-century winter counts of the Sicangu Lakotas were a catalog of clashes, small and large, with the Missouri Valley nations. An enemy they could not identify attacked them on horseback—possibly the first mounted assault they faced. "Came and attacked on horseback and stabbed a boy near the lodge," reads one account, showing an enemy soldier, again unidentified, on a rising horse, holding a gouged child in midair. The Lakotas found themselves in limbo, unable to retreat or advance. They had to fight their way in. It took years, but by the 1760s they had carved out a foothold along the Missouri by forming an expedient alliance with the Arikara Nation. Emulating their hosts, the Lakotas began to raise crops.[7]

THE LAKOTAS WOULD BECOME famous as a horse nation, but it would be another nation, far to the west, that would fully capitalize on the potential of the horse. A group of Uto-Aztecan-speaking people had slowly moved from the Great Basin to the southern plains in the sixteenth and seventeenth centuries. They represented the last wave of Uto-Aztecan migrants from the north; their predecessors had traveled hundreds of miles south, all the way into the central Valley of Mexico, where they built the vast Aztec Empire. These later migrants stopped moving earlier than the proto-Aztecs did. They separated from their parent group, the Shoshones, who moved north and settled in the southern plains, where they connected with the northward-inching horse frontier.[8]

Around 1700, this splinter group clashed with the Utes, another group of Uto-Aztecan equestrian people. The Utes controlled a large domain west of New Mexico, and they frequently raided the colony for horses and captives. The Utes called the newcomers *kumantsi*, "anyone who wants to fight me all the time," capturing the ambiguity that existed between two people of common ancestry who had been separated for generations. Recognizing their commonalities and overlapping political interests, the Utes and kumantsi—Comanches—entered into an alliance. The Utes shared their land, horses, and guns with the Comanches, ushering them into a new technological era. Within a decade, the allies were attacking New Mexico to seize more horses and captives. It was North America's first Indigenous alliance of two horse peoples, and it was conceived to contain and exploit a Spanish colony. In 1719, a distressed Spanish official demanded that "war should be made upon the Ute nation and Comanche nations, who, always united, have been committing robberies of horse herds in the name of peace."[9]

The Indigenous inhabitants of the Southwest posed a far more formidable challenge to the alliance than Spanish colonists did. The Apache nations—Lipans, Faroans, Jicarillas, Mescaleros, Carlanas, Chiricahuas Cuartelejos, Palomas, Salineros, Mimbreños, and Sierra Blancas—commanded much of the southern grasslands, having absorbed the Jumano hunter-traders into their ranks by 1715. Like the Utes and Comanches, the Apaches had built substantial horse herds, but unlike their nomadic rivals, they had also taken up systematic farming, constructing extensive irrigation works along streambeds. Apache mud houses and fields of corn, beans, squash, and pumpkins now lined the major river valleys of the southern plains. Apachería covered the most precious parts of the continental grasslands, which set the Apaches on a collision course with the Comanche-Ute alliance.

Both coalitions needed the rich soil of the river valleys for their crops, and both needed access to the region's firewood, high-calorie riparian tallgrasses, low-saline water, and shelter against freezing winter winds and snowstorms. The river valleys were the cradles of human existence in the Great Plains; humans and horses could not survive anywhere else. The Comanche-Ute alliance went to war over those river valleys, forcing their way south one valley at a time: the Arkansas, Red, Brazos, and, eventually, Canadian. The adversaries also clashed over access to New Mexico's markets, the only reliable source of guns, metal tools, and horses in the Southwest. In the end, long-range mobility, strategic flexibility, and political unity saw the Comanches and Utes through. They concentrated overwhelming force against the Apaches, shunting them to the south and west. They then attacked New Mexico, punishing the colonists for siding with the Apaches.[10]

The Comanche-Ute coalition began to mold New Mexico's northern borderlands to meet its needs. The big industry in the Southwest was the slave trade. Since the Great Southwestern Rebellion in 1680, Spanish officials had upheld the strict restrictions around slavery that protected Pueblo rights: many Pueblos had converted to Christianity, which made their enslavement illegal. To defend their authority in a province where they were a minority group, the Spanish colonists relied on *indios bárbaros*, "savage Indians," to deliver captives, and they disguised this slave traffic as *rescate*, "ransom," which entailed the idea that captured indios bárbaros could be purchased from other indios bárbaros to bring the former into the Christian fold. The slave trade became indispensable to New Mexico, and the colony exported slaves to the mining camps in Nueva Vizcaya, Coahuila, and Zacatecas, and to the tobacco plantations in Cuba. The Utes and Comanches spotted an opportunity. Before long, their mounted war parties ranged across a broadening area, raiding Jicarilla Apaches, Navajos, and Pawnees for captives. Apache women, the main targets of the slave raids, became the focal point of the Ute, Comanche, and Spanish conflict. At stake was masculine honor, the prestige of the Spanish Empire, the integrity of families and kinship networks, and, most directly, the lives of the Apache women themselves.[11]

The year 1719 was pivotal. One Spanish official complained that the Utes and Comanches "go about together for the purpose of interfering with the little barter which this kingdom has with the nations which come in to ransom. They prevent their entrance and communication with us." The Comanche-Ute alliance had New Mexico in a stranglehold, pressuring the Spanish to grant the two nations a privileged position in their markets. Another kind of report came from a Spanish missionary stationed at Geronimo de Los Taos, a frontier mission "so close to heathenism, that, as is commonly said, we are shoulder to shoulder." The Jicarillas had arrived to "ask for holy baptism." Desperate for a lifeline, they had made the Spanish colonists an irresistible offer: a Christian alliance against vicious infidels.[12]

In the fall, Antonio Valverde y Cosío, the governor of New Mexico, led six hundred Spanish troops and Pueblo auxiliaries to demolish the Comanche-Ute alliance for "the murders and robberies they have inflicted on this kingdom with their hostile invasions." Their destination was El Cuartelejo, the renowned Apache stronghold near the Arkansas Valley. As the army approached, it entered a wasteland of burned villages and cornfields; Utes and Comanches had already sacked the fort, forcing the Apaches to flee. An Apache leader warned the governor about the rapidly shifting power dynamics: "If they [the Spanish] continued to follow the said enemy they clearly risked losing all the horses, which were the chief means of defense of the kingdom." Valverde turned back and feebly announced that the Apaches "enjoyed the protection of our King and Lord" because their land "belong only to His Majesty our King and Lord Philip V."[13]

Making matters worse, the Spanish learned that the French were building a colony at La Jicarilla in the Platte Valley among the Pawnees. The French sent a message to the Spanish calling them women, in an attempt to provoke them to come out and fight. The next summer, the Spanish did exactly that and suffered a humiliating defeat: thirty-two Spanish soldiers, one-third of the strength of the Santa Fe garrison, perished, along with at least a dozen Pueblo auxiliaries—a crippling blow to Spanish ambitions in the continental interior. The Pawnee and Otoe allies of the French had done most of the fighting and killing, contributing more than the French to stopping Spain's northward expansion.[14]

The chastised Spanish adopted an increasingly defensive stance, walling themselves in in New Mexico. In 1724, Colonel Pedro de Rivera, a crown inspector who had been sent to examine the conditions of Spain's frontier garrisons in North America, recommended that the colonists should rather "conserve that which is acquired, to enjoy the fruit which has been cut, than to augment the dominions without any hope." It was at once a clear-eyed appraisal of the prevailing power relations and a massive miscalculation. The Comanches, now the leading partner of the Comanche-Ute alliance, had stolen and bred enough horses to be able to put all their people on horseback. They now hunted bison solely on horseback, riding alongside the massive, fleeing beasts and shooting them down with arrows. The Comanche Nation experienced explosive growth in wealth and ambition. A small band of hunters could deliver three hundred animals in an hour, and Comanche women became experts at curing robes and meat and at preparing pemmican—a mixture of dried bison meat, berries, and melted fat—on a vast scale.[15]

The Comanches had become uncontainable; Spain's window to suppress them had closed. The Spanish colonists turned inward, huddling behind their walls and detaching themselves from Indigenous politics in the plains. The Apaches, deprived of what little support they had received from the Spanish, abandoned the southern plains and moved farther west and south. By the 1730s, Apachería stretched from the Zuni, O'odham, and Yavapai territories all the way south into the Sierra Madres of Nueva Vizcaya and Sonora. The old Apachería became Comanchería. The Comanches now loomed large over New Mexico, monitoring it, controlling it, dwarfing it.[16]

ALL ACROSS THE CONTINENT, from the Southeast to the Southwest, from the deep interior to the Atlantic and Gulf coasts, colonial ambitions had crashed into Indigenous geographies of power. Whatever Bienville, Law, Oglethorpe, or Valverde believed or needed to believe, nothing in North America was preordained. In the early eighteenth century, the continent was still resolutely Indigenous. The English were confined to the eastern side of the Appalachians; the Spanish boasted numerous missions and forts, but their colonies were little more than glorified bridgeheads; and French colonialism remained effectively confined to the Saint Lawrence Valley and to a few weak positions in the lower Mississippi Valley.

Fundamentally, it was a matter of distance and geography. North America had become divided in two: there was the narrow and patchy colonial belt on the coastal plains, where Europeans dominated, and there was the immense Indigenous interior, where Native territories extended deep into what, to Europeans, was a great unknown. The two Americas were almost complete opposites. In the interior, the Columbian Exchange often worked to the Indians' advantage. Deadly germs were brought inland by European traders, but their impact remained limited, whereas new military technology—guns, powder, metal, and horses—became available through colonial border markets and extensive Indigenous trade networks. In a transitional belt where the Indians were neither too close to European colonies to fall under their epidemiological shadow nor too far away to reap the benefits of their commerce, several geographically privileged Indigenous regimes rose to challenge colonial expansion on their own terms. This emerging belt was where great fortunes could be amassed, and where empires were won and lost.[17]

Chapter 19

WARS TO THE END
OF THE WORLD

THE LENAPES WERE NONPLUSSED, THEN DISGUSTED
and dejected. In August 1735, the government of the Pennsylvania Colony announced stunning news: it had found a document from 1686 in which the Lenape Nation, Pennsylvania's staunchest Native ally, ceded a tract of land between the Delaware and Lehigh Valleys to the colony. The Penns—three sons of William who had inherited, one after another, his proprietorship—claimed that the scrap of paper was a deed, but the Lenape sachem Teedyuscung challenged Pennsylvania's claim to the Delaware Valley, arguing that his people had never received a payment for the 1686 land cession and thus the deed had been voided. As Pennsylvania officials chose to understand the affair, the Lenapes had agreed to give up an area extending as far as a man could walk in one and a half days—roughly forty miles. The document was debated inconclusively until Pennsylvania entered into an alliance with the Six Nations. Impressed by how completely the Iroquois controlled the Native peoples around them, the Penns felt confident in demanding that the Lenapes yield to the forty-mile limit. In the spring of 1737, two Lenape sachems—Tishcohan and Lappawinzo—assented to the walk to determine the boundaries of the area ceded to Pennsylvania.

For Pennsylvania, however, forty miles was no longer enough. The geopolitical climate had shifted, becoming even more cutthroat since Metacom's War, as English settlers kept encroaching on Indigenous domains to the west. Thomas Penn, the current proprietor of the colony, hired three expert walkers, one of whom covered more than sixty miles—running, not walking—along a meticulously cleared path, robbing the Lenapes of twelve hundred square miles of land. The Lenapes were appalled, and Teedyuscung denounced the whole affair as a fraud. Disquieted, the Penns reached out to their Iroquois allies, asking them to intervene. The Six Nations quickly enforced the land sale—a reassertion of their own authority over the smaller Native nations in the region—which in turn gave them leverage in their dealings with the English. The Iroquois were not the Penns' supplicants. When charged by the Pennsylvanians for food, the Indians were deeply insulted.[1]

Pennsylvania's infamous "Walking Purchase" marked a turning point in the history of the Indigenous continent. In the mid-eighteenth century, English colonists began to dispossess Indians more methodically. Indigenous borders, sovereignty, and lives were under unprecedented attack in the East. Buoyed by a booming economy and an influx of German, Swiss, Scottish, and Irish immigrants, southeastern Pennsylvania had seventy-three thousand European inhabitants in 1740. Philadelphia alone had become a city of ten thousand. Land—its ownership, use, division, and loss—was now a burning issue. Such established institutions as the "At the Woods' Edge Ceremony" became marginalized, and shared borderlands became contested grounds.[2]

FROM THE EARLIEST CONTACTS between Native Americans and Europeans, the Appalachian Mountains had been a great divider, stretching for fifteen hundred miles from Newfoundland into the South. The people living on the opposite sides of the variously majestic and rugged mountain range had few interactions, and there was no nation, confederacy, colony, or empire that could credibly claim to control territory on both sides. The Appalachians cut the continent's eastern half into two distinct parts. By the late 1720s, the Appalachians marked a hard border between colonial America and Indigenous America. The thirteen English colonies claimed most of the coastal plains between the Atlantic coast and the Appalachian foothills. A distinct—and, to English eyes, underdeveloped—frontier region, the "backcountry," separated the colonies from the Appala-

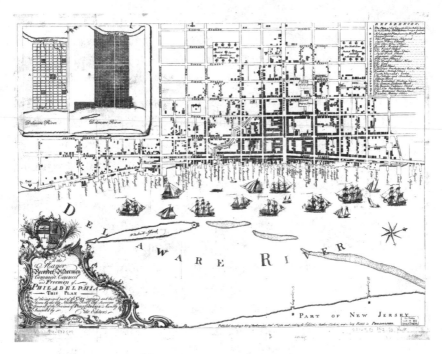

Map of Philadelphia, 1776

chians. The settlers anticipated a quick absorption of the backcountry into the British Empire, but in reality the region marked the fault line beyond which the English had no legitimate standing.

After several generations of interactions with Europeans, variously violent and peaceful, the Six Nations knew how to manage anxious, land-hungry settlers. In 1742, at a large summit in the statehouse in Philadelphia, the Onondaga sachem Canassatego addressed the Lenapes as junior allies, relegating the English to a secondary role. "Cousins: Let this Belt of Wampum serve to Chastise You," he reprimanded the Lenapes in sharply gendered language. "We conquered You, we made Women of you, you know you are Women, and can no more sell Land." Canassatego ordered them to "remove immediately" from ancestral Iroquois lands. The settlers were mere spectators of the Six Nations' power politics. The next year, another summit was held to defuse the mounting tensions between Pennsylvania and the neighboring Indians. The Six Nations envoy Zillawoolie focused on the Catawbas, promising to "persuade and charge them to be of good Behavior everywhere"—something Pennsylvania's timid settlers dared not try. The Iroquois also demanded a right to travel through Virginia as they pleased, and they reasserted their dominance over the Delaware and Ohio Valleys.[3]

Had they been present in Philadelphia, the Catawbas would have denounced the Six Nations' presumption. The Great Trading Path between the Chesapeake Bay and the Piedmont continued to channel English trading parties to Catawba towns, keeping them prosperous and powerful. As ancient residents of the Piedmont, the Catawbas thought they could simply stay put and wait for goods to flow into their towns. In exchange for their precious deerskins and furs, they received guns, powder, lead, metal tools, cloth, blankets, luxuries, and rum. Certain of the strength of their position, they were aloof to the point of becoming arrogant and outright offensive. When the talks resumed in Philadelphia in the summer of 1744, the Catawbas sent a cutting message informing the Iroquois that they "were but Women; that they [themselves] were men and double men for they had two P——s [penises]; that they could make Women of Us, and would be always at War with us."[4]

In an era when pushing the colonists back into the sea was no longer a possibility, the Catawbas kept the settlers in a state of uncertainty: Europeans feared that the Indians might launch a war any day. The colonists' nervousness about the Catawbas set that Indigenous group apart from the Iroquois and their artful diplomacy, and from the Shawnees and the strategic mobility they used to keep the settlers at a distance. The Catawbas knew that eventually they would have to adapt to new circumstances, compromise, and enter into negotiations with the Europeans, but they would hold on to their independence as long as they possibly could. They were determined to preserve Indigenous sovereignty in the face of unprecedented odds and to rebalance Indigenous power on the continent.[5]

Other nations east of the Appalachians adopted a more counterintuitive approach. They relied on accommodation and compromises that required a new mindset: Indians should embrace the colonists—at arm's length—to survive colonialism. When colonial frontiers inched toward them, they would meet the settlers on the borderlands between the two parties. This strategy demanded numbers, political gravitas, and delicate diplomacy. The Muscogee, Cherokee, and Chickasaw leaders in the Appalachian foothills and Trans-Appalachian West pursued this strategy. Tucked between French and English realms, these three Native nations were already fluent in colonial methods when the English began to push their farms and settlements uphill. The Indians left the Europeans alone, playing Louisiana, South Carolina, North Carolina, Virginia, and Pennsylvania off against each other and extracting gifts, weapons, and manufactured goods from all. The Indians were careful not to attach themselves to any single colony. The settlers thought that the Indigenous confederacies— most notably the Six Nations—had divided into pro-French and pro-English factions, but those divisions were more circumstantial than fixed. Operating in a different geopolitical landscape west of the Appalachians, the twenty-thousand-strong Choctaws divided into "Eastern," "Western," and "Sixtown" villages to engage with various colonies more flexibly.[6]

By European standards, the Muscogees, Cherokees, Chickasaws, and Choctaws were dangerously decentralized and their leaders hopelessly weak, but therein lay the genius of their political systems. Most of their leaders commanded small groups, which threw the settlers off-balance: there was no single person for the Europeans to co-opt—just a multitude of seemingly ineffectual potentates who were useless to the settlers' aims. But those leaders knew how to manage European newcomers. Old Hop, a Cherokee elder, told a visiting European that a new supply of red cloth would help him "to appear more like a man." By forcing the Europeans to compete for their trade, the Muscogees, Cherokees, Chickasaws, and Choctaws thrived. In the 1740s, the southern Indians supplied more than a hundred thousand deerskins to South Carolina markets alone, and women routinely grew enough corn for both domestic consumption and colonial markets. Ambitions swelled, and the Muscogees recruited Shawnees to "facilitate the opening a Communication that way with the Ohio and Illinois."

The Choctaw war leader Red Shoes maneuvered boldly in that maze of conflicting interests, rallying his soldiers and using his loyalty as a bargaining chip with French and English governors and merchants, whom he wanted to pull under his influence. Red Shoes was at once a freedom fighter, a go-between, and an opportunist. In 1745 he initiated negotiations—alone—with the Chickasaws and the English. When the French murdered several members of a Chickasaw peace delegation, Red Shoes spotted an opening: his soldiers killed three Frenchmen, shocking the cautious Choctaw civil leaders. Numerous Choctaw soldiers now gravitated toward Red Shoes and his radical alliance-making, which had thrown off-balance both the English and the French. Eventually, Red Shoes went too far, driving himself and the Choctaw Nation into a devastating civil war that left eight hundred of its soldiers dead. Running out of options, the French hired an assassin to kill Red Shoes; that task was accomplished in 1747.

As the Choctaws struggled, the more-than-ten-thousand-strong Muscogee Confederacy emerged as a major power in the Deep South, sending war expeditions into Spanish Florida and absorbing into its ranks Coosas, Cowetas, Yamasees, Shawnees, Alabamas, and people from other weakened nations. The English and French competed for trading privileges through shrewdly placed posts where licensed traders treated the Indians honorably; if they failed to do so, the consequences could be severe. When the French struggled to supply their Native customers, English traders filled the gap, cajoling the Choctaws, who "threw themselves Naked into our Arms, and implored our Relief, Protection and Friendship." Placating Indians with gifts in the intensely competitive environment became so commonplace that many Native leaders did not bother to personally accept the offerings, sending young men in their stead.[7]

IN THE WINTER OF 1751, Charles Langlade, an Odawa-French leader, guided Odawa, Potawatomi, and Ojibwe soldiers in an attack on the Miami town of Pickawillany. They killed thirteen Miamis and seized five English traders. Langlade proposed an exchange of captives, but the Miamis released only three Englishmen. Langlade's men captured the Miami leader Memeskia, and boiled him and ate his heart. The Odawas released the Miami women and approached the

French in Detroit with four captives and a generous supply of trade goods. The attack on Pickawillany dramatically amplified the growing tensions among the British, French, and Native Americans, accelerating the momentum toward the Seven Years' War.[8]

The intensification of colonial ambitions in the mid-eighteenth century was nowhere more evident than in the strategically central Ohio Country, a hot spot that was the continent-wide colonial-Indigenous clash in microcosm. The region offered some of the best farmland in North America, and English settlers saw it as prime real estate—a realm for commercial farming and a land speculators' paradise. For Native Americans, by contrast, the deep interior was a homeland, a hunting domain, and a stronghold against colonial expansion, and they meant to keep it so. Many of them had been displaced twice already, and they intended to stay put. They scrutinized European newcomers not only for signs of diseases but also for attitudes, proper clothing, acceptable hairstyles, and odd proclivities, all of which could broadcast humility, arrogance, or compliance. Irishmen rarely made the cut. Indians traded with the French in both the Ohio and the Illinois Countries, keeping the middle ground viable. The point where the Monongahela, Allegheny, and Ohio Rivers meet, known as the Forks of the Ohio, was a crossroads of long-distance trade networks, and it was clear that Native-European rivalries would blend into the seemingly inevitable war between Britain and France, the world's leading empires, which, for generations, had been contending for global supremacy. These mounting tensions fed directly into the Seven Years' War, the first true world war. The Ohio Country would be at the very center of it, and the violence would not stop when the Seven Years' War did. The half century between 1740 and 1815 was marked by nearly constant fighting, constituting a single transformative era in the continent's history, with Native Americans foiling European hegemonic pretensions time and again.[9]

To the southeast of the Ohio Country was another resolutely Indigenous world, where the Tuscaroras, Yamasees, Cherokees, Muscogees, and Choctaws dominated, having only recently coalesced into powerful confederacies. The Cherokees divided themselves into "Overhill," "Valley," and "Lower" settlements—a tactic that enabled

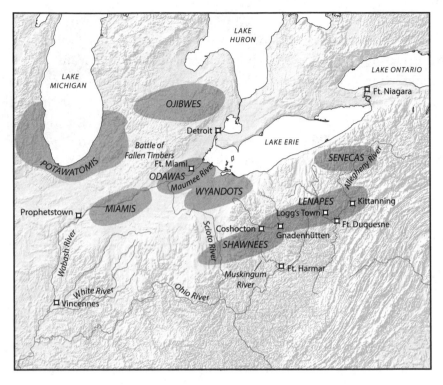

*The Indigenous Ohio Country in
the mid- and late eighteenth century*

them to play different English colonies off against one another, while simultaneously reaching out to the French. The Cherokees chose the wealthy colony of Virginia as their primary trading partner. Indigenous politics had focused for decades on containing the explosively growing English colonies east of the Appalachians—a goal that the Native nations shared with the French. By the mid-eighteenth century, there were 1.2 million English colonists on the continent. As daunting as the English influx was, it could be useful. Native Americans gained access to England's prodigious "empire of goods." The multiethnic Muscogees established trade relations with the Carolinians, securing guns, powder, lead, linen, shirts, axes, kettles, tobacco, jewelry, beads, and other desirables. They specified in detail what kind of goods they would accept and soon emerged as the dominant economic and military power in the region. For their part, the formidable Six Nations claimed the Ohio Country by the right of conquest and

*Unable to defeat Native nations in battle, colonial topographic surveys
and maps became a means to seize Indigenous land without war.
The thick cartographic depiction in this mid-eighteenth-century map
was aimed to alienate Native Americans from their land.*

considered it a foundation of their independence. Not long before, a
New York colonist had reassured his governor that "on whose side
the Iroquois Indians fall, they will cast the balance." Operating in an
intensely Indigenous world, the colonists lived in chronic fear. British
officers were adamant that they had to "out-fort, as well as out-settle"
the French, for "our colonies are in a worse condition by far than is
generally believed."[10]

What the French lacked in numbers, they more than compensated
for with the robust Indian alliance system they had secured with
extravagant generosity. From the Northeast Coast to the western
Great Lakes, and from Louisiana to the Illinois Country and all the
way north into the Ohio Valley, the French could rely on the support
of dozens of Native nations. To guarantee the survival of their North
American empire, French strategists set out to consolidate their scattered possessions into a vast arc of contiguous settlements extending
from the Gulf of Saint Lawrence through the heart of North America to the Mississippi River delta. Such a cordon would confine the

English colonies to the east and secure the interior for the French once and for all. But there was a catch: the French did not control the Ohio Valley. But fortunately for the French, the English were not in a much better position. The Muscogees and the Six Nations, not the English or French, were the dominant powers in the interior.[11]

THE SEVEN YEARS' WAR involved Indians from the very beginning. Native Americans observed the lead-up to the war, gauging how best to navigate it and perhaps benefit from it. The Shawnees started attacking the Iroquois in 1753, reaffirming their sovereignty to both the Six Nations and the Europeans. The attacks triggered further realignments, creating a chain reaction that saw Native nations reassessing their options. The Six Nations made peace with the Catawbas, hoping to end a century-long raiding war and restore stability. The Lenapes joined the French, and the Shawnees declared a "perpetual war" against Britain. French officials were elated, but the Shawnees would not be submissive allies. They would fight the British for their own reasons and in their own way, routinely rejecting French demands and pleas. Their principal ambition was to disentangle themselves from the Six Nations, which they considered a far more dangerous adversary than the British and French Empires.

The sprawling war became a crucible in which numerous Native nations redefined their relationships with European powers and their Indigenous neighbors. The war was also nearly unprecedented; only the imperial Iroquois had waged war on a subcontinental scale. The Indians kept the settlers anxious by promising alliances, military support, and trade, only to withdraw their promises when they needed the settlers to do their bidding. They created a military and diplomatic landscape that was often unreadable to Europeans.

On April 19, 1754, an untested lieutenant colonel named George Washington and the ragtag troops under his command became the first line of defense against a French invasion in the Ohio Country. At dawn on May 28, Tanaghrisson—an Iroquois leader who had been born a Catawba and, after being captured, had been raised as a Seneca—along with a dozen of his men, guided a contingent of

Virginia provincial troops under Washington through relentless rain toward Fort Duquesne, a new French fort at the Forks of the Ohio. Like other Iroquois, Tanaghrisson was offended by the French occupation of the animal-rich upper Ohio Valley, one of the most coveted regions in the interior.

Tanaghrisson—"Half King" to the British—brought Washington and his troops to a glade. The Iroquois soldiers were traveling with their families, and they urged Washington to occupy the higher ground, where the noncombatants would be safe. Washington prepared his men for an ambush on a rocky ledge above the French camp. When the French emerged from their shelters, there was a brief exchange of musket fire. Tanaghrisson's soldiers blocked the critical path, forcing the French back into a clearing where they were exposed. The French offered to surrender, but Washington, rashly, ordered his soldiers to fire. Fourteen Frenchmen were dead before Washington ordered his men to stop shooting. The captain of the French detachment, Joseph Coulon de Villiers de Jumonville, tried to explain that he had been assigned merely to defend the possessions of his sovereign, Louis XV. Tanaghrisson was not interested. "You are not yet dead, my father," he said, and he buried his hatchet in Jumonville's skull and washed his hands with the dead man's brains.

In Tanaghrisson's shadow, Washington had made his ambiguous entrance into American history. He tracked back to the Virginia provincials' encampment, at a place called the Great Meadows, and wrote reports for his superiors, informing them of mutilated French corpses. He ordered the building of a modest structure he called Fort Necessity on the Monongahela River, about sixty miles south of Fort Duquesne. Britain's lone anchor in the Trans-Appalachian West, the fort had a seven-foot-high stockade and could accommodate no more than seventy men. Washington organized a prayer within the walls. About seven weeks later, seven hundred French and Native soldiers attacked the helpless outpost. The three hundred defenders, many of them drunk, managed only weak resistance. The French-Native force killed thirty and wounded seventy before pulling back. Defeated and humiliated, Washington signed a document in which he took the blame for Jumonville's "assassination." He then led a retreat of the surviving

British troops across the Allegheny Mountains. There were no official declarations of war yet, but Tanaghrisson's surprise attack and the subsequent British capitulation had sent events spiraling. Both Britain and France prepared for a colossal clash. In the Ohio Country, Shawnees, Lenapes, and Seneca-Cayugas were already gravitating toward the French, and they launched devastating attacks along the frontiers of Pennsylvania, Virginia, and North Carolina. Hoping to create discord between the Iroquois and the English, the French told Tanaghrisson that "the English were going to divide the Land between them."[12]

The two empires had plenty of reasons to go to war. The root causes were in Europe, with its dynastic rivalries, its constantly shifting constellation of alliances, and its recurrent petty wars over Europe's many small but wealthy provinces. The two empires also competed over control of India and North America and over their resources, trying to eclipse one another in prosperity. Much depended on what they could extract from their overseas colonies. The long era of geopolitical balance, carefully forged in the Grand Settlement in Montreal in 1701 among the continent's three dominating powers—the British Empire, the French Empire, and the Iroquois League—was over.

THE IROQUOIS KNEW HIM as *Warraghiyagey*, "a man who undertakes great things." Sir William Johnson, a fabulously wealthy New York merchant and practiced backwoods go-between, had been appointed to the post of superintendent of Indian affairs for the Northern District, which effectively meant the Six Nations. Johnson had unusually strong ties to the Iroquois League. He was the common-law husband of Konwatsitsiaienni, Molly Brant, whose brother Thayendanegea, or Joseph Brant, was a leading Mohawk sachem who seemed to inhabit the European and Indigenous worlds with equal ease, entertaining visitors with sumptuous European-style dinner parties, and leading the Mohawks with traditional Iroquois values. Johnson's was one of the most important government positions in British America, and he spent vast sums on gifts, guns, food, clothing, and jewelry for the Six Nations. He may have been the most powerful European on the continent. Yet even he could not convince

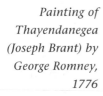

Painting of Thayendanegea (Joseph Brant) by George Romney, 1776

the Six Nations to enter into a formal military alliance with Britain. New York had been appropriating Iroquois territory for years, alienating the Six Nations.

At a conference in Albany in June 1754, Hendrick Theyanoguin, an old and scarred Mohawk sachem who had made a sensational visit to London in 1740 as an "Emperor of the Six Nations," announced that the Iroquois were happy to embrace the English but would not enter into a military alliance. He picked up a stick and, throwing it behind his back, said, "You have thus thrown us behind your back, and disregarded us, whereas the French are a subtle and vigilant people, ever using the utmost endeavors to seduce and bring our people over to them." To drive his point home, Theyanoguin explained that the governors of Virginia and New France "are both quarrelling about lands which belong to us." It was a masterful move at a critical moment, when British war prospects hung in the balance. Theyanoguin announced that the Ohio Country belonged to the Six Nations and that neither the English nor the French could enter it without the Indians' permission. Needing to secure Six Nations neutrality, Major

General Edward Braddock pledged to honor the Six Nations' sovereignty. In doing so, he gained the right of passage for nearly fifteen hundred troops, whom he would now march west.[13]

Native nations had their own reasons to fight. Lenapes, Shawnees, Odawas, Potawatomis, Eries, Wyandots, Miamis, and Iroquois had successfully navigated ever-shifting colonial wars for decades, but when the Ohio Country, an Indigenous haven between the French and British, became a war zone, Native nations had to reevaluate their options. They knew it was better to have two empires rather than one nearby; the former position spelled opportunity, the latter dependency. Most Ohio Country Indians joined the more accommodating French in fighting the British. The Six Nations allied loosely with Britain and reserved the right to decide which campaigns they would join. The formidable Muscogee Confederacy remained neutral, confident that neither empire could afford to alienate it. Teedyuscung, the Lenape sachem, kept reminding the British that his people had lost much of their land in the Walking Purchase and demanded restoration of the prepurchase borders. Such demands had traction because of the looming French threat. French officials and traders offered Native Americans political services by mediating disputes among them, and the Indians rewarded the French with their loyalty in trade and war. This connection unnerved the British, who could not match France's diplomatic and commercial reach in the interior.[14]

Ambitions and follow-through did not necessarily meet in the New World. Braddock was prickly, arrogant, and hopelessly shortsighted. In an earlier conversation with the leading Pennsylvanian Benjamin Franklin, Braddock had announced that he would take Fort Duquesne, France's military centerpiece in the Ohio Country, in three or four days. Franklin had warned him that "the only danger I apprehend of obstruction to your march is from ambuscades of Indians, who, by constant practice, are dexterous in laying and executing them." Braddock, Franklin reported, responded that "these savages may, indeed, be a formidable enemy to your raw American militia, but upon the king's regular and discipled troops, sir, it is impossible they should make an impression."[15]

Fort Duquesne supplied the Lenapes, Seneca-Cayugas, and Shawnees so generously with arms that they could be finicky and demand the light and short *fusils de chasse*, hunting rifles, fabricated at the Tulle manufactory in France. In contrast, Braddock's army included only a few Indians, and he refused to consult any of them. When the Lenape sachem Shingas asked him "what he intended to do with the Land if he Could drive the French and their Indians away," Braddock replied that "the English Should Inhabit and Inherit the Land." Taken aback, Shingas pressed the general to declare "whether the Indians that were Friends to the English might not be Permitted to Live and Trade Among the English and have Hunting Ground sufficient To Support themselves." Braddock's reply was tone-deaf: "No Savage Should Inherit the Land." Braddock was not the only blundering British official. His skeleton plan was approved by imperial officials in the royal Palace of Whitehall, who had studied maps they could not possibly understand. They expected the rivers, lakes, and roads on the way to Fort Duquesne not to belong to anybody.[16]

In the spring of 1755, Braddock launched a foray unprecedented in its size when he sent a fleet carrying four regiments to the Gulf of Saint Lawrence. London expected him to take Forts Duquesne and Niagara and consolidate the thirteen colonies into a unified political and military body. But there seemed to be little will among the British to face the Indians and their French allies in battle, for the Indians knew the terrain far better, moved faster through the thick forests, and staged terrifying ambushes. Robert Dinwiddie, the governor of Virginia and a member of a company of speculators who coveted the fertile land of the Ohio Country, was taken aback by Britain's indecision. "All North America will be lost if These Practices are tolerated," he warned. "No War can be worse to This Country than the Suffering Such Insults as These. The Truth is, the French claim almost all North America, and from whence they may drive us whenever They Please, or as soon as There shall be a Declar'd War." Edmond Atkin, the first southern superintendent of Indian affairs, reinforced the message, writing that "the Importance of Indians is now generally known and understood, a doubt remains not, that the prosperity of our Colonies on the Continent, will stand or fall with our Interest and favour among them." It was too late. The Lenapes and Shawnees had already become alienated from the British and were feeding intelligence to the French.[17]

Braddock invaded, all but blindly, a world where the Indians and the French had lived as allies and kin for generations. In the 1750s, the Ohio Country was the most viable part of the battered but persistent French-Indian middle ground. Multiethnic villages of Odawas, Lenapes, Shawnees, Kickapoos, Mascoutens, Potawatomis, Wyandots, Seneca-Cayugas, and many others filled the region with people and power: the residents could pool resources, skills, and ideas that enabled them to navigate the increasingly violent world and turn strangers into kin with generosity and sharing. Almost all of these nations had entered the middle ground with the French, and most of them still embraced the governor of New France as Onontio, a benevolent father who protected them without controlling them. This Indigenous realm was France's power base in North America. Braddock's plan was utterly detached from reality.[18]

Braddock never saw Fort Duquesne. As he marched his twenty-two hundred troops along a twelve-foot-wide military road, the column stretched for miles, making it a soft target. Arrows and bullets, seemingly coming out of nowhere, stopped Braddock's plodding column several miles away from the fort. Camouflaging themselves to blend in with the woods and thick bushes, Native and French marksmen killed and wounded nearly a thousand British soldiers, while suffering a mere forty-odd casualties. Disoriented British soldiers ended up shooting each other in the confusion. Braddock was shot in the chest and buried unceremoniously in the middle of the road. George Washington, as one of Braddock's aides-de-camp, organized his second retreat across the Alleghenies. The British world was shocked: a small group of Indians had blocked the British Empire with an effective and professional campaign. The French, for their part, were building a multinational Indigenous coalition of Shawnees, Lenapes, Odawas, Potawatomis, and Iroquois.[19]

Chapter 20

BRITISH AMERICA
BESIEGED

T HE NATIVE-FRENCH ARMY THAT DEFEATED EDWARD
Braddock was made up of more than six hundred Native soldiers
drawn from across half a continent. They were pulled together by
common enemies, shared customs, an ethos of sharing, and a deep-
seated obligation to protect allies and kin. The Indians also shared fear
and hatred of the British, who were becoming increasingly haughty as
their empire expanded into a global behemoth. The momentous victory reaffirmed to the French the value of military collaboration with
the Indians.

The British-Iroquois alliance, by contrast, was thrown into question. Britain's defeat was potentially catastrophic for the Six Nations:
the Ohio Valley was the gateway to the interior, and the Indians and
their French allies now controlled it. The frontiers separating Indians and settlers collapsed, and English settlers began to panic. British
America was completely unprepared for such a crisis. Pennsylvania
had no militia, Maryland had one company, and the House of Burgesses in Virginia, annoyed by the passivity of the other colonies, was
stingy with its military spending. Robert Hunter Morris, the governor of Pennsylvania, was quick to claim victimhood, reporting that
Braddock's defeat had left his colony "exposed to the cruel Incursions of the French and their barbarous Indians who delight in shedding human blood, and who make no distinction as to Age or Sex,
as to those that armed against them." Fear would spawn genocidal
thoughts, and then acts.

Native Americans also challenged Virginia, killing dozens of settlers, carrying countless into captivity, and rolling back its frontier.

This kind of nimble and asymmetrical warfare, in which relative military power differs significantly, threw off-balance the British military officials, who were accustomed to staged battles between mass armies in which the volume of firepower was the decisive factor. The French called it *petite guerre*, "little war." George Washington deplored the state of British frontier garrisons, having "found them very weak for want of men; but more so by indolence and irregularity. None I saw in a posture of defense." That "ruinous state of the frontiers, and the vast extent of land we have lost since this time twelve-month, must appear incredible to those who are not eye-witnesses of the desolation." Desperate to mount a forceful response to the Indigenous military superiority, British military leaders reduced their soldiers' marching load to thirty pounds, rendering them more mobile but compromising their firepower.[1]

Diminished by Native Americans, Britain's imperial project was in crisis, and shock waves reverberated across its colonies. British officials fretted over the "pernicious consequence" of the French seizing of the Ohio Country: "By the conveniency of the Ohio and its branches, they would have it in their power at any time to attack, to great advantage, either our northern or southern provinces." Britain's Native allies were disappointed and anxious. Scarouady, a prominent Oneida sachem who had trusted that an alliance with the British would protect his nation, suddenly found himself exposed. In a council in Philadelphia in August 1755, he listened to settlers complaining about "their defenseless Condition" and how "their Wives and Children are terrified to death with every the most trifling story, and are with difficulty persuaded to stay and do the Duty of their families." To Scarouady, it must have seemed that the British had lost the will to continue fighting. In mid-October the Lenapes attacked a British settlement along Penn's Creek across the Susquehanna River from Shamokin in central Pennsylvania. The incursion was revenge for the 1737 Walking Purchase.

Instead of fighting New France, whose noblemen were rapidly militarizing their colony, many British colonies began attacking their Native neighbors, hoping to capitalize on disorder. Settlers coveted Native lands for their resources and as buffer zones against Indian attacks, but they could not defeat the Indians in battle for a simple reason: the British were opportunistic looters facing highly organized Indigenous armies. Diplomacy, too, was challenging for the British. In deliberations at places like Shamokin, a multiethnic town on the Susquehanna River, Native women functioned as translators, go-betweens, traders, and healers. A British fur trader became so confused that he forgot what day of the week it was. A British soldier denounced the Virginians as "a half-starved, ragged, dirty Set" and asked "what a wild set of Creatures our English Men grow into when they lose Society." In November, Scarouady joined with Andrew Montour, a multilingual backwoodsman with Iroquois and French ancestry, to secure the Six Nations' loyalty by traveling to Shamokin. The stakes were high and the diplomacy needed to be face-to-face and frank, but half-truths, misunderstandings, and language barriers kept the settlers and Native Americans in a state of anxiety: the Indians expected the Europeans to be fluent in Indigenous metaphors and ritual language, and many were taken aback by the sheer volume of colonial documentation—and they told the British so. Robert Dinwiddie, the distressed governor of Virginia, promised "to oppose the malicious Designs of our Enemies," especially the still formidable Iroquois. He pledged to "send a great number of our Warriors to dispossess [the French] of the Lands which they have unjustly invaded."[2]

Where they could, the settlers piggybacked on Indigenous precedents. Where Britain's colonizing project was slowly unraveling, the Six Nations subordinated captive Lenapes into fictive "women" who performed farming and other forms of women's work for them. Although grasping the thickly layered metaphor only dimly, Pennsylvanians tried to appropriate the Six Nations' overlord role by simply announcing their supremacy over the Lenapes. Scarouady confronted Governor Morris as a neutral go-between and reported that the Onondaga council had "very sharply reprehended the Delawares [Lenapes] for their cruel and unbrotherly Behavior against the English." Scarouady had "urged them to repent and desist." That was not enough for Pennsylvania. In 1756, its militia attacked the Lenape town of Kittanning and killed fifty men, women, and children. Pennsylvania declared war on the Lenapes and began paying bounties for Lenape scalps.[3]

The Lenapes fought back. The sachem Shingas thought that if they stopped the English, "we may do afterwards what we please with the French, for we have [them] as it were in a sheep den, and may cut them [off] at any time." Ohio Country Indians kept attacking English settlements, forcing Pennsylvania, Maryland, and Virginia to focus on protecting their borders at a time when they should have been fighting the French. Highly mobile Native squadrons killed or captured hundreds of settlers, sending them into a chaotic retreat to the east. Soon the frontier was only a hundred miles from Philadelphia. The sudden contraction of British America became an opening for the French. General Louis-Joseph de Montcalm-Grozon, Marquis de Montcalm, planned a campaign targeting the British forts in the Great Lakes region.[4]

The war and the broader contest for dominance now followed two designs—colonial and Indigenous—that converged and diverged in an ever-shifting pattern. The Indians expected the settlers to share their technology and embrace the Indians as allies and kin, whereas the British sought to dictate to the Indians. In July 1756, the British invited some five hundred Native delegates to a summit in Easton, a dilapidated Pennsylvania town fifty miles from Philadelphia. Quaker pacifists arbitrated the talks—they were embroiled in a bitter political struggle with proprietor Thomas Penn and sought political leverage—but the Lenape sachem Teedyuscung, wearing a gold-trimmed coat, dominated the negotiations. Capitalizing on the enormous uncertainties brought by the global war, he proposed a broad peace that would involve the Six Nations and demanded a sanctuary for his people in Pennsylvania's Wyoming Valley. All participants wanted peace. Teedyuscung accepted the role of a "woman," which allowed him to become a peacemaker with the formidable Six Nations and secure Lenape entry into the alliance. He also pushed the Pennsylvanians to inspect the legality of the 1737 Walking Purchase. The Iroquois seemed to think that he was a blowhard and a fraud. Unfazed, Teedyuscung pledged to convince other Lenape sachems to deny support to the French, which in turn would open the door to another British attack on Fort Duquesne. Dangling the key to victory in front of the British, Teedyuscung, by simply the power of his words, secured guarantees of title to what all along had been Lenape land. Colonial scribes recorded everything he said, including many repetitions for emphasis—a common practice in oral societies that imparted sincerity and guaranteed accuracy. Though the final accord was concise to a fault, it established a broad peace between the Ohio Indians and the British Empire, sidelining the French. The Easton conference was one of the most significant diplomatic interventions in the Seven Years' War. With the Iroquois at least momentarily satisfied, the British could recalibrate their military strategy.[5]

The Six Nations' noninvolvement, however, denied the British a crucial ally, enabling Montcalm to press forward and seize six forts within a year. The loss of the pivotal Fort William Henry on Lake George was Britain's low point. Commanding the rivers and lands immediately to the west and south of Albany, the French-Indian alliance seemed to have thwarted the British. But then the French suddenly lost momentum. The battle at Fort William Henry had been a disaster for the British, but it also became an unexpected crisis for the French. The articles of capitulation had been negotiated, and the British soldiers were scheduled to vacate the fort, having agreed to become noncombatants for eighteen months. Montcalm, however, had not consulted his Native allies, who had not received their pay. Denied their rightful compensation, Native soldiers attacked the retreating British, killing dozens of provincial soldiers and taking several captives. Montcalm drew all the wrong conclusions about what had happened; he would never again rely on Native auxiliaries. Making matters worse, in the fall of 1757, smallpox spread from French soldiers to the Indians, devastating their towns in the interior and further alienating them from the French. Without realizing it, France had already lost the war—three years before its formal capitulation and six years before the Treaty of Paris.[6]

While the British seemed to have done almost everything wrong for three long years, from 1757 on they seemed to get almost everything right. The turn in British fortunes had much to do with the forceful William Pitt, who had become the secretary of state for the Southern Department, a role that put him in charge of Britain's war effort in North America. At Pitt's insistence, British officers continued to pursue proactive diplomacy with Indians. William Johnson used all his skills as a go-between to recruit Iroquois soldiers. The Six Nations may have become weakened, their armies comprising only eleven hundred soldiers, but they could still mobilize thousands more among the neighboring Native nations on the strength of their military power. "When we go to War," they boasted, "our manner is to destroy a Nation and there is an End of it." Backed by the domineering Iroquois League, Johnson oversaw the building of new forts and blockhouses that shielded Six Nations settlements. He effectively replaced French forts with British ones—a singular coup in the war that the Iroquois were using to preserve their dominance in the North American interior.[7]

Dangerously low on provisions for their armies, the British also reached out to the Cherokees, who had turned the Southeast into the most productive agricultural realm on the continent. The Cherokees had rebuffed European cajoling for years, carefully weighing their options, which unnerved the neighboring settlers, who blamed the Cherokees for much of the colonial-Indigenous violence in the South. Only in the fall of 1757 did Cherokee matriarchs, eager to gain access to British weapons and wares, authorize a war against the British Empire's enemies. The Cherokees pledged to "make war upon the Ohio, and spare neither the French or their Indians if they fall in our way. The hatchet we began with was but a small one, but we hope to get one of a larger size, which will enable us to do more execution than we have hitherto been able to do." The Cherokees had nurtured commercial and diplomatic ties with the English for decades, and they now brought their extensive proficiency in wilderness war into the ongoing global conflict. Cherokee leaders insisted that their alliance was with the British king, not the settlers, and they refused all British attempts to turn them into auxiliaries. Like almost all Indians who entered the war, the Cherokees fought their own war side by side with the British, using the British allies to advance their goals. They also approached the Six Nations and received wampum belts, a pledge to cooperate. By April 1758, nearly six hundred soldiers from sixteen Cherokee towns had offered military support to the British while making it clear that the alliance was one of equals. Unlike in the pays d'en haut, where creative and expedient alliances dominated, Cherokees demanded binding assurances of their sovereignty, which in turn convinced the Muscogees, Chickasaws, Catawbas, and others to join the British. As a security measure, the Cherokees kept the British in a state of uncertainty by threatening to join the French in Louisiana. They were shaping a global war through nimbly assertive foreign policy that compelled the British to remain loyal to them.[8]

The roles had reversed: suddenly, the French had a mere handful of Indigenous partners, mostly Abenakis dispossessed by the war. In June 1758 the British moved against Louisbourg, a strategically vital fortress on Île-Royale that guarded access to the Saint Lawrence Valley. Pitt named Major General James Abercrombie, a fastidious and lethargic man, the new commander in chief. Abercrombie, in turn, appointed the manifestly untried General Jeffery Amherst to lead the land operation against the fortress. The British navy blocked a Canada-bound French fleet, and Amherst managed to deliver a coup de grâce in the form of a methodical siege of Louisbourg. With five thousand casualties, it was a crippling defeat for France. British ships could now sail into the heart of New France. Abercrombie launched a seemingly suicidal attack on Fort Ticonderoga in July, conquering it. The battle marked, at long last, a return to European-style warfare for the British. Fort Frontenac fell in August after another siege, leaving French forts and trading posts in the pays d'en haut exposed. Spotting an opportunity to end the war in the South, Amherst ordered Brigadier General John Forbes to march against Fort Duquesne, bringing violence back to the Ohio Country.[9]

Terrified Virginia and Pennsylvania settlers sought refuge in the Cherokees' mountains, while Cherokee soldiers orchestrated repeated attacks against the now isolated Fort Duquesne, preventing French supply trains from reaching it. Forbes advanced cautiously. The second battle of Fort Duquesne would be nearly the opposite of the first one four years prior: where Braddock had rejected and insulted Britain's Native allies, Forbes embraced them to the point of equipping his troops with moccasins, face paint, and blankets. The British had found a common cause in a cataclysmic war against a shared enemy. The Lenapes openly ridiculed the French ambassadors' desperate efforts, kicking a war belt that they brought as though it were a snake.

Late in the war, the most significant difference between the British and the French armies was the disparity in Indigenous allies. Success and failure depended on following Native advice. When Forbes finally reached Fort Duquesne, the French and their Indian allies were already retreating. The French commander had the fort blown up— his futile effort to annoy the British.[10]

Since the spring of 1758, Pitt had asserted even more control over the British war effort. Believing that the war could not be decided on European battlefields, he moved to force an outcome in America and prepared Amherst for a decisive invasion of New France. Approximately nine hundred Six Nations soldiers joined the British in sacking Fort Niagara in June 1759. Their participation did not mean that they shared British goals and priorities, and an intense dispute broke out over the spoils. The Iroquois had not contributed to the digging of trenches or the building of fortifications, but, to the chagrin of the British, they insisted on their right to pillage the fallen fort. Johnson accommodated them. The Six Nations were fighting a parallel war over the hegemony of the Ohio Country and its people—a war that coincided only sporadically with British designs. They were not alone in their defiance. Asserting their sovereignty, the Lenapes questioned the very rationale of the war, asking the Moravian missionary Christian Frederick Post, a Pennsylvania envoy to the Indians, "Why do not you and the French fight in the old country, and on the sea? Why do you come to fight on our land? This makes everybody believe, you want to take the land from us by force, and settle it." Post knew his place. "I have not one foot of land, nor do I desire to have any," he responded. The Lenapes and Shawnees agreed to withdraw from the French alliance.[11]

The decisive British invasion of New France was a three-pronged operation, and it began in the fall of 1759, when a fleet sailed from Louisbourg up the Saint Lawrence to Quebec. Believing time was on his side, Montcalm chose not to engage, hoping that the British would not arrive before the Saint Lawrence began to freeze over. The plan backfired. The British forces moved into position faster than expected, evading Quebec's batteries, and drew the French into a battle on the plateau outside the city walls. Montcalm ordered a desperate frontal attack, and well-timed musket volleys from the British stopped it on the Plains of Abraham. The French surrendered the city on September 18—a crucial British victory that was soon muddied by events in the South, where Cherokees killed land-hungry South Carolina settlers who had wormed their way into the Indians' territory, blatantly violating Cherokee sovereignty. When the Virginia militia killed twenty-three Cherokee hostages, an open war broke out. Despite its checkered record in battling the Indians, South Carolina declared war on the mountain-dwelling Cherokees and took several hostages. When the British killed twenty-two of them, the Cherokees laid siege to Fort Loudoun. They killed and captured more than a hundred settlers as they took the fort. Led by Atagulgalu, they killed the fort's commander and twenty-two British soldiers in revenge. The Cherokee Nation's sovereignty remained effectively undiminished.[12]

The second prong of the British attack on New France came in the fall of 1760, moving through the Hudson Valley, Lake Champlain, and Richelieu Valley toward Montreal. The British blockade stopped three underprotected French supply ships, crippling France's campaign even before it got underway. In Quebec, the anxious French inhabitants waited for the masts to appear downriver. When the masts appeared flying Union Jacks, the French knew that New France was lost.

Amherst launched the third prong simultaneously with the second by pushing to Lake Ontario. The sharp edge of his army consisted of seven hundred Six Nations soldiers whose participation William Johnson had secured—to Amherst's dismay—for an extortionate £17,000. The British and Iroquois easily seized exposed French forts and descended the Saint Lawrence toward Montreal in bateaux and two armed sloops: the *Onondaga* and the *Mohawk*. The French were caught in a slowly closing vise. Amherst may have despised the Iroquois, but he knew their value. Their mere presence announced to the anxious Indians and settlers in Montreal that the fight would be quick and relatively bloodless. On September 6, 1760, Amherst received Louis-Antoine de Bougainville, the French emissary, at his headquarters in the heights around the low-lying Montreal, from where he could easily have reduced the city to ashes. Amherst told Bougainville that he had come for New France and would not "take anything less."[13]

In the south, the South Carolina militia, too, failed to defeat the Cherokees, and North Carolina and Virginia sent troops to aid the colony. In the summer of 1761, British and provincial armies retaliated by burning some twenty Cherokee towns. Guided by clan mothers, the Cherokees accepted peace and land cessions. Native American diplomacy and military might had determined the outcome of the Seven Years' War: thousands of Indians had fought alongside the British to defeat New France and banish the French from the continent. Yet, when peace came, many of them realized that North America had become a more dangerous place for them. Numerous Indigenous nations had relied on the presence of two empires to force compromises and concessions. A New York Indian affairs secretary, Peter Wraxall, had explained the logic to British policymakers: "To preserve the Balance between us and the French is the great ruling Principle of the Modern Indian Politics," he said, echoing Catawba tactics in the Piedmont. Now, that crucial strategy was all but defunct. Freed of European rivals, the British would begin to treat the Indians as subjects.[14]

IN 1761, THE OJIBWE sachem Minweweh faced British officials at Fort Michilimackinac, telling them, "The French king is our father. . . . although you have conquered the French, you have not yet conquered us! We are not your slaves. These lakes, these woods and mountains were left us by our ancestors." In the upper Mississippi Valley, an Illini soldier nudged a French officer: "Take Courage, my Father, don't abandon your children, the English will never come here as long as there is one red man." French agents needed little prodding. New France and Louisiana were no more, but there were still thousands of French traders, farmers, and officers on the continent. In the Ohio Country and the pays d'en haut, many Native nations believed that the French king's armies would soon return. The Indians maneuvered tirelessly to restore some kind of French presence in North America as a counterweight to the emboldened and expansionist Anglo-America.[15]

Their efforts were futile. The British Empire had swallowed New

France, and the French were not coming back. France's imperial offi-cials had shifted their ambitions away from the North American mainland and to the Caribbean. With the British now the only source of trade and political support, the world was off-kilter. Without an imperial counterweight, the British colonies could now dictate terms to Indigenous nations from a position of unprecedented power, and they could also play the nations off against each other, just as the Indi-ans had played the British off against the French.

George Croghan—an Irish-born borderland trader, land specu-lator, happy and heavy drinker, and now prominent British Indian agent—drastically curtailed gift-giving, demoting Native Americans from respected allies to mere lines in a ledger. The governor of Geor-gia openly extorted the Muscogees. "We can pour in Goods upon you like the Floods of a great River when it overflows," he announced, and then he warned, "You know you cannot do well without us, but we can do without you; you have tried the French and you know they can not supply your Wants." The governor asked the Muscogees to "witness the Choctaws and many other Nations on the Mississippi," who "are more like Slaves than free People." In a thinly veiled threat, he urged the Muscogees to "behave well" toward the British.[16]

The 1763 Treaty of Paris between France and Britain, signed in February of that year, made the demotion of Native Americans offi-cial by handing the lands of the Great Lakes Indians over to Britain without consulting them. With patent imperial arrogance, the treaty divided North America between Spain and Britain. Britain claimed the Mississippi Valley as a boundary. The treaty transferred half a billion acres between the Appalachians and the Mississippi River, and Spain ceded its claims to Florida and the Gulf coast. Britain now had thirty colonies in the New World—some of them tiny, others massive. Adam Smith, while writing *The Wealth of Nations*, recommended that Britain discard all its colonies, for managing an empire that extended across seven seas was too draining and costly.

The Treaty of Paris all but canceled the long-standing Indigenous strategy of playing the French and British Empires off against each other to extract concessions from both. When the Indians learned the terms, they were driven "to despair." A Shawnee sachem told the French that the Shawnees could offer the support of forty-seven villages, if the French stayed. But an exhausted France accepted the eradication of New France. France did not lament the loss of Canada: its costly Indian diplomacy had turned it into a burden for the French state. The Jesuit order left North America, and Spanish settlers in Florida evacuated in droves, heading west. French Louisiana became Spanish Louisiana. Thirteen thousand Acadians, descendants of the French immigrants who settled in Acadia from the early seventeenth century onward and survived several mass deportations, scattered across the East Coast and Louisiana, as well as Great Britain and France. The radical reshuffling left tens of thousands of people homeless and rudderless. The king of Spain, Charles III, doubted whether he should even accept Louisiana, which was filled with independent Indians, whereas the total Spanish population in North America was only about twenty-five thousand. Given how little the French had been able to do with the colony, King Charles feared that it would be a money drain. The British may have been the big winners in the Seven Years' War, but even their position was far from secure: more than a century and a half after the founding of Jamestown, their settlements were still confined to east of the Appalachians. Farther to the west, the British had claims, not possessions.[17]

IN THE EARLY SPRING OF 1763, General Amherst, now commander in chief in North America and still an Indian hater—he branded Native Americans "pernicious vermin"—refused to issue gifts to Indigenous leaders or to release Odawa war prisoners. The Odawas and their allies prepared for a war to preserve their sovereignty, civilization, and dignity. The Six Nations sent out war belts across the lower Great Lakes, urging others to join them against the British at the time corn was planted. In late spring, the Odawa war ogimaag Pontiac held councils with Anishinaabeg, Potawatomi, Lenape, Ojibwe, Shawnee, Wyandot, and Seneca-Cayuga representatives ten miles south of Fort Detroit. An astute and bold leader, Pontiac appealed to the Indians' shared fear of British aggression and to their shared sense of kinship rooted in long-standing nindoodemag lineages that covered much of the Great Lakes region. He urged them to rid the conceited and lethal British from their world.

Other Native nations mobilized as well, trying to preserve their power and sovereignty in a unipolar colonial setting in which the British could impose on Native Americans their notions of belonging and sovereignty, which revolved around hard borders and exclusive domains. The Six Nations adopted the long-standing French policy of containing British settlements in the east. Other nations confronted the British Empire directly. Slighted and vulnerable, thousands of Native soldiers joined a general war that swept across the interior from the Susquehanna Valley to the Mississippi. It was a war of survival against British settlers who pushed west and openly violated Indigenous sovereignty. British officials were powerless to stop the settlers, exposing the ad hoc nature of Britain's North American empire west of the Appalachians. The Indians also protested their radically diminished political status in postwar North America. As the war ground on, trade came to a near halt, and the critical linkages between settlers and Indians became dangerously frail. The British officers did not seem to care. They now intended to dictate to the Indians. Haughty and authoritarian, Britain kept its army in the field, while its officers snubbed Indigenous diplomatic protocols. British settlers began calling Indians "dogs" and "hogs." They thought they could simply ignore Native demands.[18]

The Indians responded in kind. In the Ohio Country, Neolin, a Lenape prophet, announced that he had journeyed to heaven, spoken to the creator, and received instructions on how to drive the White people off of Indian lands. Back on Earth, Neolin began to preach about separate creations of humanity. The Master of Life had created different kinds of people—Indians, Blacks, and Whites—for different parts of the world, but the Europeans had shattered that divine design by colonizing America. Neolin's was a message with hard racial categories. Although he drew from Christian teachings and ideas, he wanted Native Americans to denounce the European god, European goods, and European ideas about land. He wanted them to embrace a purer way of life. He even wanted Native soldiers to abandon European technology and turn back to traditional Native weaponry to ensure self-sufficiency when the war came. Neolin's plan was patient: all his soldiers were to go through seven years of training. Preaching near Fort Detroit, Neolin prophesized a new world without British settlers, diseases, and alcohol, the last of which was ruining and killing uncounted numbers of Indians. Traders pushed brandy and rum for their Native clients, and by the 1760s the total annual Native consumption of rum in the pays d'en haut may have reached 240,000 gallons. Neolin wanted the Indians to launch an otherworldly war to save themselves: "You are to return to that former happy state, in which we lived in peace and plenty, before these strangers came to disturb us, and above all, you must abstain from drinking their deadly *beson* [liquor] which they forced upon us for the sake of increasing their gains and diminishing our numbers." Neolin's message of purification reached many nations—Chippewas, Miamis, Odawas, Potawatomis, Shawnees, and Wyandots—who had prophets of their own.[19]

Chapter 21

WORLDLY AND OTHERWORLDLY WARS OF INDEPENDENCE

P ONTIAC FORCED A WORLDLY WAR TO COMPLEMENT Neolin's otherworldly one. The Odawa leader invoked the mythic Anishinaabeg hero Nanabozho, a giant shape-shifting trickster hare. The British learned through spies that the Indians believed that the empire "mean[t] to make Slaves of them, by Taking so many Posts in their Country, and that they had better Attempt Something now, to Recover their Liberty." Pontiac invited Odawas, Ojibwes, Potawatomis, and Wyandots to a council in early May 1763, where he spoke about British arrogance and the English colonists' rejection of the politics of the middle ground. Telling Neolin's story, Pontiac challenged his audience: "Why do you put up with the Whites on your lands? Is it because you can't get along without them?" Indigenous ambitions in the heart of the continent were expanding beyond mere survival.[1]

Pontiac's question was incisive: access to guns and gunpowder now decided many Indian-colonial wars in North America. Pontiac recruited three hundred soldiers and attacked Fort Detroit soon after the council, launching a war that escalated an already violence-ridden state of affairs. The Native force failed to take the heavily protected fort and settled for laying siege to it. Pontiac sent out runners to carry war belts from nation to nation, triggering attacks across the pays d'en haut. Over the course of three months, Odawas, Lenapes, Ojibwes, Shawnees, Seneca-Cayugas, and Cherokees struck British forts and garrisons, killing as many as two thousand settlers. They captured eight forts and forced the abandonment of two more. Only three forts—Pitt, Detroit, and Niagara—remained to anchor the British Empire in the interior, and each was separated from the others by four to five hundred miles; they were isolated dots in Indian country. For all practical purposes, the fort system was the empire that British forces had carved out in the West in the Seven Years' War. The allied Indians had swept most of that empire away. When rumors spread that Native soldiers had donned French uniforms and medals, British fears spiraled into panic: Pontiac was fighting to turn back time and restore the French presence to the continent. In late June of 1763, Pontiac's soldiers laid siege to the strategically critical Fort Pitt at the confluence of the Monongahela and Allegheny Rivers. Garrisons and posts fell like dominoes. The Indians killed approximately a hundred English traders. Fort Augusta, a defensive fort in the upper Allegheny region, was persistently going Native.[2]

With the British fixed in their three remaining forts, Pontiac redoubled his efforts at Fort Detroit. In the early summer, the British began sending rangers, gunships, and bateaux to the vulnerable fort. The land battle transformed into an amphibious one. The Indians, now more than eight hundred strong, attacked the incoming fleets and, with time on their side, continued their siege. Pontiac established a base two miles to the east. The Indians incapacitated a six-gun sloop and captured several smaller vessels. In the summer they stopped a supply convoy, killing or capturing some sixty men. Yet Pontiac realized he could not take the fort. The stalemate disheartened his followers, who began to leave. The Indian-hating Jeffery Amherst was emboldened: "I wish to hear of *No Prisoners*, should any of the Villains be met with in arms." The news elsewhere was less encouraging for the British: at Fort Pitt, the defenders were panicking; hundreds of settlers had sought refuge in its cramped quarters. "We are so crowded in the fort that I fear disease," the commander wrote. "The smallpox is among us."[3]

The allied Indians outside Fort Pitt's walls demanded that the British abandon the bastion. The British, alarmed by the scope of Indigenous cooperation, were becoming desperate. After long parleys, British soldiers handed the Indians two blankets and a handkerchief from their smallpox hospital, hoping for "the desired effect." Two weeks earlier, Amherst had asked Colonel Henry Bouquet in a letter, "Could it not be contrived to Send the *Small Pox* among those Disaffected Tribes of Indians? We must, on this occasion, Use Every Stratagem in Our power to Reduce them." Bouquet had written back in the affirmative, and Amherst had responded, "You will Do well to try to Inoculate the Indians by means of Blankets, as well as to try Every other method that can serve to Extirpate this Execrable Race." There was little ambiguity about what had happened: Governor-General Amherst had called for biological warfare.[4]

All along, Pontiac's watchmen, soldiers, and Native informants had been feeding him intelligence about British war plans. On July 31, leading a band of nearly 250 soldiers, Pontiac ambushed a British column at a crossing of Parent's Creek. His men fired numerous volleys into the exposed troops, killing and wounding dozens. The fight soon became known as "Bloody Run." The news of the rout electrified Indian country. The Odawas and Ojibwes sent soldiers, and the Shawnees attacked new and unauthorized British settlements west of the Appalachians, taking captives and spreading terror.[5]

THREE HUNDRED MILES to the northwest, a small Ojibwe group from the Straits of Mackinac had visited Fort Michilimackinac in early June. They had been encouraged to do so by Pontiac, who seemed to be orchestrating a significant expansion of the Indigenous war of independence. That the Ojibwe group included both women and men signaled peaceful intentions. "Everything seemed in perfect tranquillity," the commander of the fort, Major Robert Etherington, later reported. The women and some of the men stayed and rested inside the fort, while others "assembled to play ball"—lacrosse—outside the walls. They played for hours, fostering the sense of a relaxed lull, but then suddenly they threw the ball near the gate. Appearing to go after the ball, the players instead grabbed Etherington and his aide and dragged them into the woods. Inside the fort, the Native women unwrapped their blankets, took out hatchets, and handed them to the men, who killed fifteen British soldiers and a trader. The Ojibwes had issued a warning with violence.

The surviving British became captives. Tellingly, the Ojibwes let the fort's French staff be: they still hoped the French would return. Soon after, an Odawa contingent arrived. They seemed unaware of Pontiac's role in launching the attack. According to the detained Etherington, the Ojibwes "declared in council to them [the Odawas] that if they do not remove us [British] out of the fort, they will cut off all communication to this post, by which means all convoys of merchants from Montreal, La Baye, St. Joseph, and the upper posts, would perish." Threatened by the escalating war, the Ojibwes had to make difficult choices between strategic and emotional priorities: like most Indians in the pays d'en haut, they wanted to rid their lands of the haughty British, but they also needed to preserve the vital commercial lifeline at Fort Michilimackinac.[6]

THE BRITISH MIGHT HAVE won the war against Pontiac in the summer of 1763, had Amherst been more flexible and embraced Native auxiliaries. Native Americans were the key to any victories the British might win, which made William Johnson, not Amherst, the essential British official on the continent. When Amherst complained weakly about "the present disturbed state of the back settlements," Johnson offered him thirteen hundred Six Nations, Lenape, Shawnee, and Miami soldiers. Amherst was not interested. He seemed to have lost his tactical edge. Unlike in the Seven Years' War, in Pontiac's War the British troops had failed to take the initiative. The British war effort became defensive, which benefited the Indians, who could live off the land. From the perspective of British officials in London, Amherst's tentativeness had disastrously prolonged the war. The general was summoned back to England in August 1763. But the British war effort did not become any more proactive with him gone. Capturing the prevailing mindset, Benjamin Franklin wrote, "I know of nothing so liable to bring on a serious quarrel with the Indians, as invasion of their property. Let the savages enjoy their deserts in quiet." In November, nervous British officials invited nine hundred Chickasaw, Choctaw, Cherokee, and Muscogee envoys to a conference to assure them of their peaceful intentions.[7]

From London's perspective, its newly acquired American territory was both a boon and a burden. Britain's empire was a maritime empire, and it struggled to adapt to a territorial setting. London's attempted solution, the Royal Proclamation of October 1763, only complicated things. It created a boundary and a buffer zone between British and Indigenous territories along the Appalachian crest, officially dividing the continent's eastern half into two separate worlds. British officials hailed the proclamation as an instrument of peace and stability. Johnson believed it "would prove a Pax Britannica for North America"—backed by Iroquois power—but its repercussions were far more ambiguous for Native Americans. Ostensibly issued to protect Indigenous lands by prohibiting British settlers from crossing the Appalachians, the proclamation was viewed by many Native Americans as a rejection, an attempt to isolate them from the Europeans and their markets. The Mississippi Land Company, which was founded to expedite colonial settlement in the Ohio and the Mississippi Valleys and protect the colonists from "the Insults of the Savages, by the assistance of His Majesty's Forces," only further alienated the Indians. For generations, borderland trade had been a wealth-generating glue that fused Indians and Europeans together, and now they were in danger of becoming detached. When trade goods—guns, powder, lead, fabrics, kettles, metal tools, and tobacco—stopped coming, the frail thread of cooperation could snap. The French Onontio had embraced Indians as allies and kin, but the Royal Proclamation demoted them to subjects of the empire. The proclamation seemed to solidify the continent's division into two Americas—Native and non-Native—that seemed destined to exist on separate planes, inadvertently fulfilling Neolin's great ambition of separate worlds.

The Indians were caught in a quandary, struggling to balance worldly and otherworldly imperatives, and the momentum was turning against them. The French commandant of the Illinois Country refused to support the Indigenous cause in the ongoing war in the interior. Pontiac's coalition began to show signs of fatigue, and the sachem finally lifted the siege of Fort Detroit on October 10, 1763, offering a truce. "My Brother," he wrote to Major Henry Gladwin, the commander of the fort, using a potent kin metaphor, "the word

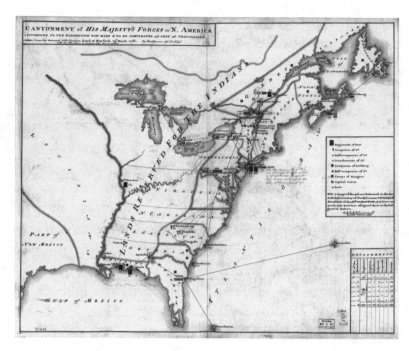

"Cantonment of His Majesty's Forces in N. America," 1766

which my father has sent to make peace I have accepted; all my young men have buried their hatchets." Pontiac wanted both sides to forgive and forget. He did not know that the fort had only a two-week supply of flour left.[8]

To capitalize on Pontiac's retreat, General Thomas Gage, the new commander in chief of British forces, envisioned a two-stage attack in the spring of 1764. The first stage was to be launched from Fort Niagara: troops would embark on a journey to Fort Detroit, where they would be within striking distance of Lenape and Shawnee towns in the Ohio Country. There, Pontiac would be brought to terms. The campaign was led by Colonel John Bradstreet, who had fourteen hundred regulars and more than six hundred Indians from the Six Nations, Odawas, Ojibwes, Nipissings, and Mississaugas, who sought to establish commerce with the British, the domineering traders after the French left the continent. The second attack was to be a direct invasion of the Ohio Country from Pennsylvania. Led by Colonel Henry Bouquet, it would include twelve hundred troops and a detachment of scouts. At the time, there were roughly thirty-eight thousand Indians in the Ohio Country.

Bradstreet's assignment overwhelmed him in the way Braddock's mission had overwhelmed its leader. With so many Native allies in his army, Bradstreet would have had to be both a commander and a diplomat. He failed in the latter capacity, treating Indians as subordinates, and he was soon reduced to helplessly recording how group after group of Native soldiers abandoned him. Bradstreet met with Odawa, Ojibwe, Wyandot, and Potawatomi envoys, who convinced the hapless colonel to sign a peace treaty with them. Bradstreet then asked Bouquet to abort his march toward the Ohio Country. Bouquet was flabbergasted: the junior officer had effectively canceled his expedition by agreeing to a treaty that was dubious at best. At Fort Detroit, Pontiac mocked the peace by flying the white French flag. Bouquet pushed ahead despite Bradstreet's request, but Shawnee, Lenape, Miami, Seneca-Cayuga, and Wyandot soldiers knew to expect him. Holding higher ground near Bushy Run Creek, the Indians paralyzed Bouquet's army with relentless musket fire. The British soldiers and officers knew now that Britain would have to negotiate its way out of complete defeat.[9]

British settlers, too, were suffering and becoming increasingly disgusted. Having borne the brunt of Native attacks, they had expected to be rewarded with land and the empire's protection. Instead, many of them had to abandon their settlements, because they were now on the wrong side of the arbitrary line created by the 1763 Royal Proclamation. If there had ever been any genuine belief in the possibility of Native-British coexistence in the Appalachian borderlands, it was destroyed by the actions of the "Paxton Boys." A vigilante group of aggrieved Scots-Irish settlers, the Paxton Boys were angered by Pontiac's War and began to spread terror in the Susquehanna Valley in the fall and winter of 1763–64, killing local Indians in an openly genocidal campaign. The Conestogas, a multiethnic group of refugee Indians, drew the Paxton Boys' spitefulness in particular. On December 14, mounted and drunken, a Paxton gang of some fifty men descended on a sleeping Conestoga town near Lancaster, Pennsylvania, murdering six people. They returned on the twenty-seventh, again fifty strong. Within fifteen minutes, they hacked fourteen Conestoga people, eight of them children, to pieces. The only reason for the killing seemed to be ingrained hatred of Indians. In 1764, five hundred Paxtonians marched into Philadelphia to bully and pressure the colony's government. In the final collapse of Pennsylvania's already frayed pacifism, the colony offered bounties for Indian scalps: $134 for a man's, $130 for a woman's, and $50 for a child's. British officials seemed powerless to stop the vigilantes, who openly defied British authorities and laws in Philadelphia, arguably Britain's most important city in North America.[10]

THE BRITISH EMPIRE in North America was in crisis, and Johnson and Gage, the leading British officers, had to formulate an exit strategy from Pontiac's War. Johnson, as expected, placed the Six Nations at the center of his vision for the future: had the Six Nations "been properly supported by us," he argued, "they would have long since put a period to the Colony of Canada." The Six Nations had expanded their power during Pontiac's War and now claimed, "in right of conquest," a vast domain that extended from the Blue Ridge Mountains to the Ohio Valley and covered most of the lower Great Lakes. Although united and emboldened through the Great League of Peace and Power, the Six Nations had never consolidated into a full-fledged military empire, but after a century of territorial expansion, they had a series of imperial moments. This was one of them.

Rather than fizzling out, Pontiac's War was transforming into a pan-Indian war. To mitigate renewed Iroquois dominance, British officials had to offer generous and regulated trade, prohibit rum traffic, and ban land sales. Johnson warned, "There is no possibility of speedily rooting out the Northern Indians, and even if practicable it would destroy our Trade." Too weak to control the situation, the British needed to keep the Indians from uniting into a single, all-powerful confederacy. "Each confederacy, with whom peace be made, should separately guarantee to the English a secure Trade and free passage thro' their several countries," Johnson advised. By treating with them separately, Johnson elaborated, "we shall prevent too strict a union amongst them."[11]

The British desire for peace only intensified when Pontiac and other Native leaders extended their operations south into the Illinois Country in 1764. The French may have signed the Treaty of Paris and relinquished their paper claims to the Illinois Country, but they did not act accordingly. They continued to cajole the Indians with gifts and goods, and their pirogue convoys, laden with guns, powder, and other necessities, kept moving up and down the Mississippi, sustaining the Indigenous war effort. The Choctaws, Tunicas, Avoyelles, and Mosopeleas now took the war directly to the British, pressuring them to end their occupation of the Illinois Country. The region became dangerous for the British, prompting the Indians to employ a trusted weapon: rumors. Soon, phantom war parties, secret stratagems, and ghost mobilizations preoccupied the British, allowing flesh-and-blood Indians to send war belts to allies along the river. Emboldened by the support of Choctaws and Illinois Country Indians, Pontiac pledged to keep fighting. So, too, would the British. In their official documents the word "tribe" began to replace the word "nation," demoting the Indians several notches down on the imagined ladder of civilizational development. In May and June, the Indians took one garrison after another, paralyzing the British war effort. Pontiac's coalition had stopped the world's greatest military power with supple warfare and diplomacy.[12]

But the war was not over. Gage went on the offensive. Few lessons having been learned, the campaign echoed the previous campaign into the interior in troubling ways. It was again a two-stage invasion led by the blundering Bradstreet and the measured Bouquet. Bradstreet's force moved first, marching toward the Great Lakes. His task was not to fight but to force submissions from the remaining warring groups. His army formed a strange procession. Bradstreet's men were mostly untrained provincials and ailing regulars, and Bradstreet kept accepting submissions from Indians, unable to verify whether they were genuine. An ambitious and delusional man, he soon saw himself as the overlord of his personal Great Lakes fiefdom. When he arrived in Detroit, Bradstreet was infuriated to find only a wampum belt from Pontiac, whom he had expected to offer submission in person. Bradstreet grabbed a hatchet and pounded the belt into pieces—an act that drained the last of the authority he had possessed among the Indians.

He abandoned his artillery and limped with his starving men back to Fort Niagara. Bouquet, in the meantime, received peace offers from the Shawnees and Lenapes. He established his headquarters on the Muskingum River in the heart of Indian country.[13]

Word of Bouquet's painstaking diplomacy spread quickly among the Ohio Indians, who, after eight years of almost constant war, yearned for normalcy. Soon there was a sincere, collective drive toward peace. Fully aware that they could not force the Indians to surrender, the British pinned their hopes on Pontiac. The powerful Wabash Confederacy of Kickapoos, Mascoutens, Miamis, Piankashaws, and Weas asked Pontiac to represent them in treaty talks with the British. It was a decisive turning point, swinging the Indigenous majority behind peace. Wabash headwomen pushed their male counterparts to "listen to the Speech of the Wives . . . [and] forget all Insults given by these Nations."[14]

Gage, a cautious man whom his men called "Old Woman," asked Johnson to organize a peace conference at Fort Niagara in early July 1764. Johnson dispatched runners across the pays d'en haut, and nineteen Native nations sent envoys to the fort. Having represented the Six Nations for years, Johnson knew how to placate them. He released several captives and asked the Indians to make peace. In return, he promised to restore trade throughout the interior and ban the sale of alcohol to restore the Indians' trust in the British after Amherst's hideous methods. Johnson distributed gifts amounting to a staggering £38,000. Through Johnson, the British Empire effectively bought peace from several Indigenous nations.[15]

Pontiac, largely sidelined since the dispiriting end of the siege of Fort Detroit, now emerged as the indispensable Native American. He shape-shifted, reinventing himself, in classic Anishinaabe shape-shifting fashion, from a nativist war ogimaag into a cooperative sachem and negotiator. Recognizing his magnetism, British officials began to praise Pontiac's wisdom and humanity, creating an image, only partially accurate, of an alliance leader and mediator. Gage described him as a shrewd man who "keeps two secretaries, one to write for him, and the other to read letters he receives, and he manages them so as to keep each of them ignorant of what is translated by the other, each of them ignorant of what is transacted by the other."

With the basic architecture of the postwar world in place, local peace councils popped up across the interior throughout the spring and summer of 1765. In early May, Indian agent George Croghan held successful talks with the Shawnees, who returned several captives, making peace possible. Native envoys made it clear that peace did not mean capitulation. In late June, Pontiac visited Fort Erie, where he smoked the calumet and shared a bottle of wine with Major Robert Rogers, and soon after, Croghan met with several nations that agreed to a general peace if trade were restored. Johnson promised Odawa, Potawatomi, Ojibwe, and Wyandot sachems a generous trade. Indigenous resistance had forced the British to accept the traditional form for their North American possessions: rather than an intrusive inland empire, it would remain a maritime one, facing east toward the Atlantic.[16]

Johnson also met with Ohio Country Indians at his estate, not far from Canajoharie, "Upper Castle" to the Mohawks. "The English have never given you cause to suspect that they would violate the faith of Treaties," he announced, fallaciously, and he told them to become "Children of the Great King" and "obey him & act in a different manner than you have hitherto done." The envoys of the other nations echoed Benavissica, pressuring the British officials to resuscitate the middle ground that had prevailed in the seventeenth and early eighteenth centuries between Native peoples and the French. The sachem wanted Johnson to assume Onontio's role as a caring father who loved and cared for his Indian allies. Johnson slipped into the role effortlessly.

Pontiac, claiming to speak for many nations, said, "My Father of France was in this country I held him by the hand and never did any bad action." He made a pledge: "I this day take you by the hand in the name of all Nations which I will acquaint." Pontiac also accepted the British king as a father. Aware of the delicacy of the situation, he insisted on only one condition: like the French before them, the British should not make any claims on the land under and around their forts in the Illinois Country. The British would be tenants in Indigenous territory. British officers accepted the demand, calculating that they could ignore it once the Indians returned to their homes. For better and for worse, the talks had revived the middle ground and its artful compromises, half-truths, and evasions. The distance between the Indians and the British was, in many ways, wider than it had been a decade earlier when the war had begun. So, too, was the distance between Britain and its American subjects. Pitt announced that "in a good cause, on a sound bottom, the force of this country can crush America to atoms."[17]

Pontiac failed to read the situation. He believed that the tattered middle ground had been resurrected, enabling him to assemble an enduring Indigenous commonwealth as a counterweight to the British Empire. But most Indians did not share his vision, resenting his fictitious status. The British stopped lavishing him with gifts, and his followers abandoned him. Sidelined and frustrated, Pontiac stabbed an Illini sachem at a peace conference in the summer of 1766, weakening his already fragile position.[18]

Chapter 22

A SECOND
CHINESE WALL

S IR WILLIAM JOHNSON WAS DYING. HE HAD BEEN the leading agent of the sole European empire in North America, and he wanted to secure his legacy in the little time he had. Pontiac traveled to Johnson Hall, Johnson's home and headquarters, in New York Colony to sign a treaty on behalf of his followers. It stipulated that the Indians "will pay all due submission and subjection so far as the same can be consistent with the Indians native rights." Quietly, Johnson had retreated from British claims of absolute sovereignty over Native Americans. Genuine peace, at long last, was possible.[1]

In November 1768, Johnson invited more than three thousand Iroquois, Lenape, Shawnee, and Seneca-Cayuga representatives to Fort Stanwix in New York to envision the postwar future. The Iroquois had preserved their neutrality for nearly the duration of the Seven Years' War, committing to the British only toward the end, when British victory was certain. Johnson, their most important ally, had experienced a meteoric rise during the war and was now preoccupied with complex diplomatic missions in the Ohio Country, where colonial land mania fueled speculation and anger among settlers and Indians alike. Johnson received orders from Whitehall to renegotiate the Six Nations' boundaries. Ahead of the conference he sent word that women would not be allowed to participate, violating centuries-old diplomatic protocols.[2]

Still, as with so many Native-colonial summits over the previous decades, the Fort Stanwix talks followed the conventions of Covenant Chain diplomacy. "I would deal with all people in their own way,"

Johnson began. "Your Ancestors have from the earliest time directed and recommended the observation of a Sett of Rules they laid down for you to follow." The British officials wiped away blood and tears with belts of wampum, and expressed concern "for the many losses" the Indians had suffered. Oneida sachem Canaghquieson responded in kind. But then, shockingly, the tone changed: Johnson revealed a new map that would drastically diminish the Iroquois domain. With the scratch of a pen, the Six Nations and other Native nations lost more than thirty thousand square miles of the Ohio Country to Britain. As compensation, the Indians would receive an amount of goods worth £10,000. A Six Nations envoy confronted Johnson, appealing to their shared history: "Now Brother, you, who know all our affairs, must be sensible that our Rights go much farther to the Southward." The British listened to the scolding and then piled goods on a table as the sachems signed the deeds. A land rush followed promptly.

The Shawnees left immediately for the Ohio Country. They reported to their allies that Johnson had admitted that the Six Nations might not have possessed the authority to execute a land transfer of such scale. The Shawnees entrenched themselves in the Ohio Valley and sent a warning that British land surveyors would not be safe. Threats, rumors, murders, and fights escalated into a war that was never declared. Serving a crumbling phantom empire, Johnson maneuvered frantically to eliminate the Shawnees and their allies. He nearly succeeded. The Shawnees retreated and turned inward. Influential Shawnee women representing different clans advocated for peace and political neutrality. When the French traders in Detroit sent war belts to the Shawnees, the women intervened. The Shawnees "dug a hole in the Ground and buried them never to rise again."[3]

The Treaty of Fort Stanwix anticipated a new world, but it was not the world that either Johnson or the Indians wanted. Land, not trade or alliances, would now define relations between Native Americans and British Americans. During the 1760s, roughly fifteen thousand immigrants—Britons, Scots, Irish, Germans, and others—arrived every year. The price of land soared, stoking uncertainty and resentment. Colonial families often had eight to twelve children, but only one of them could inherit the family holdings. The rest faced tenancy

under land barons. New England was expanding at the rate of eigh-
teen new towns per year, and thousands of New Yorkers moved into
the Mohawk and Hudson Valleys. Pennsylvanians—among them
Daniel Boone—crossed the Royal Proclamation line illegally into the
Ohio Country and floated in flatboats into lands they called Ohio
and Tennessee. General Gage, still the commander of British forces in
North America, believed systemic corruption was to blame: "Men of
Interest Abet these Encroachments."

Bursting at its seams, British America was losing its legitimacy
in Native eyes. The diplomatic middle ground, after its brief revival
during Pontiac's War, was faltering. The assertive Cherokee leader
Attakullakulla pushed British leaders to mediate grievances in the
Ohio Country where multiple Native interests clashed. Desperate
to preserve Indigenous solidarity in the Ohio Country, Shawnee,
Wabash, and Lenape headwomen pushed their male counterparts to
"forget all Insults given." It was too late for Pontiac. In 1769, a Peoria
sachem knifed him in the back in the French village of Cahokia. Pontiac may have died marginalized and misunderstood, but the legacy
of his vision for Indigenous rights and sovereignty would resonate for
generations along with those of Wahunsenacawh, Metacom, Thayendanegea, and Tecumseh.[4]

THE RIVALRIES BETWEEN INDIGENOUS nations and European
settlers had centered for generations on resources, rivers, roads, and
respect—or the lack thereof. Now land became the source of conflict.
Coexistence in the borderlands became difficult when White farmers pushed deeper into the West. Tensions mounted alarmingly when
land speculators got involved. They bought land in bulk and sold the
titles to common settlers. Allying with governors and their councils,
the speculators hoarded titles, creating a seller's market. In a desperate effort to hold on to their lands, Wappinger Indians granted parcels
to the neighboring Connecticut settlers for 999-year terms.[5]

Settlers feared that land was becoming scarce, and the repercussions were disastrous for Native Americans. In the fertile Ohio Country, six thousand Shawnees, Lenapes, and Seneca-Cayugas struggled

to hold on to their land and villages. They lived in cabins with glass windows, farmed with iron hoes and steel axes, raised pigs and cows, hunted with guns, and wore manufactured clothes. The British could have easily concluded that they were using the land "properly"—the key colonial criteria for civilization and sovereignty—but they did not. The settlers did not want Native peoples around; they wanted their land. The Royal Proclamation was a dead letter.

In 1772 the British army evacuated Fort Pitt, shuttering the region's only site of British imperial authority. The next year, settlers tried to chase Indians out of what they called Kentucky. The power vacuum had brought on a colonial land rush, inspiring an anonymous essayist to write in the *Virginia Gazette* that "not even a second Chinese Wall, unless guarded by a million soldiers, could prevent the settlement of the Lands of the Ohio and its Dependencies." General Gage had seven thousand. For his part, John Murray, fourth Earl of Dunmore, the royal governor of Virginia, had his eyes on a personal one-hundred-thousand-acre western estate. He was able to consider a massive personal land grab because there were only some fifty thousand settlers west of the Appalachians—enough to contain the Indians, but not too many to challenge his scheme. Lord Dunmore's ambitions were driven by both race and class: he wanted to rid the Ohio Country and Kentucky of both Native Americans and poor Whites.[6]

ON DECEMBER 16, 1773, a group of Bostonians dressed as Mohawk Indians, calling their actions a Tea Party, threw tea into the Boston Harbor to declare a distinct aboriginal American identity separate from the British. Native Americans soon learned how the new American identity would affect them.[7]

In the spring of 1774, Virginia backwoods thugs killed nine Seneca-Cayugas in the Ohio Country, touching off a war. It was a war that few wanted, yet it had to be fought because neither side would compromise. Dunmore dispatched two militia armies, each more than a thousand strong, to snare the Shawnees and Seneca-Cayugas, and he also recruited Black slaves as soldiers. The Indians escaped by focusing on the southern army. Shawnee and Seneca-Cayuga soldiers made their way down the Ohio on rafts, securing a position near the British. The fighting was at close range, thus favoring the Indians, who used the terrain to their advantage. The militia managed to defend its position in ferocious hand-to-hand combat, and the allied Indians executed a disciplined retreat. "The Bravest of their men made use of themselves, while others were throwing their dead into the Ohio," a British officer reported, not without admiration. The Shawnee sachem Cornstalk signed an armistice with Dunmore at Camp Charlotte, Lord Dunmore's base of operations. What would become known as Lord Dunmore's War had ended in a draw.

That was not enough for Dunmore. He pushed into the Ohio Country with Virginia militiamen and burned Shawnee and Six Nations settlements. According to the British, the Shawnees had relinquished their hunting privileges in the Ohio Country and Kentucky, but the Shawnees challenged that interpretation. Colonial treaty-making was haphazard at best. Dunmore's militia reoccupied Fort Pitt and renamed it Fort Dunmore, claiming civil and military authority under Virginia law. The West descended into anarchy. Not long after, Dunmore appeared at the Westmoreland County courthouse in Hannastown with 150 armed men. They dragged three Pennsylvania judges out of the building and marched them two hundred miles to Staunton, Virginia. Determined Indigenous resistance had turned the British against themselves.[8]

London was appalled. Parliament stopped offering land grants to settlers—an action that many saw as a betrayal and punishment. Britain simply lacked the necessary force to control events: its army had shrunk to fifty thousand, less than a third the size of the French army. In late June of 1774, Parliament passed the Quebec Act, which granted religious freedom to the province of Quebec, restored French civil law, and shifted the Ohio Valley into the province of Quebec. In the fall, twelve of the thirteen colonies—Georgia dithered—sent delegates to the First Continental Congress in Philadelphia to confront the British Empire as a single collective body. Spotting an opening, the Indians, undefeated, demanded and secured a boundary at the Ohio River in the east, which effectively nullified several western claims of the coastal colonies and posed an existential threat to settlers and land speculators along the East Coast.

The boundary, however, did not hold. Self-styled pioneers and land speculators, including Daniel Boone, were drawn to the fertile bluegrass region, where bison and other big game abounded. In March 1775, Boone blazed a footpath through the Cumberland Gap—a notch in the Appalachians—with thirty men and built the fort-like Boonesborough in the upper Kentucky Valley, where few Indigenous settlements existed. The path would soon be called the Wilderness Road. Around the same time, an ambitious North Carolinian land speculator named Richard Henderson persuaded Cherokee leaders Attakullakulla, Oconostota, and Raven to sell more than thirty-four thousand square miles of land for a handsome £10,000, and he founded the Transylvania Colony, which ran alongside the Ohio River for hundreds of miles. Henderson had openly violated both Cherokee sovereignty and the Royal Proclamation line, yet, with stunning arrogance, he hoped that Transylvania, his personal kingdom, could become the fourteenth colony of British America. Both the settlers and the Indians were now maneuvering in the interior as though the British Empire did not exist.[9]

In the spring of 1775, the Cherokees met with colonial representatives at Sycamore Shoals in the heart of their agricultural realm and prime hunting grounds. The Americans wanted the Indians to cede land, including the Cumberland Gap. Dragging Canoe, a forceful Cherokee war leader, stormed out, rejecting the colonists' offer of £10,000. The incident marked the beginning of Cherokee resistance that would last for more than half a century. Mirroring Neolin's Nativist message, some Cherokee spiritual leaders started preaching about separate creations, erecting a racial hierarchy between White and Indigenous people. By the start of the nineteenth century, the southern Indian nations had begun experimenting with pan-Indian collaboration against the self-identifying "Americans," who were staging attacks across the Southeast from the coast deep into the interior. Black slaves became collateral victims because most Indians saw them as part of the colonial machine. The Muscogees stood out by targeting plantations in the Spanish settlement of New Madrid. They thought that too many of its inhabitants were Virginians.[10]

PONTIAC'S WAR, the Treaty of Fort Stanwix, Lord Dunmore's War, and Henderson's Purchase were pieces of a larger pattern. The British, with their long history of fearing and hating Indians, were moving toward the elimination of Native peoples within and beyond their borders. That impulse had been vastly magnified by the growing crisis between Great Britain and the settlers. While the Indians and settlers had clashed in the interior, the thirteen colonies were fighting for their rights as members of the British Empire. They had protested against the Royal Proclamation, the detested Sugar and Stamp Acts, the Townsend Duties, and the Declaratory Act, the last of which asserted full British sovereignty over the colonies. They had been shocked on March 5, 1770, by what they called the Boston Massacre where British soldiers shot and killed several people, and their merchants felt abused by British tax policies. On April 18 and 19, 1775, the Battles of Lexington and Concord forced a rebellion.

Seventeen seventy-five was a critical year for Native Americans as well. In May, the committee of Tyron County, a German-speaking frontier community in western New York, complained that its settlers were uncomfortable with their Native neighbors, "whom we dread most, there being a current report through the County, that they are to be made use of in keeping us in awe." When the thirteen colonies severed ties with the British Empire a year later, the Declaration of Independence labeled Native Americans as "merciless Indian Savages," the assumption being that the Indians were loyal to the British. The enlightened Thomas Paine managed but a crude comparison on Native Americans in his radical pamphlet *Common Sense*: The "naked and untutored Indian, is less a savage than the King of Britain." John Adams advised Thomas Jefferson that "Power always follows Property." Native nations were, from the start, necessary and ambiguous actors in the war, whether on the battlefield or as props for propaganda.[11]

There would be numerous ways for Native Americans to join, evade, exit, and even benefit from the conflict. The Stockbridge Indians living in the Massachusetts borderlands volunteered to become minutemen even before the war began. Since Metacom's War in the late 1670s, they had been gradually dispossessed by the British, who took over most of the land in southwestern Massachusetts. In the 1740s, Moravian missionaries, a pietist Saxony sect that treated Indians as kin and equals, joined Christian Mahicans to run a mission in the town of Stockbridge. The chaos of the Seven Years' War and the racially charged Pontiac's War had left the Mahicans destitute. For the three hundred remaining Stockbridges, the Revolutionary War was an opportunity to win back land and disentangle themselves from the imperious Six Nations. In the spring of 1775, seventeen Stockbridge soldiers joined General George Washington's troops at Cambridge, prompting General Gage to write, "The Rebels have themselves opened the Door; they have brought down all the Savages they could against us here, who with their Rifle men are continually firing on our advanced Sentries." Where the Six Nations, Cherokees, Choctaws, and other large Native nations could rely on diplomatic prowess and sheer military power to contain colonialism, the Stockbridge Indians evaded dispossession by selectively blending in among the colonists.[12]

In late April, after the clashes at Lexington and Concord, the New England militia laid siege to Boston and its garrison. The opening of the Revolutionary War was emblematic: from the start it was a series of local wars with numerous sides. The majority of Native nations wanted nothing to do with the war, but some saw it as an opportunity to revive the strategy of playing off one colonial power against another. Some were simply swept into the conflict. Nonparticipation was almost impossible because most of the fighting took place on Indigenous land. In December 1775, the Continental Congress announced that "the Indians of St. Francis, Penobscot, Stockbridge, and Saint John's, and other tribes, may be called on in case of real necessity, and that the giving them presents is both suitable and proper." It was a measured gesture toward Native Americans—most of those listed were Christian Indians from small nations—but it soon became a general policy.[13]

Accepting that they could not prevail without Indian allies, the superior Native knowledge of the terrain, and Native weapons, especially hatchets, the Patriots reached out, as most colonial powers had, to the Six Nations. Although now much reduced in number, the Iroquois were still an essential nation, owing to their moral authority and central position between the colonial East and the Indigenous West. But the Six Nations had been neutral for decades. When a British official proclaimed in early June 1776 at Fort Niagara that a British victory was inevitable and asked the Seneca war leader Flying Crow to join the British in fighting the Patriots, Flying Crow turned him down, mockingly: "If you are so strong a Brother, and they but as a weak Boy, why ask our assistance. . . . You say they are all mad, foolish, wicked, and deceitful—I say you are so and they are wise for you want us to destroy ourselves in your War and they advise us to live in Peace." The Six Nations would not join the war. The Seneca sachem Kayashuta put it more bluntly: "We must be Fools indeed to imagine that they regard us or our Interest who want to bring us into an unnecessary War."[14]

Flying Crow's neutrality posed a dilemma to Patriots and British alike. The Continental Congress had already agreed to seek military alliances with Native Americans, and the British needed Indigenous allies to attack and defend their forts in the Great Lakes region. The British desperately wanted to avoid draining and humiliating sieges of the kind they had faced during the Seven Years' War and Pontiac's War. By relying on mobile Indigenous soldiers who knew the terrain intimately, British officers hoped to create a massive protective perimeter along the frontiers of New York, Pennsylvania, western Virginia, and Kentucky. At best, the British could isolate the Continental army on the Atlantic seaboard. At a minimum, they could force George Washington, the commander in chief of the Continental army, to divide his forces. The Six Nations, the dominant Indigenous power, were critical of the British plan.

Americans could now simply force the much-diminished Indigenous nations to provide soldiers. Proportionally, more Indians than New Englanders fought in Patriot forces in the course of the war. But the Indigenous nations of New England also displayed a subversive streak. Mohegan ministers Samson Occom and Joseph Johnson recruited followers from among the Pequots, Narragansetts, Niantics, Mohegans, and Montauks to create an independent Indigenous realm—Eeyawquit-toowauconnuck, "Brothertown"—roughly a hundred miles west of Albany. Drawing a racial line between Native "brethren" on the one hand and the British on the other, Occom and Johnson hoped to secure a protected space under Oneida auspices. Occom was superficially attached to the Patriot cause, but he condemned the aggressive methods used by both the British and the Patriots to force Indians to join them: "I am Extremely Sorry to see the White People on both Sides, to use their Influence with the poor Indians to get them on their Side, I wish they would let the poor Indians alone . . . What have they to do with your Quarrels?" Brothertown, as both a base and a movement, boosted a growing pan-Indian resistance movement against British and American imperialism.[15]

In the early spring of 1776, militant Iroquois, Shawnee, and Odawa women crafted enormous wampum belts—the largest was nine feet long—to invite other Native nations to war. That summer, Dragging Canoe ignored the Cherokee councils' wariness concerning pan-Indian resistance and accepted a war belt from the Shawnees. He planned an attack against the Americans in the western counties of both Carolinas, determined to keep settlers away from Cherokee territory in the Overhill country west of the Appalachians. Chota, the capital of the Cherokee Nation—which one colonial officer dubbed "the metropolis" of Cherokee country—emerged as a military nerve center for pro-British Shawnee, Lenape, Odawa, and Mohawk armies. Dragging Canoe led five hundred soldiers across the mountains and destroyed all colonial settlements west of the southern Appalachians. A smaller Cherokee contingent took three female captives, one of whom was Daniel Boone's teenage daughter. Instead of deterring the settlers, the attacks brought the larger war into Cherokee country. In the late summer and fall, six thousand Virginia and South Carolina militiamen invaded Cherokee territory in the Overhill country, destroying most of its forty-three towns and forcing the eight-thousand-strong Cherokee Nation to cede lands to both states. To the west, the Muscogees and Choctaws remained neutral throughout the war and retained their territories.[16]

After the war, the fledgling United States was far from safe, and it

"A Draught of the
Cherokee Country,"
by Lieutenant Henry
Timberlake, 1762

struggled to unite into a nation. The Revolutionary War was over, but both domestic and foreign tensions lasted. Farmers, urban laborers, and frontier settlers remained in rebellious mode, their livelihoods and security threatened by Indians that the new American state was too weak to subdue. The new central government was nearly crushed by war debt, Britain occupied multiple forts in the Ohio Country, U.S. money was nearly worthless, and there were only two roads—Braddock's Road and Forbes Road—that reached the Trans-Mississippi West. Geopolitically, the 1783 Treaty of Paris left the United States in limbo, failing to solve nearly all of the issues that had triggered the war, and the individual states continued to pursue independent foreign policies. The double threat of Indians and British pushed the federal government to expand its fiscal and military powers. Once committed to expansion, the new republic could capitalize on its singular advantage: its explosively growing population was approaching two million.[17]

The Chickasaws, led by Payamataha—war prophet—sided with Britain. Decades earlier, Payamataha had been wounded in battle against the French and had become a staunch ally of the British. He denounced the French, their gifts, and their artful diplomacy, and kept attacking and killing them. When he was done, he claimed to have killed forty French soldiers. He then reinvented himself as a peacemaker. A charismatic and astute leader, Payamataha mobilized the Chickasaw Nation against the French in a dual role as "head lead-ing warrior of the nation, to treat with all nations." A pragmatist, he realized that the Chickasaws, numbering only seventeen hundred, could not survive a prolonged war. He adopted the role of a diplo-mat and forged alliances with the Choctaws, Cherokees, Catawbas, and Quapaws, relying heavily on Chickasaw women, whose hospi-tality and authority made the alliances real. Payamataha was not a Nativist leader of Pontiac's ilk. His ambition was universal peace in the interior. He did not think that the world was divided into differ-ent races—Native Americans and non–Native Americans; the only meaningful divide for him was between Chickasaws and non-Chick-asaws. He kept the colonial powers at arm's length, negotiating with them through the principal chief, Mingo Houma. Remarkably, in the 1770s the Chickasaws were more securely independent than they had been in the preceding generation.[18]

IN JANUARY 1777, IN the midst of the cataclysmic war, one of the most significant turning points in American history took place, throwing almost all war strategies into question. Abruptly and shock-ingly, the Six Nations ritually extinguished their central council fire for the first time in the history of the league. Suddenly, the Iroquois Empire was no more. A disease epidemic had broken out, and the Iroquois, suffering and dying, turned against each other. Shockingly, their confederacy split into incompatible factions: the Tuscaroras aligned with the fledgling United States; the Oneidas struggled to remain neutral but eventually clashed with the Mohawks and burned their towns. The Onondagas tried to remain neutral but eventually sided with the British. The Senecas, caught in the middle, suffered heavy losses. With the Six Nations debilitated by a civil war, unprecedented strategic options became available to Americans. In 1777 the Ohio River marked a border between the American colonies on the Atlantic seaboard and the Indians in the Ohio Country. The Iroquois had contended with both Indigenous and colonial powers for four centuries, shaping the continent more profoundly than any other group or nation had done.[19]

With the Six Nations sidelined, the war shifted west, making the Ohio Country a focal point of the conflict. The Americans needed a stable West to secure their position in the East, and the Indians were in their way. The situation made Fort Niagara essential. The fort served, all at once, as military headquarters, trading post, supply depot, refugee center, council ground, and a miniature middle ground where people, ambitions, and ideas blended. It was also the headquarters of the new British superintendent of Indian affairs, Guy Johnson—Sir William's nephew—who orchestrated diplomatic maneuvers that were as ambitious as his uncle's had been. British officers supplied the Indians with guns and powder, helping Shawnee, Lenape, Seneca-Cayuga, Wyandot, and Cherokee soldiers kill hundreds of settlers in Kentucky, Pennsylvania, and western Virginia. On the American side, local militias, disgusted by the tentativeness of the official troops, assumed a larger role.[20]

Meanwhile, in the Ohio Country the Shawnees and Lenapes opened talks with the Patriots, hoping to forge an agreement under which they could coexist. The Patriots treated the Lenapes with dignity, fearing to alienate them. The Lenapes, for their part, wanted to incorporate, not eliminate, the westward-pushing Americans. The Lenape sachems White Eyes and Killbuck joined the Shawnee sachem Cornstalk at Fort Pitt to propose a political partnership, increased trade, and joint education programs. They were drawing the Americans closer in an effort to render them less dangerous. White Eyes and Killbuck sent their children to a college in New Jersey, hoping to create mutual understanding and tolerance. But they had underestimated the intensity of Indian hating among the Patriots. Vigilantes murdered Cornstalk in 1777. The Continental army quickly concluded a treaty with the Lenapes, promising the nation representation in Congress. In 1777, the Seminoles, an ethnically mixed people from Florida, attacked Fort MacIntosh in a carefully coordinated attack in East Florida. The British failed to punish the still young Seminole Nation, and the consequences would persist across several generations.

Through the first year of war, the Patriots were ineffective in both battle and diplomacy. The August 1777 fight for control of the Hudson Valley, the Battle of Oriskany—one of the bloodiest of the war—had been inconclusive, largely because the Six Nations had fought on both sides. The Oneidas and some Tuscaroras had sided with the Patriots, whereas the Mohawks, led by Thayendanegea, or Joseph Brant, had fought with the British. Molly Brant, a galvanizing moral leader who hated the Americans—they had banished her family from the Mohawk Valley—warned the Loyalists of an approaching Patriot militia. It was said that "one word from her goes farther with them than a thousand from any White Man." Knowing that only victories in battle would secure the Oneidas' future, she urged soldiers into combat and sent her brother to launch relentless attacks against American settlements in the Hudson and Susquehanna Valleys with British loyalists who called themselves "Brant's volunteers." Time was running out. Joseph Brant and the Mahican leader Hendrick Aupaumut evoked the metaphor of the "common pot" to restore balance in Indigenous spaces.

Around the same time, the Shawnees split into a militant anti-American faction and neutrals who guardedly accommodated the British. In a near-mirror image of Patriot belligerence, the allied Ohio Indians struck Kentucky settlements with methodical attacks for several years, killing people, burning crops, and forcing the now starving colonists to retreat into three small forts. Boone was captured and relented to being adopted by the Shawnee sachem Blackfish, pliantly accepting Native dominance over him. Other settlers went after Indians. In early 1778, the men under General Edward Hand shot and scalped six Lenapes and Munsees—one man, four women, and a child. Only fear and hatred could explain the atrocity. Several Lenapes joined with the Odawas, Potawatomis, and Miamis and sang war songs with them. Pennsylvania put a $100 bounty on Indian scalps. The Ohio Country had become ungovernable. The American way of waging war was amateurish, wild, and ineffective. A Loyalist mocked the Patriot war effort by noting how Indian attacks had "reduced the extensive frontier upon the Ohio, to a heap of ashes."[21]

A similar dynamic emerged in Kentucky and Pennsylvania, where several Indian nations kept attacking frontier settlements, prompting Colonel George Rogers Clark, a Virginia land surveyor and militia officer, to punish them. Having lost a number of relatives in Indian wars, Clark wanted to eradicate the Indians. He launched a personal vendetta and announced that "he expected shortly to see the whole race of Indians extirpated, that for his part he would never spare Man woman or child of them on whom he could lay his hands." It was not idle bragging. Having taken several captives, Clark marched them to a British fort and ordered them executed while the British watched the butchering from a safe distance. A young Odawa sachem, having suffered a fatal tomahawk blow to the head, pulled the weapon out of his skull and handed it to Clark, diminishing his executioner.[22]

ON JUNE 21, 1779, Spain declared war on Britain, prompting John Stuart, the British superintendent of Indian affairs for the Southern District, to work to persuade Chickasaws and Choctaws to serve as guardians of the Mississippi, patrolling the river for Patriot activity. Struggling to both recruit and defeat Native soldiers, George Washington and his cabinet launched a scorched-earth campaign against the Senecas, whom they considered the most militant of the Six Nations. In the fall, Washington mobilized five thousand troops against the nation. The campaign was a resounding success: "Forty of their towns have been reduced to ashes, some of them large and commodious, that of the Chenissee—the Genesee Castle, a Seneca stronghold—alone containing 128 houses. Their crops of corn have been entirely destroyed." The assault created five thousand refugees, who fled to the Niagara Valley, stretching out for eight miles on its banks. Hundreds died of disease and hunger. It was also a direct attack on Iroquois women, "who were the Truest Owners, being the persons who labor on the Lands." The Mohawks and Onondagas had lost vast tracts of land and gravitated even more toward the British, whereas the Oneidas acted as a buffer for the British at the head of the Mohawk River. In return, they received guarantees for their lands. Washington believed that the momentum had shifted decisively; the domain of the Six Nations "has been overrun and laid waste," he said.[23]

In the winter of 1779–80, allied Indians secured plenty of guns and powder from the British and destroyed American settlements across a vast frontier belt extending from New York in the north across Pennsylvania and western Virginia, and to Kentucky in the south and, on the east–west axis, from the Alleghenies to the Mississippi Valley. British officers hoped to shift the primary battle zone westward and provide relief to their armies operating on the Eastern Seaboard. The Ojibwes, Lenapes, Mahicans, Miamis, and Meskwakis joined the Mohawks, Onondagas, Cayugas, and Senecas in a vast British-Native alliance. These Indigenous soldiers were not auxiliaries providing supplementary support to the British army. They fought for their own reasons, with their own methods, and under their own leaders; they were waging their own war within the larger war, determined to protect their sovereignty. Their mobile soldiers relied on ambushes, retreats, regroupings, sieges, and, when necessary, frontal attacks. Whenever they provided support to British maneuvers, they expected to be rewarded. "The Indians have been accustomed to receive so very liberally, that now their Demands are quite unlimited," one British officer despaired. The Iroquois began to call Washington *Hanadagá:yas*, "Town Destroyer."[24]

British troops and pro-British Iroquois soldiers chased the Oneidas out of the Mohawk Valley, burning their villages and destroying the critical buffer zone that had shielded American settlements. Clark was in a rush because he knew that British troops under Lieutenant Governor Henry Hamilton would try to entrench themselves in the Illinois Country in early spring. To reach their destinations, the two armies had to enter the middle ground, where they could operate only by embracing Indigenous diplomacy. Rather than simply killing the Piankashaw sachem Grand Coete as his Indian-hating would have dictated, Clark appeased him. He compared the sachem to Pontiac.

Facing Native Americans whom he could not afford to alienate, Clark awkwardly announced, "It may appear otherwise to You, but [I] always thought we took the wrong method of treating with Indians, and strove as soon as possible to make myself acquainted with the French and Spanish mode which must be preferable to ours. Otherwise they could not possibly have such great influence among them." With a new mindset and proper words, Clark forged bonds with Kaskaskians, Kickapoos, and Peorias. The British militia at Fort Sackville abandoned Hamilton, and the Patriots took the fort and restored its original name, Vincennes. Every maneuver, however forceful or creative, seemed only to prolong the war. Dozens of Indigenous war expeditions left from Fort Niagara in both 1781 and 1782. At Fort Pitt, an official complained that "you could not send out your servant 100 yards without having him scalped." American power and presence in the Ohio Country were shrinking fast.[25]

While the Patriots and the British were preoccupied with the war and its many theaters of operations, smallpox had traveled in the bodies of soldiers, triggering local outbreaks in Quebec, Boston, and the Great Lakes. The pox then moved south from Quebec and north from Pensacola along the Eastern Seaboard with the marching British and Patriot armies. In 1781, the British were confident of victory and spent £100,000 to stock Forts Niagara, Detroit, and Michilimackinac with gifts for the Indians; Niagara alone treated Indians with over twenty-seven thousand gallons of rum a year. But an epidemic changed the course of the Revolutionary War when it devastated Lord Dunmore's "Ethiopian Regiment," a group of loyalist African Americans who had escaped slavery and joined the British army in a march across the South. In October, General Charles Cornwallis and the main British army were hopelessly trapped in Yorktown on the Virginia Peninsula. A promised fleet from New York had been intersected by French ships, Dunmore's Black allies were dying of the pox, and his regulars were succumbing to malaria. His army vanishing under a double pathogenic assault, Cornwallis surrendered, bringing the American Revolutionary War to an end.[26]

Britain may have exited the war, but Native Americans continued to fight. Their war of independence was still undecided, and 1782 saw some of the bitterest battling in the Ohio Valley. Shawnee, Lenape, and Seneca-Cayuga war expeditions left nearly nine hundred Kentucky settlers dead. In the pays d'en haut, British troops were still occupying forts and faced Indians who harbored nostalgia for Onontio and French traders, French gifts, and French meditation. The nostalgia was real, but it was also performative. It served to terrify British officials and force them to make concessions and keep trade goods flowing in.

In 1782, Major Arent DePeyster, the commander of Fort Detroit, apologized to his superior for the fact that the Indians "are not under better discipline." It was not for lack of trying: "I have wrought hard to endeavor to Bring them to it, but, find it impossible altogether to change their natures. I assemble them, get fair promises, and send them out, but when once out of sight the turning of a Straw may divert them from the original plan." DePeyster did not articulate it, but his report captured the fact that after twenty-five years of almost continuous war, Native Americans were still in control in the continent's interior.[27]

THE SEVEN YEARS' WAR, Pontiac's War, Lord Dunmore's War, and the Revolutionary War were to the British a single, twenty-year conflict geared at preserving their hegemony in North America and, by extension, in the Caribbean and the Atlantic. The 1783 Treaty of Paris extinguished that long-standing ambition. The thirteen colonies were severed from the British Empire and recognized as the United States of America. Native Americans had not been invited to the treaty talks, and they knew to expect an undesirable outcome. Still, when the news arrived, they were shocked and appalled. The treaty gave the United States an enormous territory between the Appalachians and the Mississippi River, including the southern Great Lakes. The United States was an instant empire, claiming lands far beyond its effective borders. The change was so abrupt that it took Jefferson, ordinarily an expeditious labeler, several years to define the new empire. He called it an "empire of liberty." For most Native Americans, it was a crude robber regime.[28]

Contemporary Europeans saw the 1783 treaty as a decisive turning point in the North American continent's history that spelled doom for Native Americans, who could no longer play rival colonial powers against one another. That view of the situation was wishful thinking. The fledgling United States may have claimed an enormous swath of Indigenous territory, but it controlled very little of it. Native Americans, allied with both Patriots and Britain, had retained their territorial supremacy in North America throughout the long war. The Great Lakes region and nearly all of the Trans-Mississippi West remained under Indigenous rule, with catastrophic consequences for the British Empire: British possessions were confined to north of the Ohio River, isolating the British from the main commercial and diplomatic networks.

In the summer of 1783, thirty-five Native nations gathered for a conference at Sandusky, a Wyandot settlement in the Ohio Country, where Joseph Brant urged them to join in an alliance against the United States through the ancient "Dish with One Spoon" law. Others directed their anger at the British. The Iroquois were "thunderstruck" when they realized that their British allies had done nothing on their behalf in Paris, limiting their territory within the boundaries of the new United States. A year later, at Fort Michilimackinac, the Ojibwe ogimaag Matchekwis branded all British "liars [and] imposters" for having "encouraged him and others to go to Canada [and] to fight and lose their Brothers and Children." Despite all his people's sacrifices, he said, the British "now despise them, and let them starve." The Seminoles, who had incorporated large numbers of fugitive slaves, shamed the British by asking them whether they now intended to sell them into slavery. For the Muscogees, Cherokees, and other southern Indians, the wars of independence would continue for generations in various forms.[29]

The wars of independence, both Indigenous and Anglo-American, that covered a half century were about respect, resources, land, and sovereignty. More abstractly, they were about legitimacy and the moral mandate to determine how war, commerce, and diplomacy were to be conducted. At the heart of the matter was the question of power—not just who should have it, but how it should be wielded in a world where Indigenous nations remained largely undefeated. By engaging selectively in wars between empires, most Native nations had preserved their independence and centrality: when the fighting ended, most of the continent was still Indigenous. Massive numbers of American settlers had crossed the Appalachians into the West, but they did not control the interior, where Native power dominated. Spain controlled a few small patches within its vast paper empire in North America—struggling settlements in the Mississippi Valley, an embryonic Indian mission project in Alta California, and the ungovernable Florida, where Indians reigned supreme. Spanish authorities tried to control the vast Louisiana Colony with five hundred troops. Crucially, Native Americans held sway in the pivotal Ohio Country where Iroquois, Seneca-Cayuga, Lenape, and Shawnee towns greatly outnumbered the colonial populations. The few American forts, garrisons, and settlements in the region were defensive enclaves.[30]

The Treaty of Paris and its repercussions, however, had only heightened the contest between the Native peoples and the settlers. The British Empire of crown soldiers and officials had been replaced by a new American empire of settlers who clamored for Native land even as they felt victimized by the Indians. Native Americans, although far from a single people, had prevailed and continued to think of themselves as sovereign nations. Where the American War of Independence had created a new sovereign nation, the Indigenous wars of independence had saved dozens of existing ones.

PART SEVEN

AMERICAN REVOLUTIONS

*(late eighteenth century to
early nineteenth century)*

Chapter 23

THE AMERICAN CRUCIBLE

T HE TALKS HAD BEEN UNDERWAY FOR SEVERAL DAYS already, and the participants were getting edgy. In the fall of 1778, with the Revolutionary War still undecided, U.S. commissioners had invited Lenape delegates to treaty talks at Fort Pitt in the heart of the Ohio Country. Both sides had delivered elaborate speeches, hoping to forge mutual understandings, and had patiently removed obstacles to peace. Yet problems remained. The commissioners felt compelled to explain Article 6 of the proposed treaty, which stated, "The Enemies of the United States have endeavored by every artifice in their power to possess the Indians in General with an opinion, that it is the design of the United States . . . to extirpate the Indians and take possession of their country." Through its new and aggressive national government, the United States had become a self-conscious settler colony that was impatient with Indigenous peoples on its claimed borders. U.S. agents were troubled by the implications of the accusation: their new nation, just two years old, had already been denounced as a genocidal behemoth, lending credence to long-lasting Native fears. The United States could not afford to carry such a reputation, because its position in the Indigenous continent was far from secure.[1]

The Seven Years' War, Pontiac's War, the Revolutionary War, and Lord Dunmore's War had positioned the Native Americans to contain the United States stalwartly. The Great Lakes region remained resolutely Indigenous, Spain was distracted by a war with Britain, and the United States was crippled by a $75 million war debt. The new Department of Finance printed so much money that it caused debilitating inflation. More than twenty-five thousand Americans had died in the wars—many of them from disease—yet wages plunged by more than twenty-five percent. Patriots abused Loyalists and confiscated their property. Sixty thousand Loyalists left the young republic, along with some fifteen thousand Black slaves and five thousand free Blacks. In Massachusetts, farmers were paying a third of their income to the state, sparking Shays' Rebellion in 1786, which forced the governor to mobilize four thousand volunteers to suppress the uprising. The United States was reeling, its moral authority in shambles.[2]

Conversely, Native Americans could take solace in the fact that they had survived three consecutive wars that shook North America in the late eighteenth century. The United States was now the dominant force east of the Mississippi, but its reach did not even extend to that attractive boundary. Britain continued to occupy forts in the interior to protect the fur trade, its most important resource in North America, but it lacked a coherent strategy for reconquest. With enduring British and Spanish presence, however diminished, Native nations could once again systematically rely on the strategies that had kept the competing colonial powers at bay. Many Native nations forged new connections to preserve their sovereignty, while American promoters and land speculators worked feverishly to lure more colonists into the Trans-Appalachian West—the vast region between the Appalachians and the Mississippi River—and especially to the fertile Ohio Country. There, people like Daniel Boone now operated as petty speculators.[3]

War-weary and nearly crushed by debt, the United States failed to properly staff its newly won forts in the interior. The upshot was that there was no effective federal oversight in the Trans-Appalachian West. The absence of overarching authority—whether American, British, or Indigenous—turned the region into a free-for-all. A genocidal massacre set the tone. In the fall of 1782, David Williamson, a wealthy Pennsylvanian militia leader known for his zeal to kill Indians, led a vigilante group to Gnadenhütten—"tents of grace"— a peaceful Lenape town where the Indians had allowed Moravian missionaries to live among them. The Americans entered carrying an English flag, and the missionaries offered them food. The vigilantes found metalware in the town and decided that the Indians must have raided American settlements. The militiamen lifted their hammers and smashed in the skulls of ninety-six children, women, and men, who kept singing a Christian hymn to the end. Many were scalped. Afterward, there was no American attempt to apologize or compensate for the massacre, which then became a declaration of war. This incident, together with other recent atrocities, especially the Paxton Boys' frenzied killing spree, brought the young United States' reputation to an all-time low.[4]

Within a year of the Gnadenhütten massacre, building on the pan-Indian Sandusky summit the previous summer, the Mohawk sachem Thayendanegea urged the Indian nations in the central Mississippi Valley and the Ohio Country to move against the United States: "Let there be Peace or War, it shall never disunite us, for our Interests are alike nor Should any Thing ever be done but by the Voice of the whole." Native nations formed what became known as the Indian Confederacy, the largest pan-Indian resistance movement in the history of North America. It had one overarching agenda: stop the United States, now a nation of four million people, from stealing Native land. The confederacy's members were committed to restoring the pre-1776 colonial borders and, in a radical measure, agreed that no nation could sell its land without the consent of the others. The member nations—Shawnees, Illinis, Miamis, Lenapes, Potawatomis, Wyandots, Odawas, Ojibwes, Piankashaws, and Wabash—agreed that all decisions had to be unanimous in order to present a unified front to the Americans. The wide-ranging Shawnees, with their deep knowledge of various colonial powers, their manifold links with distant Native nations, and their linguistic fluency, emerged as leading architects of the coalition, brokering Indigenous alliances against the savage Americans.

Alarmed, Colonel William Crawford, an old friend of George Washington, decided to attack the Indians along the Sandusky River without authorization. The Indians prevailed, captured forty Americans, and took them to Sandusky. According to one account, the Indians stripped Crawford of his clothes and told him that he would be burned. Native women put hot coals on his skin, while Crawford's pleas for a merciful bullet went ignored. Where the United States should have been cultivating alliances with Indigenous nations, most of which they had not defeated, rogue colonists and soldiers alienated nation after nation.

Blinded by land hunger and vicious racism, the Americans were fostering a dangerous climate of violence, hatred, and revenge along their badly exposed borders. The critical Fort Pitt had 110 soldiers, most of them malnourished and unpaid alcoholics. Militarily, the fort was an empty shell. The Ohio Country, one American despaired, "is in a dreadful situation, having been almost entirely overrun this Summer by the Indians; and most of the useful men having been killed." The Congress, created by the Articles of Confederation in 1781, managed to maintain only two hundred soldiers in the all-important Ohio Valley. The government was dangerously decentralized, vesting power in individual states.[5]

By contrast, a shared political philosophy founded on spiritual and prophetic nativism tightened the bonds of the Indian Confederacy's member nations, while nascent racial thinking defined Native Americans as separate from Anglo-Americans. Increasing numbers of Indians began to think of themselves as people of color, separate from Whites. Their burgeoning rebellion made the Ohio Country the focal point of Indigenous-colonial wars. It was the crucible where the continent's future would be decided, and it would see a dizzying constellation of alliances—some of them expedient, others more enduring. "Ohio" comes from *ohi:yó*, an Iroquois word for "beautiful" and "good." The region would remain so for the time being.[6]

IN THE LATE EIGHTEENTH CENTURY, an ambiguous resistance movement emerged in the southern coastal plains. The powerful Muscogees had faced both external and internal challenges for years, and had become dangerously divided. Alexander McGillivray, the son of a high-status Muscogee mother and a Scots-Irish father, played a central role in the movement. He was wealthy, having amassed Black slaves and established a plantation near Muscogee towns. He had announced that "the Crown of Spain will Gain and Secure a powerful barrier in these parts against ambitious and encroaching Americans." To erect such a barrier, he maneuvered his way into the center of the Muscogee government by dominating the clan-based police force and the Muscogee National Council. A forceful and divisive figure, McGillivray was a student of natural history, a slave trader, and a skillful diplomat who had offered his services to both the British and the Spanish, privately promising the latter to keep the Muscogees subordinate to Spain. He worked as a silent partner for the formidable Scottish trading firm Panton, Leslie & Company, supplying munitions for Muscogee soldiers, while simultaneously using his Muscogee connections to boost his own influence: he was carving a personal colony out of the Muscogee Nation. McGillivray would eventually secure much of the Florida trade for Panton, Leslie & Company and, by extension, himself. He even stood out physically: unlike most Muscogee men, he did not have tattoos.[7]

Hoboithle Micco—"Tallassee King" to the Americans—opposed McGillivray, but he, too, operated outside the Muscogee National Council. Divided as they were, the Muscogees were vulnerable to land speculators and hostile colonial officials. In 1785, Georgia absorbed large tracts of the Muscogees' land in the Treaty of Galphinton, which was negotiated by Hoboithle. A year later, the Muscogees ceded an extensive strip of land to the colony, hoping to alleviate the pressure from land-hungry colonists. The tactic failed. Believing that the federal government would be less covetous of Muscogee lands than the Georgians had been, McGillivray decided to reach out to New York, which was at that time the seat of Congress. With a retinue of thirty Muscogees, he traveled east on a horse wagon and was feted, on the president's orders, in every town along the way. McGillivray negotiated shrewdly, securing a duty-free port on the coast of Georgia, which gave him a de facto monopoly on Muscogee trade. By then, he had spent much of his political capital on his various schemes and had been rejected by many Muscogees. On his deathbed, McGillivray declared that he wanted to die as an Indian, but he left most of his possessions to his sons, violating traditional Muscogee inheritance customs.[8]

The United States had to treat Indigenous nations cautiously. Like the Americans, Native Americans had secured their independence from colonial aggression through war, and the Americans could not simply dictate terms to them, given their numbers and military power. Secure in their position, the Ohio Indians negotiated treaties with the American republic. The most consequential of them was the 1784 Treaty of Fort Stanwix, in which the divided and weakened Six Nations ceded their claims as "uncles" of the Ohio Country Indians and their lands. U.S. commissioners hastily declared the Six Nations "a subdued people," but their proclamation was wishful thinking, for the Iroquois were still a force to be reckoned with. Numbering approximately eight thousand, the Six Nations revised the treaty ten years later in the Treaty of Canandaigua, which established a government-to-government relationship between the Six Nations and the United States and recognized Iroquois claims to extensive stretches along the Niagara River. Thayendanegea insisted that the Six Nations remained "Free and Independent People."[9]

Other treaties involving the Ohio Country Indians were more fictional than real. The United States had neither defeated nor conquered the Shawnees, Wyandots, Lenapes, Odawas, Miamis, Chippewas, Potawatomis, and Kickapoos, but U.S. officials claimed the Ohio Country nonetheless. Geórgia and North Carolina had already demanded massive swaths of land in the West by the right of conquest—a rationale that was dubious at best. Spotting an opportunity, the United States claimed the Ohio Country by default. In 1787, Congress passed the Northwest Ordinance, which chartered a government for the Northwest Territory and laid out the procedure for carving U.S. states out of the Indigenous Ohio Country. A nervous Congress promised the new states an equal footing with the original states of the republic: a territory that had sixty thousand free inhabitants could apply for statehood—an accelerator of settler colonialism. U.S. authorities now expected a rapid dispossession of the Indians and an orderly expansion to the west.[10]

The U.S. government was far more concerned about White separatist schemes, such as the independent Mississippi Valley republic, than about Indigenous rights. Much of the new western land was sold to land companies in enormous blocks. In 1787, the Northwest Ordinance opened the new West to colonists who should be "robust and industrious." Tens of thousands of Americans crossed the Appalachians at multiple points, forcing Native

Competing and overlapping territorial claims in the interior in the late eighteenth century

nations to tread more carefully. The Muscogees allowed Benjamin Hawkins, a U.S. agent of Indian affairs, into their country. Hawkins, with unabashed arrogance, offered to make them civilized, which in the first instance required removing women from field work. In 1789, Henry Knox, Washington's secretary of war, launched a systematic program aimed at civilizing Indians. The plan was redundant: Native Americans were already civilized. One chagrined observer noted that the Cherokees and Chickasaws "cultivate the ground more than the other Indians."[11]

The Northwest Ordinance, the United States' effort to consolidate as a nation, had failed. The United States was too poor and weak to create new states: it simply lacked soldiers to force the Indians into adequate land cessions. In a precarious turn of events, colonists would have to be the driving force of U.S. expansion in the Ohio Country. Congress, for its part, sold much of the land that it did not own to a New Jersey syndicate. Rather than trying to remove the Indians by force, the Confederation Congress sold millions of acres to land speculators, who in turn would sell land in 160-, 640-, and 5,760-acre tracts. The strategy was obvious: once the land was sold, colonists would eradicate Native Americans on their own. Thomas Jefferson expected an imminent dispossession of Native nations in the Ohio Country, but the sales were disappointing. There were too many speculators, far too many Indians, and far too few U.S. troops. Evading the Indigenous laws that forbade non-Native men from acquiring Native land, hundreds of American men married Native women.[12]

Indigenous resistance movements were now multiplying. While the Indian Confederacy fought to the keep the Ohio Country Indigenous, in the South the Cherokees mobilized against colonists who had encroached on their domain along two distinct fronts: the southern Piedmont and the Great Appalachian Valley, a gigantic chain of ridges, escarpments, lowlands, and woodlands. The Cherokees were still reeling from the chaos of successive wars, and opportunistic land speculators had moved to carve a new state, Franklin, out of their territory. Franklin never materialized, but the Cherokees were forced to cede land—enough for Tennessee to qualify for statehood. They lost more than half of their territory. In 1792, the seven-thousand-strong Cherokee Nation retaliated by destroying White property and killing White interlopers in a series of attacks, inflicting enough damage to stop the settler invasion. Other Cherokee groups approached the Spanish in Florida and were warmly received by Governor Estevan Miró, who was in desperate need of allies to protect the fragile colony.[13]

Like the Cherokees, the neighboring Chickasaws now faced growing colonial pressure. When not coerced or manipulated by U.S. spies and traders, Chickasaw leaders were approached by Spanish envoys, who hounded them to go against the United States. The roughly two-thousand-strong nation had strived to remain neutral in the Native-colonial wars, but neutrality was becoming all but impossible. The Chickasaws also clashed with the Muscogees, Illinis, Miamis, Kickapoos, and Osages over hunting rights and all-important trading privileges. Eventually, they divided into rival factions led by two Chickasaw leaders: the U.S.-leaning Piomingo and the pro-Spanish Ugulayacabc. Piomingo made Tchitchatala, an eighty-five-by-eighty-foot fort, his base. From there he protected Chickasaw independence as "people to our selves." Much of the Southeast was securely under Indigenous sovereignty, enabling Indians and their non-Native allies to expand.[14]

The weakness of the U.S. government opened opportunities for adventurers like William Augustus Bowles, a brash, charismatic buccaneer who styled himself the emperor of the Muscogee Nation. Like McGillivray, Bowles could be useful to the Indians. He possessed an expansive diplomatic network, having escorted a Muscogee and Cherokee embassy to London in 1790 to ask for support for an independent "United States of Creeks and Cherokees." Bowles's ambitions were grander than McGillivray's, which suited the Indians well: his vision was for a sovereign state with its own armed forces and foreign policy in the Southeast. The result was the sovereign State of Muskogee, headquartered in Mikasuki, a Seminole town in the northeast corner of the Florida peninsula. It drew in large numbers of fugitive Black slaves.

Bowles worked tirelessly with Muscogees, Seminoles, and freed slaves to secure trading privileges on the Gulf coast. The allies also seized Spanish vessels off the Florida coast, and in 1800 the State of Muskogee declared war against Spain. The next year, the Seminoles, numbering only around twelve hundred, captured thirty-eight slaves from a plantation on the Saint Johns River in East Florida. The maritime war was a bold undertaking, but not sustainable. Lacking the connections to the interior forts and their essential goods—guns and powder—the overstretched State of Muskogee died with Bowles in a Havana prison in 1805. Indian power in the region endured, however. Benjamin Hawkins, the long-serving superintendent to the southern Indians, had to openly admit that he could not control the Seminoles. The scant Spanish presence in Florida, an upshot of Seminole ascendancy in the region, became a justification for the United States to annex the colony in 1821.[15]

The United States' weakness also emboldened the Indians and British to enter into alliances. Indians saw the remaining British as useful partners who could supply them, arm them, and fight the Americans alongside them, protecting the Ohio Country as a boundary between Indigenous and American domains. The British were fighting proxy wars against the United States through Native Americans, but that did not mean the Indians were pawns in Britain's lingering imperial ambitions. Limited for the most part to Canada, British America had to rely on Indigenous allies to fulfill its ambitions. The Indians needed little convincing. The Indian Confederacy and other Ohio Country nations joined forces to protect their lands, and they desperately needed British guns, powder, and lead to prevail. What was to the British a contest for prestige and position on the world stage was to Native Americans a continued war of independence. It was obvious that they could not defeat the United States in war; they were fighting to keep its aggressive colonists at arm's length. Some of them reached out to the new territorial superpower, Spain.[16]

A DELEGATION OF 260 Ohio Country Native leaders representing the Iroquois, Cherokee, Chickasaw, Choctaw, Shawnee, and Lenape Nations met with Don Francisco Zavier Cruzat, the lieutenant-governor of Spanish Upper Louisiana, in his headquarters in Saint Louis in late August of 1784. The speaker of the Indigenous coalition addressed Cruzat as "Spanish father." Then he began: "From the moment that we had the misfortune of losing our French father and learned that Spaniards were to be our neighbors, we had a great desire to know them and to establish with them a sincere friendship which would assure to us their affection. The Master of Life willed that our lands should be inhabited by the English, and that these should dominate us tyrannically, until they and the Americans, separating their interests, formed two distinct nations. That event was for us the greatest blow that could have been dealt us, unless it had been our total destruction. The Americans, a great deal more ambitious and numerous than the English, put us out of our lands, forming therein great settlements, extending themselves like a plague of locusts in the territories of the

Ohio River which we inhabit." Native peoples were adjusting to a new world where almost everything was more difficult and dangerous.[17]

Cruzat slipped easily into Onontio's vacant role. There was no other option. Spanish Louisiana was a paper colony: Spain had committed only some five hundred soldiers to patrol the huge province. Cruzat welcomed the "worthy chiefs and warriors of the six nations who at this moment offer me your hand. It is impossible to express the extreme pleasure with which I receive you in my arms as good sons whom I esteem and truly love." He contrasted Spain's accommodating policy with the Americans' increasingly aggressive treatment of Indians, regretting "the fearful condition of your villages." He invited the delegation to observe his policies and judge "whether the Spaniards deserve the evil opinion which the Americans endeavor to inspire." Echoing France's Indian policy, Cruzat invited the visitors to join an alliance in which "all the inhabitants, my children, whom you see here, and whom you treat as your brothers, will receive you in their homes as if you all belonged to our nation." It was a bravura diplomatic intervention at a moment of intense pressure. Americans were pushing into Spanish Louisiana and would soon try "fortifying themselves on certain points on the banks of the Mississippi." To have any hope of success, the Spanish needed Indian allies. Only when Cherokees, Muscogees, Choctaws, Chickasaws, and Seminoles accepted Spanish offers of cooperation would Spanish Louisiana have a shot at survival.[18]

Louisiana's Spanish became to southeastern Indians what the French had been to the many refugee Indians displaced by the Iroquois in the seventeenth century: trading partners, military allies, and fictive kin and fathers who cared for their needs. In return, the desperate Spanish gained allies who could protect the vast and fragile colony. Louisiana was a sprawling entity that covered more than eight hundred thousand square miles between the Mississippi Valley and the Rocky Mountains, yet only thirty thousand colonists resided within its borders. It was clear that Spain could never assert its sovereignty across the province. What mattered to the Spanish most was the Mississippi River, which provided access deep into the continent. The increasing centrality of the river made New Orleans the focus of the Spanish-American rivalry.[19]

Like many Indigenous nations, Spain settled on a strategy of containment when facing the United States. While the Indians tried to keep the Americans out of the interior, the Spanish tried the keep them out of New Orleans, the Gulf coast, and the Mississippi Valley. Indigenous and Spanish interests were aligned, and Spanish Louisiana became a haven for Indians. More unexpectedly, it also became a home for thousands of westward-moving American colonists who were willing to join the Spanish. Spanish officials aspired to create "a living wall of industrious citizens" through immigration from neighboring colonies. In 1787 Miró, the governor of Florida, announced, "We ought not to lose an instant and populate Louisiana with individuals who will swear a solemn oath to take up arms against any invasion attempted by Kentucky." Miró wanted citizen-soldiers, preferably Catholics, but no clergy. He admitted that the scheme was dangerous, but "circumstances force us to take this risk." Soon, twenty thousand Americans had moved into Spanish Louisiana. It was obvious that land, not any affinity for the Spanish, was the allure. Daniel Boone became entangled in land speculation and litigation and soon left Kentucky. Others came simply to loot Spanish settlements.[20]

Spanish officials invited Americans to settle also in Florida, prompting Secretary of State Jefferson to muse, in the spring of 1791, that immigration is "the means of delivering to us peaceably, what may otherwise cost us a war. . . . I wish a hundred thousand of our inhabitants would accept the invitation." Never a realistic planner, Jefferson overlooked the danger that the Spanish scheme posed to the young United States. In this feverish era of improbable stratagems, nations and empires were abstract entities at best. The Oneidas were approached by one Pierre Penet, a power-hungry French adventurer who promised to bring ten thousand French to North America to resuscitate the French Empire. That the scheme was unrealistic was evident only in hindsight. The French continued to meddle in Spanish and British plans through small interventions. The French presence was also palpable in the hundreds of stubbornly independent French voyageurs who traded with Indians in the deep interior and in the thirty-five fur trade centers in the Great Lakes region, run by French Creoles—"native-born"—offering Native nations in the interior guns, powder, kettles, beads, and other manufactured goods. Prairie du Chien in the upper Mississippi Valley became the nerve center of this exchange. Creoles had won entry by recognizing Meskwaki sovereignty in the region. Soon, intermarriages between French men and Native women solidified the settlement, with Métis women—of European and Indigenous ancestry—acting as cultural mediators. Meskwaki numbers rose dramatically. Potawatomis, Sauks, Kickapoos, Illinis, Ho-Chunks, and Iowas also traded at Prairie du Chien.

In 1792, Edmond Charles Genet, the French minister to the United States, and George Rogers Clark, the former general of the Continental army, joined with a motley crew of colonists and Kentucky ruffians in an attempt to expel Spain from the Mississippi Valley and capture New Orleans under the French flag. They aborted their expedition only when President Washington threatened to send in the army. There was a real possibility that the Trans-Mississippi West or parts of it might become French: the French Revolution in 1789 had created a nation that was supremely confident in its role and mission in the world and that possessed the resources to realize its imperial ambitions, which surpassed those of the ancien régime. French agents in North America and U.S. soldiers would continue with their stratagems.[21]

WHILE THE UNITED STATES was preoccupied with British, Spanish, and French plots, Native Americans were preoccupied with American aggression and volatility, both military and diplomatic. In late 1786, at the Wyandot settlement of Brownstown near Lake Erie, most of the member nations of the Indian Confederacy came together to stop colonial encroachments into what the Americans now called Kentucky country and the Ohio Territory. Thayendanegea evoked the common pot, the symbol of alliance, and announced, "It is certain that before Christian Nations visited this continent, we were the sole Lords of the soil." Their first task was to repeal the earlier treaties, many of which U.S. officials had negotiated with only a few, carefully selected Native leaders. "All treaties carried on with the United States," the leaders of the Indian Confederacy declared, "should be with the general voice of the whole confederacy." They also decreed that "any cession of our lands should be made in most public manner, and by the united voice of the confederacy; holding all partial treaties as void and of no effect." Defiantly and stubbornly, the Indian Confederacy combined forceful diplomacy with war, shifting from one to the other as the circumstances dictated. Now fully aware that the Northwest Ordinance was geared to divest Indians of their lands, the allies, cooperating with the British, sent a message to the U.S. Congress, rejecting the 1784–86 treaties as invalid: Native Americans had been falsely labeled as conquered people without rights. Congress refused to negotiate, and the Indian Confederacy went to war, attacking encroaching colonists across Ohio and Kentucky. Their leaders sent wampum belts to other Native nations, inviting them to join in a pan-Indian campaign to protect Indigenous sovereignty.[22]

American colonists, for their part, thought the land free for the taking, and from December 1787 to June 1788, six thousand self-styled "pioneers" pushed into the Ohio Country. They tried to treat the resident Indians with respect, but their numbers were "almost incredible," as Brigadier General Josiah Harmar reported. A year later, the United States—now equipped with a constitution and new executive departments of state, war, treasury, and justice—staged a campaign to extend its authority on both sides of the Appalachians, a feat that only the Six Nations had successfully accomplished before. The plan had two components: war against Indians in the Ohio Country and diplomacy with Indians in the South. The scheme unraveled almost immediately. U.S. agents prepared to open treaty talks with the Ohio Indians, but General Arthur St. Clair, the federal governor of the Northwest Territory, hijacked the talks, informing the Indians that they were subjugated people and had lost title to their lands.[23]

Under duress, the Wyandots, Iroquois, and Lenapes signed the Treaty of Fort Harmar in 1789, ceding large tracts of land. U.S. agents still cajoled the Six Nations—they relied on their authority to establish and preserve peace in the interior—but American officials were becoming increasingly reluctant to administer Indigenous nations through the Iroquois. Shockingly, the United States forced the Six Nations to relinquish all their claims to the Ohio Country. Coming twelve years after the quenching of their confederacy's central council fire, the loss of the Ohio Country marked the final collapse of the centuries-long Iroquois dominance in the North American interior. No other nation had done more to frustrate colonial expansion, whether French, Dutch, British, or American. The Iroquois secured reservations south of Lake Ontario, never facing removal from their ancient homelands.

Even when militarily diminished, the Six Nations' moral authority remained palpable. They demanded compensation for lost lands and pressured U.S. agents to respect their traditions. They instructed their assigned commissioner, Timothy Pickering, an austere Yankee, in their diplomatic protocols, ceremonies, and ideas of justice. A particularly charged issue was how to respond to murders. U.S. officials demanded public trials and executions, whereas the Iroquois preferred covering graves of the victims with gifts that eased pain and restored order. Eventually, Pickering concluded that the frontier colonists were "far more savage & revengeful than the Indians themselves," prompting President Washington to note that "it is in the highest degree mortifying to find that the bulk of the frontier inhabitants consider the killing of Indians in time of peace, to be no crime and that their murderers are faultless, provided they escape detection."[24]

What Washington instructed from Washington, D.C., mattered little in the interior. In the spring of 1790, St. Clair was ordered to take U.S. troops into the Ohio Country to kill Indians and seize more Indigenous territory. Like many other high-ranking officials, he hoped to force and personally benefit from land transactions. The mission did not go well. "I am very sorry to have it to remark," he informed Washington, "that they do not wear a very favorable Complexion! That the Ouabush [Wabash] Indians should have taken the Resolution to be guided entirely by those of the Miami Village, is nearly tantamount to a declaration that they will continue their Hostilities." Humiliatingly, St. Clair also had to inform the president that the American colonists "are reduced to the lowest Ebb of Poverty." Washington pledged "to impress the Indians with a strong conviction of the power of the United States." Another officer, Brigadier General Charles Scott, extended an offer of peace to the allied Indians but betrayed his anxiety by adding a clumsy threat: "Should you decline this invitation, and pursue your unprovoked hostilities . . . your warriors will be slaughtered, your towns and villages ransacked and destroyed, your wives and children carried into captivity, and you may be assured that those who escape the fury of our mighty chiefs, shall find no resting place on this side of the Great Lakes."[25]

Eager to redeem himself, St. Clair tried again in the fall of 1791, now targeting Indian settlements along the Maumee River with fourteen hundred federal soldiers. Gout-ridden, St. Clair made camp sixteen times during the march. Shawnee war leader Weyapiersenwah, or Blue Jacket, and Miami war leader Meshekinnoqquah, or Little Turtle, moved against the invaders, bringing more than a thousand Shawnee, Miami, Potawatomi, Odawa, Lenape, Sauk, Ojibwe, and Meskwaki soldiers against the Americans. The Indians attacked before dawn. They were protecting not only their land but also their children, and there could be no margin of error. A vicious fight that lasted three hours drove the U.S. soldiers into a wild retreat. The U.S. casualty rate was an astonishing 97.4 percent—the worst defeat of colonists and Americans in all the Indian wars of the colonies and the young republic. The panicked soldiers left behind most of their munitions and provisions. By the end of 1791, all the states on the Atlantic coast except Georgia had abandoned the fiction that their borders stretched to the western edge of the country at the Mississippi River. Secretary of War Henry Knox, a man not easily alarmed, warned that "the inhabitants request and demand protection; if it be not granted, seeds of disgust will be sown; sentiments of separate interests will arise out of a local situation." The position of the United States was so tenuous that it encouraged Canadian leaders to plan for an independent indigenous barrier state between U.S. and Canadian territories.[26]

To effectively wage a war on the Indian Confederacy, Washington would have needed $200,000 a year—a sum that the Treasury simply could not deliver. The enormity of the challenge seemed to overwhelm Knox, who lamented that "the United States have come into existence as a nation, embarrassed with a frontier of immense extent." He was, it seems, being intentionally oblique: it was not the frontier that caused the embarrassment, but the tens of thousands of Indians who lived there. Knox, a staunch paternalist, had little use for the rough American colonists, but he had developed sympathy for the

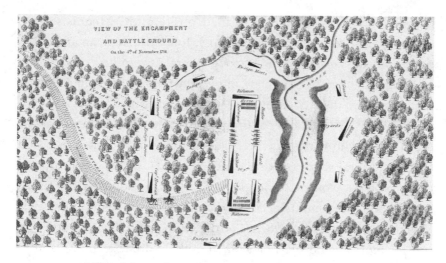

Map of General St. Clair's encampment and retreat,
November 4, 1791 (artist unknown)

Native Americans. Unlike most U.S. officials, he did not see or treat the Indians as conquered peoples. But Knox's was a minority view. The U.S. government was already planning a string of forts in the Ohio Country. "As long as Britain is suffered to retain these posts, we can never hope to succeed against the Indians," the representatives of the U.S. Congress despaired.[27]

The Indian Confederacy wasted little time in capitalizing on the United States' weakness. The Cherokee war leader Dragging Canoe sent soldiers to join the Indian Confederacy, and the following year the Muscogees informed the confederacy that "1000 Creeks would be in acts of hostility this Moon." The Indian Confederacy had established its headquarters at the Glaize, an old trading village near the confluence of the Maumee and Auglaize Rivers, where extensive cornfields and the fur trade flourished, providing a strong economic foundation for the allies. The Indian Confederacy could now operate across a vast area between the Great Lakes in the north, the Ohio Valley in the south, the Mississippi Valley in the west, and the Pennsylvania and Virginia borderlands in the east, keeping tens of thousands of colonists at bay. The Indian Confederacy was filling the power vacuum in the interior left by the fading Six Nations.

Soon, violence washed over the interior from Ohio and Kentucky to North Carolina. Confident of their position, the Miamis saw no reason to negotiate with the Americans. John Marshall, an ambitious politician who advocated for a strong federal government, feared that a settler rebellion was imminent, imperiling the young republic. Washington ordered the U.S. Army to destroy the resisting Indians and capture as many women and children as possible. Unable to defeat the allied Indians in battle, the president of the United States relied on terror and total war, targeting noncombatants, fields, orchards, and trade centers. Women's work kept the Indian Confederacy going, and the Kentucky militia decided to loot Native homes, while in Fort Washington near the confluence of the Ohio and Miami Rivers, U.S. troops imprisoned dozens of women and children, keeping them as hostages. The Americans were desperate. In April 1794, Thayendanegea met with Henry Knox, the U.S. secretary of war, and informed him that the Iroquois "are of the same opinion with the people of the United States; you consider yourselves as independent people; we, as the original inhabitants of this country, and sovereigns of the soil, look upon ourselves as equally independent, and free as any other nation or nations. This country was given to us by the Great Spirit." Numerous Native groups would have agreed.[28]

OVERWHELMED BY INDIGENOUS POWER, the United States faced a crisis that its leaders had failed to prepare for. Just as Britain had failed to consolidate its empire after the French were expelled from the interior, the United States seemed to be losing its hold on the colossal possessions it had gained in 1783. To a degree, the failure was cultural. Western colonists harbored a strong distrust of centralized government and power—a cynicism magnified by Indigenous dominance in the vast interior. The colonists did not want to be governed from a distance by a legislative body that had not armed them or kept them safe. The government's dismal record in protecting the westward-pushing colonists from Native and British attacks threatened to split the fledgling republic into eastern and western halves.

A particularly intense grievance was the government's failure to secure navigation rights on the Mississippi from Spain. The river was the gateway to Caribbean, South American, and European markets, and the western colonists thought that the government's ineptitude was denying them a fortune. Political clubs in Pennsylvania and Kentucky debated the possibility of severing their ties with the United States, and some wanted to form an independent Mississippi Valley republic. William Blount, a Tennessee senator who had invested heavily in western lands, contemplated seizing parts of Louisiana and making a separate peace with Britain. The Muscogees called him *Fushe Micco*, the "Dirt King." The Dirt King held back, but the many western colonists did not. In July 1794, the federal government imposed a tax on western Pennsylvania farmers and distillers, prompting what became known as the Whiskey Rebellion. Washington sent in thirteen thousand militiamen, and the uprising sputtered out bloodlessly, but the underlying grievances persisted, leaving frontier regions in every state south and west of New York anxious and restless.

The Whiskey Rebellion forced the hesitant U.S. government to act. Indigenous resistance, coupled with colonists' grievances, posed too grave a threat. U.S. officials invited the Ohio Indians to treaty talks, but the negotiations collapsed. Knox dispatched the alcoholic general Anthony "Mad" Wayne to lead an army against the Indian Confederacy and destroy its towns along the Maumee River west of Lake Erie. Unlike Harmar and St. Clair, Wayne did not underestimate the Indians, calling their base at Grand Glaize the "grand emporium of hostile Indians of the West," surrounded by "very extensive and highly cultivated fields and gardens" that "show the work of many hands. The margins of those beautiful rivers . . . appear like one continued village for a number of miles, both above and below this place; nor have I ever before beheld such immense fields of corn, in any part of America, from Canada to Florida." Wayne had spotted the budding multinational anti-U.S. Indigenous power in the heart of the continent. The Indians seemed far better organized and more authoritative than the Americans.[29]

The Indian Confederacy mobilized hundreds of soldiers, and the British built a new fort on the Maumee to support their Native allies. The U.S. government was spending $1 million a year to fight the Indian Confederacy—far beyond George Washington's imaginings

only a few years earlier. Realizing that he could not win a prolonged
conflict, Wayne marched his army, "The Legion of the United States,"
comprising more than three thousand troops, directly into the heart
of the Indigenous Ohio Country. It would be a dirty war. The march
set the tone: there would be no quarter, just bloodshed. U.S. troops
burned cornfields, destroyed towns, and killed women and children.
The tactic was both a strategy and a reassertion of U.S. hegemony.
When Wayne forced a battle at Fallen Timbers near Fort Miami and
won it, the Indian Confederacy was reeling.

Shawnee, Lenape, and Miami leaders focused on evacuating
women and children, abandoned their towns, and retreated down
the Maumee, seeking refuge among the British at Fort Miami. Fearing American retaliation, though, the British refused to let them in.
It was a crushing betrayal that left the Indian Confederacy exposed.
The alliance collapsed, and its members withdrew into their respective realms in the Ohio Country. Capturing something of the critical
moment, Knox wrote about "the utter extirpation of nearly all the
Indians in the most populous parts of the Union. A future historian
may mark the causes of this destruction of the human race in sable
colors." British officials in London began to fear that the Indian war
in North America was compromising Britain's war effort against the
revolutionary France.[30]

In November 1794, with seditious talk spreading among the colonists, the United States concluded the Jay Treaty with Britain. Britain
agreed to cede Forts Detroit, Michilimackinac, and Niagara to the
United States and cut all ties with the Native Americans south of the
U.S.-Canada border. The Ohio Indians' position became untenable.
Having lost British support and munitions, they could not continue
the war. In the winter of 1795, the United States sponsored treaty talks
at General Wayne's headquarters at Fort Greenville. Seeking to bring
stability to the interior, American agents tried to convince the Native
nations to make peace with the United States by offering the Indians
perpetual annuities amounting to $9,500 in return for land cessions.
The agents were obsessed with what the Indians thought of them and
wanted them to publicly acknowledge the legality of transfers of territory. For the Indians, sincerity was essential, and they scrutinized the

colonists for the smallest signs of deception or crude self-interest: the Americans were on display.

Exhausted by wars that had lasted nearly four decades, and satisfied with British support, Little Turtle and the Shawnee sachem Black Hoof agreed to a treaty, as did the Wyandot, Lenape, Shawnee, Odawa, Chippewa, Potawatomi, Miami, Kickapoo, Ojibwe, and Kaskaskia leaders. Yet when the Indians learned the specifics of the Treaty of Greenville, they were horrified. Their domain had shrunk to a swath in the northwestern corner of the Ohio Country, 150 miles north of the Ohio River. The rest—two-thirds of the Ohio Country— was opened to American settlement. The United States, emerging as a full-fledged colonial regime, also reserved the exclusive right to buy the remaining lands of the Ohio Indians.

Like Lieutenant-Governor Cruzat eleven years earlier, George Washington, in absentia, tried to assume the role of a caring "father" and to be kind and protective. The United States would be generous, offering farming tools, seeds, weapons, and education to the Indians. U.S. officials branded their generosity as a "civilization program," an Enlightenment-inspired scheme that aimed to elevate Native Americans from "savagery" to Anglo-American civilization by promoting agriculture and a sedentary lifestyle. Wisely, the officials refrained from elaborating on their plans during the Fort Greenville talks, where Little Turtle took over and challenged General Wayne. "The boundary line between the Indians and the United States," the Miami leader protested, "cuts off from the Indians a large portion of country, which has been enjoyed by my forefathers time immemorial, without molestation or dispute. The print[s] of my ancestors' houses are every where to be seen in this portion. . . . It is well known by all my brothers present, that my forefather kindled the first fire at Detroit." Tarke, a Wyandot sachem, warned the Americans that "our tomahawk remains in your head; the English gave it to me to place there."[31]

The first twenty years of the United States had been marked by nearly constant wars with Native Americans. The long fight over western lands had drained the nascent republic's coffers, absorbing nearly five-sixths of the total federal expenditure year after year. As Americans—both colonists and soldiers—clashed with Indians and grabbed their land, the United States faced a new imperial challenge: it had to articulate how to settle, integrate, and protect a realm that now covered half of the continent and contained some five million citizens. The Atlantic-centered British colonial system that the United States had inherited would no longer do. To survive, the federal nation would have to centralize all local and regional political entities under its authority. The president and federal government assumed new powers through the 1790 Trade and Intercourse Act, which authorized them to control Indian trade, evict and punish squatters on Indian lands, and monopolize treaty-making with Native Americans, excluding individual states from the process.

In 1795, Congress established a network of "factories," trading houses designed to promote peace. Government-regulated trade, the thinking went, would protect the Indians from fraud, alcohol, and abuse and help them become civilized. Years later, Jefferson captured the logic when he wrote, "Commerce is the great engine by which we are to coerce them, and not war." Factories were built across the Northwest, a dramatic change that nudged U.S. Indian policy closer to the more accommodating British one.[32]

Although paternalistic, manipulative, and disputed, the new federal initiatives brought a measure of stability to the Trans-Appalachian West. The key was steady and regulated trade, which had been the Indian Confederacy's demand throughout its existence. Indians could now rely, at least to a degree, on fair treatment. Yet those commercial privileges had to be secured through assertive foreign policy and hard bargaining: both U.S. political parties—the Federalists and the Republicans—envisioned the Ohio Country as a harmonious settler colony led by aristocrats—the Hudson of the Ohio. Soon, western colonial schemes materialized from Lake Ontario in the north to the Savannah River valley in the south. A thickening network of roads stitched individual states together, enabling them to extend their tentacles deeper into the Indigenous domains in the West. The pent-up desire for land brought a deluge of colonists to the Ohio Valley. Washington had proved not to be a protective father in the French or Spanish mold. The Indian Confederacy dissolved itself, but only temporarily. A galvanizing leader would rekindle it soon.[33]

Chapter 24

WESTERN
PROMISES

THE NACOTCHTANK, PATAWOMECK, PISCATAWAY, and Pamunkey peoples were taken aback. U.S. soldiers, engineers, and builders had infested the Potomac River valley, the homeland where their ancestors had lived for four millennia. A new city, designed by French engineer Pierre Charles L'Enfant, was slowly rising in the valley. It would be known as the "City of Washington," and it would be the seat of a new and self-conscious empire.

By the early 1790s, having claimed a prodigious contiguous territory of more than nine hundred thousand square miles, the United States was the world's fourth-largest nation, after Russia, China, and Turkey. U.S. officials felt confident enough to dictate terms to their colonial rivals. Navigation rights on the Mississippi River remained a burning issue with Spain. Fully aware that they could not contain the Americans and Native nations for long, the Spanish agreed in 1795 to the Treaty of San Lorenzo del Escorial, or Pinckney's Treaty, which set West Florida's northern boundary at the thirty-first parallel. Spain also relinquished a one-hundred-mile stretch of the Yazoo River and granted the United States duty-free transport through the port of New Orleans. Soon, American traffic on the Mississippi was booming.[1]

That commercial boon remained precarious, however, because the United States was still too weak to subjugate the Native Americans, who dominated the interior and its rivers and resources. The United States was also a risky and—to many Americans and Europeans—an unlikely political experiment. It was a democracy and thus volatile and prone to sudden swings in its priorities and policies. It was also an empire of colonists, and nearly half of its claimed territory consisted

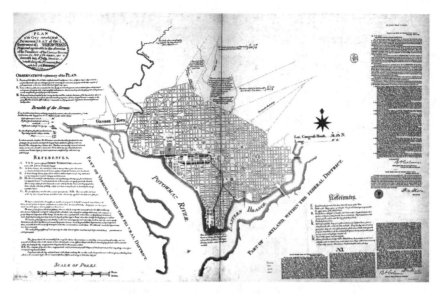

"Plan of the city intended for the permanent seat of the government of the United States," by Pierre Charles L'Enfant, 1791

of unceded Indigenous territories. There were many competing and overlapping sovereignties within its claimed borders, and numerous self-governing Indigenous nations existed within the United States as "resident foreign nations," ostensibly under U.S. sovereignty and care. In reality, the United States controlled only portions of its mammoth domain. Its borders were far from self-evident; they had to be asserted through violence, over and over again. Traveling from the nation's capital to the Illinois and Ohio Countries took approximately two months. Unlike most empires, the United States tried to govern its territories from the fringe, not from the center.[2]

Official colonial maps were clearer. Since the early 1790s, each colonial power had commanded its separate domain. Treaties granted the United States sovereignty over the Ohio Country, and colonists moved in several land rushes. Britain had secured an enormous territory north of a line that ran across the Great Lakes, and it retained Rupert's Land, a British territory that consisted of the entire Hudson Bay drainage basin and stretched to the Rocky Mountains—a foundation for a transcontinental trade system. The Gulf of Mexico had been "a Spanish lake" since 1783, shielding the Caribbean islands,

Mexico, New Mexico, and Florida against foreign intrusions. With powerful Indigenous confederacies on its side, Spain was primed to isolate the United States from the Gulf and the West. It seemed that there could be five Wests: French, British, American, Spanish, and Sioux, the last of which was the most likely.[3]

FRANCE HAD BEEN LARGELY absent from North America for more than thirty years, but it staged a comeback in the 1790s. It had managed to hold on to the eastern half of Santo Domingo, the fantastically profitable Caribbean sugar and coffee island that contained nearly half a million slaves and delivered more than 200 million livres' worth of goods to French markets each year. In 1791, France's brutal regime on the island had caused a massive slave rebellion led by Toussaint Louverture, a former slave. The revolt carried Louverture into power, shocking both Napoléon and Jefferson, along with slaveholders across the American South, who feared that the spirit of the slave rebellion would move north. The alarmed and disgusted Kentuckians threatened to leave the union.[4]

The French asked the United States, their former revolutionary ally, for help, but the U.S. government was already engaged in a rapprochement with Britain that would culminate in the Jay Treaty in 1794. Britain and France were at war; the United States had to choose sides. Rejected by the Americans, the French secured a new foothold on the continent, including ports on the Gulf coast, in part to monitor Santo Domingo. France's first consul, Napoléon Bonaparte, offered to buy Louisiana from King Charles IV of Spain, who was eager to rid himself of the money-draining colony whose colonists had failed to find profitable staples to sustain it. In the secret Treaty of San Ildelfonso in 1800, Spain handed over nearly nine percent of North America to France. In return, Napoléon would deliver the Grand Duchy of Tuscany for Spain. French strength, Charles and his advisors calculated, might achieve what Spain could not: cutting the arrogant, upstart imperial Americans down to size. The U.S. government was deeply worried: a second French Louisiana, again founded on close cooperation with the Indians, would pose a grave threat. The French could "hold forth every allurement to the inhabitants of the Trans-Alleghany settlements . . . and inveigle them by degrees into the idea of forming a separate empire." Moreover, tens of thousands of Native Americans would eagerly welcome the return of the French Onontio who could arm them, go to war alongside them, and supply them with goods by way of New Orleans.[5]

When President Jefferson learned about the land transfer, he immediately grasped that the very existence of the United States was at risk: "There is on the globe one single spot, the possessor of which is our natural and habitual enemy. It is New Orleans, through which the produce of three eighths of our territory must pass to market." For his part, Napoléon planned a campaign against Louverture with care and dispatched an armada carrying fifty thousand men across the Atlantic, only to learn soon that Louverture's army and yellow fever had thwarted the French invasion. The anxious Jefferson had already sent James Monroe as minister extraordinary to Paris in January 1803 and authorized him to buy New Orleans and as much of the Floridas as possible. Napoléon, taken aback by Louverture's success, offered instead New Orleans and all of Louisiana for a mere $15 million. On paper the Louisiana Purchase was more than a spectacular real estate transaction that promised to nearly double the size of the United States; it also handed the Americans the Mississippi Valley, the master key to North America. The great river was the spine of an enormous system of navigable tributaries that linked 1.5 million square miles of the interior to the Gulf of Mexico and Atlantic trade channels. A new American empire in the West beckoned. Jefferson announced that the Americans now had "room for all descendants to the 1,000th and 1,000th generation."[6]

In euphoric celebrations in Washington, D.C., and elsewhere, few paused to consider that almost all of the extraordinary land purchase was under Indigenous rule. Nor did the Americans acknowledge the fact that France had claimed the transferred territory only up to the Missouri-Mississippi confluence, which made the transaction all but invalid. Jefferson floated the idea of turning the Louisiana Purchase into a gargantuan Indian colony. The purchase was compromised in another way as well. What the United States had purchased from

France was the power of preemption through the Doctrine of Discovery, which gave it the exclusive right to obtain Indigenous titles either by conquest or by contract. Too weak to reduce the Indians to subjects, the United States had to negotiate contracts with sovereign Native nations. They would have to do so 222 times between 1804 and 1970, the largest cessions occurring before 1867.[7]

JEFFERSON, A POLYMATH WHO did not seem to be able to resist an opportunity to plan and make improvements—whether to Monticello or to the United States—set out to transform his nation into an agricultural and commercial giant, independent of the corrupt European empires. He also advocated for the westward expansion of slavery to alleviate the growing sectional tensions between the country's northern and southern halves. All these designs hinged on quick settlement of the West, which in turn demanded the quick dispossession of Native Americans and the assertion of U.S. sovereignty. It was clear that it could not be a military operation; by law, the size of the U.S. Army could not exceed 3,289 officers and enlisted men. The constrained army assigned a pitiful two thousand men to the Trans-Appalachian West.

Jefferson's weapon of choice was the United States' nascent civilization program, which was designed to turn Native hunters into farmers and Native women into housekeepers by providing the necessary tools and reeducation. This kind of systematic social engineering, Jefferson believed, would free up land for American colonists without war and pave the way for his ideal commonwealth of yeoman farmers. Promisingly, from his perspective, many Cherokee women welcomed the programs as an improvement, not eradication, of their ancient civilization. Kaiiontwa'kon, or Cornplanter, a prominent Seneca military leader, embraced the factory system and allowed Quakers to live in the much-diminished Seneca towns. He might have recoiled if he had known Jefferson's thoughts on the matter: "In truth the ultimate point of rest & happiness for them [the Indians] is to let our settlements and theirs meet and blend together, to intermix and become one people, incorporating themselves with us." U.S. officials calcu-

lated that implementing the civilization program among the influential Senecas would trigger a domino effect among other Native
nations. Benjamin Hawkins, the agent for the powerful Muscogees,
thought he could convince his wards to taste "the sweets of civilization" and learn "the value of property and the necessity of defending
it." The Cherokee women who gravitated to the civilization program
believed they would boost their economies and secure their territories. They seized the opportunity to acquire spinning wheels, looms,
and Anglo-American-style clothes. By the early nineteenth century,
Cherokee women owned nearly twenty thousand hogs, twenty thousand cows, more than six thousand horses, and 129 slaves.[8]

There would be, however, no domino effect. The Senecas created a counterforce that advocated resistance, not assimilation. Skaniadariyo, or Handsome Lake, Kaiiontwa'kon's alcoholic half brother
and clan relative, received four visions in 1799 and 1800. In the first
he was alone when three messengers offered him strawberries. In the
second he was in an Iroquois council house and then traveled to Sky
World and saw how Seneca hunters struggled to find game. In the
third he learned that warring and hunting were about to stop. In the
fourth, Skaniadariyo began to follow the white path that would lead
to spiritual regeneration. Where Jefferson's vision for the continent
was driven by economic and geopolitical considerations, Skaniadariyo's vision was first and foremost spiritual. His prophetic *Gaihwi:io*,
"good message," spawned the Longhouse Religion, which sought to
restore balance to the world. Skaniadariyo wanted people to be kind
to one another, abstain from alcohol, and worship properly, and those
who failed to follow his code and live virtuously were deemed to be
sinners who would spend the afterlife in an inferno. A blend of Christianity and Indigenous spirituality, Skaniadariyo's message was one of
the many new Indigenous movements that would challenge the United
States' hegemonic pretentions and insidious influence in Native lands.[9]

WHILE THE SENECAS MOUNTED a spiritual challenge to U.S.
arrogance and expansionism, the Lakotas challenged the Americans
geopolitically. In the mid-eighteenth century, having turned them-

selves into a full-fledged horse nation, the Lakotas had entrenched themselves in the middle Missouri Valley under Arikara auspices, gradually familiarizing themselves with the customs, politics, and geography of the ancient river world. The Missouri River watershed—the largest in the vast Mississippi River basin—constituted a superb transportation grid. From the west bank of the Missouri, eight inviting tributaries—the White, Bad, Cheyenne, Moreau, Grand, Cannonball, Heart, and Knife Rivers—offered multiple access points to the West and the shortgrass prairies of the High Plains. The valleys also provided reliable water, grass, and sheltering cottonwood groves for the Lakotas' growing horse herds. Drawn by crucial resources and opportunities, the Lakotas executed another leap westward. The contest over the continent was shifting to the Trans-Mississippi West.

In 1776 the Lakotas—as Indigenous explorers drawn by legends and myths in faraway lands—arrived in Pahá Sápa, the Black Hills, some three hundred miles west of the Missouri River. Pahá Sápa was an altogether extraordinary site, a singular elevation protruding from the flat grasslands, the needles of its ponderosa pines glowing black in the sun. Towering granite pillars reached to the sky, and subterranean caves seemed to extend to the very core of the world.

For the Lakotas, Pahá Sápa was the center of the world, "the heart of everything that is," the oldest part of the Earth and the place where the bison and first humans surfaced from a deep cave, guided by Iktómi, the mythological hero of the Sioux people. The Sun Dance, a ceremony of gratitude, humility, and unity, became more pivotal in the Lakotas' annual cycle, encouraging closer collaboration among the Lakota *oyátes*, or nations. The emerging coalition of Lakota oyátes was an on-again, off-again alliance, reflecting the mobile way of life of a horse people, who relied to an extraordinary degree on a single animal, the bison, for subsistence, raw materials, shelter, and spiritual fulfillment. With their Dakota, Yankton, and Yanktonai allies dominating the upper Mississippi Valley in the east, the Sioux alliance Očhéthi Šakówiŋ, the Seven Council Fires, now commanded a huge block of the North American interior. It was also in Pahá Sápa that the ancient story of Ptesáŋwiŋ, White Buffalo Calf Woman, accrued new relevance and meaning: she taught the Lakotas the Sacred Pipe

Ceremony, one of the seven vital ceremonies that kept the Očhéthi Šakówiŋ whole and powerful.

For most of the year the alliance did not exist in any concrete form, as dozens of local bands chased game, goods, and pasture in different corners of their massive domain. But every spring, Lakotas, Dakotas, Yanktons, and Yanktonais gathered at trade fairs that doubled as political conventions where major decisions were exposed to public scrutiny. These meetings, often held on the James River in the center of the Očhéthi Šakówiŋ's realm, were the foundation of the great Sioux alliance, enabling its member groups to share resources, pool information, synchronize oyáte-driven local policies, and identify dangers and opportunities. Meeting face-to-face, they smoked the calumet, reaffirming their shared identity as the formidable Seven Council Fires. This confederacy would be the foundation of Lakota and Sioux power for a century. The Sioux people could not know it, but the Očhéthi Šakówiŋ was now the most powerful Indigenous power on the continent, after the weakening of the Iroquois and Cherokees during the Seven Years' War.

American Horse, an Oglala elder, explained an entry of a very specific winter count to a U.S. Army officer, William Corbusier, in 1879. The count pinpointed the Lakota discovery of—or return to—Pahá Sápa in 1776, when Standing Bull had arrived in the mountain range. This was the first entry of the count, marking the beginning of recorded history for American Horse's people and, by extension, for the Lakota Nation. This version of Lakota history placed the Lakotas and the United States on parallel trajectories: in 1776, according to American Horse, two nations had been born in North America, both destined for discoveries of new worlds, dominance, military glory, and, finally, a terrible, violent clash with each other. American Horse may have tried to remind Corbusier about their once-respectful relationship as the two leading nations in the North American interior. He might have been appealing to a shared past to envision a shared future.[10]

The creation of a tighter Lakota alliance—within the larger Sioux Confederacy—was a sign of weakness rather than strength. Lakotas had been shunned by the Missouri Valley's Native farmers, who saw them as unwelcome rivals. They competed for prime hunting grounds, trade with Europeans, and strategic sites on the Missouri's protective riverside bluffs, and their horses and tipi settlements consumed too much grass and cottonwood. But the end of Pontiac's War in 1766 made possible a revival of the fur trade in the Trans-Mississippi West. The pent-up demand for guns, powder, lead, and metal tools now fueled intense rivalries for trading privileges in the upper Missouri Valley, where several Indigenous nations had suffered for years with unreliable access to European technology and goods. The greatest need was for gunpowder and lead: when they ran out, the Indigenous West shifted back to the Stone Age.

In the early 1770s, the Oglala Lakotas and their Yanktonai relatives attacked a town of Mandan Indian farmers and traders two hundred miles north of the regular Oglala camping grounds. "They burnt the Mandans out," an Oglala winter account recorded. The sacking of the Mandan town was a turning point, marking the beginning of a long Lakota ascendancy along the Missouri. Having found spiritual and material fulfillment in the Black Hills, the Lakotas entrenched themselves in the Missouri Valley.

The outbreak of a virulent smallpox epidemic in 1781—the same epidemic that devastated Cornwallis's army in Yorktown—was key to Lakota expansion in the upper Missouri Valley. The epidemic shocked the Lakotas, who may not have been exposed to smallpox before, but it nearly destroyed the more sedentary agricultural nations in the region. More than seventy-five percent of the Arikaras may have perished, reducing the ancient Missourian civilization to a mere shadow of its former self: the Arikara world shrank from thirty-two towns to three—"sad debris," in the words of Antoine Tabeau, an employee of the Saint Louis–based, Franco-Spanish fur-trading outfit Clamorgan, Loisel and Company. The once populous Mandans to the north of the Arikaras could now fill only three towns. The Hidatsas lost half of their people. Before the epidemic, the upper Missouri Valley had been home to tens of thousands of agrarian Indians; afterward, only eight thousand remained. The once-extensive domains of farms and towns dissolved into isolated and exposed nodes. A 1781–82 Lakota winter count reads, "Came and attacked on horseback the last time winter." It was the last successful attack by the farming Indians. The

Lakotas would eventually eliminate the weakened agrarian nations as a threat.[11]

In 1793, capitalizing on the epidemic that had dramatically weakened the Mandans, Lakotas attacked a Mandan town of fifty-eight lodges and killed almost everyone in it. The surviving Mandans fled north, desperate to put distance between themselves and the Lakotas. A two-hundred-mile stretch of the Missouri River was suddenly open before the Lakotas. They moved in, extending their Missouri domain far to the north. Their timing was auspicious.[12]

The fur trade was starting to boom like never before in the midcontinent. Commerce in the Arkansas and lower Missouri Valleys had been dominated for decades by the now nearly twenty-thousand-strong Osage Nation, which sold Spanish guns and manufactured goods westward to the Plains Indians in exchange for pelts and bison robes. Backed by the Chouteau family, the leading Saint Louis merchants who employed savvy French traders, the Osages furnished roughly fifty percent of the town's trade and reaped massive profits. The Chouteaus married into elite Osage families, embedding their partnership in kinship ties, which enabled them to facilitate commercial transactions across the midcontinent. By the early 1790s, the lower Missouri Valley was becoming overcrowded with traders. Spanish governors in Louisiana forbade trade with the Osages, but the Chouteaus persisted, siding with the Osages against the Spanish Empire. Led by Pawhuska, the Osages kept White hunters out of the Arkansas Valley, which had been the seat of Osage power for half a century. The Chouteaus, for their part, continued to send traders upriver to locate untapped fur domains. The Lakota villages stretching out along the banks of the Missouri were inevitably the traders' first stop.[13]

These commercial impulses clashed with the geopolitical ambitions of Spanish officials in Saint Louis, who agonized over imperial challenges from the north. Canadian traders had established themselves among the Mandans, diverting the upper Missouri fur trade to the north. The profit margins of Saint Louis merchants plummeted from nearly three hundred percent to twenty-five. Desperate to keep the trade alive, Spanish officials issued licenses to trade with the Indians in the upper Missouri Valley, hoping to keep the Canadian traders at bay. The stakes were enormous. If they succeeded, many believed, Spanish North America could be saved. It was an article of faith that somewhere in the upper reaches of the Missouri Valley was an all-water route to the Pacific coast—the key to a lasting Spanish Empire in the heart of the continent. But the Spanish never had a chance to find out. Franco-Spanish traders were about to crash into a Lakota barrier that they did not know existed. Like the Ohio Valley earlier, the Missouri Valley was becoming a hot spot in Native-colonial struggles.

An enterprising trader, Jacques d'Eglise, embarked upriver in 1793, aiming for Mandan country. The Lakotas stopped him three hundred miles shy of his target and confiscated most of his goods. From there on, Lakotas and Yanktons made it their policy to control the northbound trade from Saint Louis. Realizing that outright pillage risked suppressing the upriver trade altogether, the Lakotas collected tolls, forcing traders to pay for upriver access with guns, powder, lead, and other goods, turning the Missouri Valley into a tribute-yielding machine. In 1794, Jean-Baptiste Truteau, an employee of the Missouri Fur Company, embarked on a trading expedition to Mandan country far in the north, where he planned to build a fort. He was stopped by Yankton soldiers, who boarded his merchandise-laden pirogue and took him into a Lakota village upriver. There, Lakotas condemned Truteau's expedition, branding the traders who aimed to push farther upriver toward the Arikaras and Mandans as "bad men, always talking evil against them and urging that nation [Arikaras] to kill them." The gunpowder that reached Arikara and Mandan hands, the Lakotas told Truteau, "would only be used to kill Sioux." They asked Truteau to "open up the bad roads by means of large presents of merchandize," a thinly veiled demand for tribute. "This was genuine plunder," the humiliated trader carped to his journal. His list of lost merchandise anticipated the windfall that the Lakota-Yankton river policy would generate: cloth, tobacco, knives, axes, blankets, vermillion, flints, gun worms, powder, and "a proportionate number of balls." The Lakotas also wanted Truteau's help in forging a proper relationship with the governor of Spanish Louisiana and its traders. Truteau obliged. His report portrayed the Lakotas as the "greatest beaver hunters" in Spanish Louisiana.[14]

By the mid-1790s, Lakota ascendancy in the upper Missouri Valley was a recognized fact. While systematically exploiting the Franco-Spanish river traffic, the Lakotas also dominated the Native farmers in the region—Missouri Valley farmers. The Lakotas combined plundering and extortion with diplomacy and trade into a flexible economy of violence that rendered the local Whites, Arikaras, and Hidatsas fearful, deprived, and compliant. The mobile, horse-mounted Lakotas created artificial demand for their own exports by keeping the bison away from Arikara territory, reaping great profits. Tabeau noted how Lakota soldiers enclosed an Arikara town with their tipis, "forming a barrier which prevents the buffalo from coming near." Turning hunger into a weapon, the Lakotas could "fix, as they wish, the price of that which belongs to them and obtain, in exchange, a quantity of corn, tobacco, beans, and pumpkins that they demand." Although the Arikaras provided the Lakotas with the three sisters—squash, beans, and maize—for free, the Lakotas forced the Arikaras to buy bows and arrows from them, even though the Arikaras were "surrounded by woods suitable for supplying them." This "ruinous commerce" turned the surviving three thousand Arikaras into Lakota vassals. As Tabeau explained, the Lakotas saw in the Arikaras "a certain kind of serf, who cultivates for them and who, as they say, takes, for them, the place of women." The Arikara towns at the confluence of the Missouri and Grand Rivers now belonged to the Lakotas. Tabeau, sidelined, complained bitterly that the Lakotas "make the Ricaras [Arikaras] understand that I treat them [the Arikaras] as slaves."[15]

Confident of their place in the world, the Lakotas shifted shape, adjusting to the contours of the life-giving river. They entrenched themselves in strategically critical sites along the Missouri's banks, tightening their bonds. Gradually, they solidified their loose alliance into a nation, coalescing around the liquid spine of their world. They frequented the Black Hills for spiritual rejuvenation and political assemblies. Slow Buffalo, a prominent itháŋčhaŋ announced, "We are seven bands and from now on we will scatter over the world, so we will appoint one chief for each band. . . . The Mysterious One has given us this place, and now it is up to us to expand ourselves. We will name every person and everything." By the beginning of the nineteenth century, the Lakotas had adopted their sacred form as seven oyátes: Hunkpapas, Minneconjous, Oglalas, Sans Arcs, Sicangus, Sihasapas, and Two Kettles. They were now "allies against all others of mankind." Slow Buffalo dispatched other ithánčhaŋs to the east, west, and north, but not to the south. "Other people would come from that direction," he said.[16]

THE ARRIVAL OF THOSE "other people" had been in the works for years. President Jefferson was eager to secure American authority over the Louisiana Purchase, but he was vexed by the sheer size and the daunting ethnic plurality of the acquisition; he thought that the settling of Louisiana could take a thousand generations. He knew next to nothing about the loyalties of the region's Indigenous nations and feared that they might well seek alliances with British Canada in the north or New Spain in the west and south.[17]

Desperate to secure the astounding acquisition, Jefferson first planned to enlist thirty thousand American volunteers who would each receive 160 acres in return for two years of military service. In the end, he chose a leaner strategy: a small exploratory expedition that would traverse the length of the immense territory, establish alliances with the local Indians, assert U.S. sovereignty in the region, and find the fabled all-water route across the western half of the continent. Jefferson started to groom his private secretary, Meriwether Lewis, to lead the Corps of Discovery, a new unit of the United States Army, and execute the critical first plunge into the enormous domain. Lewis would have to be a soldier, a diplomat, and a natural historian all at once. Lewis, in turn, recruited William Clark, a retired army officer, as his co-commander. They hoped to find scores of docile Indians, who would supply them with food and guide them to their destination, and they were in a hurry: Jefferson feared that some foreign power might be able to claim the Pacific coast before the United States could. The nervous Jefferson unrealistically wanted to remove most eastern Indians, pushing them west of the Mississippi, where a vast trading empire would be built to channel Indigenous products, mainly furs and skins, to eastern markets.[18]

The Lakotas would shape Lewis and Clark's plans from the start. To Americans, Saint Louis was the gateway to the Trans-Mississippi West, and the Missouri River was the natural highway for colonists. That made the Lakotas, who now controlled the upper section of the river with an iron grip, the most important Native nation to win over. Jefferson had procured Truteau's journal in the fall of 1803 and had shared it with Lewis and Clark. The journal described in detail Lakota power politics in the upper Missouri Valley. According to Truteau, the Lakotas numbered "from 30. to 60,000(?) men, and abound in fire-arms"—a gross exaggeration that overestimated the Lakota population by three to six times, but also captured how thoroughly the mobile Lakotas controlled the upper Missouri Valley. It was obvious that the Americans would not be able to assert authority in Louisiana until they had won over and subdued the Lakotas. "Although you will pass through no settlements of the Sioux, you will probably meet with parties of them," Jefferson warned the co-captains. "On that nation," he stressed, "we wish most particularly to make a friendly impression, because of their immense power." Exactly what logic Jefferson and his advisors relied on when they determined that Lewis and Clark could establish American authority over the enormous acquisition with forty-some men remains unclear. But at least that figure was an improvement. Initially, Jefferson had planned to send in "twelve or fifteen men."[19]

Lewis and Clark pushed into the unknown: most available maps of the Missouri River were mere sketches. Spanish and French traders knew the interior far better than any of the Americans did, and the British in Canada were more cognizant of the power dynamics in the region than were their American rivals. Since 1799, British officials had been approaching the Lakotas, "a nation unquestionably composing the Indian Warriors in America . . . all mounted and muster about 6,000 men." Unlike the Americans, the British had learned that there was very little White people could do without accommodating the Indians.[20]

In the fall of 1803, a little over a year before Lewis and Clark's departure, the Sicangu Lakotas welcomed an embassy from the Omaha and Ponca Nations to the south. The two semisedentary agrarian peoples "urgently entreated" Black Buffalo, a Sicangu ithą́nčhaŋ who had recently been "elevated to the first rank," hoping to open trade relations with the mighty Lakotas. Instead, they became pawns in an internal Lakota power struggle. The Partisan, an ambitious rival ithą́nčhaŋ, sent six of his soldiers to abort Black Buffalo's peace with the Omahas and Poncas. They failed, and the Poncas struck back but accidentally targeted Black Buffalo's village. To save face, Black Buffalo retaliated. His soldiers killed more than half of the people in a Ponca town—perhaps as many as 150 men, women, and children—and 75 in an Omaha town. The "formerly very numerous" Poncas were now "very mild." Soon after, the Poncas and Omahas moved into a single town, which posed no challenge to Lakota interests. Lewis and Clark had no knowledge of these dramatic changes. They were entering a fluid geopolitical dynamic that they could neither understand nor manipulate. The Lakotas were consolidating their dominance over the upper Missouri Valley just ahead of the arrival of the U.S. agents of empire.[21]

The Corps of Discovery left Saint Louis on May 14, 1804. It pushed upriver in two pirogues and a fifty-five-foot keelboat armed with a bronze swivel cannon. There was no rush: the corps wanted to showcase its power and generosity to the Indians, which would take time. Lewis and Clark had brought with them 4,600 sewing needles, more than 1,500 moccasin awls, 2,800 fishhooks, 18,000 pairs of scissors, 180 polished-pewter mirrors, and 130 rolls of tobacco—all to appease and win over the Indigenous nations they were about to encounter. At Monticello, Jefferson grew increasingly anxious from the moment the expedition set off. A month after the Corps of Discovery's departure, he wrote that Lewis and Clark "must stand well" when facing the Osages and Lakotas "because in their quarter we are miserably weak." He thought the Osages were "the finest men we have ever seen" and "a great nation." Alongside the earlier idea of a massive Indian removal, Jefferson now nurtured an improbable vision of the Louisiana territory as a natural laboratory where truly enlightened men—including assimilated Indians—could become models for the rest of the world.[22]

As the Corps of Discovery pushed upriver, the first thing the Indians on their route were likely to notice was the keelboat's high mast and large sail. When the vessel inched closer, the Indians would notice a heavy, menacing-looking weapon mounted on its bow—a swivel cannon. The two pirogues followed behind. The problem for Lewis and Clark was that their appearance sent mixed messages to Indians. It was unclear whether they were soldiers or diplomats, or whether they meant to command or trade with the Native population. Lewis and Clark had extraordinary technologies and belongings, but they were obviously not like the French or Spanish traders, who were generous with their wares without demanding obedience and submission.

The Corps of Discovery faced its first real test in August, when it arrived in an Otoe-Missouria town above the Missouri-Platte confluence. Lewis and Clark were to follow an elaborate procedure authored by Jefferson: they would parade for the Indians, deliver standard speeches to explain their intentions—translated by Pierre Dorion, the corps's talented interpreter—and hand out medals to "make" chiefs. A loud shot from an air gun was to be the standard introduction. Such imperial theatrics did little to impress the Otoes. After a long break in the talks, their leader, Big Horse, made demands to the Americans. "I came here naked and I must go home naked," he complained. He had expected gifts that he could share with his followers. "A Spoon ful of your milk will qui[e]t all," he instructed the newcomers. Milk, embodying generosity, could also turn the American strangers into allies and perhaps relatives.[23]

Ten weeks later, the Corps of Discovery approached the Yanktons at the James River junction, knowing that it was crossing into the territory of the powerful Sioux Confederacy. Clark was "much engaged" in writing a speech: the last thing the captains wanted was to provoke the Yanktons with an underwhelming address. They sent the Indians a canoe laden with tobacco, corn, and iron kettles. The next morning the Yanktons paraded for the strangers in full regalia; Lewis and Clark, donning their dress uniforms, raised a flag and ordered a gun salute. Lewis delivered his standard speech about commerce, cooperation, and the Great Father in Washington, D.C., who now claimed to own the land they stood on. He then distributed gifts to prominent Yanktons, hoping to create more authoritative leaders through whom the Americans could control the Sioux Confederacy. The Yankton ithą́nčhaŋ

Shake Hand saw through the tactic. "Listen to what I say," he commanded. "I had an English medal when I went to See them, I went to the Spaniards they gave me medal and Some goods, I wish you would do the Same for my people." Half Man, another Yankton ithą́čhaŋ, warned the Americans that the "nations above will not open their ears, and you cannot I fear open them." He was referring to the increasingly powerful Lakotas. The Arikara Nation, "wearied by its losses," had tried to enter into an alliance with the Mandans and Hidatsas, but the Lakotas would not allow it. Now unsettled, Lewis and Clark decided to leave Pierre Dorion among the Yanktons as a gesture of goodwill.[24]

The Lakotas had probably learned about the incoming American expedition from their allies downriver. When the Sicangus, the southernmost Lakota oyáte, spotted the Corps of Discovery, they immediately enforced their border control by sending young swimmers to the keelboat. Using sign language, the swimmers told the Americans that two Lakota villages were nearby. A council was arranged at the mouth of the next river, the Bad. It did not go well. Meeting on a sandbar in the middle of the river, Lewis and Clark recognized Black Buffalo as "the Grand Chief," which angered the Partisan—the rival Sicangu ithą́čhaŋ—who was also present. The Sicangus on the keelboat refused to disembark, and the Partisan threatened to keep one of the expedition's pirogues as tribute. Black Buffalo grabbed the pirogue's cable, while the Partisan walked calmly over to his soldiers, who drew their bows and cocked their guns. Black Buffalo, reasserting his authority, announced that "he had warrers [sic] too." If the Americans "were to go on," he warned, his warriors would follow them and "kill and take the whole of [them] by degrees." Clark, usually a superb problem solver, now relied on crude intimidation, announcing that a letter to "their great father the president" would "have them all destroyed as it were in a moment."

Misreading the situation, Clark offered his hand to Black Buffalo, who ignored him and walked over to his own soldiers. He arranged them into position to kill the Americans, but he did not order them to fire. Black Buffalo's calm authority defused the dangerous face-off, which had come very close to ending the Lewis and Clark expedition. Black Buffalo asked that Sicangu women and children be allowed climb into the pirogue, "as they never Saw Such a one." When the women and children had boarded, Black Buffalo and two Sicangu men joined them, effectively taking over the vessel. They moved a mile upriver and anchored the boat near an island, which the humiliated Clark called "bad humered Island as we were in a bad humer." The next morning, Black Buffalo guided the Americans to the Sicangu stronghold that served as the southern bastion of the Lakota domain. Lewis and Clark were now deeply immersed in a Lakota script. They disembarked, and Lakota soldiers seated them on white buffalo robes and carried them into a ring-shaped village of roughly one hundred tipis, all of them made of luxurious tanned white buffalo robes—an Indigenous Versailles built to evoke awe. The captains were taken into a grand-council tipi, surrounded by seventy soldiers, where they were saw many symbols of the Lakotas' international reach: Omaha captives, an American flag, two Spanish flags, elaborate calumet pipes, and medicine bundles—a carefully crafted story of geopolitical and otherworldly power.[25]

The Lakotas had exposed the fiction at the center of the Corps of Discovery. Lewis and Clark tried to hold on to their conqueror narrative, in which they were asserting U.S. authority over the Missouri Valley, but in reality, the Lakotas were consolidating their supremacy over the valley in the expedition's wake. Instead of extending the American empire into the deep interior of the continent, Lewis and Clark had provoked an awe-inspiring imperial Indigenous response that foiled the Jeffersonian vision for the continent. After reaching relative safety in Mandan country near the western turn of the Missouri, the Corps of Discovery built a stockade that it grandiosely called Fort Mandan. There, Clark examined the record of the expedition so far. It was decidedly mixed. The corps may have won access to Mandan traders, but it had been thoroughly humiliated by the Lakotas. Clark wrote about the "Sioux"—he did not use "Lakota"—so often in his journal that he managed to spell "Sioux" twenty-seven different ways in his idiosyncratic orthography. Letting his hurt seep through, he branded the Lakotas as "the vilest miscreants of the savage race, and must ever remain the pirates of the Missouri." Rather than opportunistic pirates, the Lakotas were, in reality, the protectors of a newly established Indigenous hegemony.

When Lewis and Clark planned their departure upriver and then westward, they knew their next challenges would be more physical than political. They would be moving toward greater aridity and would have to navigate numerous mountain ranges that grew bigger the farther west they traveled. They needed help. In November 1804 at Fort Mandan, they met Toussaint Charbonneau, a North West Company trader, and his young, pregnant wife, Sacagawea, the daughter of a Lemhi Shoshone woman. Sacagawea had been captured in 1800 at the Three Forks of the Missouri by Hidatsas and had spent four years in captivity, until Charbonneau ransomed her. Now heading west with Lewis and Clark, she recognized key geographical features, helping to orient the captains, and when the expedition reached the navigable limits of the Missouri, she facilitated the crucial purchase of horses from Shoshone traders. Astonishingly, their leader turned out to be her brother, Cameahwait. Why Sacagawea decided to stay with the Americans is not clear, but her contributions were essential. The horses she secured made it possible for the corps to reach the Pacific. She also kept the Americans safe through her mere presence: a party that included a woman and, not long after, a baby, was seen as a peaceful one. A relieved Clark reported that "a woman with a party of men is a token of peace."[26]

Lewis and Clark were navigating an Indigenous world that they understood only dimly. While pushing upriver, they missed a major event along the Missouri: the Crows entered written history when they paraded in front of Hidatsa and Mandan Indians on the Knife River, a tributary of the Missouri. A French fur trader recorded the event. He later returned to the Crows and lavished them with axes and knives and smoked with them. With that, the Crows stepped into a shared new world of Indians and Europeans, as French allies.[27]

THE CORPS OF DISCOVERY completed its epic journey to the Pacific coast and back in less than two years, returning to Saint Louis in April 1806, having organized more than fifty conferences with Indians. The arrival of the corps was a spectacle of nationalistic fervor. The explorers returned with stories of unforeseen natural riches

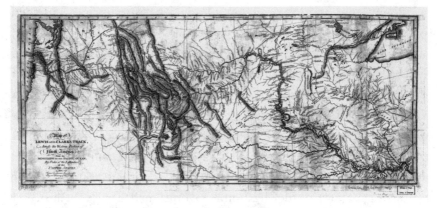

A famous 1814 map depicting Lewis and Clark's "track" across western North America from the Mississippi to the Pacific Ocean

and of the sheer scale of the continent to the west. At a celebratory dinner, Lewis and Clark were compared to Christopher Columbus, while the Missouri was branded as "a vehicle of wealth to all the nations of the world." Toasts were given to "The Commerce of the United States—The basis for the political elevation of America."[28]

During Lewis and Clark's absence, the world had changed. General James Wilkinson had launched an expedition of his own to explore the upper Mississippi Valley, partly to claim it for the United States— Canadian traders had pushed downriver for years—but mostly to carve out a fur-trading fiefdom for himself. A man of unusually malleable allegiances, Wilkinson had been known as "Agent 13" during his time as a spy in the service of Spain, working to deliver Kentucky to the Spanish Empire, and tipping off the Spanish to the Lewis and Clark expedition. After the Louisiana Purchase, Wilkinson had lobbied for himself to become governor of the territory. Jefferson gave him the job.

Whereas Lewis and Clark had contended with the Lakotas, Wilkinson reached out to their relatives, the Dakotas, who commanded much of the upper Mississippi Valley. He issued a proclamation banning British traders from the Missouri and Mississippi Valleys and sent Lieutenant Zebulon Pike up the river. Pike reached the Dakotas at the confluence of the Mississippi, Chippewa, and Saint Croix Rivers, where they were busily trapping beavers. He met with Mdewakanton Sioux leaders and proposed to build a fort and a trading post for

them. The itháŋčhaŋs Little Crow and Penichon signed a hastily formulated treaty of barely 250 words. They knew that the presence of
American traders would enable them to play British and American
traders off against each other and extract better deals from both.

Wilkinson and Pike's unauthorized maneuvering revealed how
fractured and weak the young nation was beyond the original states
in the East. Americans saw Indians as uncivilized nonstate peoples,
but in reality, Native Americans were often far better organized
than their adversaries. The Lakotas and Dakotas, along with most
Indigenous nations, had sophisticated decision-making systems that
revolved around regular nationwide councils and direct participation
by the nation's people: most Native nations made decisions based on
consensus and frequently included both women and men in the deliberations. As a result, Native Americans were able to present a unified
front to outsiders and enemies.

From 1806 on, the Lakotas methodically policed the Missouri
across a four-hundred-mile expanse, inspecting vessels and fleets and
demanding tribute payments. They sometimes staged ambushes from
subjugated Arikara towns, getting the better of American interlopers,
and they contained the United States' expansion westward, spoiling
the ambitions of such leading American entrepreneurs as John Jacob
Astor and Manuel Lisa. Controlling the Missouri was an enormously
lucrative enterprise that could have divided the Lakotas, but their
leaders were experienced in such matters, going back to their encounters with Spanish traders in the 1790s. Adhering to traditional Lakota
values, they led from the front and distributed the spoils evenly, often
depriving themselves at the expense of their followers. The reward
was loyalty, consensus, and staying power. The trajectory of the
Osage Nation was nearly the polar opposite. Lacking the numbers
and horse-powered mobility of the Lakotas, they were vulnerable to
colonial aggression. In 1808, William Clark and Pierre Chouteau—
the former a celebrated explorer, the latter a politician—met with
the Osage leaders Pawhuska and Nezuma and demanded land cessions amounting to more than eighty thousand square miles, crippling
the Osage Nation. By way of compensation, the Osages received a
U.S.-sponsored factory, the first in the Trans-Mississippi West.[29]

Chapter 25

THE WHITE DEVIL
WITH HIS
MOUTH WIDE OPEN

THE NASCENT AMERICAN REPUBLIC WAS A CHAMELEON. That was not by choice. Situated on the eastern edge of an Indigenous continent containing hundreds of Native nations, the republic had to continually adjust to the Indigenous presence and territoriality on its self-imposed borders. Every Native nation the Americans came in contact with was unique, forcing them to calibrate their foreign policies again and again. Contending with the highly mobile Lakotas was a challenge distinct from that of accommodating sedentary, farming-based Native nations and confederacies.

While the Lakotas were consolidating their dominance in the Missouri Valley, foiling American ambitions in the interior, other Native nations faced an increasingly aggressive American republic that seemed to have no regard for Native boundaries or sovereignty. American arrogance left the door ajar for British stratagems. In 1802, William Henry Harrison, the powerful governor of the Indiana Territory, warned that British agents operating out of Upper Canada were attempting to "make the Indians believe that the United States intended to destroy them with the means of small pox, which was to be communicated to them by the goods which they received from us."[1]

In 1804, Harrison—mirroring James Wilkinson's subterfuges—seized more than one thousand square miles of Native land in a fraudulent treaty, provoking Native Americans to seek Indigenous solutions to the catastrophe of colonialism. In June 1805, the Očhéthi Šakówiŋ took initiative. Evoking the "Dish with One Spoon" law, it sent war pipes to the Sauks, Meskwakis, Odawas, and Potawatomis, asking them to make peace with the Osages west of the Mississippi Valley so that they could band together to confront the "new white nation now encroaching on Our Lands." The Sioux also sent a peace pipe to the British at Fort Amherstburg at the mouth of the Detroit River and invited them to join forces with the Očhéthi Šakówiŋ against the Americans. The weakened and disgruntled Osages opted for more direct measures, proposing to U.S. officials in the Illinois Country that they would "take the warpath and pillage the silver convoys which ply between different points, as they succeeded doing some years ago." The Osages and the Chouteau family in Saint Louis created their own army of three hundred soldiers. The Osages warned George Sibley, their assigned agent, never to point with his fingers.[2]

The Shawnees would have appreciated the Osages' put-down. The U.S. government had been buying Indigenous land in the northern Ohio Country, but it failed to honor the agreed-upon annuity payments. The nascent Indigenous coalition of Sioux, Sauks, Meskwakis, Odawas, and Potawatomis moved toward war. In the spring of 1805, a disease epidemic had broken out among the Kishpoko Shawnees, fueling fear and resentment. Lalawéthika, a drunkard and failed Shawnee shaman fell into a deep, deathlike trance. In his vision he traveled to a place where he had to confront his sins. He met Meteelemelakwe, the Creator. Lalawéthika's path was now clear to him. He became Tenskwatawa—Open Door—and began to preach and heal the souls and minds of Native people as the Prophet. Drawing from the Lenape prophet Neolin's teachings and Christianity, he guided them to reject corrupting White things: alcohol, clothing, spouses, biracial children, cattle, hogs, sheep, chickens, spinning wheels, and bread. Another Shawnee holy man, Le Maigouis, denounced the Americans with particular scorn as "the scum of the great waters when it was troubled by the evil spirit, and the froth was driven into the woods by a strong east wind. They are numerous, but I hate them." Observing Meteelemelakwe's creation through a racial lens, the Prophet placed Whites and Indians in different worlds. The vital thing was to be spiritually and materially independent Indians. Tenskwatawa was obliterating the Americans from the Shawnee world with words.

To Tenskwatawa, the requirement for purity was all-encompassing, going beyond race. Wanting to protect his people from becoming dependent on foreign markets, he prohibited commercial hunting and the fur trade with colonists. He emphasized the differences between Indians and Whites and labeled Americans as other-than-human people that had emerged from the sea in the form of a great serpent. But Tenskwatawa also sought to reform his fellow Indians. He rejected polygamy and intermarriages, and he wanted his people to embrace proper gender roles embedded in male dominance. Men were to be soldiers and providers, while women were to be farmers and caregivers and removed from the public sphere. Women had been essential to the creation and survival of the generations-old middle ground between Native Americans and the French, and the Prophet's ban on women's participation in public life nearly destroyed that middle ground. Tenskwatawa's directives did not go unopposed. Beade, an ex-Moravian Indigenous prophetess, mobilized Lenape spiritualism to stamp out stealing, fornication, murder, and evil, subtly challenging the Prophet's unyielding gender regime. Tenskwatawa staged witch hunts against skeptics.[3]

Tapping into fervent Indigenous spiritualism and long-brewing animosities between Indians and Americans in the Ohio Country, Tenskwatawa met an enthusiastic audience. His message spread explosively, reaching nations from the Great Lakes deep into the continental grasslands. He prohibited individual land cessions to the United States, envisioning a vast Indigenous alliance that would present a unified front against the Americans. He made Greenville in the western Ohio Country his headquarters, launching a campaign that was at once military, religious, and spiritual. He denounced American civilization programs as a plot to reduce Indians to slavery. The Great Spirit, Aasha Monetoo, had given the Shawnees not only the land but also *mishaamis*, sacred bundles that contained the welfare of the nation and would allow the Shawnees to keep the land always.

While separating Indians from Europeans, Tenskwatawa poached elements of Christian ideology—the Devil, Heaven, and sermons— and galvanized thousands of Shawnees, Lenapes, Wyandots, Potawatomis, Kickapoos, Odawas, Ojibwes, Sauks, Ho-Chunks, and others. He had several sorcerers among the assimilated Lenapes executed, and he ordered traditional medicine bags and their spiritually laden objects destroyed because their owners were sinful. His was a total vision; he was making the world anew. To the chagrin of U.S. agents, hundreds across the Great Lakes region made pilgrimages to see and hear him. In early 1808, Tenskwatawa moved his base to Prophetstown, a new multiethnic settlement at the confluence of the Wabash and Tippecanoe Rivers. His brother, Tecumseh—"shooting star" in Shawnee—joined him there soon after. Tecumseh had fought the Europeans since he was fifteen. The brothers' mother was Muscogee, which helped the Prophet's ambitious alliance-building. A distraught Jefferson wrote Michigan's territorial governor that "if ever we are constrained to lift the hatchet against any tribe, we will never lay it down till that tribe is exterminated, or driven beyond the Mississippi." A new Indigenous alliance had emerged to continue the Indian Confederacy's mission.

At Prophetstown, a multitude of local interests and ambitions converged and mixed. It was a focal point of rumors, lies, spies, half-truths, and expedient alliances among Indians, Americans, British, and French—all of it intensified by massive consumption of alcohol, a commodity that was eclipsing all others in the Ohio Country. Prophetstown was geographically central and socially fluid—almost an ideal setting for an ambitious leader striving to elevate himself. With Tecumseh's help, Tenskwatawa sidelined local leaders and concentrated power in his hands. There was palpable tension between Tenskwatawa the zealot and Tecumseh the pragmatist; the latter continued to trade with the French, still a major presence in the Ohio Country.

In 1809, colonists panicked when rumors of imminent Indian attacks spread along the Wabash River to Vincennes, the capital of the Indiana Territory. Governor Harrison did not know what to make of it. What the Americans called the Northwest was home to nearly thirty thousand Native Americans, who were growing rapidly in numbers. Ho-Chunk, Illini, Sauk, and Meskwaki women mined lead to the tune of four hundred thousand pounds per year, which bought their people weapons, respect, and power. Such concrete and measurable success alarmed the colonists: the Indians were not disappearing. Paranoia swept across the White frontier.[4]

Having let rumors and success do their unsettling work, Tenskwa-tawa and Tecumseh prepared for war, making the most of Tecumseh's multiethnic Shawnee and Muscogee ancestry. Tecumseh, now emerging as the domineering leader, embarked on a two-thousand-mile diplomatic tour among the southern Indians to recruit allies. A three-month span of earthquakes lent his message greater urgency—the world itself seemed to be changing—and by the winter of 1811 the confederated Indians were ready. But there were fault lines among the Indians. Push-mataha, a hard-boiled Choctaw leader, denounced Tecumseh as a stranger and an agitator. Only a few Choctaws joined the movement.

Tecumseh and Tenskwatawa also reached out to the British and asked them to supply the Indians with guns and then join them in attacking the United States. Americans in the Northwest believed they were facing a full-scale Indian conspiracy. Governor Harrison warned that "unless some decisive and energetic measure is adopted to break up the combination formed by the Prophet we shall soon have every Indian tribe in this quarter allied against us." Harrison also thought that Tecumseh was "one of those uncommon geniuses which spring up occasionally and produce revolutions and overturn the established order of things." Tenskwatawa had his base fortified. Harrison mobilized his militia.

Overcome with fear, the colonists begged President James Madison for help against the emerging anti-American coalition: "The banditti under the prophet are suffered where they now are. The people have become highly irritated and alarmed." The colonists reminded the president that "the western country, sir, is indebted to your predecessor for an undeviating attachment to its prosperity." Harrison, for his part, wrote to Tenskwatawa to reassure him that "the acquirement of more land was no object with the U. States." The Indiana Territory had roughly twenty-five thousand White inhabitants and more land than "they could possibly settle." Here the Indigenous challenge to imperial Americans consisted of intensely local and relentless acts of resistance, not of the dramatic military and diplomatic maneuvers of the Six Nations, Lakotas, Cherokees, Chickasaws, Choctaws, Cataw-bas, and Comanches.[5]

While Tecumseh was still in the South, expanding the alliance and recruiting soldiers, Harrison, emboldened by Tecumseh's absence, seized the initiative. Struggling to hold on to his militia—fear-of-war fatigue was spreading rapidly among the settler-soldiers—Harrison needed to move fast. He marched an army of regulars and militia straight into Prophetstown and burned it to the ground. Suddenly deprived of his all-important local power base, Tecumseh recalibrated his ambitions. Localized violence erupted into a much larger conflict in 1812, when the United States declared war on Britain, partly because the British had allied with the Ohio Indians against the Americans. Benjamin Hawkins received reports of fanatic "prophets" who denounced all things American. The War of 1812 was a regional war between the United States and Native Americans, as well as an imperial conflict over British impressment of American sailors and British violations of U.S. maritime rights. Madison led the United States into a war against Great Britain, unrealistically confident that, with a puny navy of only sixteen vessels, the nation would prevail against the world's leading maritime power. Making matters worse, the conflict enabled large numbers of Black slaves to escape and join the British to fight the Americans.[6]

If the British-U.S. conflict was an odd one, the Native-U.S. conflict was a brutal war over territory and survival. There were hundreds of thousands of Indians in the Trans-Appalachian West, and almost all of them would become enemies of the United States if provoked. The war presented to Native peoples an opportunity to roll back colonialism while the United States was reeling under the costs of its many wars. War and treaty-making with Native Americans had become the federal budget's greatest expense and greatest failure. The Americans now faced Tecumseh's confederacy of Shawnees, Potawatomis, Kickapoos, Ho-Chunks, Menominees, Odawas, and Wyandots. The allied Indians intended to shove the Americans east of the Ohio River to establish control over the river valleys that facilitated mobilizations. The Indians' ultimate target was the pivotal Fort Detroit, which had been the starting point of Pontiac's War.

The Battle of Fort Detroit in 1812 was one of Tecumseh's finest moments. He was said to have paraded his soldiers three times around the fort, creating an illusion of a far bigger army than he actually had and tricking General William Hull into surrendering without a fight. The garrison made a humiliating and strategically disastrous retreat. Colonel Lewis Cass lamented, "We wholly left the Canadian shore and have abandoned the miserable inhabitants who depend on our will and power to protect them, to their fate." Tecumseh and his British allies then focused their efforts on Fort Meigs down the Maumee River, laying siege to the massive fortress with more than two thousand soldiers. They failed to take it, and the momentum began to turn against Tecumseh's confederacy and his British allies.[7]

ELSEWHERE, INDIGENOUS RESISTANCE MOVEMENTS turned inward, seeking to protect the core of their cultures, identities, and sovereignty. Muscogee dissidents known as Red Sticks rebelled against the wealthy Muscogee leaders who dominated the national council and who had accepted American civilization programs under Benjamin Hawkins's forceful advocacy. Led by charismatic prophet Hillis Harjo, the Red Sticks appropriated the red stick of justice for their cause and fought with red-painted war clubs, *atássas*, carrying on Tecumseh's military resistance. The Muscogee Nation split along cultural and class divides into the wealthy Upper Muscogees and poorer Lower Muscogees. The wealthy Muscogees had expanded the national council's powers, marginalizing Lower Muscogees, who felt alienated from the Muscogee Confederacy. Like Neolin and Skaniadariyo, the Red Sticks sought to purge their world of alien things— spinning wheels, forges, cattle, hogs, sheep, seed cotton, glass beads, farming tools, and bread—that symbolized the skewed concentration of power in the hands of Muscogee micos. Then they started killing Upper Muscogees and their African slaves. The Red Sticks also sought to enforce traditional Muscogee gender roles, and they targeted a White woman, Mrs. Grayson, stripping and humiliating her. Hawkins and the governors of Tennessee, Georgia, and Mississippi panicked. Desperate to contain the chaos, General Wilkinson seized Mobile to contain the Spanish in Florida.

By that point the Red Stick uprising had expanded to include not only most Muscogee towns but also Seminoles who had been

This paternalistic painting depicts Benjamin Hawkins on his plantation along the Flint River in central Georgia, showing the Muscogees—highly skilled farmers—how to use the plow.

armed by the Spanish in Pensacola. Inspired by Tecumseh, the war had acquired a palpable anti-U.S. streak. The last Indigenous victories were delivered by the Seminoles and freed African slaves, who attacked U.S. troops in Spanish Florida, keeping them out of their territory. The Seminoles and their African allies needed Spanish Florida to survive as an offset to American slave raiders, planters, and land speculators. The stakes were high because the margins for settlement were so small: ninety percent of the province was sand.[8]

In the summer of 1813, the Red Sticks lay waste to outlying plantations, and by the fall they had broadened the war from the Tennessee Valley to the Gulf coast and from the Tombigbee River to the Tallapoosa Valley. In August, hundreds of Red Sticks stormed Fort Mims and nearby Tensaw, a Muscogee town of mostly Métis, killing more than five hundred militiamen and civilians in a massacre that revealed deep fault lines among the Muscogees: they had become divided between nativists and wealthy accommodationists who disagreed over how much Americanizing their world could bear. The Red Sticks kept the colonists in a state of fear by raiding settlements, killing livestock, confiscating property, and reducing male colonists to "women"—and told them so. In October, in a desperate hand-to-hand battle against a far bigger U.S. Army on the Thames River, Tecumseh's army and his British allies suffered a complete defeat. Retreating, Tecumseh took a bullet in the chest and died immediately. He left behind a hollowed-out confederacy and a rudderless brother. The resistance died with him: Ohio's non-Native population had mushroomed to eight hundred thousand. Tenskwatawa quarreled with both Indians and British officials, and his resistance sputtered out.[9]

The British no longer had to treat Native Americans as independent peoples occupying sovereign places between the British Empire and the American republic. The Ohio Country became a settler space. Soon after Tecumseh's downfall, the last kernel of the middle ground died, marking the end to a remarkably creative and effective strand of Indigenous resistance against colonialism. With the circumstances having now come full circle, Indians became, once again, savages and strangers to Whites, and the French were outsiders.[10]

After the subjugation of the pan-Indian alliance in the Ohio Country, General Andrew Jackson, burning with ambition, set out to conquer the deeply divided Muscogees in the South. He mobilized an army of nearly three thousand U.S. troops and hundreds of Cherokee, Choctaw, and Chickasaw soldiers and descended on the Red Sticks, killing almost fifteen hundred in a genocidal campaign that culminated in an attack at Horseshoe Bend in the Mississippi Territory in which more than eight hundred Red Sticks died. In the ensuing 1814 and 1816 treaties, the Muscogees, having lost nearly two thousand soldiers, surrendered more than forty thousand square miles—a massive L-shaped swath of land in the very heart of the Indigenous South, foreshadowing the southern Indian removals to come.

At long last—and after enormous bloodshed—the United States was becoming secure. The Ohio Country had been an open wound for decades, and now the Americans had a chance to close it. The Muscogees had lost the majority of their soldiers, and Jackson—soon to become a committed Indian killer—announced that the Americans were "so carefully avoiding injustice to these tribes as even to be unjust to themselves," revealing something about the United States' warped worldview and disregard for facts. Jackson then imposed a punitive treaty on the Muscogees that echoed the genocidal cruelty of the Paxton Boys and the massacre at Gnadenhütten. The long era of wars of independence had come to an ambiguous end.[11]

FARTHER WEST, in Spanish Louisiana, Texas, and the Californias, colonialism took a different form in the face of overwhelming Indigenous power. While the United States, Britain, and France had fought for control of the continent in several wars, gaining and losing territories in an ever-changing pattern, the Spanish had been confined to the west along the Rio Grande and beyond the Rocky Mountains, slowly slipping into irrelevance. But in the second half of the eighteenth century, a modernization movement under the Enlightenment-inspired Bourbon kings gave the Spanish Empire in North America a shot of new life.

One strand of Spanish colonialism had always promoted coexistence with the Indians, who, the thinking went, could become useful subjects of the empire if properly managed. The late-eighteenth-century Bourbon reformers pushed that practice to its limits. Spanish officers now relied on scientists rather than soldiers and began collecting information about the numerous Indigenous nations on their far-flung frontiers—a crucial first step toward mutual understanding, coexistence, and peace. In their quest to civilize and pacify the unconquered Indians—indios bárbaros—the Spanish began to see Indians as "specimens" in a colossal scientific experiment aimed at creating new people in the New World. Bourbon reformers believed that an enduring Spanish Empire in North America could be built soul by soul.[12]

The grand experiment was stillborn: it crashed against concerted Indigenous resistance. The Apaches reduced Sonora to "deplorable destruction and decay," forcing the Spanish colonists to vacate their mines and settlements. Spain was simply too weak to extend its empire over the Indians, and Bourbon officials banned offensive war as too risky and counterproductive. The Spanish Jesuit order was banished from the Americas in 1767, largely because it was draining the empire's coffers and because the weakened Spanish crown coveted the order's extensive landholdings. More than two thousand Spanish Jesuits left the Americas.[13]

The costs of Spain's imperial retreat were far-reaching: Spanish colonies in both Americas would remain besieged and confined by indios bárbaros. From the 1760s on, the Spanish Empire descended into a hemispheric crisis. Repelled by the Indians, Spanish policymakers retreated to the older practice of pairing missionization with warfare. Offensive war crept back into the list of strategic options. In 1767, José de Gálvez, the dynamic minister of the Indies, sent an army of eleven hundred soldiers into Sonora to pacify the Apaches and the Seri Nation of fishers, hunters, and gatherers who lived along the arid coast on the Gulf of California. The Seris had been attacking Spanish bases in Sonora from the west, while the Apaches advanced from the east, denying the Spanish Empire a fortune: Sonora was one of the most lucrative mining districts on the continent. Gálvez's campaign was a dismal failure. Using the rugged terrain to their advantage, the Seris repelled repeated Spanish attacks from their rocky bastion in the volcanic Cerro Prieto. Two years later, Gálvez himself visited the Seris, offering them two options: peace or extermination. The Seris were not troubled. If anything, they expected the Spanish to sue for peace.[14]

That humiliating role reversal pushed the Spanish Empire to reinvent itself. The most endangered territories were elevated to the status of viceroyalties with robust budgets and bureaucracies. In 1786, Viceroy Bernardo de Gálvez, the nephew of José de Gálvez, wrote the transformative tract *Instructions for Governing the Interior Provinces of New Spain*. In yet another scheme to control the Indians, he advocated unrestricted commerce as an instrument to forge peace "by deceit." Trade, he argued, was the most effective method to subjugate the Indians. "The interest in commerce binds and narrows the desires of man," he proclaimed, "and it is my wish to establish trade with the Indians." He saw trade as a cost-effective stratagem that would quickly deliver the Indians into the Spanish fold: "We shall benefit by satisfying their desires. It will cost the king less than what is now spent in considerable and useless reinforcements of troops. The Indians cannot live without our aid. They will go to war against one another in our behalf and from their own warlike inclinations, or they may possibly improve their customs by following our good example, voluntarily embracing our religion and vassalage." Gálvez was nothing if not thorough. He authorized gun trade with the Indians and specified that the muskets should have "weak bolts without best temper," as well as long barrels that would make them cumbersome in equestrian warfare. That level of specificity was typical for the Spanish bureaucratic machine, but it also betrayed the viceroy's anxiety over the menacing Indigenous presence on New Spain's fragile frontiers, which lured in colonial rivals. Even Russia was interested, maneuvering to contest Spanish holdings in North America.[15]

Native Americans—Tlingits, Haidas, Tsimshians, Kwakiutls, Bella Coolas, Kwalhioquas, and many others—intimately knew the best sailing routes and fishing sites in North America's northwestern corner, having built, over centuries, an impressive maritime civilization that filled their coastal settlements with wealth. In 1725, an unusual vessel anchored on the Northwest Coast: Peter the Great, the Russian emperor, had sent the Danish navigator Vitus Bering to explore the region for potential colonizing ventures. Sailing south from the Kamchatka Peninsula, Bering had confirmed that there was a strait between Asia and North America, enabling Russian ships to sail south along the Northwest Coast. Although the strait was a major discovery, the Russians did not capitalize on it until the 1740s, when their fur traders entered California. Bering's discovery had engendered an enormously lucrative trade in sea otter pelts with the Indians on the Gulf of Alaska; a "New Russia" seemed a real possibility. Spanish, British, and Americans also entered the pelt business, and soon trade boomed all along the Northwest Coast, but the Russian traders treated the Indians harshly, forcing them to hunt sea otter pelts by keeping their wives hostage.[16]

The local Indians—Tlingits, Haidas, Salish, Makahs, and others—grew wealthier, and their great houses became even greater as artistic ambitions swelled to incorporate copper and other new materials. Native women produced baskets for European markets, and Native men produced pelts for Russian traders, who then sold

most of the pelts to China. Salmon was the foundation of Indigenous life in the region, yielding enormous amounts of protein and
fat. In the Columbia River, rapids and waterfalls supported massive
schools of fish, and Indians could catch jumping salmon with under-
water baskets. A single basket could yield five thousand pounds
of fish. Women dried and preserved the catch and performed the
proper rituals and ceremonies to secure future bounties. By the second half of the eighteenth century, the Indigenous Northwest had
become a part of a booming transpacific trade system on its own
terms. The greatest threat to Native peoples was not the colonists
but the diseases—smallpox, measles, tuberculosis, dysentery, and
influenza—that spread with expanding commercial networks. Outbreaks killed Europeans too, and the shared suffering gave rise to
a distinctive Pacific Northwest common ground between Native
Americans and newcomers, who shared their respective medical
and environmental knowledge.[17]

Russian successes in North America forced the Spanish to extend
their reach. Seeking silver and souls, Spanish soldiers and colonists
had sporadically ventured north from New Spain along two major
corridors: up the coast and through Nueva Vizcaya. Although they
had built only a few Pacific bases, they considered both Baja California and Alta California theirs. The Russian intrusion prompted
the Spanish crown to consolidate its North American claims. Spanish
officials sent both land and sea expeditions to Alta California and
established a mission and presidio on San Diego Bay. In early June
1770, a Spanish ship anchored in Monterey Bay and took formal possession of the new colony. The Spanish immediately embarked on
building a mission and a presidio in Monterey. The Franciscan father
Junípero Serra, a former university professor, started saving souls.[18]

Lacking soldiers and military power, the Spanish had to appeal,
once again, to Native people. The Alta California coast was inhabited by sixty thousand Indians—an unusually deep base for a colony.
As in Texas, the Spanish built a colony on an Indigenous foundation:
they constructed missions, hoping to draw the Indians into their orbit
with sacraments and the promise of eternal life. The endeavor proved

infuriatingly difficult. The potential Native converts spoke more than ninety distinct languages and lived in dozens of autonomous communities that dotted the fertile coast for hundreds of miles. They had their own deities, ceremonies, myths, hymns, and houses of worship: they already had a religion and little use for another one.

The Spanish Empire was an alliance between the Spanish crown and the church, creating a moral community of divine and natural laws, and Spanish authorities styled their empire as an open empire, tolerant of different peoples and creeds. The Franciscans believed that the world was entering the third age, the Age of the Holy Ghost, when coercion and violence were no longer needed; God's promise would be fulfilled, a New Jerusalem would become the capital of the messianic kingdom, all the people on Earth would convert, and the current world would end. That vision of nonviolent conversion reached its apogee in the Jesuit "state" of Paraguay, where some two hundred Jesuits lived—until 1767—among 150,000 Guaraní Indians. The Jesuits had rejected the feudalistic encomienda labor drafts of the wider Spanish Empire and had built a self-sufficient economy. Most missionaries had refrained from refitting sacred Indigenous spaces for Christian purposes, allowing local Native religious sites to remain visible, even as they converted large swaths of the population. But the Jesuit state was an exception. In North America the Spanish Empire was weak and vulnerable, which brewed fear and intolerance. The Spanish thought that "Indigenous religion" was an oxymoron, and if denied attempts to convert the Indians, they quickly turned to mass violence. Their overarching ambition was to bring Native Americans into their fold—peacefully if possible, but violently when facing resistance.[19]

The Franciscans in Alta California, too, denounced Indigenous customs and ways of life, and they set out to transform the Indians through methodical social engineering. Everything from body language to sexual mores and names had to be changed. The missions were total institutions where Indians were intensely controlled and cut off from their traditional lives; eventually, there would be twenty of them. The missionaries worked to stamp out Indigenous spiritu-

alism, and baptism began to replace kinship networks as a foundation of identity, fracturing an all-important stabilizing institution.
Rather than aunts, uncles, nephews, and nieces, the Indians were
now either *neofitos* or *gentils*. Lacking funds, the missionaries and
soldiers relied heavily on intimidation, whippings, burnings, and
executions to keep their subjects in line. Clothing was strictly controlled, and both women and men had to wear dresses that covered
their whole bodies. By the early 1770s, Spanish colonists were running
five mission-presidio complexes on the Alta California coast, casting
a disquieting shadow over Indigenous California. Indian children had
to attend mission schools to learn Christian doctrine, polygamy was
condemned, and divorce—a vital exit route for women in dysfunctional marriages—became more difficult. Fueling disgust and anger,
the Franciscan friars, numbering 215, meant to implant their own sexual ideology to extinguish the traditional Indigenous one.

Things came to a head on November 4, 1775, when dozens of
Kumeyaay Indians entered Mission San Diego de Alcala and asked to
be baptized. The missionaries were welcoming, and the Indians retired
for the night. The attack came in the morning. During the night, the
Kumeyaays had gathered at the ranch of a Spanish colonist where one
hundred neophytes resided. The Indians set the wooden mission on
fire. The panicked Spanish sought refuge in the other buildings of the
mission complex, but the Indians followed them, torching the buildings one after another. The Spanish at the mission were utterly isolated. Mission San Juan Capistrano, six miles away, was also burning.
In the morning, the friars found the body of Father Luis Jayme in an
arroyo, his bowels next to him. The Franciscans' grand design for
California was defunct after a year. The Indians had asserted their
sovereignty, both territorial and spiritual, and the Spanish had "come
to know their [the Indians'] power." Reluctantly, Spanish authorities
began to offer grants to colonists to shore up their mission belt. In
1785, the Kumivit Indians plotted to overthrow the Franciscans to
restore Indigenous control. They were led by Toypurina, a woman of
high status, which confused and repelled the Spanish. The uprising
was put out, and Toypurina accepted baptism, which allowed her to

remain in power. She behaved outwardly as the Franciscans expected, protecting herself and her people.[20]

THE LATE EIGHTEENTH CENTURY saw a seismic shift in Indigenous-colonial relations. The contest for land was no longer driven by raw power; colonial powers relied increasingly on law in their dealings with Indians. Law as an instrument of dispossession had been part of European colonialism from the beginning, but only in the late eighteenth century did colonial powers manage to turn it into an effective tool of conquest and control. The change was brought about by systematic treaty-making. Treaties became the United States' most effective means to divest Native Americans of their land. Between 1783 and the outbreak of the Civil War, Indigenous nations would conclude more than three hundred treaties with the U.S. government, negotiating hard and creatively. Most treaties transferred land to the United States, but they did not erase Indigenous sovereignty. Colonial maps depicted Indigenous nations boxed in their respective domains, but in reality, Native Americans could hunt, trade, wage war, and conduct diplomacy at will. Treaty-making was a delicate exercise, as much an art form as it was a psychological challenge. Many Native nations eschewed written agreements; words, songs, and dances were enough. For many Indians, peace was a mindset.[21]

Native Americans were far from defeated. They had inflicted massive damage on invading British armies, U.S. troops, and local militias, often with support from French and Spanish traders and operatives, keeping much of the western half of the continent Indigenous. The Lewis and Clark expedition, which boosted the U.S. claims to the Pacific Northwest, happened only because the Lakotas allowed it to happen. Native resistance, especially in the Ohio Country and the Great Lakes region, kept a vast segment of the continent under Indigenous rule. Between the colonial powers and the Indigenous nations, between dispossession and survival, stood the Indian Confederacy and its transmutations. Its determined resistance had a vital upshot: it bought time—decades—for the Indigenous nations in the West.

PART EIGHT

THE
AGE OF
EQUESTRIAN
EMPIRES

(nineteenth century)

Chapter 26

THE LONG
REMOVAL ERA

AMERICAN SLAVEHOLDERS IN FLORIDA WERE
appalled and terrified. Hundreds of Seminoles, Red Sticks, and
fugitive slaves had moved into northern Florida in 1815, seeking safety.
Their destination was what Americans derisively called the "Negro
Fort." After the War of 1812, the British had left the fort stocked
with arms for the Indians and their Black allies, hoping to provide
them a haven and create a thorn in the Americans' side. The fort sat
atop a steep bluff on the lower Apalachicola River, a superb location
that enabled its holders to control access to the interior and monitor
activities on the Gulf coast. Heavily armed, the fortification defied the
American settlers and soldiers who were pushing south from Georgia
and Alabama, constructing forts of their own that bore the names of
U.S. governors and generals. The forts announced the United States'
military might and its administrative authority in the aftermath of
the War of 1812, but the Negro Fort, by its mere presence, challenged
American hegemonic tendencies—the White supremacy, the exclu-
sionist racial order, the naked, in-your-face arrogance.[1]

Also in 1815, three thousand miles to the northwest, Sans Arcs
Lakotas had built dirt lodges at Peoria Bottom at the junction of the
Missouri and Bad Rivers. Soon after, they upgraded these dwellings
into wooden houses. They were preparing for the coming commercial
bonanza. Typical of postwar situations, trade was booming, and no
place on the continent boomed like the upper Missouri Valley. Tennessee and Kentucky settlers pushed into the lower Missouri Valley,
ousting the Osages, the Lakotas' only rivals. The trade shifted north,
bringing a windfall to the Lakotas. Soon, three major fur-trading

companies were competing for Lakota bison robes. The most formidable of them was John Jacob Astor's gigantic American Fur Company. Its crown jewel, Fort Tecumseh, was essentially a Lakota post: it sat on Oglala and Sicangu land.[2]

In 1822, at Prairie du Chien, a newly established borough council passed a law against White people "skulking or sneaking about after 10 oclock at night." The leaders of the Creole fur-trading community tried to police American actions and behavior. The new law had a clear racial element, but it was designed to preserve a pluralistic world. The people of Prairie du Chien were protecting what was a genuinely mixed community, in which different customs, mores, laws, and policies shaded into one another. The Creoles and their Indigenous allies were safeguarding their territorial and cultural sovereignty against the American state.[3]

Fort Tecumseh, the Negro Fort, and Prairie du Chien together reveal North America's racial and geopolitical crisis in the early nineteenth century. After many wars, the eastern Indians had not only endured but were growing rapidly, their combined population reaching one hundred thousand, and the Lakotas and other western Indians, too, could look into the future with confidence. In the summer of 1815, seven months after the Treaty of Ghent that had ended the War of 1812, U.S. officials sponsored treaty talks with western Indians at Portage des Sioux to restore order in the interior. The Lakotas had stayed out of the war, but they cared intensely about the shape of the postwar world. The Mdewakanton Dakota leader Little Crow was concerned about a geopolitical rearrangement in which the British would isolate themselves in Canada. As he lamented to a British representative, "After we have fought you, endured many hardships, lost some of our people and awakened the vengeance of our powerful neighbors, you make peace for yourselves, leaving us to obtain such terms as we can. You no longer need our services."

British officials had pledged to protect the rights of their Indian allies by creating a massive, 250,000-square-mile Indigenous buffer zone in the Northwest to curb American expansionism, but the British lacked the capacity to enforce their plans. The Battle of New Orleans late in the war had been a humiliating disaster to the British, eliminating whatever leverage they could have had against the increasingly imperial United States. The eastern Indians would have to contend with the United States by themselves. It was a daunting prospect: although the Indian population was rebounding, there were some four million Americans in the Trans-Appalachian West.[4]

Frank negotiations, artful compromises, and genuine attempts at coexistence were quickly replaced by imposed civilization programs, land surveys, and coerced land cessions camouflaged as treaties. U.S. policymakers and common citizens alike proposed various schemes to transfer land from Indians to settlers. Isaac McCoy, a zealous Baptist missionary, put forward the idea in 1823 of an "Indian Canaan," an asylum somewhere west of the Mississippi River. He called it "Aboriginia." His was not the only radical idea. Guwisguwi, or John Ross, the principal chief of the Cherokee Nation, offered a solution to the brewing crisis: President Andrew Jackson should remove all White Georgians to the west.[5]

The collision over land had accelerated with the founding of the United States, but two later decisions by President Jefferson vastly expanded the scope of the dispute. The first was his unilateral decision to buy Louisiana in 1803, which normalized enormous territorial transfers. The second came four years later, when he assigned Meriwether Lewis, the newly appointed governor of Upper Louisiana Territory, to negotiate a land transfer with the Osages. The Osage leader Pawhuska ceded eighty thousand square miles between the Missouri and Arkansas Rivers to the United States in an attempt to reach an accommodation with the Americans. The transaction was controversial, and many Osages denounced Pawhuska as a usurper. The Lenapes, too, suffered: their homelands near Cape Girardeau and New Madrid suddenly became part of U.S. territory. Yet, implausibly, Jefferson continued to believe that if Native Americans agreed to cede what he labeled as excess lands, coexistence might be possible.[6]

The massive land transfers emboldened the U.S. government to remove a group of western Cherokees into the Arkansas Territory. A few Cherokee leaders were forced to cede land, violating the Cherokee custom that prohibited individual land sales. The Cherokees created a police force, the Light Horse Guard, to protect both common and private property. Jefferson had launched the first state-sponsored Indian removal: within two years, approximately a thousand Cherokees had been removed to Arkansas against their will. Back-to-back earthquakes in 1811 and 1812 turned the region into a swampy backwater. The resident Osages saw the Cherokees as intruders. The Cherokees commenced a millenarian Ghost Dance movement.[7]

FLORIDA HAD ALWAYS BEEN a challenge to U.S. policymakers and the U.S. military. The heat, the sand, the swamps, and the ethnic jumble baffled them. Florida also made the United States vulnerable. Americans desperately wanted to secure the nation's southern frontier by putting an end to Indigenous-maroon collaboration in Florida, which posed a threat to the South's slave regime: as long as Florida remained unoccupied, escaped slaves would gravitate there. American officials were also concerned about British inroads into Florida. The British treated the Indians with calculated deference and openly acknowledged their own weakness and asked for help, calling them "ye brave Chiefs and Warriors." Both the British and the Spanish had claimed Florida, but now the United States tried to take the entire territory.

In 1816, Major General Andrew Jackson was ordered to destroy the Negro Fort, which had become a powerful symbol of Black freedom when African American soldiers occupied it. Jackson jumped at the opportunity. He wanted to demonstrate overwhelming force against Indians, Blacks, and the Spanish, which would boost his great ambition, the presidency of the United States. The five-thousand-strong Seminole Nation and its Red Stick allies warned the Americans that "if the country is checkered off, they will fight." The U.S. Army staged a three-pronged operation at the Negro Fort, involving heavy siege fortifications around the fort, an infantry attack, and an amphibious gunboat assault. The defenders, who included Muscogee and Choctaw soldiers, put up a fierce resistance, but the fort crumbled when the U.S. Gun Boat 154 fired a preheated cannonball on the fort's gunpowder magazine, causing a devastating explosion. Of the 334 defenders, 270 died in an instant.[8]

In 1818, Secretary of War John C. Calhoun sent Jackson back to Florida to put an end to the unofficial collaboration among the Seminoles, British, and Blacks that threatened American slave-raiding operations in Florida. Jackson ignored Calhoun's orders and occupied Spanish territory, giving the United States a larger presence in Florida. A year later, Spain ceded East Florida to the United States and surrendered its claims to the Pacific coast in the Adams-Onís Treaty. Pro-Spanish Seminoles declined the offer to relocate with the Spanish to Texas. The decision paid off: in 1823 the Seminoles signed the Treaty of Moultrie Creek with U.S. agents, securing a reservation that covered much of the interior peninsula. The Treaty of Payne's Landing nine years later came together under murkier circumstances. The Seminoles negotiated hard for a larger territory but seemed to have agreed to move within three years to "the Indian country"—the land lying west of the Mississippi—where they would become part of the Muscogee Nation.[9]

The Seminoles and their Black allies contested the fraudulent land cession, which triggered an undeclared war. The allies relied on guerrilla tactics that used difficult terrain—swamps, thickets, hammocks, reefs, islets, and jungles—to overwhelm the U.S. troops, whose bookstore maps were suddenly useless, rendering border-making all but futile. State-of-the-art steamboats could not navigate Florida's shallow rivers, prompting U.S. strategists to seriously consider using hot-air balloons to detect the elusive Seminoles. By the mid-1830s, the cost of the war for the United States had exceeded $20 million, more than the price of Louisiana. The Seminoles, for their part, secured munitions from Cuban maritime merchants, who coveted the Indians' rum, redfish, mullet, pompano, and grouper.

On December 29, 1835, a small Seminole outfit led by Osceola, a brilliant strategist who was born into war and raised as a Muscogee by his mother, attacked Fort King in north central Florida, killing five Americans. Osceola and his men ambushed two U.S. Army companies at Fort Brooke at the mouth of the Hillsborough River, the staging ground for deporting Seminoles from Florida. Osceola's sharpshooters killed more than fifty U.S. troops with a single volley, throwing the Americans into disarray. Only three soldiers survived. It was the opening battle in what became known as the Second Seminole War. Seminoles attacked sugar and cotton plantations and liberated Black slaves, inflicting massive losses in property and lives. They opened negotiations, only to resume their guerrilla tactics, unnerving the Americans, who feared that the joint Seminole-Black resistance could ignite a South-wide rebellion: the inclusive Seminole society was a rejection of the White southerners' racial order. Rather than disappearing or being removed, Florida's Indigenous population was growing.

WHILE THE U.S. ARMY was preoccupied with the Seminoles and the British, the Americans had grown increasingly impatient with the presence of Native Americans on their other borders as well. In the early nineteenth century, more than 123,000 Indians—far too many, in most Americans' view—lived between the Appalachians and the Mississippi River. In 1817, the Cherokee National Council, having adopted a written legal code, passed six articles that centralized power and created the Cherokee National Committee, enabling them to confront U.S. authorities more pointedly as an independent nation. The southern planters and politicians did not care. They wanted to remove every single Indian to make space for "King Cotton." The Cherokee, Muscogee, Choctaw, Chickasaw, and Seminole populations had grown rapidly, exceeding seventy thousand in total in the 1820s. They had entered into treaties with the United States, securing guarantees for their sovereignty, and they had built roads, stores, taverns, churches, fenced fields, cotton plantations, mills, and schools. Sequoyah, a brilliant Cherokee scholar, had invented a Cherokee alphabet.

Much of this was part of a calculated strategy: the Cherokees had adhered to the American standard of civilization to convince the U.S. government to let them stay in their ancestral homelands. They published newspapers and had a ninety percent literacy rate, and they were well-off, having improved the land through intensive farming. The Cherokees, along with the Chickasaws, Choctaws, and Muscogees, relied on Black slave labor, often outperforming their White neighbors in Georgia, Alabama, and Mississippi, even though their slave regimes were far less brutal. Choctaw women were able to bring more than ten thousand yards of cloth each year to the market. Such achievements spelled trouble: few things infuriated American settlers more than seeing Indians outdo them. Indian-hating became virulent across the South.[10]

White southerners, however, were also reinventing themselves: they became savvy capitalists. Eli Whitney's cotton gin had radically changed the American South starting in the 1790s, transforming the rural province into the Cotton Kingdom. By the 1820s, cotton mills dominated the southern landscape, unleashing its huge economic potential. The Deep South became the world's leading producer of raw cotton, satisfying roughly half of the global demand. Soon a new finance-insurance-shipping nexus fused southern slavery and northern capital together, creating an overpowering commercial regime. The Jeffersonian yeoman republic was reduced to a philosophical artifact. Three racially charged removals took place in this period. The first, orchestrated by southern planters, deported four hundred thousand Black slaves from the older slave states in the Upper South to newer ones in the Deep South, where they were to grow cotton. The second removal, endorsed by southern settlers and emerging cotton capitalists, aimed to purge the Cotton Kingdom of Indigenous southerners, especially the Cherokees, Chickasaws, Choctaws, and Muscogees, who owned the most fertile lands on the continent. As Whites saw it, the Indians now took up too much space, and they would be deported to a designated area in the West that became known as the Indian Territory. The third removal, organized by the U.S. government, would relocate thousands of northern Indians into the West. In a far-fetched alternative, President John Quincy Adams proposed an experiment on "benevolent colonization," which would relocate Native Americans and African Americans overseas, enabling them to nurture their own versions of civilization. Only a few Native leaders considered the scheme.[11]

The Indians resisted the removal schemes fiercely, and they had a compelling case: Congress was concerned that the supply of public land far exceeded the demand. Even in land-hungry Georgia, settlers admitted that they had too much land to farm. It was clear that the underlying motives driving Indigenous dispossession were not economic but racial. In 1821, the governor of Georgia announced that it was his ambition to replace "all the red for a white population." Three years later, Secretary of War Calhoun, without informing Congress, created the Bureau of Indian Affairs, a new division within the War Department, providing the nation with its own colonial office. Soon after, President James Monroe proposed to Congress a western sanctuary where Indigenous southerners could be relocated—his version of a humanitarian solution.[12]

Facing a program of state-sponsored ethnic cleansing, the southern Indians knew that retreating from U.S. aggression spelled dispossession and defeat. Americans recognized only one kind of civilization—their own—which meant that the Indians needed to embrace a version of that civilization if they were to survive as independent nations. The result was not only newspapers and plantations, but revised racial thinking. The Cherokee leader Guwisguwi already lived in a two-story home, had an estate of several orchards, and owned nineteen Black slaves and a ferry. He presented himself as an aristocrat and a leader, and he did it well—too well, as it turned out. Guwisguwi's prominence as a slave owner grated on his White neighbors and challenged the American ideas of uncivilized and therefore deportable Indians. Racial ideas began to creep into Cherokee marriage laws. In 1824, Cherokee leaders, mostly wealthy planters and slave owners, passed a law over the protests of Cherokee women. It declared that "intermarriages between negro slaves and indians, or whites, shall not be lawful." Violators received fifty-nine lashes on the bare back. Indian and White women who married a "negro" man slave received twenty-five lashes. Amendments to the race laws in 1825 decreed that whereas the children of Cherokee men and any free women could become Cherokee citizens, the descendants of Cherokee men and free Black women could not—a notion that made little sense in a society that otherwise defined belonging through kinship. But increasing numbers of Cherokees now viewed the world through a racial lens, even if they did not see race as an immutable personal characteristic.[13]

The Cherokee Constitution, modeled after the U.S. Constitution and ratified in July 1827, declared the Cherokees to be a sovereign people on a par with the United States. It proclaimed "the boundaries of this nation, embracing the lands solemnly guaranteed and reserved forever to the Cherokee Nation by the Treaties concluded with the United States." The Cherokees installed mechanisms to ensure that all U.S. annuity payments for ceded lands went to their National Council. The council created a bicameral legislature, partly as an effort to consolidate power and partly to broadcast Cherokee sovereignty to Georgia. The council was a forceful governing body led by a principal leader. It effectively ran the justice system and monopolized treaty-making and land sales. Guwisguwi served as the principal leader, relying on women and men who had been educated in U.S. boarding schools. Traditionalists were marginalized, and such ancient practices and institutions as revenge-driven clan justice and matrilineal inheritance were sidelined.

These and other reforms created a sovereign nation as White Americans understood it, but it did not bring the Cherokees acceptance. The Cherokees were ready to engage in nation-to-nation talks with U.S. representatives, but their cause proved futile. The Georgia assembly demanded that John Quincy Adams remove the Cherokees, and when he refused, the assembly denied Cherokee sovereignty. The parallel Chickasaw case instilled a new level of sophistication in Indigenous resistance. The Chickasaw Nation accepted a treaty that seemed to guarantee its allotments, only to be defrauded by U.S. agents and land speculators. Harboring no illusions about the trustworthiness of the American state, the Chickasaws sold their land—ten thousand square miles in all, some of it the richest on the continent—before it could be taken from them. They placed the resulting money in trust with the U.S. government, which, ironically, provided credit and liquidity to land speculators, enabling them to deliver more Native land to the market. Collusion was the speculators' favored method. Speculators assembled together, founded paper companies, and flooded the market. When prices dropped, they began to buy.[14]

Not all of the American efforts to solve the "Indian problem" were about land. In 1827, Richard Mentor Johnson, a frontier politician who had killed Tecumseh fourteen years earlier, established the Choctaw Academy, the first national Indian boarding school, on a plantation at Great Crossings in central Kentucky. It was an experimental secular school serving a pan-Indian student body, and its great mission was to "civilize" Native Americans. The Choctaws represented the majority, but the academy also attracted Dakota, Ojibwe, and Seminole students, many of them from well-to-do families. The Choctaw Academy was an attempt to narrow the cultural chasm between Americans and Native Americans through education and, eventually, assimilation, and Choctaw leaders embraced education as a means to protect their nation. The Choctaw Academy went against everything that White southerners believed. White southerners thought that treaties with the Indians were absurd, and if asked, they probably would have said the same of the academy. The funding dried up and the academy faltered. Johnson was discovered to be a sexual predator who had raped several enslaved Black women.[15]

GENERAL ANDREW JACKSON BECAME president in 1829 and announced "Indian removal"—a euphemistic term if there ever was one—as his main ambition. He did not acknowledge Indigenous sovereignty, having once argued that Congress had "the right to take it and dispose of it." Events accelerated dangerously for the Cherokees. The Georgia General Assembly strove to extend its jurisdiction over the Indians' territory, and a year later gold was found in the Dahlonega region in northern Georgia, triggering the first gold rush in American history. The land belonged to the Cherokee Nation. Jackson argued that "though lavish in its expenditures upon the subject, Government has constantly defeated its own policy, and the Indians in general, receding farther and farther to the west, have retained their savage habits." The Cherokees sent envoys to Washington, D.C., in March 1830. They stayed in Brown's Hotel, equidistant from the White House and Congress. The House of Representatives debated the expulsion of Indians from the South for two weeks before passing the Indian Removal Act by a paper-thin margin of 102–97. The Senate vote was 28–19 in favor of the act. Jackson declared that the new Indigenous domain in the West would be called the "Indian Territory."

Jackson had gotten what he wanted, but his administration had little more than a skeleton plan for how to remove eighty thousand

Indians, a number introduced by a representative from New York. An intense struggle ensued in Washington, involving pro-Native humanitarians, pro-removal government officials, and plenty of rationalizing around ethnic cleansing and extermination. President Jackson invited the Chicakasaws, Choctaws, Muscogees, and Cherokees to meet him in Franklin, Tennessee, near his plantation, but they declined. They saw through Jackson's crude power play. The Cherokees retained the former U.S. attorney general William Wirt to prepare a lawsuit. In *The Cherokee Nation v. The State of Georgia*, Wirt argued that Georgia's extension of its laws over the Cherokee Nation was unconstitutional because it violated treaties, the supreme law of the land. Wirt's primary motive was to humiliate Jackson, whom he despised. John Marshall—the chief justice of the U.S. Supreme Court—and Justice John MacLean of Ohio made the case that the Cherokee Nation was not a foreign state but a "domestic dependent nation" whose relationship with the United States was that of "a ward to his guardian." On March 18, 1831, Marshall dismissed the case because the Cherokee Nation did not possess standing to obtain judicial relief. The court framed its decision in broad terms, extending removal to all "tribes which reside within the acknowledged limits of the United States."[16]

The Supreme Court ruling may have been influenced by Jackson's bullying statement a month earlier that he would not offer the Choctaws U.S. protection against the state of Mississippi. The Cherokees tried again a year later, and Marshall ruled that the sovereignty of the Cherokee Nation was protected by a federal treaty that rendered Georgia's claims on Cherokee territory unconstitutional. Jackson had been thwarted and embarrassed by a coalition of Indians, humanitarians, evangelical Christians, and the nation's chief justice. He found the failure hard to swallow. Along with alarmed planters and southern politicians, he wanted to destroy Indigenous sovereignty in order to entrench settler sovereignty. Jackson simply ignored Marshall's ruling.

Jackson mobilized the powers of the Indian Office, and systematic mass removals began soon after. In a stark irony, U.S. civilization programs were still active when land surveyors began earmarking people for removal. The U.S. Army took over the process of deciding who should leave. Choctaw leaders, including women who were honored as "beloved people," tried to negotiate a removal treaty in 1830, but the talks failed. U.S. officers made a treaty with a minority Choctaw group that ceded 10 million acres, all of the remaining Choctaw land in Mississippi. In the winter of 1831–32, two thousand Choctaws were escorted west in a horribly underplanned operation that left them exposed to freezing weather and a new killer, cholera. In the absence of proper government oversight, White settlers and officials raped and murdered countless Native women. More than three thousand Muscogees died during their removal, triggering a yearlong on-again, off-again war that ravaged large parts of Alabama and Georgia. The Cherokees witnessed their lands being transferred to settlers through lotteries.[17]

In the midst of it all, Shoeboots, an elite Cherokee patriarch, died, leaving behind his wife Doll, who was Black, and their five children. Shoeboots and Doll had lived together for decades as master and slave. The three eldest children were not part of Shoeboots's estate and were thus legally free, but Doll was still a slave under the law, as were her two youngest children. A family divided by race and bondage struggled to become whole, but an 1824 order had outlawed Cherokee-Black intermarriages, leaving them in a racial limbo—half-free, half-slave.[18]

Also in 1824, the Shawnee prophet Tenskwatawa was at Fort Detroit, where Lewis Cass, the governor of the Michigan Territory, tried to convince him to abandon his remaining disciples and turn him into a catalyst for Shawnee removal to the West. Tenskwatawa preferred to stay put and live in the traditional Shawnee way. He kept criticizing the U.S. Indian policy, but eventually, the compassionate William Clark convinced him to accept a reservation with rich soil near Saint Louis, the American republic's gateway to the West.[19]

U.S. OFFICIALS HAD BEEN long preoccupied with the southern Indians, who dwelled in the best farming lands on the continent. But as ambitions soared, the Bureau of Indian Affairs, the formal embodiment of the American empire, began also targeting for removal the Indians in the Northwest Territory. The ninety-fifth meridian became

the "Permanent Indian Frontier," a hard race line in the heart of the
continent. It did not take long for American officials to begin policing
that line, which in their minds was dangerously porous and vague:
there was no proper plan for where the removed Indian nations would
settle. At Prairie du Chien, the Wisconsin territorial government interfered with Indigenous property rights and marriage practices in a concentrated effort to take control over Native territory. Creole women
mounted a forceful resistance, defying the American fixation on land
and uniformity by protecting ancient kinship networks and mixed
families. They relied on charity, transcultural mediation, ancient traditions of hospitality, and their expertise as healers and midwives.
At the same time in Saint Louis, Americans were tearing down the
remains of the ancient Cahokian Mound Builder civilization: Indigenous erasure had become an epidemic.[20]

The Sauks, Meskwakis, Potawatomis, Kickapoos, Iowas, Miamis,
Shawnees, Lenapes, Wyandots, Odawas, Senecas, and Anishinaabeg
were slated for deportation, which incited a determined resistance.
The Sauks, led by the sixty-five-year-old Black Hawk, had lived west
of Lake Michigan since the Iroquois had pushed them west in the late
seventeenth century. But the Sauks were vulnerable, having supposedly
signed a treaty with the United States that involved large land sales.
Despite fierce opposition from Sauk women who were determined to
protect their cornfields, Black Hawk could only watch as eighty percent of his people left for what would became known as the Indian Territory. Black Hawk hunkered down in the town of Saukenuk with his
followers. The standoff came to head in 1831 when General Edmund
P. Gaines mobilized fifteen hundred mounted militiamen. Black Hawk
fled west and crossed the Mississippi, denying the Americans their victory. The frustrated militia desecrated Native graves.

In April 1832, Black Hawk recrossed the Mississippi into the Illinois
Country, where he proclaimed sovereignty over the disputed lands. He
assembled a multinational army of eleven hundred soldiers, prompting the Americans to mobilize four thousand troops and hundreds of
mounted militiamen. It was a nasty war, with the Americans dispatch-
ing troops from Fort Atkinson to chase the Indians and massacring
women and children. The Americans thought it was necessary to bring

Warrior, an armed U.S. steamboat, up the Mississippi. On August 1, at the Bad Axe junction, the allied Indians faced a massive shelling from American cannons, and with that the war was over. By then, more than five hundred Indians had died. Black Hawk fled north. The federal government captured him and brought him to Washington, D.C. They then sent him on a tour of eastern cities as a curiosity.[21]

The 1832 conflict, which became known as the Black Hawk War, made it clear to the Indians that violent resistance against removal could achieve only so much. Native leaders reached out to sympathetic humanitarians, clergymen, and backwoodsmen. Davy Crockett denounced the 1830 Indian Removal Act as "oppression with a vengeance," and the humanitarian Edward Everett warned President Jackson that "the evil, Sir, is enormous; the violence is extreme; the breach of public faith deplorable; the inevitable suffering incalculable." Guwisguwi, John Ridge, Elias Boudinot (also known as Buck Watie), and many other Cherokee leaders fought the Removal Act in courts, in meetings with American officials, and in the pages of the *Cherokee Phoenix*—the first Native American newspaper—but they failed to reverse the act. White missionaries and reformers challenged the assimilationist policies and the notion that individual states had the right to impose regulations on Native American land. They won their case in the Supreme Court, only to witness Jackson refusing to enforce the ruling. Old fault lines within the Cherokee Nation deepened as people split into opposing parties that favored either accommodation or resistance. In 1835, the Treaty Party, a minority group of Cherokee leaders, met with U.S. officials at New Echota, the Cherokee capital. Guwisguwi and Buck Watie were among the group's leaders, and they believed that the Cherokees should accept a removal treaty before it was imposed on them. Guwisguwi signed the Treaty of New Echota on December 29, ceding all Cherokee lands east of the Mississippi to the United States for $5 million. He hoped at least to be able to shape the conditions of his people's dispossession.

Most Cherokees denounced the Treaty Party as traitors, and they categorically refused to leave their homelands. With American supporters, they petitioned the U.S. Senate to overturn the Treaty of New Echota, but the pushback from southern senators was too strong.

When Martin Van Buren, Jackson's successor as president, ordered the army to march fifteen thousand resisting Cherokees to the Indian Territory in 1838 at gunpoint, the Cherokees were too fractured to resist. As many as four thousand may have died of diseases, exposure, and polluted drinking water on their Trail of Tears. Hordes of White land speculators moved in quickly to capitalize on the Indians' deportation. The federal government charged the speculators $2.1 million below market value for the stolen Cherokee land.[22]

Removal seemed like an overwhelming endeavor, but thousands of Indians avoided being forced to the west through evasion, making themselves inconspicuous and unreachable by leaving their homelands of their own volition and retreating into hard terrain, becoming nomadic, weaponizing their deep knowledge of the terrain, and hiding in swamps, forests, and other hard-to-reach places, which they knew intimately. Some fled into the mountains and some stayed put, hiding in the blind spots of U.S. officials and soldiers. They effectively neutralized U.S. military and administrative might, preserving their sovereignty. One group of Choctaws put so much distance between themselves and the Americans that U.S. officials simply removed them from removal lists. Whenever possible, the fugitive Indians sought refuge in the South's most treacherous and spiritually significant places. With such maneuvers, they kept themselves out of the Indian Office's deportation ledger books, thereby preserving the Indigenous South: approximately twenty percent of the Native Americans targeted for removal remained in the South, humiliating the growing U.S. bureaucratic machine.[23]

The irrepressible Seminoles, too, began to feel the toll of U.S. aggression. In 1836, General Winfield Scott, one of the United States' most accomplished generals, was sent to Florida to subdue the Seminoles and force an unconditional surrender. U.S. troops unleashed Cuban bloodhounds on the Seminoles and killed and captured some twenty-four hundred people. The Muscogee strategist Osceola himself was seized in 1837 under a flag of truce. He and 237 followers were marched in chains to Fort Marion, where they were imprisoned. Osceola died at Fort Moultrie a year later. The fort's doctor severed and embalmed his head. By then, large numbers of Seminoles had retreated—strategically and deliberately—into swamps and marshes in the Everglades. By 1841, after years of jungle war on unstable terrain where soil and water often swapped places, nearly half of the four thousand U.S. troops in Florida were ill, having been exposed to exotic tropical diseases for too long. The American government announced the end of hostilities. Some four thousand Seminoles and former Black slaves had been removed to the Indian Territory. Roughly a thousand remaining Seminoles kept fighting, but by 1842, only a few hundred remained. Seminole leader Coacoochee resisted removal by leading his people to Mexico. The United States declared victory in a war that had no winners.[24]

WITH APPROXIMATELY ONE HUNDRED THOUSAND Native Americans—both southern and northern Indians—removed to the Indian Territory by the late 1840s, Indigenous America became a world of sharp and jarring contrasts. While southern and northwestern Indians were making their way to the West under duress, the Lakotas began in the 1830s to detach themselves from the Missouri Valley and also shift westward. The two journeys could hardly have been more different. Whereas the westward movement of the southern and northwestern Indians was being forced under the threat of state-sponsored violence, the Lakotas' shift to the West was simply an expansion of their homelands. For the southern Indians the westward journey was a cultural dead end. The Lakota journey signaled a new beginning.

The Lakotas were responding to the call of Ptesáŋwiŋ, White Buffalo Calf Woman, a supernatural being who offered them access to millions of bison and spiritual fulfillment. They were also responding to the magnet-like pull of Pahá Sápa, the Black Hills, the mythical birthplace of the Lakota people, where the first Lakota explorers had arrived in 1776. Geography itself seemed to summon them: from the Missouri River eight great tributaries, their banks flush with grass, cottonwood, and protective riparian forests, pointed west like fingers. The Missouri became a staging area for ambitious expeditions. The river valleys became the foundation of an expansive Lakota domain in the West. The Lakotas had taken an irreversible turn, detaching themselves from the Missouri Valley, their home for generations. It was at this point that Pahá Sápa, already a spiritual sanctuary, became the political and economic center of the Lakotas' world. Pahá Sápa stood within a unique high-altitude microclimate with generous rains, cool summers, sumptuous pastureland, and enormous bison herds. It was the sacred place where Ptesáŋwiŋ's promise of spiritual and material fulfillment could become a reality.

The Lakotas knew that Pahá Sápa was also an intensely political realm contested by several Native nations. The Lakotas would have to fight them to return to their mythical place of origin, and they suddenly found themselves at a severe disadvantage. The Kiowas, Crows, and Shoshones, whose territories stretched around the Black Hills, had become full-fledged horse people decades earlier and were determined to keep intruders out. Arapooish, a prominent Crow leader, announced that the Great Spirit had placed the Crow domain "exactly in the right place . . . to the north it is cold; the winters are long and bitter, with no grass; you cannot keep horses there, but must travel with dogs. What is a country without horses?"

When the Lakotas expanded west along the Missouri's tributaries, they clashed with several nations. Hand paintings on Pahá Sápa's rocky sides testify to the fierceness of the collision: red spots marking slain enemies; a soldier counting coup—striking an enemy with a stick to show courage; an upside-down woman, an apparent casualty of war. Lacking the large horse herds of the Crows, Shoshones, and other rivals, the Lakotas had to rely on diplomacy to secure their position. They forged an alliance with the Cheyennes and Arapahos, who had already become horse people, and pushed out the Crows, Kiowas, and Shoshones, making the Black Hills theirs. The Lakotas began wintering in Pahá Sápa.[25]

It was one of the most consequential moments in North American history. Occupying a pivotal spot in the heart of the continent, the Lakotas could now extend their reach in all directions. Pahá Sápa became a staging ground for increasingly ambitious ventures. The mounted chase became the only method for hunting bison, and Lakota soldiers raided horses from Crows, Kiowas, Poncas, Pawnees, and others. There were also millions of feral horses—progeny of strays from Spanish entradas—on the Great Plains below the North Platte River valley, and the Lakotas were exactly on that fault line. Edwin Thompson Denig, a long-serving fur trader in the West, reported on the subsequent windfall: "The wild animals were pursued from one to the other until so fatigued as to be lassoed. . . . Frequently 40 to 60 head of horses were brought home as the fruits of a single expedition." Another boon came when U.S. officials, who were eager to placate the emerging Indigenous power, vaccinated nine hundred Lakotas against smallpox during an epidemic that broke out in 1832. The Lakotas suffered a number of deaths, but the Pawnees, who had not been offered the vaccine, lost four thousand people—half of their strength. Lakota winter counts report no epidemics between 1820 and 1837. By the late 1830s, the Lakotas numbered more than eleven thousand. In 1837, smallpox returned to the Missouri Valley, devastating the Pawnees once more, but the Lakotas were largely untouched. They destroyed a grand Pawnee village, the last of its kind, with a swift mounted attack. The Lakotas now held sway over the central Great Plains and its animal wealth.[26]

Like the Comanches a century earlier, the Lakotas capitalized fully on the spectacular rewards of equestrianism: the shortcut to solar energy, the compression of space, the dramatic increase in military power, the easy access to other people and their markets. And like the Comanches, the Lakotas embraced a new way of being in the world. They constructed a hybrid economy of pastoral nomadism and bison-hunting, which demanded a carefully orchestrated annual cycle of activities that saw the Indians dispersing along protective river valleys in the cold season and distancing themselves from others. During the long winter months, the Lakotas did as little as possible, subsisting on pemmican and preserved vegetables, all prepared by women. Their principal goal through the cold months was to keep as many horses alive as possible. In spring and summer, by contrast, the Lakotas did as much as possible, gathering berries and fruit, pasturing and training horses, and stealing more horses from their enemies. Then in June, when the bison came together for the rut, the Lakotas launched communal hunts, amassing meat and fat and buffalo robes that would see them through another winter. The annual cycle culminated in the Sun

Dance, a ceremony of humility and sacrifice conducted by holy men to whom spirits had trusted sacred words. The Sun Dance restored balance in the universe and reaffirmed the unity of the Lakota people as single kindred, *takúkičhiyapi*. The Sun Dance became an annual event in the 1830s.

The Lakotas had become the dominant power in the vast continental grasslands. They had conducted brisk trade at the American Fur Company's Fort Pierre in the Platte Valley for years, but now they refused to carry their hides and pelts to the fort. They demanded that Astor's giant company—the first American business monopoly—instead build them local and movable posts. Astor relented, violating his own policy of strict centralization. Then, in the aftermath of the steamboat *Yellow Stone*'s epic trip to the Missouri-Yellowstone confluence, Astor's company bought Fort Laramie at the junction of the Laramie and North Platte Rivers and built several branch posts that were supplied by steamboats and ox-wagon caravans. All of those posts were geared to serve the Lakotas, giving them a decisive advantage over their rivals. The center of North American fur trade had shifted westward. Soon, four forts—Vrain, Vasquez, Jackson, and Lupton—rose on the upper reaches of the South Platte River. They, too, served the Lakotas. The Lakotas claimed Fort Pierre as their own.[27]

Exploiting their strategic advantages, the Lakotas moved to expel the agricultural nations—Pawnees, Omahas, and Otoes—from the river valleys of the central plains. The Lakotas needed the valleys and their resources for their growing horse herds. The winter counts for the late 1830s and early 1840s speak of an explosive surge of power and ambition: "fought the Pawnees across the ice on the North Platte"; Crazy Dog "carried the pipe around and took the war path"; "killed twenty lodges of Arapahos"; "stole two hundred horses from the Flatheads"; "Feather-in-the-Ear stole 30 spotted ponies"; "killed four lodges of Shoshone and brought home many horses." The counts for the mid- and late 1840s portray a formidable Lakota nation, safe and prosperous: "immense quantities of buffalo meat": "plenty of buffalo meat"; "much feasting." The winter counts also reveal the Lakotas' growing territorial reach. The 1848 and 1851 counts are filled with reports of clashes with the Crows, the rival horse nation that domi-

nated the Powder River country between the Black Hills and the Bighorn Mountains. The Lakotas also collided with the Assiniboines in
the northwestern plains over hunting ranges and trade outlets. They
were extending their power far into the West and the North, reinventing themselves as an empire.[28]

Despite the Lakotas' increasing reach, theirs was not a territorial
empire in the European style. It was, instead, an empire that sought
to amass people, resources, and spiritual power. Lakota armies ventured out from their core area around Pahá Sápa, capturing horses
and humans and keeping enemies out of their hunting ranges. They
now dominated the fur trade along the upper Missouri and South
Platte Valleys, and closer by, their mobile war parties kept the weakened Pawnee, Otoe, Ponca, Omaha, Arikara, Mandan, and Hidatsa
farmers under siege, stealing corn, horses, and people. In their own
villages, Lakota women processed tens of thousands of buffalo robes
a year for U.S. markets, securing munitions, clothing, and luxuries
for their people, thus safeguarding the military might and prestige of
their nation. All seven Lakota oyátes followed the same policy, keeping people and power movable and channeling both wherever they
were needed. Their maneuvers made the Lakotas appear far more formidable than they actually were, enabling them to control an oversized segment of the continent. The Lakota ascendancy rested on a
horse-powered capacity to connect and exploit key nodes: river valleys, prime bison grounds, corn-yielding Native villages, American
trading posts, and Pahá Sápa. Theirs was a kinetic empire whose
power stemmed from the systematic repetition of key political acts:
short- and long-range raids, tribute extraction, and diplomatic missions, which gave the empire an on-again, off-again character: it could
be all over the place one moment and hidden the next. The Americans
never realized its existence.

To keep their power hidden from outsiders—in their home territory, beyond imperial reach—the Lakotas needed to preserve a
sophisticated governing system. The *thióšpaye*, or local band, was the
basic political unit of the Lakota Nation. There were several dozen
thióšpayes, led by itháŋčhaŋs. Each band had a council that arbitrated
quarrels, managed relations with other villages, and authorized war.

When a council decided to move the entire band, authority shifted automatically to *wakíčuŋzas*, or deciders, and *akíčhitas*, or marshals, their faces striped black to announce their authority. At midcentury, with their power and influence expanding, the Lakotas innovated. They created two new leadership positions: *načas*, leaders who specialized in oyáte-wide affairs, and *wičháša yatáŋpikas*, shirt wearers, "highly praised men" who formed an administrative committee, a counterpart to the traditional military societies that sustained the warrior ethos. These reforms helped establish a more centralized governing system that could sustain an empire. The timing of the reform, it turned out, was propitious.[29]

AS THE LAKOTAS WERE transforming themselves into an empire, Missouri senator Thomas Hart Benton announced, in 1846, that the only empire on the continent belonged to the Americans: "The white race alone received the divine command, to subdue and replenish the earth! For it is the only race that has obeyed it [and] the only one that hunts out new and distant lands, and even a new World, to subdue and replenish. . . . The red race has disappeared from the Atlantic coast: the tribes that resisted civilization meet extinction. This is a cause of lamentation with many. For my part, I cannot murmur at what seems to be the effect of divine law." Many Americans shared Benton's views of Indigenous peoples as a doomed race, but the Lakotas would soon set them straight, making it clear that there was nothing preordained about the United States' cynical expansionism.[30]

Gold was behind the United States' latest westward encroachment. In early February of 1848, unusually rich veins were discovered at Sutter's Creek in California, setting off a rush. In 1849, twenty-seven thousand overlanders crossed the central plains along the Platte River. This intrusion was unacceptable to the Lakotas, who had executed their own westward expansion more than a decade earlier than the Americans. The Platte Valley belonged to them, and they relied on its crucial gifts: potable water, grass, cottonwood, and shelter for horses and people. Already in 1846, They Fear Even His Horses, a young Oglala itȟáŋčhaŋ, had warned the Americans about the damage they were causing along the Platte, where Oregon-bound set-tlers consumed essential resources. He wanted thuŋkašila, the Great Father—the U.S. president—to compensate the Lakotas for the harm the Americans had caused.

Instead, however, the Lakotas faced a greater catastrophe: the overlanders brought cholera with them. Every seventh Lakota died in 1848–49. The Lakotas distanced themselves from the sickly settlers, yet they kept dying. Soon there were calls to kill all the intruders. Much like the Lenape prophet Neolin a century earlier, the Lakotas began to think of White Americans as a separate category of humans: they became *wašíčus*, or White people. U.S. officials panicked. The nation's access to California gold was suddenly endangered. If the Lakotas started a war, the United States would lose it. Fort Laramie, recently reacquired by the U.S. Army, was the only military bastion of any consequence between the Rocky Mountain foothills and the Pacific coast.

The U.S. Army and government read the situation correctly, and in the spring of 1851 they sent runners to invite the Plains Indians to a peace conference at Fort Laramie. Ten thousand Indians—Lakotas, Shoshones, Arapahos, and Cheyennes—gathered at Horse Creek, near the fort. The Lakotas rode in leisurely, signaling their authority. They dominated the talks from the start. They Fear Even His Horses had made the rounds among Lakota communities, securing a strong show-ing; when the Pawnees learned about the size of the Lakota delegation, they refused to participate. For their part, U.S. officials relied on estab-lished imperial theatrics, handing out uniforms, medals, and certifi-cates denoting various military ranks. The Indian leaders would now be lieutenants and major generals, and every rank in between—a far too obvious attempt to co-opt them. The Americans also asked each nation to nominate head chiefs with whom the Indian Office could negotiate.

Believing that they had created new and accommodating lead-ers, U.S. officials moved to address the two burning issues at hand: land and borders. Colonel David Mitchell, superintendent of Indian affairs, introduced the government's plan. The midcontinent would be sliced into three blocks. The Lakotas, Crows, Mandans, Assiniboines, northern Cheyennes, and northern Arapahos would share a domain in the north; the Comanches, Kiowas, and Plains Apaches would have a domain in the south; and the southern Arapahos and southern Cheyennes would have one in the middle. The Oregon Trail in the north and the Santa Fe Trail in the south would mark the boundaries of the three Indigenous domains, thereby securing American access to gold. The scheme abolished the Permanent Indian Frontier and replaced it with racial segregation. Clear Blue Earth, the Sicangu spokesman, announced the Lakota response: "We have decided differently from you, Father, about this Chief for the nation," he proclaimed. "We want a Chief for each band, and if you will make one or two Chiefs for each band, it will be much better for you and the whites," he said, educating the Americans. "Then we will make soldiers of our young men, and we will make them good men to the whites and other Indians. But Father, we can't make one Chief." The Lakotas had seen through the U.S. scheme to interfere in Lakota politics. Clear Blue Earth had calmly rejected the American plans.[31]

Clear Blue Earth then articulated the Lakota stance: "We are a large band and we claim half of all the country . . . we can hunt anywhere." Black Hawk, the principal Oglala spokesman, reinforced the message. "If there is anything I do know," he said, "it is this country, for I was raised in it. You have split the country, and I don't like it. What we live upon, we hunt for, and we hunt from the Platte to the Arkansas." The U.S. agents had designated the Platte River as the southern border of the Lakota domain, but the Lakotas demanded the central plains all the way south to the Arkansas River by the right of conquest. "These lands once belonged to the Kiowas and the Crows," Black Hawk explained, "but we whipped these nations out of them, and in this we did what the white men do when they want the lands of the Indians." The Lakotas made it clear that they expected a two-hundred-mile southward extension of their domain. In the northern Great Plains, colonial borders would bend around Lakota borders; Americans would have to remove the Pawnees to the south to make space for the Lakotas. The United States had sided with power. Desperate to protect the Santa Fe Trail, American agents tried to convince the Comanches, Kiowas, and Plains Apaches to settle in a domain south of the Arkansas River. The Indians took the gifts, agreed to a treaty, and went on attacking the intruding wagon trains.[32]

By the middle of the nineteenth century, in the aftermath of the coerced mass removals, Indigenous America as a whole had shifted westward. Almost one hundred thousand Indians had been expelled from east of the Mississippi, spawning an entirely new Indigenous world to the river's west. The Native reservations were a sign of American weakness, not strength. The United States simply lacked the capacity to defeat and domesticate the Indians or, as its experience with the predominant Lakotas had shown, even the power to keep them at bay.[33]

Chapter 27

THE COMANCHE
ASCENDANCY

FAR TO THE SOUTH OF THE LAKOTAS LIVED ANOTHER domineering Indigenous power, the nearly forty-thousand-strong Comanches. The Comanches had gone through two expansionary phases. The first, in the early eighteenth century, had relied heavily on violence. As powerful newcomers, the Comanches had molded New Mexico's northern borderlands to meet their needs, stoking fear among local Indians and the Spanish. The second phase, in the early nineteenth century, had relied on a mix of diplomacy and coercion. The Comanches continued to attack Apache villages, take captives, and ransom them to New Mexico's slave markets, but by midcentury they had begun to teach the Spanish officers the proper ways of conducting trade. The Comanches expected the Spanish to hand out gifts to create proper relationships of amity, never haggle over prices, and never push inferior goods. Most important, the Spanish would have to establish unrestricted trade in guns, powder, and lead. If they failed to obey, mounted Comanche and Ute armies would attack New Mexico, forcing compliance.

The denizens of the thousand-year-old Taos Pueblo drew their own conclusions about the situation. As the northernmost of the Pueblo towns, Taos was a frontier community with a mixed population. Rumors started to spread that the residents of the town, Taoseños, were feeding information to the Comanches and the Utes about the movements of Spanish troops. The Taoseños seemed to have reckoned that they would be better off under Comanche auspices than under the officious Spanish regime. Alarmed, the governor of New Mexico, Joachín Codallos y Rabál, decreed that any Taoseño found more than a league from the town would be put to death. When the Comanches laid waste to the frontier settlement of Abiquiu in northern New Mexico, Codallos dispatched five hundred Spanish cavalry and Indian auxiliaries, who killed more than a hundred Comanches and Utes, took more than two hundred captives, and seized nearly a thousand horses.[1]

That defeat, paradoxically, marked the beginning of the Comanche ascendancy in the Southwest. Shaken, the Comanches reconfigured their foreign policy, reaching out to neighboring Native nations. They also approached far-ranging French traders, exchanging horses, bison robes, and captives for guns, ammunition, cloth, and other manufactured goods. The booming trade functioned as a political weapon. When Spanish officials learned that thirty-three French traders had met with Comanches near Taos, within New Mexico's borders, and sold them "plenty of muskets" in exchange for mules, they knew that the balance of power had begun to shift in the Southwest. Comanche and Ute soldiers, armed with state-of-the art muskets and iron-tipped lances, struck New Mexico's eastern borderlands with unremitting attacks, capturing horses and captives, often at night.

The involvement of French traders raised the stakes for the Spanish. In 1749, Spanish officials invited the Comanches and Lipan Apaches to talks in San Antonio. With presidial, state, and church representatives in attendance, the Comanches buried a hatchet, a lance, and a live horse in Military Plaza, making peace with the Lipans. The Spanish freed 137 Apache captives, hoping to keep the Apaches on their side. Governor Tomás Vélez Cachupín complained bitterly that "the trade that the French are developing with the Cumanches by means of Jumanes [Wichitas] will result in most serious injury to this province. Although the Cumanche nation carries on a like trade with us, coming to the pueblo of Taos . . . always, whenever the occasion offers for stealing horses or attacking the pueblos of Pecos and Galisteo, they do not fail to take advantage of it." Yet Vélez Cachupín could not close New Mexico's markets to the Comanches, for fear that doing so would shove the Indians fully into the French fold, or worse, into war. All he could do was grumble about the "perverse trade" and turn a blind eye. Hundreds of Apaches sought refuge in New Mexico, hoping to put distance between themselves and the Comanches.

Vélez Cachupín's frank report revealed New Mexico's weakness in its borderlands. The governor was resigned to securing "friendship and commerce with the Comanche tribe, diverting as much of it as possible from the French, because the Comanche tribe is the only one that could impede [French] access to that terrain and be the ruin of New Mexico." If the Spanish failed to appease the Comanches, he warned his superiors, "an extremely useful branch of trade would be lost and the French of New Orleans would acquire it in toto." New Mexico resigned to paying tribute to the Comanches to save itself: the Spanish began to pay for peace and would continue to do so for generations to come. Around 1750, Vélez Cachupín turned Taos into a Comanche market where, in the highly critical words of a Spanish visitor, "all prudence forsakes them. . . . Here, in short, is gathered everything possible for trade and barter with these barbarians in exchange for buffalo hides, and what is saddest, in exchange for Indian slaves, men and women, small and large, a great multitude of both sexes, for they are the gold and silver of the richest treasure of the governors, who gorge themselves first and with the greatest mouthfuls from this table, while the rest eat the crumbs."[2]

A rare Spanish military victory in 1751 only deepened the Comanche-Spanish rapprochement. Retaliating for a Comanche attack against the Spanish town of Pecos, Vélez Cachupín besieged three hundred Comanche soldiers in a box canyon in the Llano Estacado, a large flatland in the western High Plains, killing 112 and capturing 33. Shocked, the survivors made a wooden cross and presented it to Vélez Cachupín "with great veneration, putting it to their lips and mine." The Spanish had momentarily leveled the playing field, and the Comanches agreed to a peace with New Mexico. Vélez Cachupín recognized them as a sovereign nation in a treaty and granted them preferred access to Spanish markets. The Utes were marginalized, causing the collapse of the Comanche-Ute alliance. The Comanches, growing rapidly in numbers, had outgrown the alliance. Backed by Spain, the Comanches seized Apache lands in the northern Llano Estacado. That sequence of events set the template for Comanche foreign policy toward colonial powers for the next hundred years.[3]

BY MIDCENTURY, THE COMANCHES possessed enough horses for large-scale mounted warfare and necessary further expansion: their large population and growing horse herds demanded a larger resource base. They formed a broad alliance with Taovayas, Tonkawas, Wichitas, Hasinais, and Osages—the distraught Spanish called the allies *Norteños*—and pushed south from the Llano Estacado into the short-grass plains and their enormous herds of bison and wild horses. Forage was a major draw because Comanche horse herds needed huge amounts of grass. Their "magic dogs," descendants of desert-bred African barb horses, thrived there, boosting Comanche diets, mobility, military power, and access to markets. The Comanches radically streamlined their way of life. The mounted bison chase was now the core of their existence. Eating fish became taboo, gathering plant-based foods declined, and fowl became an emergency food eaten only when everything else failed.[4]

Boosted by horses, the Comanches set out to control the southern plains and the region's animal bounty through war. The buffalo plains were not free for the taking, and the Comanche thrust set off a long and bitter war with their old foes, the Lipan Apaches, who dominated the region, having turned many of its river valleys into a flourishing farming realm. But that agrarian success became the Lipans' undoing. Tethered to their fields, they did not stand a chance against thousands of Comanche horse soldiers. Desperate to secure Spanish aid, Lipan leaders made the kind of proposition that colonial officials could not resist: they vowed to convert to Christianity. Lipan women began carrying crosses as a sign of peace, and the Spanish built a mission-presidio complex in Apachería in the San Saba River valley, hundreds of miles to the south from New Mexico and 135 miles away from San Antonio. Three thousand Comanches visited the construction site in June 1757, taking stock; the attack came eight months later.

In mid-March 1758, an army of two thousand Norteños gathered at the gates of the mission. They informed the Spanish in the fort that "they had come with the intention of killing the Apaches." After a Comanche *paraibo*—leader—donned a French uniform, the force laid siege to the fort and set the mission's wooden buildings on fire. The defenders thought that the Indians had at least a thousand French muskets. Only eight Spanish had been killed, but the shock effect was cataclysmic. The French guns and uniforms publicized the Norteños' far-reaching diplomatic connections, and the devastation they inflicted—destroyed church ornaments, a beheaded effigy of Saint Francis, scalped and eyeless bodies placed on the church altar— bespoke a deep hatred of all things Spanish.[5]

The sacking of the San Saba Mission was a major turning point in the history of the North American West, and its shock waves reached all the way to Mexico City. The Comanches absorbed some Lipans into their ranks and banished scores to the desert lands to the west. Spanish missionaries retreated with the rest of the Lipans to new missions nearly a hundred miles south of Comanchería. Numerous Apache peoples suddenly found themselves alarmingly marginalized. Comanche *rancherías*—settlements—had become too powerful for the Apaches to challenge, and they began targeting Spanish rancherías in New Mexico and Texas. Large numbers of Lipans sought refuge in the south, settling along the Rio Grande and venturing into Coahuila. In 1760 the Pueblo town Galisteo had become "the usual theatre of the War with the Comanches, who keep this pueblo in a bad way." In Santa Fe, the Spanish were constantly on the lookout for Comanches.[6]

The Comanches were an instant territorial superpower. Comanchería now extended beyond the Arkansas River in the north, curving from there in a six-hundred-mile arc to the south, all the way to the Balcones Escarpment, where grassland steppe gives way to coastal plains. Comanchería's western boundary traced the Pecos River near the very core of New Mexico along the upper reaches of the Rio Grande. Covering approximately a quarter million miles of grassland, it was the most expansive Indigenous territory in North America by a large margin.

The vast domain made possible rapid economic growth by enabling the Comanches to sustain larger horse herds. In a world where power and survival hinged on horse wealth, to have many horses was true opulence. The Comanches could hunt more effectively and maintain a steady population increase. With their numbers nearing forty thousand, the Comanches outgrew the Norteño alliance. They pressed the advantage. Francisco Antonio Marín del Valle, Vélez Cachupín's successor as the governor of New Mexico, learned from a Comanche captive that "a barbarian has raised himself up among that nation with the appearance and accouterments of those of a little King. He has near his person a guard of armed men, pages who serve him when he mounts and dismounts from his horse, holding a canopy or shade of buffalo skins for him in which he takes his seat. All obey him." This "barbarian"—Cuerno Verde, or Green Horn—had engineered a dramatic change among the Comanches: he had a centralized Comanche power with the support of the military societies. Cuerno Verde died in battle soon after his rise, but his son assumed his position and name.[7]

Governor Marín del Valle, a vain and cautious man, misread the situation. He armed the Apaches, which posed a threat to the Comanches. The Apaches could now carry Spanish guns to kill Comanches, who did not have reliable access to European technology. Cuerno Verde the younger took the initiative and started an on-again, off-again war that continued for over a decade. His soldiers raided frontier villages, taking captives and horses and spreading fear. By the late 1770s, several New Mexico settlements lay in ruins and Texas stood paralyzed. The already puny population of Texas was plummeting, rendering the territory irrelevant. The Comanches usurped the Wichita trade along the Red and Brazos Rivers and attacked the Taovayas, absorbing large numbers of them into the Comanche ranks, while also keeping Osages, Hasinais, and Spanish out of the buffalo range. Comanche paraibos sponsored trade fairs in the upper Arkansas Valley with their northern clients. Several Native groups grew dependent on Comanche horse supply and latched onto the nation as loyal allies, orbiting around it.

The repercussions of Comanche maneuvering extended far and wide. The Utes allied with the Paiutes and relocated to the Great Basin, where they joined the Apaches, Navajos, Tohono O'odhams, and others in raiding captives for New Mexico's slave markets and extorting tolls from westbound Americans along the Old Spanish Trail. By the early nineteenth century, New Mexico was teeming with Indian slaves, mostly women and children. The slave trade was the most lucrative commerce in the Great Basin, fueling ambition, animosity, and fear. No one on the continent—not even the Comanches themselves—knew it yet, but the focal point of Indigenous resistance had shifted from the Ohio and Illinois Countries to nomadic powers in the West.[8]

THE COMANCHE ASCENDANCY SHUNTED the Spanish colonists into a shockingly abrupt fall from imagined power; as late as 1779, Spanish officials still envisioned a grand imperial future for New Mexico and Texas. Teodoro de Croix, the commandant-general of the newly established *Provincias Internas*, an enormous administrative unit of the Spanish Empire, advocated the construction of a string of outposts along the Red River—"a palladium of war" that was to became "the master-key of the north, where the friendly nations will be dealt with through mediation, the unfriendly, such as Comanches and the Osages, will be won over, or, with the help of the friendly nations, conquered." Retreating from the accommodating stance of the Bourbon officials, Croix contemplated a war of extermination against the Apaches, but he changed his mind. The Comanches posed a more acute threat to Spanish designs, and Bourbon Spain mobilized to subdue them. Juan Bautista de Anza, the new governor of New Mexico, did what few Spanish leaders had dared to do: he went to war against the Comanches.

Instead of waiting for a Spanish attack, Cuerno Verde the younger seized the initiative, leading a small party of fifty soldiers to attack Taos. In the meantime, however, Anza had already led eight hundred Spanish soldiers northeast from Santa Fe, skirting the open plains to attack a Comanche ranchería of 120 lodges in the far north of Comanchería. The Spanish killed thirty women and eighteen men and took thirty-four women captive. The survivors told Anza that it was Cuerno Verde's ranchería. Anza chased Cuerno Verde and his soldiers into a gully, neutralizing their equestrian advantage. Cuerno Verde was killed. Anza returned to Santa Fe, brandishing his defeated foe's headgear. But the real disaster was yet to come. In 1780, small-pox struck the Comanches. Sixteen thousand may have died from the same epidemic that also devastated Cornwallis's army in the East. The

Comanches turned inward and curbed their raiding operations. The mighty Comanches were suddenly ordinary and vulnerable. They opened peace talks with New Mexico in 1781.[9]

Help soon arrived from an unexpected source: the 1783 Treaty of Paris. Spain was outraged by the extension of the United States' southern border to the thirty-first parallel, which ignored Spanish claims on the Ohio-Mississippi confluence. The United States refused to compromise, leaving the Spanish in limbo. Spain's solution to the crisis also became the solution to the Comanches' crisis: this was when Spain adopted its secularized Indian policy to protect its enormous territorial holdings, offering Native nations support in the form of gifts, trade, and treaties. King Charles III appointed Bernardo de Gálvez the viceroy of New Spain. Gálvez's task was to consolidate the nine northern provinces—effectively Spain's North American West—into one gigantic buffer against the United States. As the easternmost province, Texas was critical. Gálvez assigned its governor, Domingo Cabello y Robles, to secure the frontier. Cabello vacillated. He seemed not to have the stomach to face the Comanches. He recruited Pedro Vial, an experienced Indian trader, and Francisco Xavier Chaves, a blacksmith, to approach them. Chaves had been adopted by the Comanches at the age of eight and was fluent in Comanche. Cabello dispatched the pair into Comanchería with two servants, four mules, six horses, and gifts worth four hundred pesos, a sum that could fetch three White slaves in San Antonio.[10]

In the early fall of 1785, some two hundred Comanche soldiers rode, in two lines, out of the Red River valley to meet the Spanish emissaries. The Spanish welcomed them with a multigun salute. Vial described the two Comanche envoys as "great *capitanes* of the nation, whom they listen to with much respect and attention. One is known as the Capitán de la Camisa de Hierro"—most likely the western Comanche paraibo better known as Ecueracapa—"for wearing a coat of mail that he took from an Apache *capitán*, and the other as the Capitán de la Cabeza Rapada, for having half of it in this style and the other with very long hair." Then came "another ten which they call *jefes* and which the other nations call *capitanes chiquitos*. Each one of these brought some elder Indian principales and many young men." The ranchería was the rapidly changing Comanche Nation in microcosm. The Comanches had concentrated power in the hands of tested leaders who had the necessary authority to negotiate directly with colonial powers and, if necessary, go to war. Having been humiliated by Anza in war six years earlier and devastated by smallpox, the Comanches had adopted strict border measures to be safe. They asked Vial and Chaves if they "had brought some illness that would bring death to their nation."

The Comanches convened a grand council. Vial and Chaves carried a Spanish flag into "a very large circle which all of the Indians had formed, seated on the ground as many as four deep, seeming in our opinion about 700. Surrounding the said circle were an infinity of young men, women, and children." Vial and Chaves made a bid to secure peace. They had Guersec, a Taovaya leader, announce that "it is more important to us to have friendship with the Spaniards than with the Cumanches, because our Father, the Capitan Grande of San Antonio, gives us and keeps us supplied with guns, powder, shot, pots, axes, hoes, knives, etc. . . . I let you know that it is more important for us to maintain friendship with the Spaniards than with you." Unfazed, Ecueracapa announced, "We shall remain ready to make a solid peace, once our Father, the Capitán Grande of San Antonio, accepts it wholeheartedly, making for our part only the condition that he give us passage and that he not oppose our making war against the Lipanes, our ancient enemies. And thus, we shall often go to visit our Father, the Capitán Grande of San Antonio, with confidence." The Comanches, Ecueracapa made clear, would be equal allies with the Spanish Empire. After the council concluded, Vial and Chaves escorted three Comanche paraibos to San Antonio, where Governor Cabello entertained them and then paraded them through the streets along with several Comanche women, whose presence was crucial for the peace process. The Comanches entered into a formal treaty, which merely asked them to inform the governor when they moved against the Apaches, who were still allied with Spain. To further assuage his new allies, Cabello built a 144-foot-long wattle-and-daub house for Comanche visitors in the San Antonio River valley, so that they could take their daily baths privately.[11]

In the winter of 1785, Anza met with Ecueracapa at the Big Timbers in the upper Arkansas Valley, the main center of Comanche trade. Six thousand western Comanches had gathered to witness the proceedings. A shrewd operator, Ecueracapa was fully prepared for the challenge. To ensure his election as leader of the western Comanches, he warned that "he would attach himself to the Spanish party" if denied. He had his agents assassinate Toroblanco, a militant, anti-Spanish rival paraibo, paving the way to peace with New Mexico. But Ecueracapa was not only ruthless; he was also an accomplished military strategist and a shrewd politician. Although pitiless in his domestic policy, his foreign policy ambition was peace with Spain. He had found an opening when his spies encountered an Indian who had become separated from a Spanish hunting party. The man, José Chiquito, was fluent in Spanish, and Ecueracapa decided to use him as a go-between. In January 1786, Ecueracapa executed the leader of a holdout Comanche faction that had attacked Pecos and sent word to Santa Fe of his imminent visit. He met with as many rancherías as possible, to create a broad consensus for a peace—an imperative in Comanche politics.[12]

Ecueracapa arrived in Santa Fe in late February, escorted by a column of Spanish cavalry, and rode leisurely through the main street, which was lined with spectators. He arrived at the governor's palace and dismounted. He embraced Anza. That gesture set the tone for the talks. Ecueracapa had a clear vision for a postwar world, seeking a broad peace between the Spanish Empire and the emerging Comanche Empire. The peace, he demanded, should be embedded in reciprocal trade, which required that Comanches would enjoy "free and safe passage through Pecos to Santa Fe." More alarmingly to the Spanish, Ecueracapa demanded the right to "settle and subsist a short distance from the settlements." He also wanted the Spanish and Comanches to join in a war against their "common enemies, the Apaches," expecting the Spanish to cut their ties with the remaining Apache groups on the New Mexico borderlands. Ecueracapa was proclaiming the Comanches as an empire. His envisioned geopolitical order for the American Southwest revolved around a Comanche-Spanish axis. The peace process moved to Pecos, where Anza gave Ecueracapa a staff of office.

In a symbolic gesture, Ecueracapa handed it to Tosacondata, the second-in-command: Ecueracapa was broadening the leadership of the Comanche Nation that was about to eclipse New Mexico, Spain's strongest colony in North America.

Ecueracapa had orchestrated the peace process with calm confidence, cutting Anza down to size. The governor had to improvise to reassert Spanish authority. He invited Ecueracapa to a private meeting, where he gave him "a token or credential in order that the more witnesses he had among them the better he would be able to prove his scattered rancherías that all their nation was admitted to peace." He wanted Ecueracapa, who he thought was a "remarkable genius," to "take charge of the government and absolute direction of its national interests." It was the standard Spanish method of co-opting Indigenous leaders, and Ecueracapa saw through it. Ute envoys had also been invited to Santa Fe, but Anza showed little interest in them. Ecueracapa took over the talks and made peace with the Utes. Spanish officials were overjoyed when Comanche envoys "showed a great desire to understand our language, to accommodate themselves to our customs in whatever they could imitate, even in matters of religion." The Spanish saw this as submission. It is more likely that the Comanches, who had been exposed to Christianity only fleetingly, were studying their new allies and their strange beliefs.[13]

By making treaties with the Comanches, Spanish officials believed they were creating more powerful leaders that they could negotiate with and manipulate, controlling the Indian nation from without. In reality, however, Spanish stratagems only accelerated the ongoing process of Comanche centralization. The two Cuerno Verdes had started the process, and Ecueracapa took it further, forcefully negotiating with the Spanish and other outsiders. Ecueracapa was the principal paraibo of the Kotsotekas, "buffalo eaters"—one of the three Comanche divisions—and his authority did not extend to the Yamparikas, "root eaters," and Jupes, "timber people." That kind of decentralized governing system had become obsolete in the new order, in which the Comanches dominated much of the Southwest alongside the Spanish, who were becoming the Comanches' junior allies. When Ecueracapa handed Anza's staff of office to Tosacondata, he was already fashioning a more robust governing system. Ecueracapa offered his youngest son to Anza, who pledged to treat him "as his very own." With that, Ecueracapa erased any hierarchal distance between the governor and himself. Anza then received a Navajo embassy and asked Ecueracapa to make a surprise visit "so that the Navajos, having seen them, might be moved by the fear and respect they have for this warlike nation." Anza had learned fast where power lay.[14]

Led by Ecueracapa and Tosacondata, the Comanches entered a third expansionary phase, which would consolidate their hegemony in the Southwest. This was the moment when Ecueracapa's potentially dangerous concentration of power paid off. The Comanches relied on a fluid mix of diplomacy, commerce, coercion, and co-optation to secure essential resources, and Comanche and Spanish soldiers joined forces to expel the Apaches from New Mexico's borderlands. The Spanish authorized free border trade with the Comanches, which gave rise to an ethnically diverse group of specialized traders, Comancheros.

Encouraged, the Comanches built an extensive trading system anchored in the river valleys that cut through the southern plains. Its heart was Big Timbers, a thickly wooded strip of land in the upper Arkansas Valley that offered shelter to horses during the harsh plains winters. Raising horses in the cold north was challenging, and most northern plains Indians struggled to accrue enough of them for an effective mounted chase. The Comanches, by contrast, may have possessed more than a hundred thousand horses—far more than they needed: roughly two-thirds of their mounts were surplus animals held for trade. The upper Arkansas Valley trade center became a magnet for the neighboring Indians, who replenished their herds at Comanche fairs. In exchange, the Comanches received guns, ammunition, metal weapons, and other manufactured goods that the northern nations had secured from French and British traders. The Kiowas opened their Sun Dance to the Comanches to empower their most important ally. Comanche became a trade lingua franca across the Southwest borderlands, designating a major shift in Indigenous-colonial power dynamics.

Whereas the Comanches built a more centralized nation and, eventually, an empire, the Apaches preserved the fluid and seasonally dynamic political system that had served them well before the Comanche ascendancy. The authority of the Apache leaders, *nantans*, did not typically reach beyond immediate kin groups. That horizontal governing system had served the Apaches well, enabling them to expand their resource base three hundred miles to the west of the Pecos Valley without major internal conflicts, but the rise of the Comanches rendered everything precarious. By the early nineteenth century, the combined Apache population in the southern plains was only about five thousand. Spanish officials branded the Apaches as heathens and "indomitable savages" who should be exterminated.[15]

THE SUCCESS OF the Comanches as a horse nation was founded on a deviation from the typical pattern of ecological imperialism, which had debilitated countless Indigenous nations through aggressive weeds and crowd diseases. Most native plants in the Americas had not evolved to coexist with large grazing animals, and when Eurasian fauna arrived in the sixteenth century, many of these plant species were rapidly devoured and replaced by more resilient European weeds. In the North American Great Plains, however, grasses had coevolved along with large grazers—most notably the bison—and were therefore exceptionally resilient in the face of Europe's faunal invasion. When the Comanches grasped the full extent of that advantage, they dramatically streamlined their economy and way of life. They stopped using some one hundred plants, abandoning two-thirds of their ethnobotanical tradition, and they forged trade relations with Pueblo, Pawnee, Ponca, Kansa, Wichita, and Iowa farmers to secure carbohydrates in the form of maize, squash, and beans. Comanchería became a great trade pump that channeled protein and fat out and carbohydrates in. A steady inflow of corn, beans, squash, seeds, and even baked bread from neighboring farming societies enabled the Comanches to assemble an almost ideal diet: moderate to high in protein, iron, and vitamin B_{12}; high in complex carbohydrates; and low in saturated fat, cholesterol, and sodium. Their population began to recover from the catastrophic 1780 smallpox outbreak, maintaining an upward trajectory even through multiple subsequent epidemics.[16]

At the same time, the Comanches began trading with westbound American traders operating out of Louisiana, plugging their animal-based economy into a nascent capitalist economy that could provide them with state-of-the-art weaponry and tools. The Wichitas and the Pawnees became key middlemen, feeding American manufactured goods into Comanchería and Comanche horses into Louisiana. The Omahas, still a sovereign nation, sent an embassy to Comanchería and traded nearly all their guns and ammunition for horses, which they needed to protect themselves against the Lakotas.[17]

Secure and commanding, the Comanches began to reshape the greater Southwest to meet their needs. They joined with New Mexico and Texas to force the remaining Apaches from their borders, finally eliminating them as a threat. The Spanish built eight military-run reservations—North America's first—in northern Chihuahua and Sonora to both confine and protect the Apaches. Spanish policymakers labeled the Chiricahuas *Apaches de paz*, "peaceful Apaches," and soon they made up roughly half of the southern Apache population. Spanish military leaders sought to control the Chiricahuas' horse-powered mobility by tying them to the soil, but the Chiricahuas had an agenda of their own: they treated the reservations as resource domains that could support operations outside of them.

Frustrated Spanish authorities wanted the Apaches confined. In need of revenue, they launched a cynical enterprise: they started selling Apache captives to New Spain and the Caribbean sugar islands, where Indian slaves had been in demand since Columbus inaugurated the trade. In 1791, three Chiricahua Apaches joined Spanish soldiers on a thousand-mile journey to the capital of Mexico, where they appealed to Spanish officials to return their captured relatives. Caught between the imperial Comanches and the aggressive Spanish, the Chiricahuas and other Apache divisions were reeling. They needed every single member of their nation to survive. The Chiricahua emissaries managed to redeem only one captive. The others had been sold into slavery. When war broke out between the Spanish and the southern Apaches and their Mescalero allies, one-third of the southern and Mescalero Apaches were either killed or taken captive and deported as slaves to Cuba. The violence left behind broken nations. Many more deportations to Cuba and central Mexico followed in the early nineteenth century—New Spain's version of Indian removal.[18]

The Comanches, for their part, continued to shape-shift. They lived along an ecological fault line where climatic conditions became increasingly unfavorable for animal herding, and they turned that edge into a spectacular commercial success that would make them even more powerful. Several thousand Comanches would spend much of the winter in the sheltering Big Timbers, their horses subsisting on cottonwood bark, an emergency fodder. They launched quick hunts, careful not to exert too much pressure on the bison: they wanted the beasts to stay put. They did not allow visitors to hunt bison, preferring to feed any guests themselves. Senior wives were in charge of households, managing slave labor, trading with outsiders, and overseeing child-rearing. Under the paraibos' leadership, women assumed a larger role in horse-herding, which scandalized many non-Native observers. A visitor stated that "marriage among the Comanches is a purchase which the man makes, rather than a contract between two individuals." It was a blinkered observation that nonetheless illuminated an Indigenous nation reinventing itself as an empire, with women's labor as its engine.[19]

AFTER YEARS OF POLITICAL turmoil and war with the Spanish Empire, in 1821 Mexico broke away and established itself as an independent nation. Agustín de Iturbide, the leader of the Royalist forces, was proclaimed the emperor of Mexico. He faced an alarming situation in the north, where the Comanches had reduced Texas to a client colony. Texas's weakness seemed to open the door to the United States to move in and take it. In 1822, the Comanche paraibo Guonique was invited to attend Iturbide's coronation and "was liberally entertained with his retinue." The Comanches were now San Antonio's preferred Native allies.[20]

Mexico's largesse bought a few years of relative calm, but from the mid-1820s on, the Comanches—allied with the Kiowas—were again moving south in search of horses and captives. They raided Texas, New Mexico, Coahuila, and Chihuahua, unnerving Mexican

An 1834 painting by George Catlin depicting mounted Comanche soldiers meeting U.S. dragoons as they placed themselves between the Americans and their tipi village, enforcing strict border control to keep enemies and pathogens out of Comanche territory

officials, who felt powerless in the face of "the savage hordes that infest the northern frontier." Comanche and Kiowa soldiers reduced Mexico's northern colonies to a thoroughfare for their southbound armies. The Mexican government seemed utterly unable to protect its citizens, the overwhelming majority of whom were now Anglo-Americans who had been migrating into Texas since the 1790s, lured by generous land grants.[21]

The Comanches' capacity for war alarmed the Texans, alienating them from the seemingly weak Mexican Republic. In early March 1836, at Washington-on-the-Brazos, delegates from more than forty Texas communities severed their ties with Mexico. Sam Houston, as the first president of the Lone Star Republic, tried to stabilize relations with the Comanches through trade, but he lost the 1838 election to Mirabeau B. Lamar, a true Indian hater. Indians were branded "red niggers," and Lamar waged a vicious war against the Comanches. In

March 1840 a group of Comanches visited San Antonio, with a single White captive in tow. The Comanches held numerous Texans in captivity, and freeing only one of them incensed the Texans. The Texans shot thirty-five Comanches point-blank in the town plaza and streets. After the massacre, Potsanaquahip—Buffalo Hump—led his soldiers down the Guadalupe River valley to the Gulf coast, where they sacked the towns of Victoria and Linnville in what became known in Texas frontier lore as the Great Raid. Texas volunteers ambushed the returning Comanches, killing 140 men, women, and children.

Texan aggression backfired. The Comanches joined forces with two ambitious Saint Louis traders, Charles and William Bent, and asked them to build a trading post near the Big Timbers in northern Comanchería. A walled, two-story adobe bastion, Bent's Fort was massive. In 1840 the Comanches, Kiowas, Cheyennes, and Arapahos forged an alliance in the "Great Peace." Through Bent's Fort and its eastern connections, the Comanches had radically expanded their commercial sphere. Lamar lost the 1841 election to Houston, who invited the Comanches to peace talks. To unsettle the Texans, Potsanaquahip delayed his response. When he did emerge, he demanded a boundary line that gave the Comanches all of Texas except for a 125-mile belt along the Gulf coast. Houston signed away half of Texas's claimed territory to the Comanches. Texas was utterly exposed.[22]

The Comanches had demoted Texas and could now shape the Southwest to meet their needs. Bent's Fort became the northern anchor of the Comanche Empire and its allies. It was a vital supply depot where the four Great Peace nations secured guns, ammunition, horses, metal tools, blankets, and other necessities. Comanchería was soon bursting at its seams. The horse herds of the four allies had exceeded Comanchería's carrying capacity, forcing a difficult choice: either reduce their herds or expand again. The Comanches did not seek war, but they could not accept smaller herds; the Comanches' individual and collective power hinged on horse wealth. The Comanches turned south and went to war with Mexico for horses, grass, and captives. Raiding, already a major enterprise, was about to become an industry. The Comanches carried scores of Mexican captives into Comanchería to tend to their growing horse herds. Slavery became a substantial institution within the Comanche world, but it was not rigidly structured or managed. A large number of slaves were eventually adopted into Comanche households. They were called *kwuhupus*, "my captives."[23]

THE STAGING GROUND for the Texas- and Mexico-bound operations was Big Spring, a pool of artesian water near the headwaters of the Colorado River. From there, two trunk lines took Indigenous armies to the Rio Grande, where the two lines branched into four, taking them deep into Mexico. By the mid-1840s, Comanche armies were operating in the Mexican tropics, and their expeditions resembled seasonal migrations. Their main destination was Bolsón de Mapimí, a vast bowl-like desert plateau, where streams drained not to the sea but toward the plateau's center, nurturing rich plant and animal life. Bolsón became a self-sustaining Comanche colony on foreign soil. "In the fall and winter season," an American visitor wrote, Comanches "enjoy uninterrupted possession of a wide extent of country, whence they make their sallies into the heart of Mexico." The Mexicans thought the Comanches were led by "captains" and "generals" who enforced strict discipline, and they were not far off: "When the march is in war formation," another observer noted, "the scouts and spies ride ahead, then the chief of the tribe at the front of his people, with the women staying behind. If the enemy makes a surprise attack on a trail camp the women protect their offspring, if necessary with bows and knives, fighting to the death if they cannot take flight." The expansionist American Democratic Party had dreamt of a United States that would encompass Sonora, but it was the Comanches and Kiowas who made such an ambition a reality, even if impermanently.

Between 1834 and 1847, the Comanches and their Kiowa allies dispatched more than forty major expeditions into Mexico, each involving at least a hundred soldiers. In their slipstream, the Wichitas raided the increasingly aggressive Texans for horses, captives, and revenge, and to the northwest, the Chiricahuas and Tohono O'odhams began making forays of their own into Mexico: the Apaches de paz reservation experiment had unraveled, and for the Chiricahuas, long-distance raiding was a means both to acquire captives and to evade Comanche and Kiowa aggression. Pushing south from their desert strongholds, the Chiricahuas used rugged terrain to their advantage, making themselves hard to find and defeat. Sonora and Chihuahua were soon tottering. The Apache attacks divided two Mexican states: Chihuahua generally allowed the Apaches to move unopposed through its territory into Sonora. The Apaches "left our frontiers depopulated," José Aguilar, the governor of Sonora, despaired. There may have been a dose of envy when he reported that the villages of the Gileño Papagos in Sonora "are placed close together, almost in professional military fashion, to facilitate their defense against the Apache." Texas officials thought that the Comanches saw the Mexicans as "their stockkeepers and out of which nation they procure slaves." In a world where power hinged on horse wealth, that was true opulence.[24]

The Comanches raided Mexico for portable wealth—horses and captives—but on a deeper level they sought to save energy, grass, and labor. Mexico had become an ecological safety valve: every person and every horse the Comanches brought with them transformed into a crucial conservation of natural resources in Comanchería. With each pilfered horse, the Comanches got more than the animal itself; they also extracted, after the fact, the years of labor and the millions of calories that had gone into bringing that animal to maturity. Through raiding, the Comanches forced an unequal division of labor and ecological exchange between Comanchería and Mexico.[25]

The raids also helped create new connections. The northward flow of Mexican wealth enabled the Comanches to expand their trade networks. They approached the removed southeastern Indians in the Indian Territory in the West. There was violence at first, but the Cherokees adapted to the new conditions quickly, rebuilding dynamic communities that boasted farms, plantations, salt mines, ferries, mercantile shops, and 126 public schools, entering a "golden age." After the Comanches forged commercial ties with the removed southeastern Indians, Comanche trade in the Indian Territory boomed with the increasingly prosperous Cherokees. On the borderlands of Comanchería and the Indian Territory, two of the continent's most influential Indigenous nations came together.[26]

Boosted by new trade outlets, the Comanches reached their apogee in the 1840s. By then, every tenth Native American may have been Comanche. The Americans did not know that, and even if they had, they would have been at a loss to explain it. Their grid of war trails extended mainly to the south, covering much of Chihuahua, Coahuila, Nuevo León, Tamaulipas, Durango, Zacatecas, and San Luis Potosí, and reducing huge chunks of Mexico to a Greater Comanchería, an extractive imperial landscape on foreign soil. The Comanches faced very little resistance from Mexican soldiers. In Tamaulipas, villages petitioned to be exempted from military service. Panicking, Mexican officials started paying locals and mercenaries for Apache scalps. It was an exact business: only crowns with both ears were accepted. Saltillo, Chihuahua, and Coahuila began paying tribute to the Comanches to survive, and they became client states. When returning back north, the Comanches regularly sold some of their animal and human booty in New Mexico for guns and manufactured goods. The Comanche tide had splintered the Mexican Republic into numerous small entities that were each preoccupied with their own survival. Left largely unopposed, Comanche campaigns peaked in 1846 and 1847, with more than a thousand soldiers trekking into Mexico each year. The 1846 expedition attacked the city of Querétaro, only 135 miles north of Mexico City. Such was the Comanches' ambition, power, and momentum that the Comanche Empire burst out of the North American continent into Mesoamerica.[27]

The Comanches were an empire with a difference. They ranged widely but ruled lightly, seeking resources and loyalty, not unconditional submission or sameness. They allowed Spanish and Mexican colonies to linger as formally independent but economically subservient entities, extracting resources from them without draining them completely. As nomads, they did not want direct control over foreign societies; instead, they sought access to foreign resources—horses, cattle, and captives, which, in a sense, took the place of landed property. The Comanches turned mobility into an imperial strategy, using horses to compress time and distance, bringing remote resources near while keeping violence at bay. Like the emerging Lakota Empire, theirs was a kinetic empire. Observed from the urban vantage points of New Mexico, Texas, or Zacatecas, the Comanches were every-where and nowhere, alternating between different activities and fusing them into a protean economy of violence that left the colonists exposed. The Comanches' ascendancy rested not on territorial control but on a capacity to connect vital economic and ecological nodes: trade corridors, grassy river valleys, grain-producing peasant villages, and tribute-paying colonial capitals. Adhering to an imperial ethos different from that of the United States and the European nations on the continent, the Comanches represented the pinnacle of Indigenous power in North America.

Chapter 28

THE LAKOTA
SHIELD

WHILE THE COMANCHES WERE PROJECTING THEIR might deep into Mexico, the Americans were divided over how to expand their republic. In 1836, slave-owning Anglo-American emigrants in Texas and elite Tejanos—ethnically Mexican inhabitants—formed an expedient alliance and seceded from Mexico. President Antonio López de Santa Anna marched six thousand soldiers to San Antonio and attacked the Alamo, an old Franciscan mission now manned by Texans, killing two hundred defenders, only to soon suffer a crushing defeat by American forces. Texas became an independent republic, although it did not much want to remain one: the Comanche threat was too acute. But President James K. Polk pushed ahead with his expansionist agenda and proposed to annex all of the disputed Oregon Country and end the joint U.S.-British occupation of the territory, which had been in place since 1818 and had fueled constant disputes. Britain flatly rejected the offer. By then the Mexican campaign was already underway, and in the summer of 1845, Polk proposed to annex only the portion of Oregon below the forty-ninth parallel. Yet between the annexation of Texas in 1845 and the Mexican Cession, the United States had increased its territory by sixty-six percent within three years.

The United States was now an imperial nation that saw peoples and places as movable pieces on maps. Capturing the zeitgeist, John Louis O'Sullivan, a journalist, famously encouraged Americans to embrace their God-given mission to spread democracy and civilize lesser peoples. That, he insisted, was America's "manifest destiny." Mexico, "imbecile and distracted," was destined to lose California,

he argued, ignoring the fact that the United States itself was distracted by a growing sectional crisis over slavery. Many Americans
advocated for expansion, but they were not unified: many southerners promoted a Caribbean-based slaveholding empire, whereas
northerners desired Hawaii and Canada. Some Americans wanted to
annex the entire Western Hemisphere.[1]

A more realistic but no less cynical exercise took place in the White
House in February 1848. President Polk was perusing maps with
his cabinet, trying to determine how much of Mexico they should
absorb. The United States had declared war on the Mexican Republic in April 1846 and had won, as expected, with ease. On the eve of
the war, much of northern Mexico was already in ruins: U.S. troops
had marched south in the footsteps of the Comanches, Kiowas, and
Apaches, who had turned vast segments of Mexico's heartland into an
economically feeble, politically fragmented, and psychologically shattered world that was ripe for conquest. U.S. officers in the field had
consulted Comanche soldiers who were still raiding in Mexico, mining their expertise on how to subjugate and kill Mexicans. However
distinct the two empires were, in northern Mexico U.S. expansion
was the direct heir to Comanche power.[2]

Polk and his cabinet quickly capitalized on Mexico's weakness. The
Nueces Strip and the San Francisco Bay were obvious spoils, setting
Mexico's northern boundary at latitude 37° north. The real question
was Mexico's southern boundary. Some wanted the border at latitude
25° north, which happened to be the southern extent of the Comanche
reach. Polk wanted the California coast above anything else; some of
his advisors wanted all of Mexico. But Mexico had not yet officially
surrendered, and in the 1848 Treaty of Guadalupe Hidalgo, the United
States took only Alta California and New Mexico. The Mexican Cession totaled 525,000 square miles, increasing the size of the United
States by fifteen percent. In losing Texas, the Mexican Republic had
lost half of its territory. With the stroke of a pen, Mexico's Far North
became the American Southwest. Yet fear of the Comanches lingered.
Between 1849 and 1852, the overwhelmed U.S. Army built eight
military forts on Comanchería's eastern border to keep the Comanches away, turning inward. The Texans were terrified of the Coman-

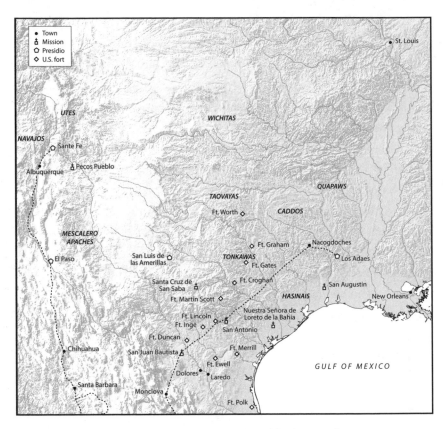

Texas surrounded by Indians in the mid-nineteenth century

ches. They had reason to be: the Mexican government was soliciting
Comanches to join it in a war against the United States.[3]

THE UNITED STATES' EXPANSIONIST burst—mightily boosted
by rising capitalism—was a dark moment for many Native Americans
in the West. The western half of the continent was still overwhelmingly Indigenous, which was unacceptable to Polk and most Americans, who wanted unhindered access to California and its gold, its
fertile land, and its Pacific connections. The U.S. government believed
that treaties and reservations had pacified the Indians and secured
American dominance from ocean to ocean. That was wishful thinking. The federal bureaucracy was completely unprepared for its task
of managing tens of thousands of Indians living far from American

settlements. Most Native nations were assigned a single U.S. officer to oversee their government-issued annuities, their "civilization"
process, and their eventual absorption into the U.S. body politic as
reformed peoples.

Taking advantage of the skeletal U.S. governance in Indian lands,
speculators, settlers, timber thieves, whiskey traders, and other
opportunists pushed into reservations. In the recently acquired California, Whites focused on banishing the Indians, and then on killing them. U.S. agents deported as many Native Americans as they
could to small concentration camps. The land, supremely fertile and
laced with gold, was too good for the Indians. Things came to a
head in 1847 in the valley of the Walla Walla River, a tributary of the
Columbia. The Cayuse Indians, already disgusted by unfair trading
practices and growing traffic along the Oregon Trail, believed that
the local missionaries working among them, Narcissa and Marcus
Whitman, were poisoning them. The Cayuses attacked the mission,
killed fourteen people, and took fifty-three prisoners. The Americans responded with a wild killing spree that led to a genocide across
hundreds of local massacres, abductions, murders, and rapes, leaving
a staggering number of people—between 9,492 and 16,094—dead.
The genocide coincided with epidemics—first measles and then
smallpox. In 1846, there had been 150,000 California Indians; in
1860, only 35,000 remained.[4]

IN A STRIKING CONTRAST to the murderous American aggression
in California, the Hudson's Bay Company, a massive joint-stock mer-
chandizing corporation that claimed the lands from the Rocky Mountains to the West Coast, opened trade relations with the Makahs in
Neah Bay near Puget Sound in 1851. Two years later, the U.S. Congress organized the Washington Territory, and settlers began pouring
in, threatening Makah sovereignty. The Makahs adjusted to the settler invasion by signing the Treaty of Neah Bay in 1855, while making
it clear that they would punish any violators of their sovereignty. A
delicate common ground took hold, helped by contrasting ambitions:
the Americans wanted access to the towering forests of the North-

west, while the Makahs wanted access to the sea and its resources. For them, control over maritime spaces was far more important than control over land. The sea was, and is, "their country." The Treaty of Neah Bay enabled the Makahs to hold on to their all-important fishing rights into the mid-twentieth century.[5]

A year before the Neah Bay treaty and fifteen hundred miles to the east, a Minneconjou Lakota, High Forehead, had killed a stray cow belonging to a Mormon emigrant on the Oregon Trail. Lieutenant John Grattan, a committed Indian hater, took it as an opportunity to "crack it to the Sioux." He boasted that he could bring the Lakotas to their knees with thirty men. Trying to avoid bloodshed, the Lakotas warned the Americans that they could "easily overcome any party or number that may be sent against them." Grattan pushed into a Lakota village with twenty-nine men and two cannons. The Lakotas refused to negotiate, and Grattan fired his cannons—but missed his target. The Lakotas killed all the U.S. soldiers. What Americans came to call the Grattan Massacre revealed deep deficiencies in the United States' Indian policy: it was haphazard, shortsighted, racist, and prone to antagonize. Only three months earlier, Congress had passed the Kansas-Nebraska Act, which allowed American emigrants to claim vast tracts of land in those territories through the doctrine of "popular sovereignty" and make their own laws without federal oversight.[6]

The Lakotas went to war, attacking immigrant trains and U.S. Army patrols in the Platte Valley. Simultaneously to the south, the Cheyennes, Arapahos, Utes, and three Apache divisions—Jicarillas, Mescaleros, and Chiricahuas—ambushed settlers along the Oregon Trail, which skirted their territories. The federal government's design for a subjugated Indigenous America was in tatters after only five years. But the United States was no longer the same nation that the Lakotas, Cheyennes, and others had known before the Mexican-American War. It now held vast possessions far in the West, and it was determined to pacify the lands in between. To subdue the Lakotas, the War Department dispatched General William Harney, the nation's most accomplished Indian fighter, who had chased pirates in Louisiana and conceived riverine tactics that helped vanquish the Seminoles in Florida. He now marched against the Lakotas with six hundred men—a tenth of the nation's regular army—under his command. He held perfunctory talks with Lakota and Cheyenne leaders at Ash Hollow on the lower North Platte on September 2, 1855. The attack came the next morning, in the midst of another parley. Harney's dragoons forced a fluid, fast-moving fight that unfolded over five miles. Eighty-six Lakotas and Cheyennes were massacred. Recognizing the power of the supremely mobile Lakotas, however, Harney agreed to a treaty that confirmed the status quo.[7]

The Harney massacre only hardened Lakota resistance. In 1857, all of the Lakota oyátes met near Bear Butte at the northern edge of Pahá Sápa to determine how to keep the Americans out of their world. The debates lasted several days, until a consensus was reached. The Americans would be allowed to travel along the Platte and send ships up the Missouri, but all lands to the north and west were now closed to them. Only traders could enter Lakota territory. The Lakotas knew that Pahá Sápa contained rich veins of gold, and they also knew the Americans' thirst for it. They decreed that any Indian who told Americans about the gold would be executed. The Lakotas were entrenching themselves in Pahá Sápa. They had learned how to effectively herd the notoriously unherdable bison, securing a dependable food source in the heart of their empire.[8]

The Lakotas were not alone in resisting U.S. encroachments. In 1857, the Dog Soldiers, members of a new militant Cheyenne division in the central plains, confronted Colonel Edwin Sumner, who was leading the First Cavalry to attack them. The Dog Soldiers threatened Americans' access to western gold, which was simply unacceptable to the U.S. government and army. Sumner's force burned two hundred lodges and killed several Dog Soldiers. Two years later, Thomas Twiss, the Bureau of Indian Affairs agent for the Lakotas, Cheyennes, and Arapahos, told those nations that the bison were "now all destroyed" and that the U.S. president would "send his white families to build houses and settle on farms in these valleys." The Dog Soldiers claimed the western half of the central plains between the Arkansas and Platte Rivers as their sovereign domain, a safe haven that had been secured by truces, treaties, and kinship politics. Whereas the Cheyenne government, the Council of Forty-Four, focused on preserving peace, the Dog Soldiers went to war to keep their world inviolate. They shunned American traders and, if offered goods, burned them. The Sicangu and Oglala Lakotas, along with the Kiowas, often joined the Dog Soldiers in attacking settler convoys and gold seekers, expanding the alliance to cover much of the central and northern plains. Women from these nations entered into exogamous marriages, creating a broad kinship network to strengthen the military alliance.[9]

The Navajos, too, fought back against American incursions. In the fall of 1858, in a misguided campaign, U.S. soldiers invaded Canyon de Chelly, "the seat of the supreme power of the Navajo tribe." The Navajos retaliated in April 1860 by sending nearly a thousand soldiers to attack Fort Defiance, the westernmost U.S. Army post in the New Mexico Territory. The battle ended in a draw, which was symptomatic: the U.S. Army was reacting to events rather than driving them, and the results were disastrous. The Navajos kept attacking U.S. Army columns, fending off U.S. troops, who in turn targeted horses and sheep in an effort to destroy the Navajos' pastoral economy. At the same time, Coyotero Apaches attacked American ranches in the Sonoita Valley, facing feeble resistance and running off with oxen.

U.S. officials summoned the already famed Chiricahua leader Cochise to a parley from a nearby camp at the Apache Pass between the Dos Cabezas and Chiricahua Mountains in early 1861. Outrageously, the Americans accused Cochise of the attacks on the ranches and imprisoned him. They put him in a tent; he slashed it and escaped. He was now determined to fight the Americans for as long as it took to defeat them. Making matters worse, U.S. troops attacked a Chiricahua stronghold in the Apache Pass, sparking a sporadic war with the Chiricahuas that would last twenty-five years. Cochise's Chiricahuas went on the offensive, extending their operations deep into the West. The U.S. Army was overwhelmed by the seemingly multiplying small wars against Indigenous nations, even as a civil war seemed more inevitable by the day. In Texas, according to one anxious officer, "the whole frontier wishes to engage in expeditions against the Comanche."[10]

———————

ESTABLISHED IN 1849, the Minnesota Territory had experienced explosive growth, and it was home to 150,000 settlers less than a decade later. Dakota oyátes had ceded their richest farming lands along the Minnesota River in return for a reservation and fifty years of annuities. When Minnesota became a state in 1858, the 1849 treaty proved to be an illusion. Using hunger as a weapon, U.S. officials in Washington had forced Dakota ithą́nčhaŋs to sign a treaty that gave the richest portion of their reservation to Minnesota. A federal mandate assigned a small group of American traders to manage the Dakotas' annuities, but the corrupt men pocketed most of the funds. When German settlers began to encroach on their lands, the Dakotas prepared for war in the shadow of the American Civil War. The Dakota leader Little Crow, in an apparent last-ditch effort to avoid bloodshed, approached trader Andrew Myrick and asked for help. The American refused. "So far as I am concerned," he announced through an interpreter, "if they are hungry, let them eat grass." The Dakotas went to war. Myrick was their first target. His severed head was found with its mouth filled with grass.[11]

The Dakotas were in a fight for survival. Their soldiers moved along the Minnesota River, butchering domesticated animals, burning farms, taking hostages, and killing about five hundred settlers. Major General John Pope, fresh from having lost the Second Battle of Bull Run, where more than fifteen thousand soldiers under his command had been killed, wounded, or captured, or were missing, sought to redeem himself by exterminating the Dakotas. Denying their humanity, he announced that "they are to be treated as maniacs or wild beasts." The Dakotas, hoping to appease the Americans, released 269 captives. The gesture was to no avail. Pope imprisoned almost two thousand Dakota women, children, and men at Fort Snelling. Four hundred Dakotas were indicted for atrocities against Whites. Ad hoc military tribunals condemned 303 to death, but Abraham Lincoln allowed only those found guilty of rapes or massacres to be executed. On December 26, 1862, in the frontier town of Mankato, thirty-eight Dakotas and biracial persons were escorted onto a collapsible platform, where they were noosed and dropped. In that same year, Congress passed the Homestead Act, which entitled every U.S. citizen to 160 acres of federal land west of the Mississippi—an accelerator of Indigenous dispossession.[12]

The mass roundups and the mass execution were a warning: Indigenous nations now faced an administrative behemoth capable of inflicting enormous harm. The hangings, the termination of treaties, and the sheer ethnic hating galvanized the Očhéthi Šakówiŋ, Seven Council Fires—the Sioux alliance—to rebel. As an empire themselves, the Lakotas were the sharp edge of the Sioux resistance. Allied with the Cheyennes and Arapahos, the Lakotas confronted invading U.S. soldiers in a vast theater of war between the Red and Minnesota Rivers to the east and the Little Missouri to the west. Inkpáduta, a Wahpekute Dakota, along with the Hunkpapa leaders Sitting Bull and Gall, assembled an army of sixteen hundred horse soldiers that moved swiftly from target to target, keeping U.S. troops in a state of uncertainty. The first clash took place at the thickly forested Killdeer Mountain just north of the Little Missouri River. To the Lakotas, it was the "first fight with white men." The U.S. Army had been thwarted, but the Americans claimed victory nonetheless.[13]

Sioux warfare followed a logic that was strange to the Americans, who aimed simply to kill Indians. By contrast, for the Lakotas every fight that did not result in large-scale loss of life for their side increased their odds of winning. The Americans were operating in an alien environment, struggling to sustain themselves, and Lakota maneuvers drew them farther and farther from their forts. Eventually, the allied Indians lured the Americans into the Little Missouri Badlands, a bone-dry labyrinth of rock, where they could pick off soldier after soldier from buttes and side canyons. The U.S. Army had not only failed to subdue the Lakotas; it had also created an enemy that it could not afford to face. In the summer of 1864, Lakota, Cheyenne, and Arapaho horse soldiers attacked Americans—soldiers, overlanders, prospectors—across a massive war zone extending from Minnesota to the Rocky Mountains, much of it uncharted by the Americans. A frustrated Colonel John Chivington attacked a peaceful Cheyenne village at Sand Creek with seven hundred Colorado Volunteers. They murdered more than 150 people, mostly women, children, and elderly. One American killed a pregnant woman, cut her open, and scalped the fetus. Others decorated themselves with body parts. When later asked about the brutality, Chivington deadpanned, "Nits make lice." Soon after, U.S. troops attacked the Shoshones in Utah without an official order and killed more than two hundred people. It was not the first massacre that the Shoshones had suffered at American hands. From the Indigenous perspective, the Civil War seemed more and more like a war of empire.[14]

During the period between the incidents at Mankato and Sand Creek, the United States had become a genocidal regime. In early 1865, the Cheyennes, Arapahos, and Lakotas retaliated, burning nearly every ranch, way station, and settlement along the South Platte. The Lakotas also attacked steamboats and unauthorized forts in the upper Missouri Valley, warning that they would "destroy all the whites in the country." With the Civil War still raging, the War Department, at long last, accepted that there was no military solution to the crisis. U.S. officials proposed treaty talks, hoping to reconstruct the horse nations. But while treaties were being negotiated along the Missouri, the War Department began to build forts north of the Platte along the Bozeman Trail in the summer of 1866; gold had been discovered in the Montana Territory. Red Cloud, a noted Oglala shirt wearer emerged as the leader of resistance alongside They Fear Even His Horses, a prominent Oglala civil leader. Lakota, Cheyenne, and Arapaho soldiers systematically harassed the U.S. troops who were building the forts along the exposed trail. But the soldiers would not leave, and Red Cloud prepared for war.

In December 1866, Captain William J. Fetterman allegedly announced that he would ride through the entire Sioux Nation with eighty men. When Fetterman moved to attack, Crazy Horse, a lucid tactician and a shirt wearer, formulated his battle plan. He led a decoy party that lured Fetterman and his eighty-one soldiers into a trap on a high ridge near Fort Kearny. There the allied Indians converged on the U.S. forces and killed every one of them in a fluid and punishing running fight. "They killed 100 white men at Phil Kearney [Fort Kearny]," records the Oglala winter count for the year. Later, when

Americans inspected the battleground, they found ears, noses, teeth, fingers, hands, and feet placed on rocks. It was a warning, issued by the Lakota Empire.[15]

The Lakotas and their allies had won what became known as Red Cloud's War. The United States proposed peace talks, now as a defeated party. In April 1867, U.S. envoys approached the Lakotas. Red Cloud waited until all forts along the Bozeman Trail were dismantled before agreeing to a cease-fire. The Americans were negotiating from a position of weakness, and the 1868 Treaty of Fort Laramie reflected that. It recognized Lakota hegemony in the northern Great Plains, transferred tens of thousands of square miles that had belonged to other Native nations, and granted the Lakotas generous hunting privileges outside the Great Sioux Reservation, which covered roughly forty-eight thousand square miles. The treaty also designated the lands east of the Bighorn Mountains and north of the North Platte as "unceded Indian territory," but it did not define the northern boundary of this unceded territory, leaving the door open to further Lakota expansion.[16]

In October 1867, the Cheyennes, led by Black Kettle, signed the Medicine Lodge Treaty with U.S. representatives. Only a month later, Lieutenant Colonel George Custer, burning with ambition, attacked Black Kettle's village on the Washita River, killing dozens of solders and women and children. U.S. Indian policy was misguided, vicious, and incompetent all at once, entangling the nation in unnecessary wars that only weakened its authority in the critical midsection of the continent. All in all, it was a massive miscalculation that would quickly come to haunt the U.S. Army. The central plains became dangerous to Americans, and soon a U.S. official complained that the Kiowas and Comanches "have been doing much of this wrong. I shall however, continue to exert myself to prevent these acts of violence." The Americans were making far too many enemies.[17]

BY THE EARLY 1870s, the Lakotas were raiding horses in Crow country, purchasing guns and ammunition from Canadian Métis traders, and, most urgently, searching for bison. The herds were dwindling rapidly under intense commercial hunting by both Americans and Indians, driving the Lakotas to expand their empire. They pushed simultaneously into Canada and far to the south, where they clashed again with the Pawnees. But their main thrust was to the west. There, they kept the U.S. Army away from the Powder River Country, extending their empire all the way to the Little Bighorn River. They denounced the U.S. president as a "white fool and a dog, without eyes and brains," because he did not seem to know how to listen. Frightened U.S. agents began channeling annuity goods earmarked for the Crows to the Lakotas. Soon the Lakotas dominated "the larger part of" the Crow reservation—a stinging embarrassment to the U.S. authorities.[18]

If the Lakotas were becoming increasingly assertive, so, too, was the United States. While the U.S. Army was fighting the Lakotas, Cheyennes, Arapahos, and Shoshones, Colonel Kit Carson applied constant pressure on the Jicarilla Apaches in the upper Rio Grande valley. The Jicarillas retaliated by killing livestock for food and capturing intruders. In 1863, Carson led the New Mexico Volunteers against the Mescalero Apaches, defeating them and forcing them into a reservation in Bosque Redondo in the Pecos Valley. He then targeted the Navajos for removal and marched three-fourths of them into Bosque Redondo in the "Long Walk"—which was actually a series of removals. Like the South and the North, the West, too, had a removal era that extended into the 1860s. Nine thousand Navajos became prisoners of war, and U.S. officers confiscated one hundred thousand sheep from Navajo rancherías. The Navajos spent four harrowing years in internment next to their Mescalero enemies, while the Southwest remained a tinderbox. The Utes and Apaches ignored their treaties with the United States and kept raiding New Mexico, now a U.S. territory. In 1868, a high-powered Indian Peace Commission was assigned to pacify the American West by negotiating treaties with the Native nations. Moved by Navajo suffering and alarmed by the "very great expense to the government" of the internment, the commissioners allowed the Navajos to return to their traditional homeland, Dinétah, in the Four Corners region, amid their four sacred mountains.

The scarring Bosque Redondo experience had pushed the Navajos to reinvent themselves as the Navajo Nation in order to present a unified front to Americans. Upon returning to Dinétah, the Navajos thrived almost immediately. They revived their pastoral economy of sheep-, goat-, and horse-herding, and by 1870 their population had reached fifteen thousand. In stark contrast to the Dakota experience in Minnesota, they expanded their reservation. Between 1878 and 1886, five additions quadrupled the Navajo territory, and the Navajo Nation was never targeted for allotment, the forced subdivision of communal landholdings. At more than twenty-seven thousand square miles, the Navajo Nation reservation remains North America's largest Indigenous domain by a wide margin.

While the Navajos secured their own relative safety, the numerous Apache groups relied on traditional raiding economies and descending on American settlements for livestock and captives. The few and scattered U.S. forts in the Southwest were powerless to stop them, and distressed American officials relied on whippings, hostage-taking, and hangings, turning peaceful leaders such as Cochise, Mangas Coloradas, and Geronimo into staunch enemies. Geronimo hated the Mexicans, who had killed his wife, mother, and three children in an attack on their camp. Cochise complained that he had lived with unfulfilled U.S. promises for fifteen years.

Like the Comanches, the Apaches sent war expeditions deep into Mexico, taking captives, stealing food, attacking towns and mining camps, ambushing mail stagecoaches, and evading U.S. troops, who tended to struggle on the unfamiliar terrain south of the border. Local U.S. officials lacked the power to negotiate binding treaties with the Apaches, and the U.S. Army was too weak to subdue the decentralized nation; U.S. troops were forced to chase the Apaches under the doctrine of hot pursuit. It was a stinging humiliation for the Americans. In the Treaty of Guadalupe Hidalgo, the United States had agreed to prevent Native incursions into Mexico. Unlike the Comanches, the many Apache nations never unified into a single alliance or empire, but their localized organization served them well: their raids would continue.[19]

The Civil War was officially over, but Texas remained in a rebellious mode—yet another embarrassment to the United States. The overwhelmed Lone Star State had fought both northern armies and Indians, and the largest U.S.-Indian battle during the Civil War had taken place at Adobe Walls, the Bent family's satellite post in Texas, where some thirteen hundred Comanches and Kiowas led by Quanah Parker, the galvanizing mixed-blood war leader, and Isatai, a young medicine man, routed Kit Carson's troops and Ute scouts. It was the Kiowas' first major engagement with the U.S. Army. Desperate to end the fighting, the Indian Peace Commission opened treaty talks with the Comanches. Since the end of the Mexican-American War in 1848, the Comanches had gone into a steep decline owing to a catastrophic drought in the southern plains: grasses withered, and their empire vanished into hot air. Taking advantage of the Comanches' plight, U.S. agents made an offer: cede 140,000 square miles, accept a fifty-five-hundred-square-mile reservation in the Indian Territory, and allow military forts to be built in Comanchería in return for annuity payments. It was an insult and a betrayal. The Comanches rejected the land cession but signed the Treaty of Medicine Lodge in 1867, which recognized their traditional hunting privileges in the southern plains. To the Comanches, hunting privileges *were* ownership. Although diminished, they were still a force that Americans could not ignore. U.S. officials expected the Comanches to grow crops and live in peace; the Comanches made their Mexican captives do most of the tilling. They also raided Navajos, Choctaws, Cherokees, and Lenapes in the Indian Territory. Like the Iroquois before them, even in decline the Comanches could terrify outsiders and impose their will.[20]

U.S. officials failed to see that, and the American colossus crashed, all but blindly, against a nomad wall. The Civil War and its staggering number of casualties had relegated Native Americans to a secondary threat. Capitalizing on the suffering and distracted American state, the Comanches were able to recover in peace. The Southwest was suddenly up for grabs. The Comanches revived their raiding economy, and soon they were taking horses and captives across Texas and into Mexico. By the late 1860s the Comanche sphere of influence stretched eight hundred miles from north to south and five hundred miles from east to

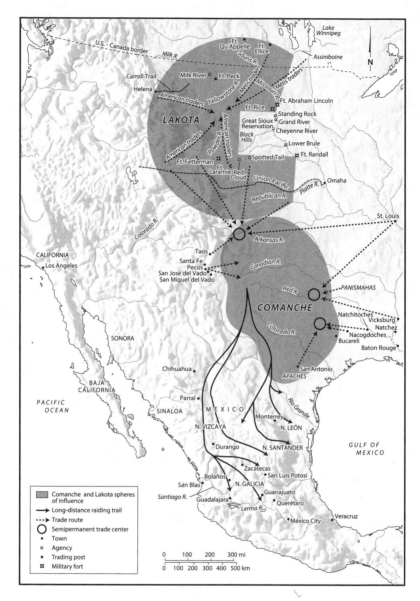

The Comanche and Lakota Empires in
the mid- and late nineteenth century

west. The Comanches sold massive numbers of stolen Texas longhorns to Comancheros, reaping huge profits that enabled them to arm themselves against the Americans. A U.S. agent deemed the Comanches "the most, wild, treacherous, warlike, and brutal of all other Indians."

Had the contemporaries placed the Comanches and the Lakotas in the same frame, they may have realized that they raided—separately—from the Mexican tropics to the Canadian border.[21]

U.S. officials were putting out fires all across the West. After four centuries of colonialism, the extent of Indigenous power was still staggering. While the Cherokees were reasserting their sovereignty against U.S. presumption, the Comanches and Lakotas alone had extended their dominions over an enormous chunk of the continent and much of the American West. Like the Lakotas farther north, the Comanches were expanding again, now alongside and within the American state. The United States managed to weaken the Comanches only after 1872, when the Kansas Pacific Railway enabled professional hunters—generously sponsored by the U.S. Army—to kill buffalo on an industrial scale and ship the robes to the East. The hunts were spectacularly wasteful and nearly exterminated the southern-plains bison. In 1874, Isatai, a young Comanche with powerful *puha*—sacred power—announced that he could raise the dead and render Comanche soldiers bulletproof, thereby starting a movement. Such male-dominated rituals enabled men to gain authority, status, and followers when going to war. When the Kiowas and Cheyennes joined the movement, American authorities began to panic. Led by Tonkawa scouts, U.S. troops chased the Comanches to the Palo Duro Canyon, where they trapped most of the fifteen hundred surviving Comanches. The Americans did not need to kill any of them. They just killed their horses.[22]

THE LONG CONTEST for the North American West revolved around powerful nations, large confederacies, and long-drawn-out wars involving massive numbers of soldiers. The Comanches, Lakotas, Cheyennes, and Apaches kept the United States at arm's length for decades, protecting their own territories and, inadvertently, the territories of a multitude of smaller Native nations. North America had always been an intensely connected Indigenous continent where every battle and every war caused a range of adjustments—political, territorial, cultural, and spiritual. That dynamism itself served as a vast protective shield: it made the Indigenous West all but indecipherable to Americans.

The West was, in its essence, a spatial challenge, and the U.S. Army formulated a spatial solution to it. General Ulysses S. Grant had become president in 1869 on his reputation as the hero of the Civil War, but he chose a nonmilitary approach to the Indian question. It was called the "Peace Policy." Grant's government decided to isolate the Indians from settlers by moving them into tightly protected reservations managed by churches, which jumped at the opportunity: they had been offered a substantial captive audience. The scheme was a debacle. Denominations competed for souls, undermining what was to be a unified policy. Wars not only continued but escalated, and soon the West was once again a battleground. The government found itself spending $144,000 a day to fight Plains Indians. General Philip Sheridan would later marvel at how "no other army in the world has such a difficult line to keep in order," and he boasted that "no other nation in the world would have attempted reduction of these wild tribes and occupation of their country with less than 60,000 to 70,000 men, while the whole force employed and scattered over the enormous region . . . never numbered more than 14,000 men." The United States was becoming an imperial nation without borders.[23]

Yet another massacre, this one in southeastern Arizona in 1871, revealed the United States' vicious, inconsistent, and failed Indian policy. On April 30, sixty miles from Tucson, a vigilante group of Americans, Tohono O'odham Indians, and Mexicans marched in darkness toward Aravaipa Canyon to the northeast of Tucson. Each group in the coalition had its own motive for being there. The Americans wanted to acquire the land and curb Apache mobility, which was the Indians' most important strategy for resisting colonial aggression. The Mexicans wanted to put an end to the Apache raids, and the Tohono O'odhams had spotted an opportunity to diminish the enemies with whom they had fought for generations. They all descended on the Pinal and Aravaipa Apaches, killing 144 people in their sleep in a slaughter that became known as the Camp Grant Massacre. Seven people faced trial in Tucson. They were found not guilty.[24]

The Apaches' transhemispheric mobility was a danger and an

embarrassment to the United States, but the federal government had already taken measures to confine the Apaches and other intractable Native Americans. By the early 1870s, the United States boasted a transcontinental railroad grid, a coast-to-coast telegram network, and countless bridges that together enabled the army to stage fast and massive mobilizations. Fortified by powerful infrastructure—a long-distance train had an average of twenty ten-ton railcars—the government could, at long last, negotiate from a position of strength. Cochise and other Apache leaders negotiated hard and fast, knowing that time was not on their side: the next round of talks was bound to be more difficult. The resulting treaties established reservations for many Apache groups, and U.S. officials consulted the Apaches on their locations. Most Apaches welcomed the reservations as shields against the U.S. military and as winter bases. By the late 1870s, there were five Apache reservations in the American Southwest. Two of them had been built next to U.S. Army forts, revealing the officials' anxiety over Apache resistance. When a U.S. government inspector visited the Chiricahuas in 1875, he found them well armed and well stocked with horses.[25]

At the Warm Springs Reservation in the Northwest, south of the Columbia River, U.S. officials adopted a stern, bureaucratic approach to the "Apache problem." The Chiricahuas, led by the nearly eighty-year-old Nana, now faced American officials who meant not to erase them but to reduce them to lines in ledger books. "Ration cards were issued to the heads of each family and lists were kept in the office," the Chiricahuas remembered. "We camped about the mill until Saturday—Issue Day—when we took our places at the end of the long line of Mescaleros, filed past the window, and were given meat, flour, sugar, and coffee." But the Apaches would not live confined and monitored. They continued their age-old raiding operations and used the reservations as supply depots.[26]

AT A GRAND SUMMIT in the Powder River Country in 1869, the Lakotas embraced *iwaštegla*, a new political philosophy recognizing that they would have to eventually coexist with the Americans. Crazy

Horse, the consummate Oglala soldier, and Sitting Bull, the galvanizing, uncompromising war leader of the northern Lakotas, refrained from war, hoping to buy time and adapt to the inevitable melding of Lakota and American worlds.

Since the routing of Captain Fetterman and his men in 1868, Red Cloud, the Lakota military leader, had become a diplomat advocating peace. He visited Washington, D.C., in 1870, dining in the White House and observing the gargantuan bureaucratic and military might of the post–Civil War United States with majestic detachment. The Mandans, Hidatsas, Arikaras, Assiniboines, Crows, and Blackfoot had accepted reservations in the upper Missouri Valley, and the Comanches were struggling under a long drought, making the Lakota Empire the last best hope of the Indigenous continent. In 1872, on another journey to Washington, D.C., Red Cloud negotiated hard with the U.S. government over annuities and local agencies on Lakota lands, variously charming and disparaging the Americans. Iwaštegla did not mean capitulation; on the contrary, it aimed to bring the United States closer and to secure access to its prodigious resources. That the Lakotas accepted government agencies in their territory was a sign of confidence, not weakness: the agencies provided goods, clothing, and weapons, which the U.S. government had agreed to supply after losing Red Cloud's War. Well armed and assertive, the Lakotas expanded their empire across the northern plains in a quest to secure enough bison for themselves. They pushed the Crows, Utes, Shoshones, and Flatheads out of their way, and they expected the Americans to respect their position.

Once more, gold came between the Lakotas and the Americans. A U.S. Army expedition led by George Armstrong Custer found traces of gold in the Black Hills in 1874, setting off a rush. While the Comanches, under Quanah Parker, were fighting a desperate defensive war against the Americans, the Lakotas emerged as the main protagonists of Indigenous resistance. The Americans pressured the Lakotas to either sell or lease the hills, threatening to cancel their annuities and demanding them to "perform labor." Disgusted, the Lakotas and their allies went to war to protect the sacred Pahá Sápa and their sovereignty and rights. The Lakota Empire snapped into action.

The Lakotas may have lacked the United States' military-technological might—railroads, steamboats, machine guns—but they had accumulated a vast amount of knowledge of the U.S. Army's tactics and weaknesses. The Lakotas had three galvanizing leaders who had fought the Americans for more than a decade: Red Cloud and Crazy Horse, who were both Oglalas, and Sitting Bull, who was a Hunkpapa and lived to the north of the Oglalas. Crazy Horse was a brilliant tactician who thought he was only good for war, while Sitting Bull was an electrifying spiritual leader who mobilized the northern Lakotas for war by ritually giving flesh, cutting himself fifty times before collapsing. Red Cloud refrained from battle, residing in his agency and keeping diplomatic channels open, should the Lakotas need to negotiate their way out of the war.

The Lakotas fought an American army to a standstill in the Battle of Rosebud in early 1876, neutralizing General Sheridan's pincer movement aimed at corralling the Lakotas and their Cheyenne allies. A confusing lull ensued. The Lakotas used it to mobilize. Their horse soldiers emerged from the Great Sioux Reservation and converged along the Little Bighorn River, which the Lakotas called the Greasy Grass. The Lakotas had monitored the U.S. mobilization along the Yellowstone River, which was boosted by a paddle steamer. When the Americans attacked, the Lakotas and their allies were ready. They repelled the first American wave, thereby foiling Sheridan's two-arm pincer maneuver. The Indians seized the initiative, forcing a fluid and fragmented battle that played to their strengths and left the Americans disoriented. In a decisive, creative maneuver, Crazy Horse led a band of soldiers nearly a mile downstream along the Little Bighorn, outflanking the Americans. Soon there were fewer than one hundred American soldiers alive, Custer among them. They shot their horses and huddled together on a small round hill, knowing they would die. The Indians maneuvered effectively, closing in, and axing and clubbing the Americans down. They "did not take a single soldier prisoner, but killed all of them; none were left alive for even five minutes." The Indians thrust an arrow into Custer's penis, sending him into the afterlife diminished.[27]

The Lakotas had won an overwhelming and galvanizing victory, but they would lose the war. The humiliating defeat in the United States' centennial year required a colossal response. Editorials compared Custer's "hill of death" to Golgotha and demanded retribution. The U.S. Army, now supercharged by capitalism, railroads, and the telegram, launched a series of winter attacks and imprisoned key leaders. Crazy Horse resisted arrest and was killed by a bayonet thrust near his cabin. Sitting Bull escaped north and crossed the "Medicine Line," a one-hundred-mile stretch of the U.S.-Canada border that seemed to stop U.S. soldiers like magic. A vengeful Congress seized Pahá Sápa, willfully violating the Treaty of Fort Laramie, and the army launched attacks to force the horse nations into reservations, eliminating their most important asset, mobility. The sheer vastness of the Trans-Mississippi West had helped the equestrian Indigenous powers for decades, allowing them to put distance between the Americans and themselves. But mobility on the continent now belonged to the Americans, whose railroads had ushered in a modern corporate world centered on Wall Street, where Indians had no place. By annihilating space with rail lines, the United States could shrink the West to a manageable size, while the railroad tracts and trains disturbed the all-important migrations of the bison herds. In late 1876, Spotted Tail, a prominent Sicangu Lakota leader, met with U.S. authorities and a Muscogee Indian delegation in the Indian Territory and lamented how "my country is covered with gold. I have made a bargain with the great father to sell it, because the white men came to take it. . . . All the people are poor. My land is covered with gold and I must have to pay for it."[28]

As the United States' most formidable foe, the Lakotas had unintentionally bought time for other Indigenous nations in their struggles against the imperial Americans. Led by Quanah Parker, Comanches continued to raid Mexican wagon trains, kill American bison hunters, and steal American horses, keeping the southern plains in a state of uncertainty that allowed them hold on to to their traditional way of life. The enduring power of the Lakotas and Comanches in the North American West looped back across the continent, helping smaller Indigenous nations to survive. Yet by 1877 the war was over. The United States unleashed its prodigious power—embodied by repeating carbines, transcontinental railroads, and explosively proliferating post offices that disseminated the continent's most precious commodity: intelligence. Suddenly exposed, Parker and the Comanches had to settle in a reservation. Congress appropriated $200,000 for forts in Yellowstone Country and launched another systematic winter campaign against the Lakotas and Cheyennes. "Custer's Avengers" brought down the great Lakota-Cheyenne alliance within a year. The next—and final—campaign would not be so straightforward.[29]

THE NEZ PERCES had lived in relative peace in their capacious high-altitude homeland on the Columbia Plateau between the Spokane and Snake Rivers, where they had access to streams teeming with fish and grasslands fringed by animal-rich forests. It was a superior realm for horse-breeding, and the Nez Perces became a formidable horse nation. Shielded by the towering mountain ranges that ringed their territory, the Nez Perces had been able to keep the Americans at bay until the late 1850s, when U.S. officials opened negotiations with the Columbia Plateau nations: looking past the Indians, the United States sought access to the Pacific through Puget Sound and encouraged immigration by shifting land to American settlers through treaties with Indians and new western states.

The Nez Perces staged a dramatic arrival at the talks that echoed the Lakotas' arrival at the Fort Laramie parley in the spring of 1851. After contentious negotiations and expedient misunderstandings, the Walla Wallas, Umatillas, Cayuses, Yakamas, and Nez Perces agreed to treaties and reservations. But in 1860, gold was discovered on the Nez Perce reservation, provoking a long struggle among Indians, local officials, and the U.S. Army. The United States imposed unfavorable treaties on the Nez Perces, while land-hungry settlers nibbled at the margins of the reservation. By the mid-1870s, hemmed in by the Washington and Idaho territories and the state of Oregon, the Nez Perces faced U.S. officials who demanded obedience and threatened to remove the Indians from their lands.[30]

The Nez Perces, led by Chief Joseph, or Thunder Rolling Down the Mountain, went to war. The first clash with U.S. troops, along Clearwater Creek in June 1877, was an exception: the only prolonged battle in a war that featured large-scale maneuvers, sustained volleys, and repeated charges. The fight was inconclusive, and soon after, the Nez Perces decided to leave their homelands. The U.S. Army pursued them, and from then on the Nez Perces conducted a mobile war, which they had perfected over several decades. A seemingly endless series of skirmishes, routs, and regroupings ensued, as the Nez Perces kept moving away from the U.S. Army's maneuver warfare that aimed to incapacitate them through shock attacks. The Nez Perces launched a massive and highly coordinated campaign that enabled them to hold on to two thousand horses, dozens of dogs, and several villages. In mid-September, eight hundred Nez Perces, led by Chief Joseph, broke for Canada, crossing the Continental Divide three times to reach the Medicine Line along the 49th parallel. They traveled fifteen hundred miles in 115 days before U.S. forces caught them, a mere forty miles away from asylum. The U.S. Army apprehended the Nez Perces and handed them over to the Indian Office, which would see to their removal to the Indian Territory. The last official military engagement between the United States and North America's Indigenous peoples was over.[31]

INDIGENOUS NATIONS COULD no longer win wars against the American leviathan. That did not mean that North America was no longer an Indigenous continent, or that the Indians were doomed. The western half of the continent was speckled with large reservations, and the eastern half with numerous smaller ones. Indigenous territories may have shrunk, and the Indigenous population had plummeted, but large domains remained under Native control in the West, where there were many nations that had never been defeated or dispossessed by the United States. Now, however, U.S. expansionism was facilitated by a menacing chain reaction: when one Native nation was subjugated, another one became exposed, making it possible for the Americans to channel their forces against one nation at a time. Native peoples were forced to rely on the weapons of the weak: mobility, evasion, invisibility, and quiet defiance.

The Eastern Shoshones, a formidable horse people, had dominated parts of the Rocky Mountains, Columbia Plateau, Wyoming

Basin, and Great Plains since the mid-seventeenth century, contending intermittently with the Blackfoot, Yakamas, Walla Wallas, Crees, Nez Perces, and Umatillas. The high-altitude setting protected them against colonial intrusions: few American settlers wanted to reside in the mountains, where they were isolated and farming was difficult. When emigrants did begin to pour west in the 1850s, the Shoshones sought refuge in the Wyoming Basin. They treated the American overlanders gently, bartering with them and feeding them, but eschewed formal political pacts, preferring fleeting face-to-face encounters. The Mormon leader Brigham Young, serving as the superintendent of Indian affairs for the Utah Territory, complained that the Shoshones "are so broken up into small bands, that it is impossible to tell with any degree of accuracy their numbers." He wanted them to "not depend on hunting for living, but to settle on good localities where they could raise grain." Young tried to render the Shoshones visible, manageable, and productive. The Shoshones flatly ignored him. Being inconspicuous kept them safe. But when Mormon settlers pushed into their territory, the Shoshones retaliated by killing and wounded dozens of them. In 1863, Union forces intervened, murdering several hundred Shoshones in what became known as the Bear River Massacre. The Mormons looked for other ways to extract wealth from local Indians. Considering bondage natural, and branding both Africans and Indians as "dark and loathsome," they began to buy large numbers of Indian children.[32]

Like the Shoshones, the Blackfoot, nestled in the Rocky Mountain foothills, kept a measured distance from imperial powers, limiting their interactions with Whites to the fur trade: for generations they allowed the Hudson's Bay Company to maintain posts in their borderlands because the company sought trade, not land, and operated as a surrogate government that mediated relations between the Indians and the settlers. The Blackfoot skirmished with the British and Americans but avoided full-scale wars. Like their neighboring Shoshones and unlike other large Native nations, they were not directly in the way of American expansion: few colonists wanted to settle in the Rockies, which they saw solely as an obstacle to cross. The Blackfoot thrived in this colonial blind spot for a century and a half. But by the early 1870s, coexistence had become tenuous. Ancient multi-ethnic kinship networks could no longer sustain common worlds in the face of the influx of White settlers and racism. In late January 1870, prompted by a single revenge killing, two hundred mounted U.S. troops descended on the Piikani band of the Blackfoot Confederacy on the Marias River. Within an hour, approximately two hundred Blackfoot women, children, and men were dead. The massacre had its roots in American expansionism and persistent Indigenous presence near American settlements. Many Blackfoot retreated to Canada for refuge, but they did not find it. Like the United States, Canada had developed a settler mindset. In 1867 the Canadian colonies had united into the Dominion of Canada, in large part to boost westward expansion.[33]

Far to the north of the Medicine Line, Native peoples could still find refuge in the cold. There, in the Canadian subarctic, Indians were able to coexist and cooperate with Europeans, mostly unbothered by American settlers. The Canadian fur conglomerates—the Hudson's Bay Company and the North West Company—embraced Native hunters and trappers as valuable allies. The stakes were high—the northern fur trade was a prodigious industry with more than six hundred trading posts, large and small—with Crees, Gros Ventres, Ojibwes, Chippewas, Assiniboines, and others vying intensely over trading privileges. The Canadian subarctic endured as an Indigenous world. It was not an Indigenous paradise; the contest for furs, guns, and merchandise fueled chronic animosities, collisions, and open wars. But those wars were conducted on Indigenous terms, emphasizing negotiation over coercion and kinship ties over hard borders.[34]

The Métis kept their distance from the dominion, extending the all-important trade networks from their base at the Red River Colony, which the Hudson's Bay Company had bestowed on them in 1811. Highly mobile people, the Métis produced massive amounts of bison robes and pemmican for both fur companies. The Métis ranged broadly, shifting from bison-rich grasslands to parklands and beaver-rich woods and rivers, skirting colonial centers. They traded with the Hudson's Bay Company's great rival, the North West Company, and crossed the U.S.-Canada border at will, challenging the assumed authority of both nation-states. The Métis' kinship networks were nearly continental in scope, making them a formidable force in a world where nation-states were becoming the norm. In 1869 the Dominion of Canada miscalculated by absorbing Rupert's Land, the vast territory around Hudson Bay and in the northern grasslands.

The Métis rose up. Louis Riel, their leader, asserted the sovereignty of the Métis and insisted that land transactions should be conducted between the Red River Colony and Canada and not between Canada and the Hudson's Bay Company. Canada retreated from its position and recognized Métis claims. The Métis' victory was sullied almost immediately, however. In 1870 a devastating smallpox epidemic, coupled with the government's careless attitude toward its treaty obligations, caused a population catastrophe that cleared much of the Canadian West for settlers.[35]

The Apaches took the strategy of evasion further than any other people. They shifted constantly in and out of their assigned reservations, raided settlements for captives, and then retreated into the mountains or deep canyons. They visited their assigned reservations mostly for supplies and new recruits. When pressed by larger U.S. forces, they found safe haven in Mexico or in difficult terrain, and if they were forced to fight, their guerrilla tactics often left the enemy confused and without a target to strike. When pursued, the Apaches polluted water sources and set fires to slow down American troops. If those measures failed, they fortified their camps with rock emplacements and breastworks to hold back the Americans. They dispersed and came together again, using mirrors and smoke signals to communicate. When moving in large groups, they followed a precise marching line with a central body protected by advance, rear, left, and right guards. From the American perspective, the Apaches were all over the map, yet nowhere to be seen. Evasion was only secondarily a military strategy. Its main purpose was to enable the Apaches to stay put and live in peace in their desert strongholds and enjoy the fruits of their operations: spacious tipis, large herds of horses, and captives, as well as mule loads of water jugs, metal utensils, and clothing. As evasion became entrenched, Apache women became active combatants; they organized war parties and exacted vengeance in battle. Lozen, a Chiricahua prophet, became a forceful leader of women and men.[36]

Both U.S. and Mexican authorities needed the Apaches pacified: the Indians' persistent cross-border raids thwarted settlement and crippled commerce. Both governments were still paying bounties for Apache scalps—Chihenne leader Victorio's would fetch $2,000—but that only stiffened Apache resistance. The U.S.-Mexico border was essentially meaningless to the Apaches, who breezed across it easily. In the early 1870s the United States established a reservation for the Chiricahuas on the U.S.-Mexico border. The reservation immediately became a staging ground for Chiricahua excursions deep into Mexico and led to the abandonment of several mines, farms, and haciendas by Mexicans.

The U.S. Army sent in General George Crook, who, with the crucial help of friendly Apache scouts, forced the Chiricahuas into the San Carlos Reservation in east-central Arizona by 1877. From then on, the Apaches found themselves increasingly hemmed in by the two nation-states. Their evasive tactics had bought them years of freedom, but they could no longer win battles, let alone wars, against the United States and the Mexican state. The Americans now wanted all Indians confined, pacified, and fixed in space. Crook was assigned to bring in Geronimo, the embodiment of Indigenous resistance and of Americans' failure to secure the continent. In 1882, the United States and Mexico formed a pact that allowed cross-border pursuit of Apaches. Stripped of their sanctuaries across boundaries, the Apaches were soon reeling.

After years on the run, Geronimo finally surrendered in 1886 in Skeleton Canyon, just north of the border. He had only eighty people with him. They were put on a train that took them to Florida, where Geronimo, still deemed dangerous, was sent to Fort Pickens, a military fort three miles away from the others. His requests to return to the West went ignored. Not long after Geronimo's transfer to Florida, the Chiricahuas were removed again, now to Fort Sill in Oklahoma, where they spent twenty years as prisoners of war in wretched conditions. John Gregory Bourke, an aspiring American ethnologist, conducted interviews with Apache women at Fort Sill. In the blink of an eye, the Apaches had become objects of study.[37]

Bourke wanted to rescue Apache lore before it vanished, but he failed to realize that Apache history and traditions did not need his rescue efforts. Every Apache group possessed a comprehensive record of its past, told and retold by elders, and those records would survive removals, the vicious arrogance of U.S. agents, the innate racism of American civilization programs, and, as the nineteenth century drew to a close, the cynical neglect of the United States. Bourke's attempt to repossess Apache culture ran up against a far more powerful historical force: Apache resilience.

Epilogue

REVENGE AND REVIVAL

I N THE LONG AFTERMATH OF THE BATTLE OF THE LIT-
tle Bighorn, the Indian Office criminalized the Sun Dance in 1882,
creating a gaping spiritual void in numerous Native nations. In the
winter of 1889, the Lakotas heard of a new religion, the Ghost Dance,
preached by Wovoka, a Northern Paiute holy man. Lakota envoys
rode trains to Nevada to learn firsthand from the prophet. A blend
of millenarian and modern elements, the Ghost Dance seemed to
offer Indians the tools to survive in a rapidly changing world, and it
began to fill the emptiness left by the U.S. government's ban on the
Sun Dance. In the winter of 1889–90, the Lakotas started to dance,
desperate to bring bison and their dead relatives back. The Americans
still feared the Lakotas, and the Lakota agents panicked, mistaking
the forward-looking Ghost Dance movement for an anti-White conspiracy. The army mobilized against the dancers and trapped a group
of them at Wounded Knee Creek. The Seventh Cavalry, Custer's former regiment, occupied the higher ground and began shooting at the
exposed people below. At least 270 died, and at least 170 of the dead
were women and children. It was revenge for the humiliation fourteen
years earlier. Twenty soldiers involved in the massacre were awarded
the Congressional Medal of Honor.[1]

The apocalyptic Wounded Knee Massacre was a sign of American weakness and fear. When the Indian wars came to an end in
1877, the United States was simultaneously imperious and exhausted.
Since the founding in 1776, there had been more than sixteen hundred official military engagements with Native Americans. Moreover,
while fighting Indians, the United States had descended into a drain-

ing and demoralizing Civil War that had claimed as many as 750,000 American lives. When peace finally came, the United States committed to completing not one but two reconstructions, of the American South and of the Indigenous West. The United States had suffered a hundred-year-long crisis of authority, and it was determined to assert its hegemony. Compared to the reconstruction of the American South, which involved conciliatory elements, the Indigenous reconstruction was, on the whole, harsh and vindictive, featuring more "civilization programs," boarding schools designed to "kill the Indian to save the man," and land policies that labeled Indigenous territories "surplus land." Richard Henry Pratt, the founder of the Carlisle Indian Industrial School, wondered why the United States did not simply absorb the remaining Indians and eradicate their cultures—and he actually cared about the Indians.[2]

Like many other settler states throughout history, the United States tried to immobilize and contain Indigenous peoples within its borders. The Indian Office was sidelined by zealous liberal reformers, evangelical Christians, ranchers, western settlers, and railroad boosters who all wanted to see Indian reservations gone. Indigenous leaders were marginalized, and their time-honored governing systems, societies, ceremonies, dances, and feasts—the things that made Indians Indians—were either suppressed or banned. The backlash was vast and overwhelming, revealing how powerfully Native Americans had stood their ground against White settlers and how effectively they had thwarted colonialism. There was a direct link between the Indigenous success and Americans' sense of vulnerability and scale of vengeance.[3]

The four-hundred-year struggle to keep the continent Indigenous had stretched colonists from the European powers, and then the United States, to the breaking point again and again. The enormous range of Native nations and the sheer depth and multiplicity of their resistance had frustrated the colonists, if it did not kill them. Some nations relied on naked force and numbers to corral and punish colonial powers, while others sought alliances with them. Some forged ties to other Native nations and reinvented themselves as confederacies. The most powerful nations and confederacies—the Six Nations of the Iroquois Confederacy, the Indian Confederacy, the

Wyandots, Lakotas, Comanches, Muscogees, Cherokees, and Semi-noles—defeated the colonists in battle repeatedly and controlled the diplomatic proceedings that followed. They possessed the authority, savvy, and will to dictate terms to the Spanish, French, British, and U.S. empires. The Iroquois were the dominant imperial power in the heart of North America for generations, and in the early nineteenth century the Comanches and Lakotas built empires of their own, in part to survive colonialism. Instead of fighting these Indigenous pow-ers, the colonists placated them. They desperately wanted to be allies and not enemies. They sided with power.

Smaller Native nations relied on more nuanced and delicate tac-tics. Rather than confronting colonial powers directly in battle, they evaded them by making themselves small and inconspicuous, using the striking environmental variety of North America. The Cataw-bas, Shoshones, Utes, Nez Perces, Blackfoot, Seminoles, and others found refuge in deserts, mountains, and swamps, evading the set-tler empires that struggled with difficult and strange terrain, while the Shawnees, "the greatest travellers in America," countered colo-nial displacement with a highly organized Indigenous diaspora. In the lower Mississippi Valley, the petites nations made themselves into forceful regional powers through strategic mobility, calculated violence, and expedient alliances, keeping just ahead of the imperial gaze of the surrounding colonial empires. The Catawba population had fallen to 110 in the mid-1820s, but 110 proved to be enough for the nation to survive.[4]

Indigenous power in North America reached its apogee in the mid- to late nineteenth century, which, at first glance, appears coun-terintuitive. This was the period when the United States emerged onto the world stage with its "monstrous contiguous economic ter-ritories," inspiring awe and fear in Germany and fueling an impres-sion as the "greatest menace" in Italy. Subduing independent Native nations and erasing their sovereignty seemed to the imperial United States a straightforward problem of plying its overwhelming military might and technological advances, including railroads. But the Indig-enous nations, too, reinvented themselves, in part as a response to the rising American empire. The Comanches forged an empire that reduced much of the Mexican Republic to an extractive hinterland, enabling them to reign over an oversized section of the hemisphere. The Lakotas, relying on their equestrian mobility, their broad alliance network, and their generations-long experience of blocking colonial ambitions, emerged as the leading, though inadvertent, guardians of the Indigenous continent. Over a period of seven decades, they foiled U.S. expansion again and again, protecting in the process scores of smaller and more vulnerable nations. There is no way to measure the lives saved, but given the palpable genocidal tendencies of the American settlers, the Lakota Empire's protective presence may have been the most significant single entity keeping the continent Indigenous. Seen from the Indigenous perspective, Custer's Last Stand was neither an aberration nor an atrocity; it was expected and necessary. Looking east from the North American West, the history of North America emerges as a single story of resolute resistance that kept much of the continent Indigenous for generations.[5]

Native peoples carry on the legacy of the long history of resistance. In truth, Native Americans have fought colonialism for more than five centuries, not four, opposing and foiling numerous imperial designs and keeping the continent Indigenous into the twentieth and twenty-first centuries. They have turned to a vast range of strategies, shifting fluidly from diplomacy and war to appeasement and evasion. Merely surviving has been difficult. In the 1890s the number of remaining Indians was 250,000—a terrifyingly low figure that reveals the enormity of U.S. genocidal campaigns. American expansion had diminished North America's Indigenous population by seventy percent.[6]

But 250,000 was enough to sustain a revival. Today, many Native nations and communities are rapidly growing in numbers. The continent is speckled with hundreds of Native nations that preserve Indigenous sovereignty and nationhood. Each of them embodies the centuries-long Indigenous resistance to colonial violence and expansion, whether Spanish, French, British, Dutch, Canadian, or American. The colonists, after all, would have absorbed every inch of North America if not denied by the continent's Indigenous inhabitants.

A present-day map of Indian reservations in North America captures the story of the Indigenous continent. Canada has hundreds of reserves, most of them small, belonging to a single "band"—a centralized system that differs drastically from the United States' removal policy that created the Indian Territory in 1830. In 2016, half of Canada's First Nation peoples lived in reserves that were fairly evenly distributed among the provinces, with the heaviest concentration on the Pacific coast. South of the forty-ninth parallel, things are different. The East Coast and the coastal plains south of the Chesapeake Bay were violently contested from the seventeenth century on, and these regions are now nearly devoid of reservations. So, too, are the places where Indigenous nations faced Americans in the time of high U.S. imperialism in the late eighteenth and early nineteenth centuries: the Ohio Country, the Deep South, and Texas. The largest reservations in the United States are in the West and belong to Navajos, Utes, Comanches, Tohono O'odhams, Oglala Lakotas, Hunkpapa Lakotas, Sihasapa Lakotas, Eastern Shoshones, Northern Arapahos, and Crows. All of those nations fought colonial powers for generations to protect their territory and sovereignty. There are also thick clusters of reservations in the Great Lakes region, where Indigenous resistance forced the colonists to respect Native ways, cooperate, and acknowledge Indigenous authority.[7]

The Ojibwe writer David Treuer argues that when it comes to views of the continent's wilderness, "America has succeeded in becoming more Indian over the past 245 years rather than the other way around." It is a comment on the enduring and often unseen impact of Indigenous culture. But beyond Treuer's specific claim, it is worth pausing to consider just how recent the United States, and its ascendancy, are. The four hundred years of colonialism that followed Columbus's arrival failed to extinguish Indigenous sovereignty in North America. It was only 130 years ago, a brief span when compared to the long precontact history of Indigenous America, that the United States could claim to have subjugated a critical mass of Native Americans. Iroquois power lasted from the sixteenth century deep into the nineteenth century, making the Iroquois Nation older and more historically central than the United States. On an Indigenous timescale, the United States is a mere speck.

Set against the deep history of the Indigenous continent, American history looks fundamentally different. So does the American present. Today, sovereign Indigenous America persists in the dynamism of modern Native communities, in the endurance of traditional ways of life, and in the continuation and evolution of the primary Indian response to colonialism: resistance.[8]

ACKNOWLEDGMENTS

MANY PEOPLE HELPED ME DURING THE RESEARCH AND writing of this book, and it is my great pleasure to thank them. Fred Anderson, Rani Andersson, Juliana Barr, James Belich, Lance Blythe, Patrick Bottiger, Paul Conrad, Jane Dinwoodie, François Furstenberg, Daniel Green, Patrick Griffin, Mandy Izadi, Paul Kelton, John Kessell, Matthew Kruer, Sami Lakomäki, Joy Porter, Charles Prior, Andrés Reséndez, Nancy Shoemaker, Coll Thrush, Camilla Townsend, and Samuel Truett generously gave their time to talk about this project and read parts of the manuscript, and they made it better with their insights. James Merrell read the entire manuscript and offered detailed and shrewd criticism; I am deeply indebted to him for his advice. My editor, Daniel Gerstle, improved the book vastly with his perceptive feedback. I am grateful to Zeba Arora for her work with the images. It was wonderful to work again with Bill Nelson on the maps. I also want to thank my agent, Geri Thoma, for her support, enthusiasm, and wisdom. I owe a large debt of gratitude to my copy editor, Stephanie Hiebert, who not only improved the manuscript enormously but also taught me a lot about writing. I want to thank Kaspar Supinen and Lidia Supinen for their insights and support. As always, Veera Supinen helped me immensely with her sheer brilliance.

I first tested some of the ideas and arguments of *Indigenous Continent* in an essay titled "The Shapes of Power: Indians, Europeans, and North American Worlds from the Seventeenth to the Nineteenth Century," published in *Contested Spaces of Early America*, ed. Juliana Barr and Edward Countryman (Philadelphia: University of Pennsylvania Press, 2014). I am very grateful for the feedback of the other contributors and everybody who participated in the manuscript workshop before that volume was published. In particular, I would like to extend my thanks to Matthew Babcock, Juliana Barr, Ned Blackhawk, Edward Countryman, Chantal Cramaussel, Brian DeLay, Elizabeth Fenn, Allan Freer, Raúl José Mandrini, Cynthia Radding, Birgit Brander Rasmussen, Alan Taylor, and Samuel Truett.

NOTES

ABBREVIATIONS

AHR   *American Historical Review*

ARCIA   U.S. Department of the Interior, *Annual Report of the Commissioner of Indian Affairs* (Washington, DC: Government Printing Office), University of Wisconsin–Madison Libraries, UW-Digitized Collections, Documents Relating to Native American Affairs, http://digicoll.library.wisc.edu/cgi-bin/History/History-idx? type=browse&scope=HISTORY.COMMREP.

ARI   Colin G. Calloway, *The American Revolution in Indian Country: Crisis and Diversity in Native American Communities* (New York: Cambridge University Press, 1995).

BR   Daniel K. Richter, *Before the Revolution: America's Ancient Pasts* (Cambridge, MA: Belknap Press of Harvard University Press, 2011).

CE   Pekka Hämäläinen, *The Comanche Empire* (New Haven, CT: Yale University Press, 2008).

CW   Fred Anderson, *Crucible of War: The Seven Years' War and the Fate of Empire in British North America, 1754–1766* (New York: Vintage, 2000).

EW   Jon Parmenter, *The Edge of the Woods: Iroquoia, 1534–1701* (East Lansing: Michigan State University Press, 2010).

HAC   R. Cole Harris, ed., *Historical Atlas of Canada*, vol. 1, *From the Beginning to 1800* (Toronto: University of Toronto Press, 1987).

IALT   Charles J. Kappler, ed., *Indian Affairs: Laws and Treaties* (Washington, DC: Government Printing Office, 1929), 4 vols.

JAH   *Journal of American History*

JLCE   Gary E. Moulton, ed., *Journals of the Lewis & Clark Expedition* (Lincoln: University of Nebraska Press, 1983–2001), 13 vols.

JP   *The Papers of Sir William Johnson* (Albany: University of the State of New York, 1921–65), 14 vols.

JR   *The Jesuit Relations and Allied Documents*, ed. Reuben Gold Thwaites (Cleveland, OH: Burrows, 1896–1901), 73 vols.

LA   Pekka Hämäläinen, *Lakota America: A New History of Indigenous Power* (New Haven, CT: Yale University Press, 2019).

MG   Richard White, *The Middle Ground: Indians, Empires, and Republics in the Great Lakes Region, 1650–1815* (New York: Cambridge University Press, 1991).

MPCP   Samuel Hazard, ed., *Minutes of the Provincial Council of Pennsylvania from the Organization to the Termination of the Proprietary Government* (Harrisburg, PA: Theophilus Fenn, 1838), 6 vols.

MPHC   *Michigan Pioneer Historical Society: Collections and Researchers* (Lansing, MI: The Society, 1877–1929), 40 vols.

NEQ   *New England Quarterly*

NOT   Claudio Saunt, *A New Order of Things: Property, Power, and the Transformation of the Creek Indians, 1733–1816* (New York: Cambridge University Press, 1999).

NWA   Colin G. Calloway, *New Worlds for All: Indians, Europeans, and the Remaking of Early America* (Baltimore: Johns Hopkins University Press, 1998).

NYCD   John Romeyn Brodhead, *Documents Relative to the Colonial History of the State of New York; Procured in Holland, England, and France*, ed. F. B. O'Callaghan (Albany, NY: Weed, Parsons, 1853–87), 15 vols.

OBK   Lisa Brooks, *Our Beloved Kin: A New History of King Philip's War* (New Haven, CT: Yale University Press, 2018).

OL   Daniel K. Richter, *The Ordeal of the Longhouse: The Peoples of the Iroquois League in the Era of European Colonization* (Chapel Hill: University of North Carolina Press, 1992).

PNAS   *Proceedings of the National Academy of Sciences of the United States of America*

SA   D. W. Meinig, *The Shaping of America: A Geographical Perspective on 500 Years of History* (New Haven, CT: Yale University Press, 1986–2005), 4 vols.

SFNA   David J. Weber, *Spanish Frontier in North America* (New Haven, CT: Yale University Press, 1992).

SG   Jeremy Ostler, *Surviving Genocide: Native Nations and the United States from the American Revolution to Bleeding Kansas* (New Haven, CT: Yale University Press, 2019).

WHC   *Collections of the State Historical Society of Wisconsin*, ed. Lyman C. Draper and Reuben G. Thwaites (Madison, WI: The Society, 1855–1911), 20 vols.

WMQ   *William and Mary Quarterly*

WUH   Gregory Evans Dowd, *War under Heaven: Pontiac, the Indian Nations, and the British Empire* (Baltimore: John Hopkins University Press, 2002).

YSF   Candace S. Greene and Russell Thornton, eds., *The Year the Stars Fell: Lakota Winter Counts at the Smithsonian* (Washington, DC: Smithsonian National Museum of Natural History, 2007).

INTRODUCTION: THE MYTH OF COLONIAL AMERICA

1.   I borrowed "infinity of nations" from Michael Witgen, *An Infinity of Nations: How the Native New World Shaped Early America* (Philadelphia: University of Pennsylvania Press, 2012).

A NOTE ON TERMINOLOGY AND STYLE

1.   Nancy Shoemaker, "2019 Presidential Address: Sameness and Difference in Ethnohistory," *Ethnohistory* 67, no. 4 (October 2020): 537–49.

CHAPTER 1: THE WORLD ON THE TURTLE'S BACK

1.   Alice B. Kehoe, *North American Indians: A Comprehensive Account*, 2nd ed. (Englewood Cliffs, NJ: Prentice Hall, 1992), 1–11; Stuart J. Fiedel, "Older Than We Thought: Implications of Corrected Dates for Paleoindians," *American Antiquity* 64 (January 1999): 95–115; Jennifer Raff, *Origin: A Genetic History of the Americas* (New York: Twelve, 2022).
2.   J. V. Moreno-Mayar, L. Vinner, P. de Barros Damgaard, C. de la Fuente, J. Chan, J. P. Spence, M. E. Allentoft, et al., "Early Human Dispersals within the Americas," *Science* 362, no. 6419 (2018), https://doi.org/10.1126/science.aav2621; Todd J. Braje, Tom D. Dillehay, Jon M. Erlandson, Richard G. Klein, and Torben C. Rick, "Finding the First Americans," *Science* 358, no. 6363 (November 2017): 592–94; Fen Montaigne, "The Fertile Shore," *Smithsonian Magazine*, January/February 2020, https://www.smithsonianmag.com/science-nature/how-humans-came-to-americas-180973739. There is considerable disagreement about the dates; some scientists believe that people reached Monte Verde as early as thirty-two thousand years ago.

For the debate, see Charles C. Mann, *1491: New Revelations of the Americas before Columbus*, 2nd ed. (New York: Vintage, 2011), 182–96; Matthew R. Bennett, David Bustos, Jeffrey S. Pigati, Kathleen B. Springer, Thomas M. Urban, Vance T. Holliday, Sally C. Reynolds, et al., "Evidence of Humans in North America during the Last Glacial Maximum," *Science*, no. 6562 (September 24, 2021): 1528–31.

3.   Lisa Ford, *The Common Pot: The Recovery of Native Space in the Northwest* (Minneapolis: University of Minnesota Press, 2008), 2–3; William N. Fenton, "This Island, the World on the Turtle's Back," *Journal of American Folklore* 75 (October–December 1962): 283–300; Dean R. Snow, *The Iroquois* (Malden, MA: Blackwell, 1994), 3–4; Daniel P. Barr, *Unconquered: The Iroquois League at War in Colonial America* (Westport, CT: Praeger, 2006), 3.

4.   George Bird Grinnell, "Pawnee Mythology," *Journal of American Folklore* 6 (April–June 1893): 114–30.

5.   James Mooney, *Myths of the Cherokee* (Washington, DC: Government Printing Office, 1902), 240.

6.   Richard Erdoes and Alfonso Ortiz, ed., *American Indian Myths and Legends* (New York: Pantheon, 1984), 496–99 ("Now," 498–99).

7.   Scott Momaday, *The Way to the Rainy Mountain* (Albuquerque: University of New Mexico Press, 1969), 17.

8.   Louise Lamphere, "Symbolic Elements in Navajo Ritual," *Southwestern Journal of Anthropology* 25 (Autumn 1969): 279–305; Gladys A. Reichard, "Distinctive Features of Navaho Religion," *Southwestern Journal of Anthropology* 1 (Summer 1946): 210–13; Gary Witherspoon, "The Central Concepts of Navajo World View," *Linguistics* 12, no. 119 (1974): 41–60; Gary Witherspoon, *Navajo Kinship and Marriage* (Chicago: University of Chicago Press, 1975), 15–22, 68–69.

9.   Alice Beck Kehoe, *North America before the European Invasions* (New York: Longman, 2002), 9; Robert N. Zeitlin and Judith Francis Zeitlin, "The Paleoindian and Archaic Cultures of Mesoamerica," in *The Cambridge History of the Native Peoples of the Americas*, vol. 2, *Mesoamerica*, ed. Richard E. Adams and Murdo J. MacLeod (New York: Cambridge University Press, 2000), 45–121, esp. 51–53.

10. Vine Deloria Jr., *Red Earth, White Lies: Native Americans and the Myth of Scientific Fact* (New York: Scribner, 1995); Mathias vom Hau and Guillermo Wilde, "'We Have Always Lived Here': Indigenous Movements, Citizenship and Poverty in Argentina," *Journal of Development Studies* 46, no. 7 (2010): 1283–1303; Erdoes and Ortiz, ed., *American Indian Myths and Legends*, xiv. For a forceful argument of the centrality of land in American history, see Roxanne Dunbar-Ortiz, *An Indigenous Peoples' History of the United States* (Boston: Beacon Press, 2014).

11. Clark Wissler and D. C. Duvall, *Mythology of the Blackfoot Indians*, Anthropological Papers of the American Museum of Natural History, vol. 2, pt. 1 (New York: The Trustees, 1908), 121–33; Donald K. Grayson and David J. Meltzer, "A Requiem for North American Overkill," *Journal of Archaeological Science* 30 (May 2003): 585–93; Jacquelyn L. Gill, John W. Williams, Stephen T. Jackson, Katherine B. Lininger, and Guy S. Robinson, "Pleistocene Megafaunal Collapse, Novel Plant Communities, and Enhanced Fire Regimes in North America," *Science* 326, no. 5956 (November 2009): 1100–1103; Gary Haynes, ed., *American Megafaunal Extinctions at the End of the Pleistocene* (New York: Springer, 2009).

12. Jeff M. Martin, Jim I. Mead, and Perry S. Barboza, "Bison Body Size and Climate Change," *Ecology and Evolution*, May 2018, 4564–74; Stuart J. Fiedel, *Prehistory of the Americas*, 2nd ed. (Cambridge: University of Cambridge Press, 1992), 143–46.

13. Fiedel, *Prehistory of the Americas*, 66; J. E. McClellan III and H. Dorn, *Science and Technology in World History* (Baltimore: Johns Hopkins University Press, 2006), 11; John C. Whittaker, Devin B. Pettigrew, and Ryan J. Grohsmeyer, "Atlatl Dart Velocity: Accurate Measurements and Implications for Paleoindian and Archaic Archaeology," *PaleoAmerica* 3, no. 2 (2017): 161–81.

14. Kehoe, *North American Indians*, 403.

15. Joshua L. Reid, *The Sea Is My Country: The Maritime World of the Makahs, an Indigenous Borderlands People* (New Haven, CT: Yale University Press, 2015), 4–12; Steven W. Hackel, *Children of Coyote, Missionaries of Saint Francis: Indian-Spanish Relations in Colonial California, 1769–1850* (Chapel Hill: University of North Carolina Press, 2005), 17–20; Colin Calloway, *One Vast Winter Count: The Native American West before Lewis and Clark* (Lincoln: University of Nebraska Press, 2003), 45–50; Kehoe, *North American Indians*, 429–34.

16. Kehoe, *North American Indians*, 434–57; Allan Greer, "Commons and Enclosure in the Colonization of North America," *AHR* 117, no. 2 (April 2012): 370.

CHAPTER 2: THE EGALITARIAN CONTINENT

1. J. M. J. De Wet, J. R. Harlan, and C. A. Grant, "Origin and Evolution of Teosinte (*Zea mexicana* [Schrad.] Kuntze.)," *Euphytica* 20, no. 2 (1971): 255–65; Andrew Sluyter and Gabriela Dominguez, "Early Maize (*Zea mays* L.)," *PNAS* 103 (January 2006): 1147–51.

2. D. R. Piperno and K. V. Flannery, "The Earliest Archaeological Maize (*Zea mays* L.) from Highland Mexico: New Accelerator Mass Spectrometry Dates and Theory Implications," *PNAS* 98 (February 2001): 2101–3; Robert M. Rosenswig, "Sedentism and Food Production in Early Complex Societies of the Soconusco, Mexico," *World Archaeology* 38 (June 2006): 330–55.

3. Steadman Upham, Richard S. MacNeish, Walton C. Galinat, and Christopher M. Stevenson, "Evidence concerning the Origin of Maiz de Ocho," *American Anthropologist* 89 (June 1987): 410–19.

4. J. H. Garrison Wilkes, "Maize and Its Wild Relatives," *Science* 177 (September 1972): 1071–77; M. Jensen, "Native American Women and Agriculture: A Seneca Case Study," *Sex Roles* 3, no. 5 (1977): 423–41; C. Margaret Scarry, "Crop Husbandry Practices in North America's Eastern Woodlands," in *Case Studies in Environmental Archaeology*, ed. Elizabeth Reitz, C. Margaret Scarry, and Sylvia J. Scudder (New York: Springer, 2008), 391–404.

5. Paul S. Martin, "Prehistory: Mogollon," in *Southwest*, ed. Alfonso Ortiz, vol. 9 of *Handbook of North American Indians*, ed. William Sturtevant (Washington, DC: Smithsonian Institution, 1979), 61–74; George J. Gumerman and Emil W. Haury, "Prehistory: Hohokam," in *Southwest*, ed. Ortiz, 75–90; Suzanne K. Fish and Paul R. Fish, "Prehistoric Landscapes of the Sonoran Desert Hohokam," *Population and Environment* 13 (Summer 1992), 269–83; *BR*, 15–17; Thomas C. Windes and Dabney Ford, "The Chaco Wood Project: The Chronometric Reappraisal of Pueblo Bonito," *American Antiquity* 61 (April 1996): 295–310.

6. Kevin Rafferty, "The Virgin Anasazi and the Pan-southwestern Trade System, A.D. 900–1150," *Kiva* 56, no. 1 (1990): 324; Timothy A. Kohler and Kathryn Kramer Turner, "Raiding for Women in the Pre-Hispanic Northern Pueblo Southwest?" *Current Anthropology* 47 (December 2006): 1035–45; Alice B. Kehoe, *North American Indians: A Comprehensive Account*, 2nd ed. (Englewood Cliffs, NJ: Prentice Hall, 1992), 120–22; Amanda J. Landon, "The 'How' of the Three Sisters: The Ori-

gins of Agriculture Mesoamerica and the Human Niche," *Nebraska Anthropologist* 40 (2008): 110–24; *BR*, 19–20.

7.   Carrie Heitman, "Houses Great and Small: Reevaluating the 'House' in Chaco Canyon, New Mexico," in *The Durable House: House Society Models in Archaeology*, ed. Robin A. Beck Jr., Occasional Paper 35 (Carbondale, IL: Center for Archaeological Investigations, Southern Illinois University), 248–72.

8.   Jon L. Gibson, *The Ancient Mounds of Poverty Point: A Place of Rings* (Gainesville: University Press of Florida, 2001); Jenny Ellerbe and Siena M. Greenlee, *Poverty Point: Revealing the Forgotten City* (Baton Rouge: Louisiana State University Press, 2015).

9.   Sarah E. Baires, "Cahokia's Rattlesnake Causeway," *Midcontinental Journal of Archeology* 39, no. 2 (2014): 145–62.

10. The literature on Cahokia is vast and growing. I relied especially on Sarah E. Baires, *Land of Water, City of the Dead: Religion and Cahokia's Emergence* (Tuscaloosa: University of Alabama Press, 2017); Timothy R. Pauketat, *Cahokia: Ancient America's Great City on the Mississippi* (New York: Viking, 2009); and Biloine Whiting Young and Melvin L. Flower, *Cahokia: The Great Native American Metropolis* (Urbana: University of Illinois Press, 2000).

11. Young and Fowler, *Cahokia*, 192; Mary Beth D. Trubitt, "Mound Building and Prestige Goods Exchange: Changing Strategies in the Cahokia," *American Antiquity* 65 (October 2000): 669–90; Kathryn M. Koziol, "Performances of Imposed Status: Captivity in Cahokia," in *Bioarchaeology of Violence*, ed. Debra L. Martin, Ryan P. Harrod, and Ventura R. Pérez (Gainesville: University Press of Florida, 2012), 227–28; Samuel E. Munoz, Kristine E. Gruley, Ashtin Massie, David A. Fike, Sissel Schroeder, and John W. Williams, "Cahokia's Emergence and Decline Coincided with Shifts of Flood Frequency on the Mississippi River," *PNAS* 112 (May 2015): 6319–24; Larry V. Benson, Timothy R. Pauketat, and Edward R. Cook, "Cahokia's Boom and Bust in the Context of Climate Change," *American Antiquity* 74 (July 2009): 467–83. For the Little Ice Age in general, see Brian Fagan, *The Little Ice Age: How Climate Made History, 1300–1850*, rev. ed. (New York: Basic Books, 2019).

12. Ruth M. Van Dyke, "Memory, Meaning, and Masonry: The Late Bonito Chacoan Landscape," *American Antiquity* 69 (July 2004): 423–27; Nancy M. Mahoney, Michael A. Adler, and James W. Kendrick, "The Changing Scale and Configuration of Mesa Verde Communities," *Kiva*, Fall 2000, 67–90; Julie Zimmermann Holt, "Rethinking the Ramey State: Was Cahokia the Center of a Theater State?" *American Antiquity* 74 (April 2009): 231–54.

13. *BR*, 30–31; Lynn S. Teague, "Prehistory and the Traditions of the O'Odham and Hopi," *Kiva* 58, no. 4 (1993): 435–54; Don Watson, *Indians of the Mesa Verde* (Ann Arbor, MI: Cushing Malloy, 1953), 136.

14. Paul E. Minnis and Michael E. Whalen, *Discovering Paquimé* (Tucson: University of Arizona Press, 2016), 23–52; Dean R. Snow, *Archaeology of Native North America* (New York: Routledge, 2009), 123.

15. Kehoe, *North American Indians*, 124–26; Richard E. W. Adams, *Prehistoric Mesoamerica* (Norman: University of Oklahoma Press, 1991), 301–7; Jorge E. Hardoy, *Pre-Columbian Cities* (London: Routledge, 1973), 58; Terence N. D'Altroy, *The Incas* (Chichester, UK: Wiley, 2014), 174–76; Robert J. Sharer, *Maya Civilization* (Westport, CT: Greenwood, 2009), 100–107.

16. Celina Campbell and Ian D. Campbell, "The Little Ice Age and Neutral Faunal Assemblages, *Ontario Archaeology* 49 (1989): 13–33; Sam White, *A Cold Welcome: The Little Ice Age and Europe* (Cambridge, MA: Harvard University Press,

2017), 109–31; David Wishart, *An Unspeakable Sadness: The Dispossession of the Nebraska Indians* (Lincoln: University of Nebraska Press, 1994), 4; Elizabeth A. Fenn, *Encounters at the Heart of the World: A History of the Mandan People* (New York: Hill and Wang, 2014), 8–26; Colin Calloway, *One Vast Winter Count: The Native American West before Lewis and Clark* (Lincoln: University of Nebraska Press, 2003), 109–10; *BR*, 30–36; Geoff Cunfer, "The Decline and Fall of the Bison Empire," in *Bison and People on the North American Great Plains: A Deep Environmental History*, ed. Geoff Cunfer and Bill Waiser (College Station: Texas A&M University Press, 2016), 8–9; Dan Flores, "Reviewing the Iconic Story: Environmental History and Demise of the Bison," in *Bison and People on the North American Great Plains*, 39.

17. Liz Bryan, *The Buffalo People: Pre-contact Archaeology on the Canadian Plains* (Surrey, BC: Heritage House, 2005), 69; Beth R. Ritter, "Piecing Together the Ponca Past: Reconstructing Degiha Migrations to the Great Plains," *Great Plains Quarterly* 22 (Fall 2002): 271–84; Elliott West, *The Contested Plains: Indians, Goldseekers, and the Rush to Colorado* (Lawrence: University Press of Kansas, 1998), 36–41; George Bird Grinnell, *Blackfoot Lodge Tales: The Story of a Prairie People* (Lincoln: University of Nebraska Press, 1962), 228; Jack W. Brink, *Imagining Head-Smashed-In: Aboriginal Buffalo Hunting on the Northern Plains* (Edmonton, AL: Athabasca University Press, 2008).

18. Benjamin Madley, "Reexamining the American Genocide Debate: Meaning, Historiography, and New Methods," *AHR* 120 (February 2015): 98–99.

CHAPTER 3: BLIND CONQUESTS

1. Brian Fagan, *The Little Ice Age: How Climate Made History, 1300–1850*, rev. ed. (New York: Basic Books, 2019); Philip Blom, *Nature's Mutiny: How the Little Ice Age of the Long Seventeenth Century Transformed the West* (New York: Liveright, 2019); Chris Wickham, *Framing the Middle Ages: Europe and the Mediterranean, 400–800* (Oxford: Oxford University Press, 2005); Peter Brown, *The World of the Late Antiquity, AD 150–750* (London: Thames & Hudson, 1971; repr., New York: W. W. Norton, 1989); Gerald A. J. Hodgett, *A Social and Economic History of Medieval Europe* (London: Methuen, 1972), 185–98; *BR*, 38–41.

2. For the rise of fiscal military states, see Charles Tilly, *Coercion, Capital, and European States, AD 990–1992* (Malden, MA: Blackwell, 1990); and Geoffrey Parker, *The Military Revolution: Military Innovation and the Rise of the West, 1500–1800*, 2nd ed. (Cambridge: Cambridge University Press, 1990), 16–44.

3. For a small selection of key works, see Fernand Braudel, *Civilization and Capitalism, 15th–18th Century*, vol. 2, *The Wheels of Commerce* (Berkeley: University of California Press, 1992); J. H. Elliott, *Spain, Europe and the Wider World 1500–1800* (New Haven, CT: Yale University Press, 2009); and Joseph F. O'Callaghan, *Reconquest and Crusade in Medieval Spain* (Philadelphia: University of Pennsylvania Press, 2003).

4. J. H. Parry, *The Spanish Seaborne Empire* (Berkeley: University of California Press, 1966), 39–42; Alfred W. Crosby, *Ecological Imperialism: The Biological Expansion of Europe, 900–1900* (New York: Cambridge University Press, 1986), 70–92; John E. Kicza, "Patterns in Early Spanish Overseas Expansion," *WMQ* 49 (April 1992): 233–38.

5. Henry Vignaug, *Toscanelli and Columbus: The Letter and Chart of Toscanelli on the Route to the Indies by Way of the West, Sent in 1474 to the Portuguese, Fernam Martins, and Later On to Christopher Columbus* (New York: E. P. Dutton, 1902); Carl Ortwin Sauer, *The Early Spanish Main* (Berkeley: University of Califor-

nia Press, 1966), 12–16 ("from successor," 16); Gene Rhea Tucker, "Place-Names, Conquest, and Empire: Spanish and Amerindian Conceptions of Place in the New World" (PhD dissertation, University of Texas at Arlington, 2011), 101–10; J. H. Elliott, *Imperial Spain, 1469–1716* (London: Edward Arnold, 1963), 45–76.

6.   Andrés Reséndez, *The Other Slavery: The Uncovered Story of Indian Enslavement in America* (Boston: Houghton Mifflin Harcourt, 2016), 35–36; Samuel Eliot Morison, *Admiral of the Ocean Sea: A Life of Christopher Columbus* (1942; repr., New York: Little, Brown, 1991), esp. 33–34, 63–65, 183–286.

7.   Crosby, *Ecological Imperialism*, 100; Morison, *Admiral of the Ocean Sea*, 389–494; Sauer, *Early Spanish Main*, 23–35, 71; Jace Weaver, "The Red Atlantic: Transoceanic Cultural Exchanges," *American Indian Quarterly* 35 (Summer 2011): 426.

8.   Sam White, *A Cold Welcome: The Little Ice Age and Europe* (Cambridge, MA: Harvard University Press, 2017), 9–10; Molly A. Walsh, "Enslaved Pearl Divers in the Sixteenth Century Caribbean," *Slavery and Abolition* 31 (September 2010): 345–62; Kicza, "Patterns," 243. For population decline, see Massimo Livi-Bacci, "The Depopulation of Hispanic America after the Conquest," *Population and Development Review* 32 (June 2006): 199–232; Russell Thornton, *American Indian Holocaust and Survival: A Population History since 1492* (Norman: University of Oklahoma Press, 1987), 3–47; D. S. Jones, "Virgin Soils Revisited," *WMQ* 60 (October 2003): 703–42.

9.   *SA*, 1:8–9.

10.   James Lockhart, *Spanish Peru: A Colonial Society, 1532–1560* (Madison: University of Wisconsin Press, 1968), 13–37; John Hemming, *The Conquest of the Incas* (New York: Harcourt, 1970); Timothy J. Yaeger, "Encomienda or Slavery? The Spanish Crown's Choice of Labor Organization in Sixteenth-Century Spanish America," *Journal of Economic History* 55 (December 1995): 842–49; Hugh Thomas, *Conquest: Cortes, Montezuma, and the Fall of Old Mexico* (New York: Simon and Schuster, 1993), 175–250, 358; Ross Hassig, *Mexico and the Spanish Conquest*, 2nd ed. (Norman: University of Oklahoma Press, 2006), esp. 65–124.

11.   Alfred W. Crosby Jr., *The Columbian Exchange: Biological and Cultural Consequences of 1492* (Westport, CT: Greenwood, 1972); Elliott, *Imperial Spain*, 77–163; *SA*, 1:11–17; Timothy R. Walton, *The Spanish Treasure Fleets* (Sarasota, FL: Pineapple, 1994).

12.   Andrés Reséndez, *A Land So Strange: The Epic Journey of Cabeza de Vaca* (New York: Basic Books, 2007), 21–23; Bartolomé de las Casas, *A Short Account of the Destruction of the Indies*, trans. and ed. Nigel Griffin (New York: Penguin, 1992), 14.

CHAPTER 4: TERRA NULLIUS

1.   *SFNA*, 33–34; John L. Kessell, *Spain in the Southwest: A Narrative History of Colonial New Mexico, Arizona, Texas, and California* (Norman: University of Oklahoma Press, 2002), 4–13; T. Frederick Davis, "Ponce de Leon's Second Voyage and Attempt to Colonize Florida," *Florida Historical Society Quarterly* 14 (July 1935): 55; Patricia Seed, *Ceremonies of Possession in Europe's Conquest of the New World, 1492–1640* (New York: Cambridge University Press, 1995), 13.

2.   John H. Hann, "Political Leadership among the Natives of Spanish Florida," *Florida Historical Quarterly* 71 (October 1992): 188–93; Jane Landers, "Social Control on Spain's Contested Frontier," in *Choice, Persuasion, and Coercion: Social Control on Spain's North American Frontiers*, ed. Jesús F. de la Teja and Ross Frank (Albuquerque: University of New Mexico Press, 2005), 27; Victor D. Thompson, Michael H.

Marquardt, Michael Savarese, Karen J. Walker, Lee A. Newson, Isabelle Lulewich, Nathan R. Lawres, Amanda D. Roberts Thompson, Allan R. Bacon, and Christopher A. Walser, "Ancient Engineering of Fish capture in Southwest Florida," *PNAS* 117 (April 2020): 8374–81; *SFNA*, 34; *NWA*, 33.

3. Andrés Reséndez, *The Other Slavery: The Uncovered Story of Indian Enslavement in America* (Boston: Houghton Mifflin Harcourt, 2016), 16, 40–45.

4. Russell Thornton, *American Indian Holocaust and Survival: A Population History since 1492* (Norman: University of Oklahoma Press, 1987), 65.

5. Andrés Reséndez, *A Land So Strange: The Epic Journey of Cabeza de Vaca* (New York: Basic Books, 2007), 43–48; *SFNA*, 42–43.

6. Reséndez, *Land So Strange*, 64, 76–110.

7. Reséndez, *Land So Strange*, 91–102.

8. Álvar Núñez Cabeza de Vaca, *Relation of Alvar Núñez Cabeza de Vaca*, trans. Buckingham Smith (Albany, NY: J. Munsell, 1871), 38 ("continual").

9. Cabeza de Vaca, *Relation*, 39 ("appear"); Reséndez, *Land So Strange*, 103–6, 111–31, 133–67.

10. Reséndez, *Land So Strange*, 133–67.

11. George Parker Winship, "The Coronado Expedition, 1540–1542," in *The Fourteenth Annual Report of the Bureau of Ethnology* (Washington, DC: Government Printing Office, 1896), 351–52; *SA*, 1:87.

12. Percy M. Baldwin, "Fray Marcos de Niza and His Discovery of the Seven Cities of Cibola," *New Mexico Historical Review* 1, no. 2 (April 1926): 193–223 ("Our Lord," "no one," 217); *SFNA*, 45–46; "Vázquez de Coronado's Letter to the King, October 20, 1541," in *Documents of the Coronado Expedition, 1539–1542: "They Were Not Familiar with His Majesty, nor Did They Wish to Be His Subjects"*, ed. and trans. Richard Flint and Shirley Cushing Flint (Albuquerque: University of New Mexico Press, 2005), doc. 26 ("grander towns," "ate out of").

13. "Vázquez de Coronado's Letter to the Viceroy, August 3, 1540," in *Documents of the Coronado Expedition, 1539–1542*, ed. and trans. Flint and Flint, doc. 19 ("This"); *SFNA*, 46–48.

14. George Parker Winship, trans. and ed., *The Journey of Coronado, 1540–1542* (New York: A. S. Barnes, 1904), 226–36, 243 ("fishes as big," "under a great tree," 243); *NWA*, 93–94; Richard Flint, "Juan Troyano, the Eighth *de Oficio* Witness," in Flint, *Great Cruelties Have Been Reported: The 1544 Investigation of the Coronado Expedition* (Albuquerque: University of New Mexico Press, 2002), 169–73; George P. Hammond and Agapito Rey, eds. and trans., *Narratives of the Coronado Expedition* (Albuquerque: University of New Mexico Press, 1940), 1:189 ("to a place").

15. *SFNA*, 49.

16. Alfred W. Crosby, *Ecological Imperialism: The Biological Expansion of Europe, 900–1900* (New York: Cambridge University Press, 1986), 71–103; John E. Kicza, "Patterns in Early Spanish Overseas Expansion," *WMQ* 49 (April 1992): 229–53; Heather Miyano Kopelson, "Women, Gender, Families, and States," in *Cambridge History of America and the World*, ed. Eliga Gould, Paul Mapp, and Carla Gardina Pestana (New York: Cambridge University Press, 2021), 444–45.

17. Barnard Ship, *The History of DeSoto and Florida: Or, Record of Fifty-Six Years, from 1512–1568* (Philadelphia: Robert M. Lindsay, 1851), 287–97, 608 ("the son of the sun," 608); James F. Barnett, *The Natchez Indians* (Jackson: University Press of Mississippi, 2007), 3–5; Ann F. Ramenofsky, *Vectors of Death: The Archaeology of European Contact* (Albuquerque: University of New Mexico Press, 1987), 7; Robin A. Beck, *Chiefdoms, Collapse, Coalescence in the Early American South*

(Cambridge: Cambridge University Press, 2013), 23, 66; *NWA*, 95; Jon T. Coleman, *Nature Shock: Getting Lost in America* (New Haven, CT: Yale University Press, 2020), 14–19.

18. Juliana Barr, "There's No Such Thing as 'Prehistory': What the Longue Durée of Caddo and Pueblo History Tells Us about Colonial America," *WMQ* 74 (April 2017): 208–10; Timothy K. Perttula, *The Caddo Nation: Archaeological and Ethnohistoric Perspectives* (Austin: University of Texas Press, 1992), 85. There are no exact sources on Pueblo population, and "hundred thousand" comes from John Kessell, email to the author, June 21–22, 2020. Also see Ann M. Malkovich, "Historic Population of the Eastern Pueblos: 1540–1910," *Journal of Anthropological Research* 41 (Winter 1985): 401–26.

19. *SFNA*, 80–81; "The Articles of Agreement Which the Viceroy, Don Luís de Velasco, Made with Don Juan de Oñate, Governor and Captain-General of the Provinces of New Mexico," in *Historical Documents Relating to New Mexico, Nueva Vizcaya, and Approaches Thereto, to 1773*, ed. Charles W. Hackett (Washington, DC: Carnegie Institution, 1923–37), 1:273; Ramón A. Gutiérrez, *When Jesus Came, the Corn Mothers Went Away: Marriage, Sexuality, and Power in New Mexico, 1500–1846* (Stanford, CA: Stanford University Press, 1991), xxiii; George Peter Hammond and Agapito Rey, "Act of Taking Possession of New Mexico," in Hammond and Rey, *Don Juan de Oñate, Colonizer of New Mexico, 1595–1628* (Albuquerque: University of New Mexico Press, 1953), 1:335 ("from the leaves"); Kessell, *Spain in the Southwest*, 75–80. For *Requirimiento*, see Seed, *Ceremonies of Possession*, 69–72, 96–97.

20. Hammond and Rey, *Don Juan de Oñate*, 1:470 ("Castilian whoremongers"); "Relation of Provinces Discovered in the Year 1598 by Don Juan de Oñate, Governor of the Provinces of New Mexico," in *New Mexico in 1602: Juan de Montoya's Relation of the Discovery of New Mexico*, ed. George P. Hammond and Agapito Rey (Albuquerque, NM: Quivira Society, 1938), 44–47 ("this offence," 47); *SFNA*, 84–86; Kessell, *Spain in the Southwest*, 80–81; Nan A. Rothschild, *Colonial Encounters in a Native American Landscape* (Washington, DC: Smithsonian Institution, 2003), 54.

21. Hammond and Rey, *Narratives of the Coronado Expedition*, 1:459 ("If you").

22. Marc Simmons, *The Last Conquistador: Juan de Oñate and the Settling of the Far Southwest* (Norman: University of Oklahoma Press, 1991), 179–80; John L. Kessell, *Kiva, Cross, and Crown: The Pecos Indians and New Mexico, 1540–1840* (Washington, DC: National Park Service, 1979), 85.

23. *SFNA*, 82.

CHAPTER 5: THE POWHATAN EMPIRE

1. Frederick A. Ober, *John and Sebastian Cabot* (New York: Harper, 1908), 101 ("so great," "they sometimes"); *SA*, 1:50.

2. Rainer Baehre, "Newfoundland's West Coast and the Gulf of St. Lawrence Fishery, ca. 1755–83," in *The Greater Gulf: Essays on the Environmental History of the Gulf of St. Lawrence*, ed. Claire Elizabeth Campbell, Edward MacDonald, and Brian Payne (Montreal, QC: McGill-Queen's University Press, 2019), 71–73.

3. Samuel Eliot Morison, *The Great Explorers: The European Discovery of America* (New York: Oxford University Press, 1978), 94–96; Bruce M. Trigger, *Natives and Newcomers: Canada's "Heroic Age" Reconsidered* (Montreal, QC: McGill-Queen's University Press, 1985), 124.

4. *SA*, 1:50–51, 56–57; David Hackett Fischer, *Champlain's Dream: The European Founding of North America* (New York: Simon and Schuster, 2008), 112–13; James

H. Merrell, "'The Customes of Our Countrey': Indians and Colonists in Early America," in *Strangers within the Realm: Cultural Margins of the First British Empire*, ed. Bernard Bailyn and Philip D. Morgan (Chapel Hill: University of North Carolina Press, 1991), 121; *Dictionary of Canadian Biography*, s.v. "Donnacona," accessed March 28, 2020, http://www.biographi.ca/en/bio/donnacona_1E.html.

5. André Vachon, *Dreams of Empire: Canada before 1700*, trans. John F. Flinn (Ottawa, ON: Public Archives of Canada, 1982), 23, plate 7 ("all mainlands," "did not dare"), courtesy of Public Records Office, London, England: Chancery, Warrants for the Great Seal, ser. 2, C 82/146, no. 6; *SA*, 1:51, 55.

6. *BR*, 95; Benjamin Woolley, *Savage Kingdom: Virginia and the Founding of English America* (London: Harper Press, 2007), 8 ("wicked Lutheran sect"); "Francisco López de Mendoza Grájales's Account of the Conquest of Florida, 1565," in *Interpreting a Continent: Voices from Colonial America*, ed. Kathleen DuVal and John DuVal (Lanham, MD: Rowman & Littlefield, 2009), 233–40 ("being Lutherans," 240). For land as a commodity, see Daniel K. Richter, *Facing East from Indian Country: A Native History of Early America* (Cambridge, MA: Harvard University Press, 2001), 54–55.

7. Trigger, *Natives and Newcomers*, 127; David Childs, *Invading America: The English Assault on the New World, 1497–1630* (Barnsley, UK: Seaforth, 2012), 192–94; Jane Landers, "Social Control on Spain's Contested Frontier," in *Choice, Persuasion, and Coercion: Social Control on Spain's North American Frontiers*, ed. Jesús F. de la Teja and Ross Frank (Albuquerque: University of New Mexico Press, 2005), 27–30; Charles E. Bennett, "A Copy of a Letter Coming from Florida, Sent to Rouen and Then to M. D'Everon, Together with the Plan and Picture of the Fort Which the French Built There [1564]," and "Description of the Land and Sea Animals and Monstrous Beasts Encountered on the Island of Florida," in Bennett, *Laudonnière & Fort Caroline: History and Documents* (Tuscaloosa: University of Alabama Press, 2001), 70–74 ("the latest," "prodigious," 74).

8. *SFNA*, 60–75; Sarah M. S. Pearsall, "'Having Many Wives' in Two American Rebellions: The Politics of Households and the Radically Conservative," *AHR* 118 (October 2013): 1001–2, 1011–14; Robert Allen Matter, "Missions in the Defense of Spanish Florida, 1566–1710," *Florida Historical Quarterly* 54 (July 1975): 19–20; J. Michael Francis and Kathleen M. Kole, *Murder and Martyrdom in Spanish Florida: Don Juan and the Guale Uprising of 1597*, American Museum of Natural History Anthropological Papers 95 ([New York]: American Museum of Natural History, 2011), https://core.ac.uk/download/pdf/18228437.pdf.

9. Nicholas Canny, "Origins of Empire: An Introduction," in *Origins of Empire: British Overseas Enterprise to the Close of the Seventeenth Century*, ed. Canny, Oxford History of the British Empire, vol. 1 (New York: Oxford University Press, 1998), 3–4; Anthony Padgen, "The Struggle for Legitimacy and the Image of Empire in the Atlantic to c. 1700," in *Origins of Empire*, 51; Richard Hakluyt, *A Discourse concerning Western Planting*, ed. Leonard Woods (1584; repr., Cambridge: John Wilson, 1877), 48, 95, 154, 158 ("upon the mouths," 95; "the Spanishe King," 154; "enlarge the glory," "plant sincere religion," 158); Timothy Sweet, "Economy, Ecology, and Utopia in Early Colonial Promotional Literature," *American Literature* 71 (September 1999): 399–427.

10. Arthur Barlowe, *The First Voyage Made to the Coasts of America, with Two Barks, Wherein Were Captains M. Philip Amadas and M. Arthur Barlowe, Who Discovered Part of the Country Now Called Virginia, Anno 1584. Written by One of the Said Captaines, and Sent to Sir Walter Ralegh, Knight, at Whose Charge and Direc-*

tion, the Said Voyage Was Set Forth (1584; repr., Boston: Directors of the Old South Work, 1898), 4–5 ("The manner," "hee never,"4; "would defend," 5).

11. Nicholas P. Canny, "The Ideology of English Colonization: From Ireland to America," *WMQ* 30 (October 1973): 575–98; John Locke, *Second Treatise of Government*, ed. C. B. Macpherson (1778; repr., Indianapolis, IN: Hackett, 1980), 36, 311 ("vacant places," 311); Andrew Lipman, *The Saltwater Frontier: Indians and the Contest for the American Coast* (New Haven, CT: Yale University Press, 2015), 35–37.

12. Michael Leroy Oberg, *The Head in Edward Nugent's Hand: Roanoke's Forgotten Indians* (Philadelphia: University of Pennsylvania Press, 2008), 57–73 ("very fast," 73); David J. Silverman, *Red Brethren: The Brothertown and Stockbridge Indians and the Problem of Race in Early America* (Ithaca, NY: Connell University Press, 2010), 13; Karen Ordahl Kupperman, *Roanoke: The Abandoned Colony*, 2nd ed. (Lanham, MD: Lowman & Littlefield, 2007), 71–86.

13. Kathleen Donegan, *Seasons of Misery: Catastrophe and Colonial Settlement in Early America* (Philadelphia: University of Pennsylvania Press, 2014), 21–68; Childs, *Invading America*, 68–71; Oberg, *Head in Edward Nugent's Hand*, 81–100, 113; Andrew Lawner, "It Was America's First English Colony. Then It Was Gone," *National Geographic*, June 2018, https://www.nationalgeographic.com/magazine/2018/06/lost-colony-roanoke-history-theories-croatoan; David B. Quinn, *Set Fair for Roanoke: Voyages and Colonies* (Chapel Hill: University of North Carolina Press, 1985), 368–75.

14. *SFNA*, 75. For mercantilism, see Mark Blaug, *The Early Mercantilists: Thomas Mun, 1571–1641, Edward Misselden, 1608–1634, and Gerard De Malynes, 1586–1623* (Cheltenham, UK: Edward Elgar, 1991); John P. Appleby, "War, Politics, and Colonization, 1558–1625," in *Origins of Empire*, ed. Nicholas Canny, 65.

15. Helen C. Rountree, *Pocahontas, Powhatan, Opechancanough: Three Indian Lives Changed by Jamestown* (Charlottesville: University of Virginia Press, 2005), 53–60; Alan Taylor, *American Colonies* (New York: Viking, 2001), 136. For the broader Powhatan world and knowledge of colonial powers and intrusions, see Charlotte M. Gradie, "The Powhatans and the Spanish Empire," in *Powhatan Foreign Relations, 1500–1722*, ed. Helen C. Rountree (Charlottesville: University Press of Virginia, 1993), 154–72. For a forceful argument on water-based colonialism, see Lauren A. Benton, *A Search for Sovereignty: Law and Geography in European Empires* (New York: Cambridge University Press, 2010). For the performative dimension of Powhatan warfare, see Frederic W. Gleach, *Powhatan's World and Colonial Virginia: A Conflict of Cultures* (Lincoln: University of Nebraska Press, 1997), 43–54; George R. Stewart, *Names on the Land: A Historical Account of Place-Naming in the United States* (New York: Random House, 1945), 23 ("at a big river").

16. Helen C. Rountree, *Pocahontas's People: The Powhatan Indians of Virginia through Four Centuries* (Norman: University of Oklahoma Press, 1990), 3–28; Gleach, *Powhatan's World and Colonial Virginia*, 33; NWA, 95–96; Patricia Seed, *Ceremonies of Possession in Europe's Conquest of the New World, 1492–1640* (New York: Cambridge University Press, 1995), 16–23; John Smith, *The Generall Historie of Virginia, New England and the Summer Isles with the Names of the Adventurers, Planters, Governours from Their First Beginning Anno: 1584 to This Present 1624* (London: I. D. and I. H., 1629), 1:37–38 ("the form," 37; "is a law," 38); Martin D. Gallivan, "Powhatan's Werowocomoco: Constructing Place, Polity, and Personhood in the Chesapeake, C.E. 1200–C.E. 1609," *American Anthropologist* 109 (March 2007): 85–100; Helen C. Rountree and E. Randolph Turner, "The Evolution of the

Powhatan Paramount Chiefdom in Virginia," in *Chiefdoms and Chieftaincy in the Americas*, ed. E. M. Redmond (Gainesville: University Press of Florida, 1998), 265–96; James Axtell, "The Rise and Fall of the Powhatan Empire," in Axtell, *After Columbus: Essays in the Ethnohistory of Colonial North America* (New York: Oxford University Press, 1988), 189; Ethan A. Schmidt, "Cockacoeske, Weroansqua of the Pamunkeys, and Indian Resistance in Seventeenth-Century Virginia," *American Indian Quarterly* 36 (Summer 2012): 292–94, 297–98. There have been numerous views on how to label the Powhatan regime. See Gleach, *Powhatan's World and Colonial Virginia*, 22–24. The Powhatans were led by powerful mamanatowicks, who commanded a web of towns, many of them forcefully subjugated, and "empire" seems the most accurate term. For Powhatan's ambitions, see *BR*, 125.

17. Camilla Townsend, *Pocahontas and the Powhatan Dilemma* (New York: Hill and Wang, 2004), 52–60; Rountree, *Pocahontas, Powhatan, Opechancanough*, 113–14; John Smith, *A True Relation of Virginia* (1608; repr., Boston: I. Tappe, 1606), 66–73 ("how well," 73); Helen C. Rountree, "Powhatan Indian Women: The People Captain John Smith Barely Saw," *Ethnohistory* 45 (Winter 1998): 1–29; *BR*, 125–26.

18. Smith, *Generall Historie*, 35 ("three great"); Captain John Smith, *Travels, History of Virginia: The True Travels, Adventures and Observations of Captain John Smith* (Cambridge 1908; rpt. 2011), 117 ("upon the top," "neare sixty foot"). For the saltiness of the James River and the Chesapeake Bay, see Charles C. Mann, *1493: How Europe's Discovery of the Americas Revolutionized Trade, Ecology and Life on Earth* (London: Granta, 2011), 45; and Carville V. Earle, "Environment, Disease, and Mortality in Early Virginia," in *The Chesapeake in the Seventeenth Century: Essays on Anglo-American Society*, ed. Thad W. Tate and David L. Ammerman (Chapel Hill: University of North Carolina Press, 1979), 96–122.

19. John Smith, *A Description of New-England* (London: Humfrey Lownes, for Robert Clerke, 1616), 17; Smith, *Generall Historie*, 31, 44 ("to be seen," 31; "Our drink," 44).

20. James P. P. Horn, *A Land as God Made It: Jamestown and the Birth of America* (New York: Basic Books, 2005), 189–90; Smith, *Generall Historie*, 53 ("There was"); Allan Greer, "Commons and Enclosure in the Colonization of North America," *AHR* 117 (April 2012): 372–73; Helen C. Rountree, "The Powhatans and the English: A Case of Multiple Conflicting Agendas," in *Powhatan Foreign Relations*, ed. Rountree, 183–90; Sam White, *A Cold Welcome: The Little Ice Age and Europe* (Cambridge, MA: Harvard University Press, 2017), 114; Joseph Stromberg, "Starving Settlers in Jamestown Colony Resorted to Cannibalism," *Smithsonian Magazine*, April 30, 2013, https://www.smithsonianmag.com/history/starving-settlers-in -jamestown-colony-resorted-to-cannibalism-46000815.

21. Donegan, *Seasons of Misery*, 34, 69–116.

22. Townsend, *Pocahontas and the Powhatan Dilemma*, 13, 85–88, 111–13, 129–30, 135–58; Richter, *Facing East from Indian Country*, 41–51; *BR*, 126–27; Heather Miyano Kopelson, "Women, Gender, Families, and States," in *Cambridge History of America and the World*, ed. Eliga Gould, Paul Mapp, and Carla Gardina Pestana (New York: Cambridge University Press, 2021), esp. 442; Appleby, "War, Politics, and Colonization," 73. For Pocahontas's other names, see Townsend, *Pocahontas and the Powhatan Dilemma*, chaps. 1 and 7.

23. Gleach, *Powhatan's World and Colonial Virginia*, 210; Virginia DeJohn Anderson, *Creatures of Empire: How Domesticated Animals Transformed Early America* (Oxford: Oxford University Press, 2002), 177–79, 188; Smith, *Generall Historie*, 144 ("few or none"); Edward Waterhouse to the Honorable Companie of Virginia, in *Records of the Virginia Company of London, 1606–26*, ed. Susan Kingsbury (Wash-

ington, DC: Government Printing Office, 1906–1985), 3:551, 557 ("that fatal," 551; "conquering," 557); Jay Miller, "Blending Worlds," in *The Native Americans: An Illustrated History*, ed. Betty Ballantine and Ian Ballantine (Atlanta, GA: Turner, 1993), 186 ("eat up").

24. Council of Virginia to Virginia Company in London, January 30, 1623/4, and Council of Virginia to the Earl of Southampton and Company of Virginia, December 2, 1624, in *Records of the Virginia Company*, ed. Kingsbury, 4:450, 508 ("We have," 450; "a plentiful," 508).

25. John Winthrop, *Winthrop's Journal: "History of New England," 1630–1649*, ed. James Kendall Hosmer (New York: Scribner's, 1908), 2:167 ("the English"); Robert Beverley, *The History of Virginia, in Four Parts* (1705; repr., Richmond, VA: J. W. Randolph, 1855), 48–49 ("The subtle Indians," "uneasy," 48; "His eyelids," 49); Taylor, *American Colonies*, 134–36. For Powhatan tactics, see James D. Rice, "War and Politics: Powhatan Expansionism and the Problem of Native American Warfare," *WMQ* 77 (January 2020): esp. 24.

26. Robert Beverley, *The History and Present State of Virginia: A New Edition* (Chapel Hill: University of North Carolina Press, 2013), 48.

27. Joyce Lorimer, ed., *English and Irish Settlement on the Amazon, 1540–1646*, ser. 2 (1989; repr., New York: Routledge, 2018), esp. chap. 2; Taylor, *American Colonies*, 136; Anderson, *Creatures of Empire*, 107–13; Adrian van der Donck, *A Description of New Netherland*, 1655, trans. Diederick Willem Goedhuys (Lincoln: University of Nebraska Press, 2008); April Lee Hatfield, "Geography, Law, and Anglo-Spanish Relations in the Western Caribbean and Southeastern North America" (paper, WMQ-EMSI workshop, 2006). For the relative weakness of the English state in a global context, see Allison Games, *The Web of Empire: English Cosmopolitans in an Age of Expansion, 1560–1660* (New York: Oxford University Press, 2008).

CHAPTER 6: WARS AT THE WATER'S EDGE

1. Margaret Ellen Newell, "Indian Slavery in Colonial New England," in *Indian Slavery in Colonial America*, ed. Alan Gallay (Lincoln: University of Nebraska Press, 2009), 35–36; *OBK*, 8-9; John Smith, *A Description of New-England* (London: Humfrey Lownes, for Robert Clerke, 1616), 5.

2. Adrian van der Donck, *A Description of New Netherland*, trans. Diederick Willem Goedhuys (Lincoln: University of Nebraska Press, 2008), 7–8; Christopher Bilodeau, "The Paradox of Sagadahoc: The Popham Colony, 1607–1608," *Early American Studies* 12, no. 2 (2014): 1–35; David Childs, *Invading America: The English Assault on the New World, 1497–1630* (Barnsley, UK: Seaforth, 2012), 261–62.

3. John S. Marr and John T. Cathey, "New Hypothesis for Cause of Epidemic among Native Americans, New England, 1616–1619," *Emerging Infectious Diseases* 16 (February 2020): 281–86; "A Relation or Journal of a Plantation Settled at Plymouth in New England, and Proceedings Thereof, 1622," in Massachusetts Historical Society, *Collections of the Massachusetts Historical Society* (Boston: Munroe and Francis, 1802), 8:221 ("a great deal"); [Robert Cushman], "Reasons and Considerations Touching the Lawfulness of Removing Out of England into the Parts of America," in *Remarkable Providences, 1600–1760*, ed. John Demos (New York: George Braziller, 1972), 1:28 ("Our land"); Andrew Lipman, *The Saltwater Frontier: Indians and the Contest for the American Coast* (New Haven, CT: Yale University Press, 2015), 101; David Silverman, *This Land Is Their Land: The Wampanoag Indians, Plymouth Colony, and the Troubled History of Thanksgiving* (New York: Bloomsbury, 2019),

169–71; William Bradford and Edward Winslow, "Journal," in Alexander Young, *Chronicles of the Pilgrim Fathers of the Colony of Plymouth, from 1602 to 1625*, 2nd ed. (Boston: Charles C. Little & James Brown, 1844), 189–90, 202–13; Michael Freeman, "Puritans and Pequots: The Question of Genocide," *NEQ* 68 (June 1995): 282–83; Richard Middleton and Anne Lombard, *Colonial America to 1763*, 4th ed. (Malden, MA: Blackwell, 2011), 80–83. For the New England Puritan mindset, see Perry Miller, *The New England Mind: The Seventeenth Century* (Cambridge, MA: Harvard University Press, 1939).

4.   Robert Cushman, "The State of the Colony, and the Need of Public Spirit in the Colonists," and "Reasons and Considerations Touching the Lawfulness of Removing Out of England into the Parts of America," in Alexander Young, *Chronicles of the Pilgrim Fathers of the Colony of Plymouth, from 1602 to 1625* (Boston: Charles C. Little and James Brown, 1841), 243, 265 ("God did," 243; "The country," 265); Virginia DeJohn Anderson, *Creatures of Empire: How Domesticated Animals Transformed Early America* (Oxford: Oxford University Press, 2002), 144–45; Christine M. DeLucia, *Memory Lands: King Philip's War and the Place of Violence in the Northeast* (New Haven, CT: Yale University Press, 2018), 36. For the Wampanoag communal ethic, see David J. Silverman, *Faith and Boundaries: Colonists, Christianity and Community among the Wampanoag Indians of Martha's Vineyard, 1600–1871* (New York: Cambridge University Press, 2005), 183–84.

5.   Patricia Seed, *Ceremonies of Possession in Europe's Conquest of the New World, 1492–1640* (New York: Cambridge University Press, 1995), 16–17; Mark Peterson, *The City-State of Boston: The Rise and Fall of an Atlantic Power, 1630–1865* (Princeton, NJ: Princeton University Press, 2019), 11–13; Allan Greer, *Property and Dispossession: Natives, Empires and Land in Early Modern North America* (Cambridge: Cambridge University Press, 2018), 194–97; Christopher Tomlins, *Freedom Bound: Law, Labor, and Civic Identity in Colonizing English America, 1580–1865* (Cambridge: Cambridge University Press, 2006), 175–77.

6.   *SA*, 1:41–42; Wim Klooster, "The Dutch Atlantic," in *Four Centuries of Dutch-American Relations, 1609–2009*, ed. Hans Krabbendam, Cornelis A. van Minnen, and Giles Scott-Smith (Albany: State University of New York Press, 2009), 63–73; Simon Hart, *The Prehistory of the New Netherland Company: Amsterdam Notarial Records of the First Dutch Voyages to the Hudson* (Amsterdam: City of Amsterdam Press, 1959), 17–21.

7.   Matthew R. Bahar, *The Strom of the Sea: Indians and Empires in the Atlantic's Age of Sail* (New York: Oxford University Press, 2018), 17–37, 40–41, 67–69, 101–3; Lynn Ceci, "The Value of Wampum among the New York Iroquois: A Case Study in Artifact Analysis," *Journal of Anthropological Research* 38 (Spring 1982): 97–107; Kenneth M. Morrison, *The Embattled Northeast: The Elusive Ideal of Alliance in Abenaki* (Berkeley: University of California Press, 1984), 75–77, 103–5; David Graeber, *Debt: The First 5000 Years* (New York: Melville House, 2011), 131–36; *BR*, 141–42, 157–60; *OL*, 85; Gail D. MacLeitch, *Imperial Entanglements: Iroquois Change and Persistence on the Frontiers of Empire* (Philadelphia: University of Pennsylvania Press, 2011), 35–36; Sarah M. S. Pearsall, *Polygamy: An Early American History* (New Haven, CT: Yale University Press, 2019), 108–10.

8.   David D. Hall, *A Reforming People: Puritanism and the Transformation of Public Life in New England* (Chapel Hill: University of North Carolina Press, 2011), 36–39, 80–82, 177–83; Alfred A. Cave, "The Pequot Invasion of Southern New England: A Reassessment of the Evidence," *NEQ* 62 (March 1989): 27–33; Margaret Ellen Newell, *Brethren by Nature: New England Indians, and the Origins of American*

Slavery (Ithaca, NY: Cornell University Press, 2015), 20; William Wood, *Wood's New-England Prospect* (Boston: John Wilson, 1865), 70 ("women-like men"). For Pequot political organization, see William A. Starna, "The Pequots in the Early Seventeenth Century," in *Pequots in Southern New England: The Fall and Rise of an American Indian Nation*, ed. Laurence M. Hauptman and James D. Wherry (Norman: University of Oklahoma Press, 1990), 33–47.

9.   John Winthrop to Sir Simonds D'Ewes, July 21, 1634, in *The Winthrop Papers*, ed. Allyn Bailey Forbes (Boston: Massachusetts Historical Society, 1943), 3:171–72.

10.   John Underhill, *Newes from America; or, A New and Experimentall Discoverie of New England; Containing, a Trve Relation of Their War-like Proceedings These Two Yeares Last Past, with a Figure of the Indian Fort, or Palizado*, ed. Paul Royster (1638), Electronic Texts in American Studies, Libraries at University of Nebraska-Lincoln, https://digitalcommons.unl.edu/cgi/viewcontent.cgi?article=1037&context=etas, 2–3 ("the blood," 3).

11.   Ronald Dale Karr, "'Why Should You Be So Furious?': The Violence of the Pequot War," *JAH* 85 (December 1998): 890–91; Underhill, *Newes from America*, 8, 13–15 ("gave fire," 13; "made many," 14; "all they found," 14–15); John Winthrop, *A Journal of the Transactions and Occurrences in the Settlement of Massachusetts and the Other New-England Colonies, from the Year 1630 to 1644* (Hartford, CT: Elisha Babcock, 1790), 124 ("join against"); Roger Williams, *The Complete Writings of Roger Williams* (1644; repr., Eugene, OR: Wips & Stock, 2007), 1:31 ("the Pequots").

12.   Lipman, *Saltwater Frontier*, 133–37.

13.   Lipman, *Saltwater Frontier*, 135–36; Alfred A. Cave, *The Pequot War* (Amherst: University of Massachusetts Press, 1996), 63–68.

14.   John Mason, *A Brief History of the Pequot War* (Boston: S. Kneeland, 1736), 5–8 ("two Forts," 6; "Such a dreadful," 8); "Journal of the Proceedings of the Congress Held at Albany, in 1754," in *Collections of the Massachusetts Historical Society*, 3rd ser., vol. 5 (Boston: John H. Eastburn, 1836), 25 ("fought").

15.   Underhill, *Newes from America*, 2, 35–36, 38 ("insolent," 2; "it may be," 35; "Sometimes," 36; "Our *Indians*," 38); Andrew Lipman, "'A Meanes to Knitt Them Togeather': The Exchange of Body Parts in the Pequot War," *WMQ* 65 (January 2008): 3–28 ("cried *mach it*," 19).

16.   Donck, *Description of New Netherland*, 5 ("are not aware").

17.   *BR*, 136–42, 159–60; Oliver A. Rink, *Holland on the Hudson: An Economic and Social History* (Ithaca, NY: Cornell University Press, 1986), 118; Daniel P. Barr, *Unconquered: The Iroquois League at War in Colonial America* (Westport, CT: Praeger, 2006), 5–6, 31–33; Middleton and Lombard, *Colonial America to 1763*, 113–14; Eric E. Jones, "Population History of the Onondaga and Oneida Iroquois, A.D. 1500–1700," *American Antiquity* 75 (April 2010): 387–407; Newell, *Brethren by Nature*, 22; Donck, *Description of New Netherland*, 14–15; Jaap Jacobs, *The Colony of New Netherland: A Dutch Settlement in Seventeenth-Century America* (Leiden, Netherlands: Brill, 2005), 76–77; Timothy Walker, "European Ambitions and Early Contacts: Diverse Styles of Colonization, 1492–1700," in *Converging Worlds: Communities and Cultures in Colonial America*, ed. Louise A. Breen (New York: Routledge, 2012), 33–34; William A. Starna and José António Brandão, "From the Mohawk-Mahican War to the Beaver Wars: Questioning the Pattern, *Ethnohistory* 51 (Fall 2004): 737; Lipman, *Saltwater Frontier*, 25–26, 117–21.

18.   Evan Haefeli, "Kieft's War and the Cultures of Violence in Colonial America," in *Lethal Imagination: Violence and Brutality in American History*, ed. Michael A.

Bellesiles (New York: New York University Press, 1999), 17–31; Lipman, "'Meanes to Knitt Them Togeather,'" 14.

19. "Declaration of Harmen Meyndertsen van den Bogaert and Others respecting an Attack by the Raritan Indians," in *New York Historical Manuscripts: Dutch*, vol. 2, *Registrar of the Provincial Secretary, 1642–1647*, ed. and trans. Arnold J. F. Van Laer (Baltimore: Genealogical Publishing, 1974), 409 ("instead of," "began to scoff," "all armed"); *NWA*, 98.

20. David Pietersz. de Vries, "Korte historiael ende journaels aenteyckeninge," in *Original Narratives of Early American History*, vol. 8, *Narratives of New Netherland, 1609–1664*, ed. J. Franklin Jameson (New York: Scribner's, 1909), 227–28 ("A great shrieking," 227; "Infants," "some with," "in the same," 228).

21. Haefeli, "Kieft's War," 32–35.

22. Jacobs, *Colony of New Netherland*, 78–79 ("the poor," "all together"); Charles Gehring, ed. and trans., *Correspondence, 1647–1653*, New Netherlands Documents (Syracuse, NY: Syracuse University Press, 2000), xx ("within a cannon shot"); Wayne Bodle, "The Middle Colonies," in *Converging Worlds*, ed. Breen, 227.

23. Alden T. Vaughan, *New England Frontier: Puritans and Indians, 1620–1675*, 3rd ed. (Norman: University of Oklahoma Press, 1995), 95 ("exercised," "except"); *OBK*, 32. For the centrality of guns in Native American warfare, trade, and diplomacy, see David J. Silverman, *Thundersticks: Firearms and the Violent Transformation of Native America* (Cambridge, MA: Harvard University Press, 2016).

CHAPTER 7: THE PEQUOTS SHALL NO MORE BE CALLED PEQUOTS

1. Michael Leroy Oberg, *Uncas: First of the Mohegans* (Ithaca, NY: Cornell University Press, 2003), 38–39; Yasuhide Kawashima, *Igniting King Philip's War: The John Sassamon Murder Trial* (Lawrence: University Press of Kansas, 2002).

2. Alden T. Vaughan, *New England Frontier: Puritans and Indians, 1620–1675*, 3rd ed. (Norman: University of Oklahoma Press, 1995), 155–57; Michael Parker, *John Winthrop: Founding the City upon a Hill* (New York: Routledge, 2014), 90–91; "Articles of Agreement between the English in Conneticutt and the Indian Sachems," September 21, 1638, Yale Digital Collections, http://findit.library.yale.edu/catalog/digcoll:2389 ("shall no more"); Michael L. Fickes, "'They Could Not Endure That Yoke': The Captivity of Pequot Women and Children after the War of 1637," *NEQ* 73 (March 2000): 60–61; Christine M. DeLucia, *Memory Lands: King Philip's War and the Place of Violence in the Northeast* (New Haven, CT: Yale University Press, 2018), 290–95; "Treaty of Hartford, Articles of Agreement between the English in Connecticut in 1638," Venture Smith's Colonial Connecticut, accessed November 23, 2021, https://venturesmithcolonialct.org/library/treaty-of-hartford-1638 ("as soon as").

3. Michael Leroy Oberg, "'We Are All the Sachems from East to West': A New Look at Miantonomi's Campaign of Resistance," *NEQ* 77 (September 2004): 478–99; Andrew Lipman, *The Saltwater Frontier: Indians and the Contest for the American Coast* (New Haven, CT: Yale University Press, 2015), 161–63; John W. De Forest, *History of the Indians of Connecticut* (Hartford, CT: Wm. Jas Hamersley, 1852), 153–200. I have read De Forest's detailed *History* against the grain. Instead of seeing Uncas as self-centered opportunist, I have examined his actions as a sachem, a leader of his people. The picture that emerges is different.

4. *SA*, 1:153; Robert D. Mitchel, "American Origins and Regional Institutions: The Seventeenth-Century Chesapeake," *Annals of the Association of American Geographers* 73 (September 1983): 413; Stephen Warren, *The Worlds the Shawnees Made:*

Migration and Violence in Early America (Chapel Hill: University of North Carolina Press, 2014), 85–88.

5. BR, 129; Richard Hakluyt, ed., *The Principall Nauigations, Voiages, and Discoueries of the English Nation* (London: George Ralph Newberie, 1589), 723; Bruce M. Trigger, *Natives and Newcomers: Canada's "Heroic Age" Reconsidered* (Montreal, QC: McGill-Queen's University Press, 1985), 135–37, 147–48.

6. David Hackett Fischer, *Champlain's Dream: The European Founding of North America* (New York: Simon and Schuster, 2008), 42–60; Patricia Seed, *Ceremonies of Possession in Europe's Conquest of the New World, 1492–1640* (New York: Cambridge University Press, 1995), 64–65.

7. Samuel de Champlain, *The Works of Samuel de Champlain*, ed. H. P. Biggar (Toronto: Champlain Society, 1922–36), 1:137 ("secure"); Champlain, *Works*, 2:99–100 ("shot straight," 99; "astonished," 100); P. F. X. de Charlevoix, *History and General Description of New France*, trans. and ed. John Gilmary Shea (New York: Francis P. Harper, 1900), 2:7–9; Fischer, *Champlain's Dream*, 5:227–80; NWA, 92–93; Daniel P. Barr, *Unconquered: The Iroquois League at War in Colonial America* (Westport, CT: Praeger, 2006), 20; JR, 1:109.

8. OL, 6–7, 31–39; Bruce G. Trigger, *Children of Aataentsic: A History of the Huron People to 1660* (Montreal, QC: McGill-Queen's University, 1987), 27–31; NWA, 36; Colin Calloway, *One Vast Winter Count: The Native American West before Lewis and Clark* (Lincoln: University of Nebraska Press, 2003), 220. For early trade with Europeans, see EW, 10–11.

9. Barr, *Unconquered*, 31.

10. JR, 6:297 ("The Beaver does," "It makes kettles," "making sport"); Champlain, *Works*, 6:197 ("of both sexes"); Charlevoix, *History and General Description*, 41; Allan Greer, *Property and Dispossession: Natives, Empires and Land in Early Modern North America* (Cambridge: Cambridge University Press, 2018), 154–61.

11. Sarah M. S. Pearsall, "Native American Men—and Women—at Home in Plural Marriages," *Gender & History* 27 (November 2015): 591–610; Greer, *Property and Dispossession*, 154.

12. Charlevoix, *History and General Description*, 41; Samuel de Champlain, "Abstract of the Discoveries in New France, 1631," in *NYCD*, 9:1 ("do not deny").

13. JR, 10:77 ("his body," "master," "he would").

14. SA, 1:50–51.

CHAPTER 8: THE RISE OF THE FIVE NATIONS LEAGUE

1. OL, 9–17, 30–31; Leanne Simpson, "Looking after Gdoo-naaganinaa: Precolonial Nishnaabeg Diplomatic and Treaty Relationships," *Wicazo Sa Review* 23 (Fall 2008): 29–42.

2. Nancy Shoemaker, "Introduction," in *Negotiators of Change: Historical Perspectives on Native American Women*, ed. Shoemaker (New York: Routledge, 1995), 7–8; Shoemaker, "Kateri Tekakwitha's Tortuous Path to Sainthood," in *Negotiators of Change*, 61–62; Judith Brown, "Economic Organization and the Position of Women among the Iroquois," *Ethnohistory* 17 (Summer 1970): 151–67 ("nothing," 153); OL, 1, 30–49; Timothy J. Shannon, *Iroquois Diplomacy on the Early American Frontier* (New York: Viking Penguin, 2008), 23–30; José António Brandão, ed., *Nation Iroquoise: A Seventeenth-Century Ethnography of the Iroquois* (Lincoln: University of Nebraska Press, 2004), 63 ("He then"); JR, 51:237 ("Their policy"); Robert Launay, "Lafitau Revisited: American 'Savages' and Universal History," *Anthropologica* 52, no. 2 (2010): 340–41.

3. Chad L. Anderson, *The Storied Landscape of Iroquoia: History, Conquest, and Memory in the Native Northwest* (Lincoln: University of Nebraska Press, 2020), 137–38.

4. *OL*, 55–57; *JR*, 5:203 ("had always," "had assisted," "he himself").

5. John Winthrop to Sir Simonds D'Ewes, July 24, 1634, Papers of John Winthrop Family, 1537–1990, in Massachusetts Historical Society, *Publications of the Colonial Society of Massachusetts*, vol. 7, *Transactions: 1900–1902* (Boston: The Society, 1905), 71–72 ("I am still," 71); *BR*, 162.

6. *JR*, 15:41 ("yet know"); *OL*, 58–59; Matthew Dennis, *Cultivating a Landscape of Peace: Iroquois Encounters in Seventeenth-Century America* (Ithaca, NY: Cornell University Press, 1993), esp. 85–91.

7. *JR*, 26:57 ("All the people"); *MG*, 1–23; P. F. X. de Charlevoix, *History and General Description of New France*, trans. and ed. John Gilmary Shea (New York: Francis P. Harper, 1900), 209.

8. Arnoldus Montanaus, *Description of New Netherland* (Amsterdam, 1671), 117 ("streaked"); *OL*, 94–95; Lois M. Feister, "Linguistic Communication between the Dutch and Indians in New Netherland, 1609–1664," *Ethnohistory* 20 (Winter 1973): 36–37.

9. *JR*, 27:249–51 ("as a mark," 249; "We have," 251).

10. *JR*, 27:257, 261 ("There," 257; "be but one," 261).

11. *JR*, 41:79 ("the fury," "the very end"); Michael Witgen, *An Infinity of Nations: How the Native New World Shaped Early America* (Philadelphia: University of Pennsylvania Press, 2012), 19–21; Heidi Bohaker, "'Nindoodemag': The Significance of Algonquian Kinship Networks in the Eastern Great Lakes Region, 1600–1701," *WMQ* 63 (January 2006): 23–52; *EW*, 80; Allan Greer, *Property and Dispossession: Natives, Empires and Land in Early Modern North America* (Cambridge: Cambridge University Press, 2018), 146.

12. *MG*, 1–23; Charlevoix, *History and General Description*, 209.

13. Daniel P. Barr, *Unconquered: The Iroquois League at War in Colonial America* (Westport, CT: Praeger, 2006), 15; *OL*, 31–38; *EW*, 290; *JR*, 24:295 ("skilled in handling"); *JR*, 44:61–63, 191 ("must not take," "must prevent," "in sight of," 191). For a broader view of ritualistic and real cannibalism, see Carla Cevasco, "This Is My Body: Communion and Cannibalism in Colonial New England and New France," *NEQ* 89 (December 2016): 556–86; Henry R. Schoolcraft, *Notes on the Iroquois: Or Contributions to American History, Antiquities, and General Ethnology* (New York: Bartlett & Welford, 1846), 29, 51 ("their nationality," 29; "a body cut," 51).

14. *JR*, 41:79 ("all the four"); *JR*, 42:55 ("My brothers").

15. *JR*, 44:61–63, 213 ("Were one," 63); *JR*, 45:213 ("it is beyond").

16. *JR*, 44:117–19; *JR*, 45:189 ("Everywhere," 189); *JR*, 46:205 ("If they"); *JR*, 47:107 ("filled with fire"); "Instructions for Sieur Gaudais Sent by the King to Canada," in *NYCD*, 9:9–10 ("all the French," 10); *OL*, 98–99. For the *filles du roi*, see Peter Gagné, *King's Daughters and Founding Mothers: Filles du Roi, 1663–1673* (Pawtucket, RI: Quinton, 2001).

17. *OL*, 85; Johannes Megapolensis, "A Short Account of the Mohawk Indians, Their Country, Language, Stature, Dress, Religion, and Government, Thus Described and Recently, August 26, 1644," in *In Mohawk Country: Early Narratives of a Native People*, ed. Dean R. Snow, Charles T. Gehring, and William A. Starna (New York: Syracuse University Press, 1996), 41 ("the Principal"); "Marie de L'Incarnation to Her Son, 1667," in *Interpreting a Continent: Voices from Colonial America*, ed.

Kathleen DuVal and John DuVal (Lanham, MD: Rowman & Littlefield, 2009), 195; "Propositions Made by Mohawk Sachems," October 19, 1659, in *NYCD*, 13:122 ("it is very wrong," "dogs," "rascals, "live with them").

CHAPTER 9: ENEMIES OF THE FAITH

1. *JR*, 34:25 ("perceived").
2. *JR*, 34:27 ("The Iroquois," "Overwhelmed").
3. *JR*, 34:141 ("My children").
4. Allan Greer, "Introduction," in *The Jesuit Relations: Natives and Missionaries in Seventeenth-Century North America*, ed. Greer (Boston: Bedford/St. Martin's, 2000), 3–12; Allan Greer, *Mohawk Saint: Catherine Tekakwitha and the Jesuits* (New York: Oxford University Press, 2015), 75. For Jesuits as empire-builders, see Bronwen McShea, *Apostles of Empire: The Jesuits and New France* (Lincoln: University of Nebraska Press, 2019).
5. *JR*, 34:25, 123–25 ("marked," "enemies of the Hurons," 123; "This village," 125); Thomas J. Craughwell, *Death in the Wilderness: The Harrowing Story of the Eight Martyrs of North America* (New York: Penguin, 2017); "A Veritable Account of the Martyrdom and Blessed Death of Father Jean Breboeuf and of Father Gabriel L'Alemant, in New France, in the Country of the Hurons, by the Iroquois, Enemies of Faith," in *Jesuit Relations and Allied Documents: A Selection*, ed. S. R. Mealing (McGill-Queen's University Press, 1978), https://www.jstor.org/stable/j.ctt7zt2f2 ("enemies of the faith").
6. *JR*, 34:137, 197, 205, 207, 217 ("lest they," "scattering," 197; "infested," 207); *JR*, 35:59, 79, 107 ("in the sight," 59; "flung themselves," 77; "to find death," 79).
7. *JR*, 35:81, 89, 163, 189 ("to make some," 81; "the spirit," 163; "My pen," 189); *JR*, 35:283; *JR*, 36:191.
8. Bruce G. Trigger, *Children of Aataentsic: A History of the Huron People to 1660* (Montreal, QC: McGill-Queen's University, 1987), 789; *JR*, 35:211; *JR*, 36:119, 123, 133–37, 143, 165 ("coming," 143; "would be," 165).
9. *JR*, 37:111.
10. *JR*, 40:157 ("At last," "the Iroquois," "this change").
11. Robert Michael Morrissey, *Empire by Collaboration: Indians, Colonists, and Governments in Colonial Illinois Country* (Philadelphia: University of Pennsylvania Press, 2015), 31–32; Trigger, *Children of Aataentsic*, 795–96; Daniel K. Richter, "Iroquois versus Iroquois: Jesuit Missions and Christianity in Village Politics, 1642–1686," *Ethnohistory* 32 (Winter 1985): 3; *JR*, 41:55–57 ("to separate," 55; "in as great," 57).
12. *JR*, 44:205 ("the Iroquois"); *HAC*, 86 ("were not able"); Allan Greer, *Property and Dispossession: Natives, Empires and Land in Early Modern North America* (Cambridge: Cambridge University Press, 2018), 368–71; James Pritchard, *In Search of Empire: The French in the Americas, 1670–1730* (Cambridge: Cambridge University Press, 2004), 153–54; Alan Taylor, *American Colonies* (New York: Viking, 2001), 113; Claiborne A. Skinner, *The Upper Country: French Enterprise in the Colonial Great Lakes* (Baltimore: Johns Hopkins University Press, 2008), 15–16.
13. Gilles Havard and Cécile Vidal, *Histoire de l'Amérique Française* (Paris: Flammarion, 2005), 413–35; *JR*, 49:141–43 ("Savages," 141; "the Iroquois," 143).
14. *OL*, 99–104.
15. Richard Aquila, *The Iroquois Restoration: Iroquois Diplomacy on the Colonial Frontier, 1701–1754* (Detroit, MI: Wayne State University Press, 1983), 40–41; *EW*, 128–32; *HAC*, plate 37.

16. *JR*, 54:275, 281 ("It is a stroke," 275); *JR*, 55:35 ("little Church," "admirable"); David L. Preston, *The Texture of Context: European and Indian Settler Communities on the Frontiers of Iroquoia, 1667–1783* (Lincoln: University of Nebraska Press, 2009), 27–29; Greer, *Property and Dispossession*, 182.

17. *OL*, 134–37; *EW*, 148–49; Eric Hinderaker, *The Two Hendriks: Unraveling a Mohawk Mystery* (Cambridge, MA: Harvard University Press, 2010), 32–33; *HAC*, 87.

18. *EW*, 149–50.

19. Lawrence H. Leder, ed., *The Livingston Indian Records, 1666–1723* (Gettysburg, PA, 1956), 45–46, 51 ("We are one," 45–46; "our Castles," 51); Five Nations, *Propositions Made by the Five Nations of Indians to His Excellency Richard Earl of Bellomont* (New York, 1698), 4 ("unto the utmost").

20. Louis Hennepin, *A New Discovery of a Vast Country in America*, ed. Reuben Gold Thwaites (Chicago: A. C. McClurg, 1903), 1:47–48 ("Village," 47; "lying," "*Indian Corn*," 48).

21. *HAC*, 86–87; Carolyn Podruchny, *Making the Voyager World: Travelers and Traders in the North American Fur Trade* (Lincoln: University of Nebraska Press, 2006), 21–25. For a comprehensive work on coureurs de bois, see Gilles Havard, *Histoire des coureurs de bois: Amerique du Nord, 1600–1840* (Paris: Les Indes Savantes, 2016).

22. *JR*, 62:155–57, 223 ("After they have," 155; "undertaking," 155–57; "obtained," 157; "The terror," 223); M. l'abbé De Belmont, *Histoire Du Canada* (1840), 12–17 ("than putting" [*que de mettre Onontio á la Chaudière*], 14). For a broader context, see J. F. Lee, *Masters of the Middle Waters: Indian Nations and Colonial Ambitions along the Mississippi* (Cambridge, MA: Harvard University Press, 2019).

23. *EW*, 169; M. de la Barre to M. de Seignelay, November 4, 1683, in *NYCD*, 9:201–10 ("the bravest," 201; "They will not," 202; "Advanced," 210).

24. Isaac Joslin Cox, ed., *The Journeys of Réné Robert Cavelier, Sieur de La Salle* (New York: Allerton, 1922), 1:12 ("they would not"); *EW*, 159–61 ("Christian Indians," "flesh and blood," 161); William Hand Browne, ed., *Archives of Maryland* (Baltimore: Maryland Historical Society, 1896), 15:176 ("scour the heads").

25. For a detailed analysis of these dynamics, see *OL*, 105–61.

26. Louis Hennepin, *Description of Louisiana* (New York: John G. Shea, 1880), 267; *EW*, 162–64, 286.

27. For the Iroquois playoff policy, see Daniel K. Richter, *Facing East from Indian Country: A Native History of Early America* (Cambridge, MA: Harvard University Press, 2001), 164. Lefevre de La Barre to the King, November 4, 1683, in *Découvertes et établissements des Français dans l'ouest et dans le sud de l'Amérique septentrionale (1614–1754): Mémoires et documents originaux*, pt. 5, *Première formation d'une chaine de postes entre le Fleuve Saint-Laurent et le Golfe du Mexique (1683–1724)*, ed. Pierre Margry (Paris: D. Jouaust, 1883), 7 ("the sole" [*lá seuls maistres du commerce*]); *JR*, 62:223 ("completely ruined").

28. *EW*, 140–45; *JR*, 62:175 ("reputation," "Journeys"); "Letter of Father Claude Chauchetiere, respecting the Iroquois Mission of Sault St. François Xavier, near Montreal," October 14, 1682, in *JR*, 62:165–89. I have relied on Greer, *Mohawk Saint*, here.

29. Nancy Shoemaker, "Kateri Tekakwitha's Tortuous Path to Sainthood," in *Negotiators of Change: Historical Perspectives on Native American Women*, ed. Shoemaker (New York: Routledge, 1995), 61–62.

30. *JR*, 62:163 ("lack of any," "They are now"); *EW*, 128, 146.

CHAPTER 10: THE POWER OF WEAKNESS

1.   *JR*, 62:155–63 ("render," 155; "destroying," "all the trade," 159; "This is a war," 161); *HAC*, 87.

2.   *HAC*, plate 36.

3.   "Relation of the Events of the War, and State of the Affairs in Canada, October 30, 1688, in *NYCD*, 9:388–90 ("spread," "The facility," 390).

4.   *OL*, 105–32; *JR*, 54:263–65 ("Let Onnontio," 263; "For whom," 263–65).

5.   *JR*, 49:227–31 (" 'Great Onnontio,' " 227–29; "the greatest," 231).

6.   *MG*, 20–21; Michael Witgen, *An Infinity of Nations: How the Native New World Shaped Early America* (Philadelphia: University of Pennsylvania Press, 2012), 93–94. For the Wyandots, see Kathryn Magee Labelle, *Dispersed but Not Destroyed: A History of the Seventeenth-Century Wendat People* (Vancouver, BC: UBC Press, 2013).

7.   *JR*, 54:191–93 ("Their manners," "him with"); *JR*, 51:53 ("a language"); *JR*, 55:167–69 ("A general League"); Witgen, *Infinity of Nations*, 66–68.

8.   *JR*, 54:191 ("the Iroquois"); *JR*, 58:255–57 ("a nation," "the common," "even pushed," "ten of," "massacre," 255; "stirred up," 257). For the Iroquois as hammer, see *MG*, 11.

9.   Claude Charles Le Roy, Bacqueville de la Potherie, *History of the Savage People Who Are Allies of New France*, in *The Indian Tribes of the Upper Mississippi Valley and Region of the Great Lakes*, ed. Emma H. Blair (Cleveland, OH: Arthur H. Clark, 1911–12), 1:343–47 ("take possession," 343; "if they would," 346; "as his own children," "If any enemies," 347).

10.   "Lettre du Sieur Du Lhut à M. le Comte de Frontenac," April 5, 1679, in *Découvertes et établissements des Français dans l'ouest et dans le sud de l'Amérique septentrionale (1614–1754): Mémoires et documents originaux*, pt. 6, *Exploration des affluents du Missisipi et découverte des Montagnes Rocheuses (1679–1754)*, ed. Pierre Margry (Paris: D. Jouaust, 1886), 30 ("a nursery for beaver" [*pépinière de castors*]); *MG*, 78–82; "Lettre du Père Enjalran à Lefèvre de la Barre, gouverneur de la Nouvelle-France," August 26, 1683, in *Découvertes et établissements*, pt. 5, *Première formation d'une chaine de postes entre le Fleuve Saint-Laurent et le Golfe du Mexique (1683–1724)*, ed. Margry (Paris: D. Jouaust, 1883), 5; *JR*, 65:241; *HAC*, plate 38; Helen Hornbeck Tanner, *Atlas of Great Lakes Indian History* (Norman: University of Oklahoma Press, 1986), map 6; "The Voyage of St. Cosme, 1698–99," in *Early Narratives of the Northwest, 1634–1699*, ed. Louise Phelps Kellogg (New York: Scribner's, 1917), 344. For the gun trade, see *MG*, 136.

11.   *MG*, ix–x, 99–104.

12.   Bacqueville de la Potherie, *History of the Savage People*, 1:354–66 ("Listen," "foremost," "What child," 354; "Vomit up," "believe," 355).

13.   Nicolas Perrot, *Memoir on the Manners, Customs, and Religion of the Savages of North America*, in *Indian Tribes of the Upper Mississippi Valley*, ed. Blair, 1:262 ("arrogant"); David Andrew Nichols, *People of the Inlands Sea: Native Americans in the Great Lakes Region, 1600–1870* (Athens: Ohio University Press, 2018), esp. 3; Daniel K. Richter, *Facing East from Indian Country: A Native History of Early America* (Cambridge, MA: Harvard University Press, 2001), 66.

14.   This is a synopsis of Richard White's book *The Middle Ground: Indians, Empires, and Republics in the Great Lakes Region, 1650–1815* (Cambridge: Cambridge University Press, 1991).

15.   *JR*, 55:203–5 ("We availed," 203; "free access," 205); Erik R. Seeman, "Reading Indians' Deathbed Scenes: Ethnohistorical and Representational Approaches," *JAH* 88 (June 2001): 17–47.

16. "Extract from a Letter by Du Luth," April 12, 1684, in *WHC*, 16:118–20 ("made accusations," "This confrontation," "Seeing," "It is enough," 118; "to put them," "to treat," "I believed," 119; "If I were not," 120); Witgen, *Infinity of Nations*, 202–11.

17. *WHC*, 16:121 ("baptize," "six collars").

18. Susan Sleeper-Smith, "Women, Kin and Catholicism: New Perspectives on the Fur Trade," *Ethnohistory* 47 (Spring 2000): 425–28.

19. Witgen, *Infinity of Nations*, 55; "Mémoire du sieur Greyselon Du Lhut adressé à Monsieur le Marquis de Seignelay," in *Découvertes et établissements*, ed. Margry, 6:22 ("make peace" [*faire la paix avec les Nadouesioux, leurs communs ennemis*]); "Lettre du sieur Du Lhut à M. le Comte de Frontenac," April 5, 1679, 27–30. For an excellent reconstruction of the peace process, see Witgen, *Infinity of Nations*, 143–48.

20. Bacqueville de la Potherie, *History of the Savage People*, 1:367–72 ("bathing it," 368; "this was," "give suck," "They found," 372); *LA*, 38–41. For population estimates, see Pierre-Esprit Radisson, *Voyages of Peter Esprit Radisson: Being an Account of His Travels and Experiences among the North American Indians, from 1652 to 1684* (Boston: Prince Society, 1885), 219–20; and Perrot, *Memoir*, 170. All estimates of Sioux numbers are educated guesses. Gary Clayton Anderson argues that the total Sioux population may have reached thirty-eight thousand in 1650. See Anderson, *Kinsmen of Another Kind: Dakota-White Relations in the Upper Mississippi Valley, 1650–1862* (1984; repr. Lincoln: University of Nebraska Press, 1997), 16–19.

21. Perrot, *Memoir*, 1:365 ("settle near," "He was going").

CHAPTER 11: THE ENGLISH AS A LITTLE CHILD

1. James Pritchard, *In Search of Empire: The French in the Americas, 1670–1730* (Cambridge: Cambridge University Press, 2004),16; Mark F. Boyd, "Enumeration of the Florida Spanish Missions in 1675," *Florida Historical Quarterly* 27, no. 2 (1948): 181–88; *SFNA*, 90, 101–3; *HAC*, plate 38; Sylvia Van Kirk, *Many Tender Ties: Women in Fur-Trade Society, 1670–1870* (Norman: University of Oklahoma Press, 1980), 9–73.

2. Nancy H. Steenburg, "Murder and Minors: Changing Standards in the Criminal Law in Connecticut," in *Murder on Trial: 1602–2002*, ed. Robert Asher, Lawrence B. Goodheart, and Alan Rogers (Albany: State University of New York Press, 2005), 131, n. 3.

3. *OBK*, 107–9; Daniel K. Richter, *Facing East of Indian Country: A Native History of Early America* (Cambridge, MA: Harvard University Press, 2001), 100–101; Russell Bourne, *Red King's Rebellion: Racial Politics in New England, 1675–1678* (New York: Oxford University Press, 1991), 89. In calling the English colonies "settler societies," I am relying on Patrick Wolfe's conceptualization; see Wolfe, "Settler Colonialism and the Elimination of the Native," *Journal of Genocide Research* 8 (December 2006): esp. 387. There is a range of views on the applicability of settler colonialism in early American history; see "Forum: Settler Colonialism in Early American History," *WMQ* 76 (July 2019): 361–450.

4. Nathaniel B. Shurtleff, ed., *Records of the Colony of New Plymouth, in New England* (Boston: William White, 1855), 3–4:192 ("damage done," "according to").

5. Alan Taylor, *American Colonies* (New York: Viking, 2001), 202. For the Puritan view of the soul, see Elizabeth Reis, "The Devil, the Body, and the Feminine Soul in Puritan New England," *JAH* 82 (June 1995): 15–36. For the Half-Way Covenant, see Jenny Hale Pulsipher, *Subjects unto the Same King: Indians, English, and the Contest for Authority* (Philadelphia: University of Pennsylvania Press, 2005), 89–91.

6.   Harold W. Van Lonkhuyzen, "A Reappraisal of the Praying Indians: Acculturation, Conversion, and Identity at Natick, Massachusetts," *NEQ* 63 (September 1990): 396–428; David J. Silverman, *Faith and Boundaries: Colonists, Christianity and Community among the Wampanoag Indians of Martha's Vineyard, 1600–1871* (New York: Cambridge University Press, 2005), 63–64; Virginia DeJohn Anderson, "King Philip's Herds: Indians, Colonists, and the Problem of Livestock in Early New England," *WMQ* 51 (October 1994): 601–6; Jill Lepore, *The Name of War: King Philip's War and the Origins of American Identity* (New York: Knopf, 1998), 35; Pulsipher, *Subjects unto the Same King*, 74; James Axtell, *Invasion Within: The Contest of Cultures in Colonial North America* (New York: Oxford University Press, 1985), 140–45, 179; *NWA*, 74–76.

7.   *OBK*, 4–5, 72–88. For a detailed study of Martha's Vineyard, the missionaries, and Native views and tactics, see Silverman, *Faith and Boundaries*, esp. 16–89.

8.   Mark Peterson, *The City-State of Boston: The Rise and Fall of an Atlantic Power, 1630–1865* (Princeton, NJ: Princeton University Press, 2019), 125–38; Wendy Warren, *New England Bound: Slavery and Colonization in Early America* (New York: Liveright, 2016), 9; Margaret Ellen Newell, *Brethren by Nature: New England Indians, and the Origins of American Slavery* (Ithaca, NY: Cornell University Press, 2015), 6; Stephen Warren, *The Worlds the Shawnees Made: Migration and Violence in Early America* (Chapel Hill: University of North Carolina Press, 2014), 67–70.

9.   "The Charter of the Colony of the Massachusetts Bay in New England, 1628–9," in *Records of the Governor and Company of the Massachusetts Bay in New England*, ed. Nathaniel B. Shurtleff (Boston: William White, 1853), 1:3–4 ("sea to sea," 3); Jean M. O'Brien, *Dispossession by Degrees: Indian Land and Identity in Natick, Massachusetts* (New York: Cambridge University Press, 1997), 40–42; William Cronon, *Changes in the Land: Indians, Colonists, and the Ecology of New England* (New York: Hill and Wang, 1983), esp. 48–53, 54–75, 108–39; Anderson, "King Philip's Herds."

10.   *OBK*, 21–23, 31, 121–31; Warren, *New England Bound*, esp. 9–14, 11–28, 36–64; Newell, *Brethren by Nature*, 133–54, 211–36 ("in any part," 215); O'Brien, *Dispossession by Degrees*, 42.

11.   *OBK*, 27–54; Francis Jennings, *The Invasion of America: Indians, Colonialism, and the Cant of Conquest* (Chapel Hill: University of North Carolina Press, 1975), 288–90.

12.   *OBK*, 67–71, 131–34.

13.   Lepore, *Name of War*, 30–32, 39; Newell, *Brethren by Nature*, 95–96; *OBK*, 63–64, 118–24; Increase Mather, *A Brief History of the Warr with the Indians in New-England* (Boston: John Foster, 1676), 10–11 ("but one reason," He was," 11); Mather, *Brief History*, 12 ("Thus did").

14.   Lepore, *Name of War*, 22–25; John Easton, "A Relation of the Indian War, by Mr. Easton, of Rhode Island, 1675," ed. Paul Royster, Faculty Publications, UNL Libraries, Libraries at University of Nebraska-Lincoln, 2–8 ("would do no harm," 3; "they had done," 4; "All English," "they had been," 5–6; "had let them," 6; "for 40 years," 8), https://digitalcommons.unl.edu/libraryscience/33.

15.   *OBK*, 131–47; Daniel R. Mandell, *King Philip's War: Colonial Expansion, Native Resistance, and the End of Indian Sovereignty* (Baltimore: Johns Hopkins University Press, 2010), 48–50.

16.   *OBK*, 147–61, 177–78; Easton, "Relation of the Indian War," 8 ("from all"); Mandell, *King Philip's War*, 48–59, 74–85.

17.   *OBK*, 130, 236–37; Mandell, *King Philip's War*, 64–71; Scott Weidensaul, *The First*

Frontier: The Forgotten History of Struggle, Savagery and Endurance in Early America (Boston: Houghton Mifflin, 2012), 163; O'Brien, *Dispossession by Degrees*, 17 ("*Nqussutam*").

18. *OBK*, 236–47; Christine DeLucia, "The Memory Frontier: Uncommon Pursuits of Past and Place in the Northeast after King Philip's War," *JAH* 98 (March 2012): 980–81; Linford D. Fisher, "'Dangerous Designes': The 1676 Barbados Act to Prohibit New England Indian Slave Importation," *WMQ* 71 (January 2014): 99–124; Margaret Ellen Newell, "Indian Slavery in Colonial New England," in *Indian Slavery in Colonial America*, ed. Alan Gallay (Lincoln: University of Nebraska Press, 2009), 46; Mather, *Brief History*, 34–37 ("a strange," 37). For Massachusetts impressment practices, see Kyle Zelner, *A Rabble in Arms: Massachusetts Towns and Militiamen during King Philip's War* (New York: New York University Press, 2009).

19. *OBK*, 271–72, 274; Lepore, *Name of War*, 105.

CHAPTER 12: METACOM'S CHALLENGE

1. "A Short Accompt of the Generall Concerns of New Yorke from October 1674 to November 1677," in *NYCD*, 3:254–55 ("row boats," 255).

2. Richard Middleton and Anne Lombard, *Colonial America to 1763*, 4th ed. (Malden, MA: Blackwell, 2011), 189–90; "Council Minutes," April 16, 1675, and "Propositions of the Mohawks to Governor Colve and His Answers, May 22, 1674," in *NYCD*, 13:479–80, 483 ("always been," 479; "encouraged," "not to molest," 483); Increase Mather, *A Brief History of the Warr with the Indians in New-England* (Boston: John Foster, 1676), 38 ("as Spies"); James David Drake, *King Philip's War: Civil War in New England, 1675–1676* (Amherst: University of Massachusetts Press, 1999), 174; Eric B. Shultz and Michael J. Tobias, *King Philip's War: The History and Legacy of America's Forgotten Conflict* (Woodstock, VT: Countryman, 1999), 183–84; William Berkeley to [Secretary Thomas Ludwell?], February 16, 1676, Henry Coventry Papers, vol. 77, folio 56, Library of the Marquis of Bath at Longleat, Wilts, England, Bodleian Library ("the infection," "would be rid").

3. *OBK*, 272–75; Erik R. Seeman, *Death in the New World: Cross-Cultural Encounters, 1492–1800* (Philadelphia: University of Pennsylvania Press, 2010), 178; Charles L. Lincoln, ed., *Narratives of the Indian War* (New York: Scribner's, 1913), 86 ("deriding"); Steven D. Neuwirth, "The Images of Place: Puritans, Indians, and the Religious Significance of the New England Frontier," *American Art Journal* 18 (1986): 47–51.

4. Mather, *Brief History*, 40–47 ("God had let," 47); *OL*, 135–36; Jill Lepore, *Name of War: King Philip's War and the Origins of American Identity* (New York: Knopf, 1998), 112–14; Alan Taylor, *American Colonies* (New York: Viking, 2001), 201; *OBK*, 286–95, 305–7, 320–21.

5. Mather, *Brief History*, 60–62 ("The Heathen," 60); *OBK*, 307–24; Drake, *King Philip's War*, 168–69; Daniel R. Mandell, *King Philip's War: Colonial Expansion, Native Resistance, and the End of Indian Sovereignty* (Baltimore: Johns Hopkins University Press, 2010), 134–35; Guy Chet, *Conquering the American Wilderness: The Triumph of European Warfare in the Colonial Northeast* (Amherst: University of Massachusetts Press, 2003), 45.

6. James H. Merrell, "'The Customes of Our Countrey': Indians and Colonists in Early America," in *Strangers within the Realm: Cultural Margins of the First British Empire*, ed. Bernard Bailyn and Philip D. Morgan (Chapel Hill: University of North Carolina Press, 1991), 121; Colin G. Calloway, *The Western Abenakis of Vermont, 1600–1800: War, Migration, and the Survival of an Indian People* (Norman: Univer-

sity of Oklahoma Press, 1990), 76–89; Increase Mather, *An Earnest Exhortation to the Inhabitants of New-England* (Boston: John Foster, 1676), 12 ("Farms and"). I am grateful to Matthew Kruer for advice on contemporary currencies.

7. *The Soveraignty and Goodness of God, Together with the Faithfulness of His Promises Displayed: Being a Narrative of the Captivity and Restauration of Mrs. Mary Rowlandson* (Boston: I. Fleet, 1720), 69 ("our perverse"); Lepore, *Name of War*, 48–52.

8. *BR*, 291–94. For Andros, see Mary Lou Lustig, *The Imperial Executive in America: Sir Edmund Andros, 1637–1714* (Madison, NJ: Fairleigh Dickinson University Press, 2002), 15–18; Middleton and Lombard, *Colonial America*, 182–86.

9. Mary Beth Norton, *In the Devil's Snare: The Salem Witchcraft Crisis of 1692* (New York: Vintage, 2002), 98–111; James Weems, "A Short Account of the Losse of Pemiquid Fort in New England August 3d 1689," Colonial Office Papers, Public Record Office, London 5/855, f76 ("have all"); *BR*, 312–13; Middleton and Lombard, *Colonial America*, 182–89; Mark Peterson, *The City-State of Boston: The Rise and Fall of an Atlantic Power, 1630–1865* (Princeton, NJ: Princeton University Press, 2019), 181; John Emerson, "A Faithful Account of Many Wonderful and Surprising Things Which Happened in the Town of Glocester, in the Year 1692," in *Narratives of the Indian Wars, 1675–1699*, ed. Charles H. Lincoln (New York: Scribner's, 1913), 246–47 ("real French," 246–47; "Molestation," 247).

10. Stacy Schiff, *The Witches: Salem, 1692* (New York: Little, Brown, 2015), 15–19, 53–60, 93, 124; Norton, *In the Devil's Snare*, 44–140; Louise A. Breen, "Judgment at Salem: War, Witchcraft, and Empire," in *Converging Worlds: Communities and Cultures in Colonial America*, ed. Breen (New York: Routledge, 2012), 281–391. For the wider context of witch trials, see John Demos, *Entertaining Satan: Witchcraft and the Culture of Early New England* (Oxford: Oxford University Press, 1982); Virginia DeJohn Anderson, "New England in the Seventeenth Century, in *Origins of Empire: British Overseas Enterprise to the Close of the Seventeenth Century*, ed. Nicholas Canny, Oxford History of the British Empire, vol. 1 (New York: Oxford University Press, 1998), 207.

CHAPTER 13: VIRGINIA'S CIVIL AND UNCIVIL WARS

1. Wilcomb E. Washburn, "Governor Berkeley and King Philip's War," *NEQ* 30 (September 1957): 373 ("The New England"); Kevin Butterfield, "Puritans and Religious Strife in the Early Chesapeake," *Virginia Magazine of History and Biography* 109, no. 1 (2001): 5–36.

2. Edmund S. Morgan, *American Slavery, American Freedom: The Ordeal of Colonial Virginia* (New York: W. W. Norton, 1975), 185–95, 215–49; Kathleen M. Brown, *Good Wives, Nasty Wenches, and Anxious Patriarchs: Gender, Race, and Power in Colonial Virginia* (Chapel Hill: University of North Carolina Press, 1996), 319–66; Lorena S. Walsh, *From Calabar to Carter's Grove: The History of a Virginia Slave Community* (Williamsburg: University of Virginia Press, 2000); Warren M. Billings, *Sir William Berkeley and the Forging of Colonial Virginia* (Baton Rouge: Louisiana State University Press, 2004), 174–209.

3. Warren M. Billings, "The Causes of Bacon's Rebellion: Some Suggestions," *Virginia Magazine of History and Biography* 78 (October 1970): 409–35; James D. Rice, *Nature and History in the Potomac Country: From Hunter-Gatherers to the Age of Jefferson* (Baltimore: Johns Hopkins University Press, 2009), 108–42. For enduring fear and anxiety along the East Coast, see Karen Ordahl Kupperman, *Indians and English: Facing Off in Early America* (Ithaca, NY: Cornell University Press, 2000).

4. James D. Rice, *Tales from a Revolution: Bacon's Rebellion and the Transformation of Early America* (New York: Oxford University Press, 2012), 4–7; Matthew Kruer, "Bloody Minds and Peoples Undone: Emotion, Family, and Political Order in the Susquehannock-Virginia War," *WMQ* 74 (July 2017): 416–17.

5. Richard J. S. McCracken, "Susquehannocks, Brulé, and Carantouannais: A Continuing Research Problem," *Bulletin and Journal of Archaeology for New York State* 91 (1985): 46–48; April Lee Hatfield, *Atlantic Virginia: Intercolonial Relations in the Seventeenth Century* (Philadelphia: University of Pennsylvania Press, 2004), 199–200; Kruer, "Bloody Minds and Peoples Undone," 417–21; James D. Rice, "Bacon's Rebellion in Indian Country," *JAH* 101 (December 2014): 733–35; John Berry and Francis Moryson, "A True Narrative of the Rise, Progresse, and Cessation of the Late Rebellion in Virginia, Most Humbly and Impartially Reported by His Majestyes Commissioners Appointed to Enquire into the Affaires of the Said Colony," in *Narratives of the Insurrections, 1675–1690*, ed. Charles M. Andrews (New York: Scribner's, 1915), 107–8 ("approaching calamity," 108); Rice, *Tales from a Revolution*, 30–31, 36; Matthew Kruer, email to the author, May 2020.

6. *BR*, 268.

7. Kruer, "Bloody Minds and Peoples Undone," 419–20; Alan Taylor, *American Colonies* (New York: Viking, 2001), 149–50.

8. "Bacon's Declaration in the Name of the People 30 July 1676," American History from Revolution to Reconstruction and Beyond, http://www.let.rug.nl/usa/documents/1651-1700/bacons-declaration-in-the-name-of-the-people-30-july-1676.php ("having protected"); "Mr. Bacon's Acct of Their Troubles by Ye Indians, July 18, 1676," *WMQ* 9 (July 1900): 2, 8 ("wee destroyed", 2; "satisfaction," "soe enraged," "came home," 8); Warren M. Billings, ed., *Papers of Sir William Berkeley, 1605–1677* (Richmond: Library of Virginia, 2007), 516; Rice, "Bacon's Rebellion," 746.

9. Berry and Moryson, "True Narrative," 114–15; "Mrs. Bacon to Sister of Nathaniel Bacon, June 29, 1676," *WMQ* 9 (July 1900): 4 ("I am sure").

10. Kruer, "Bloody Minds and Peoples Undone," 429–30; L. Scott Philyaw, *Virginia's Western Visions: Political and Cultural Expansion on an Early American Frontier* (Knoxville: University of Tennessee Press, 2004), 7–9; Taylor, *American Colonies*, 149–51; Marcia Brownell Bready, "A Cavalier in Virginia—The Right Hon. Sir Wm. Berkeley, His Majesty's Governor," *WMQ* 18 (October 1909): 28, 123–30 ("old fool," 28); Stephen Saunder Webb, *1676, the End of American Independence* (New York: Knopf, 1984), 75–76.

11. *JR*, 59:251 ("utterly defeated," "Their insolence"); *OL*, 135–42; Gail D. MacLeitch, *Imperial Entanglements: Iroquois Change and Persistence on the Frontiers of Empire* (Philadelphia: University of Pennsylvania Press, 2011), 40–41. For a theoretical discussion of gender metaphors, see Nancy Shoemaker, "An Alliance between Men: Gender Metaphors in Eighteenth-Century American Indian Diplomacy East of the Mississippi," *Ethnohistory* 46 (Spring 1999): esp. 241. For "forest diplomacy," see Claudia B. Haake, "Appeals to Civilization and Customary 'Forest Diplomacy': Arguments against Removal in Letters Written by the Iroquois, 1830–1857," *Wicazo Sa Review* 30 (Fall 2015): 100–128.

12. "Treaty between Virginia and the Indians, 1677: Articles of Peace between the Most Mighty Prince & Our Dread Soveraigne Lord Charles the II by the Grace of God King of Greate Brittaine France, and Ireland Defender of the Ffaith &c: And the Severall Indian Kings and Queens &c Assentors and Subscribers Hereunto Made and Concluded at the Camp of Middle Plantation, May: 1677; Being the Day of the Most Happy Birth & Restauration of Our s'd Soveraigne Lord, and in the

XXIX Yeare of His Said Ma'ties Reigne," *Virginia Magazine of History and Biography* 14 (January 1907): 290–94 ("Indian Kings," 290; "each Indian," 293; "every Indian," 294); Martha W. McCartney, "Cockacoeske, Queen of Pamunkey: Diplomat and Suzeraine," in *Powhatan's Mantle: Indians in the Colonial Southeast*, ed. Peter H. Wood, Gregory A. Waselkow, and M. Thomas Hatley (Lincoln: University of Nebraska Press, 1989), 173–95.

13.   Taylor, *American Colonies*, 266–69; J. H. Elliott, *Empires of the Atlantic World: Britain and Spain in America, 1492–1830* (New Haven, CT: Yale University Press, 2006), 212; *EW*, 170–71; Stephen Warren, *The Worlds the Shawnees Made: Migration and Violence in Early America* (Chapel Hill: University of North Carolina Press, 2014), 158; Eric Hinderaker, *Elusive Empires: Constructing Colonialism in the Ohio Valley, 1673–1800* (New York: Cambridge University Press, 1997), 103–5; Daniel K. Richter, "Land and Words: William Penn's Letter to the Kings of the Indians," in Richter, *Trade, Land, Power: The Struggle for Eastern North America* (Philadelphia: University of Pennsylvania Press, 2013), 135–54.

14.   *OL*, 150–53; Baron de Lahontan, *New Voyages to North-America*, ed. Reuben Gold Thwaites (1703 English ed.; repr., Chicago: A. C. McClurg, 1905), 1:78–82 ("The Warriors," "was to ruin," "I have express," 78; "French who," "upon the end," "joyn," 79; "Onontio," "I must," 80; "we are born," 82); "Abstract of Proposalls of the Onoundages and Cayouges Sachims at New Yorke," August 2, 1684, in *NYCD*, 3:347 ("protect them"); "Abstract of the Proposalls of the Onoundages and Cayouges Sachems at New York, 2. August," in *The Documentary History of the State of New-York*, ed. E. B. O'Callaghan (Albany, NY: Weed, Parsons, 1849), 1:400–401 ("Penn's people," 402).

15.   *EW*, 175–79; M. de Denonville to M. de Seignelay, September 9, 1686, in *NYCD*, 9:295–98 ("I am very sorry," 295; "The Iroquois," "the Colony," 298).

CHAPTER 14: THE GREAT SOUTHWESTERN REBELLION

1.   "Declaration of Pedro Naranjo of the Queres Nation, December 19, 1681," and "Autos Drawn Up as a Result of the Rebellion of the Christian Indians, August 9, 1680," in *Revolt of the Pueblo Indians of New Mexico and Otermin's Attempted Reconquest, 1680–1682*, ed. Charles Wilson Hackett, trans. Charmion Clair Shelby (Albuquerque: University of New Mexico Press, 1942), 2:3–4, 245–49 ("all the nations," 3–4). For Po'pay and runners, see Andrés Reséndez, *The Other Slavery: The Uncovered Story of Indian Enslavement in America* (Boston: Houghton Mifflin Harcourt, 2016), 152–55.

2.   Alonso de Benavides, *A Harvest of Reductant Souls: Fray Alonso de Benavides's History of New Mexico*, trans. and ed. Baker H. Morrow (Albuquerque: University of New Mexico Press, 1996), 39–41 ("land was," 41); *SFNA*, 92–100; Andrew L. Knaut, *The Pueblo Revolt of 1680: Conquest and Resistance in Seventeenth-Century New Mexico* (Norman: University of Oklahoma Press, 1997), 17–52. For the Chichimeca War, see Philip Wayne Powell, *Soldiers, Indians, and Silver: The Northward Advance of New Spain* (Berkeley: University of California Press, 1952).

3.   Ramón A. Gutiérrez, *When Jesus Came, the Corn Mothers Went Away: Marriage, Sexuality, and Power in New Mexico, 1500–1846* (Stanford, CA: Stanford University Press, 1991), 108–12; Henry R. Voth, *The Traditions of the Hopi*, Field Columbian Museum Publication 96, Anthropological Series, no. 8 (Chicago, 1905), 268–69.

4.   Alonso de Benavides, *Revised Memorial of 1634* (Albuquerque: University of New Mexico Press, 1945), 171 ("to take"); James Brooks, *Captives and Cousins: Slavery,*

Kinship, and Community in the Southwest Borderlands (Chapel Hill: University of North Carolina Press, 2002), 50–51.

5. J. H. Elliott, *Empires of the Atlantic World: Britain and Spain in America, 1492–1830* (New Haven, CT: Yale University Press, 2006), 190–91; *NWA*, 30; *SFNA*, 122–26, 130; Reséndez, *Other Slavery*, 125–29, 158–59; Gutiérrez, *When Jesus Came*, 4–10.

6. Fray Juan Bernal to the Tribunal, Santo Domingo, April 1, 1669, in *Historical Documents Relating to New Mexico, Nueva Vizcaya, and Approaches Thereto, to 1773*, ed. Charles W. Hackett (Washington, DC: Carnegie Institution, 1923–37), 3:272 ("a great many"); James E. Ivey, "'The Greatest Misfortune of All': Famine in the Province of New Mexico, 1667–1672," *Journal of the Southwest* 36 (Spring 1994): 81–87.

7. Ned Blackhawk, *Violence over the Land: Indians and Empires in the Early American West* (Cambridge, MA: Harvard University Press, 2006), 24–32; Gary Clayton Anderson, *The Indian Southwest, 1580–1830: Ethnogenesis and Reinvention* (Norman: University of Oklahoma Press, 1999), 22–27, 105–11; Gutiérrez, *When Jesus Came*, 107.

8. Ivey, "'Greatest Misfortune of All,'" 87–89; Anderson, *Indian Southwest*, 15–29. For a comprehensive work on the Jumanos, see Nancy Parrott Hickerson, *The Jumanos: Hunters and Traders of the Southern Plains* (Austin: University of Texas Press, 1994).

9. Samuel Truett, *Fugitive Landscapes: The Forgotten History of the U.S.-Mexico Borderlands* (New Haven, CT: Yale University Press, 2006), 25–27; Anderson, *Indian Southwest*, 21–27; J. Charles Kelly, "The Historic Indian Pueblos of La Junta de los Rios," *New Mexico Historical Review* 27 (October 1952): 265–68; Paul Conrad, *The Apache Diaspora: Four Centuries of Displacement and Survival* (Philadelphia: University of Pennsylvania Press, 2021), 23.

10. Gutiérrez, *When Jesus Came*, 10–36; Reséndez, *Other Slavery*, 158–66; Conrad, *Apache Diaspora*, 17–19.

11. Charles Wilson Hackett, "The Revolt of the Pueblo Indians of New Mexico in 1680," *Quarterly of the Texas State Historical Association* 15 (October 1911): 98–102; James F. Brooks, "Women, Men, and Cycles of Evangelism in the Southwest Borderlands, A.D. 750 to 1750," *AHR* 118 (June 2013): 738–64.

12. "Antonio Otermín Describes the Pueblo Revolt," in *Interpreting a Continent: Voices from Colonial America*, ed. Kathleen DuVal and John DuVal (Lanham, MD: Rowman & Littlefield, 2009), 254 ("How could"); Hackett, "Revolt of the Pueblo Indians of New Mexico in 1680," 103–44 ("to the greater," 143); Conrad, *Apache Diaspora*, 29–30, 75; *SFNA*, 135; Reséndez, *Other Slavery*, 167–71.

13. Hackett, "Revolt of the Pueblo Indians of New Mexico in 1680," 105–30; John L. Kessell, *Kiva, Cross and Crown: The Pecos Indians and New Mexico, 1540–1840* (Washington, DC: National Park Service, 1979), 231–37. For the anti-Spanish and anti-Christian character of the revolt, see Gutiérrez, *When Jesus Came*, 134–36; and Matthew J. Liebmann, *Revolt: An Archeological History of Pueblo Resistance and Revitalization in 17th Century New Mexico* (Tucson: University of Arizona Press, 2012), 29–82.

14. Tracy Brown, "Tradition and Change in Eighteenth-Century Pueblo Indian Communities," *Journal of the Southwest* 46 (Autumn 2004): 463–500; *SFNA*, 136.

15. Conrad, *Apache Diaspora*, 77.

16. Jack D. Forbes, *Apache, Navajo, and Spaniard* (Norman: University of Oklahoma Press, 1960), 292–311. For a comprehensive study of the Spanish reconquest, see Man-

uel Espinosa, *Crusaders of Río Grande: The Story of Diego de Vargas and the Reconquest and Refounding of New Mexico* (Chicago: Institute of Jesuit History, 1942).

17. Diego de Vargas to the Conde de Galve, May 20, June 2 and 3 (two letters), 1694, and October 14, in *Blood on the Boulders: The Journals of Don Diego de Vargas, New Mexico, 1694–97*, ed. John L. Kessell, Rick Hendricks, and Meredith D. Dodge (Albuquerque: University of New Mexico Press, 1998), 242–66, 416–19 ("over the dwelling," 265); Angélino Chavez, *Our Lady of Conquest* (Santa Fe: Historical Society of New Mexico, 1948), 21–28; Kessell, *Kiva, Cross, and Crown*, 252–67; David Roberts, *The Pueblo Revolt: The Secret Rebellion That Drove the Spaniards Out of the Southwest* (New York: Simon and Schuster, 2005), 182–91.

18. *SFNA*, 139–41; Gutiérrez, *When Jesus Came*, 143–46, 156–57.

19. Conrad, *Apache Diaspora*, 77.

20. Colin Calloway, *One Vast Winter Count: The Native American West before Lewis and Clark* (Lincoln: University of Nebraska Press, 2003), 177–85.

21. "Diary of Juan de Ulibarrí to El Cuartelejo, 1706," in *After Coronado: Spanish Exploration Northeast of New Mexico, 1696–1727*, ed. and trans. Alfred Barnaby Thomas (Norman: University of Oklahoma Press, 1935), 61; Brooks, "Women, Men, and Cycles of Evangelicalism," esp. 739.

CHAPTER 15: HOLDING THE LINE

1. Francis Nicholson, "Catawba Deerskin Map," Library of Congress, accessed October 22, 2021, https://www.loc.gov/resource/g3860.ct000734/?r=-0.0335,-0.023,1.773,0.764,0 ("the English Path"); Mary Elizabeth Fitts, "Mapping Catawba Coalescence," *North Carolina Archeology* 55 (2006): 8–14; James H. Merrell, "The Racial Education of the Catawba Indians," *Journal of Southern History* 50 (August 1984): 363–65 ("Nothings," 365); John Lawson, *A New Voyage to Carolina; Containing the Exact Description and Natural History of That Country: Together with the Present State Thereof* (London, 1709), 44 ("our Landlord"); James H. Merrell, "'Our Bond of Peace': Patterns of Intercultural Exchange in the Carolina Piedmont, 1650–1750," in *Powhatan's Mantle: Indians in the Colonial Southeast*, ed. Peter H. Wood, Gregory A. Waselkow, and M. Thomas Hatley (Lincoln: University of Nebraska Press, 1989), 282; Joshua Piker, *Okfuskee: A Creek Indian Town in Colonial America* (Cambridge, MA: Harvard University Press, 2004), 38–39; Nancy Shoemaker, "How Indians Got to Be Red," *AHR* 102 (June 1997): 625–44; J. F. Lee, *Masters of the Middle Waters: Indian Nations and Colonial Ambitions along the Mississippi* (Cambridge, MA: Harvard University Press, 2019), 84–86.

2. Bradley J. Dixon, "'His One Netev Ples': The Chowans and the Politics of Native Petitions in the Colonial South," *WMQ* 76 (January 2019): 41–74.

3. Richard Middleton and Anne Lombard, *Colonial America to 1763*, 4th ed. (Malden, MA: Blackwell, 2011), 149; Lawson, *New Voyage to Carolina*, 241, 244, 251 ("absolute Lords," 241; "in so remote," "among so many," "Savages," 251); Thomas C. Parramore, "The Tuscarora Ascendancy," *North Carolina Historical Review* 59 (October 1982): 307–26; James Atkinson, *Splendid Land, Splendid People: The Chickasaw Indians to Removal* (Tuscaloosa: University of Alabama Press, 2003), 30–32.

4. Kathryn E. Holland Braund, "Guardians of Tradition and Handmaidens to Change: Women's Roles in Creek Economic and Social Life during the Eighteenth Century," *American Indian Quarterly* 14 (Summer 1990): 239–58; Theda Perdue, *Cherokee Women: Gender and Culture Change, 1700–1835* (Lincoln: University of Nebraska

Press, 1998), 38; Michelene E. Pesantubbee, *Choctaw Women in a Chaotic World: The Clash of Cultures in the Colonial Southeast* (Albuquerque: University of New Mexico Press, 2005), 175; John Archdale, *A New Description of That Fertile and Pleasant Carolina* (1707; repr., Charleston, SC: A. E. Miller, 1822), 14 ("Charles-Town"); *NOT*, 39–42; Felicity Donohoe, "'Decoying Them Within': Creek Gender Identities and the Subversion of Civilization," in *Native Diasporas: Indigenous Identities and Settler Colonialism in the Americas*, ed. Gregory D. Smithers and Brooke N. Newman (Lincoln: University of Nebraska Press, 2014), 187–88.

5.   U.S. Census Bureau, *Historical Statistics of the United States, Colonial to 1975*, bicentennial ed. (Washington, DC: U.S. Department of Commerce, Bureau of the Census, 1975), 2:1168, https://www2.census.gov/prod2/statcomp/documents/CT1970p2-13.pdf.

6.   For the epidemic and the broader historical context, see Paul Kelton, *Epidemics and Enslavement: Biological Catastrophe in the Native Southeast, 1492–1715* (Lincoln: University of Nebraska Press, 2007), 101–60.

7.   Andrew Preston, *Sword of the Spirit, Shield of Faith: Religion in American War and Diplomacy* (New York: Anchor, 2012), 51–54; Alejandra Dubcovsky, "Defying Indian Slavery: Apalachee Voices and Spanish Sources in the Eighteenth-Century Southeast," *WMQ* 75 (April 2018): 295–322; Alan Gallay, *The Indian Slave Trade: The Rise of the English Empire in the American South, 1670–1717* (New Haven, CT: Yale University Press, 2002), 135–40, 144–54; John H. Hahn, *Apalachee: The Land between the Rivers* (Gainesville, FL: LibraryPress@UF, 2017), 15; *NWA*, 102; Stephen Warren, *The Worlds the Shawnees Made: Migration and Violence in Early America* (Chapel Hill: University of North Carolina Press, 2014), 81 ("warrior paths").

8.   Coll Thrush, *Indigenous London: Native Travelers at the Heart of Empire* (New Haven, CT: Yale University Press, 2016), 73–76; *OL*, 201–2.

9.   South Carolina Board of Commissioners of the Indian Trade, *Journals of the Commissioners of the Indian Trade: September 20, 1710–August 29, 1718*, ed. W. L. McDowell, Colonial Records of South Carolina, ser. 2, The Indian Books (Columbia: South Carolina University Press, 1955), 56.

10. H. R. McIlwaine, ed., *Executive Journals of the Council of Colonial Virginia*, vol. 3, *(May 1, 1705–October 23, 1721)* (Richmond, VA: Davis Bottom, 1928), 291; Gallay, *Indian Slave Trade*, 275–77, 283–302; Verner W. Crane, *The Southern Frontier, 1670–1732* (Durham, NC: Duke University Press, 1929), 158–61; *OL*, 238–39; *NWA*, 103; Taylor, *American Colonies*, 233.

11. James H. Merrell, *Indians' New World: Catawbas and Their Neighbors from European Contact through the Era of Removal* (Chapel Hill: University of North Carolina Press, 1989), 68–75; Merrell, "'Our Bond of Peace,'" 285–86; Steven J. Oatis, *A Colonial Complex: South Carolina's Frontiers in the Era of the Yamasee War* (Lincoln: University of Nebraska Press, 2004), 210 ("50 Nations"); Crane, *Southern Frontier*, 162–72; Steven C. Hahn, *The Invention of the Creek Nation, 1670–1763* (Lincoln: University of Nebraska Press, 2004), 82, 94–96; Amanda Hall, "The Persistence of Yamasee Power and Identity at the Town of San Antonio de Pocotalaca, 1716–1752," in *Yamasee Indians: From Florida to South Carolina*, ed. Denise I. Bossy (Lincoln: University of Nebraska Press, 2018), 221–23; Christina Snyder, *Slavery in Indian Country: The Changing Face of Captivity in Early America* (Cambridge, MA: Harvard University Press, 2010), 76.

12. Gary Nash, *Red, White, and Black: Peoples of Early North America* (Englewood Cliffs, NJ: Prentice-Hall, 1974), 123; Gallay, *Indian Slave Trade*, 337–41; James

H. Merrell, "'Their Very Bones Shall Fight': Catawba-Iroquois Wars," in *Beyond the Covenant Chain: The Iroquois and Their Neighbors in Indian North America*, ed. Daniel K. Richter and James H. Merrell (Philadelphia: University of Pennsylvania Press, 1987), 124. For go-betweens, see James H. Merrell, *Into the American Woods: Negotiations on the Pennsylvania Frontier* (New York: W. W. Norton, 1999); Jane T. Merritt, "Metaphor, Meaning, and Misunderstanding: Language and Power on the Pennsylvania Frontier," in *Contact Points: American Frontiers from the Mohawk Valley to the Mississippi*, ed. Andrew R. L. Cayton and Fredrika J. Teute (Chapel Hill: University of North Carolina Press, 1998), 60–87; William B. Hart, "Black 'Go-Betweens,' and the Mutability of 'Race,' 'Status,' and Identity on New York's Pre-Revolutionary Frontier," in *Contact Points*, ed. Cayton and Teute, 88–113; Judith Carney, "The African Origins of Carolina Rice Culture," *Ecumene* 7 (April 2000): 125–49; Piker, *Okfuskee*, 22–26; Alejandra Dubcovsky, *Informed Power: Communication in the Early American South* (Cambridge, MA: Harvard University Press, 2016), 198.

13. Patrick Gordon to James Oglethorpe, June 15, 1732, in *Pennsylvania Archives*, ed. Samuel Hazard et al. (Philadelphia: Joseph Severns et al.), ser. 1, vol. 1 (1851–53): 322 ("I doubt not," "constantly"); Phinizy Spalding, "Oglethorpe, William Stephens, and the Origin of Georgia Politics," in *Oglethorpe in Perspective: Georgia's Founder after Two Hundred Years*, ed. Phinizy Spalding and Harvey H. Jackson (Tuscaloosa: University of Alabama Press, 1889), 80–98; D. Andrew Johnson, "Displacing Captives in Colonial South Carolina: Native American Enslavement and the Rise of the Colonial State after the Yamasee War," *Journal of Early American History* 7 (July 2017): 115–40.

14. The Landholders of Georgia to James Oglethorpe, n.d., in *Collections of the Georgia Historical Society* (Savannah: The Society, 1842), 2:166 ("the ancient"); Benjamin Martyn, *Reasons for Establishing the Colony of Georgia* (London: Printed for W. Meadows, at the Angel in Cornhill, 1733), 3; *SA*, 1:181–82; James Edward Oglethorpe, *A New and Accurate Account of the Provinces of South-Carolina and Georgia* (London: J. Worrall, 1732), 13 ("must at all Times").

15. Martyn, *Reasons for Establishing*, 6–15; William B. O. Peabody, "Life of James Oglethorpe, the Founder of Georgia," in *Lives of James Otis and James Oglethorpe*, Library of American Biography, vol. 12 (Boston: Charles C. Little and James Brown, 1844), 241 ("secret enemies"); Ralph Gray and Betty Wood, "The Transition from Indentured to Involuntary Servitude in Colonial Georgia," *Explorations in Economic History* 13, no. 4 (1976): 353–66; Kathryn E. Holland Braund, "The Creek Indians, Blacks, and Slavery," *Journal of Southern History* 57 (November 1991): 605–9; Rodney M. Baine, "Indian Slavery in Colonial Georgia," *Georgia Historical Quarterly* 79 (Summer 1995): 418–24; "Oglethorpe's Treaty with the Lower Creek Indians," *Georgia Historical Quarterly* 4 (March 1920): 14; Jace Weaver, "The Red Atlantic: Transoceanic Cultural Exchanges," *American Indian Quarterly* 35 (Summer 2011): 422–23. For intimate ties among the colonists and Muscogees, see Bryan C. Rindfleisch, *George Galphin's Intimate Empire: The Creek Indians, Family, and Colonialism Early America* (Tuscaloosa: University of Alabama Press, 2019).

16. Theda Perdue, "Cherokee Relations with the Iroquois in the Eighteenth Century," in *Beyond the Covenant Chain*, ed. Richter and Merrell, 136; Peter H. Wood, "Circles in the Sand: Perspectives on the Southern Frontier at the Arrival of James Oglethorpe," in *Oglethorpe in Perspective*, ed. Spalding and Jackson, 9; William Stephens to the Trustees, January 19 and February 27, 173⅞, Stephens to Harman

Verelst, January 19, 173⅞, Thomas Causton to the Trustees, March 1, 1737–8, James Oglethorpe to Joseph Jekyll, September 19, Oglethorpe to Trustees, September 19, 1738, in *The Colonial Records of the State of Georgia*, vol. 22, *Original Papers, Correspondence, Trustees, General Oglethorpe and Others: 1737–1740*, pt. 1, *1737–1739* (Atlanta, GA: Chas. P. Byrd, 1913), 69–110, 251, 252 ("past Danger," 110; "this Province," 251; "the Parliament," 252). For the centrality of gadugi, see Julie Reed, *Serving the Nation: Cherokee Sovereignty and Social Welfare, 1800–1907* (Norman: University of Oklahoma Press, 2016).

17. "Oglethorpe's Treaty," *Georgia Historical Quarterly*, 2–9 ("The English," 7–8; "Rightful," 9); Piker, *Okfuskee*, 1–12.

18. William Stephens to Harman Verelst, May 27, 1738, James Pierce to Verelst, July 14, 1738, William Bull to Lords of Trade, July 20, 1738, Causton to Trustees, August 26, 1738, Oglethorpe to Jekyll, September 19, 1738, and Oglethorpe to Trustees, September 19, 1738, in *Original Papers, Correspondence, Trustees*, pt. 1:175, 193, 212–16, 231, 251–53 ("10,000 Fighting men," 193; "The poor People," 251; "the Misery," 253).

19. Patrick Tailfer, *A True and Historical Narrative of the Colony of Georgia* (Charles Town: P. Timothy, for the authors, 1741), 20 ("The First Thing"); *NOT*, 46; John R. Wunder, "'Merciless Indian Savages' and the Declaration of Independence: Native Americans Translate the Ecunnaunuxulgee Document," *American Indian Law Review* 25 (2000/2001): 65–92 ("Ecunnaunuxulgee," 66); Louis DeVorsey Jr., "Indian Boundaries in Colonial Georgia," *Georgia Historical Quarterly* 54 (Spring 1970): 63–78.

20. U.S. Census Bureau, *Historical Statistics*, 1168; James H. Merrell, "'The Customes of Our Countrey': Indians and Colonists in Early America," in *Strangers within the Realm: Cultural Margins of the First British Empire*, ed. Bernard Bailyn and Philip D. Morgan (Chapel Hill: University of North Carolina Press, 1991), 117–56; Merrell, *Indians' New World*, 77; Jean O'Brien, "Divorced from the Land: Accommodation Strategies of Indian Women in Eighteenth-Century New England," in *Gender, Kinship, and Power: A Comparative and Interdisciplinary History*, ed. Mary Jo Maynes, Ann Waltner, Brigitte Soland, and Ulrike Strasser (New York: Routledge, 1996), 319–33; William Cronon, *Changes in the Land: Indians, Colonists, and the Ecology of New England* (New York: Hill and Wang, 1983), 159–70; Virginia DeJohn Anderson, "King Philip's Herds: Indians, Colonists, and the Problem of Livestock in Early New England," *WMQ* 51 (October 1994): 601–24; Ruth Wallis Herndon and Ella Wilcox Sekatau, "The Right to a Name: The Narragansett People and Rhode Island Officials in the Revolutionary Era," *Ethnohistory* 44 (Summer 1997): 440–43; Margaret Ellen Newell, "Indian Slavery in Colonial New England," in *Indian Slavery in Colonial America*, ed. Alan Gallay (Lincoln: University of Nebraska Press, 2009), 33–66; Warren, *Worlds the Shawnees Made*, 101–2 ("fifty guns"); Pekka Hämäläinen, "The Shapes of Power: Indians, Europeans, and North American Worlds from the Seventeenth to the Nineteenth Century," in *Contested Spaces of Early America*, ed. Juliana Barr and Edward Countryman (Philadelphia: University of Pennsylvania Press, 2014), 31–68. For "modern Indian politics," see Merrell, *Indians' New World*, 134–66.

CHAPTER 16: THEY SMELLED LIKE ALLIGATORS

1. Gilles Havard and Cécile Vidal, *Histoire de l'Amérique Française* (Paris: Flammarion, 2005), 105–8; David W. Miller, *The Forced Removal of American Indians from the Northeast: A History of Territorial Cessions and Relocations, 1620–1854*

(Jefferson, NC: McFarland, 2011), 36; Robert Michael Morrissey, *Empire by Collaboration: Indians, Colonists, and Governments in Colonial Illinois Country* (Philadelphia: University of Pennsylvania Press, 2015), 32–34, 40.

2. Morrissey, *Empire by Collaboration*, 32–36; Zenobius Membré, "Narrative of the Adventures of La Salle's Party at Fort Crevecoeur, in Illinois," in *The Journeys of Réné Robert Cavelier, Sieur de La Salle*, ed. Isaac Joslin Cox (New York: Allerton, 1922), 106–30; Count de Frontenac to the King, November 6, 1679, in *NYCD*, 9:129 ("immense"); *JR*, 62:10 ("killed and ate"); "M. Du Chiesnau's Memoir on the Western Indians, &," in *Pennsylvania Archives*, ed. Samuel Hazard et al. (Philadelphia: Joseph Severns et al.), ser. 2, vol. 6 (1852): 9 ("took no more," "who were very"); Statistics Canada, "Early French Settlements (1605 to 1691)," accessed January 22, 2012, https://www150.statcan.gc.ca/n1/pub/98-187-x/4064812-eng.htm.

3. Count de Frontenac to the King, November 2, 1681, and "M. Du Chesneau's Memoir on the Western Indians," in *NYCD*, 9:147 ("that we do not," "a want of power").

4. Pierre Talon and Jean Talon, "Voyage to the Mississippi through the Gulf of Mexico," Ann Linda Bell, trans., in *La Salle, the Mississippi, and the Gulf: Three Primary Documents*, ed. Mary Christine Morkovsky and Patricia Galloway, trans. Bell and Robert S. Weddle (College Station, TX: Texas A&M University Press, 1987), 225–58; Daniel H. Usner Jr., *Indians, Settlers, and Slaves in a Frontier Exchange Economy: The Lower Mississippi Valley before 1783* (Chapel Hill: University of North Carolina Press, 1992), 14–15. For the character of La Salle, see Peter H. Wood, "La Salle: Discovery of a Lost Explorer," *AHR* 89 (April 1984): 323.

5. Paul W. Mapp, *The Elusive West and the Contest for Empire, 1713–1763* (Chapel Hill: University of North Carolina Press, 2011), 194–232.

6. Havard and Vidal, *Histoire de l'Amérique Française*, 110–12; *HAC*, 87; *EW*, 247–63, 287; Timothy J. Shannon, *Iroquois Diplomacy on the Early American Frontier* (New York: Viking Penguin, 2008), 46; *OL*, 180–89; David L. Preston, *The Texture of Contact: European and Indian Settler Communities on the Frontiers of Iroquoia, 1667–1783* (Lincoln: University of Nebraska Press, 2009), 87; "An Account of the Most Remarkable Occurrences in Canada from the Departure of the Vessels," in *NYCD*, 9:678–87 ("are left," 687); Gail D. MacLeitch, *Imperial Entanglements: Iroquois Change and Perspective on the Frontiers of Empire* (Philadelphia: University of Pennsylvania Press, 2011), 37; Frank McLynn, *1759: The Year Britain Became the Master of the World* (New York: Atlantic Monthly, 2005), 27.

7. Gilles Havard, *The Great Peace of Montreal of 1701: French-Native Diplomacy in the Seventeenth Century* (Montreal: McGill-Queen's University Press, 2001), 111–78; James H. Merrell, "'Their Very Bones Shall Fight': Catawba-Iroquois Wars," in *Beyond the Covenant Chain: The Iroquois and Their Neighbors in Indian North America*, ed. Daniel K. Richter and James H. Merrell (Philadelphia: University of Pennsylvania Press, 1987), 118–33 ("Peace," 120); *EW*, 287; Michael Witgen, *An Infinity of Nations: How the Native New World Shaped Early America* (Philadelphia: University of Pennsylvania Press, 2012), 274–76; Richard Aquila, *The Iroquois Restoration: Iroquois Diplomacy on the Colonial Frontier, 1701–1754* (Detroit, MI: Wayne State University Press, 1983), 205–10; Thomas R. Berger, *A Long and Terrible Shadow: White Values, Native Rights in the Americas, 1492–1992* (Vancouver, BC: Douglas & McIntyre, 1991), 60 ("the five Iroquois").

8. For a detailed study of the raid, see Evan Haefeli and Kevin Sweeney, *Captors and Captives: The French and Indian Raid on Deerfield* (Amherst: University of Massachusetts Press, 2003). For Kanenstenhawi, see John Demos, *The Unredeemed Captive: A Family Story from Early America* (New York: Alfred Knopf, 1994).

9. Brett Rushforth, *Bonds of Alliance: Indigenous and Atlantic Slaveries in New France* (Chapel Hill: University of North Carolina Press, 2012), esp. 193–253; Tiya Miles, *The Dawn of Detroit: A Chronicle of Slavery in the City of the Straits* (New York: New Press, 2017), 39–46; Havard and Vidal, *Histoire de l'Amérique Française*, 413–35; *HAC*, plates 46, 47.

10. Pierre Le Moyne d'Iberville, *Iberville's Gulf Journals*, trans. and ed. Richebourg Gaillard McWilliams (Tuscaloosa: University of Alabama Press, 1981), 17–105; Jean-Baptiste Bénard de La Harpe, "Historical Journal of the Establishment of the French Louisiana," in *Historical Collections of Louisiana*, ed. B. F. French (New York: D. Appleton, 1851), 3:12–19; Joe Bassette Wilkins, "La Moyne de d'Iberville, Pierre," in *Colonial Wars of North America, 1512–1763: An Encyclopedia*, ed. Alan Gallay (1996; repr., New York: Routledge, 2015), 378–79.

11. Patricia K. Galloway, "Choctaws at the Border of the Shatter Zone: Spheres of Exchange and Spheres of Social Value," in *Mapping the Mississippian Shatter Zone: The Colonial Indian Slave Trade and Regional Instability in the American South*, ed. Robbie Ethridge and Sheri M. Shuck-Hall (Lincoln: University of Nebraska Press, 2009), 333–56; Pierre Margry, ed., *Découvertes et établissements des français dans l'ouest et dans le sud de l'Amérique Septentrionale (1614–1754): Mémoires et documents originaux*, pt. 4, *(1694–1703)* (Paris: D. Jouaust, 1880), 517–19 ("an air of" [*air de Iroquois et les manières de gens de guerre*], 519); James Atkinson, *Splendid Land, Splendid People: The Chickasaw Indians to Removal* (Tuscaloosa: University of Alabama Press, 2003), 59–60.

12. Carl J. Ekberg, *French Roots in the Illinois Country: The Mississippi Valley Frontier in Colonial Times* (Urbana: University of Illinois Press, 2000), 54–58.

13. Robert Michael Morrissey, "The Power of the Ecotone: Bison, Slavery, and the Rise and Fall of the Grand River of Kaskaskia," *JAH* 102 (December 2015): 667–91; Havard and Vidal, *Histoire de l'Amérique Française*, 132; Daniel P. Barr, *Unconquered: The Iroquois League at War in Colonial America* (Westport, CT: Praeger, 2006), 81; *MG*, 160.

14. *MG*, 82–90, 149–54; *OL*, 223–24; Brett Rushforth, "Slavery, the Fox Wars, and the Limits of Alliance," *WMQ* 63 (January 2006): 57–65; Joseph Marest to Philippe de Rigaud, Marquis de Vaudreuil, June 4, 1708, Francois Clairambault D'Aigremont, letter, November 14, 1708, and Philippe de Rigaud and Jacques Raudot, "Report of the Colonies," November 14, 1708, in *Historical Collections. Collections and Researches Made by the Pioneer and Historical Society of Michigan* (Lansing, MI: The Society, 1904), 33:383–87, 404–6, 431–46; Witgen, *Infinity of Nations*, 288–95; "Charlevoix's journal historique," in *WHC*, 16:417–18 ("great damage," 417).

15. Havard and Vidal, *Histoire de l'Amérique Française*, 131–32; James Pritchard, *In Search of Empire: The French in the Americas, 1670–1730* (Cambridge: Cambridge University Press, 2004), 25–26, 44; David MacDonald, *Lives of Fort Charters: Commandants, Soldiers, and Civilians in French Illinois, 1720–1770* (Carbondale: Southern Illinois University Press, 2016), 37; J. F. Lee, *Masters of the Middle Waters: Indian Nations and Colonial Ambitions along the Mississippi* (Cambridge, MA: Harvard University Press, 2019), 92; Sophie White, *Wild Frenchmen and Frenchified Indians: Material Culture and Race in Colonial Louisiana* (Philadelphia: University of Pennsylvania Press, 2012), 28; Light Townsend Cummins, Judith Kelleher Schafer, Edward F. Haas, Michael L. Kurtz, Bennett H. Wall, and John C. Rodrigue, *Louisiana: A History*, ed. Wall and Rodrigue, 6th ed. (Malden, MA: Wiley Blackwell, 2014), 40; Usner, *Indians, Settlers, and Slaves*, 31–32; Mathé Allain, *Not Worth a Straw: French Colonial Policy and the Early Years of Louisiana* (Lafayette: Center for Louisiana Studies, 1988), 67–68.

16. Richard White, *The Roots of Dependency: Subsistence, Environment, and Social Change among the Choctaws, Pawnees, and Navajos* (Lincoln: University of Nebraska Press, 1983), 48–49; Antonio de la Mothe Cadillac and Pierre Liette, *The Western Country in the 17th Century: The Memoirs of Lamothe Cadillac and Pierre Liette*, ed. Milo Milton Quaife (ca. 1702; repr., Chicago: Lakeside Press, 1947), 78 ("a large number," "deserves to be," "alone decides"); Jeffrey P. Brain, "The Natchez 'Paradox,'" *Ethnology* 10 (April 1971): 215–22.

17. Usner, *Indians, Settlers, and Slaves*, 27–29; Daniel H. Usner Jr., *American Indians in the Lower Mississippi Valley: Social and Economic Histories* (Lincoln: University of Nebraska Press, 1998), 23; Gilles Havard, "'Protection' and 'Unequal Alliance': The French Conception of Sovereignty over Indians in New France," in *French and Indians in the Heart of North America, 1630–1815*, ed. Robert Englebert and Guillaume Teasdale (East Lansing: Michigan State University Press, 2013), 113–38.

18. Havard and Vidal, *Histoire de l'Amérique Française*, 392–93; Kathleen DuVal, *The Native Ground: Indians and Colonists in the Heart of the Continent* (Philadelphia: University of Pennsylvania Press, 2006), 778–82.

19. DuVal, *Native Ground*, 79–83, 104–7; Kathleen DuVal, "Living in the Reordered World, 1680–1763," in *The Oxford Handbook of American Indian History*, ed. Frederick E. Hoxie (New York: Oxford University Press, 2016), 58–59; Lee, *Masters of the Middle Waters*, 165–67.

20. Jean-Baptiste Bienville to the Council, February 1, 1723, in *Mississippi Provincial Archives, 1704–1734: French Dominion*, ed. and trans. Dunbar Kowland and A. G. Sanders (Jackson: Press of the Mississippi Department of Archives and History, 1927–84), 3:343 ("to put these"); James Adair, *The History of the American Indians* (London: Printed for Edward and Charles Dilly, 1775), 260 ("The Old men").

21. Jean-Bernard Bossu, *Travels in the Interior of North America, 1752–1762*, trans. and ed. Seymour Feiler (Norman: University of Oklahoma Press, 1962), 83–84 ("who were half," "smelled like," 84). For Bourgmont, see A. P. Nasatir, ed., *Before Lewis and Clark: Documents Illustrating the History of the Missouri, 1785–1804* (1952; repr., Lincoln: University of Nebraska Press, 1990), 2:12–22; and Elliott West, *The Essential West: Collected Essays* (Norman: University of Oklahoma Press, 2012), 137–41.

22. DuVal, *Native Ground*, 104–10; "Memoir on Indians by Kerlérec," in *Mississippi Provincial Archives*, ed. and trans. Kowland and Sanders, 5:206; Willard H. Rollings, *The Osage: An Ethnohistorical Study of Hegemony on the Prairie-Plains* (Columbia: University of Missouri Press, 1992), 127–33; Colin Calloway, *One Vast Winter Count: The Native American West before Lewis and Clark* (Lincoln: University of Nebraska Press, 2003), 363, 381 ("the Osages," 381); Lee, *Masters of the Middle Waters*, 167–71.

23. Elizabeth Ellis, "The Natchez War Revisited: Violence, Multinational Settlements, and Indigenous Diplomacy in the Lower Mississippi Valley," *WMQ* 77 (July 2020): 455–63; Mary Ann Wells, *Native Land: Mississippi, 1540–1798* (Jackson: University Press of Mississippi, 1994), 119–21; Usner, *Indians, Settlers, and Slaves*, 70–72; Usner, *American Indians in the Lower Mississippi Valley*, 24–25; Patricia D. Woods, "The French and the Natchez Indians in Louisiana: 1700–1731," *Louisiana History* 19 (Autumn 1978): 432–34; Havard and Vidal, *Histoire de l'Amérique Française*, 301–5.

24. Ellis, "Natchez War Revisited," 1 ("The colony"); Usner, *Indians, Settlers, and Slaves*, 46–47, 70–76; Daniel H. Usner Jr., "Indian-Black Relations in Colonial and Antebellum Louisiana," in *Slave Cultures and the Cultures of Slaves*, ed. Stephan Palmié (Knoxville: University of Tennessee Press, 1995), 151; Daniel H. Usner Jr., "From African Captivity to American Slavery: The Introduction of Black Laborers

to Colonial Louisiana," *Louisiana History* 20 (Winter 1979): 40; Rushforth, "Slavery, the Fox Wars," 72–80; Witgen, *Infinity of Nations*, 293–95; R. David Edmunds and Joseph L. Peyser, *The Fox Wars: The Mesquakie Challenge to New France* (Norman: University of Oklahoma Press, 1993), 159; Charles de la Boiche de Beauharnois and Gilles Hocquart to the French Minister, November 2, 1730, in *WHC*, 17:113, 167 ("total destruction," 113; "the last blow," 167").

25. Kathleen DuVal, "Indian Intermarriage and Métissage in Colonial Louisiana," *WMQ* 65 (April 2008): 267–304; Ellis, "Natchez War Revisited," 442.

26. *Mississippi Colonial Archives: French Dominion*, ed. Patricia Galloway, rev. ed. (Baton Rouge, LA: Louisiana State University Press, 1984), 4:262 ("none of those"); Wells, *Native Land*, 161 ("the bulwark"); Usner, *Indians, Settlers, and Slaves*, 76–81.

27. "Relation du sieur St. Pierre, commandant au poste des Sioux, jointe à la lettre de M. le Marquis de Beauharnois," October 14, 1737, in *Découvertes et établissements des Français dans l'ouest et dans le sud de l'Amérique septentrionale (1614–1754): Mémoires et documents originaux*, pt. 6, *Exploration des affluents du Mississipi et découverte des Montagnes Rocheuses (1679–1754)*, ed. Pierre Margry (Paris: D. Jouaust, 1886), 577 ("with reflection and design" [*avec reflexion et dessein*]); "Paroles d'un chef renard adressées à Coulon de Villiers," MG1-C11A, F-49, fols. 521–521v, Library and Archives Canada; Constant le Marchand de Lignery to Beauharnois, August 30, 1728, in *WHC*, 17:33–34; Beauharnois to the French Minister, May 19, 1729, July 21, 1729, and October 1, 1731, in *WHC*, 17:62–63, 139–41; Charles des Champs de Boishébert to Beauharnois, February 28, 1732, in *WHC*, 17:148–52; "Report of Trade for 1732," in *WHC*, 17:167–69 ("caused," 167); "Réponse de Beauharnois aux paroles des Sioux, Sakis, Renards, Puants, Sauteux de la Pointe de Chagüamigon et Folles-Avoines," July 28, 1742, Library and Archives Canada, MG1-CiiA, C-2394, fol. 236v ("My Children" [*Mes enfans, comme je vois nûs, je vous donne de quoy vous couvrir*]); Rushforth, *Bonds of Alliance*, 193–94.

28. *LA*, 76–78.

CHAPTER 17: AN INFINITY OF RANCHERÍAS

1. Henri Joutel, *Joutel's Journal of La Salle's Last Voyage, 1684–7* (Albany: Joseph McDonough, 1906), 159–61; F. Todd Smith, *The Caddo Indians: Tribes at the Convergence of Empires, 1542–1854* (College Station: Texas A&M University Press, 1995), 21–37.

2. Debbie S. Cunningham, ed., "The Domingo Ramón Diary of the 1716 Expedition into the Province of the Tejas Indians: An Annotated Translation," *Southwestern Historical Quarterly* 107 (July 2006): 39–66 ("an infinity," 65; "I named," 66).

3. *SFNA*, 161–67; James L. McCorkle Jr., "Los Adaes and the Borderlands Origins of East Texas," *East Texas Historical Journal* 22, no. 2 (1984): 3–12; Juliana Barr, "A Diplomacy of Gender: Rituals of First Contact in the 'Land of the Tejas,'" *WMQ* 61 (July 2004): esp. 396; Gary Clayton Anderson, *The Indian Southwest, 1580–1830: Ethnogenesis and Reinvention* (Norman: University of Oklahoma Press, 1999), 94.

4. Juliana Barr, "Geographies of Power: Mapping Indian Borders in the Early Southwest," *WMQ* 68 (January 2011): 11 ("as well beaten"); Barr, "Diplomacy of Gender," 405; Jean-Baptiste Bénard de La Harpe, "Historical Journal of the Establishment of the French Louisiana," in *Historical Collections of Louisiana*, ed. B. F. French (New York: D. Appleton, 1851), 3: 9–10 ("neither").

5. Richard White, *The Roots of Dependency: Subsistence, Environment, and Social Change among the Choctaws, Pawnees, and Navajos* (Lincoln: University of

Nebraska Press, 1983), 53–56; Juliana Barr, "Beyond Their Control: Spaniards in Native Texas," in *Choice, Persuasion, and Coercion: Social Control on Spain's North American Frontiers*, ed. Jesús F. de la Teja and Ross Frank (Albuquerque: University of New Mexico Press, 2005), 160.

6. Gilles Havard and Cécile Vidal, *Histoire de l'Amérique Française*, 305–6; Daniel H. Usner, *Indians, Settlers, and Slaves in a Frontier Exchange Economy: The Lower Mississippi Valley before 1783* (Chapel Hill: University of North Carolina Press, 1992), 81–85, 88; Michael McDonnell, *Masters of Empire: Great Lakes and the Making of America* (New York: Hill and Wang, 2015), 130–31; Arrell M. Gibson, *The Chickasaws* (Norman: University of Oklahoma Press, 1971), 50–53 ("entire destruction," 50); J. F. Lee, *Masters of the Middle Waters: Indian Nations and Colonial Ambitions along the Mississippi* (Cambridge, MA: Harvard University Press, 2019), 89–90, 100–109; James Atkinson, *Splendid Land, Splendid People: The Chickasaw Indians to Removal* (Tuscaloosa: University of Alabama Press, 2003), 38, 43–44, 58–60, 68.

7. Richard Campanella, *Time and Place in New Orleans: Past Geographies in the Present Day* (Gretna, LA: Pelican, 2002), 54; *SA*, 1:197; Michael Witgen, *An Infinity of Nations: How the Native New World Shaped Early America* (Philadelphia: University of Pennsylvania Press, 2012), 302–8; Colin Calloway, *One Vast Winter Count: The Native American West before Lewis and Clark* (Lincoln: University of Nebraska Press, 2003), 298; Bill Moreau, "The Death of Père Aulneau, 1736: The Development of Myth in the Northwest," *CCHA Historical Studies* 69 (2003): 54–60; Arthur J. Ray, *Indians in the Fur Trade: Their Role as Trappers, Hunters, and Middlemen in the Lands Southwest of Hudson Bay, 1660–1870* (Toronto: University of Toronto Press, 1998), 59–60.

8. Lawrence J. Burpee, *The Search for the Western Sea: The Story of the Exploration of North-Western America* (New York: D. Appleton, 1908); James Pritchard, *In Search of Empire: The French in the Americas, 1670–1730* (Cambridge: Cambridge University Press, 2004), 3; Richard Middleton and Anne Lombard, *Colonial America to 1763*, 4th ed. (Malden, MA: Blackwell, 2011), 377, 396; *LA*, 67–70.

9. Elizabeth Ellis, "Petite Nation with Powerful Networks: The Tunics in the Eighteenth Century," *Louisiana History* 58 (Spring 2017): 136–40; Elizabeth N. Ellis, "The Many Ties of the Petites Nations: Relationships, Power, and Diplomacy in the Lower Mississippi Valley, 1685–1785" (PhD dissertation, University of North Carolina, 2015), 38–52, 96–142.

10. Sami Lakomäki, *Gathering Together: The Shawnee People through Diaspora and Nationhood, 1600–1870* (New Haven, CT: Yale University Press, 2014), 13–24.

11. Lakomäki, *Gathering Together*, 24–29; Isaac Joslin Cox, ed., *The Journeys of Réné Robert Cavalier, Sieur de La Salle* (New York: Allerton, 1922), 1:277–83 ("were not," "in the most," 283); *MG*, 49 ("would be devoid"); Charles Callender, "Shawnee," in *Northeast*, ed. Bruce G. Trigger, vol. 15 of *Handbook of North American Indians*, ed. William C. Sturtevant (Washington, DC: Smithsonian Institution, 1978), 623.

12. Lakomäki, *Gathering Together*, 73, 101; Stephen Warren and Randolph Noe, "'The Greatest Travelers in America': Shawnee Survival in the Shatter Zone," in *Mapping the Mississippian Shatter Zone: The Colonial Indian Slave Trade and Regional Instability in the American South*, ed. Robbie Ethridge and Sheri M. Shuck-Hall (Lincoln: University of Nebraska Press, 2009), 165–67; Frederick Webb Hodge, ed., *Handbook of North American Indians North of Mexico* (Washington, DC: Smithsonian, 1912), 2:536.

13. Warren and Noe, "'Greatest Travelers in America,'" 169–76; Samuel Hazard, ed., *Hazard's Register of Pennsylvania* (Philadelphia: W. F. Geddes, 1828), 1:190 ("liberty," "without fear"); Lakomäki, *Gathering Together*, 30–36; Stephen Warren, *The Worlds the Shawnees Made: Migration and Violence in Early America* (Chapel Hill: University of North Carolina Press, 2014), 84, 92; Gail D. MacLeitch, *Imperial Entanglements: Iroquois Change and Persistence on the Frontiers of Empire* (Philadelphia: University of Pennsylvania Press, 2011), 28; "Council Held at Philadelphia, June 23, 1711," in *MPCP*, 2:533–34 ("if hereafter," 534); John Lawson, *A New Voyage to Carolina; Containing the Exact Description and Natural History of That Country: Together with the Present State Thereof* (London, 1709), 42 ("famous"). For racial reclassification, see Theda Perdue, "American Indian Survival in South Carolina," *South Carolina Historical Magazine* 108 (July 2007): 218–19.

14. "Council Held at Philadelphia," July 12, 1720, in *MPCP*, 3:94 ("William Penn," "with their friend"); "Journal of a Mission to Onondaga," in *NYCD*, 5:376 ("abandoned"); "Conference between Governor Hunter and the Indians," September 14, 1714, in *NYCD*, 5:387, 571 ("as our Children," 387; "are the balance," "the ruin," 571).

15. Lakomäki, *Gathering Together*, 38–45; William Burnet to the Lords of Trade, November 21, 1722, "Conference between Governor Burnet and the Indians," August 27, 1722, and "Answer of Mahikanders or River Indians to William Burnet," August 22, 1722, in *NYCD*, 5:655–63 ("would never molest," 657; "We now," 663); Warren, *Worlds the Shawnees Made*, 14; Susan Sleeper-Smith, *Indigenous Prosperity and American Conquest: Indian Women of the Ohio River Valley, 1690–1792* (Williamsburg, VA: Omohundro Institute of Early American History and Culture, 2018), 13–16, 44–46.

16. Edmond Atkin to the Lords Commissioners of Trade and Plantations, May 30, 1755, in *Indians of the Southern Frontier*, ed. Wilbur R. Jacobs (Columbia: University of South Carolina Press, 1954), 65 ("Stout," "lived," "withdrew," "settled").

17. Paul Kelton, *Epidemics and Enslavement: Biological Catastrophe in the Native Southeast, 1492–1715* (Lincoln: University of Nebraska Press, 2007), 182–84, 191–92; Christina Snyder, *Slavery in Indian Country: The Changing Face of Captivity in Early America* (Cambridge, MA: Harvard University Press, 2010), 74–75; Gregory A. Waselkov, *Old Mobile Archaeology* (Tuscaloosa: University of Alabama Press, 1999), 44–46; John H. Hann, *Apalachee: The Land between the Rivers* (Gainesville: University Presses of Florida, 1988), 227–85.

18. James H. Merrell, *Indians' New World: Catawbas and Their Neighbors from European Contact through the Era of Removal* (Chapel Hill: University of North Carolina Press, 1989), 49–91; Robin A. Beck Jr., "Catawba Coalescence and the Shattering of the Carolina Piedmont, 1540–1676," in *Mapping the Mississippian Shatter Zone*, ed. Ethridge and Shuck-Hall, 138.

19. Merrell, *Indians' New World*, 92–133; John Lawson, *The History of Carolina, Containing the Exact Description and Natural History of That Country* (London: W. Taylor at the Ship, and F. Baker at the Black Boy, in Pater Roster Row, 1714), 71, 232 ("very large," 71; "great," 232); Charles L. Heath, "Catawba Militarism: Ethnohistorical and Archaeological Overviews," *North Carolina Archaeology* 53 (2004): 81–83.

20. Malinda Maynor Lowery, *The Lumbee Indians: An American Struggle* (Chapel Hill: University of North Carolina Press, 2028), 19–47; Adolph L. Dial and David K. Eliades, *I Know: A History of the Lumbee Indians* (Syracuse, NY: Syracuse University Press, 1996), 1–5.

21. James H. Merrell, "The Racial Education of the Catawba Indians," *Journal of*

Southern History 50 (August 1984): 367–73; Merrell, *Indians' New World*, 555; Martha M. Bentley, "The Slaveholding Catawbas," *South Carolina Historical Magazine* 92 (April 1991): 85–92; H. R. McIlwaine, ed., *Executive Journals of the Council of Colonial Virginia*, vol. 3, *(May 1, 1705–October 23, 1721)* (Richmond, VA: Davis Bottom, 1928), 442–43.

CHAPTER 18: MAGIC DOGS

1. Pekka Hämäläinen, "The Rise and Fall of Plains Indian Horse Cultures," *JAH* 90 (December 2003): 835–53; *YSF*, 74.

2. Ryan Hall, *Beneath the Backbone of the World: Blackfoot People and the North American Borderlands, 1720–1877* (Chapel Hill: University of North Carolina Press, 2020), 13–26; David Thompson, *David Thompson's Narrative of His Explorations in Western America, 1784–1812*, ed. J. B. Tyrrell (Toronto: Champlain Society, 1916), 328–30 ("The Peegans," 328; "By this time," 330).

3. Thompson, *David Thompson's Narrative*, 334–35 ("We pitched," "as the leaves," "We all," 334; "The terror," 335); Kathleen DuVal and John DuVal, eds., *Interpreting a Continent: Voices from Early America* (Lanham, MD: Rowman & Littlefield, 2009), 131 ("was killed").

4. Colin Calloway, *One Vast Winter Count: The Native American West before Lewis and Clark* (Lincoln: University of Nebraska Press, 2003), 267; Vaclav Smil, *Energy in Nature and Society: General Energetics of Complex Systems* (Cambridge: Massachusetts Institute of Technology, 2008), 80.

5. Elliott West, *The Contested Plains: Indians, Goldseekers, and the Rush to Colorado* (Lawrence: University of Kansas Press, 1998), 34–54; Dan Flores, *Caprock Canyons: Journeys into the Heart of the Southern Plains* (Austin: University of Texas Press, 1990), 382 ("the primary").

6. John C. Ewers, *The Blackfeet: Raiders on the Northwestern Plains* (Norman: University of Oklahoma Press, 1958), 23–24.

7. *LA*, 57–61, 86–87 ("Came and attacked," 59).

8. *CE*, 21–24.

9. Marvin K. Opler, "The Origins of Comanche and Ute," *American Anthropologist* 45 (January–March 1943): 155–58; Thomas W. Kavanagh, "Comanche," in *The Plains*, ed. Raymond J. DeMallie, vol. 13 of *Handbook of North American Indians*, ed. William C. Sturtevant (Washington, DC: Smithsonian Institution, 2001), pt. 2:902; "Opinion of Ensign Bernardo Casillas," August 19, 1719, in *After Coronado: Spanish Exploration Northeast of New Mexico, 1696–1727*, ed. and trans. Alfred Barnaby Thomas (Norman: University of Oklahoma Press, 1935), 104 ("war"). For the changing Ute-Comanche dynamics, see Ned Blackhawk, *Violence over the Land: Indians and Empires in the Early American West* (Cambridge, MA: Harvard University Press, 2006), 35–36.

10. *CE*, 28–33; Manuel San Juan de la Cruz to Marqués de Valero, 1719, in *After Coronado*, ed. Thomas, 138.

11. Juliana Barr, *Peace Came in the Form of a Woman: Indians and Spaniards in the Texas Borderlands* (Chapel Hill: University of North Carolina Press, 2007), 160–76; Blackhawk, *Violence over the Land*, 21–40; James Brooks, *Captives and Cousins: Slavery, Kinship, and Community in the Southwest Borderlands* (Chapel Hill: University of North Carolina Press, 2002), 30–40; Andrés Reséndez, *The Other Slavery: The Uncovered Story of Indian Enslavement in America* (Boston: Houghton Mifflin Harcourt, 2016), 212; Max L. Moorhead, "Spanish Deportation of Hostile Apaches:

The Policy and the Practice," *Arizona and the West* 17 (Autumn 1975): 205–22; David J. Weber, *Bárbaros: Spaniards and Their Savages in the Age of Enlightenment* (New Haven, CT: Yale University Press, 2005), 150.

12. "Opinion of Captain Miguel de Coca," August 19, 1719, in *After Coronado*, ed. Thomas, 105 ("go about"); Cruz to Valero, 1719, in *After Coronado* ("ask for," "so close," 138).

13. Log and Itinerary of Antonio Valverde Cosío in His Campaign against the Utes and Comanches, 1719, Bancroft Library, University of California, Berkeley, BANC MSS P-E 43, 1, 17, 22 ("the murders," 1; "If they," 17; "enjoyed," 22).

14. Antonio Valverde y Cosío, "Diary of a Campaign . . . against Ute and Comanche Indians, 1719," in *After Coronado*, ed. Thomas, 110–19; Blackhawk, *Violence over the Land*, 43–44.

15. Pedro de Rivera to Casa Fuerte, September 26, 1727, in *After Coronado*, ed. Thomas, 214 ("conserve").

16. *CE*, 35–38.

17. Pekka Hämäläinen, "The Politics of Grass: European Expansion, Ecological Change, and Indigenous Power in the Southwest Borderlands," *WMQ* 67 (April 2010), 173–208. For European exploration and lack of familiarity with the North American interior, see Paul W. Mapp, *The Elusive West and the Contest for Empire, 1713–1763* (Chapel Hill: University of North Carolina Press, 2011), 166–201.

CHAPTER 19: WARS TO THE END OF THE WORLD

1. Francis Jennings, *The Ambiguous Iroquois Empire: The Covenant Chain Confederation of Indian Tribes with English Colonies* (New York: Norton, 1984), 328–40; *OL*, 274; James Logan to the Proprietaries, June 25, 1735, in *Pennsylvania Archives*, ed. Samuel Hazard et al. (Philadelphia: Joseph Severns et al.), ser. 2, vol. 7 (1876–90, 1896): 178; *A Treaty of Friendship Held with the Chiefs of the Six Nations, at Philadelphia, in September and October, 1736* (Philadelphia: Printed and sold by B. Franklin, 1737), 13.

2. Susan E. Klepp, "Demography in Early Philadelphia, 1690–1860," *Proceedings of the American Philosophical Society* 133 (June 1989): 95; James H. Merrell, *Into the American Woods: Negotiations on the Pennsylvania Frontier* (New York: W. W. Norton, 1999), 20, 35–37; Matthew C. Ward, "The 'Peaceable Kingdom' Destroyed: The Seven Years' War and the Transformation of the Pennsylvania Backcountry," *Pennsylvania History* 74 (Summer 2007): 261.

3. "Council Held at the Proprietors," July 12, 1742, in *MPCP*, 4:579–80 ("Cousins," 579; "remove," 580); "Council Held at Philadelphia," April 23, 1743, in *MPCP*, 4:668 ("persuade"); Judith Ridner, "Building Urban Spaces for the Interior: Thomas Penn and the Colonization of Eighteenth-Century Pennsylvania," in *Early American Cartographies*, ed. Martin Brückner (Chapel Hill: University of North Carolina Press, 2012), 309; Gunlög Fur, *A Nation of Women: Gender and Colonial Encounters among Delaware Indians* (Philadelphia: University of Pennsylvania, 2009), 164; Richard Aquila, *Iroquois Restoration: Iroquois Diplomacy on the Colonial Frontier, 1701–1754* (Detroit, MI: Wayne State University Press, 1983), 223–24.

4. "[Meeting] in the Court House Chamber at Lancaster, June 30, 1744," in *MPCP*, 4:721 ("were"); Nancy Shoemaker, "An Alliance between Men: Gender Metaphors in Eighteenth-Century American Indian Diplomacy East of the Mississippi," *Ethnohistory* 46 (Spring 1999): 241.

5. James H. Merrell, *Indians' New World: Catawbas and Their Neighbors from*

European Contact through the Era of Removal (Chapel Hill: University of North Carolina Press, 1989), 161–66.

6. Richard White, *The Roots of Dependency: Subsistence, Environment, and Social Change among the Choctaws, Pawnees, and Navajos* (Lincoln: University of Nebraska Press, 1983), 65; *NWA*, 120; Daniel K. Richter, *Facing East from Indian Country: A Native History of Early America* (Cambridge, MA: Harvard University Press, 2001), 169–71; Claudio Saunt, "'Domestick . . . Quiet Being Broke': Gender Conflict among the Creek Indians in the Eighteenth Century," in *Contact Points: American Frontiers from the Mohawk Valley to the Mississippi*, ed. Andrew R. L. Cayton and Fredrika J. Teute (Chapel Hill: University of North Carolina Press, 1998), 156.

7. Kathryn E. Holland Braund, *Deerskins and Duffels: The Creek Indian Trade with Anglo-America, 1685–1815* (Lincoln: University of Nebraska Press, 1993), 70–71, 97; Theda Perdue, *Cherokee Women: Gender and Culture Change, 1700–1835* (Lincoln: University of Nebraska Press, 1998), 65–72; Woody Holton, *Forced Founders: Indians, Debtors, Slaves, and the Making of the American Revolution in Virginia* (Chapel Hill: University of North Carolina Press, 1999), 5 ("to appear"); Verner W. Crane, *The Southern Frontier, 1670–1732* (Durham, NC: Duke University Press, 1929), 161; Edmond Atkin, *Indians of the Southern Colonial Frontier*, ed. Wilbur R. Jacobs (Columbia: University of South Carolina Press, 1954), 22–29, 61, 66 ("threw," 23–24; "facilitate," 66); White, *Roots of Dependency*, 61.

8. David Treuer, *The Heartbeat of Wounded Knee: Native America from 1890 to the Present* (New York: Riverhead, 2019), 49–50.

9. *CW*, 16–18; Elizabeth A. Perkins, "Distinctions and Partitions amongst Us: Identity and Interaction in the Revolutionary Ohio Valley," in *Contact Points: American Frontiers from the Mohawk Valley to the Mississippi*, ed. Andrew R. L. Cayton and Fredrika J. Teute (Chapel Hill: University of North Carolina Press, 1998), 205–34. For the Ohio Valley as a "hot spot," see François Furstenberg, "The Significance of the Trans-Appalachian Frontier in Atlantic History," *AHR* 113 (June 2008): 650–52.

10. Allan Greer, *The People of New France* (Toronto: University of Toronto Press, 1997), 19; Alan Taylor, *American Colonies* (New York: Viking, 2001), 426 ("on whose side"); Richter, *Facing East from Indian Country*, 174–75; *WUH*, 26; *State of the British and French Colonies in America* (London: A. Millar, 1755), 37 ("out-fort").

11. Richter, *Facing East from Indian Country*, 169–70.

12. "Trent's Journal," in *History of Colonel Henry Bouquet and the Western Frontiers of Pennsylvania, 1747–1764*, ed. Mary Carson Darlington (n.p., 1920), 21 ("the English"); *CW*, 5–7, 12, 50–65; David L. Preston, *Braddock's Defeat: The Battle of the Monongahela and the Road to Revolution* (Oxford: Oxford University Press, 2015), 26–30, 33; Robert L. O'Connell, *Revolutionary: George Washington at War* (New York: Random House, 2019), 24 ("You are not").

13. Alan Taylor, *The Divided Ground: Indians, Settlers, and the Northern Borderland of the American Revolution* (New York: Vintage, 2006), 3; Gail D. MacLeitch, *Imperial Entanglements; Iroquois Change and Persistence on the Frontiers of Empire* (Philadelphia: University of Pennsylvania Press, 2011), 65–68; *BR*, 377–78; "Meeting in the Court House of Albany," July 2, 1754, in *NYCD*, 6:869–70 ("You have thus," 869; "are both," 870). For the unveiling of Theyanoguin's identity, see Barbara J. Sivertsen, *Turtles, Wolves, and Bears: A Mohawk Family History* (Bowie, MD: Heritage Books, 1996); and Eric Hinderaker, *The Two Hendricks: Unraveling a Mohawk Mystery* (Cambridge, MA: Harvard University Press, 2010), 238–41.

14. *ARI*, 6–7; *MG*, 240–68; *WUH*, 27.

15. Benjamin Franklin, *Autobiography of Benjamin Franklin*, ed. John Bigelow (London: J. B. Lippincott, 1868), 310–11 ("the only," 310–11; "these savages," 311).

16. Preston, *Braddock's Defeat*, 151; Beverly W. Bond Jr., "The Captivity of Charles Stuart, 1755–57," *Mississippi Valley Historical Review* 13 (June 1926): 63 ("what he," "the English," "whether," "No Savage"); Matthew C. Ward, *Breaking the Backcountry: Seven Years' War in Virginia and Pennsylvania, 1754–1765* (Pittsburgh, PA: University of Pittsburgh Press, 2004), 40–41; John Mack Faragher, *A Great and Noble Scheme: The Tragic Story of the Expulsion of the French Acadians from Their American Homeland* (New York: W. W. Norton, 2005), 297.

17. *CW*, 67 ("All"); Edmond Atkin, "The Appalachian Frontier: The Edmond Atkin Report and Plan of 1755," in *Voices of the Old South: Eyewitness Accounts, 1521–1861*, ed. Alan Gallay (Athens: University of Georgia Press, 1994), 46 ("the Importance"); Gregory Evans Dowd, "'Insidious Friends': Gift Giving and the Cherokee-British Alliance,'" in *Contact Points*, ed. Cayton and Teute, 125.

18. *MG*, 186–89.

19. Colin G. Calloway, *The Indian World of George Washington: The First President, the First Americans, and the Birth of the Nation* (New York: Oxford University Press, 2018), 110–12; Preston, *Braddock's Defeat*, 165–215, 282–83.

CHAPTER 20: BRITISH AMERICA BESIEGED

1. *CW*, 106–7; David L. Preston, *Braddock's Defeat: The Battle of the Monongahela and the Road to Revolution* (Oxford: Oxford University Press, 2015), 148–49; Matthew C. Ward, *Breaking the Backcountry: Seven Years' War in Virginia and Pennsylvania, 1754–1765* (Pittsburgh, PA: University of Pittsburgh Press, 2004), 39–40, 44–45; George Washington to Robert Dinwiddie, November 9, 1756, and Washington to John Robinson, November 9, 1756, in *Writings of George Washington*, 39 vols., ed. John C. Fitzpatrick (Washington, DC: Government Printing Office, 1931–39), 1:494, 505 ("found them," 494; "ruinous state," 505); "Council Held at Philadelphia," July 24, 1755, and "Council Held at Philadelphia," August 22, 1755, in *MPCP*, 6:486 ("exposed"). For *petite guerre*, see Bruce Buchan, "Pandours, Partisans, and Petite Guerre: The Two Dimensions of Enlightenment Discourse on War," *Intellectual History Review* 23, no. 3 (2013): 329–47; and Preston, *Braddock's Defeat*, 84.

2. *State of the British and French Colonies in North America* (London: A. Millar, 1755), 4 ("pernicious consequence," "By the conveniency"); *CW*, 106–7; Allan Greer, *Property and Dispossession: Natives, Empires and Land in Early Modern North America* (Cambridge: Cambridge University Press, 2018), 170–71; Ward, *Breaking the Backcountry*, 39–40, 44–45; "At a Council Held at Philadelphia," August 22, 1755, in *Colonial Records of Pennsylvania*, ed. Samuel Hazard (Harrisburg, PA: Theo. Fenn, 1851), 6:590; "Minutes of the Provincial Council," in *Colonial Records of Pennsylvania*, ed. Hazard, 6:590 ("their Wives," "their defenseless Condition"); Preston, *Braddock's Defeat*, 86–87 ("a half-starved," 86; "what a wild set," 87); James H. Merrell, "Shamokin, 'the Very Seat of the Prince of Darkness': Unsettling the Early American History," in *Contact Points: American Frontiers from the Mohawk Valley to the Mississippi*, ed. Andrew R. L. Cayton and Fredrika J. Teute (Chapel Hill: University of North Carolina Press, 1998), 16–59; Jane T. Merritt, "Metaphor, Meaning, and Misunderstanding: Language and Power on the Pennsylvania Frontier," in *Contact Points*, ed. Cayton and Teute, 62, 73; Ruth Ann Denasi, "The Penn's Creek Massacre and the Captivity of Marie le Roy and Barbara Leininger," *Pennsylvania History* 74 (Summer 2007): 307–32; John H. Merrell, *Into*

the American Woods: Negotiations on the Pennsylvania Frontier (New York: W. W. Norton, 1999), 48, 186–236; "Governor Dinwiddie to the Sachems and Warriors of the Great Nations of Cherokees and Catawbas," November 4, 1754, in *The Official Records of Robert Dinwiddie, Lieutenant-Governor of the Colony of Virginia, 1751–1758*, comp. R. A. Brock (Richmond: Virginia Historical Society, 1883), 1:391, 395 ("send a great," 391," to oppose," 395).

3.   "Council Held in the Council Chamber," April 3, 1756, in *MPCP*, 7:70–71 ("very sharply," "urged," 71); Jay Miller, "The Delaware as Women: A Symbolic Solution," *American Ethnologist* 1 (August 1974): 507–8; Roger M. Carpenter, "From Indian Women to English Children: The Lenni-Lenape and the Attempt to Create a New Diplomatic Identity," *Pennsylvania History* 74 (Winter 2007): 1–20; Jeffrey Ostler, "'To Extirpate the Indians': An Indigenous Consciousness of Genocide in the Ohio Valley and Lower Great Lakes, 1750s–1810," *WMQ* 72 (October 2015): 596; Scott Weidensaul, *The First Frontier: The Forgotten History of Struggle, Savagery and Endurance in Early America* (Boston: Houghton Mifflin, 2012), 354–57.

4.   Daniel P. Barr, "'A Road for Warriors': The Western Delawares and the Seven Years War," *Pennsylvania History* 73 (Winter 2006): 20 ("we may do"); *CW*, 135–37; *SG*, 187.

5.   Preston, *Braddock's Defeat*, 80–81, 159–60; *HAC*, plate 42; Gunlög Fur, *A Nation of Women: Gender and Colonial Encounters among Delaware Indians* (Philadelphia: University of Pennsylvania, 2009), 179–80; Robert Daiutolo Jr., "The Role of Quakers in Indian Affairs during the French and Indian War," *Quaker History* 77 (Spring 1988): 4–5; "Minutes of Conferences, Held with the Indians, at Easton, in the Months of July and November, 1756," Evans Early American Imprint Collection, accessed December 15, 2020, https://quod.lib.umich.edu/e/evans/N06248.0001 .001/1:2.7?rgn=div2;view=fulltext; Merrell, *Into the American Woods*, 239; James H. Merrell, "'I Desire All That I Have Said . . . May Be Taken Down Aright': Revisiting Teedyuscung's 1756 Treaty Council Speeches," *WMQ* 63 (October 2006): 778–82.

6.   *CW*, 152–56, 185–201.

7.   Gail D. MacLeitch, *Imperial Entanglements: Iroquois Change and Persistence on the Frontiers of Empire* (Philadelphia: University of Pennsylvania Press, 2011), 66–77; Daniel Claus to Johnson, April 5, 1756, in *JP*, 2:439 ("When we").

8.   Gregory Evans Dowd, "'Insidious Friends': Gift Giving and the Cherokee-British Alliance," in *Contact Points*, ed. Cayton and Teute, 114–15, 120–23; Theda Perdue, *Cherokee Women: Gender and Culture Change, 1700–1835* (Lincoln: University of Nebraska Press, 1998), 88; *CW*, 238; Paul Kelton, "The British and Indian War: Cherokee Power and the Fate of Empire in North America," *WMQ* 69 (October 2012): 766–76; "At a Meeting of Three Mohawk Chiefs, Two Seneca Sachems and Two Cherokee Indians," September 12, 1757, in *NYCD*, 7:325 ("make war"); Theda Perdue, "Cherokee Relations with the Iroquois in the Eighteenth Century," in *Beyond the Covenant Chain: The Iroquois and Their Neighbors in Indian North America*, ed. Daniel K. Richter and James H. Merrell (Philadelphia: University of Pennsylvania Press, 1987), 136–37.

9.   *HAC*, plate 42; *CW*, 250–68; *NWA*, 108; Dowd, "'Insidious Friends,'" 114–20.

10.   *CW*, 227–33, 258, 267–83; Colin G. Calloway, *Indian World of George Washington: The First President, the First Americans, and the Birth of the Nation* (New York: Oxford University Press, 2018), 125–26. I am drawing here from Kathleen DuVal, *Independence Lost: Lives on the Edge of the American Revolution* (New York: Random House, 2015), 293. The central argument of DuVal's book is that "independence depended on others" in the American Revolutionary War.

11. *CW*, 330–39; "The Reply of the Six Nations to Johnson's Speech," April 16, 1759, in *NYCD*, 7:386–94; "Journal of the Siege of Fort Niagara," in *NYCD*, 10:977–90; "The Journal of Christian Frederick Post, from Philadelphia to the Ohio," in *Early Western Travels, 1748–1846*, ed. Reuben Gold Thwaites (Cleveland, OH: Arthur H. Clark, 1904), 1:214 ("Why do not," "I have not"); Merrell, "Shamokin," 42.

12. *CW*, 355–65, 457–68. For what became known as the Anglo-Cherokee War, see John Oliphant, *Peace and War on the Anglo-Cherokee Frontier, 1756–63* (Baton Rouge. Louisiana State University Press, 2001).

13. *CW*, 387–409; *HAC*, plate 42; Tom Hatley, *The Dividing Paths: Cherokees and South Carolinians through the Revolutionary Era* (New York: Oxford University Press, 1995), 119–56; P. M. Hamer, "Fort Loudoun in the Cherokee War," *North Carolina Historical Review* 24 (October 1925): 442–58; Perdue, *Cherokee Women*, 96; William R. Nester, *"Haughty Conquerors": Amherst and the Great Indian Uprising of 1763* (Westport, CT: Praeger, 2000), 2 ("take anything less").

14. Peter Wraxall, *An Abridgement of the Indian Affairs: Contained in Four Folio Volumes, Transacted in the Colony of New York, from the Year 1678 to the Year 1751*, ed. Charles Howard McIlwain (Cambridge, MA: Harvard University Press, 1915), 220 ("To preserve).

15. Gilles Havard and Cécile Vidal, *Histoire de l' Amérique Française* (Paris: Flammarion, 2005), 677 ("Take Courage"; my translation); Alexander Henry, *Alexander Henry's Travels and Adventures in the Years 1760–1776*, ed. Milo Milton Quaife (Chicago: R. R. Donnelley, 1921), 43 ("The French king"); Gregory Evans Dowd, "The French King Wakes Up in Detroit: 'Pontiac's War' in Rumor and History," *Ethnohistory* 37 (Summer 1990): 254–59.

16. Merrell, *Into the American Woods*, 81–82, 100; George Croghan to Henry Bouquet, December 10, 1762, in *Sir Jeffery, 1st Baron Amherst, Official Papers, 1740–1783* (London: World Microfilm Publications, 1979), microfilm, reel 30, 216–17; "Council Held in the Council Chamber at Savannah," January 4, 1763, in *The Colonial Records of the State of Georgia*, vol. 9, *Proceedings and Minutes of the Governor and Council from January 4, 1763, to December 2, 1766* (Atlanta, GA: Franklin-Turner, 1907), 13–14 ("you know," 13–14; "We can," "witness," "behave well," 14).

17. Rich Atkinson, *The British Are Coming: The War for America* (New York: Henry Holt, 2019), 6–7, 13; Colin G. Calloway, *A Scratch of a Pen: 1763 and the Transformation of North America* (New York: Oxford University Press, 2006), 37, 112–16, 133, 150–64; Alan Taylor, "The People of British America, 1700–75," *Orbis* 47 (Spring 2003): 247–61; Havard and Vidal, *Histoire de l' Amérique Française*, 677–78; George Croghan to H. Bouquet, March 19, 1763, Bouquet Papers, Add. Mss 21,649, fol. 87–88v., Reel 25, British Library, London, England ("to despair"); John Mack Faragher, *A Great and Noble Scheme: The Tragic Story of the Expulsion of the French Acadians from Their American Homeland* (New York: W. W. Norton, 2005).

18. Charles E. Cleland, *Rites of Conquest: The History of and Culture of Michigan's Native Americans* (Ann Arbor: University of Michigan Press, 1992), 131 ("pernicious vermin"); François Furstenberg, "The Significance of the Trans-Appalachian Frontier in Atlantic History," *AHR* 113 (June 2008): 651–52; *WUH*, 101, 118–20; Heidi Bohaker, "'Nindoodemag': The Significance of Algonquian Kinship Networks in the Eastern Great Lakes Region, 1600–1701," *WMQ* 63 (January 2006): 23–52.

19. Alfred A. Cave, "The Delaware Prophet Neolin: A Reappraisal," *Ethnohistory* 46 (Spring 1999): 265–90; *WUH*, 92–105; *CW*, 536–37; Peter C. Mancall, *Deadly Medicine: Indians and Alcohol in Early America* (Ithaca, NY: Cornell University Press, 1995), 53–54; Walter S. Dunn, *Frontier Profit and Loss: The British Army and the*

Fur Traders, 1760–1764 (Westport, CT: Greenwood, 1998), 178–89; Rob Harper, *Unsettling the West: Violence and State Building in the Ohio Valley* (Philadelphia: University of Pennsylvania Press, 2018), 43; Anthony F. C. Wallace, *The Death and Rebirth of the Seneca* (New York: Knopf, 1970), 120 ("You are to").

CHAPTER 21: WORLDLY AND OTHERWORLDLY WARS OF INDEPENDENCE

1. *WUH*, 12–15, 64–65; Michael Witgen, *An Infinity of Nations: How the Native New World Shaped Early America* (Philadelphia: University of Pennsylvania Press, 2012), 65; Heidi Bohaker, "'Nindoodemag': The Significance of Algonquian Kinship Networks in the Eastern Great Lakes Region, 1600–1701," *WMQ* 63 (January 2006): 23–51; Robert Rogers to Johnson, October 7, 1763, in *JP*, 10:871–72; Henry Gladwin to Jeffery Amherst, April 20, 1763, in *JP*, 4:95 ("mean[t] to make"); "Journal or Narrative of a Conspiracy of the Indians against the English, and the Siege of Fort Detroit by Four Different Tribes (Beginning) May 7, 1763," in *Journal of Pontiac's Conspiracy 1763*, ed. M. Agnes Burton (Detroit: Clarence Monroe Burton, 1912), 18–20; "Pontiac's Speech to an Ottawa, Potawatomi, and Huron Audience, 1764," in *Interpreting a Continent: Voices from Colonial America*, ed. Kathleen DuVal and John DuVal (Lanham, MD: Rowman & Littlefield, 2009), 79–83 ("Why do you," 81).

2. Richard Middleton, "Pontiac: Local Warrior or Pan-Indian Leader?" *Michigan Historical Review* 32 (Fall 2006): 1–32; James Piecuch, "French and Indian War," in *Converging Worlds: Communities and Cultures in Colonial America*, ed. Louise A. Breen (New York: Routledge, 2012), 576; *WUH*, 124–25; James H. Merrell, "Shamokin, 'the Very Seat of the Prince of Darkness': Unsettling the Early American History," in *Contact Points: American Frontiers from the Mohawk Valley to the Mississippi*, ed. Andrew R. L. Cayton and Fredrika J. Teute (Chapel Hill: University of North Carolina Press, 1998), 40–41.

3. Tiya Miles, *Dawn of Detroit: A Chronicle of Slavery in the City of the Straits* (New York: New Press, 2017), 36–37; *WUH*, 132–35; Amherst to Bouquet, June 23, 1763, in *MPHC*, 19:203 ("I wish"); Melanie Armstrong, *Germ Wars: The Politics of Microbes and America's Landscape of Fear* (Oakland: University of California Press, 2017), 36 ("We are").

4. Elizabeth A. Fenn, "Biological Warfare in Eighteenth-Century North America: Beyond Jeffery Amherst," *JAH* 86 (March 2000): 1553–57 ("the desired effect," 1554; "Could it not," 1555; "You will," 1556–57).

5. *WUH*, 135–45.

6. Robert Etherington to Henry Gladwin, June 12, 1763, in *WHC*, 7:162–63 ("Everything," "assembled," "declared," 163).

7. Amherst to the Earl of Egremont, July 23, 1763, in *NYCD*, 7:529 ("the present"); Benjamin Franklin, *Works of Benjamin Franklin* (Philadelphia: Childs and Peterson, 1840), 4:318 ("I know"); James Atkinson, *Splendid Land, Splendid People: The Chickasaw Indians to Removal* (Tuscaloosa: University of Alabama Press, 2003), 89.

8. François Furstenberg, "The Significance of the Trans-Appalachian Frontier in Atlantic History," *AHR* 113 (June 2008): 653–54; *CW*, 547–48; Colin G. Calloway, *A Scratch of a Pen: 1763 and the Transformation of North America* (New York: Oxford University Press, 2006), 75, 97 ("My Brother," 75; "would prove," 97); "Mississippi Land Company Articles of Agreement, 3 June 1763," Founders Online, National Archives, accessed January 4, 2022, https://founders.archives.gov/documents/Washington/02-07-02-0134, ("the Insults").

9. William R. Nester, *"Haughty Conquerors": Amherst and the Great Indian Upris-*

ing of 1763 (Westport, CT: Praeger, 2000), 212–13; Celia Barnes, *Native American Power in the United States, 1783–1795* (Madison, NJ: Fairleigh Dickinson University Press, 2003), 19; *WUH*, 151–68.

10. *WUH*, 177–79; Woody Holton, *Forced Founders: Indians, Debtors, Slaves, and the Making of the American Revolution in Virginia* (Chapel Hill: University of North Carolina Press, 1999), 3–38; James H. Merrell, *Into the American Woods: Negotiations on the Pennsylvania Frontier* (New York: W. W. Norton, 1999), 285–87; Kevin Kenny, *Peaceable Kingdom Lost: The Paxton Boys and the Destruction of William Penn's Holy Experiment* (New York: Oxford University Press, 2009), 1–2; Alan Taylor, *American Revolutions: A Continental History, 1750–1804* (New York: W. W. Norton, 2016), 60.

11. Johnson to the Lords of Trade, November 13, 1763, and January 20, 1764, in *NYCD*, 7:573–80, 600 ("been properly," "in right," 573; "There is no," "Each," "we shall," 600).

12. *WUH*, 77–78, 168–73. For rumors, see *WUH*, 63, 142.

13. *CW*, 619–25.

14. *CW*, 625–31; Holton, *Forced Founders*, 15 ("listen to").

15. Johnson to Cadwallader Colden, August 23, 1764, in *JP*, 4:511–14; Claudio Saunt, *West of the Revolution: An Uncommon History of 1776* (New York: W. W. Norton, 2014), 166.

16. *MG*, 300; *WUH*, 229–31; Francis Parkman, *The Conspiracy of Pontiac and the Indian War after the Conquest of Canada*, 10th ed. (New York: Little, Brown, 1895), 1:255–56 ("keeps two"). For Anishinaabe shape-shifting, see Witgen, *Infinity of Nations*, 367–68.

17. *MG*, 303–7; "Proceedings of Sir William Johnson with the Ohio Indians, July 4, 1765, in *NYCD*, 7:750 ("The English," "Children," "obey him"); Robert Rogers to Johnson, June 28, 1766, in *JP*, 12:120; "Proceedings of Sir William Johnson with Pondiac and Other Indians," July 23, 1766, in *NYCD*, 7:784, 854–59 ("My Father," 784; "I this day," 858); The Duke of Grafton to Mr. Pitt, January 18, 1766, in *The Correspondence of William Pitt, Earl of Chatham*, ed. William Stanhope (London: John Murray, 1838), 2:372 ("in a good cause").

18. *MG*, 313.

CHAPTER 22: A SECOND CHINESE WALL

1. "Proceedings of Sir William Johnson with the Ohio Indians, July 4, 1765," in *NYCD*, 7:754 ("will pay"); *MG*, 307.

2. Gail D. MacLeitch, *Imperial Entanglements: Iroquois Change and Persistence on the Frontiers of Empire* (Philadelphia: University of Pennsylvania Press, 2011), 227; Timothy J. Shannon, *Iroquois Diplomacy on the Early American Frontier* (New York: Viking Penguin, 2008), 167–69.

3. *MG*, 351–65; "Proceedings of Sir William Johnson with the Indians at Fort Stanwix to Settle a Boundary Line," 1768, in *NYCD*, 8:111–20 ("for the many losses," 114; "I would," "Now Brother," 116); Woody Holton, *Forced Founders: Indians, Debtors, Slaves, and the Making of the American Revolution in Virginia* (Chapel Hill: University of North Carolina Press, 1999), 10; Reuben Gold Thwaites and Louise Phelps Kellogg, eds., *The Revolution in the Upper Ohio, 1775–1777* (Madison: Wisconsin Historical Society, 1908), 58 ("dug a hole"); Rob Harper, *Unsettling the West: Violence and State Building in the Ohio Valley* (Philadelphia: University of Pennsylvania Press, 2018), 33–34; Sami Lakomäki, *Gathering Together: The Shawnee People*

through Diaspora and Nationhood, 1600–1870 (New Haven, CT: Yale University Press, 2014), 96–101.

4.   Alan Taylor, *American Revolutions: A Continental History, 1750–1804* (New York: W. W. Norton, 2016), 56, 67–69; Gage to Johnson, November 9, 1767, in *JP*, 12:379 ("Men of Interest"); *MG*, 313, 323–39; Patrick Griffin, *The American Leviathan: Empire, Nation, and Revolutionary Frontier* (New York: Hill and Wang, 2007), 125–26; Stephen Aron, *How the West Was Lost: The Transformation of Kentucky from Daniel Boone to Henry Clay* (Baltimore: Johns Hopkins University Press, 1996), 30–31, 55; Harper, *Unsettling the West*, 48–55, 64–65; Claudio Saunt, *West of the Revolution: An Uncommon History of 1776* (New York: W. W. Norton, 2014), 17–23; Holton, *Forced Founders*, 15 ("forget all Insults given").

5.   Edward R. Lambert, *History of New Haven before and after the Union with Connecticut* (New Haven, CT: Hitchcock & Stafford, 1838), 96.

6.   Taylor, *American Revolutions*, 68, 73–74; Aron, *How the West Was Lost*, 21–23; Harper, *Unsettling the West*, 47–49; "A Friend to the True Interests of Britain in America," *Virginia Gazette*, January 14, 1773 ("not even"); *SG*, 53–54; Griffin, *American Leviathan*, 98–99.

7.   Philip J. Deloria, *Playing Indian* (New Haven, CT: Yale University Press, 1998), 27–37.

8.   William Christian to William Preston, October 15, 1774, John Floyd to William Preston, October 16, 1774, and Isaac Shelby to John Shelby, October 16, 1774, in *Documentary History of Dunmore's War, 1774*, ed. Reuben Gold Thwaites and Louise Phelps Kellogg (Madison: Wisconsin Historical Society, 1905), 261–75 ("The Bravest," 275); Matthew L. Rhoades, "Blood and Boundaries: Virginia Backcountry Violence and the Origins of the Quebec Act, 1758–1775," *West Virginia History* 3 (Fall 2009): 1–22.

9.   Griffin, *American Leviathan*, 125–26; Aron, *How the West Was Lost*, 30–31, 35–37; Rich Atkinson, *The British Are Coming: The War for America* (New York: Henry Holt, 2019), 24; Harper, *Unsettling the West*, 48–55, 64–65; Saunt, *West of the Revolution*, 17–23; Alan Taylor, *The Divided Ground: Indians, Settlers, and the Northern Borderland of the American Revolution* (New York: Vintage, 2006), 80–81.

10. Christina Snyder, *Slavery in Indian Country: The Changing Face of Captivity in Early America* (Cambridge, MA: Harvard University Press, 2010), 156–67.

11. William W. Campbell, *Annals of Tryon County, or the Border Warfare of New-York* (New York: J. & J. Harper, 1831), 35 ("whom we dread"); Thomas Paine, *Common Sense* (Philadelphia: W. & T. Bradford, 1776), 142 ("naked"); "From John Adams to James Sullivan, 26 May 1776," Founders Online, National Archives, accessed September 12, 2020, https://founders.archives.gov/documents/Adams/06-04-02-0091 ("Power"). For Adams's views on Indians, see Daniel H. Usner, "'A Savage Feast They Made of It': John Adams and the Paradoxical Origins of Federal Indian Policy," *Journal of the Early Republic* 33 (Winter 2013): 607–41.

12. David J. Silverman, *The Red Brethren: The Brothertown and Stockbridge Indians and the Problem of Race in America* (Ithaca, NY: Cornell University Press, 2010), 25, 72, 88–101; *ARI*, 85–93 ("The Rebels," 93).

13. Worthington Chauncey Ford and Gaillard Hunt, eds., *Journals of Continental Congress, 1774–1789* (Washington, DC: Government Printing Office, 1905), 401 ("the Indians"); Sami Lakomäki, email to the author, October 15, 2020.

14. Ronald Wright, *Stolen Continents: Five Hundred Years of Conquest and Resistance in the Americas* (Boston: Houghton Mifflin, 1992), 138–39; *NWA*, 110; William R. Nester, *The Frontier War for American Independence* (Mechanicsburg, PA:

Stackpole, 2004), 103 ("If you"); *ARI*, 28–34; J. Almon, ed., *The Remembrancer, or Impartial Repository of Public Events for the Year 1776*, vol. 3, pt. 3 (London: J. Almon, 1776), 53–54 ("We must").

15. Taylor, *American Revolutions*, 252; Samson Occom to John Thornton, 1777, in Harold Blodgett, *Samson Occom* (Hanover, NH: Dartmouth College Publications, 1935), 164–65 ("I am"); Linford D. Fisher, "Religion, Race, and the Formation of Pan-Indian Identities in the Brothertown Movement, 1700–1800," in *Native Diasporas: Indigenous Identities and Settler Colonialism in the Americas*, ed. Gregory D. Smithers and Brooke N. Newman (Lincoln: University of Nebraska Press, 2014), 151–86; Anthony Wonderley, "Brothertown, New York History, 1785–1796," *New York History* 81 (October 2000): 457–92.

16. Harper, *Unsettling the West*, 86; Aron, *How the West Was Lost*, 35–39; *ARI*, 182–200; *SG*, 59, 189; Henry Timberlake, *Memoirs, 1756–1765* (Johnson City, TN: Watauga, 1927), 58 ("the metropolis").

17. François Furstenberg, "The Significance of the Trans-Appalachian Frontier in Atlantic History," *AHR* 113 (June 2008): 660; Alan Taylor, *The Civil War of 1812: American Citizens, British Subjects, Irish Rebels, and Indian Allies* (New York: Alfred A. Knopf, 2010), 27. For growing state power, see Sveinn Jóhannesson, " 'Securing the State': James Madison, Federal Emergency Powers, and the Rise of the Prerevolutionary America," *JAH* 104 (September 2017): 364; William H. Bergman, *The American National State and the Early West* (New York: Cambridge University Press, 2012); and Arthur Whitaker, *The Spanish-American Frontier, 1783–1795* (New York: Houghton Mifflin, 1927), 1–5.

18. Kathleen Duval, *Independence Lost: Lives on the Edge of the American Revolution* (New York: Random House, 2015), 14–23; Jason Herbert, "To Treat with All Nations: Invoking Authority in the Chickasaw Nation, 1783–1795," *Ohio Valley History* 18, no. 1 (Spring 2018): 35 ("head leading warrior").

19. "Draft for the Governor General of Canada, the Duke of Connaught, by Duncan Scott, Deputy Superintendent General of Indian Affairs," n.d., National Archives of Canada, Indian Affairs, vol. 2284, 57, 169–71; *ARI*, 33–34; J. David Lehman, "The End of the Iroquois Mystique: The Oneida Land Cession Treaties of the 1780s," *WMQ* 47 (October 1990): 525.

20. *ARI*, 129–41; Matthew Dennis, *Seneca Possessed: Indians, Witchcraft, and Power in the Early American Republic* (Philadelphia: University of Pennsylvania Press, 2010), 35–36; Karim M. Tiro, "A 'Civil' War? Rethinking Iroquois Participation in the American Revolution," *Explorations in Early American Culture* 4 (2000): 148–65; Griffin, *American Leviathan*, 130; Harper, *Unsettling the West*, 100–18.

21. *The Public Statutes at Large of the United States of America*, vol. 7, ed. Richard Peters (Boston: Charles C. Little and James Brown, 1856), 13–15; Peter Cozzens, *Tecumseh and the Prophet: The Shawnee Brothers Who Defied a Nation* (New York: Penguin, 2020), 74; Aron, *How the West Was Lost*, 35–49; Sarah M. S. Pearsall, "Women in the American Revolution War," in *Oxford Handbook of the American Revolution*, ed. Jane Kamensky and Edward G. Gray (New York: Oxford University Press, 2012), 279–80 ("one word," 279); Kevin Kokomoor, " 'Burning & Destroying All before Them': Creeks and Seminoles on Georgia's Revolutionary Frontier," *Georgia Historical Quarterly* 98 (Winter 2014): 312–13; John Bowman to Edward Hand, December 12, 1777, in *Frontier Defense on the Upper Ohio, 1777–1778*, ed. Reuben Gold Thwaites and Louise Phelps Kellogg (Madison: Wisconsin Historical Society, 1912), 181–83; Jane T. Merritt, "Native Peoples in the Revolutionary War," in *Oxford Handbook of the American Rev-*

olution, ed. Kamensky and Gray, 242; Lakomäki, *Gathering Together*, 109–12; *ARI*, 205–7; Susan Sleeper-Smith, *Indigenous Prosperity and American Conquest: Indian Women of the Ohio River Valley, 1690–1792* (Williamsburg, VA: Omohundro Institute of Early American History and Culture, 2018), 215–19; *SG*, 61; Griffin, *American Leviathan*, 160 ("reduced").

22. "Journal of Joseph Bowman," in *Collections of the Illinois State Historical Library* (Springfield: Trustees of the Illinois State Historical Library, 1915–1940), 8:159; Ben Kiernan, *Blood and Soil: A World History of Genocide and Extermination from Sparta to Darfur* (New Haven, CT: Yale University Press, 2009), 321–22 ("he expected," 322).

23. Daniel P. Barr, *Unconquered: The Iroquois League at War in Colonial America* (Westport, CT: Praeger, 2006), 144–63; *ARI*, 222–25; Janice Potter-MacKinnon, *While the Women Only Wept: Loyalist Refugee Women in Eastern Ontario* (Montreal, QC: McGill-Queen's University Press, 1993), 49, 67–68; George Washington, "General Orders, 17 Oct., 1779," in *The Papers of George Washington. Revolutionary War Series*, vol. 22, *1 August–21 October 1779*, ed. Benjamin L. Huggins (Charlottesville: University of Virginia Press, 2013), 448, 741 ("has been overrun," 448; "Forty," 741); Pearsall, "Women in the American Revolution War," 279–80 ("who were," 280); Gregory Evans Dowd, *Groundless: Rumors, Legends, and Hoaxes on the Early American Frontier* (Baltimore: Johns Hopkins University Press, 2015), 181–83; Dennis, *Seneca Possessed*, 36–37; Taylor, *American Revolutions*, 256; Max M. Mintz, *Seeds of Empire: The American Revolutionary Conquest of the Iroquois* (New York: New York University Press, 1999), 117.

24. Griffin, *American Leviathan*, 128–29; Barbara Graymont, *The Iroquois in the American Revolution* (Syracuse, NY: Syracuse University Press, 1972), 230–33; *MG*, 403–7; Haldimand to Arent De Peyster, August 10, 1780, *MPHC*, 10:416 ("The Indians"); Alan Michelson, "*Hanödaga:yas* (Town Destroyer) and Mantle," *Third Text* 32 (2018): 689–92.

25. George Rogers Clark to Mason, November 19, 1779, in *WHC*, 8:123–24 ("It may appear"); *ARI*, 140–42; Griffin, *American Leviathan*, 160 ("you could not"). For broader context, see *MG*, 368–75.

26. Taylor, *American Revolutions*, 254; Frederick Haldimand to Richard B. Lernoult, July 23, 1779, in *MPHC*, 10:345; Elizabeth Fenn, *Pox Americana: The Great Smallpox Epidemic of 1775–82* (New York: Hill and Wang, 2001), 126–31; Elizabeth A. Fenn, *Encounters at the Heart of the World: A History of the Mandan People* (New York: Hill and Wang, 2014), 163; John McNeill, *Mosquito Empires: Ecology and War in the Greater Caribbean, 1620–1914* (New York: Cambridge University Press, 2010), 197–234; Ashley Jackson, *The British Empire: A Very Short Introduction* (Oxford: Oxford University Press, 2013), 72.

27. Griffin, *American Leviathan*, 138–41, 156–61; *MG*, 396–412; Peyster to Haldimand, January 26, 1782, in *MPHC*, 10:547–48 ("are not," "I have wrought," 548).

28. Amy S. Greenberg, "US Expansionism during the Nineteenth Century: 'Manifest Destiny,'" in *The Oxford World History of Empire*, ed. Peter Fibiger Bang, C. A. Baily, and Walter Scheidel (New York: Oxford University Press, 2021), 1014–15. For continuities, see Thomas Bender, *A Nation among Nations: America's Place in World History* (New York: Hill and Wang, 2006), 79–87.

29. *ARI*, 273–76; Colin G. Calloway, "Suspicion and Self-Interest: The British-Indian Alliance and the Peace of Paris," *Historian* 48 (November 1985): 51–57; Daniel Robertson to Secretary Matthews, September 6, 1784, in *MPHC*, 11:453 ("liars," "encouraged," "now despise"). For the "Dish with One Spoon," see Lisa Ford, *The*

Common Pot: The Recovery of Native Space in the Northwest (Minneapolis: University of Minnesota Press, 2008), 106–62.

30. Frank G. Speck, "The Delaware Indians as Women: Were the Original Pennsylvanians Politically Emasculated?" *Pennsylvania Magazine of History and Biography* 70 (October 1946): 377–89; Saunt, *West of the Revolution*, 167.

CHAPTER 23: THE AMERICAN CRUCIBLE

1. "Treaty with the Delawares: 1778," Avalon Project, Yale Law School, Lillian Goldman Law Library, accessed May 22, 2020, https://avalon.law.yale.edu/18th_century/del1778.asp ("The Enemies"). For the United States as a violent regime, see Patrick Griffin, *The American Leviathan: Empire, Nation, and Revolutionary Frontier* (New York: Hill and Wang, 2007).

2. Maya Jasanoff, *Liberty's Exiles: The Loss of America and the Remaking of the British Empire* (New York: Harper, 2011), 6–9; Alan Taylor, *American Revolutions: A Continental History, 1750–1804* (New York: W. W. Norton, 2016), 366–67.

3. James H. Merrell, "American Nations, Old and New: Reflections on Indians and the Early Republic," in *Native Americans and the Early Republic*, ed. Frederick E. Hoxie, Ronald Hoffman, and Peter J. Albert (Charlotte: University Press of Virginia, 1999), 336–37; *SA*, 1:358–61; Stephen Aron, *How the West Was Lost: The Transformation of Kentucky from Daniel Boone to Henry Clay* (Baltimore: Johns Hopkins University Press, 1996), 73–74.

4. Griffin, *American Leviathan*, 168–75; Peter R. Silver, *Our Savage Neighbors: How Indian War Transformed Early America* (New York: W. W. Norton, 2008), 267–69; Rob Harper, *Unsettling the West: Violence and State Building in the Ohio Valley* (Philadelphia: University of Pennsylvania Press, 2018), 135–41; Gunlög Fur, *A Nation of Women: Gender and Colonial Encounters among Delaware Indians* (Philadelphia: University of Pennsylvania, 2009), 156–57.

5. Max M. Mintz, *Seeds of Empire: The American Revolutionary Conquest of the Iroquois* (New York: New York University Press, 1999), 175 ("Let there be"); Taylor, *American Revolutions*, 261–62; Griffin, *American Leviathan*, 164–65, 168–70, 173 ("is in," 173); Silver, *Our Savage Neighbors*, 278–82.

6. Elizabeth Mancke, "The Ohio Country and Indigenous Geopolitics in Early Modern North America, circa 1500–1760," *Ohio Valley History* 18 (Spring 2018): 7; Sami Lakomäki, *Gathering Together: The Shawnee People through Diaspora and Nationhood, 1600–1870* (New Haven, CT: Yale University Press, 2014), 116–17, 122–24; Patrick Bottiger, *Borderland of Fear: Vincennes, Prophetstown, and the Invasion of the Miami Homeland* (Lincoln: University of Nebraska Press, 2016), 36–37; *NOT*, 234.

7. *NOT*, 70–77; John Walton Caughey, *McGillivray of the Creeks* (Norman: University of Oklahoma Press, 1938), 66 ("the Crown").

8. *SA*, 1:354; *NOT*, 79–89; J. Leitch Wright Jr., "Creek-American Treaty of 1790: Alexander McGillivray and the Diplomacy of the Old Southwest," *Georgia Historical Quarterly* 51 (December 1967): 385–87; Anthony F. C. Wallace, *Jefferson and the Indians: The Tragic Fate of the First Americans* (Cambridge, MA: Belknap Press of Harvard University Press, 1999), 220.

9. "Treaty with the Six Nations: 1784," Avalon Project, Yale Law School, Lillian Goldman Law Library, accessed February 21, 2020, https://avalon.law.yale.edu/18th_century/six1784.asp; Harper, *Unsettling the West*, 167, 170; *SG*, 186. For the Six Nations as "uncles," see Frank G. Speck, "The Delaware Indians as Women: Were

the Original Pennsylvanians Politically Emasculated?" *Pennsylvania Magazine of History and Biography* 70 (October 1946): 384; Gregory Ablavsky, "Species of Sovereignty: Native Nationhood, the United States, and International Law, 1783–1795," *JAH* 106 (December 2019): 598 ("Free"); Barbara Graymont, *The Iroquois in the American Revolution* (Syracuse, NY: Syracuse University Press, 1972), 281 ("a subdued people").

10. Bethel Saler, *The Settlers' Empire: Colonialism and State Formation in America's Old Northwest* (Philadelphia: University of Pennsylvania Press, 2015), 13–40; "Locating Settler Colonialism in Early American History," *WMQ* 76 (July 2019): 444; *SA*, 1:342–43.

11. *SA*, 1:355–59; *NOT*, 139; Robbie Ethridge, *Creek Country: The Creek Indians and Their World* (Chapel Hill: University of North Carolina Press, 2003), 119; Jeffrey Washburn, "Directing Their Own Change: Chickasaw Economic Transformation and Civilization Plan, 1750s–1830s," *Native South* 13 (2020): 94–111 ("cultivate," 95); Peter S. Onuf, *Statehood and Union: A History of the Northwest Ordinance* (Bloomington: Indiana University Press, 1987), 58 ("robust").

12. *MG*, 416–17; *SG*, 187–88; "Treaty with the Wyandot, etc., 1785," "Treaty with the Six Nations, 1784," "Treaty with the Cherokee, 1785," "Treaty with the Choctaw, 1786," "Treaty with the Chickasaw, 1786," in *IALT*, 2:5, 8–23; Eric Hinderaker, *Elusive Empires: Constructing Colonialism in the Ohio Valley, 1673–1800* (New York: Cambridge University Press, 1997), 247–49; Kathleen DuVal, "Indian Intermarriage and Métissage in Colonial Louisiana," *WMQ* 65 (April 2008): 300.

13. *ARI*, 205–9; *SA*, 1:351, 354; Jon W. Parmenter, "Dragging Canoe (Tsi'ya-gûnsi'ni): Chickamauga Cherokee Patriot," in *The Human Tradition in the American Revolution*, ed. Nancy L. Rhoden and Ian K. Steele (Wilmington, DE: SR Books, 2000), 128–31; Tiya Miles, "The Narrative of Nancy, a Cherokee Woman," *Frontiers* 29 (2008): 59–80; *SG*, 189.

14. *ARI*, 213–43 ("people," 243); *SG*, 189; James Atkinson, *Splendid Land, Splendid People: The Chickasaw Indians to Removal* (Tuscaloosa: University of Alabama Press, 2003), 64.

15. Jane G. Landers, *Atlantic Creoles in the Age of Revolutions* (Cambridge, MA: Harvard University Press, 2010), 99–102; Gilbert C. Din, "William Augustus Bowles on the Gulf Coast, 1787–1803: Unraveling a Labyrinthine Conundrum," *Florida Historical Quarterly* 89 (Summer 2010): 11; Lyle N. McAlister, "William Augustus Bowles and the State of Muskogee," *Florida Historical Quarterly* 40 (April 1962): 325–26; *NOT*, 205–12, 220; Tribal Historic Preservation Office, available at: http://www.stofthpo.com/History-Seminole-Tribe-FL-Tribal-Historic-Preservation-Office.html, accessed Feb. 2, 2020. For Muscogee nationalism, see Evan Nooe, "Common Justice: Vengeance and Retribution in Creek Country," *Ethnohistory* 82 (April 2005); and Amy S. Greenberg, "US Expansionism during the Nineteenth Century: 'Manifest Destiny,'" in *The Oxford World History of Empire*, ed. Peter Fibiger Bang, C. A. Baily, and Walter Scheidel (New York: Oxford University Press, 2021), 1020–21 ("United States of Creeks").

16. François Furstenberg, "Significance of the Trans-Appalachian Frontier in Atlantic History," *AHR* 113 (June 2008): 651–60; *SA*, 1:355; Secretary of War, "Report," January 15, 1791, in *American State Papers, Class II. Indian Affairs* (Washington, D.C: Gales and Seaton, 1832), 1:112; Taylor, *American Revolutions*, 333.

17. Gervasio Cruzat y Cóngora to Estevan Rodriguez Miró, August 23, 1784, in *Spain in the Mississippi Valley, 1765–1794: Post War Decade, 1782–1794*, ed. Lawrence Kinnaird (Washington, DC: Government Printing Office, 1946), 117 ("Spanish father,"

"From the moment"); Furstenberg, "Significance of the Trans-Appalachian Frontier," 655. For the rupture of what James Belich calls the "Anglo-world," see Belich, *Replenishing the Earth: The Settler Revolution and the Rise of the Anglo-Worlds, 1783–1939* (New York: University of Oxford Press, 2009), esp. 48–57.

18. Cruzat to Miró, August 23, 1784, and Bernardo del Campo to José Moñino Floridablanca, December 11, 1783, in *Spain in the Mississippi Valley*, ed. Kinnaird, 118–19 ("worthy," "the fearful," "all the inhabitants," "whether," 118; "fortifying," 119); David J. Weber, *Bárbaros: Spaniards and Their Savages in the Age of Enlightenment* (New Haven, CT: Yale University Press, 2005), 204–8; Claudio Saunt, *West of the Revolution: An Uncommon History of 1776* (New York: W. W. Norton, 2014), 167.

19. Furstenberg, "Significance of the Trans-Appalachian Frontier," 656–57.

20. Taylor, *American Revolutions*, 346 ("a living wall," "circumstances"); Alan Taylor, "Remaking Americans: Louisiana, Upper Canada, and Texas," in *Contested Spaces of Early America* (Philadelphia: University of Pennsylvania Press, 2014), 212 ("We ought"); Aron, *How the West Was Lost*, 82–86.

21. Jefferson to Washington, April 2, 1791, in *The Papers of Thomas Jefferson*, ed. Julian P. Boyd (Princeton, NJ: Princeton University Press, 1982), 20:97 ("the means"); Alan Taylor, *The Divided Ground: Indians, Settlers, and the Northern Borderland of the American Revolution* (New York: Vintage, 2006), 214–19; Carolyn Podruchny, *Making the Voyager World: Travelers and Traders in the North American Fur Trade* (Lincoln: University of Nebraska Press, 2006), 5; Lucy Eldersveld Murphy, *Great Lakes Creoles: A French Community in the Northern Borderlands, Prairie du Chien, 1750–1860* (New York: Cambridge University Press, 2014), 24–30.

22. Peter Cozzens, *Tecumseh and the Prophet: The Shawnee Brothers Who Defied a Nation* (New York: Penguin, 2020), 65; Celia Barnes, *Native American Power in the United States, 1783–1795* (Madison, NJ: Fairleigh Dickinson University Press, 2003), 72 ("It is certain"); James E. Seelye and Steven A. Littleton, eds., *Voices of the American Indian Experience*, vol. 1, pt. B, *1716–1826* (Santa Barbara, CA: Greenwood, 2013), 165 ("All treaties," "any cession"). For the common pot, see Lisa Brooks, *The Common Pot: The Recovery of Native Space in the Northeast* (Minneapolis: University of Minnesota Press, 2008).

23. Griffin, *American Leviathan*, 199–200; Alan S. Brown, "The Role of the Army in Western Settlement: Josiah Harmar's Command, 1785–1790," *Pennsylvania Magazine of History and Biography* 93 (April 1969): 173 ("almost incredible"); Bottiger, *Borderland of Fear*, 33–37.

24. Furstenberg, "Significance of the Trans-Appalachian Frontier," 660–63; "Treaty with the Six Nations," January 9, 1789, in *IALT*, 2:18–19; *SG*, 322–25; Timothy J. Shannon, *Iroquois Diplomacy on the Early American Frontier* (New York: Viking Penguin, 2008), 207–9; Taylor, *Divided Ground*, 241–46; "Timothy Pickering to Washington, December 4, 1790," Founders Online, National Archives, accessed May 16, 2019, https://founders.archives.gov/documents/Washington/05-07-02-0014 ("far more savage," "it is in the highest degree").

25. Lakomäki, *Gathering Together*, 126; "To George Washington from Arthur St. Clair, 1 May 1790," Founders Online, National Archives, accessed July 4, 2020, https://founders.archives.gov/documents/Washington/05-05-02-0239; "Proclamation on the Treaty of Fort Harmar, 29 September 1789," Founders Online, National Archives, accessed July 9, 2020, https://founders.archives.gov/documents/Washington/05-04-02-0076 ("I am very sorry"); Clarence Edwin Carter and John Porter Bloom, eds., *The Territorial Papers of the United States*, vol. 2, *The Territory Northwest of the River Ohio, 1787–1803* (Washington, DC: U.S. Government Printing Office,

1934), 245 ("are reduced"); "Instructions to Brigadier General Charles Scott, March 9, 1791," in *American State Papers, Class II. Indian Affairs*, 1:129 ("to impress"); Charles Scott, "To the Various Tribes of Piankeshaws, and All the Nations of Red People, Lying on the Waters of the Wabash River, June 5, 1791," in *American State Papers, Class II. Indian Affairs*, 1:133 ("Should you decline").

26. Harper, *Unsettling the West*, 167; Colin G. Calloway, *The Victory with No Name: The Native American Defeat of the First American Army* (New York: Oxford University Press, 2014), 3; Bottiger, *Borderland of Fear*, 36–37; Taylor, *American Revolutions*, 404; Secretary of War, "Report," January 15, 1791, in *American State Papers, Class II. Indian Affairs*, 1:113 ("the inhabitants").

27. Secretary of War, "Report," January 22, 1791, in *American State Papers, Class II. Indian Affairs*, 1:113 ("the United States"); Taylor, *Divided Ground*, 238–39; Joseph D. Ibbotson, "Samuel Kirkland, the Treaty of 1792, and the Indian Barrier State," *New York History* (October 1938): 374–91; *Annals of Congress*, House of Representatives, 2nd Cong., 1st Sess., January 26, 1792, 338 ("As long as").

28. Helen Hornbeck Tanner, "The Glaize in 1792: A Composite Indian Community," *Ethnohistory* 25 (Winter 1978): 15–39; Andrew R. L. Cayton, *The Frontier Republic: Ideology and Politics in the Ohio Country, 1780–1825* (Kent, OH: Kent State University Press, 1986), 38–39; Cozzens, *Tecumseh and the Prophet*, 81–87; Parmenter, "Dragging Canoe," 128–31; James Wilkinson to Washington, September 6, 1792, in "Extracts of Correspondence on Indian Affairs, October 1792," Founders Online, National Archives, https://founders.archives.gov/documents/Washington/05-11-02 -0164, accessed September 18, 2020 ("1000 Creeks"); William H. Bergman, *The American National State and the Early West* (New York: Cambridge University Press, 2012), 75; Bottiger, *Borderland of Fear*, 37; Susan Sleeper-Smith, *Indigenous Prosperity and American Conquest: Indian Women of the Ohio River Valley, 1690– 1792* (Williamsburg, VA: Omohundro Institute of Early American History and Culture, 2018), 243–79; "Reply of the Six Nations," April 24, 1794, in *American State Papers, Class II. Indian Affairs*, 1:481 ("are of the same").

29. *SA*, 1:351–53; Thomas P. Slaughter, *The Whiskey Rebellion: Frontier Epilogue to the American Revolution* (New York: Oxford University Press, 1986), 117, 164–69; Taylor, *Divided Ground*, 291–92; Anthony Wayne to the Secretary of War, August 15, 1794, and Henry Knox to George Washington, December 29, 1794, in *American State Papers, Class II. Indian Affairs* 1:490, 544 ("grand emporium," "very extensive," "show the work," 490).

30. Calloway, *Victory with No Name*, 97–98; J. F. Lee, *Masters of the Middle Waters: Indian Nations and Colonial Ambitions along the Mississippi* (Cambridge, MA: Harvard University Press, 2019), 213; Gordon S. Wood, *Empire of Liberty: A History of the Early Republic, 1789–1815* (New York: Oxford University Press, 2009), 135–39; Gregory H. Nobles, *American Frontiers: Cultural Encounters and Continental Conquest* (New York: Hill & Wang, 1997), 99–132; Knox to Washington, December 29, 1794, in *American State Papers, Class II. Indian Affairs*, 1:544 ("the utter"); *SG*, 110.

31. Lakomäki, *Gathering Together*, 126–30; Witgen, "A Nation of Settlers: The Early American Republic and the Colonization of the Northwest Territory," *WMQ* 76 (July 2019): 397–99; Furstenberg, "Significance of the Trans-Appalachian Frontier," 668; *MG*, 467–48; Andrew R. L. Cayton, "'Noble Actors' upon 'the Theatre of Honour': Power and Civility in the Treaty of Greenville," in *Contact Points: American Frontiers from the Mohawk Valley to the Mississippi*, ed. Cayton and Fredrika J. Teute (Chapel Hill: University of North Carolina Press, 1998), 235–39; Bottiger, *Borderland*

of Fear, 38–39; *SA*, 1:353–55; Reginald Horsman, *Race and Manifest Destiny: The Origins of American Racial Anglo-Saxonism* (Cambridge, MA: Harvard University Press, 1986); Greenberg, "US Expansionism," 1014–15; Cayton, *Frontier Republic*, 39; "Treaty with the Tribes of Indians, Aug. 9, 1795," in *American State Papers, Class II. Indian Affairs*, 1:570–71 ("The boundary," 570; "our tomahawk," 571).

32. Wallace, *Jefferson and the Indians*, 206–14; David Andrew Nichols, *Engines of Diplomacy: Indian Trading Factories and the Negotiation of American Empire* (Chapel Hill: University of North Carolina Press, 2016), 32, 69–88; Anne F. Hyde, *Empires, Nations, Families: A History of the North American West, 1800–1860* (Lincoln: University of Nebraska Press, 2011), 243; Bergman, *American National State and the Early West*, 172–74; Thomas Jefferson to Meriwether Lewis, August 21, 1808, in "From Thomas Jefferson to Meriwether Lewis, 21 August 1808," Founders Online, National Archives, accessed December 12, 2020, https://founders .archives.gov/documents/Jefferson/99-01-02-8555 ("Commerce").

33. *SA*, 1:348–49, 355–60; Reginald Horsman, *Expansion and American Indian Policy, 1783–1812* (East Lansing: Michigan State University Press, 1967), 53–65; Bernard W. Sheehan, *Seeds of Extinction: Jeffersonian Philanthropy and the American Indian* (New York: W. W. Norton, 1973), 45–65; Cayton, *Frontier Republic*, 56.

CHAPTER 24: WESTERN PROMISES

1. *SFNA*, 289; *SA*, 2:6–7.

2. *SA*, 1:367–69. For travel times, see J. F. Lee, *Masters of the Middle Waters: Indian Nations and Colonial Ambitions along the Mississippi* (Cambridge, MA: Harvard University Press, 2019), 181 ("resident foreign nations").

3. William Lytle Schurz, "The Spanish Lake," *Hispanic American Historical Review* 5 (May 1922): 181–94; Pekka Hämäläinen, "How Native Americans Shaped Early America," in *Cambridge History of America and the World*, ed. Eliga Gould, Paul Mapp, and Carla Gardina Pestana (New York: Cambridge University Press, 2021), 199.

4. Gilles Havard and Cécile Vidal, *Histoire de l'Amérique Française* (Paris: Flammarion, 2005), 704–11; Hämäläinen, "How Native Americans Shaped Early America," 199–200.

5. *New York Daily Advertiser*, February 12, 1802 ("hold forth").

6. Thomas Jefferson to Robert R. Livingston, April 18, 1802 ("There is"), Thomas Jefferson, "Draft of First Inaugural," March 4, 1801 ("room for all"), Thomas Jefferson Papers at the Library of Congress, ser. 1, General Correspondence, 1651–1827, https://www.loc.gov/item/mtjbib011277; Stanley Elkins and Eric McKitrick, *The Age of Federalism: The Early American Republic, 1788–1800* (New York: Oxford University Press, 1995), 406–30; Robert L. Paquette, "Revolutionary Saint Domingue in the Making of Territorial Louisiana," in *A Turbulent Time: The French Revolution and the Greater Caribbean*, ed. David Barry Gaspar and David Patrick Geggus (Bloomington: Indiana University Press, 1997), 204–25.

7. Robert Lee, "Accounting for Conquest: The Price of the Louisiana Purchase in Indian Country," *JAH* 103 (March 2017): 912–42; Nicholas Guyatt, "'The Outskirts of Our Happiness': Race and the Lure of Colonization in the Early Republic," *JAH* 95 (March 2009): 995; Kent McNeil, "The Louisiana Purchase: Indian and American Sovereignty in the Missouri Watershed," *Western Historical Quarterly* 50 (Spring 2019): 17–42.

8. Christa Dierksheide, "'The Great Improvement and Civilization of That Race': Jefferson and the 'Amelioration' of Slavery, ca. 1770–1826," *Early American Studies* 6 (Spring 2008): 165–97; Anthony F. C. Wallace, *Jefferson and the Indians: The*

Tragic Fate of the First Americans (Cambridge, MA: Belknap Press of Harvard University Press, 1999), 216; Jack D. L. Holmes, "Benjamin Hawkins and United States Attempts to Teach Farming to Southeastern Indians," *Agricultural History* 60 (Spring 1986): 216–32; *NOT,* 164 ("the sweets," "the value"); "From Thomas Jefferson to Benjamin Hawkins, 18 February 1803," Founders Online, National Archives, accessed November 29, 2020, https://founders.archives.gov/documents/Jefferson/01 -39-02-0456 ("In truth"); Theda Perdue, *Cherokee Women: Gender and Culture Change, 1700–1835* (Lincoln: University of Nebraska Press, 1998), 116–17, 122, 152.

9. Anthony F. C. Wallace, *The Death and Rebirth of the Seneca* (New York: Knopf, 1970), esp. 233–53; Elisabeth Tooker, "On the Development of the Handsome Lake Religion," *Proceedings of the American Philosophical Society* 133 (March 1989): 35–50; Arthur C. Parker, "The Code of Handsome Lake, the Seneca Prophet," *Education Department Bulletin* 530 (November 1912).

10. Claudio Saunt, *West of the Revolution: An Uncommon History of 1776* (New York: W. W. Norton, 2014), 149–51.

11. *LA,* 95–96; Pierre-Antoine Tabeau, *Tabeau's Narrative of Loisel's Expedition to the Upper Missouri,* ed. Annie Heloise Able (Norman: University of Oklahoma Press, 1939), 123–124 ("sad debris"); Raymond J. DeMallie, Douglas Parks, and Robert Vezina, eds., *A Fur Trader on the Upper Missouri: The Journal and Description of Jean-Baptiste Truteau, 1794–1796,* trans. Mildred Mott Wedel, Raymond J. DeMallie, and Robert Vezina (Lincoln: University of Nebraska Press, 2017), 177–79; Elizabeth A. Fenn, *Encounters at the Heart of the World: A History of the Mandan People* (New York: Hill and Wang, 2014), 166; *YSF,* 95, 103 ("They burnt," 95; "Came, 103").

12. *YSF,* 118–20; *LA,* 99.

13. Louis F. Burns, *A History of the Osage People* (Tuscaloosa: University of Alabama Press, 2004), 242; *SA,* 2:15; Lee, *Masters of the Middle Waters,* 158–60, 170–71, 179–81; Saunt, *West of the Revolution,* 180; Anne F. Hyde, *Empires, Nations, and Families: A History of the North American West, 1800–1860* (Lincoln: University of Nebraska Press, 2011), 239–40.

14. "Extract from the Journals of the Voyage of J-Bte Truteau," in *Fur Trader on the Upper Missouri,* ed. DeMallie, Parks, and Vezina, 103–7 ("bad men," "would only," 103; "open up," "This was," 105; "a proportionate," 107); Thomas Jefferson to Meriwether Lewis, November 16, 1803, Thomas Jefferson Papers at the Library of Congress, ser. 1, General Correspondence, 1651–1827, http://www.loc.gov/resource/mtj1 .029_0512_0513 ("greatest").

15. *Tabeau's Narrative,* 130–31, 138 ("a certain kind," 130; "forming," "fix," "surrounded," "ruinous commerce," 131; "make the Ricaras," 138).

16. Raymond J. DeMallie, ed., *The Sixth Grandfather: Black Elk's Teachings Given to John G. Neihardt* (Lincoln: University of Nebraska Press, 1984), 307–8 ("We are," 307; "Other people," 308); Steven Sabol, *"The Touch of Civilization": Comparing American and Russian Internal Colonization* (Boulder: University Press of Colorado, 2017), 62; James R. Walker, *The Lakota Society,* ed. Raymond J. DeMallie (Lincoln: University of Nebraska Press, 1992), 125 ("allies").

17. Peter S. Onuf, "The Revolution of 1803," *Wilson Quarterly* 27 (Winter 2003): 24.

18. *SA,* 2:14–16; "From Thomas Jefferson to John Jay, 23 August 1785," Founders Online, National Archives, accessed January 12, 2021, https://founders.archives .gov/documents/Jefferson/01-08-02-0333; Christian B. Keller, "Philanthropy Betrayed: Thomas Jefferson, the Louisiana Purchase, and the Origins of Federal Indian Removal Policy," *Proceedings of the American Philosophical Society* 144 (March 2000): 33–66.

19. *SA*, 1:60; Thomas Jefferson to Meriwether Lewis, November 6, 1803, and January 22, 1804, in *Letters of the Lewis and Clark Expedition with Related Documents, 1783–1854*, ed. Donald Jackson (Urbana: University of Illinois Press, 1962), 138, 166 ("from 30. to 60.000," 138; "Although," 166); "Journal of Jean Baptiste Truteau on the Upper Missouri, 'Premiere Partie,' June 7, 1794–March 26, 1795," *AHR* 19 (January 1914): 299–333; Thomas Jefferson to Congress, January 18, 1803, https://tile.loc.gov/storage -services/service/mss/mtj//mtj1/027/027_0841_0844.pdf ("twelve or fifteen men").

20. Prideaux Selby to Peter Russell, January 23, 1799, in *WHC*, 18:460 ("a nation").

21. *Tabeau's Narrative*, 99–100, 110 ("elevated," "formerly," 99; "very mild," "urgently entreated," 110); *JLCE*, 3:399.

22. Jefferson to Robert Smith, July 13, 1804, Thomas Jefferson Papers at the Library of Congress, ser. 1, General Correspondence, 1651–1827, https://www.loc.gov/ resource/mtj1.030_1058_1058 ("must stand well," "because," "the finest," "a great nation"); Joseph J. Ellis, *American Sphinx: The Character of Thomas Jefferson* (New York: Alfred A. Knopf, 1996), 246–53; John D. Seelye, *Beautiful Machine: Rivers and the Republican Plan, 1755–1825* (New York: Oxford University Press, 1991), 193–209; *LA*, 129.

23. *JLCE*, 2:438–41, 487–93 ("I came here," 491; "a Spoon ful," 492); James P. Ronda, *Lewis and Clark among the Indians* (Lincoln: University of Nebraska Press, 1984), 21–23.

24. *JLCE*, 3:21, 29–30 ("much engaged," 21; "Listen," 29; "nations above," 30); *Tabeau's Narrative*, 127 ("wearied").

25. *JLCE*, 3:111–14, 139 ("the Grand Chief," 111; "bad humered," 114; "Were to go on," "kill and take," 139); John Ordway, "Sergeant Ordway's Journal," in *The Journals of Captain Meriwether Lewis and Sergeant John Ordway*, ed. Milo M. Quaife (Madison: State Historical Society of Wisconsin, 1916), 138–39 ("he had warriers," "their great," "as they never Saw," 139).

26. James P. Ronda, "Appendix: A Note on Sacagawea," in *Lewis and Clark among the Indians*, Journals of the Lewis and Clark Expedition Online, accessed September 6, 2020, https://lewisandclarkjournals.unl.edu/item/lc.sup.ronda.01.appendix; *JLCE*, 5:23, 114 ("a woman with," 23); *JLCE*, 3:418 ("the vilest"); *LA*, 139–43.

27. Frederick E. Hoxie, *Parading through History: The Making of the Crow Nation in America, 1805–1935* (New York: Cambridge University Press, 1995), 30–37.

28. "Arrival of Lewis and Clark at St. Louis," *Western World*, October 1, 1806, quoted in James P. Ronda, "St. Louis Welcomes and Toasts the Lewis and Clark Expedition: A Newly Discovered Newspaper Account," in *Explorations into the World of Lewis & Clark*, ed. Robert A. Saindon (Scituate, MA: Digital Scanning Inc., 2003), 3:1280–81 ("a vehicle," "The Commerce").

29. Robert J. Miller, *Native America, Discovered and Conquered: Thomas Jefferson, Lewis & Clark, and Manifest Destiny* (Westport, CT: Praeger, 2006), 104–7; Jared Orsi, *Citizen Explorer: The Adventurous Life of Zebulon Pike* (New York: Oxford University Press, 2014), 95–103; "General Wilkinson's Proclamation," August 24, 1805, National Archives Microfilm Publications, no. 222, Letters Received by the Secretary of War, Unregistered Series, 1789–1860, roll 2, unregistered file.

CHAPTER 25: THE WHITE DEVIL WITH HIS MOUTH WIDE OPEN

1. William Henry Harrison to Sec. of War, February 19, 1802, in *Governors Messages and Letters: Messages and Letters of William Henry Harrison Concluded, John Gibson, Thomas Posey*, ed. Logan Esarey (Indianapolis: Indiana Historical Commission, 1922), 1:38 ("make the Indians").

2.   Gregory Evans Dowd, *A Spirited Resistance: The North American Indian Struggle for Unity, 1745–1815* (Baltimore: Johns Hopkins University Press, 1992), esp. 29; *MG*, 512 ("new white nation"); Anne F. Hyde, *Empires, Nations, and Families: A History of the North American West, 1800–1860* (Lincoln: University of Nebraska Press, 2011), 245–50; "Marquis of Casa-Calvo, May 28, 1804," in Pierre-Antoine Tabeau, *Tabeau's Narrative of Loisel's Expedition to the Upper Missouri*, ed. Annie Heloise Able (Norman: University of Oklahoma Press, 1939), 241 ("take the warpath").

3.   Sami Lakomäki, *Gathering Together: The Shawnee People through Diaspora and Nationhood, 1600–1870* (New Haven, CT: Yale University Press, 2014), 143–44; *MG*, 502–9; *WUH*, 272; "Extract from a Talk Delivered at Le Maiouitinong, Entrance of Lake Michigan, by the Indian Chief Le Maigouis, or the Trout, May 4, 1807," in *State Papers and Public Documents of the United States* (Boston: T. B. Wait, 1817), 8:435 ("the scum"); R. David Edmunds, *Tecumseh and the Quest for Indian Leadership* (Boston: Little, Brown, 1984), 71–72; Gregory A. Waselkov, *A Conquering Spirit: Fort Mims and the Redstick War of 1813–1814* (Tuscaloosa: University of Alabama Press, 2006), 74–77; Daniel K. Richter, *Facing East from Indian Country: A Native History of Early America* (Cambridge, MA: Harvard University Press, 2001), 230.

4.   Sara Mohammedi, "The Interpretation of Christianity by American Prophets," *Indigenous Nations Studies Journal* 3 (Fall 2002): 71–88; "From Thomas Jefferson to Henry Dearborn, 28 August 1807," Founders Online, National Archives, accessed January 5, 2021, https://founders.archives.gov/documents/Jefferson/99-01-02-6267 ("if ever"); Adam Jortner, *The Gods of Prophetstown: The Battle of Tippecanoe and the Holy War for the American Frontier* (New York: Oxford University Press, 2011); Peter Cozzens, *Tecumseh and the Shawnee Prophet: The Shawnee Brothers Who Defied a Nation* (New York: Penguin, 2020), 48; Patrick Bottiger, *Borderland of Fear: Vincennes, Prophetstown, and the Invasion of the Miami Homeland* (Lincoln: University of Nebraska Press, 2016), 114–16, 140–43; *SG*, 187–88.

5.   Bottiger, *Borderland of Fear*, 74, 82–92; Edmunds, *Tecumseh and the Quest*, 223; Lakomäki, *Gathering Together*, 143–50; Gordon S. Wood, *Empire of Liberty: A History of the Early Republic, 1789–1815* (New York: Oxford University Press, 2009), 675; John Sudgen, *Tecumseh: A Life* (New York: Henry Holt, 1997), 215 ("one of those"); Christina Snyder, *Great Crossings: Indians, Settlers, and Slaves in the Age of Jackson* (New York: Oxford University Press, 2017), 35; Harrison to Secretary of War, July 10, 1811, and "Petition to James Madison, President of the United States, July 31, 1811," in *Governors Messages and Letters*, ed. Esarey, 1:532, 534, 540 ("unless," 532; "the acquirement," "they could," 534; "the western," "The banditti," 540).

6.   Wood, *Empire of Liberty*, 659–62; Kathryn E. Holland Braund, ed., "Introduction," in *Tohopeka: Rethinking the Creek War and the War of 1812* (Tuscaloosa: University of Alabama Press, 2012), 3. For Black runaway slaves, see Alan Taylor, *The Internal Enemy: Slavery and War in Virginia, 1772–1832* (New York: W. W. Norton, 2013).

7.   Hyde, *Empires, Nations, and Families*, 235–36; Bernard W. Sheehan, *Seeds of Extinction: Jeffersonian Philanthropy and the American Indian* (New York: W. W. Norton, 1973), 121; Lewis Cass to Return J. Meigs, August 12, 1812, in *Documents Relating to the Invasion of Canada and the Surrender of Detroit, 1812*, ed. E. A. Cruikshank (Ottawa: Government Printing Bureau, 1912), 137 ("We wholly"); Bottiger, *Borderland of Fear*, 137–39; Alan Taylor, "The War of 1812 and the Struggle for the Continent," in *The World of the Revolutionary American Republic: Land,*

Labor, and the Conflict for a Continent, ed. Andrew Shankman (New York: Routledge, 2014), 250; *NOT*, 237–48; Rembert W. Patrick, *Florida Fiasco: Rampant Rebels on the Georgia-Florida Border, 1810–1815* (Athens: University of Georgia Press, 1954), 29–30, 179–82.

8. Claudio Saunt, "'Domestick . . . Quiet Being Broke': Gender Conflict among the Creek Indians in the Eighteenth Century," in *Contact Points: American Frontiers from the Mohawk Valley to the Mississippi*, ed. Andrew R. L. Cayton and Fredrika J. Teute (Chapel Hill: University of North Carolina Press, 1998), 151–74; *NOT*, 249–72; Patrick, *Florida Fiasco*, 29–30, 179–82; Waselkov, *Conquering Spirit*, 86, 96–97.

9. Waselkov, *Conquering Spirit*, 96–100, 140; Saunt, "'Domestick,'" 151–54; *NOT*, 264–67; Dowd, *Spirited Resistance*, 155.

10. R. Douglas Hurt, *The Ohio Frontier: Crucible of the Old Northwest, 1720–1830* (Bloomington: Indiana University Press, 1996), 340–44; Cozzens, *Tecumseh and the Prophet*, 398–419; *MG*, 523.

11. Hurt, *Ohio Frontier*, 375; Susan M. Abram, "Cherokees in the Creek War: A Band of Brothers," in *Tohopeka: Rethinking the Creek War and the War of 1812*, ed. Kathryn E. Holland Braund (Tuscaloosa: University of Alabama Press, 2012), 135; Andrew Jackson to William H. Crawford, June 10, 1816, in *American State Papers, Class II. Indian Affairs* (Washington, DC: Gales and Seaton), 2:111 ("so carefully"); Richter, *Facing East from Indian Country*, 233.

12. David J. Weber, *Bárbaros: Spaniards and Their Savages in the Age of Enlightenment* (New Haven, CT: Yale University Press, 2005), 5, 31–41.

13. D. A. Brading, *The First America: The Spanish Monarchy, Creole Patriots, and the Liberal State, 1492–1867* (New York: Cambridge University Press, 1991), 499; Weber, *Bárbaros*, 72–75, 109–10 ("deplorable," 75).

14. Weber, *Bárbaros*, 143–44.

15. Bernardo de Gálvez, *Instructions for Governing the Interior Provinces of New Spain 1786*, trans. and ed. Donald E. Worcester (Berkeley, CA: Quivira Society, 1951), 40–42, 48–49 ("by deceit," 40; "We shall," 41; "The interest," 42; "weak bolts," 49); Weber, *Bárbaros*, 179–220.

16. Alan Taylor, *American Colonies* (New York: Viking, 2001), 446–48; Colin Calloway, *One Vast Winter Count: The Native American West before Lewis and Clark* (Lincoln: University of Nebraska Press, 2003), 399.

17. *SFNA*, 237–38; *NWA*, 48–49; Jennifer Seltz, "Epidemics, Indians, and Border-Making in the Nineteenth-Century Northwest," in *Bridging National Borders in North America: Transnational and Comparative Histories*, ed. Benjamin H. Johnson and Andrew Graybill (Durham, NC: Duke University Press, 2010), 91–100; Joseph E. Taylor, *Making Salmon: An Environmental History of Northwest Fisheries* (Seattle: University of Washington Press, 1999), 13–17; Richard White, *The Organic Machine: The Remaking of the Columbia River* (New York: Hill and Wang, 1995), 16–22.

18. *SFNA*, 246; Albert Hurtado, *Intimate Frontiers: Sex, Gender, and Culture in Old California* (Albuquerque: University of New Mexico Press, 1999), 1–6; Steven W. Hackel, *Children of Coyote, Missionaries of Saint Francis: Indian-Spanish Relations in Colonial California, 1769–1850* (Chapel Hill: University of North Carolina Press, 2005), 28–29.

19. J. H. Elliott, *Empires of the Atlantic World: Britain and Spain in America, 1492–1830* (New Haven, CT: Yale University Press, 2006), 204–18; Michael Kammen, *Mystic Chords of Memory: The Transformation of Tradition in American Culture* (New York: Vintage, 1991), 208; Walter Nonneman, "On the Economics of the Socialist Theocracy of the Jesuits in Paraguay (1609–1767), in *The Political Econ-*

omy of Theocracy, ed. Mario Ferrero and Ronald Wintrobe (New York: Palgrave Macmillan, 2009), 119–20.

20. Lisbeth Haas, *Saints and Citizens: Indigenous Histories of Colonial Missions and Mexican California* (Berkeley: University of California Press, 2014), 55–80; Jennifer M. Spear, "Beyond the Native/Settler Divide in Early California," *WMQ* 76 (July 2019), 361–68; Claudio Saunt, *West of the Revolution: An Uncommon History of 1776* (New York: W. W. Norton, 2014), 59–64; *SFNA*, 249–50; Felipe Neve to Antonio María Bucareli, February 26, 1777, in Edwin A. Beilharz, *Felipe de Neve, First Governor of California* (San Francisco: California Historical Society, 1971), 83; James A. Sandos, "Social Control within Missionary Frontier: Alta California, 1760–1821," in *Choice, Persuasion, and Coercion: Social Control on Spain's North American Frontiers*, ed. Jesús F. de la Teja and Ross Frank (Albuquerque: University of New Mexico Press, 2005), 253–64; Taylor, *American Colonies*, 458 ("come to know").

21. Stuart Banner, *How the Indians Lost Their Land: Law and Power on the Frontier* (Cambridge, MA: Harvard University Press, 2005), 3–9; Colin G. Calloway, *Pen and Ink Witchcraft: Treaties and Treaty Making in Colonial America* (New York: Oxford University Press, 2013), 1–11; Max M. Edling, *A Hercules in the Cradle: War, Money, and the American State* (Chicago: Chicago University Press, 2014), 7–8.

CHAPTER 26: THE LONG REMOVAL ERA

1. Matthew J. Clavin, *The Battle of Negro Fort: The Rise and Fall of a Fugitive Slave Community* (New York: New York University Press, 2019), 1–2; *NOT*, 273–74. In titling this chapter, I took my cue from *SG*, 191, 361–64.

2. *YSF*, 157–61.

3. Lucy Eldersveld Murphy, *Great Lakes Creoles: A French Community in the Northern Borderlands, Prairie du Chien, 1750–1860* (New York: Cambridge University Press, 2014), 65–66.

4. Paul Williams, *The Dakota Conflict and Its Leaders, 1862–1865: Little Crow, Henry Sibley and Alfred Sully* (Jefferson, NC: McFarland, 2020), 143 ("After"); Alan Taylor, *The Civil War of 1812: American Citizens, British Subjects, Irish Rebels, and Indian Allies* (New York: Alfred A. Knopf, 2010), 413–21; Clavin, *Battle of Negro Fort*, 16; François Furstenberg, "The Significance of the Trans-Appalachian Frontier in Atlantic History," *AHR* 113 (June 2008): 675; *SG*, 190.

5. Nicholas Guyatt, *Bind Us Apart: How Enlightened Americans Invented Racial Segregation* (New York: Basic Books, 2016), 317–18; Claudio Saunt, *Unworthy Republic: The Dispossession of Native Americans and the Road to Indian Territory* (New York: W. W. Norton, 2020), 3–11.

6. J. F. Lee, *Masters of the Middle Waters: Indian Nations and Colonial Ambitions along the Mississippi* (Cambridge, MA: Harvard University Press, 2019), 217–19; Nicholas Guyatt, "'The Outskirts of Our Happiness': Race and the Lure of Colonization in the Early Republic," *JAH* 95 (March 2009): 994.

7. Sean M. Theriault, "Party Politics during the Louisiana Purchase," *Social Science History* 30 (Summer 2006): 293–324; Theda Perdue, "The Conflict Within: The Cherokee Power Structure and Removal," *Georgia Historical Quarterly* 73 (Fall 1989): 471–73; S. Charles Bolton, "Jeffersonian Indian Removal and the Emergence of Arkansas Territory," *Arkansas Historical Quarterly* 62 (Autumn 2003): 253–71; John P. Bowes, "American Indian Removal beyond the Removal Act," *Native American and Indigenous Studies* 1 (Spring 2014): 65–87; Anthony F. C. Wallace,

Jefferson and the Indians: The Tragic Fate of the First Americans (Cambridge, MA: Belknap Press of Harvard University Press, 1999), 206; Kathleen DuVal, *The Native Ground: Indians and Colonists in the Heart of the Continent* (Philadelphia: University of Pennsylvania Press, 2006), 199–205; William G. McLoughlin, "New Angles of Vision on the Cherokee Ghost Dance Movement of 1811–1812," *American Indian Quarterly* 5 (November 1979): 315–45.

8. Clavin, *Battle of Negro Fort*, 104, 113–14, 121–26 ("ye brave," "if the country," 104); Frank Lawrence Owsley Jr. and Gene A. Smith, *Filibusters and Expansionists: Jeffersonian Manifest Destiny, 1800–1821* (Tuscaloosa: University of Alabama Press, 1997), 111; *SG*, 189.

9. Jon Meacham, *American Lion: Jackson in the White House* (New York: Random House, 2008), 35–36; *SFNA*, 299–300; John K. Mahon, "The Treaty of Moultrie Creek," *Florida Historical Quarterly* 40 (April 1962): 350–72; John K. Mahon, "Two Seminole Treaties: Payne's Landing, 1832, and Ft. Gibson, 1833," *Florida Historical Quarterly* 41 (July 1962): 1–21.

10. Tiya Miles, *Ties That Bind: The Story of an Afro-Cherokee Family in Slavery and Freedom* (Berkeley: University of California Press, 2016), 103–5; *SG*, 189; Anne F. Hyde, *Empires, Nations, and Families: A History of the North American West, 1800–1860* (Lincoln: University of Nebraska Press, 2011), 229–31; Saunt, *Unworthy Republic*, 41–47, 54; Christina Snyder, *Slavery in Indian Country: The Changing Face of Captivity in Early America* (Cambridge, MA: Harvard University Press, 2010), 90–93; Guyatt, " 'Outskirts of Our Happiness,' " 1003.

11. Joshua D. Rothman, *Flush Times and Fever Dreams: A Story of Capitalism and Slavery in the Age of Jackson* (Athens: University of Georgia Press, 2012), 3–4; Walter Johnson, *River of Dark Dreams: Slavery and Empire in the Cotton Kingdom* (Cambridge, MA: Belknap Press of Harvard University Press, 2013), 1–45, 245–30; Sven Beckert, *Empire of Cotton: A Global History* (New York: Alfred A. Knopf, 2014), 102–4; Edward E. Baptist, *The Half Has Never Been Told: Slavery and the Making of American Capitalism* (New York: Basic Books, 2014), 3–38, 175–85; *SG*, 189; Guyatt, " 'Outskirts of Our Happiness.' " For northern Indian removal, see John P. Bowes, *Land Too Good for Indians: Northern Indian Removal* (Norman: University of Oklahoma Press, 2016).

12. Saunt, *Unworthy Republic*, 31–33 ("all the red," 33); *SA*, 2:80–81. For the Bureau of Indian Affairs as a colonial office, see Brian DeLay, "Indian Politics, Empire, and the History of American Foreign Relations," *Diplomatic History* 39 (November 2015): 935.

13. Miles, *Ties That Bind*, 104; Theda Perdue, *Cherokee Women: Gender and Culture Change, 1700–1835* (Lincoln: University of Nebraska Press, 1998), 155–57; Fay A. Yarbrough, *Race and the Cherokee Nation: Sovereignty in the Nineteenth Century* (Philadelphia: University of Pennsylvania Press, 2008), 25–32; Fay A. Yarbrough, "Legislating Women's Sexuality: Cherokee Marriage Laws in the Nineteenth Century, *Journal of Social History* 38 (Winter 2004): 385–406 ("intermarriages"); Barbara Krauthammer, *Black Slaves, Indian Masters: Slavery, Emancipation, and Citizenship in the Native American South* (Chapel Hill: University of North Carolina Press, 2013), 39.

14. Miles, *Ties That Bind*, 109–12; "Constitution of the Cherokee Nation," *Cherokee Phoenix* 1, no. 1 (February 21, 1828), https://www.wcu.edu/library/DigitalCollections/CherokeePhoenix/Vol1/no01/constitution-of-the-cherokee-nation-page-1-column-2a-page-2-column-3a.html, ("the boundaries"); M. Amanda Moulder, "Cherokee

Practice, Missionary Intentions: Literacy Learning among Early Nineteenth-Century Cherokee Women," *Indigenous Ethnic Rhetorics* (September 2011): 75–96; Theda Perdue, "Traditionalism in the Cherokee Nation: Resistance to the Constitution of 1827," *Georgia Historical Quarterly* 66 (Summer 1982): 159–70; Emilie Connolly, "Panic, State Power, and Chickasaw Dispossession," *Journal of the Early Republic* 40 (Winter 2020): 683–89; Saunt, *Unworthy Republic*, 205.

15. For an incisive study of the Choctaw Academy, see Christina Snyder, *Great Crossings: Indians, Settlers, and Slaves in the Age of Jackson* (New York: Oxford University Press, 2017).

16. Andrew Jackson to James Monroe, March 4, 1817, in *The Papers of Andrew Jackson*, ed. Harold D. Moser, David R. Hoth, and George H. Hoemann (Knoxville: University of Tennessee Press, 1994), 95 ("the right"); Andrew Jackson, "First Annual Message to Congress, December 8, 1829," in *Documents of United States Indian Policy*, ed. Francis Paul Prucha, 3rd ed. (Lincoln: University of Nebraska Press, 1975), 47 ("though lavish"); DeLay, "Indian Politics, Empire," 936; Saunt, *Unworthy Republic*, 69–77, 86, 97–100; *SG*, 249–50; Miles, *Ties That Bind*, 132; John Faragher, "More Motley than Mackinaw: From Ethnic Mixing to Ethnic Cleansing on the Frontier of the Lower Missouri, 1783–1833," in *Contact Points: American Frontiers from the Mohawk Valley to the Mississippi, 1750–1830*, ed. Andrew Cayton and Frederika Teute (Chapel Hill: University of North Carolina Press, 1998), 305; Michael L. Oberg, "William Wirt and the Trials of Republicanism," *Virginia Magazine of History and Biography* 99, no. 3 (July 1991): 312–14; "The Cherokee Nation vs. The State of Georgia, Supreme Court, January, 1831 Term," accessed November 24, 2021, https://www.sfu.ca/~palys/USSC1831CherokeevGeorgia.htm, ("domestic," "a ward," "tribes which reside").

17. Lisa Ford, *Settler Sovereignty: Jurisdiction and Indigenous People in America and Australia, 1788–1836* (Cambridge, MA: Harvard University Press, 2010), 3–4, 130, 155–56, 175–82; Krauthammer, *Black Slaves, Indian Masters*, 38–39; Saunt, *Unworthy Republic*, 124–70; John T. Ellisor, *The Second Creek War: Interethnic Conflict and Collusion on a Collapsing Frontier* (Lincoln: University of Nebraska Press, 2010), 47–181. For Choctaw women, see Michelene E. Pesantubbee, *Choctaw Women in a Chaotic World: The Clash of Cultures in the Colonial Southeast* (Albuquerque: University of New Mexico Press, 2005), 2. For rapes and murders of Native women, see Sarah Deer, *The Beginning and End of Rape: Confronting Sexual Violence in Native America* (New York: Oxford University Press, 2015), esp. 68–71.

18. Miles, *Ties That Bind*, 7–8, 130–32.

19. Peter Cozzens, *Tecumseh and the Prophet: The Shawnee Brothers Who Defied a Nation* (New York: Penguin, 2020), 427–33.

20. *SA*, 4:158; Murphy, *Great Lakes Creoles*, 148–86; Lee, *Masters of the Middle Waters*, 230–32. For northern Indian removal, see Bowes, *Land Too Good for Indians*, esp. 78–210.

21. Lucy Eldersveld Murphy, "Autonomy and the Economic Roles of the Fox-Wisconsin River Region, 1763–1832," in *Negotiators of Change: Historical Perspectives on Native American Women*, ed. Nancy Shoemaker (New York: Routledge, 1995), 72; *SG*, 297–320; James H. Merrell, "American Nations, Old and New: Reflections on Indians and the Early Republic," in *Native Americans and the Early Republic*, ed. Frederick E. Hoxie, Ronald Hoffman, and Peter J. Albert (Charlotte: University Press of Virginia, 1999), 338. For a comprehensive study of the Black Hawk war, see Patrick J. Jung, *The Black Hawk War of 1832* (Norman: University of Oklahoma Press, 2007).

22. Jeremiah Evarts, ed., *Speeches on the Passage of the Bill for the Removal of Indians*

Delivered in the Congress of the United States (Boston: Perkins and Marvin, 1830), 253, 299 ("oppression," 253; "the evil," 299); Daniel Walker Howe, *What God Hath Wrought: The Transformation of America, 1815–1848* (New York: Oxford University Press, 2007), 352–57, 414–16; Saunt, *Unworthy Republic*, 201–26, 256–66; Theda Perdue and Michael D. Green, *The Cherokee Nation and the Trail of Tears* (New York: Viking, 2008), 137–39; Matthew T. Gregg, "Shortchanged: Uncovering the Value of Pre-removal Cherokee Property," *Chronicles of Oklahoma* 3 (2009): 320–30.

23. Jane Dinwoodie, "Evading Indian Removal in the American South," *JAH* 108 (June 2021): 17–41.

24. Nathaniel Millet, *The Maroons of Prospect Bluff and Their Quest for Freedom in the Atlantic World* (Gainesville: University Press of Florida, 2013), 239–49; Snyder, *Slavery in Indian Country*, 224–26; Dinwoodie, "Evading Indian Removal," 30–31; *SA*, 2:89–90; Jack E. Davis, *The Gulf: The Making of an American Sea* (New York: W. W. Norton, 2017), 12–22; Saunt, *Unworthy Republic*, 239–42, 281–98, 305–6. For Florida's geography and its geopolitical repercussions, see Michele Currie Navakas, *Liquid Landscape: Geography and Settlement at the Edge of Early America* (Philadelphia: University of Pennsylvania Press, 2017); *SG*, 284; Susan A. Miller, *Coacoochee's Bones: A Seminole Saga* (Lawrence: University Press of Kansas, 2003).

25. Washington Irving, *The Adventures of Captain Bonneville: In the Rocky Mountains and the Far West* (New York: G. P. Putnam's Sons, 1868), 240 ("exactly"); *LA*, 164–69; Claudio Saunt, *West of the Revolution: An Uncommon History of 1776* (New York: W. W. Norton, 2014), 158–75.

26. Alan J. Osborn, "Ecological Aspects of Equestrian Adaptations in Aboriginal North America," *American Anthropologist* 85 (September 1983): 568–70; Elliott West, *The Contested Plains: Indians, Goldseekers, and the Rush to Colorado* (Lawrence: University Press of Kansas, 1998), 70–71; Edwin Thompson Denig, *Five Indian Tribes of the Upper Missouri: Sioux, Arickaras, Assiniboines, Crees, Crows*, ed. John Ewers (Norman: University of Oklahoma Press, 1961), 17 ("The wild"); J. Diane Pearson, "1851 Cass and the Politics of Disease: The Indian Vaccination Act of 1832," *Wicazo Sa Review* 18 (Autumn 2003): 9–35; David Wishart, *An Unspeakable Sadness: The Dispossession of the Nebraska Indians* (Lincoln: University of Nebraska Press, 1994), 80–81; *LA*, 186–87; *YSF*, 202–3; Kingsley M. Bray, "Teton Sioux: Population History, 1655–1881," *Nebraska History* 75 (1994): 179.

27. *LA*, 160–63, 168–73.

28. *YSF*, 200–218 ("fought the Pawnees," 200; "carried the pipe," 204; "killed twenty," "stole two hundred," 208; "Feather-in-the-Ear," 209; "killed four lodges," 213; "plenty," "much feasting," 217; "immense quantities," 218).

29. *LA*, 193–207.

30. William M. Meigs, *The Life of Thomas Hart Benton* (Philadelphia: J. B. Lippincott, 1904), 309–10 ("The white race").

31. *Missouri Republican*, November 2, 1851 ("We have decided").

32. *Missouri Republican*, November 2, 1851 ("We are"); *Missouri Republican*, November 9, 1851 ("If there is," "These lands"); "Treaty with the Sioux—Sisseton and Wahpeton Bands, 1851," "Treaty with the Sioux—Mdewakanton and Wahpakoota Bands, 1851," "Treaty of Fort Laramie with Sioux, etc., 1851," "Treaty with the Comanche, Kiowa, and Apache, 1853," in *IALT*, 2:588–96, 600–602.

33. Saunt, *Unworthy Republic*, 314; Richard White, *"It's Your Misfortune and None of My Own": A New History of the American West* (Norman: University of Oklahoma Press, 1991), 91–93; U.S. Department of the Interior, Census Office, *Report on Indian and Indians Not Taxed in the United States* (Washington, DC: Govern-

ment Printing Office, 1894), 15–16; Benjamin Madley, *An American Genocide: The United States and the California Indian Catastrophe, 1846–1873* (New Haven, CT: Yale University Press, 2016), 3–12.

CHAPTER 27: THE COMANCHE ASCENDANCY

1. *CE*, 38–42, 240; James Brooks, *Captives and Cousins: Slavery, Kinship, and Community in the Southwest Borderlands* (Chapel Hill: University of North Carolina Press, 2002), 64.

2. *CE*, 42–50 ("plenty of muskets", 43); Robert Ryal Miller, ed., "New Mexico in Mid-eighteenth Century: A Report Based on Governor Vélez Cachupín's Inspection," trans. Miller, *Southwestern Historical Quarterly* 79, no. 2 (October 1975): 173 ("the trade," "perverse trade," "friendship," "an extremely useful"); Paul Conrad, *The Apache Diaspora: Four Centuries of Displacement and Survival* (Philadelphia: University of Pennsylvania Press, 2021), 88–89; Juliana Barr, *Peace Came in the Form of a Woman: Indians and Spaniards in the Texas Borderlands* (Chapel Hill: University of North Carolina Press, 2007), 174–75; "Report of the Reverend Father Provincial, Fray Pedro Serrano, to the Most Excellent Señor Viceroy, the Marquis of Cruillas. In regard to the *Custodia* of New Mexico. In the Year 1761," in *Historical Documents Relating to New Mexico, Nueva Vizcaya, and Approaches Thereto, to 1773*, ed. Charles W. Hackett (Washington, DC: Carnegie Institution, 1923–37), 3:486–87 ("all prudence").

3. *CE*, 45–48; Conrad, *Apache Diaspora*, 80–94; Tomás Vélez Cachupín to Juan Francisco de Güemes Padilla y Horcasitas, conde de Revillagigedo I, November 27, 1751, in *The Plains Indians and New Mexico, 1751–1778: A Collection of Documents Illustrative of the Eastern Frontier of New Mexico*, ed. and trans. Alfred Barnaby Thomas (Albuquerque: University of New Mexico Press, 1940), 73 ("with great").

4. *CE*, 48–58.

5. *CE*, 59–60; Barr, *Peace Came*, 175–85; "Deposition of Joseph Gutiérrez," in *San Sabá Papers: A Documentary Account of the Founding and Destruction of the San Sabá Mission*, ed. Lesley Bird Simpson, trans. Paul D. Nathan (1959; repr., Dallas, TX: Southern Methodist University Press, 2000), 43 ("they had come"); Juan M. Romero de Terreros, "The Destruction of the San Sabá Apache Mission: A Discussion of the Casualties," *Americas* 60 (April 2004): 617–27.

6. Eleanor B. Adams, "Bishop Tamarón's Visitation of New Mexico," *New Mexico Historical Review* 28 (October 1953): 212 ("the usual theatre"); Conrad, *Apache Diaspora*, 108–9; Barr, *Peace Came*, 185–86.

7. The population figure comes from compilation contemporary estimates that each focus on one segment of Comanchería. See J. Gaignard, "Journal of an Expedition up the Red River, 1773–1774," in *Athanase de Mézières and the Louisiana-Texas Frontier, 1768–1780*, ed. Herbert Eugene Bolton (Cleveland, OH: Arthur H. Clark, 1914), 2:83–100; Francisco Xavier Ortiz to Juan Bautista de Anza, May 20, 1786, in *Forgotten Frontiers: A Study of the Spanish Indian Policy of Don Juan Bautista de Anza, Governor of New Mexico, 1777–1787: From the Original Documents in the Archives of Spain, Mexico, and New Mexico*, ed. and trans. Alfred Barnaby Thomas (Norman: University of Oklahoma Press, 1932), 321–24, esp. 323; "List of Comanches Who Came to Make Peace in New Mexico, 1786," in *Forgotten Frontiers*, ed. and trans. Thomas, 325–27; Curtis D. Tunnell and W. W. Newcomb Jr., *A Lipan Apache Mission: San Lorenzo de la Santa Cruz, 1762–1771* (Austin: Texas Memorial

Museum, 1969), 167–72; Pedro Vermín de Mendinueta to Viceroy, June 18, 1767, in *Plains Indians and New Mexico*, ed. and trans. Thomas, 167 ("a barbarian").

8. John L. Kessell, *Kiva, Cross, and Crown: The Pecos Indians and New Mexico, 1540–1840* (Albuquerque: University of New Mexico Press, 1987), 385; Ned Blackhawk, *Violence over the Land: Indians and Empires in the Early American West* (Cambridge, MA: Harvard University Press, 2006), 102–44; Juliana Barr, "Beyond Their Control: Spaniards in Native Texas," in *Choice, Persuasion, and Coercion: Social Control on Spain's North American Frontiers*, ed. Jesús F. de la Teja and Ross Frank (Albuquerque: University of New Mexico Press, 2005), 150; Brooks, *Captives and Cousins*, 73–74; CE, 98–103; Natale A. Zappia, *Traders and Raiders: The Indigenous World of the Colorado Basin, 1540–1859* (Chapel Hill: University of North Carolina Press, 2014), 66–68.

9. Mézières to Juan María Vicencio, Barón de Ripperdá, July 4, 1772, in *Athanase de Mézières*, ed. Bolton, 1:297–303; Elizabeth A. Fenn, *Pox Americana: The Great Smallpox Epidemic of 1775–82* (New York: Hill and Wang, 2001), 146–66, 211–15; Elizabeth A. H. John, ed., "Inside the Comanchería, 1785: The Diary of Pedro Vial and Francisco Xavier Chaves," trans. Adan Benavides Jr., *Southwestern Historical Quarterly* 98, no. 1 (July 1994): 37–38, 49; CE, 99–100 ("a palladium of war," 99; "the master-key," 100).

10. CE, 112–13; Douglas W. Richmond, "Africa's Initial Encounter with Texas: The Significance of Afro-Tejanos in Colonial Tejas, 1528–1821," *Bulletin of Latin American Research* 26 (April 2007): 204.

11. John, "Inside the Comanchería," 37–46 ("great *captitanes*," "another ten," "had brought," 37; "a very large," 39; "it is more important," 44; "We shall," 46); CE, 117; Juliana Barr, "Geographies of Power: Mapping Indian Borders in the Early Southwest," *WMQ* 68 (January 2011): 38. For Camisa de Hierro as Ecueracapa, see Thomas W. Kavanagh, *The Comanches: A History, 1706–1875* (Lincoln: University of Nebraska Press, 1996), 119–21.

12. Pedro Garrido y Duran, "An Account of the Events Which Have Occurred in the Provinces of New Mexico and concerning Peace Conceded to the Comanche Nation and Their Reconciliation with the Utes since November 17 of the Last Year and July of the Current [1786]," in *Forgotten Frontiers*, ed. and trans. Thomas, 295–96 ("he would," 295); CE, 118–19.

13. CE, 107, 120–23; Garrido, "Account of the Events," 300–302 ("settle and subsist," 300; "free and safe," 300–301; "common enemies," "a token," 301; "remarkable genius," "take charge," 302; "showed," 317–18").

14. Garrido, "Account of the Events," 314 ("as his very own"); Pedro Garrido Duran, "Account Received of What Was Done in the Province of New Mexico by Governor Don Juan Bautista de Anza . . . ," *Forgotten Frontiers*, ed. and trans. Thomas, 348 ("so that").

15. CE, 125–64; Pekka Hämäläinen, "The Politics of Grass: European Expansion, Ecological Change, and Indigenous Power in the Southwest Borderlands," *WMQ* 67 (April 2010): 186; Gary Clayton Anderson, *The Indian Southwest, 1580–1830: Ethnogenesis and Reinvention* (Norman: University of Oklahoma Press, 1999), 116–27; Conrad, *Apache Diaspora*, 115–26 ("indomitable savages," 126); Jennifer Graber, *Religion and the Struggle for the American West* (New York: Oxford University Press, 2018), 23.

16. Brooks, *Captives and Cousins*, 78; Hämäläinen, "Politics of Grass," 180, 187; Dan Flores, "Bison Ecology and Bison Diplomacy: The Southern Plains from 1800 to 1850," *JAH* 78 (September 1991): 471; Andrew C. Isenberg, *The Destruction of the*

Bison: An Environmental History, 1750–1920 (New York: Cambridge University Press, 2000), 22–23. For ecological imperialism, see Alfred W. Crosby, *Ecological Imperialism: The Biological Expansion of Europe, 900–1900* (New York: Cambridge University Press, 1986).

17. *CE*, 152; Grant Foreman, *Advancing the Frontier, 1830–1860* (Norman: Oklahoma University Press, 1933), 172; M. Duval to William L. Marcy May 31, 1847, in *Letters Received by the Office of Indian Affairs, 1824–1881: Seminole Agency, 1824–1876* (Washington, DC: National Archives, 1956), microfilm, reel 801, 47–48.

18. Conrad, *Apache Diaspora*, 113–67, 176–77. For Apache reservations, see Matthew Babcock, *Apache Adaptation to Hispanic Rule* (Cambridge: Cambridge University Press, 2016); and Samuel Truett, *Fugitive Landscapes: The Forgotten History of the U.S.-Mexico Borderlands* (New Haven, CT: Yale University Press, 2006), 27–28.

19. Jean Louis Berlandier, *The Indians of Texas in 1830*, ed. John C. Ewers, trans. Patricia Reading Leclercq (Washington, DC: Smithsonian Institution, 1969), 118 ("marriage"); *CE*, 240–50.

20. "Treaty with the Comanche," December 13, 1822, in *Documents of American Indian Diplomacy: Treaties, Agreements, and Conventions, 1775–1979*, comp. Vine Deloria and Raymond DeMallie (Norman: University of Oklahoma Press, 1999), 150–52; "Delegation from the Comanche Nation to the Mexican Congress," in *Papers concerning Robertson's Colony in Texas*, comp. and ed. Malcolm McLean (Austin: University of Texas Press, 1974–93), 4:428 ("was liberally"); *CE*, 190–92.

21. "Tadeo Ortiz de Ayala and the Colonization of Texas 1822–33," *Southwestern Historical Quarterly* 32 (July 1928): 32 ("the savage).

22. *CE*, 207–18; Gary Clayton Anderson, *The Conquest of Texas: Ethnic Cleansing in the Promised Land, 1820–1875* (Norman: University of Oklahoma Press, 2005), 173–81; Pekka Hämäläinen, "The Shapes of Power: Indians, Europeans, and North American Worlds from the Seventeenth to the Nineteenth Century," in *Contested Spaces of Early America*, ed. Juliana Barr and Edward Countryman (Philadelphia: University of Pennsylvania Press, 2014), 63.

23. *CE*, 250–55.

24. Brian DeLay, *War of a Thousand Deserts: Indian Raids and the U.S. Mexican War* (New Haven, CT: Yale University Press, 2008), 61–62, 117–19, 274–88; Truett, *Fugitive Landscapes*, 14–16, 22, 29, 41, 48, 187 ("left our frontiers," 29); *CE*, 224–29; John Russell Bartlett, *Personal Narrative of Explorations and Incidents in Texas, New Mexico, California, Sonora, and Chihuahua, Connected with the United States and Mexican Boundary Commission, during the Years 1850, '51, '52, and '53* (New York: D. Appleton, 1854), 2:386 ("In the fall"); Amy S. Greenberg, "US Expansionism during the Nineteenth Century: 'Manifest Destiny,'" in *The Oxford World History of Empire*, ed. Peter Fibiger Bang, C. A. Baily, and Walter Scheidel (New York: Oxford University Press, 2021), 1028–29; Berlandier, *Indians of Texas in 1830*, 82 ("When the march"); F. Todd Smith, *The Wichita Indians: Traders of Texas and the Southern Plains* (College Station: Texas A&M University Press, 2000), 145–53; Jennifer Bess, "The Tohono O'odham 'Attack' on El Plomo: A Study in Sovereignty, Survivance, Security, and National Identity at the Dawn of the American Century," *Western Historical Quarterly* 51 (Summer 2020): 143–44; Kieran McCarty, "Sonorans Plan a New Frontier: The 1849 Report of Governor José Aguilar," *Journal of Arizona History* 39 (Winter 1998): 381 ("are placed"); "Report of Standing Committee on Indian Affairs, Oct, 12, 1837," in *The Indian Papers of Texas and Southwest, 1825–1916*, ed. Dorman H. Winfrey and James M. Day (1966; repr., Austin: Texas State Historical Association, 1995), 1:24 ("their stockkeepers").

25. Hämäläinen, "Politics of Grass."

26. Hämäläinen, "Politics of Grass," 196–98; Tiya Miles, *Ties That Bind: The Story of an Afro-Cherokee Family in Slavery and Freedom* (Berkeley: University of California Press, 2016), esp. 71–79; *CE*, 152–56; Rennard Strickland and William M. Strickland, "Beyond the Trail of Tears: One Hundred Fifty Years of Cherokee Survival," in *Cherokee Removal: Before and After*, ed. William L. Anderson (Athens: University of Georgia Press, 1991), 112–15.

27. *CE*, 227–32; Ralph A. Smith, "Indians in American-Mexican Relations before the War of 1846," *Hispanic American Historical Review* 43 (February 1963): 46; DeLay, *War of a Thousand Deserts*, 159–60, 270–73; Lance R. Blyth, *Chiricahua and Janos: Communities of Violence in the Southwestern Borderlands, 1680–1880* (Lincoln: University of Nebraska Press, 2012), 132–33; Ralph A. Smith, "The Scalp Hunter in the Borderlands, 1835–1850," *Arizona and the West* 6 (Spring 1964): 20.

CHAPTER 28: THE LAKOTA SHIELD

1. Richard White, *"It's Your Misfortune and None of My Own": A New History of the American West* (Norman: University of Oklahoma Press, 1991), 76–77; Andrés Reséndez, *Changing National Identities at the Frontier: Texas and New Mexico, 1800–1850* (New York: Cambridge University Press, 2005), 164–70; John O'Sullivan, *United States Magazine and Democratic Review* 17 (July–August 1845): 5 ("imbecile and distracted"); Nicholas Guyatt, *Providence and the Invention of the United States, 1607–1876* (New York: Cambridge University Press, 2007), 216–19; Amy S. Greenberg, "US Expansionism during the Nineteenth Century: 'Manifest Destiny,'" in *The Oxford World History of Empire*, ed. Peter Fibiger Bang, C. A. Baily, and Walter Scheidel (New York: Oxford University Press, 2021), 1013. For capitalism-driven U.S. expansion, see Walter Johnson, *River of Dark Dreams: Slavery and Empire in the Cotton Kingdom* (Cambridge, MA: Belknap Press of Harvard University Press, 2013); and Matthew Karp, *This Vast Southern Empire: Slaveholders at the Helm of American Foreign Policy* (Cambridge, MA: Harvard University Press, 2016).

2. Brian DeLay, *War of a Thousand Deserts: Indian Raids and the U.S. Mexican War* (New Haven, CT: Yale University Press, 2008), 253–73.

3. David J. Weber, *The Mexican Frontier, 1821–1846: The American Southwest under Mexico* (Albuquerque: University of New Mexico Press, 1982), 274; DeLay, *War of a Thousand Deserts*, 288–89; Natale A. Zappia, *Traders and Raiders: The Indigenous World of the Colorado Basin, 1540–1859* (Chapel Hill: University of North Carolina Press, 2014), 101–11; *SA*, 2:145–53; M. L. Crimmins, "The First Line of Army Posts Established in West Texas in 1849," *West Texas Historical Association Year Book* 19 (1943): 121; *CE*, 301.

4. David Igler, *The Great Ocean: Pacific Worlds from Captain Cook to the Gold Rush* (New York: Oxford University Press, 2013), 99–128; White, *"It's Your Misfortune"*, 90–94, 99–100; Susan Lee Johnson, *Roaring Camp: The Social World of the California Gold Rush* (New York: W. W. Norton, 2000), 59–60, 220–22; Benjamin Madley, *An American Genocide: The United States and the California Indian Catastrophe, 1846–1873* (New Haven, CT: Yale University Press, 2016), esp. 12, 59–132, 346; Sarah Deer, *The Beginning and End of Rape: Confronting Sexual Violence in Native America* (New York: Oxford University Press, 2015), 67; Cameron Addis, "The Whitman Massacre: Religion and Manifest Destiny on the Columbia Plateau, 1809–1858, *Jour-*

nal of the Early Republic 25 (Summer 2005): 221–58; Jennifer M. Spear, "Beyond the Native/Settler Divide in Early California," *WMQ* 76 (July 2019): 427–43.

5. Joshua L. Reid, *The Sea Is My Country*, 88–163, 211, 272–73; *SA*, 2:119, 210–11.

6. George E. Hyde, *Red Cloud's Folk* (1937; repr., Norman: University of Oklahoma Press, 1975), 72 ("crack it"); Charles Page to W. Hoffman, May 28, 1855, and Ed. Johnson to Hoffman, October 10, 1855, Sen. Ex. Doc. 91, 34th Cong., 1st Sess., 11; Alfred J. Vaughan to Alfred Cumming, March 21, 1854, in *Letters Received by the Office of Indian Affairs, 1824–1881: Upper Missouri Agency, 1824–1874; 1852–1864* (Missoula: University of Montana—Missoula, Mansfield Library, 1956), microfilm, roll 885 ("easily"); David J. Wishart, *An Unspeakable Sadness: The Dispossession of the Nebraska Indians* (Lincoln: University of Nebraska Press, 1994), 101–40; Anne F. Hyde, *Empires, Nations, and Families: A History of the North American West, 1800–1860* (Lincoln: University of Nebraska Press, 2011), 478–80.

7. *LA*, 227–30; Robert M. Utley, *Frontiersmen in Blue: The United States Army and the Indian, 1848–1865* (Lincoln: University of Nebraska Press, 1967), 146–53.

8. C. K. Warren, *Preliminary Report of the Explorations in Nebraska and Dakota in the Years 1855-'56-'57* (Washington, DC: Government Printing Office, 1875), 18–20, 51–52.

9. Elliott West, *The Contested Plains: Indians, Goldseekers, and the Rush to Colorado* (Lawrence: University Press of Kansas, 1998), 194–201; Thomas Twiss, "Proceedings of a Council," September 18, 1859, Sen. Ex. Doc. 35, 36th Cong., 1st Sess., 7 ("now all destroyed," "send his white"); Paul Conrad, *Apache Diaspora: Four Centuries of Displacement and Survival* (Philadelphia: University of Pennsylvania Press, 2021), 190.

10. Utley, *Frontiersmen in Blue*, 161–63, 167–72; Samuel Truett, *Fugitive Landscapes: The Forgotten History of the U.S.-Mexico Borderlands* (New Haven, CT: Yale University Press, 2006), 47–49; Conrad, *Apache Diaspora*, 190; Megan Kate, *The Union, the Confederacy, and Native Peoples in the Fight in the West* (New York: Scribner, 2020), 46; Claudia B. Haake, "Resistance and Removal: Yaqui and Navajo Identities in the Southwest Borderlands," in *Native Diasporas: Indigenous Identities and Settler Colonialism in the Americas*, ed. Gregory D. Smithers and Brooke N. Newman (Lincoln: University of Nebraska Press, 2014), 237, 267–72; T. H. Espy to Sam Houston, February 15, 1860, in *The Indian Papers of Texas and the Southwest, 1825–1916*, ed. Dorman H. Winfrey and James M. Day (1966; repr., Austin: Texas State Historical Association, 1995), 4:9 ("the whole frontier"); Andrés Reséndez, *The Other Slavery: The Uncovered Story of Indian Enslavement in America* (Boston: Houghton Mifflin Harcourt, 2016), 242 ("the seat").

11. "Treaty with the Sioux—Sisseton and Wahpeton Bands, 1851," "Treaty with the Sioux—Mdewakanton and Wahpakoota Bands," "Treaty with the Sioux—Mendawakanton and Wahpahoota Bands, 1858," "Treaty with the Sioux—Sisseeton and Wahpaton Bands, 1858," in *IALT*, 2:588–93, 781–89; Barbara T. Newcombe, "'A Portion of the American People': The Sioux Sign a Treaty in Washington in 1858," *Minnesota History* 45 (Fall 1976): 82–96; Gary Clayton Anderson, *Kinsmen of Another Kind: Dakota-White Relations in the Upper Mississippi Valley, 1650–1862* (1984; repr. Lincoln: University of Nebraska Press, 1997), 177–260; Waziyaṭawiŋ Angela Wilson, *Remember This!: Dakota Decolonization and the Eli Taylor Narratives* (Lincoln: University of Nebraska Press, 2005), 5–6; Winifred W. Barton, *John P. Williams: A Brother to the Sioux* (New York: Fleming H. Revell, 1919), 49–50 ("So far as," 49).

12. H. H. Sibley to Alex Ramsey, August 20, 1862, and John Pope to Sibley, September 28, 1862, in *Minnesota in the Civil and Indian Wars*, comp. and ed., Board of Commissioners (St. Paul, MN: Pioneer Press, 1893), 2:257 ("they are"); Alvin M. Josephy, *The Civil War in the American West* (New York: Viking, 1991), 133–39; Eric Foner, *The Fiery Trial: Abraham Lincoln and American Slavery* (New York: W. W. Norton, 2010), 261. For a comprehensive account of the U.S.-Dakota war, see Gary Clayton Anderson, *Massacre in Minnesota: The Dakota War, the Most Ethnic Conflict in American History* (Norman: University of Oklahoma Press, 2019).

13. Ned Blackhawk, *Violence over the Land: Indians and Empires in the Early American West* (Cambridge, MA: Harvard University Press, 2006), 226–66; *YSF*, 255 ("first fight"). For the changing character of the United States, see Jerome J. Rockwell, *Indian Affairs and the Administrative State in the Nineteenth Century* (Cambridge: Cambridge University Press, 2010), 217–45; Max M. Edling, *A Hercules in the Cradle: War, Money, and the American State* (Chicago: University of Chicago Press, 2014); and Steven Hahn, *A Nation without Borders: The United States and Its World in an Age of Civil Wars, 1830–1910* (New York: Viking, 2016).

14. *LA*, 255–64; "Henry Halleck to John Pope, November 3, 1864," *South Dakota Historical Collections* 8 (1916): 348–49; Ari Kelman, *A Misplaced Massacre: Struggling over the Memory of Sand Creek* (Cambridge, MA: Harvard University Press, 2013), xi, 22–24; Brigham D. Madsen, *Glory Hunter: A Biography of Patrick Edward Connor* (Salt Lake City: University of Utah Press, 1990), 78–80. For the United States as an imperial nation, see Hahn, *Nation without Borders*; and Robert G. Thrower, "Causalities and Consequences of the Creek War," in *Tohopeka: Rethinking the Creek War and the War of 1812*, ed. Kathryn E. Holland Braund (Tuscaloosa: University of Alabama Press, 2012), 24 ("Nits make lice").

15. J. R. Hanson to D. S. Stanley, May 24, 1867, Letters Received by HQS, Department of Dakota, 1866–1877, M1734, National Archives, roll 1 ("destroy all"); White, *"It's Your Misfortune"*, 96–97; Kingsley M. Bray, *Crazy Horse: A Lakota Life* (Norman: University of Oklahoma Press, 2006), 98–102; N. B. Buford to E. M. Stanton, June 6, 1867, National Archives and Records Service, Record Group 393, "Special Files" of Headquarters, created by the Military Division of the Missouri, Relating to Military Operations and Administration, 1863–1885, M1495; *YSF*, 259 ("They killed"); *LA*, 280.

16. *LA*, 281–93.

17. *ARCIA*, 1867, 314–15 ("have been doing"). For what would later be called the Washita Massacre, see Stan Hoig, *The Battle of the Washita: The Sheridan-Custer Indian Campaign 1867–1869* (Lincoln: University of Nebraska Press, 1976).

18. *LA*, 303, 322–32; *ARCIA*, 1870, 208 ("white fool"); Frederick E. Hoxie, *Parading through History: The Making of the Crow Nation in America, 1805–1935* (New York: Cambridge University Press, 1995), 80–82, 100–107; Dexter E. Clapp to Edward P. Smith, September 10, 1877, in *ARCIA*, 1875, 303 ("the larger part of").

19. White, *"It's Your Misfortune"*, 99–101; Megan Kate Nelson, *The Three-Cornered War: The Union, the Confederacy, and Native Peoples in the Fight for the West* (New York: Scribner, 2020), 196; "Report to the President by the Indian Peace Commission, January 7, 1868," accessed December 1, 2020, http://history.furman .edu/[SXB]benson/docs/peace.htm, 110 ("very great"); James Brooks, *Captives and Cousins: Slavery, Kinship, and Community in the Southwest Borderlands* (Chapel Hill: University of North Carolina Press, 2002), 331–32; Reséndez, *The Other Slavery*, 242–44; Peter Cozzens, *The Earth Is Weeping: The Epic Story of the Indian*

Wars for the American West (London: Atlantic, 2016), 380–91; Peter Iverson, *Diné: A History of the Navajos* (Albuquerque: University of New Mexico Press, 2002), 60–73; Robert M. Utley, *Geronimo* (New Haven, CT: Yale University Press, 2012), 27; Alice L. Baumgartner, "The Line of Positive Safety: Borders and Boundaries in the Rio Grande Valley, 1848–1880," *JAH* 101 (March 2015): 1106–22; Conrad, *Apache Diaspora*, 187; Lance R. Blyth, *Chiricahua and Janos: Communities of Violence in the Southwestern Borderlands, 1680–1880* (Lincoln: University of Nebraska Press, 2012), 155–86.

20. Hampton Sides, *Blood and Thunder: An Epic of the American West* (New York: Doubleday, 2006), 372–77; Jennifer Graber, *Religion and the Struggle for the American West* (New York: Oxford University Press, 2018), 69; *CE*, 308–9, 319–25.

21. *CE*, 313–30; Pekka Hämäläinen, "Reconstructing the Great Plains," *Journal of the Civil War Era* 6 (December 2016): 493; *ARCIA*, 1866, 145 ("the most").

22. David La Vere, *Contrary Neighbors: Southern Plains and Removed Indians in Indian Territory* (Norman: University of Oklahoma Press, 2000), 167–76; Jennifer Graber, *The Gods of Indian Country: Religion and the Struggle for the American West* (New York: Oxford University Press, 2018), 109–12; *CE*, 336–41; Juliana Barr, *Peace Came in the Form of a Woman: Indians and Spaniards in the Texas Borderlands* (Chapel Hill: University of North Carolina Press, 2007), 207–8.

23. P. E. Sheridan to E. D. Townsend, October 25, 1878, in *Report of the Secretary of War, 1878* (Washington, DC: Government Printing Office, 1878), 1: 10, 33 ("no other nation," 10; "no other army," 33); Mark Wahlgren Summers, *The Ordeal of Reunion: A New History of Reconstruction* (Chapel Hill: University of North Carolina Press, 2014), 181–82; David E. Wilkins, *American Indian Sovereignty and the U.S. Supreme Court: The Masking of Justice* (Austin: University of Texas Press, 1997), 12; Ron Chernow, *Grant* (London: Head of Zeus, 2017), 657–59. For Grant's vision, see Ulysses S. Grant, "First Annual Message," December 6, 1869, in *A Compilation of the Messages and Papers of the Presidents*, comp. James D. Richardson (New York: Bureau of National Literature, 1897–1922), 9:3993. For the larger context, see Hahn, *Nation without Borders*.

24. Karl Jacoby, *Shadows at Dawn: An Apache Massacre and the Violence of History* (New York: Penguin, 2008).

25. Conrad, *Apache Diaspora*, 190–98; Sam Truett, "Borderlands and Border Crossings," in *Cambridge History of America and the World*, ed. Jay Sexton and Kristin Hoganson (Cambridge: Cambridge University Press, 2021), 2:594–616. For infrastructure, see William Adler, *Engineering Expansion: The U.S. Army and Economic Development, 1787–1860* (Philadelphia: University of Pennsylvania Press, 2021). For railroads, see James Belich, *Replenishing the Earth: The Settler Revolution and the Rise of the Anglo-Worlds, 1783–1939* (New York: University of Oxford Press, 2009), 107–8.

26. Eve Ball, *In the Days of Victorio: Recollections of a Warm Springs Apache* (Tucson: University of Arizona Press, 1970), 25–26 ("Ration cards").

27. *SA*, 4:159; *LA*, 299–330, 351–70; "Red Horse Account," in *Lakota and Cheyenne: Indian Views of the Great Sioux War, 1876–1877*, comp. and ed. Jerome A. Greene (Norman: University of Oklahoma Press, 1994), 37 ("did not take").

28. Richard Slotkin, *The Fatal Environment: The Myth of the Frontier in the Age of Industrialization, 1800–1890* (Norman: University of Oklahoma Press, 1985), 458 ("hill of death"); *LA*, 370–73; Beth LaDow, *The Medicine Line: Life and Death on an American Borderland* (New York: Routledge, 2001), 40–42, 65–66; Richard

White, *Railroaded: The Transcontinentals and the Making of Modern America* (New York: W.W. Norton, 2011), esp. 59–62, 134–39, 496–98; *The Indian Journal, December 7, 1876, re: visit of the Sioux Indian Territory*, University of Oklahoma Libraries Western History Collection, accessed January 22, 2021, https://digital .libraries.ou.edu/cdm/ref/collection/creek/id/6 ("my country").

29. Hermann Lehmann, *Nine Years among the Indians, 1870–1879: The Story of the Captivity and Life of a Texan among the Indians* (1927; repr., University of New Mexico Press, 1993), 75–90; Thom Hatch, *The Last Days of George Armstrong Custer* (New York: St. Martin's Press, 2015), 203–13; *LA*, 370–73; David D. Smits, "The Frontier Army and the Destruction of the Buffalo: 1865–1883," *WHQ* 25 (Autumn 1994): 312–38. For the postal offices, see Cameron Blevins, *Paper Trails: The US Post and the Making of the American West* (New York: Oxford University Press, 2021).

30. Elliott West, *The Last Indian War: The Nez Perce Story* (New York: Oxford University Press, 2009), 60–70.

31. West, *Last Indian War*, 98–155, 243–99; LaDow, *Medicine Line*, 71; Francis Haines, "Chief Joseph and the Nez Perce Warriors," *Pacific Northwest Quarterly* 45 (January 1954): 1–7.

32. Adam R. Hodge, *Ecology and Ethnogenesis: An Environmental History of the Wind River Shoshones, 1000–1868* (Lincoln: University of Nebraska Press, 2019), 116–37, 212, 238–39; Dale L. Morgan, "Shoshonean Peoples and the Overland Trails: Frontiers of the Utah Superintendency of Indian Affairs," ed. Richard L. Saunders (Logan: Utah State University Press, 2007), 209 ("are so broken," "not depend"); Reséndez, *Other Slavery*, 266–75.

33. For this summary of Blackfoot history, I relied on Ryan Hall, *Beneath the Backbone of the World: Blackfoot People and the North American Borderlands, 1720–1877* (Chapel Hill: University of North Carolina Press, 2020). For the Marias River massacre and its larger context, see Andy Graybill, *The Red and the White: A Family Saga of the American West* (New York: Liveright, 2013).

34. Theodore Binnema, *Common and Contested Ground: A Human and Environmental History of the Northwestern Plains* (Norman: University of Oklahoma Press, 2001), 106–96; *HAC*, plate 62.

35. Truett, "Borderlands," 871–73; Daschuk, *Clearing the Plains: Disease, Politics of Starvation and the Loss of Aboriginal Life* (Regina, SK: University of Regina Press, 2013), 99–126; *SA*, 2:69–71. For a comprehensive study of the pemmican trade, see George Colpitts, *Pemmican Empire: Food, Trade, and the Last Bison Hunts in the North American Plains* (New York: Cambridge University Press, 2014).

36. Robert N. Watt, "Victorio's Military and Political Leadership of the Warm Springs Apaches," *War in History*, November 2011, 457–94; Eve Ball, *Indeh, an Apache Odyssey* (Norman: University of Oklahoma Press, 1980), 2–9; "Lozen: An Apache Woman Warrior," in *Sifters: Native American Women's Lives*, ed. Theda Perdue (New York: Oxford University Press, 2001), 98–103.

37. Truett, *Fugitive Landscapes*, 57–61, 179–226; Conrad, *Apache Diaspora*, 224–50; Cozzens, *Earth Is Weeping*, 362–79.

EPILOGUE: REVENGE AND REVIVAL

1. Jeffrey Ostler, *The Plains Sioux and U.S. Colonialism from Lewis and Clark to Wounded Knee* (Cambridge: Cambridge University Press, 2004), 222–29; Jerry Green, "The Medals of Wounded Knee," *Nebraska History* 75 (Summer 1994):

200–208. For the broader context of the Ghost Dance and its modernizing, forward-looking thrust, see Louis S. Warren, *God's Red Son: The Ghost Dance Religion and the Making of Modern America* (New York: Basic Books, 2017).

2.   J. David Hacker, "Census-Based Count of the Civil War Dead," *Civil War History* 57 (December 2011): 307–48; Pekka Hämäläinen, "The Shapes of Power: Indians, Europeans, and North American Worlds from the Seventeenth to the Nineteenth Century," in *Contested Spaces of Early America*, ed. Juliana Barr and Edward Countryman (Philadelphia: University of Pennsylvania Press, 2014), 65; Richard White, *The Republic for Which It Stands: The United States during Reconstruction and the Gilded Age, 1865–1896* (New York: Oxford University Press, 2017), 604–5. For the two simultaneous reconstructions, which Elliot West calls "the Greater Reconstruction," see West, "Reconstructing Race," *Western Historical Quarterly* 34 (April 2003), 6–26; Philip J. Deloria, "From Nation to Neighborhood: Land, Policy, Culture, Colonialism, and Empire in U.S.-Indian Relations," in *The Cultural Turn in U.S. History: Past, Present, and Future*, ed. James W. Cook, Lawrence B. Clickman, and Michael O'Malley (Chicago: University of Chicago Press, 2008), 364; K. Tsianina Lomawaima and Jeffrey Ostler, "Reconsidering Richard Henry Pratt: Cultural Genocide and Native Liberation in an Era of Racial Oppression," *Journal of American Indian Education* 57 (Spring 2018): 79–100 ("kill the Indian," 79).

3.   Richard Henry Pratt, "The Advantages of Mingling Indians with the Whites," in *Americanizing the American Indians: Writings by the "Friends of the Indian" 1880–1900*, ed. Francis Paul Prucha (Cambridge, MA: Harvard University Press, 1973), 260–71.

4.   *SG*, 186; Sami Lakomäki, *Gathering Together: The Shawnee People through Diaspora and Nationhood, 1600–1870* (New Haven, CT: Yale University Press, 2014), 15 ("the greatest").

5.   Sven Beckert, "American Danger: United States Empire, Eurafrica, and the Territorialization of Industrial Capitalism, 1870–1950," *AHR* 122 (October 2017): 1137–70 ("monstrous," "greatest menace," 1137). For genocide, ethnic cleansing, and massacres, see Ned Blackhawk, *Violence over the Land: Indians and Empires in the Early American West* (Cambridge, MA: Harvard University Press, 2006); Ari Kelman, *Misplaced Massacre: Struggling over the Memory of Sand Creek* (Cambridge, MA: Harvard University Press, 2013); Gary Clayton Anderson, *Conquest of Texas: Ethnic Cleansing in the Promised Land, 1820–1875* (Norman: University of Oklahoma Press, 2005); Karl Jacoby, *Shadows at Dawn: An Apache Massacre and the Violence of History* (New York: Penguin, 2008); and Andy Graybill, *The Red and the White: A Family Saga of the American West* (New York: Liveright, 2013).

6.   Benjamin Madley, "Reexamining the American Genocide Debate: Meaning, Historiography, and New Methods," *AHR* 120 (February 2015): 1. The seventy percent figure comes from *SG*, 12.

7.   Russell Thornton, *American Indian Holocaust and Survival: A Population History since 1492* (Norman: University of Oklahoma Press, 1987), 43; *The Canadian Encyclopedia*, s.v. "Indigenous Peoples in Canada," accessed January 4, 2021, https://www.thecanadianencyclopedia.ca/en/article/aboriginal-people; World Population Review, "Native American Population, 2021," accessed May 12, 2021, https://worldpopulationreview.com/state-rankings/native-american-population.

8.   I am drawing here from David Treuer, *The Heartbeat of Wounded Knee: Native America from 1890 to the Present* (New York: Riverhead Books, 2019); and David Treuer, "Return the National Parks to the Tribes," *Atlantic*, May 2021 ("America has").

ILLUSTRATION CREDITS

Page 69: University of Oxford
Page 71: Boston Public Library
Page 72: Sutro Library
Page 81: New York Public Library
Page 91: Division of Rare and Manuscript Collections, Cornell University Library
Page 122: Library and Archives Canada
Page 184: John Mackenzie Burke
Page 194: Library of Congress Geography and Map Division
Page 205: Library of Congress Prints and Photographs Division
Page 211: Library of Congress Geography and Map Division
Page 261: Library of Congress Geography and Map Division
Page 267: Library of Congress Geography and Map Division
Page 271: National Gallery of Canada
Page 294: Library of Congress Geography and Map Division
Page 346: Library of Congress Geography and Map Division
Page 364: Library of Congress Geography and Map Division
Page 373: Greenville County Museum of Art
Page 424: Smithsonian American Art Museum

Maps by Bill Nelson

INDEX

Page numbers in *italics* refer to illustrations and maps.
Page numbers beginning at 467 refer to notes.